W9-CMQ-868

The Poems of T. S. Eliot

Volume I

Collected Poems 1909–1962
Uncollected Poems
The Waste Land: An Editorial Composite

Commentary

Volume II

Old Possum's Book of Practical Cats
Anabasis
Other Verses
Noctes Binanianæ
Improper Rhymes

Commentary
Textual History

By T. S. Eliot

THE COMPLETE POEMS AND PLAYS

verse

COLLECTED POEMS 1909–1962
PRUFROCK AND OTHER OBSERVATIONS
THE WASTE LAND AND OTHER POEMS
FOUR QUARTETS
SELECTED POEMS
THE WASTE LAND:
A Facsimile and Transcript of the Original Drafts
edited by Valerie Eliot
INVENTIONS OF THE MARCH HARE:
Poems 1909–1917
edited by Christopher Ricks
THE ARIEL POEMS
THE WASTE LAND
OLD POSSUM'S BOOK OF PRACTICAL CATS

plays

MURDER IN THE CATHEDRAL
THE FAMILY REUNION
THE COCKTAIL PARTY
THE CONFIDENTIAL CLERK
THE ELDER STATESMAN

literary criticism

THE SACRED WOOD
SELECTED ESSAYS
THE USE OF POETRY AND THE USE OF CRITICISM
TO CRITICIZE THE CRITIC
ON POETRY AND POETS
SELECTED PROSE OF T. S. ELIOT
edited by Frank Kermode
THE COMPLETE PROSE OF T. S. ELIOT: THE CRITICAL EDITION
Volume 1: Apprentice Years, 1905–1918
edited by Jewel Spears Brooker and Ronald Schuchard
Volume 2: The Perfect Critic, 1919–1926
edited by Anthony Cuda and Ronald Schuchard

social criticism

NOTES TOWARDS THE DEFINITION OF CULTURE

letters

THE LETTERS OF T. S. ELIOT
Volume 1: 1898–1922
Volume 2: 1923–1925
edited by Valerie Eliot and Hugh Haughton
Volume 3: 1926–1927
Volume 4: 1928–1929
Volume 5: 1930–1931
Volume 6: 1932–1933
Volume 7: 1934–1935
edited by Valerie Eliot and John Haffenden

The Poems of
T. S. ELIOT

Volume II

Practical Cats and Further Verses

Edited by

Christopher Ricks and Jim McCue

Farrar, Straus and Giroux
New York

Farrar, Straus and Giroux
120 Broadway, New York 10271

All writings by T. S. Eliot copyright © 2015 by Set Copyrights Limited
Introduction, commentary, and editorial material
copyright © 2015 by Christopher Ricks and Jim McCue
All rights reserved
Printed in the United States of America
Published by arrangement with Houghton Mifflin Harcourt
Publishing Company and Faber & Faber Ltd
Originally published in 2015 by Faber & Faber Ltd, Great Britain
First American paperback edition, 2018

Library of Congress Control Number: 2018947122
ISBN 978–0–374–23514–7

Designed by Paul Luna
Typeset by Donald Sommerville

Our books may be purchased in bulk for promotional,
educational, or business use. Please contact your local
bookseller or the Macmillan Corporate and Premium Sales
Department at 1–800–221–7945, extension 5442, or by e-mail at
MacmillanSpecialMarkets@macmillan.com.

www.fsgbooks.com
www.twitter.com/fsgbooks • www.facebook.com/fsgbooks

3 5 7 9 10 8 6 4 2

Contents · Volume II

CONTENTS · VOLUME II

An Autobiographical Sketch

Sent to M. A. Frank-Duchesne, 5 November 1945

My family, since its removal from England in 1669, has always been settled in or near Boston, Massachusetts. It has therefore been associated for some generations with the Unitarian sect and with Harvard University. My grandfather, as a minister of Unitarianism, went out to St. Louis, Missouri in 1837 to found the first Unitarian church west of the Mississippi River: but though he was extremely active in public life there, and amongst other activities founded a local university, Boston remains the family *foyer*. The seventeenth-century background is of course strongly Puritan–Calvinistic.

I spent my early years in St. Louis, was later at school in Massachusetts and at Harvard. My interests there were chiefly literary, and as an undergraduate at Harvard I began to write verse under the influence of Baudelaire and Laforgue, and read widely amongst other French poetry. On taking my degree at Harvard I spent a year in Paris, following lectures at the Sorbonne and the Collège de France, and fell under the influence of Bergson. I returned to Harvard to study philosophy, with the intention of making my career in that pursuit. I also took up the study of Sanskrit and Pali, as Indian thought had always had a strong attraction for me; and I thought of proceeding to the study of comparative religion. At this period the influence of Bergson was succeeded by the influence of F. H. Bradley. Consequently, I spent a year at Oxford working on Plato and Aristotle under Bradley's greatest disciple, Harold Joachim. But for the outbreak of war in 1914 I should probably have spent some time also in Germany studying Greek philosophy; and I was attracted at that time by the work of such philosophers at Husserl and Meinong.

I had never been able to get any of my verse published; and the first recognition I received was from Mr. Ezra Pound, whom I met in London in 1915. This encouragement turned my mind to poetry again; and on ending my year at Oxford I remained in London. For a time I was a schoolmaster, then for eight years in a bank in the City. During this period my interests were exclusively literary, though I occasionally reviewed philosophical books. My first book of verse appeared in 1917, and my first volume of literary essays in 1920. I joined the newly formed publishing firm of Faber & Gwyer (since, Faber & Faber) in 1925.

I had always had a lively interest in anthropology and the study of religions. The early work of Maritain made a deep impression on me, and I began reading discursively in theology. In 1927 I was received into the Church of England. My interest in Christian sociology had developed since that time, partly through association with the Christendom group of writers, and partly through association with the activities of Dr. J. H. Oldham. In more recent years still, I have interested myself in political philosophy, and have returned to the reading of Edmund Burke. I was naturalised as a British subject in 1927. My chief function is to write verse, and verse plays, and to publish the poetry of other writers: everything else I do is a *Nebenfach* [ancillary study]. My theological standpoint is that of what is called the "Anglo-Catholic" movement in the Church of England.

Table of Dates

1920   FEB: *Ara Vos Prec* published by the Ovid Press; *Poems* published by Knopf, NY. 15 AUG: Meets Joyce in Paris. NOV: *The Sacred Wood* published.

1921   Leave of absence from Lloyds Bank for treatment for a nervous breakdown. OCT–NOV: in Margate, writing *The Waste Land*. NOV–DEC: Completes draft of the poem while in Lausanne for treatment with Dr. Roger Vittoz.

1922   JAN: Pound and Eliot work together on *The Waste Land*, first in person in Paris, then in correspondence. OCT: Publication of *The Waste Land* in the *Criterion*, a journal edited by TSE until its closure in 1939 in the face of the Second World War. In New York, the poem is published in the *Dial*, and TSE is awarded the Dial Prize of $2,000. DEC: *The Waste Land* published in volume form by Boni & Liveright, NY, with the Hogarth Press edition following in Britain in SEPT 1923.

1925   Joins Faber & Gwyer (later Faber & Faber). NOV: Faber publishes *Poems 1909–1925*, which includes *The Hollow Men*.

1926   Clark Lecturer at Trinity College, Cambridge. Rejected as candidate for a Research Fellowship at All Souls, Oxford.

1927   JUNE: Baptised, and then confirmed the following day. Becomes godfather to Tom Faber. *Journey of the Magi* published (first of TSE's Ariel Poems). Naturalised as a British citizen.

1928   NOV: Preface to *For Lancelot Andrewes* declares that "The general point of view may be described as classicist in literature, royalist in politics, and anglo-catholic in religion."

1929   10 SEPT: Death of TSE's mother. 27 SEPT: *Dante*.

1930   APR: *Ash-Wednesday*. MAY: *Anabasis*.

1932   SEPT: *Selected Essays 1917–1932*. DEC: *Sweeney Agonistes*.

1932–33 Lectures in America, including Charles Eliot Norton Lectures at Harvard and Page-Barbour Lectures at U. Virginia. Earliest recordings. Having decided not to return to Vivien, TSE lodges with his priest and with friends until the end of the Second World War.

1934   FEB: *After Strange Gods* (the Page-Barbour Lectures). MAY: *The Rock*, a pageant for the Forty-Five Churches Fund, staged at Sadler's Wells.

1935   MAY: *Murder in the Cathedral* performed at Canterbury Cathedral.

1936   APR: *Collected Poems 1909–1935* includes *Burnt Norton*.

1937   MAY: Visits Austria and (briefly) Germany, on holiday.

1938   Vivien Eliot committed to an asylum.

1939   MAR: *The Family Reunion* produced at the Westminster Theatre. OCT: *Old Possum's Book of Practical Cats*.

1940   MAR: *East Coker*.

1941   FEB: *The Dry Salvages*.

1942   OCT: *Little Gidding*.

1943   MAY: *Four Quartets* published in New York, with the British edition following in OCT 1944.

Glossary

blind-ruled	impressed with rules but without ink
braced	with added brackets or square brackets not in themselves intended as punctuation (often for further consideration)
cognate	ribbon and carbon copies from the same act of typing and therefore textually identical unless annotated or edited (see *reciprocal*)
draft	preliminary manuscript or typescript
excised leaves	leaves removed, for instance from the *March Hare* Notebook, and not accompanying the original
eye-skip	omission caused by eye of copyist or compositor jumping to a later repetition of words (such as "The nymphs are departed", *The Waste Land* [III] 175, 179)
indented	(of an individual line) set to the right of the left-hand margin of the poem
inset	(of a group of lines) set to the right of the left-hand margin of the poem
laid in	of extraneous leaves introduced into a manuscript volume such as the *March Hare* Notebook but not bound as part of it
orphan	the first line of a paragraph set as the last line of a page or column
overtyped	typed in the same position so as to supersede what originally appeared
part	a division of a poem marked by the author with a numeral
quad-ruled	printed with vertical and horizontal lines forming rectangles
reciprocal	of typescripts in which the two or more pages are a mixture of cognate ribbon copies and carbons, and which together would constitute the complete ribbon copy and the complete carbon
scored	marked with a vertical line in the margin
section	a division of the text of a book ("The section of 'Occasional Poems' was introduced in *1963*")
separately	constituting an entire book, pamphlet or broadsheet
stepped	arranged on more than one line; unless specified, each step beginning where the previous ends
variant	difference in the text; within TSE's poems, unless otherwise specified, variants are differences from the main text of the present edition (see Textual History)
widow	a last word or short last line of a paragraph falling at the top of a page or column

Abbreviations and Symbols

ANQ	*American Notes and Queries*
AraVP	*Ara Vos Prec* (Ovid Press, 1920)
Ariel	Faber Ariel Poem pamphlets (standard editions)
Ash-Wed	*Ash-Wednesday* (Faber, 1930)
Beinecke	Beinecke Library, Yale University
BL	British Library
BN	*Burnt Norton* pamphlet (1941)
Composition FQ	Helen Gardner, *The Composition of "Four Quartets"* (Faber, 1978)
del.	delete, deleted
DS	*The Dry Salvages* pamphlet (1941)
EC	*East Coker* pamphlet (1940)
ed.	edition, editor, edited (by)
EinC	*Essays in Criticism*
ELH	*English Literary History*
ELN	*English Language Notes*
Fr.	French
Ger.	German
Houghton	Houghton Library, Harvard University
Inf.	*Inferno* (Dante)
King's	Modern Archive Centre, King's College, Cambridge
L.	Latin
LG	*Little Gidding* pamphlet (1942)
Magdalene	Library of Magdalene College, Cambridge
March Hare	*Inventions of the March Hare*
MLN	*Modern Language Notes*
MLR	*Modern Language Review*
ms	manuscript
N&Q	*Notes and Queries*
NEW	*New English Weekly*
NY	New York
NYPL	New York Public Library
OED	The Oxford English Dictionary (2nd ed., 1989, with online updates)
Oxf Bk of English Verse	*The Oxford Book of English Verse* ed. A. T. Quiller-Couch (1900)
PMLA	*Publications of the Modern Language Association of America*
Purg.	*Purgatory* (Dante)
repr.	reprint, reprinted

RES	*Review of English Studies*
rev.	revised
Sw. Ag.	*Sweeney Agonistes* (Faber, 1932)
Texas	Harry Ransom Center, University of Texas at Austin
TLS	*Times Literary Supplement*
tr.	translation, translated (by)
ts	typescript
U.	University, University of
VE	Valerie Eliot
WLComposite	composite text of the drafts of *The Waste Land* (present edition)
WLFacs	*The Waste Land: A Facsimile and Transcript of the Original Drafts including the Annotations of Ezra Pound* ed. Valerie Eliot (1971)

Abbreviated titles are detailed in Volume I, Index of Identifying Titles for Prose by T. S. Eliot. Abbreviated titles for TSE's poetic works are detailed in this volume, in the Textual History headnote, 3. KEY TO EDITIONS.

Abbreviated titles for works by other authors are detailed in Volume I, in the Bibliography.

Quotations from OED retain its abbreviations.

SYMBOLS

|	line break, used in quotations from verse
||	stanza break, used in quotations from verse
ⅽ	informal ampersand, used in quotations from manuscript
+	"and in derived text" (of a reading within a poem, or a poem within editions)
¶	new paragraph
> or <	line space (used at the foot of a page in the poems)
[]	enclosing a date not specified by the author or publisher
^	insertion, used to indicate where additional material was to be placed
...	ellipsis (raised), used to indicate omissions made by the editors of the present edition
...	ellipsis (baseline), used in quotation where the ellipsis is present in the original
..	ellipsis in entries quoted from OED
||	used to separate different readings within textual history collations; see, in this volume, Textual History headnote, 2. NOTATION
~	to indicate a range of instances most of which, but not necessarily all, have a certain feature; see Textual History headnote, 2. NOTATION

T.S. ELIOT

OLD POSSUM'S

BOOK

OF

PRACTICAL

CATS

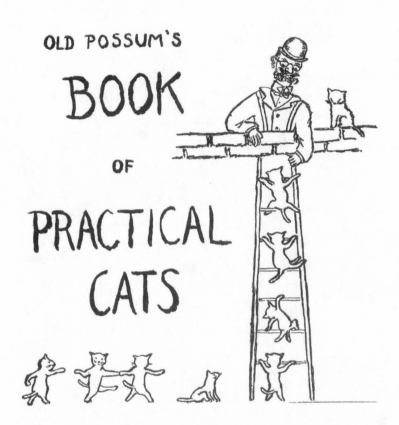

FABER AND FABER LIMITED

Preface

This Book is respectfully dedicated to those friends
who have assisted its composition by their encour-
agement, criticism and suggestions: and in par-
ticular to Mr. T. E. Faber, Miss Alison Tandy, Miss
Susan Wolcott, Miss Susanna Morley, and the Man
in White Spats.

O. P.

The Naming of Cats

The Naming of Cats is a difficult matter,
    It isn't just one of your holiday games;
You may think at first I'm as mad as a hatter
    When I tell you, a cat must have THREE DIFFERENT NAMES.
First of all, there's the name that the family use daily,   5
    Such as Peter, Augustus, Alonzo or James,
Such as Victor or Jonathan, George or Bill Bailey—
    All of them sensible everyday names.
There are fancier names if you think they sound sweeter,
    Some for the gentlemen, some for the dames: 10
Such as Plato, Admetus, Electra, Demeter—
    But all of them sensible everyday names.
But I tell you, a cat needs a name that's particular,
    A name that's peculiar, and more dignified,
Else how can he keep up his tail perpendicular,   15
    Or spread out his whiskers, or cherish his pride?
Of names of this kind, I can give you a quorum,
    Such as Munkustrap, Quaxo, or Coricopat,
Such as Bombalurina, or else Jellylorum—
    Names that never belong to more than one cat.   20
But above and beyond there's still one name left over,
    And that is the name that you never will guess;
The name that no human research can discover—
    But THE CAT HIMSELF KNOWS, and will never confess.
When you notice a cat in profound meditation,   25
    The reason, I tell you, is always the same:
His mind is engaged in a rapt contemplation
    Of the thought, of the thought, of the thought of his name:
        His ineffable effable
        Effanineffable   30
Deep and inscrutable singular Name.

The Old Gumbie Cat

I have a Gumbie Cat in mind, her name is Jennyanydots;
Her coat is of the tabby kind, with tiger stripes and leopard
   spots.
All day she sits upon the stair or on the steps or on the mat:
She sits and sits and sits and sits—and that's what makes a
   Gumbie Cat!

5   But when the day's hustle and bustle is done,
    Then the Gumbie Cat's work is but hardly begun.
    And when all the family's in bed and asleep,
    She slips down the stairs to the basement to creep.
    She is deeply concerned with the ways of the mice—
10 Their behaviour's not good and their manners not nice;
    So when she has got them lined up on the matting,
    She teaches them music, crocheting and tatting.

I have a Gumbie Cat in mind, her name is Jennyanydots;
Her equal would be hard to find, she likes the warm and
   sunny spots.
15 All day she sits beside the hearth or on the bed or on my hat:
She sits and sits and sits and sits—and that's what makes a
   Gumbie Cat!

    But when the day's hustle and bustle is done,
    Then the Gumbie Cat's work is but hardly begun.
    As she finds that the mice will not ever keep quiet,
20 She is sure it is due to irregular diet;
    And believing that nothing is done without trying,
    She sets straight to work with her baking and frying.
    She makes them a mouse-cake of bread and dried peas,
    And a *beautiful* fry of lean bacon and cheese.

>

I have a Gumbie Cat in mind, her name is Jennyanydots;   25
The curtain-cord she likes to wind, and tie it into sailor-knots.
She sits upon the window-sill, or anything that's smooth and flat:
She sits and sits and sits and sits—and that's what makes a
    Gumbie Cat!

But when the day's hustle and bustle is done,
Then the Gumbie Cat's work is but hardly begun.   30
She thinks that the cockroaches just need employment
To prevent them from idle and wanton destroyment.
So she's formed, from that lot of disorderly louts,
A troop of well-disciplined helpful boy-scouts,
With a purpose in life and a good deed to do—   35
And she's even created a Beetles' Tattoo.

So for Old Gumbie Cats let us now give three cheers—
On whom well-ordered households depend, it appears.

Growltiger's Last Stand

GROWLTIGER was a Bravo Cat, who travelled on a barge:
In fact he was the roughest cat that ever roamed at large.
From Gravesend up to Oxford he pursued his evil aims,
Rejoicing in his title of 'The Terror of the Thames'.

5   His manners and appearance did not calculate to please;
His coat was torn and seedy, he was baggy at the knees;
One ear was somewhat missing, no need to tell you why,
And he scowled upon a hostile world from one forbidding eye.

The cottagers of Rotherhithe knew something of his fame;
10   At Hammersmith and Putney people shuddered at his name.
They would fortify the hen-house, lock up the silly goose,
When the rumour ran along the shore: GROWLTIGER'S ON
        THE LOOSE!

Woe to the weak canary, that fluttered from its cage;
Woe to the pampered Pekinese, that faced Growltiger's rage;
15   Woe to the bristly Bandicoot, that lurks on foreign ships,
And woe to any Cat with whom Growltiger came to grips!

But most to Cats of foreign race his hatred had been vowed;
To Cats of foreign name and race no quarter was allowed.
The Persian and the Siamese regarded him with fear—
20   Because it was a Siamese had mauled his missing ear.

Now on a peaceful summer night, all nature seemed at play,
The tender moon was shining bright, the barge at Molesey lay.
All in the balmy moonlight it lay rocking on the tide—
And Growltiger was disposed to show his sentimental side.

25   His bucko mate, GRUMBUSKIN, long since had disappeared,
For to the Bell at Hampton he had gone to wet his beard;

And his bosun, TUMBLEBRUTUS, he too had stol'n away—
In the yard behind the Lion he was prowling for his prey.

In the forepeak of the vessel Growltiger sate alone,
Concentrating his attention on the Lady GRIDDLEBONE.   30
And his raffish crew were sleeping in their barrels and their bunks—
As the Siamese came creeping in their sampans and their junks.

Growltiger had no eye or ear for aught but Griddlebone,
And the Lady seemed enraptured by his manly baritone,
Disposed to relaxation, and awaiting no surprise—   35
But the moonlight shone reflected from a hundred bright blue eyes.

And closer still and closer the sampans circled round,
And yet from all the enemy there was not heard a sound.
The lovers sang their last duet, in danger of their lives—
For the foe was armed with toasting forks and cruel carving knives.   40

Then GILBERT gave the signal to his fierce Mongolian horde;
With a frightful burst of fireworks the Chinks they swarmed aboard.
Abandoning their sampans, and their pullaways and junks,
They battened down the hatches on the crew within their bunks.

Then Griddlebone she gave a screech, for she was badly skeered;   45
I am sorry to admit it, but she quickly disappeared.
She probably escaped with ease, I'm sure she was not drowned—
But a serried ring of flashing steel Growltiger did surround.

The ruthless foe pressed forward, in stubborn rank on rank;
Growltiger to his vast surprise was forced to walk the plank.   50
He who a hundred victims had driven to that drop,
At the end of all his crimes was forced to go ker-flip, ker-flop.

Oh there was joy in Wapping when the news flew through the land;
At Maidenhead and Henley there was dancing on the strand.
Rats were roasted whole at Brentford, and at Victoria Dock,   55
And a day of celebration was commanded in Bangkok.

The Rum Tum Tugger

The Rum Tum Tugger is a Curious Cat:
If you offer him pheasant he would rather have grouse.
If you put him in a house he would much prefer a flat,
If you put him in a flat then he'd rather have a house.
5   If you set him on a mouse then he only wants a rat,
If you set him on a rat then he'd rather chase a mouse.
Yes the Rum Tum Tugger is a Curious Cat—
    And there isn't any call for me to shout it:
        For he will do
10   As he do do
            And there's no doing anything about it!

The Rum Tum Tugger is a terrible bore:
When you let him in, then he wants to be out;
He's always on the wrong side of every door,
15   And as soon as he's at home, then he'd like to get about.
He likes to lie in the bureau drawer,
But he makes such a fuss if he can't get out.
Yes the Rum Tum Tugger is a Curious Cat—
    And it isn't any use for you to doubt it:
20   For he will do
        As he do do
            And there's no doing anything about it!

The Rum Tum Tugger is a curious beast:
His disobliging ways are a matter of habit.
25   If you offer him fish then he always wants a feast;
When there isn't any fish then he won't eat rabbit.
If you offer him cream then he sniffs and sneers,
For he only likes what he finds for himself;
So you'll catch him in it right up to the ears,

If you put it away on the larder shelf. 30
The Rum Tum Tugger is artful and knowing,
The Rum Tum Tugger doesn't care for a cuddle;
But he'll leap on your lap in the middle of your sewing,
For there's nothing he enjoys like a horrible muddle.
Yes the Rum Tum Tugger is a Curious Cat— 35
    And there isn't any need for me to spout it:
      For he will do
      As he do do
    And there's no doing anything about it!

The Song of the Jellicles

Jellicle Cats come out to-night,
Jellicle Cats come one come all:
The Jellicle Moon is shining bright—
Jellicles come to the Jellicle Ball.

5 Jellicle Cats are black and white,
Jellicle Cats are rather small;
Jellicle Cats are merry and bright,
And pleasant to hear when they caterwaul.
Jellicle Cats have cheerful faces,
10 Jellicle Cats have bright black eyes;
They like to practise their airs and graces
And wait for the Jellicle Moon to rise.

Jellicle Cats develop slowly,
Jellicle Cats are not too big;
15 Jellicle Cats are roly-poly,
They know how to dance a gavotte and a jig.
Until the Jellicle Moon appears
They make their toilette and take their repose:
Jellicles wash behind their ears,
20 Jellicles dry between their toes.

Jellicle Cats are white and black,
Jellicle Cats are of moderate size;
Jellicles jump like a jumping-jack,
Jellicle Cats have moonlit eyes.
25 They're quiet enough in the morning hours,
They're quiet enough in the afternoon,
Reserving their terpsichorean powers
To dance by the light of the Jellicle Moon.

>

Jellicle Cats are black and white,
Jellicle Cats (as I said) are small;   30
If it happens to be a stormy night
They will practise a caper or two in the hall.
If it happens the sun is shining bright
You would say they had nothing to do at all:
They are resting and saving themselves to be right   35
For the Jellicle Moon and the Jellicle Ball.

Mungojerrie and Rumpelteazer

Mungojerrie and Rumpelteazer were a very notorious couple of cats.
As knockabout clowns, quick-change comedians, tight-rope
    walkers and acrobats
They had an extensive reputation. They made their home in Victoria
    Grove—
That was merely their centre of operation, for they were incurably
    given to rove.
They were very well known in Cornwall Gardens, in Launceston
5   Place and in Kensington Square—
They had really a little more reputation than a couple of cats can
    very well bear.

    If the area window was found ajar
    And the basement looked like a field of war,
    If a tile or two came loose on the roof,
10   Which presently ceased to be waterproof,
    If the drawers were pulled out from the bedroom chests,
    And you couldn't find one of your winter vests,
    Or after supper one of the girls
    Suddenly missed her Woolworth pearls:
15 Then the family would say: 'It's that horrible cat!
It was Mungojerrie—or Rumpelteazer!'—And most of the time they
    left it at that.

Mungojerrie and Rumpelteazer had a very unusual gift of the gab.
They were highly efficient cat-burglars as well, and remarkably
    smart at a smash-and-grab.
They made their home in Victoria Grove. They had no regular
    occupation.
They were plausible fellows, and liked to engage a friendly
20   policeman in conversation.
>

When the family assembled for Sunday dinner,
With their minds made up that they wouldn't get thinner
On Argentine joint, potatoes and greens,
And the cook would appear from behind the scenes
And say in a voice that was broken with sorrow: 25
'I'm afraid you must wait and have dinner *tomorrow*!
For the joint has gone from the oven—like that!'
Then the family would say: 'It's that horrible cat!
It was Mungojerrie—or Rumpelteazer!'—And most of the time they
    left it at that.

Mungojerrie and Rumpelteazer had a wonderful way of working   30
    together.
And some of the time you would say it was luck, and some of the
    time you would say it was weather.
They would go through the house like a hurricane, and no sober
    person could take his oath
Was it Mungojerrie—or Rumpelteazer? or could you have sworn that
    it mightn't be both?

And when you heard a dining-room smash
Or up from the pantry there came a loud crash   35
Or down from the library came a loud *ping*
From a vase which was commonly said to be Ming—
Then the family would say: 'Now which was which cat?
It was Mungojerrie! AND Rumpelteazer!'—And there's nothing at all
    to be done about that!

Old Deuteronomy

Old Deuteronomy's lived a long time;
    He's a Cat who has lived many lives in succession.
He was famous in proverb and famous in rhyme
    A long while before Queen Victoria's accession.
5   Old Deuteronomy's buried nine wives
    And more—I am tempted to say, ninety-nine;
And his numerous progeny prospers and thrives
    And the village is proud of him in his decline.
At the sight of that placid and bland physiognomy,
10   When he sits in the sun on the vicarage wall,
The Oldest Inhabitant croaks: 'Well, of all . . .
    Things . . . Can it be . . . really! . . . No! . . . Yes! . . .
      Ho! hi!
      Oh, my eye!
15   My sight may be failing, but yet I confess
I *believe* it is Old Deuteronomy!'

Old Deuteronomy sits in the street,
    He sits in the High Street on market day;
The bullocks may bellow, the sheep they may bleat,
20   But the dogs and the herdsmen will turn them away.
The cars and the lorries run over the kerb,
    And the villagers put up a notice: ROAD CLOSED—
So that nothing untoward may chance to disturb
    Deuteronomy's rest when he feels so disposed
25   Or when he's engaged in domestic economy:
    And the Oldest Inhabitant croaks: 'Well, of all . . .
    Things . . . Can it be . . . really! . . . No! . . . Yes! . . .
      Ho! hi!
      Oh, my eye!

I'm deaf of an ear now, but yet I can guess   30
That the cause of the trouble is Old Deuteronomy!'

Old Deuteronomy lies on the floor
   Of the Fox and French Horn for his afternoon sleep;
And when the men say: 'There's just time for one more,'
   Then the landlady from her back parlour will peep   35
And say: 'Now then, out you go, by the back door,
   For Old Deuteronomy mustn't be woken—
I'll have the police if there's any uproar'—
   And out they all shuffle, without a word spoken.
The digestive repose of that feline's gastronomy   40
   Must never be broken, whatever befall:
And the Oldest Inhabitant croaks: 'Well, of all . . .
   Things . . . Can it be . . . really! . . . Yes! . . . No! . . .
     Ho! hi!
     Oh, my eye!   45
My legs may be tottery, I must go slow
And be careful of Old Deuteronomy!'

Of the Awefull Battle of the Pekes and the Pollicles
Together with some Account
of the Participation
of the Pugs and the Poms, and
the Intervention of the Great Rumpuscat

The Pekes and the Pollicles, everyone knows,
Are proud and implacable passionate foes;
It is always the same, wherever one goes.
And the Pugs and the Poms, although most people say

5   That they do not like fighting, will often display
Every symptom of wanting to join in the fray.
And they
         Bark bark bark bark
         Bark bark BARK BARK

10   Until you can hear them all over the Park.

Now on the occasion of which I shall speak
Almost nothing had happened for nearly a week
(And that's a long time for a Pol or a Peke).
The big Police Dog was away from his beat—

15   I don't know the reason, but most people think
He'd slipped into the Bricklayer's Arms for a drink—
And no one at all was about on the street
When a Peke and a Pollicle happened to meet.
They did not advance, or exactly retreat,

20   But they glared at each other, and scraped their hind feet,
And started to
         Bark bark bark bark
         Bark bark BARK BARK
         Until you could hear them all over the Park.

\>

Now the Peke, although people may say what they please,　　25
Is no British Dog, but a Heathen Chinese.
And so all the Pekes, when they heard the uproar,
Some came to the window, some came to the door;
There were surely a dozen, more likely a score.
And together they started to grumble and wheeze　　30
In their huffery-snuffery Heathen Chinese.
But a terrible din is what Pollicles like,
For your Pollicle Dog is a dour Yorkshire tyke,
And his braw Scottish cousins are snappers and biters,
And every dog-jack of them notable fighters;　　35
And so they stepped out, with their pipers in order,
Playing *When the Blue Bonnets Came Over the Border*.
Then the Pugs and the Poms held no longer aloof,
But some from the balcony, some from the roof,
Joined in　　40
To the din
With a
　　　　Bark bark bark bark
　　　　Bark bark BARK BARK
　　Until you can hear them all over the Park.　　45

Now when these bold heroes together assembled,
The traffic all stopped, and the Underground trembled,
And some of the neighbours were so much afraid
That they started to ring up the Fire Brigade.
When suddenly, up from a small basement flat,　　50
Why who should stalk out but the GREAT RUMPUSCAT.
His eyes were like fireballs fearfully blazing,
He gave a great yawn, and his jaws were amazing;
And when he looked out through the bars of the area,
You never saw anything fiercer or hairier.　　55
And what with the glare of his eyes and his yawning,
The Pekes and the Pollicles quickly took warning.

He looked at the sky and he gave a great leap—
And they every last one of them scattered like sheep.

60   *And when the Police Dog returned to his beat,*
      There wasn't a single one left in the street.

Mr. Mistoffelees

You ought to know Mr. Mistoffelees!
The Original Conjuring Cat—
(There can be no doubt about that).
Please listen to me and don't scoff. All his
Inventions are off his own bat.   5
There's no such Cat in the metropolis;
He holds all the patent monopolies
For performing surprising illusions
And creating eccentric confusions.
　　At prestidigitation   10
　　　　And at legerdemain
　　He'll defy examination
　　　　And deceive you again.
The greatest magicians have something to learn
From Mr. Mistoffelees' Conjuring Turn.   15
Presto!
　　Away we go!
　　　　And we all say: OH!
　　　　　Well I never!
　　　　　Was there ever   20
　　　　　A Cat so clever
　　　　　　As Magical Mr. Mistoffelees!

He is quiet and small, he is black
From his ears to the tip of his tail;
He can creep through the tiniest crack,   25
He can walk on the narrowest rail.
He can pick any card from a pack,
He is equally cunning with dice;
He is always deceiving you into believing
That he's only hunting for mice.   30

He can play any trick with a cork
    Or a spoon and a bit of fish-paste;
If you look for a knife or a fork
    And you think it is merely misplaced—
35   You have seen it one moment, and then it is *gawn!*
But you'll find it next week lying out on the lawn.
    And we all say: OH!
        Well I never!
        Was there ever
40   A Cat so clever
            As Magical Mr. Mistoffelees!

His manner is vague and aloof,
You would think there was nobody shyer—
But his voice has been heard on the roof
45   When he was curled up by the fire.
And he's sometimes been heard by the fire
When he was about on the roof—
(At least we all *heard* somebody who purred)
Which is incontestable proof
50   Of his singular magical powers:
    And I have known the family to call
Him in from the garden for hours,
    While he was asleep in the hall.
And not long ago this phenomenal Cat
55   Produced *seven kittens* right out of a hat!
    And we all said: OH!
        Well I never!
        Did you ever
        Know a Cat so clever
60   As Magical Mr. Mistoffelees!

Macavity: The Mystery Cat

Macavity's a Mystery Cat: he's called the Hidden Paw—
For he's the master criminal who can defy the Law.
He's the bafflement of Scotland Yard, the Flying Squad's despair:
For when they reach the scene of crime—*Macavity's not there!*

Macavity, Macavity, there's no one like Macavity,   5
He's broken every human law, he breaks the law of gravity.
His powers of levitation would make a fakir stare,
And when you reach the scene of crime—*Macavity's not there!*
You may seek him in the basement, you may look up in the air—
But I tell you once and once again, *Macavity's not there!*   10

Macavity's a ginger cat, he's very tall and thin;
You would know him if you saw him, for his eyes are sunken in.
His brow is deeply lined with thought, his head is highly domed;
His coat is dusty from neglect, his whiskers are uncombed.
He sways his head from side to side, with movements like a snake;   15
And when you think he's half asleep, he's always wide awake.

Macavity, Macavity, there's no one like Macavity,
For he's a fiend in feline shape, a monster of depravity.
You may meet him in a by-street, you may see him in the square—
But when a crime's discovered, then *Macavity's not there!*   20

He's outwardly respectable. (They say he cheats at cards.)
And his footprints are not found in any file of Scotland Yard's.
And when the larder's looted, or the jewel-case is rifled,
Or when the milk is missing, or another Peke's been stifled,
Or the greenhouse glass is broken, and the trellis past repair—   25
Ay, there's the wonder of the thing! *Macavity's not there!*

<

And when the Foreign Office find a Treaty's gone astray,
Or the Admiralty lose some plans and drawings by the way,
There may be a scrap of paper in the hall or on the stair—
30   But it's useless to investigate—*Macavity's not there!*
And when the loss has been disclosed, the Secret Service say:
'It *must* have been Macavity!'—but he's a mile away.
You'll be sure to find him resting, or a-licking of his thumbs,
Or engaged in doing complicated long division sums.

35   Macavity, Macavity, there's no one like Macavity,
There never was a Cat of such deceitfulness and suavity.
He always has an alibi, and one or two to spare:
At whatever time the deed took place—MACAVITY WASN'T
     THERE!
And they say that all the Cats whose wicked deeds are widely
     known
40   (I might mention Mungojerrie, I might mention Griddlebone)
Are nothing more than agents for the Cat who all the time
Just controls their operations: the Napoleon of Crime!

Gus: The Theatre Cat

Gus is the Cat at the Theatre Door.
His name, as I ought to have told you before,
Is really Asparagus. That's such a fuss
To pronounce, that we usually call him just Gus.
His coat's very shabby, he's thin as a rake,   5
And he suffers from palsy that makes his paw shake.
Yet he was, in his youth, quite the smartest of Cats—
But no longer a terror to mice and to rats.
For he isn't the Cat that he was in his prime;
Though his name was quite famous, he says, in its time.   10
And whenever he joins his friends at their club
(Which takes place at the back of the neighbouring pub)
He loves to regale them, if someone else pays,
With anecdotes drawn from his palmiest days.
For he once was a Star of the highest degree—   15
He has acted with Irving, he's acted with Tree.
And he likes to relate his success on the Halls,
Where the Gallery once gave him seven cat-calls.
But his grandest creation, as he loves to tell,
Was Firefrorefiddle, the Fiend of the Fell.   20

'I have played', so he says, 'every possible part,
And I used to know seventy speeches by heart.
I'd extemporize back-chat, I knew how to gag,
And I knew how to let the cat out of the bag.
I knew how to act with my back and my tail;   25
With an hour of rehearsal, I never could fail.
I'd a voice that would soften the hardest of hearts,
Whether I took the lead, or in character parts.
I have sat by the bedside of poor Little Nell;
When the Curfew was rung, then I swung on the bell.   30

In the Pantomime season I never fell flat,
And I once understudied Dick Whittington's Cat.
But my grandest creation, as history will tell,
Was Firefrorefiddle, the Fiend of the Fell.'

35   Then, if someone will give him a toothful of gin,
He will tell how he once played a part in *East Lynne*.
At a Shakespeare performance he once walked on pat,
When some actor suggested the need for a cat.
He once played a Tiger—could do it again—
40   Which an Indian Colonel pursued down a drain.
And he thinks that he still can, much better than most,
Produce blood-curdling noises to bring on the Ghost.
And he once crossed the stage on a telegraph wire,
To rescue a child when a house was on fire.
45   And he says: 'Now, these kittens, they do not get trained
As we did in the days when Victoria reigned.
They never get drilled in a regular troupe,
And they think they are smart, just to jump through a hoop.'
And he'll say, as he scratches himself with his claws,
50   'Well, the Theatre's certainly not what it was.
These modern productions are all very well,
But there's nothing to equal, from what I hear tell,
     That moment of mystery
     When I made history
55   As Firefrorefiddle, the Fiend of the Fell.'

Bustopher Jones: The Cat about Town

Bustopher Jones is *not* skin and bones—
In fact, he's remarkably fat.
He doesn't haunt pubs—he has eight or nine clubs,
For he's the St. James's Street Cat!
He's the Cat we all greet as he walks down the street   5
In his coat of fastidious black:
No commonplace mousers have such well-cut trousers
Or such an impeccable back.
In the whole of St. James's the smartest of names is
The name of this Brummell of Cats;   10
And we're all of us proud to be nodded or bowed to
By Bustopher Jones in white spats!

His visits are occasional to the *Senior Educational*
And it is against the rules
For any one Cat to belong both to that   15
And the *Joint Superior Schools.*
For a similar reason, when game is in season
He is found, not at *Fox's,* but *Blimp's;*
But he's frequently seen at the gay *Stage and Screen*
Which is famous for winkles and shrimps.   20
In the season of venison he gives his ben'son
To the *Pothunter's* succulent bones;
And just before noon's not a moment too soon
To drop in for a drink at the *Drones.*
When he's seen in a hurry there's probably curry   25
At the *Siamese*—or at the *Glutton;*
If he looks full of gloom then he's lunched at the *Tomb*
On cabbage, rice pudding and mutton.

<

So, much in this way, passes Bustopher's day—
30   At one club or another he's found.
It can cause no surprise that under our eyes
He has grown unmistakably round.
He's a twenty-five pounder, or I am a bounder,
And he's putting on weight every day:
35   But he's so well preserved because he's observed
All his life a routine, so he'll say.
And (to put it in rhyme) 'I shall last out my time'
Is the word of this stoutest of Cats.
It must and it shall be Spring in Pall Mall
40   While Bustopher Jones wears white spats!

Skimbleshanks: The Railway Cat

There's a whisper down the line at 11.39
When the Night Mail's ready to depart,
Saying 'Skimble where is Skimble has he gone to hunt the
    thimble?
We must find him or the train can't start.'
All the guards and all the porters and the stationmaster's
    daughters   5
They are searching high and low,
Saying 'Skimble where is Skimble for unless he's very nimble
Then the Night Mail just can't go.'
At 11.42 then the signal's nearly due
And the passengers are frantic to a man—   10
Then Skimble will appear and he'll saunter to the rear:
He's been busy in the luggage van!
      He gives one flash of his glass-green eyes
         And the signal goes 'All Clear!'
      And we're off at last for the northern part   15
         Of the Northern Hemisphere!

You may say that by and large it is Skimble who's in charge
Of the Sleeping Car Express.
From the driver and the guards to the bagmen playing cards
He will supervise them all, more or less.   20
Down the corridor he paces and examines all the faces
Of the travellers in the First and in the Third;
He establishes control by a regular patrol
And he'd know at once if anything occurred.
He will watch you without winking and he sees what you are
    thinking   25
And it's certain that he doesn't approve
Of hilarity and riot, so the folk are very quiet
When Skimble is about and on the move.

You can play no pranks with Skimbleshanks!
30   He's a Cat that cannot be ignored;
So nothing goes wrong on the Northern Mail
When Skimbleshanks is aboard.

Oh it's very pleasant when you have found your little den
With your name written up on the door.
35   And the berth is very neat with a newly folded sheet
And there's not a speck of dust on the floor.
There is every sort of light—you can make it dark or bright;
There's a button that you turn to make a breeze.
There's a funny little basin you're supposed to wash your face in
40   And a crank to shut the window if you sneeze.
Then the guard looks in politely and will ask you very brightly
'Do you like your morning tea weak or strong?'
But Skimble's just behind him and was ready to remind him,
For Skimble won't let anything go wrong.
45   And when you creep into your cosy berth
And pull up the counterpane,
You are bound to admit that it's very nice
To know that you won't be bothered by mice—
You can leave all that to the Railway Cat,
50   The Cat of the Railway Train!

In the middle of the night he is always fresh and bright;
Every now and then he has a cup of tea
With perhaps a drop of Scotch while he's keeping on the watch,
Only stopping here and there to catch a flea.
55   You were fast asleep at Crewe and so you never knew
That he was walking up and down the station;
You were sleeping all the while he was busy at Carlisle,
Where he greets the stationmaster with elation.
But you saw him at Dumfries, where he summons the police
60   If there's anything they ought to know about:

When you get to Gallowgate there you do not have to wait—
For Skimbleshanks will help you to get out!
    He gives you a wave of his long brown tail
      Which says: 'I'll see you again!
    You'll meet without fail on the Midnight Mail   65
      The Cat of the Railway Train.'

The Ad-dressing of Cats

You've read of several kinds of Cat,
And my opinion now is that
You should need no interpreter
To understand their character.
You now have learned enough to see
That Cats are much like you and me
And other people whom we find
Possessed of various types of mind.
For some are sane and some are mad
And some are good and some are bad
And some are better, some are worse—
But all may be described in verse.
You've seen them both at work and games,
And learnt about their proper names,
Their habits and their habitat:
But
     How would you ad-dress a Cat?

So first, your memory I'll jog,
And say: A CAT IS NOT A DOG.

Now Dogs pretend they like to fight;
They often bark, more seldom bite;
But yet a Dog is, on the whole,
What you would call a simple soul.
Of course I'm not including Pekes,
And such fantastic canine freaks.
The usual Dog about the Town
Is much inclined to play the clown,
And far from showing too much pride
Is frequently undignified.

He's very easily taken in—   30
Just chuck him underneath the chin
Or slap his back or shake his paw,
And he will gambol and guffaw.
He's such an easy-going lout,
He'll answer any hail or shout.   35

Again I must remind you that
A Dog's a Dog—A CAT'S A CAT.

With Cats, some say, one rule is true:
Don't speak till you are spoken to.
Myself, I do not hold with that—   40
I say, you should ad-dress a Cat.
But always keep in mind that he
Resents familiarity.
I bow, and taking off my hat,
Ad-dress him in this form: O CAT!   45
But if he is the Cat next door,
Whom I have often met before
(He comes to see me in my flat)
I greet him with an OOPSA CAT!
I've heard them call him James Buz-James—   50
But we've not got so far as names.
Before a Cat will condescend
To treat you as a trusted friend,
Some little token of esteem
Is needed, like a dish of cream;   55
And you might now and then supply
Some caviare, or Strassburg Pie,
Some potted grouse, or salmon paste—
He's sure to have his personal taste.
(I know a Cat, who makes a habit   60
Of eating nothing else but rabbit,

And when he's finished, licks his paws
So's not to waste the onion sauce.)
A Cat's entitled to expect
These evidences of respect.
And so in time you reach your aim,
And finally call him by his NAME.

So this is this, and that is that:
And there's how you AD-DRESS A CAT.

65

Cat Morgan Introduces Himself

I once was a Pirate what sailed the 'igh seas—
    But now I've retired as a com-mission-aire:
And that's how you find me a-takin' my ease
    And keepin' the door in a Bloomsbury Square.

I'm partial to partridges, likewise to grouse,   5
    And I favour that Devonshire cream in a bowl;
But I'm allus content with a drink on the 'ouse
    And a bit o' cold fish when I done me patrol.

I ain't got much polish, me manners is gruff,
    But I've got a good coat, and I keep meself smart;   10
And everyone says, and I guess that's enough:
    'You can't but like Morgan, 'e's got a kind 'art.'

I got knocked about on the Barbary Coast,
    And me voice it ain't no sich melliferous horgan;
But yet I can state, and I'm not one to boast,   15
    That some of the gals is dead keen on old Morgan.

So if you 'ave business with Faber—or Faber—
    I'll give you this tip, and it's worth a lot more:
You'll save yourself time, and you'll spare yourself labour
    If jist you make friends with the Cat at the door.   20

MORGAN.

Old Possum's Book of Practical Cats: Commentary

1. Possum   2. *Old Possum's Book of Practical Cats*   3. Composition
4. Broadcasts   5. Publication   6. With and Without Illustrations
7. TSE's Recording   8. Apropos of *Practical Cats* by Valerie Eliot

1. POSSUM

OED: "To play possum: to feign, dissemble; to pretend illness: in allusion to the opossum's habit of feigning death when threatened or attacked · · · (orig. *U.S.*)", from 1822. (L. *possum* = I am able to.)

Writing to Father Martingale on 30 Jan 1930, TSE claimed to have been "nourished in my childhood on the Natural History of the Revd. Mr. Wood". Wood published many such books for different readerships. *The Illustrated Natural History* (2 vols, 1872) on the Opossum:

> It is a voracious and destructive animal, prowling about during the hours of darkness, and prying into every nook and corner · · · Although it is such an adept at "'possuming," or feigning death, it does not put this ruse into practice until it has used every endeavour to elude its pursuers, and finds that it has no possibility of escape. It runs sulkily and sneakingly forward, looking on every side for some convenient shelter, and seizing the first opportunity of slipping under cover · · · there are none so prone to entangle themselves in difficulties as the over-artful. They must needs travel through crooked byeways, instead of following the open road, and so blunder themselves stupidly and sinuously into needless peril, from which their craftiness sometimes extricates them, it is true, but not without much anxiety and apprehension. When captured it is easily tamed, and falls into the habit of domestication with great ease. It is, however, not very agreeable as a domestic companion, as it is gifted with a powerful and very unpleasant odour.

TSE to Pound, 19 July 1922, while planning the *Criterion*: "I have decided not to put any manifestoe in the 1st number, but adopt a protective colour for a time until suspicion is lulled. What do you think of 'The Possum' for a title?" In 1928: "I have made bold to unite these occasional essays · · · to refute any accusation of playing 'possum. The general point of view may be described as classicist in literature, royalist in politics, and anglo-catholic in religion", *For Lancelot Andrewes*, Preface. A letter to Dorothy Pound dated 11 Aug [1925] is perhaps the earliest to be signed "Possum", which was the signature also to TSE's letter in *NEW* 14 June 1934, headed *The Use of Poetry* and ending "I am going to set round the chimbly and have a chaw terbacker with Miss Meadows and the gals; and then I am going away for a 4tnight where that old Rabbit can't reach me with his letters nor even with his post cards. I am, dear Sir, Your outraged, POSSUM". "I confess that I cannot see why we should take such pains to produce a race of men, millennia hence, who will only look down upon *us* as apes, lemurs or opossums", *Literature and the Modern World* (1935).

Levy 29 reports TSE as saying "It was Ezra Pound, you know, who dubbed me 'Old Possum'." TSE: "'Possum' is a nickname given me by Ezra Pound with reference to Brere Possum in *The Stories of Uncle Remus*" (by Joel Chandler Harris), *Northrop Frye corrigenda* (1963). The Uncle Remus stories were adapted for the stage as *Brer Rabbit* by Mabel Dearmer, with music by Martin Shaw (who later composed the music for *The*

Rock), and performed at the Little Theatre in 1914 and again in Liverpool in 1915–16 (Shaw archive). TSE of Booker T. Washington: "an interview from Booker T. | Entitled 'Up from Possum Stew!' | Or 'How I set the nigger free!'", *Ballade pour la grosse Lulu* 10–12. To Polly Tandy, 23 Dec 1941: "I read Uncle Remus aloud here: a bit rusty with the lingo I am, but it sounds allright to those who have never heard the real thing." In addition to Old Possum, other forms appear in letters and inscriptions, such as "T. P." (Tom Possum) and the punning "O. Possum".

After *Practical Cats*, TSE used Old Possum again for a series of plates, in the manner of Edward Lear's Nonsense Botany (Faber archive). TSE sent these to Geoffrey and Enid Faber, in an envelope of 12 Feb 1940 marked "ORDER YOUR SPRING PLANTS NOW. See Inside", and another addressed to "Mrs. Faber, | The Herbaceous Border". The first six spoof botanical plates, drawn by him in ink and with elaborate descriptions, were headed "OLD POSSUM'S BOOK OF 'Flowers shown to the Children'", and the last two, drawn and watercoloured by TSE, were of "OLD POSSUM'S 'CHILDREN SHOWN TO THE FLOWERS' (including "Plate 1. Possum Pie").

2. *OLD POSSUM'S BOOK OF PRACTICAL CATS*

Old Moore's Almanac (1700–), a book of astrological prophecies, was an established annual bestseller. Practical guides, another publishing stalwart, included *Audels Handy Book of Practical Electricity* (1924), and pet books included *A Practical Guide on the Diseases, Care and Treatment of the Angora Cat* (1899).

TSE's *Practical* may invoke the earliest recorded sense: OED II 5: "That practises art or craft; crafty, scheming, artful. *Obs.*" with sole example from 1570. TSE's *The Columbiad* st. 48 begins "King Bolo's big black bastard Kween | (That practickle Bacchante)". See TSE to Tom Faber, 7 May 1931, in headnote to *The Practical Cat*. To Pound, 12 Feb [1935], declining to start a libel case: "you aint Practical · · · Old Ike Carver of Mosquito Cove was Practical · · · Podesta again you aint Practical." 22 Dec 1936, referring to Buddhist scriptures: "remember what is stated in the Digha Nikaya: that the Practical Cat (Dirghakarna) has no Theories".
    When the BBC was planning a broadcast of poems by TSE for Christmas 1937, TSE wrote to Ian Cox, 30 Nov: "Very well: I agree with you that it would be best to confine yourselves to cats for the Christmas programme · · · I suggest that the heading had better be *Practical Cats*, as that term is much more comprehensive than *Jellicle* · · · I must also demand a fee from the BBC for the reading, and I am likely to ask more for unpublished poems than I should for poems previously published." (Five poems were broadcast, but in reply to a request from J. R. Ackerley of the *Listener*, TSE wrote, 13 Dec: "I am sorry to appear ungracious, but I really would prefer that none of the Cat poems should be published until I am able to make a book of them. It seems to me that one by itself looks rather silly, whereas a number together might, I hope, appear to have some reason for existence.") To Pound, "Childermass 1937": "Best wishes for the New Year from [*signed*] TP | Ole Possum & his Performin Practical Cats".
    On 30 Oct 1937, TSE sent Geoffrey Faber an immensely elaborate "Provisional Order of Proceedings for Mr. & Mrs. Faber's 20th Anniversary", which began and ended with salvos of 20 giant crackers, and included: "9.30am: Arrival of Old Possums Gift: two duralumin wheel chairs, fitted with trafficators etc" and "1.00 LUNCH: Lobster,

champagne, cheese (20 yrs. old) and practical jokes." The crackers were a memory of a boardroom practical joke, which TSE had relayed to Hayward on 19 Sept 1935: "We can confidently recommend the new giant crackers on sale at Hamley's at prices ranging from eighteen pence to half-a-crown. One of these petards was hoisted at Messrs. Faber & Faber's Book Committee yesterday, on the occasion of the return of the Chairman from the grouse moors. While the attention of the Committee was distracted, at the tea interval, by the presentation of a large chocolate cake bearing an inscription WELCOME, CHIEF!, the cracker was produced from under the table and successfully fired. It exploded with a loud report, and scattered about the room multi-coloured festoons, some of which draped themselves on the chandelier, others on the head of the Chairman. At this point another novelty, called 'Snake-in-the-grass', was introduced: one of them escaped and set fire to the festoons. After the conflagration had been extinguished the business of the committee was resumed, and an enjoyable time was had by all." Writing to Hayward on 2 Jan 1936, TSE mentioned exploding cigarettes. (The Chairman was "genially tolerant of the practical jokes and horse play with which some of us, in the early days, would occasionally disorganise the meeting", *Geoffrey Faber 1889–1961* 17–18.) Thanking Enid Faber, 14 Sept 1938, for a holiday spent in Wales, TSE wrote: "And it is most pleasant to think that we are to meet again for the evening of Monday the 19th and Harold Lloyd, so I hope nothing will go wrong meanwhile, and so I will close." (Harold Lloyd's new comedy film was *Professor Beware*.)

W. H. Auden: "In Eliot the critic, as in Eliot the man, there is a lot, to be sure, of a conscientious church-warden, but there was also a twelve-year-old boy, who likes to surprise over-solemn wigs by offering them explosive cigars, or cushions which fart when sat upon. It is this practical joker who suddenly interrupts the church-warden to remark that Milton or Goethe are no good", *T. S. Eliot, O.M.: A Tribute* in *Listener* 7 Jan 1965.

TSE's four godchildren were: Tom Faber (b. 1927), Alison Tandy (b. 1930), Susanna Morley (b. 1932) and Adam Roberts (b. 1940); see note to Preface. For TSE's understanding of his responsibilities, see letter to K. de B. Codrington, 18 Sept 1934.

In 1940, Polly Tandy, wife of the museum curator and broadcaster Geoffrey Tandy, was considering whether to evacuate their children Richard and Alison to America. TSE wrote to her, 3 July 1940 (opening as though a BBC broadcast): "This is Possum speaking · · · A line in haste, to say that if you and Geoffrey should change your minds, I have relatives in America who wish, and others who ought to be made to, take British children. *I* can't advise, and I don't think I ought to take that responsibility anyhow · · · but if you DID decide that America was the best place, I would keep the cables hot telegraphing about it."

3. COMPOSITION

"Lear and Carroll wrote for children, but for particular friends of theirs. Children like their works, but this is only incidental; our adult enjoyment is what really matters", *Mr. Eliot Sets his Audience Puzzle in Lecture* (1933).

Acknowledging his brother's detective novel *The Rumble Murders* (1932), TSE wrote, 3 May: "I am quite sure that I could never write a detective story myself; my only possible resource for adding to my income would be to write children's verses or stories, having had a little success in writing letters to children (and illustrating them of course)."

To Virginia Woolf, 16 Aug 1933, after his lecture tour in the US: "I have since my return [from America] been living quietly in the country, playing Patience, observing the habits of finches and wagtails, composing nonsense verse." This followed the publication of *Five-Finger Exercises* in January, and may refer to the beginnings of *Practical Cats*.

To Aurelia Hodgson, 25 Mar 1934, sending the lyric "When I was a lad what had almost no sense" from *The Rock* (67–68): "I have been working very hard · · · and have been writing no end of verses not poetry for a Paggeant which is to be produced in June · · · When this is done I have a Nonsense Book which I have been working on by fits and starts." To Parker Tyler, Galleon Press, NY, 5 Apr 1934: "I have literally nothing to show, by which I should care to be judged, that is to say, I have only a few scraps of more or less humorous verse of no interest as poetry." On 2 Feb 1936 he told his Aunt Susie that he had "a speech and two essays to write, and to prepare my book of nonsense verse", but sending his *Collected Poems 1909–1935* to John Cournos, 8 Apr, he wrote: "As for the nonsense poems, I fear that those are indefinitely postponed."

The earliest appearance of cats in his writing had been in *Fireside* No. 4, where a page is devoted to the headline "FAT QUAKER CATS" and a comic drawing of a cat. After their father's death, TSE wrote to his brother Henry, 29 Feb 1919: "I find that I think more of his own youthful possibilities that never came to anything: and yet with a great deal of satisfaction; his old-fashioned scholarship! his flute-playing, his drawing. Two of the Cats that I have seem to me quite remarkable."

Before and after the publication of *Practical Cats*, the creatures and these poems were a recurrent topic in TSE's correspondence with the Tandys. To Polly Tandy, 4 Nov 1934: "So far in my experience there are cheifly 4 kinds of Cat the Old Gumbie Cat the Practical Cat the Porpentine Cat and the Big Bravo Cat; I suspect that yours is a Bravo Cat by the look of things." 9 Dec 1936: "When a Cat adopts you, and I am not superstitious at all I don't mean only Black cats there is nothing to be done about it except to put up with it and wait until the wind changes." (See headnote to *The Practical Cat*.) To Enid Faber, 16 Aug 1937: "My black cat (Tumblecat) has turned up again: he really belongs next door." Postcard to Geoffrey Tandy, 2 Aug 1938:

> ?????I waited for you till 6.20??????
> ??????????at Gordon's????????????
> ??????????and you did not come???
> ??????????and, for the matter of that
> ??????What is a Tantamile Cat?????
>   tp.

For "Tantomile" as a name for a witch's cat, see Valerie Eliot in 8. APROPOS OF PRACTICAL CATS (below). TSE to Polly Tandy, 12 Sept 1949: "our housekeeper being in the hospital · · · now we have her cat on our hands which is I am sorry to say a Tantamile Cat if ever there was one".

In June 1935, TSE listed among "all I can bother with" of his publications, "*Pollicle Dogs and Jellicle Cats* (unfinished at this time)", *Harvard College Class of 1910, Seventh Report* (1935). The Faber catalogue for Spring 1936 then listed for publication:

Mr. Eliot's Book of Pollicle Dogs and Jellicle Cats as Recited to Him by the Man in White Spats:

> Mr. Eliot informs the Publishers that his book of Children's Verses should be completed by Easter, 1936. If this statement (for which the Publishers accept no responsibility) proves to be true, the book will certainly be published this year with the least possible delay. There is no doubt that Mr. Eliot is writing it; for several of the poems, illustrated by the author, have been in private circulation in the Publishers' various families for a considerable time, and at least one of them has been recorded on the gramophone. (*N.B.*—There is only one record in this country, and there is believed to be another in America. Applications for duplicates will be thrown into the wastepaper basket.) Mr. Eliot intends to illustrate the book himself; but it is not yet possible to be sure that reproduction of the illustrations will be within the scope of any existing process. No announcement can, therefore, be made about the price of this book, but every endeavour will be made to keep it within reason.
>
> (*Gallup* E6b)

The recording was of TSE's INVITATION TO ALL POLLICLE DOGS & JELLICLE CATS TO COME TO THE BIRTHDAY OF THOMAS FABER from 1931 (see "Other Verses"). It survives on a cylinder at the British Library.

On 6 Mar 1936, TSE sent *Pollicle Dogs and Jellicle Cats* to Geoffrey Faber, along with a typed memorandum "(Take your time over it)" and (separately) three pencil sketches:

> I am more and more doubtful of my ability to write a successful book of this kind, and I had rather find out early that I can't do it, than waste a lot of time for nothing. And this sort of thing is flatter if it *is* flat, than serious verse [*addition*: can be]. Nobody wants to make a fool of himself when he might be better employed.
>
> I append the *introductory verses* and three rough sketches. I should have to do them much larger to get in any refinement of expression, and naturally I can't draw difficult things like stools in a hurry. The idea of the volume was to have different poems on appropriate subjects, such as you already know, recited by the Man in White Spats. They would be of course in a variety of metres and stanzas, *not* that of the narrative which connects them. After this opening there would only be *short* passages or interludes between the Man in White Spats and myself. At the end they all go up in a balloon, self, Spats, and dogs and cats.
>
> > "Up up up past the Russell Hotel,
> > Up up up to the Heaviside Layer."
>
> There are several ways in which this might be a failure. The various Poems (how many should there be?) might not be good enough. The matter such as here attached may be not at all amusing: a book simply of collected animal poems might be better. Finally, the contents and general treatment may be too mixed: there might be a part that children wouldn't like and part that adults wouldn't like and part that nobody would like. The *mise-en-scène* may not please. There seem to be many more ways of going wrong than of going right.

The Heaviside layer is an ionized layer in the upper atmosphere able to reflect long radio waves (OED). William Empson: "Their arch of promise the wide Heaviside layer | They rise above a vault into the air", *Doctrinal Point* (in *Poems*, 1935). TSE: "What ambush lies beyond the heather | And behind the Standing Stones? | Beyond the Heaviside Layer | And behind the smiling moon?", *The Family Reunion* II iii (*Raine* 98). When TSE spoke on Yeats at Harvard in March 1933, *The Cat and the*

Moon (about "Black Minnaloushe") was among the poems he discussed. For "Jellicle Moon" see note to *Song of the Jellicles* 28.

To Enid Faber, 21 Feb 1938: "When I have cleared up these Cats (labouring over two more, but I fear the vein is exhausted) I shall be able to turn my mind to the great Sherlock Holmes play."

To Christina Morley, 7 Apr 1938: "Miss Evans has plenty to do, because she is typing out my Complete Cats, which will presently be offered to Faber & Faber."

To Mrs. F. M. McNeille, 31 Jan 1939: "at the present moment I cannot help you by providing you with a text of the poems you mention. I fear that it will be impossible to submit these to the criticism of tutorial classes until they have been published, which I hope may be in the autumn. At the moment, the Pollicle Dogs have been suppressed, and the Jellicle Cats are in the melting pot; and until they have assumed their final shape after this ordeal, I fear that they must remain in seclusion."

Some of the Possum poems appear to have been written concurrently. The earliest certain indication of each appears below, some from dates of posting. Those with asterisks do not appear in *Old Possum's Book of Practical Cats*, but can be found in the present edition in "Uncollected Poems". See also *Cat's Prologue* [Apr?] 1934 in "Other Verses".

7 Jan 1936	*The Naming of Cats*	to Tom Faber
6 Mar 1936	*Pollicle Dogs and Jellicle Cats* *	to Geoffrey Faber
before 10 Nov 1936	*The Old Gumbie Cat*	to Alison Tandy
20 Nov 1936	*The Marching Song of the Pollicle Dogs* *	to Polly Tandy (mentioned)
21 Nov 1936	*Growltiger's Last Stand*	to Bonamy Dobrée (mentioned)
6 Jan 1937	*The Rum Tum Tugger*	to Alison Tandy
25 Jan 1937	*The Song of the Jellicles*	to John Hayward
12 Sept 1937	*How to Pick a Possum* *	to Alison Tandy
21 Oct 1937	*Mungojerrie and Rumpelteazer*	to Alison Tandy
15 Nov 1937	*Old Deuteronomy*	to Enid Faber & Alison Tandy
15 Nov 1937	*The Practical Cat* *	to Alison Tandy
[uncertain]	*The Awefull Battle of the Pekes and the Pollicles*	to Tandy family
[uncertain]	*Mister Mistoffelees*	to Tandy family
8 Dec 1937	*Macavity: The Mystery Cat*	to Geoffrey Tandy (BBC)
8 Dec 1937	*Skimbleshanks: The Railway Cat*	to Geoffrey Tandy
8 Dec 1937	*The Ad-dressing of Cats*	to Geoffrey Tandy
6 Feb 1938	*Gus: The Theatre Cat*	to Enid Faber
28 Feb 1938	*Bustopher Jones: The Cat about Town*	to Enid Faber
[uncertain]	*Billy M'Caw: The Remarkable Parrot* *	to Tandy family
30 Oct 1944	*Cat Morgan Introduces Himself*	to Mary Trevelyan (quoted)

In conversation with Donald Hall, *Paris Review* (1959):

> INTERVIEWER: Do you write anything now in the vein of *Old Possum's Book of Practical Cats* or *King Bolo*?

ELIOT: Those things do come from time to time! I keep a few notes of such verse, and there are one or two incomplete cats that probably will never be written. There's one about a glamour cat. It turned out too sad. This would never do. I can't make my children weep over a cat who's gone wrong. She had a very questionable career, did this cat. It wouldn't do for the audience of my previous volume of cats. I've never done any dogs. Of course dogs don't seem to lend themselves to verse quite so well, collectively, as cats. I may eventually do an enlarged edition of my cats. That's more likely than another volume. I did add one poem, which was originally done as an advertisement for Faber and Faber [*Cat Morgan Introduces Himself*]. It seemed to be fairly successful. Oh, yes, one wants to keep one's hand in, you know, in every type of poem, serious and frivolous and proper and improper. One doesn't want to lose one's skill.

Pollicle Dogs was a corruption, in the style of Edward Lear, of "poor little dogs". Jellicle Cats, a corruption of "dear little cats". W. S. Gilbert: "White Cat · · · sly ickle · · · White Cat", *The Precocious Baby* in *Bab Ballads*. (In *Prairie Schooner* Spring 1960, "Felix Clowder" quizzed "Jellicle" as "either a deliberately sly shortening of *Evangelical* or an accurate rendition of middle-class speech"; in *the Review* Nov 1962, John Fuller suggested *angelical*.) TSE addressed letters to Polly Tandy as "Dear Pollicle ma'am" or simply "Dear Pollicle". At Christmas 1937, he suggested to her a labrador puppy as a possible Christmas present for the children. The epithet came to mean "dog", as when TSE wrote to Alison Tandy, 20 Dec 1940 about the household where he was lodging for Christmas: "There are also two dogs · · · There is also a small pollicle which is Australian, and another pollicle is expected by post from Devon." Similarly, "Tantamile" was first a kind of Cat, then (as "Tantomile") a name for a witch's cat. "Morgan" may have become a generic name for staff (see headnote to *Cat Morgan Introduces Himself*). In the letters to Bonamy Dobrée containing Improper Rhymes, "Wux" is a name, a prefix, a version of "worse" and an indeterminate part of speech with indeterminate meaning. See note to *East Coker* II 41, "grimpen".

4. BROADCASTS

Nearly two years before publication in book form, five of the *Practical Cats* were broadcast by the BBC at Christmas ("Regional: Saturday, 25th December, 1937: 2.30–2.45 p.m"). *Radio Times* 17 Dec: "*Practical Cats*. For some time past Mr. Eliot has been amusing and instructing the offspring of some of his friends in verse on the subject of cats. These poems are not of the kind that have been usually associated with his name, and they have not yet been published. With his permission, some of them have been arranged into a programme, and they will be read by Geoffrey Tandy." (TSE to Hamilton Marr of the BBC, 6 Dec: "I wish this fee of 10 guineas to be added to the payment to Mr. Geoffrey Tandy for reading the poems, and not to be sent to me.") TSE may have been reluctant to read these poems himself, although he had often broadcast on the BBC (see Michael Coyle's *T. S. Eliot's Radio Broadcasts, 1929–63: A Chronological Checklist* in *T. S. Eliot and Our Turning World*, ed. Jewel Spears Brooker, 2001). Asked to select from Vaughan, Herbert and Crashaw for broadcasting, TSE wrote to George Barnes, 14 Aug 1936: "The difficulty of suiting the poems to the time is the greatest, because another reader might read one or another poem, or all the poems, more quickly or more slowly than I should read them myself. I know from experience that a considerable variation in the matter of time is possible. The B.B.C. people ought to know by now what my voice is like, and I have been given to understand that they do not like it. In any case I am not going to undergo another voice test."

The broadcast was a great success. Tandy to TSE, 23 Jan 1938: "I hope you've been properly informed of the repeat performance of *Practical Cats* on Saturday next." TSE to Ezra Pound, 28 Jan: "you bein a radio fan must keep your ear open for *Ole Possum's Popular Lectures on Cats* in the *Childrens Hour*." To Henry Eliot, 17 Feb: "There is to be a broadcast of some more Cats, London Regional on April 7th at 9.30 p.m. Greenwich time, for anybody who has a radio set that will take it" (this too was a repeat).

On 25 June 1938 a 20-minute programme of *Cats Mostly Practical* was broadcast by Tandy (for Bret Harte, *The Heathen Chinee and Other Poems Mostly Humorous*, see note to *Of the Awefull Battle of the Pekes and the Pollicles* 25–26). *Radio Times* 17 June: "On Christmas Day and at the end of April and May were broadcast selections from a series of poems on cats which T. S. Eliot has written for the amusement and instruction of his friends' children. These poems proved such excellent broadcasting material and were so well received that another selection is to be broadcast of poems of a kind not usually associated with the name of their author. They have not yet been published." A third broadcast of *Pollicles and Jellicles: Tales of Cats and Dogs in Verse* followed on 7 Oct 1939. (To Ian Cox, 18 Feb: "your new programme might have the original title of *Pollicle Dogs and Jellicle Cats*, as you have put both of them in. How does that strike you?") *Radio Times* 29 Sept 1939: "Before Christmas Day 1937, when the first selection was broadcast, nobody would have associated a set of cheery, yet at the same time profound, verses on the subjects of dogs and cats with the name of T. S. Eliot. Nevertheless the author of *The Waste Land* has written such verses, originally for the amusement of his friends' children. The great war between the Pollicle Dogs and the Jellicle Cats is a hilarious epic, and makes ideal broadcasting from the lips of Geoffrey Tandy, whom T. S. Eliot selected to read these poems in the past."

Although they are secretarial copies, Tandy's scripts represent the form of the poems as first made public (see Textual History). The earliest batch has before the poems a page of scribbled notes (possibly in TSE's hand):

1. Now to begin with it's very important to understand about *The Naming of Cats*.
2. Most cats are practical, which is why we have chosen this title; but you might [*omission*] to know first what it means for a cat to be practical.
3. Some cats are more practical than others, and they are practical in different ways. Now I'm going to tell you about three kinds of cat.
    The first is the Bravo Cat; and I'll tell you the history of one Bravo Cat, who[se] name was Growltiger [*poems*].

5. PUBLICATION

With a covering letter signed "Faithfully yours, O. Possum" (King's), TSE submitted his typescript to Faber & Faber on 18 Apr 1938.

OLD POSSUM'S BOOK OF
PRACTICAL CATS
with pixtures supplied by
The Man in White Spats

consists of the first 11 poems in the book, along with "early drafts of two poems, & unpublished material, including Old Possum's Letter to the Publishers and his parodies of readers' reports ascribed to members of the firm of Faber & Faber Ltd." (King's). In Book Committee meetings, Anne Ridler reported, "Though he might appear not to listen he was well aware of the foibles of his colleagues both senior and junior, and when he proffered his *Practical Cats* to the Committee, produced with it a series of mock reports on the script, parodying the style of each member. Mine, I recall, was scathing in tone and peppered with parentheses" (*Working for T. S. Eliot* 9). The submission letter is addressed as though from the Swinburne and Watts-Dunton household:

The Pines,
Putney, S.W.15.
18th April, 1938.

Messrs. Faber & Faber,
  Publishers,
    24 Russell Square, W.C.1.

Dear Sirs,

    I enclose herewith stamps for the return of the enclosed poems. The publishers to whom I have previously offered them all tell me that the only firm which publishes poetry is Faber & Faber. Is this true? If so, I shall take your rejection as final.

    I must explain that these poems are meant to be illustrated; and that, if you should look upon them with a not unfavourable eye, my friend the Man in White Spats is prepared to sumbit specimen illustrations. If you should consider the poems worthy of publication, or alternatively if you should wish to publish them, and should approve of the speciment illustrations, then I suggest a royalty of 10% and an advance on royalty of £25 to be paid not to me but to my friend the Man in White Spats.

    I enclose some opinions on the enclosed poems.

Faithfully yours,

O. Possum

(The letter has "Ack." (Acknowledged) added at the head, and "not enclosed P. S." pencilled against "stamps". "P. S." was probably a secretary. "P. E. S." below?)

Report on PRACTICAL CATS.

I have had this manuscript for six weeks and haven't had a minute in which to look at them, so I bring them back.

R. de la M.

(Richard de la Mare was one of the founding directors of Faber. TSE has underlined "them" with "query 'it'? A. B.", as though by the meticulous Anne Bradby, later Ridler.)

Report on PRACTICAL CATS.

These poems are apparently the product of some member of the would-be Chelsea intelligentsia of the Blue Cockatoo variety. Personally, I find them pretentious, and cannot recommend publication. They might sell. I think they should be read through carefully with a view to the possibility of libel, that is, if you think seriously of publishing them. In view of the attitude of Colonel James Moriarty on a previous occasion, and the likelihood of legal proceedings, I think that one of these poems should be omitted. That is, if you decide to publish them. Personally, I think that the author should be seen and encouraged to offer us his next book, on the understanding that we might publish this book subsequently if his next book proved a success. I think a second opinion is needed. Would Mr. Morley look at this ms.?

A. P.

(Alan Pringle was best known as Lawrence Durrell's editor. The Blue Cockatoo Restaurant, Cheyne Walk, was popular with artists. For Conan Doyle's Moriarty and legal proceedings, see headnote to *Macavity: The Mystery Cat*.)

Report on PRACTICAL CATS.

Mrs. Crawley was delighted with the first two or three that she read, but after a time she found that she couldn't get on with them. So I started at the other end and very much enjoyed the two or three that I read, but when I had worked back to about the middle I found my attention wandering. Since then I have spoken to Minchell and rung up Sampson Low and been on the telephone to Blackie's, and everybody agrees that the market for Cats is pretty dead. If we could get the author to do a book on Herrings, I believe I could interest the trade in Hull, Grimsby and Lossiemouth.

[Unsigned]

(For W. J. Crawley, the sales manager who ran the children's list, see headnote to *For W. J. Crawley* in "Other Verses". Sampson Low had published *The English Catalogue of Books* since 1835, and also published children's books such as the *Rupert Bear* series. Blackie's also published many children's books.)

Report on PRACTICAL CATS.

This book purports to be a systematic account of the varieties of Cat. It begins by an explanation (which seems to me out of place) of how to name a Cat. Thence it proceeds to give descriptions, in a facetious vein, or so I believe the author believes it to be (for the humour is rather forced, and at times, it seems to me, misplaced) of several kinds of Cat. One might complain at this point that the description of Cats is by no means exhaustive: nevertheless the author at the end appears to be under the impression that he has described every kind of Cat. As for the poems themselves (I should explain at this point that they are written in verse) they exhibit every kind of catachresis and clevelandism; they abound in marinisms and gongorisms; they exhibit every wire-drawn perversity that human ingenuity can distort into the most tortured diabolism.

A. B.

(OED "catachresis": "Improper use of words; application of a term to a thing which it does not properly denote; abuse or perversion of a trope or metaphor". "Clevelandism" is not in OED, but in her historical novel *They Were Defeated* (1932), Rose Macaulay wrote: "you don't manage the conceited, metaphysical style well ··· when you try and Clevelandise, not only Cleveland but young Cowley leave you a mile behind". For TSE to Bradby on his intention to "do something in the style of Cleveland or Benlowes, only better", see headnote to *East Coker*, 4. AFTER PUBLICATION. OED "Marinism": "The affected style of writing characteristic of the

Italian poet Giovanni Battista Marini (*d.* 1625)". "Gongorism": "An affected type of diction and style introduced into Spanish literature in the 16th century by the poet Gongora y Argote".)

Report on PRACTICAL CATS.

Here's a book that F. & F. ought to publish, Frank: I think I could get Heinemann's to do it, but it's much more F. & F. stuff. O. P. is the real surrealist poet we have been waiting for; he's going to knock Gascoyne and Barker stiff; and what's more, he needs the money. If F. & F. don't see the point, I despair of modern society. There are enough complexes in this book to keep all of Freud's disciples busy for a generation. Ludo and Thomas send you their love. Yrs.

H. R.

(Herbert Read to the Faber director Frank V. Morley. As an editor as well as a writer, Read had influence with publishers including Heinemann. TSE to Morley, [6 Jan] 1943: "Herbert and I control the poetry market between us." Ludo was Read's second wife, Margaret Ludwig, and Thomas was their first child. In 1936, Read had been involved in the International Surrealist Exhibition and edited the Faber volume *Surrealism*. His experiment *The Green Child* was read in 1935 for Faber by TSE, who wrote that he was attempting a "Sykes Davies surrealists or whimsical vein which doesnt suit him". David Gascoyne and Hugh Sykes Davies were surrealist poets. Gascoyne's translation of André Breton's *What is Surrealism?* was published by Faber (1936). George Barker joined the firm's poetry list with *Poems* (1935), which was followed by *Calamiterror* (1937) and many other volumes. For TSE's parody of a surrealist poem, see *A Proclamation*, written in 1937.)

A further report is set differently on the page from those preceding and may not be by TSE (see below):

Report on PRACTICAL CATS.

I take it that the author is as much of an authority on Cats as he claims to be. If that is so, the Committee has to consider whether what I see in the poems is really there or not; and if it is there, whether anyone else will want to read them. That I think is antecedently improbable. What the poems convey to me is the sense of a particular Cat in a particular place at a particular time; and here I must warn the Committee against approaching these Cats from the standpoint of Thomas Gray, Old Mother Tabbyskins, or the callow polyps of the Faber Book of Animal Verse. Nor is it to use my report as an excuse for avoiding a second opinion.

(This is stamped "21 Apr 1938", with "Came with no covering letter -- ? Miss Stoneman, G.M.R." and "? T.S.E., P.E.S." at head and, in TSE's hand, "? perhaps F.V.M." at foot. Gray's *Ode on the Death of a Favourite Cat Drowned in a Tub of Gold Fishes* was published in 1748. *Mother Tabbyskins*, a moral tale, in *Child-World* by Menella Bute Smedley and Elizabeth Anna Hart (1869). There was no *Faber Book of Animal Verse*. Miss Stoneman was a Faber secretary.)

6. WITH AND WITHOUT ILLUSTRATIONS

Obtaining illustrations for *Practical Cats* caused delays. The day after John Hayward sent a letter containing a light-hearted drawing, TSE wrote to him, 29 Jan 1937: "Ere. I didn't know you was such a accomplished Illustrater. Maybe you are the appointed

Illustrater for my Popular Lectures on Cats. Wd. you care to submit a few speccimim illustrations? In combitition with Mr. F. V. Morley, who thinks he can do it." Along with the two pencil and ink drawings by TSE which appeared on the jacket of *1939*, King's has thirteen cartoonish drawings by Hayward (selections shown in *Granta* May 1978 and *Quarto* June 1981). However, TSE and Faber tried to commission illustrations from Ralph Hodgson, who let them down (see John Harding, *Dreaming of Babylon: The Life and Times of Ralph Hodgson*, 2008, 154–58). TSE discussed the matter during Hodgson's visit to Britain in 1938, and a letter from TSE of 13 Sept 1938 is illustrated with a large cat drawing. In 1932 the Hodgsons named a puppy "Pickwick", and in Feb 1939 TSE sent the Fabers and the Hodgsons a mock exam paper entitled "Pickwick Paper (Advanced)", on which the final question was: "(To be attempted only by Mr. Ralph Hodgson) Having in mind the four cats in the wheelbarrow, what are you doing about the Depicting of Cats?" TSE to Mrs Muller, 9 Feb 1939: "The canon of *Practical Cats* has now been fixed and there are only a few slight textual emendations to be made. What is awaited is an illustrator. My friend Mr. Ralph Hodgson, the poet, is supposed to be engaged in preparing designs to submit; but as he is 4000 miles away, and I have no control over him, there is no knowing whether anything will come of it." On 8 Apr 1939, TSE sent a telegram to Hodgson in Madison, Wisconsin: "EASTER GREETINGS FROM POSSUM STOP URGENT NEED INTERIM REPORT CATS YOUR FINANCIAL INTEREST AND MINE". On 5 May, Hodgson wrote to Geoffrey Faber: "I haven't made a start on Possum's Cats for many reasons: The chief being that we haven't found a suitable house to settle down in yet ··· I believe I have a good enough eye for cats to justify my undertaking this work—but not in my inner consciousness: therefore I must have cats about me to study and proper conscience for their wellbeing ··· I trust all this isn't as tedious to read as it is unpleasant to write, for I regard it as a high honour to be asked to illustrate the Possum's Immortal Cats, but after all the fun of doing it—or attempting it—is the thing, and that is possible only with my feet up on the mantel piece, as the saying is." Faber replied on 2 June: "Clearly you won't be able to collect the necessary models in time to illustrate the first edition, which we have now decided to do without illustrations this autumn. May we announce it as 'With illustrations missing by Ralph Hodgson'? Perhaps an illustrated edition might follow later."

The first edition, published 5 Oct 1939, had no illustrations except drawings by TSE on the jacket. The front panel shows a bearded Old Possum, in bowler hat and stiff collar, leaning over a wall against which stands a ladder, up which a procession of cats is scrambling. (On the jacket of the copy TSE presented to Enid and Geoffrey Faber, he wrote at the foot of the ladder: "O.P. pinxit". See headnote to *INVITATION TO ALL POLLICLE DOGS & JELLICLE CATS*. For a bearded TSE in 1937, see note to *Ash-Wednesday* I unadopted title.) The rear panel shows Old Possum roller-skating with the Man in White Spats (who wears morning dress and a top hat). "Unillustrated" reprints continued as a cheaper alternative to those with pictures.

1939 jacket material:

> It is more than three years since we announced a book of children's verses by Mr. Eliot under the title of *Pollicle Dogs and Jellicle Cats*.
>
> We have sometimes been accused, by members of the public who have complained that this book was not obtainable through their booksellers, of having invented it out of our own heads. This accusation is baseless. Many of the poems have been in private circulation for some years; and their privileged recipients (of ages varying between six

and twelve) have exerted the strongest possible pressure upon the author in favour of more general publication.

In resisting this pressure Mr. Eliot is believed to have been fortified by a growing desire for the company of *cats*, and a growing perception that it would be impolite to wrap them up with *dogs*. The cat poems, however, are now numerous enough to make a book by themselves.

TSE to Geoffrey Faber, 27 July 1939: "I am sorry that you took my comments on the cat blurb quite so seriously. No objection to the blurb as a whole: but you will perhaps understand the author's apprehensions. It is harder to judge of a blurb about one's own book than it is even about one's own blurbs: going through my own depressed me, but I couldn't think of any improvements. I was so anxious that the Cats should flourish, if at all, on their own merits, and not as a TSE curio, that I would have asked that it be published anonymously had I thought that fair to the publishers; it is *intended* for a NEW public, but I am afraid cannot dispense with the old one."

Harcourt Brace press advertisement: "T. S. Eliot's friends often receive anonymous poems (which they can usually identify), and very often these poems concern cats— not dear little cats but practical cats. The poems about cats have now been collected for the benefit of a wider audience of Mr. Eliot's friends. *PRACTICAL CATS*. There are a few cats of Mr. Eliot's own design on the jacket."

US 1939 jacket material: "Mr. T. S. Eliot's intimate friends receive from time to time typewritten verses which are apparently anonymous but which are always identifiable. The poems which concern cats are presented here."

Hayward acknowledged the illustrated *Practical Cats* on 20 Nov 1940. On the title page: "NICOLAS BENTLEY | drew the pictures"; these included full colour plates. TSE to Hayward, 25 Nov: "I am glad you can speak so favourably of the Bentley drawings: they were rather a shock to me at first, but I am beginning to get used to them. Bentley's intuition of the feline is not mine; but the only distinct failures now seem to me to be Macavity and Gus. He is hardly the perfect Tenniel for my purpose, if I may say that without appearing presumptuous." (In Mar 1942 Hayward commented to Frank Morley that Mervyn Peake would have been a better choice.) TSE to Polly Tandy, 12 Dec 1940: "I am glad you find that the illustrated Cats improve with acquaintance, they have done so with me. I didnt like them at all at first, and I still think Macavity and Gus are a Pity. You are right, of course, about Contemplation: but perhaps we know too much about Cats to be quite in touch with vulgar opinion, and perhaps something a little more popular is wanted." (The plate illustrating *The Naming of Cats*—"His mind is engaged in rapt contemplation"—appears to show a cat with a sore head.) The first paperback edition, in 1962, "with decorations by NICOLAS BENTLEY", retained the "tail pieces" but not the colour plates, which were reserved for the hardback until 1976.

"Books by T. S. Eliot" flyer, *c.* 1948: "This is a collection of poems about Cats which were written for the amusement and instruction of Mr. Eliot's particular young friends. It has also delighted other young people, and elder folk who appreciate virtuosity in jingling. The cheaper edition is decorated only by cover designs by the author; the edition illustrated by Nicolas Bentley gives a visual realisation of

Mr. Eliot's Cats and their capers, which will supply the defect of imagination of the least imaginative reader."

7. TSE'S RECORDING

To Frederick C. Packard Jr., initiator of Vocarium Records at Harvard, 22 Nov 1955: "True, I have never recorded any 'Cats'. Other people have wished me to do so, but I have not given any encouragement for the reason that there are not very many of these poems, and I am afraid that a recording might interfere with the sales of the book, from which I derive more profit · · · What I should be prepared to do, would be to record two or three of the cats for your archives, on the understanding that no record would be sold, and that no public use would be made of the recording."

The whole book was recorded in 1957 as *T. S. Eliot reads Old Possum's Book of Practical Cats*, under the auspices of the British Council; released by Argo in 1959. Recording sleeve: "Apology. We had prepared erudite notes for this record, but they appear to have been intercepted on the way to the printers by—Macavity."

Additionally, *Macavity: The Mystery Cat* was recorded by TSE in Nov 1959 in Chicago as part of a celebration of *Poetry* magazine.

Other recordings include the reading by Robert Donat, with music by Alan Rawsthorne, released in 1956, and a reading by John Gielgud and Irene Worth released in 1983.

*

Practical Cats has been adapted to musical purposes more than once. *New York Times*, 27 Aug 1954: "Although there is no new T. S. Eliot play this year in Edinburgh, the first musical novelty of the festival, *Practical Cats*, depends largely on the poet for its success. Described as an 'entertainment for Children', this work consists of six settings from *Old Possum's Book of Practical Cats* preceded by a brief overture. Mr Eliot's verses were brilliantly declaimed by Alvar Lidell, well known British broadcaster, while the full-scale orchestral accompaniment was performed by the British Broadcasting Corporation's Scottish Orchestra under Ian Whyte."

The musical *Cats* by Andrew Lloyd-Webber opened in 1981 in London and in 1982 on Broadway, running for 21 and 18 years respectively.

8. APROPOS OF *PRACTICAL CATS* BY VALERIE ELIOT

(The following note from *Cats: The Book of the Musical* is taken from the version prepared for the American production. The version in the original British printing of 1981 was shorter and not illustrated by drawings.)

> In an early poem, *The Love Song of J. Alfred Prufrock*, T. S. Eliot likened the yellow fog of St. Louis to a cat

> > that rubs its back upon the window-panes,
> > The yellow smoke that rubs its muzzle on the window-panes,
> > Licked its tongue into the corners of the evening,
> > Lingered upon the pools that stand in drains,
> > Let fall upon its back the soot that falls from chimneys,
> > Slipped by the terrace, made a sudden leap,
> > And seeing that it was a soft October night,
> > Curled once about the house, and fell asleep . . .

> He also remarked that "The great thing about cats is that they possess two qualities to an extreme degree—dignity and comicality".

> "I am glad you have a cat", TSE wrote to his godson, Tom Faber, on 20th January 1931, "but I do not believe it is so remarkable a cat as My cat . . . There never was such a Lilliecat.

> > ITS NAME IS
> > J E L L Y O R U M

> and its one Idea is to be

> > USEFUL!!

> FOR Instance

> IT STRAIGHTENS THE PICTURES

> IT DOES THE GRATES

> LOOKS INTO THE LARDER TO SEE
> WHAT'S NEEDED —

> AND INTO THE DUSTBIN TO SEE
> THAT NOTHING'S WASTED —

> and yet

IT IS SO LILLIE AND
SMALL THAT

IT CAN SIT ON MY EAR!
(Of course I had to draw my Ear rather
Bigger than it Is to get
the Lilliecat onto it).

I would tell you about our Cus Cus Praps except that I can't Draw
Dogs so well as Cats, Yet; but I mean to . . . "

This was the first occasion on which Old Possum revealed himself. When Tom was four
TSE suggested that all Pollicle Dogs and Jellicle Cats should be

INVITED to Come
With a Flute & a Fife & a Fiddle & Drum
With a Fiddle, a Fife, & a Drum & a Tabor
To the Birthday Party of THOMAS ERLE FABER!

Then there was "a very Grand Cat . . . a Persian Prince and it is Blue because it has Blue
Blood, and its name was MIRZA MURAD ALI BEG but I said that was too Big a Name for
such a Small Flat, so its name is *wiskuscat*. But it is sometimes called The MUSICAL BOX
because it makes a noise like singing and sometimes COCKALORUM because it Looks
like one. (Have you ever seen a Cockalorum? Neither have I)". In April 1932 Tom learnt
that "the Porpentine cat has been in bed with Ear Ache so the Pollicle Dog stopped At
Home to Amuse it by making Cat's Cradles".

TSE was always inventing suitable cat names, as he was often asked for them by
friends and strangers. I remember "Noilly Prat" (an elegant cat); "Carbucketry"
(a knock-about cat); "Tantomile" (a witch's cat); he also liked "Pouncival" with its *Morte
d'Arthur* flavour, and "Sillabub", a mixture of silly and Beelzebub.

Most of the poems were written between 1936 and 1938. "I have done a new
cat, modelled on the late Professor Moriarty but he doesn't seem very popular: too
sophisticated perhaps . . . " TSE wrote to Frank Morley. This will surprise today's many
admirers of *Macavity*. Although he confided to Enid Faber on 8th March 1938 that "The
Railway Cat (L.M.S.) is rather stuck", a week later the poem was finished. *Skimbleshanks*
is based on Kipling's *The Long Trail* just as *The Marching Song of the Pollicle Dogs* was
written to the tune of *The Elliots of Minto*. *Grizabella the Glamour Cat* is an unpublished
fragment of which only the last eight lines were written because TSE realised she was
developing along the lines of Villon's *La Belle Heaulmière* who fell on evil days and he
felt it would be too sad for children.

About this time, when he was driving to the country, he and the driver began
discussing their respective dogs. The chauffeur wishing to make clear that his was a
mongrel said, "He is not what you would call a consequential dog." This so delighted
TSE that he resolved to write a book of Consequential Dogs to match the Practical Cats.
But, alas, it was never done. During the war when he was living with friends in Surrey
he remarked of the temporary absence of a noisy pug, "When does '. . . that fatall and
perfidious Bark | Built in th'eclipse, and rigg'd with curses dark . . .' return to us?"
(Milton). [*Lycidas* 100–101.]

Although Faber & Faber announced "Mr. Eliot's book of *Pollicle Dogs and Jellicle Cats*"
in their 1936 Spring catalogue, TSE had run into difficulties over his general approach.
"The idea of the volume was to have different poems on appropriate subjects · · · recited

by the Man in White Spats ··· At the end they all go up in a balloon, self, Spats, and dogs and cats.

> Up up up past the Russell Hotel,
> Up up up to the Heaviside Layer."

Three more years, as his publisher put it, brought "a growing perception that it would be impolite to wrap cats up with dogs" and the realisation that the book would be exclusively feline ···

Old Possum's Book of Practical Cats was published in England on 5th October 1939 in an edition of 3005 copies at 3/6d with TSE's drawings on the front cover and the dust-wrapper. He was nervous about its reception. His verse play *The Family Reunion* had appeared in March and *The Idea of a Christian Society* was due in three weeks. "It is intended for a NEW public", he informed Geoffrey Faber, "but I am afraid I cannot dispense with the old one." He need not have worried. "*Cats* are giving general satisfaction", the Sales Manager reported shortly afterwards, while the *Manchester Guardian* said they partook "of the infinite variety of human nature". Today they are a minor classic and have been translated into a dozen languages ···

P.S. Whenever he was unwell or could not sleep, TSE would recite the verses under his breath.

––––––––

Preface] TSE to Enid Faber, 12 July 1939:

> Now about the dedication of *Cats*. I had thought of putting something like the following:
>
>> The Author wishes to thank several friends for their suggestions, criticism and encouragement: particularly Mr. T. E. Faber, Miss Alison Tandy, Miss Susan Wolcott, and the Man in White Spats.
>
> (Some two or three were composed for the second, and the third is a small American cousin who *thinks* that they were written for her). Then it occurred to me that Tom has arrived at years of maturity at which he might not be pleased by having his name associated with anything so juvenile. In that case, the dedication will be omitted altogether. My second doubt was whether I ought to include Susanna: but as she was not the cause of any of the poems, and so far as I know has never seen them, and I don't know whether she would like them, I don't want to. And the form would have to be one of straight dedication instead of acknowledgement.

the Man in White Spats: although Susanna Morley believed that this was her father (BBC *Arena*, 2009), Hayward's copy of the first British edition is inscribed "to John Hayward Esqr—the original Man in White Spats—only begetter of Bustopher Jones and Skimbleshanks, this from his ob^t. oblgd. servt. O.P. 3.x.39". (The front of the jacket is initialled "O.P. fecit", referring to the drawings.) Hayward's copy of the illustrated edition is also inscribed: "for the Man in White Spats: John Hayward from T.S.E. 14.11.40". *Smart* 102: "When Hayward told him of his youthful infatuation with Dagmar [Erhardt] and how he had chosen a pair of his father's white spats to impress her, these became fixed in Eliot's imagination ··· Eliot wrote when Hayward sent him his cat sketches. (In fact Hayward was very disappointed when they were turned down for the dust-jacket, signing himself, 'l'homme aux guêtres blancs'.)" However, the verse letter *I am asked by my friend, the Man in White Spats* (sent to Alison Tandy, see "Uncollected Poems") mentions "his Budgerigars and his prize Cockatoo", which suggests Ralph Hodgson, who was addressed as "The Man in White Spats" in a letter to him of 28 Oct 1938 (see Harding, *Dreaming of Babylon* 157). The copy of *How to Pick a Possum* sent to Alison Tandy, 12 Sept 1937, is subscribed "THE MAN IN WHITE SPATS". So this was a compound dandy. *Punch* had given its opinion *About White Spats* on 22 July 1925: "Some men, it is true, wear white spats because of their power to arrest attention; and it must be confessed that they have a certain usefulness in this respect. White spats draw the eye of an observer down to the feet, and, though feet are seldom much of an attraction in themselves, there is undoubtedly a type of man whose feet are less trying to the eye than his upper parts." Jellicle cats (which "are black and white", *Song of the Jellicles* 5) often have "white socks".

The Naming of Cats

OED "Tom" 6: "The male of various beasts and birds; perh. first for a male cat", with 1791, "Cats .. Of titles obsolete, or yet in use, Tom, Tybert, Roger, Rutterkin, or Puss." Wyndham Lewis gave a warning in *Mr. Zagreus and the Split-Man* in *Criterion* Feb 1924 (*Harmon 1976a*):

> "Never change the barbarous names given by god to each and all," you read in the spurious AVESTA compiled at Alexandria;
> "Because there are names possessing an unutterable efficacity! . . ."
> "Beginning with the stock-in-trade of the Phap: the name you utter is not the name. The UNNAMED is the principle of heaven and of earth. But the name is an abortion and a tyranny: and you do not have to ascend into the sky, with the TAO, or allege anything more than a common cat, for that. Name a cat and you destroy it! 'Not knowing his name I call him TAO' · · ·"

The Apes of God (1930) 341

TSE to Polly Tandy, 3 July 1935: "Your news is noted, and I look forward to attempting to photograph the remarkable cats, although I don't understand why one of them should be called Dolabella. Nevertheless I have always maintained that a cat's name should have at least 3 syllables, except in exceptional circumstance." Dolabella is a male character in *Antony and Cleopatra*. E. Martin Browne recalled another Shakespearean cat: "A few years after *The Book of Practical Cats* was written, we acquired a female cat of very questionable lineage. My wife, who was at the time playing Hamlet's mother, christened her Gertrude. When Eliot next came to our flat and met her, he enquired her name. Gertrude would not do: a cat's name must have at least three syllables · · · I looked at her white 'shirt-front' and suggested Ermyntrude as a substitute; this was accepted", *Browne* 312. (For "Cats with short names", see note to *The Song of the Jellicles* 1.)

TSE's correspondence with the Tandy family includes undated lists of "some good names" and "some bad names" (BL Add. 71004, fols. 152–53). Since the good include "Blandina", "Crispiniana" and "Emerentiana", they are more probably for cats than for daughters.

The Naming of Cats is known first from a letter to TSE's godson, Tom Faber, 7 Jan 1936 (*ts*, Valerie Eliot collection):

Dear Tom,

> While lying in bed getting better and better,
> I hope you'll have time for perusing this letter,
> Inasmuch as my friend, the Man in White Spats,
> Asks me to convey
> In a personal way
> This poem he composed on

THE NAMING OF CATS

> The naming of cats is a difficult matter,
>   It isn't just one of your holiday games;
> You may think at first I'm as mad as a hatter,
>   But I tell you, a Cat must have THREE DIFFERENT NAMES.
> First of all, there's the name that the servants use daily,
>   Such as Peter, Alonzo, or Betty or James,
> Such as Victor, or Jonathan, George or Bill Bailey—
>   All of them practical everyday names.
> There are fancier names if you think they sound sweeter,
>   Some for the gentlemen, some for the dames:
> Such as Plato, Admetus, Electra, Demeter—
>   But all of them practical everyday names.
> But, I tell you, a Cat needs a name that's particular,
>   A name that's peculiar, and more dignified,
> Else how can he keep up his ears perpendicular,
>   Or smooth out his whiskers, or tickle his pride?
> Of names of this kind, I can give you a quorum,
>   Such as Munkustrap, Quaxo, or Capricopat,
> Such as Bombalurina, or else Jellylorum—
>   Names that never belong to more than one Cat.
> But above and beyond, there's still one name left over,
>   And that is the name that you never will guess;
> The name that no human research can discover—
> But BUT B UT
> BUT the *Cat himself knows*, and will never confess.
> When you notice a Cat in profound meditation,
>   The reason, I tell you, is always the same;
> His mind is engaged in intense contemplation
>   Of the thought, of the thought, of the thought of his NAME.
>   Not his everyday name,
>   Not his personal name,
> But just his ineffable
>   Effanineffable
> Deep and inscrutable singular Name.
>
> Now that's what my friend, the Man in White Spats,
> Has asked me to tell you, about names of Cats.
> I don't know myself, so I will not endorse it,
> For what's true in Yorks may be falsehood in Dorset.

He may be quite right and he may be quite wrong,
But for what it is worth, I will pass it along.
For passing the time it may be an expedient,
He remains, as do I, your obliged and obedient
Servant, now and in years to come.

Your afexnate

Uncle Tom

Title Naming: "the meaning of a name always goes beyond and binds together the contexts in which it has been used", *The Validity of Artificial Distinctions* (1914).

1 **The Naming of Cats is a difficult matter**: "The choice of bowl is a serious matter", *How to Prepare a Salad* (1936).

2 **holiday games**: Washington Irving: "in Greenwich Park I was witness to the old holiday games of running down hill; and kissing in the ring", *Buckthorne* in *Tales of a Traveller.*

4 **three different names**: Roman names had three parts, the *prænomen*, from a limited traditional range; *nomen*, common to members of a clan; and *cognomen*, a nickname, physical description or occupation, often with an element of humour. To Frank Morley [7 Feb 1940], on the birth of his daughter: "You know that a daughter should have three different names: one of which must be the name of a Saint. Viz. Sophia Theresa Read. I have looked into the matter and find that if she was born yesterday the Saint is Titus: that does not seem helpful." On niceties of naming, see note to the title *The Love Song of J. Alfred Prufrock.*

6 **Augustus**: this name is not in the version of the poem sent to Tom Faber (above); nor is it the full name of Gus the Theatre Cat ("His name, as I ought to have told you before, | Is really Asparagus", 2–3).

11 **Admetus, Electra, Demeter**: respectively, one of the Argonauts; daughter of Agamemnon; earth-mother goddess. For TSE explaining Greek to a god-daughter, see headnote to *Old Deuteronomy.*

18 **Quaxo, or Coricopat**: perhaps related to *Paxo* (the spiced stuffing) and *coriander*. ("co co rico", *The Waste Land* V 392.)

19 **Bombalurina**: perhaps *bombastic* + *ballerina*. TSE enjoyed compound words. Having mistyped "operations on winder front" in a letter to John Hayward, 12 Apr 1943, he added a note: "wider and windier".   **Jellylorum**: see letter to Tom Faber, 20 Jan 1931, quoted in headnote, 8. APROPOS OF *PRACTICAL CATS* by Valerie Eliot.

28 **the thought, of the thought, of the thought**: Joyce: "Thought is the thought of thought", *Ulysses* episode II (Nestor). For Nietzsche's "an *appearance of appearance*", see note to *Oh little voices of the throats of men* 15, 21–22.

29 **ineffable effable**: Longfellow: "These effable and ineffable impressions of the mysterious world", *The Divine Tragedy* (1871) II ii.   **ineffable**: "Towards the unconscious, the ineffable, the absolute", *Afternoon* 9. To John Hayward, 21 July 1942, on Robert Nichols: "He sent me a copy of his *Selected Poems*. What one thinks about them is not only ineffable but unthinkable: but I managed to write him a letter about them."

29–31 **ineffable** ··· **Name**: the Hebrew divine name too sacred to be spoken, commonly represented as "Jehovah"; see OED. Joyce: "the Name Ineffable, in heaven hight, K. H.", *Ulysses* episode IX (Scylla and Charybdis), with, in the same paragraph, "The life esoteric is not for ordinary person. O.P. must work off bad karma first." K.H. = Kristos Hiesos (Christ Jesus). O.P. = ordinary person (as opposed to Old Possum).

The Old Gumbie Cat

To Tom Faber, 28 Dec 1931: "NOW I must tell you about my Cat. You Remember that we had a black & white Jellicle Cat that lived with us? Well, it got to staying out Nights and trying to be a Big Bravo Cat and it took to visiting Neighbours and then it began to complain of the Food and saying it didn't like Dried Haddock & Kippers and why wasn't there more Game even when there was no Game in Season, so finally it went to live somewhere else. So then I advertised for Another Cat to come and Board with us, and now we have a Beautiful Cat which is going to be a Good Old Gumbie Cat in Time."

To Alison Tandy, 10 Nov 1936 (after *Growltiger's Last Stand*): "The last Cat I wrote about, was such a Boastful Brutal Beastly Bloody Bad Pirate, that you may think that I am a kittenthrope, or Hater of Cats; but such is not the Case. On the contrary. So I hasten to tell you about another Kind of Cat, to my knowledge, that is wholly admirable. It is THE OLD GUMBIE CAT [*poem*] So now! nobody can say that I am UNAPPRECIATIVE of Cats."

2 **Her coat is of the tabby kind**: Gray: "Demurest of the tabby kind", *Ode on the Death of a Favourite Cat* 4. TSE to William Force Stead, 3 Dec 1937: "I have read your essay on Two Poets and Two Cats with enjoyment. I am afraid however that in its present form it is either too light or too heavy for *The Criterion*. As a general essay comparing the life of Christopher Smart with that of Thomas Gray, it is informative but more suitable for such a review as *English*. What I like, and what is quite new, is the comparison of Smart's admirable cat poem with that of Gray. You say that the poem of Smart is still unpublished and unknown: it would be very jolly for *The Criterion* to have an essay on this poem, including large chunks of the text (for I take it that the whole poem is much too long to publish in this way), and comparing it with Gray's 'Selima'. But with all deference, it seems to me that you praise Gray's poem much too highly. It has always seemed to me a piece of very prim and frigid wit, and the fact that it was not his own cat, but Horace Walpole's, is no excuse. It would be a bad poem, I think, if it were about a china cat, but about a real cat it is unforgivable. Smart has real feeling for cats, and Gray has none. Anyway, you may or may not feel inclined to make a different paper of it." Stead had discovered the manuscript of Smart's *Jubilate Agno* and published it in 1939 as *Rejoice in the Lamb*. TSE on Smart: "His poem about cats is to all other poems about cats what the Iliad is to all other poems on war", *Walt Whitman and Modern Poetry* (1944). For many a cat, see *Five-Finger Exercises*. TSE several times quotes Kipling, "What Mirza Murad Ali Beg's book is to all other books · · ·"; see note to the title V. *Lines for Cuscuscaraway and Mirza Murad Ali Beg*.

7 *variant* **fambly:** jokey spelling frequent in TSE's letters to the Tandys. To Bonamy Dobrée, 31 Dec 1935: "Frank Flint · · · says I pronounce it *fambly*, but that is just a gesture of superiority." Joyce: "Any brollies or gumboots in the fambly?" *Ulysses* episode XIV (The Oxen of the Sun).

8, 27, 38 **the basement · · · the window-sill · · · households** (8 *has variant* **tucks up her skirts · · · the kitchen**): "basement kitchens · · · housemaids · · · muddy skirts", *Morning at the Window* 1, 3, 7.

10 **behaviour's not good · · · manners not nice:** TSE associated the Unitarianism that he rejected with the nice: "those who are born and bred to be nice people will always prefer to behave nicely, and those who are not will behave otherwise in any case: and this is surely a form of predestination", *The "Pensées" of Pascal* (1931).

12 **tatting:** lace knitting.

38 **well-ordered households:** Edward Irving: "this is the ordinance of God's providence, that blessings many and precious should attend upon dutiful and well-ordered households", *The Last Days* (1828) 528; the locution became common among Victorians.

Growltiger's Last Stand

To Bonamy Dobrée, 21 Nov 1936, offering poems for his daughter: "Would Georgina whom God preserve be interested in my two latest poems or not? I mean *Growltiger's Last Stand* (picaresque) and *The Old Gumbie Cat* (domestic) or not?" (There is no evidence that Georgina was sent the poems.) The use of rhyming fourteeners for this naval verse resembles *The Fall of Admiral Barry*, in TSE's letters to Pound 30 Aug and 22 Oct 1922 (see note to 21–22, and *For below a voice did answer, sweet in its youthful tone* in "Improper Rhymes").

Title **Growltiger's Last Stand:** Custer's Last Stand, at the Battle of the Little Bighorn, June 1876, was the most prominent action of the Great Sioux War.

Unadopted epigraph **"He was no better than a Pirate":**—Sir John Simon, replying to a Question in the House during the Debate on the Growltiger Incident: Eva March Tappan imagined Queen Elizabeth addressing Sir John Hawkins: "'They tell me you are no better than a pirate,' she said, bluntly", *In the Days of Queen Elizabeth* (1902) ch. 12.

1 **Bravo:** OED: "a daring villain, a hired soldier or assassin; 'a man who murders for hire' (Johnson); a reckless desperado."   **travelled on:** to Richard de la Mare, 6 Feb 1945: "There is a line I want to change in the Practical Cats, if there is ever another printing of that. The first line of *Growltiger* ought to be 'travelled on a barge' instead of 'lived upon a barge'" (Faber archive). Emended in 4th imp. of the illustrated ed. (1946).

3–4 **Oxford · · · aims · · · Thames:** Arnold's "story of the Oxford scholar": "the sparkling Thames · · · divided aims", *The Scholar-Gipsy* 202, 204.

4 **"The Terror of the Thames":** *Henry VI Pt. I* I iv, of Talbot: "Here, said they, is

the Terror of the French". The locution became formulaic, as in *Quantrell: The Terror of the West* by "Alouette" (1866).

5 **did not calculate to please** (*variant*: **he was hardly made to please**): "Whose constant care is not to please | But to", *East Coker* IV 8–9.

6 **torn and seedy** (*variant*: **rough and shaggy**) · · · **baggy at the knees**: "Apeneck Sweeney spreads his knees", *Sweeney Among the Nightingales* 1.

15 **Woe to the bristly bandicoot**: J. G. Wood's *The Illustrated Natural History* (1859) described the fur of the Long-Nosed Bandicoot as "very harsh to the touch." Carroll: "shun | The frumious bandersnatch!" *Jabberwocky* 7–8 (in *Through the Looking-Glass* ch. I). See notes to 52 and 53–56.

21–22 **Now on a peaceful summer night, all nature seemed at play, | The tender moon was shining bright, the barge at Molesey lay**: moonlight on the eve of battle, a commonplace since Homer *Iliad* VIII.   **all nature seemed at play**: formulaic, as in Mary Rankin: "Autumn was in her glory drest— | All nature seemed at play", *The Prismatic Rainbow* in D. R. Good, *The Daughter of Affliction* (1858).

22 **the barge at Molesey lay**: Tennyson: "At Flores in the Azores Sir Richard Grenville lay", *The Revenge: A Ballad of the Fleet* 1. TSE to Pound, 22 Oct 1922: "'In old Manila harbour, the Yankee wardogs lay, | 'The stars ⍺ stripes streamed overhead, ⍺ the band began to play' (From *The Fall of Admiral Barry*)."

22, 26–28 **Molesey** · · · **the Bell** · · · **the Lion**: TSE knew the area of Hampton-on-Thames, where the Tandys lived. The Bell is in East Molesey, with a Lion close by in Teddington. To Polly Tandy, 31 Dec 1935: "best wishes for the New Year to the Licensee of the Bell". To Hayward, 15 Apr [1936]: "You may communicate with me at this address, by addressing your letters to 'White Cargo' c/o the Licensee the Bell, Hampton-on-Thames." TSE's facetious "Pickwick Paper (Advanced)", sent to the Fabers and Hodgsons in Feb 1939, includes a section about traditional pubs.

22, 24, 41–42 **tender** · · · **his sentimental side** · · · **fierce Mongolian** · · · **Chinks**: "the illusion of the hard boiled. Even Mr. Ernest Hemingway—that writer of tender sentiment, and true sentiment · · · has been taken as the representative of hard boiling · · · only another defence mechanism adopted by the world's babies; if the Chinese bandits ever discover that they are hard boiled I shall have to infer that the oldest civilization in the world has reverted to · · · puerility", *A Commentary* in *Criterion* Apr 1933.

25 **bucko**: OED: "*Naut. Slang.* a. A blustering, swaggering, or domineering fellow; sometimes used as a term of address. Also attrib. or as adj. = blustering, swaggering, bullying; esp. in phr. bucko mate", from 1883: "no sailor will deny that a 'bucko mate' is not sometimes useful".

27 **bosun**: pronounced *bozun* in TSE's recording.

29 **sate**: as if rhyming with *fate* in TSE's recording. See *A Cooking Egg* 1.

32 **sampans**: OED: "A Chinese word meaning 'boat', applied by Europeans in the China seas to any small boat of Chinese pattern."   **junks**: OED *n.*3: "the common type of native sailing vessel in the Chinese seas".

37 **And closer still and closer**: Macaulay: "And louder still and louder | Rose from the darkened field | The braying of the war-horns, | The clang of sword and

shield", *The Battle of Lake Regillus* XIV, *Lays of Ancient Rome*. In TSE's third-year class at school, Macaulay's *Lays* were prescribed reading (Smith Academy yearbook, 1901–02), and a copy appears in *TSE's books: Bodleian list* (1934). A. C. Benson: "Wider still and wider shall thy bounds be set", *Land of Hope and Glory*.

40 **toasting forks and cruel carving knives**: Carroll: "They pursued it with forks and hope; | They threatened its life", *The Hunting of the Snark* Fit the Fifth.

41 **GILBERT**: OED: "*Obs. rare.* A proper name used as the appellation of a male cat (cf. Tom). Usually shortened to Gib." The name was changed in productions of *Cats* after the first to "Genghis". For "Jenghiz Khan", see note to *The wind sprang up at four o'clock* 12, "Tartar".

41–42 **fierce Mongolian horde · · · swarmed**: "Who are those hooded hordes swarming | Over endless plains", *The Waste Land* [V] 368–69 (see note).

42 **Chinks**: OED "Chink": "A Chinaman (derogatory)", from 1901.

43 **pullaways**: sole citation of this sense in OED ("pull-"). "In the midst of the sea, like a tough man of war, | Pull away, pull away, yo ho there!" *The Land in the Ocean* in Dibdin's *Songs, Naval and National* (1841).

47 **I'm sure she was not drowned**: *The Ballad of the House Carpenter* (American ballad, based on a Scottish original): "They had not been at sea three weeks, | And I'm sure it was not four, | When the vessel it did spring a leak, | And it sank to rise no more!" (quoted for instance in Bayard Taylor, *The Story of Kennet*, 1866, 417).

48–50 **flashing steel · · · vast surprise**: Pope: "his shining sword · · · view the slain with vast Surprise", *The First Book of Statius His Thebais* 725–27, the locutions becoming formulaic in battle poetry.

49–50 **rank on rank · · · walk the plank**: Meredith: "he looked, and sank. | Around the ancient track marched, rank on rank, | The army of unalterable law", *Lucifer in Starlight*. For TSE's use of Meredith's last line, see note to *Cousin Nancy* 13.

52 **to go ker-flip, ker-flop**: Carroll: "The vorpal blade went snicker-snack! | He left it dead", *Jabberwocky* 18–19.   **ker-flip, ker-flop**: OED "ker-": "*U.S. vulgar* · · · The first element in numerous onomatopœic or echoic formations intended to imitate the sound or the effect of the fall of some heavy body", citing *The Adventures of Huckleberry Finn* (1884) "ker-*blam*!"; J. Runciman *Skippers & Shellbacks* (1885) "They hoists him over and lets him go ker-whop"; H. G. Wells (1935) "And plump back ker-splosh! into the sea!"; with TSE the only citation for "ker-flip, ker-flop".

53–56 **joy · · · Victoria Dock · · · day · · · Bangkok**: Carroll: "'And hast thou slain the Jabberwock? | Come to my arms, my beamish boy! | O frabjous day! Callooh! Callay!' | He chortled in his joy", *Jabberwocky* 21–24.

The Rum Tum Tugger

Title **Rum Tum**: OED: "[A fanciful formation.]" 1: "*dial.* A jovial diversion or prank." 3: "Used in imitation of a regular rhythmic sound", quoting Joyce, "Of all the glad new year, mother, the rum tum tiddledy tum", *Ulysses* episode III (Proteus).

(A rum-tum is a boat, and so is a tug.)   *Tugger*: OED: "One who tugs or pulls with force; *spec.* one who pulls in a tug-of-war." A. A. Milne's Tigger figures in *Winnie-the-Pooh* (1926).

1 **a Curious Cat**: curiosity killed the cat, proverbial. ("Man's curiosity", *The Dry Salvages* V 16; see note.)

9–10 **For he will do | As he do do**: Dickens, *Our Mutual Friend* bk. I ch. X (Valerie Eliot, *WLFacs* 125):

> "And *other* countries," said the foreign gentleman. "They do how?"
> "They do, Sir," returned Mr. Podsnap, gravely shaking his head; "they do—I am sorry to be obliged to say it—*as* they do."

11 **And there's no doing anything about it**: TSE to Frank Morley, "Friday" [after Feb 1938]: "a longstanding engagement · · · fixed by Mabel · · · and theres no doing anything about it".

16 **He likes to lie in the bureau drawer**: "bureau drawer", *Goldfish* IV 6, at the line-end.

24–26 **habit · · · he won't eat rabbit**: see note to *The Ad-dressing of Cats* 60–61.

25 **If you offer him fish then he always wants a feast**: for a cat that "began to complain of the Food and saying it didn't like Dried Haddock & Kippers", see letter to Tom Faber, 28 Dec 1931, in headnote to *The Old Gumbie Cat*.   **fish · · · feast**: to I. A. Richards, 1 Mar 1934: "Friday March 10th will do for me as well as any other night. The only difficulty being the limitation of a fish diet." To Richard Jennings, 21 Nov 1939: "Friday is fish or eggs."

The Song of the Jellicles

1 *Jellicle*: recalling Edward Lear's nonsense word "runcible" from *The Owl and the Pussy-Cat* (see 28). To Polly Tandy, 21 May 1935:

> As for those Cats with short names they may wag their tails at Mr. Kipling. But I bet half a Crown he will outlive the pair of them and
>
> > Jellicle cats & dogs all must
> > Like cocktail mixers, come to dust.

(Kipling: "How at Bankside, a boy drowning kittens | Winced at the business; whereupon his sister— | Lady Macbeth aged seven—thrust 'em under | Sombrely scornful", *The Craftsman* 13–16; included in *A Choice of Kipling's Verse*. *Cymbeline* IV ii: "Golden lads and girls all must, | As chimney-sweepers come to dust.")

1–4 *come out to-night · · · come one come all · · · The Jellicle Moon is shining bright · · · come to the Jellicle Ball*: "Boys and girls come out to play, | The moon doth shine as bright as day · · · Come with a whoop and come with a call, | Come with a good will or not at all", nursery rhyme.   *come one come all*: traditional rhetoric since Scott. See letter to Tom Faber, Easter 1931, "if ALL the Pollice Dogs & Jellicle Cats came (and of course they all *would* come)", quoted in note to *INVITATION TO ALL POLLICLE DOGS & JELLICLE CATS TO COME TO THE BIRTHDAY OF THOMAS FABER* (in "Other Verses").

5 **Jellicle Cats are black and white**: to Tom Faber, 28 Dec 1931: "You Remember that we had a black & white Jellicle Cat that lived with us?" (see headnote to *The Old Gumbie Cat*).

7 **merry and bright**: "One finger one thumb · · · We'll all be merry and bright", nursery rhyme.

8 **caterwaul**: OED *v.* 1: "*intr.* Of cats: To make the noise proper to them at rutting time", first cit. from Chaucer.

18 **toilette**: pronounced *twa-lette* in TSE's recording. *Fowler* "toilet, -ette": "The word should be completely anglicized in spelling & sound (not –*e'tte*, nor twahle't)."

27 **terpsichorean**: the Muse Terpsichore presided over dancing. Pronounced *terp-si-korèan* in TSE's recording.

28 **To dance by the light of the Jellicle Moon**: Lear: "They danced by the light of the moon, | The moon, | The moon, | They danced by the light of the moon", *The Owl and the Pussy-Cat*. TSE: "When cats are maddened in the moonlight dance", *To Walter de la Mare* 19. "Under the light of the silvery moon", *Suite Clownesque* III 7 (and see note for the vaudeville sketch "School Boys and Girls").

Mungojerrie and Rumpelteazer

To Alison Tandy, 21 Oct 1937: "Some time ago I mentioned in a letter that I was meaning to write a Poem about TWO Cats, named Mungojerrie and Rumpelteazer—and here it is. You may not like it, because those two Cats have turned out to be even Worse than I expected."

Verso of envelope to "Mrs. Tandy herself" enclosing "Letter in English: from T. Possum", postmarked 3 Nov 1939: "How would *Wuxaboots* do as a Name for that Intruder Cat?" On "Wux" see letter to Bonamy Dobrée, 10 May 1927 in "Improper Rhymes"; "-aboots" perhaps from *Puss in Boots* or from markings on the cat.

Title **Rumpelteazer**: in Grimms' fairy tale, the dwarf Rumpelstiltskin takes his name from "Rumpelstilt", a goblin who makes rattling noises with posts.

Unadopted note on the author **By the Author of** | "*The Fantasy of Fonthill: or, Betjeman's Folly*" | **and** | "*John Foster's Aunt*": see *Noctes Binanianæ*, headnote to *Ode to a Roman Coot*. John Foster also figures in TSE's comic lines quoted in the note to *Sweeney Erect* 40.

3–4 **reputation · · · centre of operation**: of another double act: "a disreputable part of town · · · police · · · long after the centre of misery had been engulphed in his cell", *Eeldrop and Appleplex* I (1917). "centre of formalities", *Mandarins* 1 12 (see note). "F. M.": "the uproar · · · has its centre in the kitchen, but gradually it spreads · · · crashing of china · · · flinging of a heavy saucepan", *Diary of the Rive Gauche* I (1925) ("dining room smash · · · from the pantry there came a loud crash", 34–35).

3–5 **Victoria Grove · · · Cornwall Gardens · · · Launceston Place · · · Kensington**

Square: residential streets between Kensington High Street and Cromwell Road. TSE moved into two rented rooms in nearby Emperor's Gate in Apr 1937.

14 **Woolworth**: OED: "The name of the retailing company (orig. sixpenny store) F. W. Woolworth ··· used *attrib.* to designate low-priced goods regarded as typical of its merchandise", from 1931, with Auden in 1932. MacNeice had previously had "search in Heaven's Woolworth's for a soul", *Middle Age* in *Blind Fireworks* (1929). TSE to Roy Campbell, 26 Jan 1946, of a line about Penguin books in his poem *Talking Bronco*: "The line 'That Woolworthiser of ideas and theories' must be preserved at all costs." (Penguin published TSE's *Selected Poems* in 1948.)

17 **gift of the gab**: OED: "a talent for speaking, fluency of speech". Richardson's *New English Dictionary* (1835–37) specified "the gift of speaking plausibly ··· making the best of a bad cause" (see *N&Q* 27 Apr 1867). Regarded by *Partridge* as "low colloquial", so at odds with the refined district.

18 **cat-burglars**: OED: "a burglar who enters by extraordinarily skilful feats of climbing" (1907).

22 *variant* **the man that's inner**: OED "inner" 3. Phr. *the inner man*: "The inner or spiritual part of man", with Milton: "This attracts the soul, | Governs the inner man", *Paradise Regained* II 477–78. b. *humorously*: "The stomach or 'inside', esp. in reference to food."

Old Deuteronomy

To Alison Tandy, 15 Nov 1937: "I have written a number of Poems about Cats, and I thought it was time to write a Poem about a Very Old Cat; because he has only forty or fifty years more to live, and I wanted him to have the glory of a Poem about him now while he could appreciate it. Why is he called Old Deuteronomy? Well, you see, that is Greek, and it means 'second name'—at least, it means as near that as makes no difference, though perhaps not quite that; and you see when he was young he had quite an ordinary name, but when he became quite old—I mean about forty-eight or nine—the people thought that he deserved a Distinction, or a grander name, so that is the name they gave him. So will close. Your fexnite | Possum." In 1937 Alison Tandy turned seven. TSE had recently turned 49. Deuteronomy derives from δεύτερο [*deutero*] = second + νόμος [*nomos*] = law, and the Book of Deuteronomy is so named because it repeats the Decalogue and most of the laws in Exodus. But instead of Deutero-nomy TSE playfully divides the word as Deuter-onomy: δεύτερ [*deuter*] second + όνομα [*onoma*] name. For similar playfulness with Greek, see note to *Mr. Eliot's Sunday Morning Service* 32 and Pound's comment on "polymath". TSE to Polly Tandy, 4 Oct 1943: "Your two daughters progress in the Arts, which I am pleased to see (you know that Painting in Water Colours and Sketching are among my requirements for the Education of Young Ladies—I hope, by the way, that Alison is now beginning Greek with Fr. Kenton, it is high time)."

5 **buried nine wives**: combining the cat's traditional nine lives with Henry VIII's six wives?

6 **ninety-nine:** Luke 15: 7: "Joy shall be in heaven over one sinner that repenteth, more than over ninety and nine just persons, which need no repentance."

11 **Oldest Inhabitant:** human, as opposed to feline in the poem. OED "oldest" 3: "*Phr. oldest inhabitant*; freq. in joc. use", with first citation from Hawthorne's *The Scarlet Letter* (1850). But earlier are *Notes on the Month* in *The New Monthly Magazine* (1826): "It is difficult to take up a country-newspaper at some seasons of the year, without encountering a venerable personage under this title, whose business it is never to remember anything. He has never seen the like of a drought or a harvest · · · 'Well, of all the sights'—'Well, never in my born days did I see'—'Well, I don't believe within the memory of man!'" And Hawthorne again: "that twin brother of Time · · · hand-and-glove associate of all forgotten men and things,—the Oldest Inhabitant · · · 'But my brain, I think,' said the good old gentleman, 'is getting not so clear as it used to be'", *A Select Party* in *Mosses from an Old Manse* (1846); "The 'Oldest Inhabitant' seems to live, move, and have his being in the newspapers · · · The 'Oldest Inhabitant,' however, is only cited as an authority when he does not remember", *Graham's Illustrated Magazine* Jan 1857. W. W. Jacobs (1863–1943): "The oldest inhabitant of Claybury sat beneath the sign of the 'Cauliflower' and gazed with affectionate, but dim, old eyes in the direction of the village street", *In the Family* (1906). (TSE: "my sight may be failing", 15). Eden Phillpotts, *The Oldest Inhabitant*, stage comedy, 1934.

Several references to TSE and a misquotation of *Preludes* in G. K. Chesterton's *An Apology for Buffoons* in *London Mercury* June 1928 caused TSE to write to Chesterton on 2 July in protest. Chesterton replied, 4 July, that he had intended his "nonsense · · · to be quite amiable, like the tremulous badinage of the Oldest Inhabitant in the bar parlour, when he has been guyed by the brighter lads of the village" (*Letters 4* 201–202).

23 **untoward:** pronounced *untòrd* in TSE's recording.

25 ^ 26] The rhyme scheme suggests that a line is missing, ending with a rhyme for "of all" as in the first and third stanzas. In *1939* and *1953* such a line would have appeared at the head of the poem's second page, but none is present in known drafts.

33 **Fox and French Horn:** although it had closed in the 1920s or 1930s, this was probably the historic pub in Clerkenwell, the name of which was listed among "Curious Compounds" in G. A. Tomlin's *Pubs* (1922).

38 **I'll have the police if there's any uproar:** "And what with the Station it being so near", *Billy M'Caw: The Remarkable Parrot* 6.

Of the Awefull Battle of the Pekes and the Pollicles

Title] Abbreviated on contents pages to *The Pekes and the Pollicles*. Samuel Johnson's youthful translation of *Battle of the Pygmies and Cranes*, from Addison's mock-heroic Greek poem, was first published in *MLR* Jan 1936.   **Together with some Account:** John Evelyn, *Numismata: A Discourse of Medals, Antient and Modern. Together with some Account of Heads and Effigies · · · To which is added a Digression concerning Physiognomy* (1697), the turn becoming common.

4–6 say ⋯ display ⋯ fray: the first triplet in Johnson's *The Battle of the Pygmies and Cranes* rhymes "array ⋯ fray ⋯ day".

8–10 Bark bark ⋯ bark bark ⋯ hear: "KNOCK KNOCK KNOCK", *Sweeney Agonistes: Fragment of an Agon* 169 and 170. "Hark! now I hear them   scratch scratch   scratch", *Dirge* 17.

10 Until you can hear them all over the Park: "All cheering until you could hear us for miles", *Mr. Pugstyles* 48.

16 Bricklayer's Arms (*variant* Wellington Arms): the oldest pub in Putney, the Bricklayer's Arms was licensed under the Duke of Wellington's Beer Act (1830).

19 They did not advance, or exactly retreat: "Unable to fare forward or retreat", *Animula* 26.

25–26 Peke ⋯ a Heathen Chinese: Bret Harte: "The heathen Chinee is peculiar | Which the same I would rise to explain", *Plain Language from Truthful James* (1870).

33 dour: pronounced *do-er* in in TSE's recording.   **tyke:** OED: "A nickname for a Yorkshireman: in full *Yorkshire tyke.* (Perhaps originally opprobrious; but now accepted ⋯ It may have arisen from the fact that in Yorkshire *tyke* is in common use for *dog*)."

34 braw: OED: "Sc. form of *brave*, in old pronunciation".

37 *When the Blue Bonnets Came Over the Border*: Walter Scott's poetic celebration of the Jacobite army on the march in 1745. For the ferocity of the Scottish Pollicle, see *The Marching Song of the Pollicle Dogs* 31–40.

51 GREAT RUMPUSCAT: to Mary Trevelyan, 18 Nov 1944:

> I think I ate something which was unsympathetic a few days ago.

> In the year that King Uzziah died,
> Rumpuscat felt bad inside.

(Requies-cat?) Isaiah 6: 1: "In the year that king Uzziah died I saw also the Lord sitting upon a throne". (As King of Jerusalem for 52 years, he was stricken by the Lord with leprosy for permitting sacrificial rituals: 2 Kings 15: 2–5.)

52 His eyes were like fireballs fearfully blazing: to Hayward, 23 June 1944: "the eye of the small pekinese had popped out while it was being given medicine. That is one of the unpleasant features of these unpleasant little animals. Eventually the vet got the eye back again and the dog is reported to be seeing with it: but from now on I shall always be uncomfortable to be in the same room with one of these wretched creatures, for fear of its eye coming out."

59 scattered like sheep: Matthew 9: 36: "scattered abroad, as sheep."

Mr. Mistoffelees

Title Mistoffelees: *Mister* + *Mephistopheles.* (For "a mixture of silly and Beelzebub", see headnote to volume, 8. APROPOS OF *PRACTICAL CATS* BY VALERIE ELIOT.)

2 Conjuring: OED "conjure" III: "To invoke by supernatural power, to effect by magic or jugglery" and 5a: "To call upon, constrain (a devil or spirit) to appear or do one's bidding, by the invocation of some sacred name or the use of some 'spell'." Marlowe: "Faustus, thou art conjuror laureate | That canst command great Mephistophilis", *Dr. Faustus* I iii (1604 text), with "conjure" and "conjuring" throughout the play.

4–5 **All his | Inventions are off his own bat**: OED "off his own bat", originally from cricket, also "*fig.* solely by his own exertions" (citing this poem). For "It's my own invention", see headnote to "Uncollected Poems", 3. *INVENTIONS OF THE MARCH HARE*.

10–11 **At prestidigitation | And at legerdemain**: OED "prestidigitation": "Slight of hand, legerdemain". The awkwardness for cats is evident in the etymologies (*preste*, nimble + *digitus*, finger; and *léger de main*, light of hand).

28 **cunning**: see note to *Verses to Honour and Magnify Sir Geoffrey Faber Kt.* 4.

Macavity: The Mystery Cat

Geoffrey Tandy to TSE 6 Feb 1938: "Report on MACAVITY: THE MYSTERY CAT. The *General Impression* is entirely favourable. It has been read to Mr Richard Tandy and Miss Alison Tandy who received it very well and said that they liked it very much. Mr Richard Tandy observed that 'it's like Growltiger, but not so rough and tumble'. Of the corpus known to him he places *Old Deuteronomy* and *The Old Gumbie Cat* second. He says he would like to hear about other Kinds of Cat. He does not find any troublesome obscurity in *Macavity*. Miss Alison Tandy, examined separately, expressed herself well pleased with *Macavity*; but exhibited the same preferences and order of merit as her brother. On Moral Grounds I regret to see that, unlike Growltiger, the criminal seems to escape the due reward of his deeds." Geoffrey Tandy queried 12, 23 and 27–31 (see below) and then concluded "I think it 'sounds' well" (BL Add. 71003 fol.8).

TSE to Frank Morley, 17 Feb 1938: "I have done a new Cat, modelled on the late Prof. Moriarty, but he doesn't seem very popular: too sophisticated perhaps."

Macavity was reprinted in Herbert Read's anthology *The Knapsack: A Pocket-book of Prose and Verse* (1939).

Conan Doyle on Professor Moriaty: "He is the Napoleon of crime, Watson. He is the organiser of half that is evil and of nearly all that is undetected in this great city · · · He does little himself. He only plans. But his agents are numerous and splendidly organised · · · The agent may be caught · · · But the central power which uses the agent is never caught—never so much as suspected", *The Final Problem* in *The Memoirs of Sherlock Holmes*, the story alluded to throughout the poem. (Byron: "Was reckoned a considerable time, | The grand Napoleon of the realms of rhyme", *Don Juan* XI lv.) Most of the parallels between specific lines and *The Final Problem* were identified by H. T. Webster and H. W. Starr in *Baker Street Journal* Oct 1954. Priscilla Preston: "The humour is increased if one realizes that Macavity is modelled on a particular villain, Professor Moriarty, the most sinister of all of Sherlock Holmes's opponents. Mr Eliot intended this relationship to be recognized by the reader. [*Footnote*: Confirmed in a letter of 28 Nov 1956]", *MLR* July 1959. Katharine Loesch also noted similarities, *N&Q* Jan 1959.

A note signed by Anne Bradby [Ridler], probably dating from 1937, and preserved by Hayward at King's, describes *"John O'London's Weekly* ringing up to tell me severely that Mr. Eliot had cribbed from Conan Doyle, and their not being able to understand that he did it on purpose." This probably referred to the borrowing in *Murder in the Cathedral* of a short dialogue from another Sherlock Holmes story, *The Musgrave Ritual*, pointed out by Elizabeth Jackson in the *Saturday Review of Literature* 25 Jan 1941.

This borrowing was remarked again by Grover Smith in *N&Q* 2 Oct 1948, and letters to the *TLS* of 19 and 26 Jan, and 23 Feb 1951. Another letter, on 28 Sept 1951, quoted TSE himself: "My use of the *Musgrave Ritual* was deliberate and wholly conscious." When solicitors then complained on behalf of the Conan Doyle Estate, Faber was obliged to seek legal advice. TSE then suggested that he should "state his willingness to print an acknowledgement · · · in the next edition of the play in which the words from *The Musgrave Ritual* appear. He will then re-write the passage referred to so that it is no longer based on *The Musgrave Ritual*. There would therefore in fact never be any acknowledgement, because the new passage would be inserted before the book is reprinted" (Peter du Sautoy to Field, Roscoe & Co., 8 Aug 1952, Faber archive). Apparently no further action was taken by the Conan Doyle Estate.

Charles Monteith on TSE's loyalty to Holmes: "As evidence of his continuing enthusiasm he extracted from his wallet a formidable stack of membership cards from Sherlock Holmes societies all over the United States: the Speckled Band of Cincinnati, the Brooklyn Red-headed League, the Silver Blazes of Minnesota, more than a dozen. 'The old lady,' he said observing the pile with mild surprise, 'shows her medals'", *Eliot in the Office* (Faber archive). For "the great Sherlock Holmes play", see headnote 3. COMPOSITION, above.

Durrell, of an occasion soon after publication of *Four Quartets*: "At the mention of the name [Conan Doyle] he lit up like a torch · · · 'I flatter myself,' he said,—and this is the nearest to an immodesty that I had ever heard him go—'that I know the names of everyone, even the smallest character.' Two minutes afterward he found he could not recall the name of one of Conan Doyle's puppets. His annoyance was comical. He struck his knee with irritation and concentrated. It would not come. Then he burst out laughing at himself · · · 'By the way,' he said anxiously, 'I trust that you, as a genuine Holmes fan, noticed the reference to him in *Burnt Norton*.' I had not. He looked shocked and pained. 'Really not?' he said. 'You do disappoint me deeply. A clear reference to *The Hound of the Baskervilles*. I refer to the 'great Grimpen Marsh,' do you recall? Yes, then I remembered; but I had forgotten that it features in the Holmes story. 'But listen, Eliot, with all this critical work on your sources, has nobody mentioned it?' His eye lit up like the eye of a zealot. 'Not yet,' he said under his breath. 'They haven't twigged it. 'But please don't tell anyone, will you?' I promised to keep his secret." (The "grimpen" occurs in *East Coker* II 41; the error was probably Durrell's.)

TSE's enjoyment of detective novels, spoofs and riddling came together in a message to John Hayward [6 Jan 1936]: "THE SUPPLY OF GAME FOR LONDON IS GOING STEADILY UP. HEAD KEEPER HUDSON, WE BELIEVE, HAS BEEN NOW TOLD TO RECEIVE ALL ORDERS FOR FLY-PAPER, AND FOR PRESERVATION OF YOUR HEN PHEASANT'S LIFE." On [20 Jan 1939] he sent Hayward a cutting:

HE KNOWS THE CAT SLAYER

From our own correspondent Ipswich, Monday.

Such is the cunning of Holbrook's cat-slayer that it may take three months to bring him to justice and completely solve the riddle of the vanishing cats.

After a week-end of investigations, William Coombs, called the "Inspector Hornleigh of the pet world" has returned to the London headquarters of Our Dumb Friends' League, his brief case packed with documentary evidence including an anonymous letter.

Mr. Coombs is confident that he knows the identity of the cat-killer.

"But bringing a successful prosecution is a different matter," he told ex-Serviceman John Lamb, leader of the Holbrook cat lovers. "However, we are determined to see the thing through, and if necessary we shall send an investigator down here for three months."

"He was wonderful," Mr. Lamb told me to-day. "Talking to him was like consulting Sherlock Holmes, and things which I had regarded as immaterial he recognised immediately as important clues."

The whole village is pinning its faith on the Inspector.

Title **Macavity**: Ronald A. MacAvity attended Milton Academy two years behind TSE (*Stayer*). ***The Mystery Cat***: "The Mr. E. Cat"? (*Bevis*).

1 **Hidden Paw**: E. D. E. N. Southworth's adventure novel *The Hidden Hand* (serial, 1859; book, 1888) was often dramatised. Conan Doyle: *Spiritualists and the Hidden Hand*, letter to the editor, *Daily Express* 4 May 1925.

2 **who can defy the law**: Conan Doyle: "some deep organizing power which forever stands in the way of the law", *The Final Problem*.

3 **Flying Squad**: formed in 1919 and so-called (informally) for its brief to range across London in pursuit of professional criminals.

4–31 **when** (*eight times in all*): Kipling: "And when the Thing that Couldn't has occurred", *The Song of the Banjo* 19; see note to *Portrait of a Lady* I 15–19.

6 **he breaks the law of gravity**: Kipling: "Laws of gravitation scorning", *La Nuit Blanche* 11.

6, 8 **he breaks the law of gravity · · · Macavity's not there**: Henry James: "not finding him present when by all the laws and the logic of life he should *be* present · · · he is definitely *not there*", notes for *The Sense of the Past* (pub. with the novel in 1917).

11–13 **he's very tall and thin · · · his eyes are sunken in. | His brow is deeply lined with thought, his head is highly domed**: Conan Doyle: "His appearance was quite familiar to me. He is extremely tall and thin, his forehead domes out in a white curve, and his two eyes are deeply sunken in this head · · · His shoulders are rounded from much study", *The Final Problem*.

12 **for**: queried by Tandy, but unchanged (see headnote).

15 **He sways his head from side to side, with movements like a snake**: Conan

Doyle: "his face protrudes forward, and is forever slowly oscillating from side to side in a curiously reptilian fashion · · · He rose also and looked at me in silence, shaking his head sadly", *The Final Problem*. TSE: "The great snake · · · awakens in hunger and moving his head to right and to left prepares for his hour to devour", *Choruses from "The Rock"* X 7–8.

23 **The jewel-case is rifled**: Geoffrey Tandy on the draft reading "the jewels have been rifled": "A box, a safe or a bag can be rifled; but can jewels?"

23–29 **rifled · · · stifled · · · a Treaty's gone astray · · · a scrap of paper**: Conan Doyle: "Is there a crime to be done, a paper to be abstracted, we will say, a house to be rifled, a man to be removed—the word is passed to the Professor", *The Final Problem*.

26 **Ay, there's the wonder of the thing**: Conan Doyle: "Aye, there's the genius and the wonder of the thing!" *The Final Problem*. "Aye there's the rub", *Hamlet* III i, thence colloquial (Shawn Worthington, personal communication).

27–28 **Foreign Office find a Treaty's gone astray, | Or the Admiralty lose some plans**: as in Conan Doyle's *The Adventure of the Naval Treaty* and *The Adventure of the Bruce-Partington Plans*. Holmes's "interference in the matter of the 'Naval Treaty'" is also alluded to in *The Final Problem*.

27–31] Geoffrey Tandy queried: "Do you like Foreign Office, Admiralty and Secret Service as plural nouns?" The lines remained unchanged.

29 **a scrap of paper in the hall or on the stair**: Conan Doyle: "As I took it up a small square of paper upon which it had lain fluttered down on to the ground", *The Final Problem*.

33–34 **You'll be sure to find him · · · doing complicated long division sums**: Conan Doyle: "endowed by nature with a phenomenal mathematical faculty · · · no possible connection will ever be traced between the gentleman upon whose front teeth I have barked my knuckles and the retiring mathematical coach, who is, I dare say, working out problems upon a black-board ten miles away", *The Final Problem*.

41–42 **nothing more than agents**: Conan Doyle: "He does little himself. He only plans. But his agents are numerous and splendidly organized", *The Final Problem*.

42 **the Napoleon of Crime**: Conan Doyle: "He is the Napoleon of crime, Watson", *The Final Problem*. TSE to Hayward, 2 Jan 1936: "Your true Napoleon of crime, John, never descends to such commonplace devices." To Hayward, 17 Aug 1942: "the Napoleon of Cinematography, Mr. George Hoellering".

Gus: The Theatre Cat

To Geoffrey Tandy, 10 Feb 1938: "I fear that if Gus is too antiquated for a young man like you, it will be completely unintelligible to a youngster like [Ian] Cox."

2 **as I ought to have told you before**: "my sister, of whom I have told you before", *Pollicle Dogs and Jellicle Cats* 38.

16 **Irving · · · Tree:** actor-managers Sir Henry Irving (1838–1905) and his rival in Shakespeare, Sir Herbert Beerbohm Tree (1852–1917). TSE was introduced on 28 Oct 1934 to Sir Henry's grandson, the theatrical designer Laurence Irving, who was involved in commissioning *Murder in the Cathedral* and designed the set. At Christmas 1957, TSE gave a copy of *Henry Irving* by Laurence Irving (Faber, 1957) to the producer of all of his own plays, E. Martin Browne.

16 *variant* **Benson:** Sir Frank Benson (1858–1939) acted with Tree before becoming an actor-manager and reviving many neglected Shakespeare plays. TSE met him on 5 July 1934.

17–18 **his success · · · gave him seven cat-calls:** as though cries of "Encore". OED "cat-call" 1: "A squeaking instrument, or kind of whistle, used esp. in play-houses to express impatience or disapprobation." 2: "The sound made by this instrument or an imitation with the voice", citing Johnson: "Should partial cat-calls all his hopes confound", Prologue to *Irene*.

20 **Firefrorefiddle, the Fiend of the Fell:** Milton's Hell and the fallen angels: "the parching air | Burns frore, and cold performs th'effect of fire", *Paradise Lost* II 595–96.   **the Fiend of the Fell:** feline equivalent of Conan Doyle's Hound of the Baskervilles. Scott: "It was the Spirit of the Flood that spoke, | And he called on the Spirit of the Fell", *The Lay of the Last Minstrel* I 103–104.

23 **to gag:** in the Victorian theatre, to interpolate spontaneous material when performing (see OED *n.* 1, 3).

25 **I knew how to act with my back and my tail:** the rhetorical stiffness of Victorian theatre was gradually supplanted by new schools of acting such as those of F. Matthias Alexander (Alexander technique) and Constantin Stanislavski (Method acting), emphasizing the body's expressiveness.

27, 29 **the hardest of hearts · · · Little Nell:** Oscar Wilde (attrib.) on Dickens's character in *The Old Curiosity Shop*: "One would have to have a heart of stone to read the death of little Nell without dissolving into tears of laughter."

30 **When the Curfew was rung, then I swung on the bell:** Rose Hartwick Thorpe's *Curfew Must Not Ring Tonight* (1867) tells how, with her sweetheart condemned to die when the curfew sounds, Bessie grasps the bell's tongue:

> Out she swung,—far out. The city seemed a speck of light below,—
> There 'twixt heaven and earth suspended, as the bell swung to and fro.
> And the sexton at the bell-rope, old and deaf, heard not the bell,
> Sadly thought that twilight curfew rang young Basil's funeral knell.

A favourite for recitations, the poem was also made into three silent films (Barbara Lauriat, personal communication).

32 **Dick Whittington's Cat:** "I am the Cat who was Dick Whittington's", *Cat's Prologue* 9 ("Other Verses").

35 **toothful:** OED 1: "As much as would fill a tooth; a small mouthful, esp. of liquor", from 1774.

36 *East Lynne:* melodramatic novel by Mrs. Henry Wood, 1861, soon adapted for the stage; filmed 1916.

37–38 **At a Shakespeare performance he once walked on pat · · · the need for a**

cat: *King Lear* I ii: EDMUND: "And pat he comes like the catastrophe of the old comedy." *The Merchant of Venice* IV i: "Why he, a harmless necessary cat".

39–40 **a Tiger · · · Which an Indian Colonel pursued down a drain:** Conan Doyle: Colonel Sebastian Moran "was always a man of iron nerve, and the story is still told in India how he crawled down a drain after a wounded, man-eating tiger", *The Empty House* (*Priscilla Preston*).

44 **when a house was on fire:** melodramas such as Boucicault's *The Poor of New York* (1857) showed burning buildings on stage for the first time.

45–48 **"Now these kittens, they do not get trained | As we did · · · jump through a hoop:** *Hamlet* II ii, ROSENCRANTZ: "there is, sir, an eyrie of children, little eyases, that cry out on the top of question; and are most tyrannically clapped for't; these are now the fashion".

Bustopher Jones: The Cat about Town

In the copies of *Old Possum's Book of Practical Cats* in which he wrote *emendations A* and *emendations B*, TSE noted the original (alternative) readings "One club that he's fixed on's the Wormwood and Brixton" and "Joint Correctional Schools" (13, 16). In the copy of *1939* that contains *emendations C* he also identified: *Fox's* = Brooks's; *Blimp's* = White's; *Stage and Screen* = Garrick; *Pothunter's* = Orleans; *Drones* = Boodle's; *Siamese* = Oriental; *Tomb* = Athenæum. Against *Glutton* he wrote "?" The other clubs were perhaps *Senior Educational* = Oxford and Cambridge; *Joint Superior Schools* = Public Schools; *Glutton* = Beefsteak. Facetious names were evidently in vogue, for on 25 Feb 1930 TSE invited Dobrée to lunch at "the Low Society Club".

To Hayward, 22 Oct 1940, after bombing of the Oxford and Cambridge Club: "The O. & C. has now been patched up · · · but its atmosphere is unrestful because it has given refuge to three other clubs which are in a worse way, and the mixture of types is disturbing." [2 Feb] 1942: "I think of trying to join the Garrick, because it does not appear to be crowded with supernumerary wartime feeders, because it still has a certain proportion of male staff, because it still is possible to entertain guests there in a *cabinet particulier*, useful also for ladies (not les girls) and because I am told by Ashley Dukes that H. G. Wells is not, as I had thought, a member · · · You would have liked the Authors' Club · · · as much like a club as one floor of an office building can be: the food is poor, the members are musty. I still have not placed the Authors: it was a snowy day, and some of the most eminent, e.g. Sir Wm. Beach Thomas, did not turn up. There was a stout Colonial Office man named Sir. Wm. Dawe; there was a whimsical man with a little white beard who talked to me about his cat. The atmosphere is that of Brothers of the Pen: rather more refined brothers than frequent the pothouse called the Savage, and rather more antiquated brothers, dug out of suburban retirement, than the brethren of the Savile." TSE resigned from the O & C, his earliest London club, in Dec 1957, after more than 25 years, because he no longer used it, but maintained his memberships of the Garrick and Athenæum and also listed "several dining clubs, the Burke Club (political), All Souls' Club (religious)" and numerous overseas memberships, in *Harvard College Class of 1910, Fiftieth Anniversary Report* (1960). In 1930 he was also using the Royal

Societies Club in St. James's. He had been clubbable since his Harvard days, when he joined the Southern Club, the Digamma (Fox Club), the Signet Society and the Stylus Club.

Title **Bustopher**: Mustapha (Arab.) = "the Chosen One". (Christopher = Christ-bearer.)

7 **mousers · · · trousers**: pronounced *mouzers · · · trouzers* in TSE's recording.

7–10 **well-cut trousers · · · Brummell**: Beau Brummell (1778–1840), *arbiter elegantiarum* of Regency Mayfair, credited with establishing men's fitted suits, including full-length trousers.

12 **in white spats**: for "the original Man in White Spats—only begetter of Bustopher Jones and Skimbleshanks", see note to TSE's Preface.

14–16 **it is against the rules | For any one Cat to belong both to that | And the *Joint Superior Schools***: "Mr. Beaumont Pease has recently been elected to the captaincy of the Royal & Ancient Golf Club of St. Andrew's. He is also captain of the Royal St. George's Golf Club, and therefore will hold the two offices concurrently", reporting the dinner of the British Bankers' Association, *A Commentary* in *Criterion* July 1931. (Properly, "St Andrews" with no apostrophe.)   **it is against the rules · · · Cat · · · Schools**: "Mary had a little lamb · · · it followed her to school one day, | That was against the rule; | It made the children laugh and play | To see a lamb at school", nursery rhyme.

17 **when game is in season**: for a cat that asked "why wasn't there more Game even when there was no Game in Season", see letter to Tom Faber, 28 Dec 1931, in headnote to *The Old Gumbie Cat*. "He always knows what game is in season", *The Practical Cat* 18.

21 **venison · · · ben'son**: pronounced *ven'zon · · · ben'zon* in TSE's recording. This pronunciation of "venison" is the first of three in OED, which recommends the pronunciation *benn-is'n*. (TSE initially wrote "benison".) TSE rhymes "benison · · · Tennyson" in *An Exhortation* 6, 8 (see note).

37 *variant* **to put it in rhyme: "I shall last out my time"**: Bustopher's "time" rhymes only internally with "rhyme" itself, an effect made more visible by TSE's bracketing of "(to put it in rhyme)" in his emendations (first printed in *1964 pbk*). See Textual History.

39 **Pall Mall**: (pronounced *pal mal*), the smart avenue that is home to several London clubs. See note to *Montpelier Row* author's Notes 13.

Skimbleshanks: The Railway Cat

To Alison Tandy, 2 Mar 1938: "I am trying to do a Poem about a Railway Train Cat, and if I can do it I will send it to you in due course." To Hayward on the same day: "I am plodding on with the Railway Cat, and have produced one good line, viz.: 'All the guards and all the porters and the superintendent's daughters—'." To Enid Faber, 8 Mar 1938: "The Railway Cat (L.M.S.) is rather stuck." (The West Coast line to Scotland run by the London, Midland and Scottish Railway, 1923–48, was at this time in competition with the East Coast line of the London and North Eastern Railway. The six-and-a-half hour Coronation Scot service was introduced by the L.M.S.

in 1937.) A "Supplementary Agenda" by TSE (dated by Hayward 14 Mar 1938 and beginning with "A Night at the Flicks") includes "Railway Cats". This may indicate that TSE was reading the poem to Hayward, or consulting him about it. *Smart* 12, on Hayward's fascination with trains: "a party piece in later life was a vigorous full-voiced imitation of steam engines". (For Hayward as "only begetter" of this poem, see note to Preface, "the Man in White Spats".)

To Geoffrey Faber, 29 Oct 1937: "Having just arrived from Edinburgh by the Night Mail, your Agent has the honour to submit the following report · · · P.S. One does feel a Swell leaving by sleeping car and walking up and down the station platform in a dinner jacket." The term "Night Mail" could apply to any train carrying mail, including those with sleeping cars, as well as specifically to Travelling Post Offices, which were devoted entirely to mail and had onboard sorting offices. A Travelling Post Office is the subject of the 1936 documentary film *Night Mail*, which begins: "8.30pm, weekdays and Sundays, the down Postal Special leaves Euston for Glasgow, Edinburgh and Aberdeen". For Auden's poem *Night Mail* (1935), commissioned for the film, see *The English Auden* ed. Edward Mendelson (1977) 290–92. (OED "down" c: "Of a train or coach: Going 'down', i.e. away from the central or chief terminus; in Great Britain, from London.")

1–3 **There's a whisper down the line · · · Saying "Skimble, where is Skimble":** Kipling: "There's a whisper down the field where the year has shot her yield · · · Singing: 'Over then, come over'", *The Long Trail* 1, 3 (in *A Choice of Kipling's Verse*) (G. Schmidt, *N&Q* Dec 1970).   **11.39:** "Trains from Bristol, Cardiff, Manchester, Stoke, Liverpool and Birmingham bring a thousand bags of mails for the north between 10.57 and 11.39pm", *Night Mail* (commentary).

3 **hunt the thimble:** children's party game.

5 **porters · · · daughters:** "O the moon shone bright on Mrs. Porter | And on her daughter", *The Waste Land* [III] 199–200.

12 **busy in the luggage van:** TSE, 23 Dec 1963: "When I was a boy and we travelled by train from St. Louis to the East, I was always apprehensive. I always feared that it would pull out in front of our eyes, or that my father, busy with seeing the luggage put aboard, would miss the train", reported *Levy* 135.

14 **the signal goes "All Clear!":** Kipling: "And it's 'All clear aft'", *The Long Trail* 43.

15 **off at last for the northern part:** Kipling: "It's North you may run", *The Long Trail* 13.

18 **Sleeping Car Express:** to Hayward, 30 Apr 1943, on a trip to Edinburgh: "the journey, with a first class sleeping compartment to oneself, is as pleasant as ever: all my life Sleeping Cars have spelled Romance to me."

19 **bagmen:** OED 2a: "*spec.* A commercial traveller. (*Somewhat depreciatory*)" with "A traveller—I mean a bagman, not a tourist—arriving with his samples at a provincial town" (1865). TSE: "An undernourished bagman", *Dearest Mary* | *Je suis très affairé* 4. To William Empson, 24 July 1936: "I was travelling back from Derby last week, and sat opposite two Midland bagmen". Dickens, *Pickwick Papers* ch. XIV includes "a Tale told by a Bagman".

22 **in the First and in the Third:** Victorian railways had First, Second and Third Class accommodation. The companies were obliged by law to provide Third

Class, so when the poorest coaches were upgraded in the 1870s to reduce the number of classes, it was Second that was nominally abolished. First and Third were finally renamed First and Second in 1956.

27 **hilarity:** pronounced *hylarity* in TSE's recording of 1957.

38 **button · · · to make a breeze:** air-conditioning was first introduced on overnight trains (in the US) in 1932.　　**button:** the emendation from "handle" may reflect changes in sleeper cars. The early fittings were handles to be turned.

61 **Gallowgate:** TSE is unlikely to have visited this run-down area of east Glasgow. It had formerly had two stations, but neither was on the main line from London.

The Ad-dressing of Cats

On TSE's 1957 recording of *Practical Cats*, this is the last poem, following *Cat Morgan Introduces Himself* (there as *Morgan, the Commissionaire Cat*).

20–21 **Now Dogs pretend they like to fight · · · bite:** Isaac Watts: "Let dogs delight to bark and bite, | For God hath made them so; | Let bears and lions growl and fight, | For 'tis their nature too · · · But, children, you should never let | Such angry passions rise", *Against Quarrelling.*

22–23 **A Dog is · · · a simple soul:** "Issues from the hand of God, the simple soul", *Animula* 1.

37 **A Dog's a Dog — a cat's a cat:** Burns: "A man's a man for a' that", *Is There for Honest Poverty* (refrain).

45 **o cat!:** recalling the declension of Latin nouns, vocative form.

49 **oopsa cat!:** "OOPSA! The Practical Cat", *The Practical Cat* 16.

50 **James Buz-James:** A. A. Milne: "James James | Morrison Morrison | Weatherby George Dupree", *Disobedience* in *When We Were Very Young* (1924). TSE used Messrs. James & James, a firm of solicitors, during the 1930s, and Buz is a name within the law thanks to Dickens's Mr. Serjeant Buzfuz, counsel for the plaintiff in Bardell v. Pickwick (see note to unadopted headings to Parts I and II of *The Waste Land*: "HE DO THE POLICE IN DIFFERENT VOICES"). The Victorian judge and legal historian James Fitzjames Stephen was an uncle of Virginia Woolf's. Ford Madox Ford (previously Hueffer) died in June 1939.

51 **we've not got so far as names:** to Herbert Read, 22 Mar 1943: "Who is this strange lady friend of Peter Gregory's, who called me by my first name after half an hour's acquaintance?" See note to *Five-Finger Exercises* V 1 on dropping the "Mister".

57 **Strassburg Pie:** duck foie gras wrapped in bacon and baked in a puff pastry loaf.

60–61 **habit | Of eating nothing else but rabbit:** TSE in 1955–56: "Our housekeeper has her problems with Pettipaws! The previous cat I had, named Wiscus, was a fussy eater, too! · · · Pettipaws, who dominates this establishment and whose insistence on eating nothing but rabbit is going to bring us to penury", *Levy* 69, 76. TSE: "a matter of habit · · · won't eat rabbit", *The Rum Tum Tugger* 24–26.

Cat Morgan Introduces Himself

First printed in *Faber Book News*, with a note: "Morgan's verses may be reproduced without his permission." Published in *The Bookseller*, 13 Oct 1951. Reprinted after Morgan's death as a broadside by Donald Gallup (E2g) in 1953. A copy of this was autographed "pp. Exors. of the late Sir Henry Morgan. T. S. Eliot" (Bonhams, 28 Mar 2006). Added to *Practical Cats* in 1953, but not to American editions until the paperback of 1968.

In the recording, where this poem is entitled *Morgan, the Commissionaire Cat*, TSE begins, as though answering the telephone: "Morgan speaking · · ·"

To Hayward, 3 Mar 1944: "a black cat has recently added itself to the society of 24 and 23 Russell Square, which is a great comfort". 14 Apr: "this week I have been alone (with occasional visits from Cat Morgan) doing my own charring". To Hope Mirrlees [Oct 1944]: "Morgan has sat on my lap for a short time every evening, both times smelling strongly of fish. He is getting so fat that he has to stop for breath going up stairs."

To Christina Morley, 27 Apr 1945: "The most remarkable addition to the staff is Cat Morgan, the ex-pirate (now the commissionaire: there is a poem about him)." To Polly Tandy, 22 May 1945: "I am glad to say that the first person to greet me on my return to Russell Square, late at night, was Cat Morgan the Commissionaire. Did I ever send you the poem he wrote?"

Morley Kennerley to the Faber directors, 2 Oct 1951: "Much to my surprise and delight Mr. Eliot handed me last night a poem about Morgan. I have only just had time to read the poem and have dictated the attached this morning without any thought whatsoever, for I simply haven't had time. Will you please revise this and add your own bright ideas. This note is to be roneod and sent out to the press (our bulletin list with the new catalogue); therefore I don't think the note should be too erudite." Kennerley's dictated note became the first page of *Faber Book News*, sent to trade and press with the catalogue:

> The front cover of Faber & Faber's new Autumn and Winter catalogue bears an attractive drawing by Margaret Wolpe of the portico of 24, Russell Square. Even some of the firm's directors had not noticed that the railings, as shown, are on one side Victorian—on the other Georgian. On the back cover you will find a

> He is advancing to take up his favourite seat, cuddled up against and protected by the door-scraper. Morgan, for that is his name, is the Faber & Faber cat. He has for some time been much interested in the re-building and re-decorating of the two Faber

buildings, for he was present when the flying bomb, which did so much damage, landed just across the road in Russell Square. Many who have been attracted by

obviously an animal of great character, have asked for information about him. We felt it impertinent to attempt to supply such data ourselves. One of the firm's directors, having a special affection for Morgan, who comforted him during the trying nights of fire-watching, offered to approach Morgan personally about his lives, and Morgan, with some show of affected diffidence, handed him the following a few days ago. We were astonished to find the biographical note written in verse, but perhaps this is not surprising if one considers the literary atmosphere in which he has passed so much of his life, and the many visiting poets at whose feet he has sat. Morgan says that the present shortage of paper is a triviality compared to the shortage of fish which he lived through some years ago, but he is sympathetic to the problems of others and has so arranged his natural history that the first and last verses form an entity when printed by themselves.

TSE to C. St. B. Seale, 10 July 1952, replying to a request to reprint the poem in *The Animals' Magazine*: "I would only ask that you should also print a note to the effect that this venerable animal died on the morning of July 7th, 1952 in spite of all that veterinary science and domestic care could do for him, of extreme old age." *The Animals' Magazine* Sept 1952 duly complied (identifying the poem as written "through the pen of T. S. Eliot, O.M.").

To Robert L. Beare, 12 Nov 1958: "The broadsheets of *Cat Morgan's Apology* were printed primarily for circulation amongst the Directors and Staff of Faber & Faber, who had known Cat Morgan personally. The poem was originally composed as advertising matter for the firm. Subsequently Cat Morgan has died and the value of the broadsheets has risen in consequence · · · You are correct in assuming that the poem appeared first on the mimeographed sheets, to be circulated to booksellers."

Title **Morgan**: TSE to Hayward, 13 Oct 1936, of the Oxford and Cambridge Club: "I had a good welcome at the club to-day Morgan said now sir I have got a new chef who cooks the roast beef the way you like it and Smith the Strangers Room Steward came in and said we have a consignment of Old Cheshire from Mr. Hutchinson · · · which I think you will appreciate." To Hope Mirrlees, 12 Sept [1941]: "I am chiefly worried at the moment by hearing that Morgan may be taken from her [Mappie Mirrlees] · · · I imagine that the difficulty about these female chauffeur-gardeners is their ambiguous place between the drawing room and the servants' hall."

1 **Pirate**: Peter du Sautoy to John Ferrone, 2 Apr 1968: "Eliot used to call the cat Captain Morgan, after the famous pirate, but it was in fact a stray that became our caretaker's pet and was really called something quite ordinary like Tibbles."

Privateer and pirate Admiral Sir Henry Morgan (1635?–88) was notorious for his raids on settlements on the Spanish Main.

3, 4 **ease · · · Bloomsbury Square**: "Leicester Square · · · ease", *Paysage Triste* 7, 13 (at line ends). Faber & Gwyer moved to 24 Russell Square on 28 Dec 1925.

7 **on the 'ouse**: OED "house" *n.*[1] c: "on the house: at the expense of the tavern, saloon, etc. (orig. *U.S.*)", with *Kansas City* (Missouri) *Times & Star*, 1889, then 1934.

9 **I ain't got much polish, me manners is gruff**: *Fowler* ("be"), on *a(i)n't* for *isn't*: "an uneducated blunder · · · But it is a pity that *a(i)n't* for *am not*, being a natural construction & supplying a real want, should shock us as though tarred with the same brush · · · there is no abbreviation but *ain't I?* for *am I not?* or *am not I?* · · · the speaker's sneaking affection for the *ain't I* that he (or still more she) fears will convict him of low breeding."

12 *variant* **'e's got a good 'art**: to Mary Trevelyan, 30 Oct 1944, enclosing *Four Quartets*: "I can't tell you what a wonderful letter that was, and I am sending you me 4tets this week, and my prattle is no return for such a letter, but remember that like Cat Morgan I have a good Heart really and a serious side to him."

13 **Barbary Coast**: north African coast renowned for piracy and slavery.

14 **melliferous**: mellifluous, melodious, odoriferous. "vociferous · · · fumiferous", *The Triumph of Bullshit* 17–21.

17 **Faber—or Faber**: when Faber & Gwyer was reorganised in 1929, Geoffrey Faber proposed a variety of names. Although he was the only member of his family on the board, he played the dual role of chairman and principal director, and the name chosen was Faber & Faber.

Anabasis

CHANSON
SONG

ANABASE
ANABASIS

CHANSON
SONG

CHANSON

Il naissait un poulain sous les feuilles de bronze. Un homme mit des baies amères dans nos mains. Étranger. Qui passait. Et voici qu'il est bruit d'autres provinces à mon gré . . . 'Je vous salue, ma fille, sous le plus grand des arbres de l'année.'

* * *

Car le Soleil entre au Lion et l'Étranger a mis son doigt dans la bouche des morts. Étranger. Qui riait. Et nous parle d'une herbe. Ah! tant de souffles aux provinces! Qu'il est d'aisance dans nos voies! que la trompette m'est délice et la plume savante au scandale de l'aile! . . . 'Mon âme, grande fille, vous aviez vos façons qui ne sont pas les nôtres.'

* * *

Il naquit un poulain sous les feuilles de bronze. Un homme mit ces baies amères dans nos mains. Étranger. Qui passait. Et voici d'un grand bruit dans un arbre de bronze. Bitume et roses, don du chant! Tonnerre et flûtes dans les chambres! Ah! tant d'aisance dans nos voies, ha! tant d'histoires à l'année, et l'Étranger à ses façons par les chemins de toute la terre! . . . 'Je vous salue, ma fille, sous la plus belle robe de l'année.'

SONG

Under the bronze leaves a colt was foaled. Came such an one   i
who laid bitter fruit in our hands. Stranger. Who passed. Here
comes news of other provinces to my liking.—'Hail, daughter!
under the tallest tree of the year.'

* * *

For the Sun enters the sign of the Lion and the Stranger   ii
has laid his finger on the mouth of the Dead. Stranger. Who
laughed. And tells us of an herb. O from the provinces blow
many winds. What ease to our way! how the trumpet rejoices
my heart and the feather revels in the scandal of the wing! 'My
Soul, great girl, you had your ways which are not ours.'

* * *

Under the bronze leaves a colt had been foaled. Came such   iii
an one who laid this bitter fruit in our hands. Stranger. Who
passed. Out of the bronze tree comes a great bruit of voices.
Roses and bitumen, gift of song, thunder and fluting in the
rooms. O what ease in our ways, how many tales to the year, and
by the roads of all the earth the Stranger to his ways . . . 'Hail,
daughter! robed in the loveliest robe of the year.'

ANABASE

I

Sur trois grandes saisons m'établissant avec honneur, j'augure bien du sol où j'ai fondé ma loi.

Les armes au matin sont belles et la mer. A nos chevaux livrée la terre sans amandes

nous vaut ce ciel incorruptible. Et le soleil n'est point nommé, mais sa puissance est parmi nous

et la mer au matin comme une présomption de l'esprit.

Puissance, tu chantais sur nos routes nocturnes! . . . Aux ides pures du matin que savons-nous du songe, notre aînesse?

Pour une année encore parmi vous! Maître du grain, maître du sel, et la chose publique sur de justes balances!

Je ne hélerai point les gens d'une autre rive. Je ne tracerai point de grands

quartiers de villes sur les pentes avec le sucre des coraux. Mais j'ai dessein de vivre parmi vous.

Au seuil des tentes toute gloire! ma force parmi vous! Et l'idée pure comme un sel tient ses assises dans le jour.

* * *

. . . Or je hantais la ville de vos songes et j'arrêtais sur les marchés déserts ce pur commerce de mon âme, parini vous

invisible et fréquente ainsi qu'un feu d'épines en plein vent.

Puissance, tu chantais sur nos routes splendides! . . . 'Au délice du sel sont toutes lances de l'esprit . . . J'aviverai du sel les bouches mortes du désir!

ANABASIS

I

I have built myself, with honour and dignity have I built myself   i
on three great seasons, and it promises well, the soil whereon I
have established my Law.

   Beautiful are bright weapons in the morning and behind us   ii
the sea is fair. Given over to our horses this seedless earth

     delivers to us this incorruptible sky. The Sun is not named   iii
but his power is amongst us

      and the sea at morning like a presumption of the mind.   iv

   Power, you sang as we march in darkness . . . At the pure ides   v
of day what know we of our dream, older than ourselves?

   Yet one more year among you! Master of the Grain, Master of   vi
the Salt, and the commonwealth on an even beam!

   I shall not hail the people of another shore. I shall not trace   vii
the great

     boroughs of towns on the slopes with powder of coral. But I   viii
have the idea of living among you.

   Glory at the threshold of the tents, and my strength among   ix
you, and the idea pure as salt holds its assize in the day light.

* * *

   . . . So I haunted the City of your dreams, and I established in   x
the desolate markets the pure commerce of my soul, among you

     invisible and insistent as a fire of thorns in the gale.   xi

   Power, you sang on our roads of splendour . . . 'In the delight   xii
of salt the mind shakes its tumult of spears . . . With salt shall
I revive the dead mouths of desire!

Qui n'a, louant la soif, bu l'eau des sables dans un casque,
  je lui fais peu crédit au commerce de l'âme . . .' (Et le soleil n'est
point nommé, mais sa puissance est parmi nous.)

Hommes, gens de poussière et de toutes façons, gens de négoce
et de loisir, gens des confins et gens d'ailleurs, ô gens de peu de
poids dans la mémoire de ces lieux; gens des vallées et des plateaux
et des plus hautes pentes de ce monde à l'échéance de nos rives;
flaireurs de signes, de semences, et confesseurs de souffles en Ouest;
suiveurs de pistes, de saisons, leveurs de campements dans le petit
vent de l'aube; ô chercheurs de points d'eau sur l'écorce du monde;
ô chercheurs, ô trouveurs de raisons pour s'en aller ailleurs,
  vous ne trafiquez pas d'un sel plus fort quand, au matin, dans un
présage de royaumes et d'eaux mortes hautement suspendues sur les
fumées du monde, les tambours de l'exil éveillent aux frontières
  l'éternité qui bâille sur les sables.

* * *

. . . En robe pure parmi vous. Pour une année encore parmi vous.
'Ma gloire est sur les mers, ma force est parmi vous!
  A nos destins promis ce souffle d'autres rives et, portant au delà
les semences du temps, l'éclat d'un siècle sur sa pointe au fléau des
balances . . .'
  Mathématiques suspendues aux banquises du sel! Au point
sensible de mon front où le poème s'établit, j'inscris ce chant de tout
un peuple, le plus ivre,
  à nos chantiers tirant d'immortelles carènes!

He who has not praised thirst and drunk the water of the   xiii
sands from a sallet

I trust him little in the commerce of the soul . . .' (And the   xiv
Sun is not named but his power is amongst us.)

Men, creatures of dust and folk of divers ways, people of   xv
business and of leisure, men from the marches and those from
beyond, O men of little weight in the memory of these lands;
people from the valleys and the uplands and the highest slopes
of this world to the ultimate reach of our shores; Scenters of
signs and seeds, and confessors of the western winds, followers
of trails and of seasons, breakers of camp in the little dawn wind,
seekers of watercourses over the wrinkled rind of the world,
O seekers, O finders of reasons to be up and be gone,

you traffic not in a salt more strong than this, when at morning   xvi
with omen of kingdoms and omen of dead waters swung high
over the smokes of the world, the drums of exile waken on the
marches

Eternity yawning on the sands.   xvii

* * *

. . . In a single robe and pure, among you. For another year,   xviii
among you. 'My glory is upon the seas, my strength is amongst
you!

To our destiny promised this breath of other shores, and there   xix
beyond the seeds of time, the splendour of an age at its height
on the beam of the scales . . .'

Mathematics hung on the floes of salt! there at the sensitive   xx
point on my brow where the poem is formed, I inscribe this
chant of all a people, the most rapt god-drunken,

drawing to our dockyards eternal keels!   xxi

II

Aux pays fréquentés sont les plus grands silences, aux pays fréquentés de criquets à midi.

Je marche, vous marchez dans un pays de hautes pentes à mélisses, où l'on met à sécher la lessive des Grands.

Nous enjambons la robe de la Reine, toute en dentelle avec deux bandes de couleur bise (oh! que l'acide corps de femme sait tacher une robe à l'endroit de l'aisselle!)

Nous enjambons la robe de Sa fille, toute en dentelle avec deux bandes de couleur vive (ah! que la langue du lézard sait cueillir les fourmis à l'endroit de l'aisselle!)

Et peut-être le jour ne s'écoule-t-il point qu'un même homme n'ait brûlé pour une femme et pour sa fille.

Rire savant des morts, qu'on nous pèle ces fruits! ... Eh quoi! n'est-il plus grâce au monde sous la rose sauvage?

Il vient, de ce côté du monde, un grand mal violet sur les eaux. Le vent se lève. Vent de mer. Et la lessive

part! comme un prêtre mis en pièces ...

II

In busy lands are the greatest silences, in busy lands with the   i
locusts at noon.

I tread, you tread in a land of high slopes clothed in balm,   ii
where the linen of the Great is exposed to dry.

We step over the gown of the Queen, all of lace with two   iii
brown stripes (and how well the acid body of a woman can stain
a gown at the armpit).

We step over the gown of the Queen's daughter, all of lace   iv
with two bright stripes (and how well the lizard's tongue can
catch ants at the armpit).

And perhaps the day does not pass but the same man may   v
burn with desire for a woman and for her daughter.

Knowing laugh of the dead, let this fruit be peeled for us! ...   vi
How, under the wild rose is there no more grace to the world?

Comes from this side of the world a great purple doom on   vii
the waters. Rises the wind, the sea-wind. And the linen exposed
to dry

scatters! like a priest torn in pieces ...   viii

III

A la moisson des orges l'homme sort. Je ne sais qui de fort a parlé sur mon toit. Et voici que ces Rois sont assis à ma porte. Et l'Ambassadeur mange à la table des Rois. (Qu'on les nourrisse de mon grain!) Le Vérificateur des poids et des mesures descend les fleuves emphatiques avec toute sorte de débris d'insectes
    et de fétus de paille dans la barbe.

Va! nous nous étonnons de toi, Soleil! Tu nous as dit de tels mensonges!... Fauteur de troubles, de discordes! nourri d'insultes et d'esclandres, ô Frondeur! fais éclater l'amande de mon œil! Mon cœur a pépié de joie sous les magnificences de la chaux, l'oiseau chante: 'ô vieillesse!...', les fleuves sont sur leurs lits comme des cris de femmes et ce monde est plus beau
    qu'une peau de bélier peinte en rouge!

Ha! plus ample l'histoire de ces feuillages à nos murs, et l'eau plus pure qu'en des songes, grâces, grâces lui soient rendues de n'être pas un songe! Mon âme est pleine de mensonge, comme la mer agile et forte sous la vocation de l'éloquence! L'odeur puissante m'environne. Et le doute s'élève sur la réalité des choses. Mais si un homme tient pour agréable sa tristesse, qu'on le produise dans le jour! et mon avis est qu'on le tue, sinon
    il y aura une sédition.

Mieux dit: nous t'avisons, Rhéteur! de nos profits incalculables. Les mers fautives aux détroits n'ont point connu de juge plus étroit! Et l'homme enthousiasmé d'un vin, portant son cœur farouche et bourdonnant comme un gâteau de mouches noires, se prend à dire de ces choses: '... Roses, pourpre délice: la terre vaste à mon désir, et qui en posera les limites ce soir?... la violence au cœur du sage,

III

Man goes out at barley harvest. I know not what strong voice   i
has been heard on my roof. And here at my door are seated these
Kings. And the Ambassador eats at the table of the Kings. (Let
them be fed on my grain!) The Assayer of Weights and Measures
comes down the imposing rivers, with every sort of remains of
dead insects
    and bits of straw in his beard.   ii

    Come, we are amazed at you, Sun! You have told us such lies!   iii
. . . Instigator of strife and of discord! fed on insults and slanders,
O Slinger! crack the nut of my eye! my heart twittered with joy
under the splendour of the quicklime, the bird sings 'O great
age!' the streams are in their beds like the cries of women and
this world has more beauty
    than a ram's skin painted red!   iv

    Ha! ampler the story of the leaf shadows on our walls, and the   v
water more pure than in any dream, thanks thanks be given it for
being no dream! My soul is full of deceit like the agile strong sea
under the vocation of eloquence! The strong smells encompass
me. And doubt is cast on the reality of things. But if a man shall
cherish his sorrow—let him be brought to light! and I say, let
him be slain, otherwise
    there will be an uprising.   vi

    Better said: we notify you, Rhetorician! of our profits beyond   vii
reckoning. The seas erring in their straits have not known a
narrower judge! And man inspired by wine, who wears his heart
savage and buzzing like a swarm of black flies, begins to say such
words as these: '. . . Roses, purple delight; the earth stretched
forth to my desire—and who shall set bounds thereunto, this
evening? . . . violence in the heart of the sage, and who shall set

et qui en posera les limites ce soir? . . .' Et un tel, fils d'un tel, homme
pauvre,

    vient au pouvoir des signes et des songes.

    'Tracez les routes où s'en aillent les gens de toute race, montrant
cette couleur jaune du talon: les princes, les ministres, les capitaines
aux voix amygdaliennes; ceux qui ont fait de grandes choses, et
ceux qui voient en songe ceci ou cela . . . Le prêtre a déposé ses lois
contre le goût des femmes pour les bêtes. Le grammairien choisit le
lieu de ses disputes en plein air. Le tailleur pend à un vieil arbre un
habit neuf d'un très beau velours. Et l'homme atteint de gonorrhée
lave son linge dans l'eau pure. On fait brûler la selle du malingre et
l'odeur en parvient au rameur sur son banc,

    elle lui est délectable.'

    A la moisson des orges l'homme sort. L'odeur puissante
m'environne, et l'eau plus pure qu'en Jabal fait ce bruit d'un autre âge
. . . Au plus long jour de l'année chauve, louant la terre sous l'herbage,
je ne sais qui de fort a marché sur mes pas. Et des morts sous le sable
et l'urine et le sel de la terre, voici qu'il en est fait comme de la bale
dont le grain fut donné aux oiseaux. Et mon âme, mon âme veille a
grand bruit aux portes de la mort—Mais dis au Prince qu'il se taise:
à bout de lance parmi nous

    ce crâne de cheval!

bounds thereunto, this evening? . . .' and upon such an one, son of such an one, a poor man,

    devolves the power of signs and visions.   viii

'Trace the roads whereon take their departure the folk of all ix races, showing the heel's yellow colour: the princes, the ministers, the captains with tonsillar voices; those who have done great things, and those who see this or that in a vision. . . . The priest has laid down his laws against the depravities of women with beasts. The grammarian chooses a place in the open air for his arguments. On an old tree the tailor hangs a new garment of an admirable velvet. And the man tainted with gonorrhoea washes his linen in clean water. The saddle of the weakling is burnt and the smell reaches the rower on his bench,

    it is sweet in his nostrils.'   x

Man goes out at barley harvest. The strong smells encompass xi me, and the water more pure than that of Jabal makes sound of another age . . . On the longest day of the bald year, praising the earth under grass, I know not what being of strength has followed my pace. And the dead under the sand and the urine and the salt of the earth, it is done with these as with the husks whereof the grain was given to the fowls. And my soul, my soul keeps loud vigil at the portals of death—But say to the Prince to be still: on the point of a lance, amongst us,

    this horse's skull!   xii

IV

C'est là le train du monde et je n'ai que du bien à en dire— Fondation de la ville. Pierre et bronze. Des feux de ronces à l'aurore
    mirent à nu ces grandes
    pierres vertes et huileuses comme des fonds de temples, de latrines,
        et le navigateur en mer atteint de nos fumées vit que la terre, jusqu'au faîte, avait changé d'image (de grands écobuages vus du large et ces travaux de captation d'eaux vives en montagne).

        Ainsi la ville fut fondée et placée au matin sous les labiales d'un nom pur. Les campements s'annulent aux collines! Et nous qui sommes là sur les galeries de bois,
    tête nue et pieds nus dans la fraîcheur du monde,
        qu'avons-nous donc à rire, mais qu'avons-nous à rire, sur nos sièges, pour un débarquement de filles et de mules?
        et qu'est-ce à dire, depuis l'aube, de tout ce peuple sous les voiles?— Des arrivages de farines! ... Et les vaisseaux plus hauts qu'Ilion sous le paon blanc du ciel, ayant franchi la barre, s'arrêtaient
        en ce point mort où flotte un âne mort. (Il s'agit d'arbitrer ce fleuve pâle, sans destin, d'une couleur de sauterelles écrasées dans leur sève.)

    Au grand bruit frais de l'autre rive, les forgerons sont maîtres de leurs feux! Les claquements du fouet déchargent aux rues neuves des tombereaux de malheurs inéclos. O mules, nos ténèbres sous le sabre de cuivre! quatre têtes rétives au nœud du poing font un vivant corymbe sur l'azur. Les fondateurs d'asiles s'arrêtent sous un arbre et les idées leur viennent pour le choix des terrains. Ils m'enseignent le sens et la destination des bâtiments: face honorée, face muette; les galeries de latérite, les vestibules de pierre noire et

IV

Such is the way of the world and I have nothing but good to say   i
of it.—Foundation of the City. Stone and bronze. Thorn fires at
dawn
    bared these great   ii
    green stones, and viscid like the bases of temples, of latrines,   iii
    and the mariner at sea whom our smoke reached saw that   iv
the earth to the summit had changed its form (great tracts of
burnt-over land seen afar and these operations of channelling
the living waters on the mountains).

    Thus was the City founded and placed in the morning under   v
the labials of a clear sounding name. The encampments are razed
from the hills! And we who are there in the wooden galleries,
    head bare and foot bare in the freshness of the world,   vi
    what have we to laugh at, but what have we to laugh at, as we   vii
sit, for a disembarkation of girls and mules?
    and what is there to say, since the dawn, of all this people   viii
under sail?—Arrivals of grain! . . . And the ships taller than Ilion
under the white peacock of the sky, having crossed the bar,
hove to
    in this deadwater where floats a dead ass. (We must ordain   ix
the fate of this pale meaningless river, colour of grasshoppers
crushed in their sap.)

    In the great fresh noise of the yonder bank, the blacksmiths   x
are masters of their fires! The cracking of whips in the new
streets unloads whole wainsful of unhatched evils. O mules, our
shadows under the copper sword! four restive heads knotted to
the fist make a living cluster against the blue. The founders of
asylums meet beneath a tree and find their ideas for the choice
of situations. They teach me the meaning and the purpose of
the buildings: front adorned, back blind; the galleries of laterite,

les piscines d'ombre claire pour bibliothèques; des constructions très fraîches pour les produits pharmaceutiques. Et puis s'en viennent les banquiers qui sifflent dans leurs clefs. Et déjà par les rues un homme chantait seul, de ceux qui peignent sur leur front le chiffre de leur Dieu. (Crépitements d'insectes à jamais dans ce quartier aux détritus!)... Et ce n'est point le lieu de vous conter nos alliances avec les gens de l'autre rive; l'eau offerte dans les outres, les prestations de cavalerie pour les travaux du port et les princes payés en monnaie de poissons. (Un enfant triste comme la mort des singes— sœur aînée d'une grande beauté—nous offrait une caille dans un soulier de satin rose.)

... Solitude! l'œuf bleu que pond un grand oiseau de mer, et les baies au matin tout encombrées de citrons d'or!—C'était hier! L'oiseau s'en fut!

Demain les fêtes, les clameurs, les avenues plantées d'arbres à gousses et les services de voirie emportant à l'aurore de grands morceaux de palmes mortes, débris d'ailes géantes ... Demain les fêtes,

les élections de magistrats du port, les vocalises aux banlieues et, sous les tièdes couvaisons d'orage,

la ville jaune, casquée d'ombre, avec ses caleçons de filles aux fenêtres.

* * *

... A la troisième lunaison, ceux qui veillaient aux crêtes des collines replièrent leurs toiles. On fit brûler un corps de femme dans les sables. Et un homme s'avança à l'entrée du Désert—profession de son père: marchand de flacons.

the vestibules of black stone and the pools of clear shadow for libraries; cool places for wares of the druggist. And then come the bankers blowing into their keys. And already in the streets a man sang alone, one of those who paint on their brow the cipher of their god. (Perpetual crackling of insects in this quarter of vacant lots and rubbish.) ... And this is no time to tell you, no time to reckon our alliances with the people of the other shore; water presented in skins, commandeering of cavalry for the dock-works and princes paid in currency of fish. (A child sorrowful as the death of apes—one that had an elder sister of great beauty—offered us a quail in a slipper of rose-coloured satin.)

 ... Solitude! the blue egg laid by a great sea-bird, and the   xi
bays at morning all littered with gold lemons!—Yesterday it was!
The bird made off!

 Tomorrow the festivals and tumults, the avenues planted   xii
with podded trees, and the dustmen at dawn bearing away
huge pieces of dead palmtrees, fragments of giant wings ...
Tomorrow the festivals,

 the election of harbour-masters, the voices practising in the   xiii
suburbs and, under the moist incubation of storms,

 the yellow town, casque'd in shade, with the girls' waist cloths   xiv
hanging at the windows.

* * *

 ... At the third lunation, those who kept watch on the hill-   xv
tops folded their canvas. The body of a woman was burnt in the
sands. And a man strode forth at the threshold of the desert—
profession of his father: dealer in scent-bottles.

V

Pour mon âme mêlée aux affaires lointaines, cent feux de villes avivés par l'aboiement des chiens . . .

Solitude! nos partisans extravagants nous vantaient nos façons, mais nos pensées déjà campaient sous d'autres murs:

'Je n'ai dit à personne d'attendre . . . Je vous hais tous avec douceur . . . Et qu'est-ce à dire de ce chant que vous tirez de nous? . . .'

Duc d'un peuple d'images à conduire aux Mers Mortes, où trouver l'eau nocturne qui lavera nos yeux?

Solitude! . . . Des compagnies d'étoiles passent au bord du monde, s'annexant aux cuisines un astre domestique.

Les Rois Confédérés du ciel mènent la guerre sur mon toit et, maîtres des hauteurs, y établissent leurs bivacs.

Que j'aille seul avec les souffles de la nuit, parmi les Princes pamphlétaires, parmi les chutes de Biélides! . . .

Ame jointe en silence au bitume des Mortes! cousues d'aiguilles nos paupières! louée l'attente sous nos cils!

La nuit donne son lait, qu'on y prenne bien garde! et qu'un doigt de miel longe les lèvres du prodigue:

'. . . Fruit de la femme, ô Sabéenne! . . .' Trahissant l'âme la moins sobre et soulevé des pures pestilences de la nuit,

je m'élèverai dans mes pensées contre l'activité du songe; je m'en irai avec les oies sauvages, dans l'odeur fade du matin! . . .

—Ha! quand l'étoile s'anuitait au quartier des servantes, savions-nous que déjà tant de lances nouvelles

poursuivaient au désert les silicates de l'Eté? 'Aurore, vous contiez . . .' Ablutions aux rives des Mers Mortes!

Ceux qui ont couché nus dans l'immense saison se lèvent en foule sur la terre—se lèvent en foules et s'écrient

que ce monde est insane! . . . Le vieillard bouge des paupières dans la lumière jaune; la femme s'étire sur son ongle;

V

For my soul engaged in far-off matters, an hundred fires revived   i
in towns by the barking of dogs . . .

Solitude! our immoderate partisans boasted of our ways, but   ii
our thoughts were already encamped beneath other walls:

'I have told no one to wait . . . I hate you all, gently . . . And   iii
what is to be said of this song that you elicit from us? . . .'

Leader of a people of dreams to be led to the Dead Seas, where   iv
shall I find the water of night that shall bathe our eyes?

Solitude! . . . squadrons of stars pass the edge of the world,   v
enlisting from the kitchens a homely star.

The Confederate Kings of Heaven make war over my roof and,   vi
lords of the high places, set there their bivouacs.

Let me go alone with the airs of the night, among the   vii
pamphleteering Princes, among the falling Bielides! . . .

Soul united in silence to the bitumen of the Dead! our eyelids   viii
sewn with needles! praised be the waiting under our eyelids!

The night gives its milk, O take heed! let a honeyed finger   ix
touch the lips of the prodigal:

'. . . Fruit of woman, O Sabaean! . . .' Betraying the least sober   x
soul and roused from the pure pestilences of night,

in my thoughts I will protest against the activity of dream; I   xi
shall be off with the wild geese, in the stale smell of morning! . . .

Ah when the star was benighted in the servant-girls' quarters,   xii
did we know that already so many new spears

pursued in the desert the silicates of Summer? 'Dawn, you   xiii
were saying . . .' Ablutions on the banks of the Dead Seas!

Those who lay naked in the immense season arise in crowd   xiv
on the earth—arise in crowds and cry out

that this world is mad! . . . The old man stirs his eyelids in the   xv
yellow light; the woman extends herself from nail to nail;

et le poulain poisseux met son menton barbu dans la main de l'enfant, qui ne rêve pas encore de lui crever un œil . . .

'Solitude! Je n'ai dit à personne d'attendre . . . Je m'en irai par là quand je voudrai . . .'—Et l'Étranger tout habillé

de ses pensées nouvelles, se fait encore des partisans dans les voies du silence: son œil est plein d'une salive,

il n'y a plus en lui substance d'homme. Et la terre en ses graines ailées, comme un poète en ses propos, voyage . . .

and the sticky colt thrusts his bearded chin into the hand of   xvi
the child, who has not yet, in dreams, stolen one of his eyes . . .

'Solitude! I have told no one to wait . . . I shall go away in that   xvii
direction when I wish . . .'—And the Stranger clothed

in his new thoughts, acquires still more partisans in the ways   xviii
of silence: his eye is full of a sort of saliva,

there is no more substance of man in him. And the earth in   xix
its winged seeds, like a poet in his thoughts, travels . . .

VI

Tout-puissants dans nos grands gouvernements militaires, avec nos
filles parfumées qui se vêtaient d'un souffle, ces tissus,
    nous établîmes en haut lieu nos pièges au bonheur.

    Abondance et bien-être, bonheur! Aussi longtemps nos verres où
la glace pouvait chanter comme Memnon...

    Et fourvoyant à l'angle des terrasses une mêlée d'éclairs, de
grands plats d'or aux mains des filles de service fauchaient l'ennui
des sables aux limites du monde.

    Puis ce fut une année de souffles en Ouest et, sur nos toits lestés
de pierres noires, tout un propos de toiles vives adonnées au délice
du large. Les cavaliers au fil des caps, assaillis d'aigles lumineuses
et nourrissant à bout de lances les catastrophes pures du beau
temps, publiaient sur les mers une ardente chronique:

    Certes! une histoire pour les hommes, un chant de force pour les
hommes, comme un frémissement du large dans un arbre de fer!
... lois données sur d'autres rives, et les alliances par les femmes
au sein des peuples dissolus; de grands pays vendus à la criée sous
l'inflation solaire, les hauts plateaux pacifiés et les provinces mises
à prix dans l'odeur solennelle des roses...

    Ceux-là qui en naissant n'ont point flairé de telle braise, qu'ont-ils
à faire parmi nous? et se peut-il qu'ils aient commerce de vivants?
'C'est votre affaire et non la mienne de régner sur l'absence...' Pour
nous qui étions là, nous produisîmes aux frontières des accidents
extraordinaires, et nous portant dans nos actions à la limite de nos
forces, notre joie parmi vous fut une très grande joie:

    'Je connais cette race établie sur les pentes: cavaliers démontés
dans les cultures vivrières. Allez et dites à ceux-là: un immense
péril a courir avec nous! des actions sans nombre et sans mesure,
des volontés puissantes et dissipatrices et le pouvoir de l'homme
consommé comme la grappe dans la vigne... Allez et dites bien:
nos habitudes de violence, nos chevaux sobres et rapides sur les

VI

Omnipotent in our great military governments, with our scented   i
girls clad in a breath of silk webs,

    we set in high places our springes for happiness.   ii

    Plenty and well-being, happiness! For so long the ice sang in   iii
our glasses, like Memnon . . .

    And deflecting a crossing of lights to the corners of terraces,   iv
great chargers of gold held up by the handmaidens, smote the
weariness of the sands, at the confines of the world.

    Then came a year of wind in the west and, on our roofs   v
weighted with black stones, all the business of bright cloths
abandoned to the delight of wide spaces. The horsemen on the
crest of the capes, battered by luminous eagles, and feeding on
their spear-tips the pure disasters of sunshine, published over
the seas a fiery bulletin:

    Surely a history for men, a song of strength for men, like a   vi
shudder from afar of space shaking an iron tree! . . . laws enacted
upon other shores, alliances by marriage in the midst of dissolute
peoples, great territories auctioned away beneath the inflation
of the Sun, the highlands subdued and the provinces priced in
the solemn odour of roses . . .

    They who at birth have not sniffed such embers, what have   vii
they to do with us? Can they have commerce with the living? 'It
is your business, not mine, to rule over absence . . .' For us who
were there, we caused at the frontiers exceptional accidents, and
pushing ourselves in our actions to the end of our strength, our
joy amongst you was a very great joy:

    'I know this race settled on the slopes, horsemen dismounted   viii
among the food crops. Go say to them: a great risk to run with us!
deeds innumerable unmeasured, puissant and destructive wills,
and the power of man absorbed like the cluster in the vine . . . Go
and say truly: our habits of violence, our horses abstemious and

semences de révolte et nos casques flairés par la fureur du jour . . .
Aux pays épuisés où les coutumes sont à reprendre, tant de familles à
composer comme des encagées d'oiseaux siffleurs, vous nous verrez,
dans nos façons d'agir, assembleurs de nations sous de vastes
hangars, lecteurs de bulles à voix haute, et vingt peuples sous nos
lois parlant toutes les langues . . .

'Et déjà vous savez l'histoire de leur goût: les capitaines pauvres
dans les voies immortelles, les notables enfouie venus pour nous
saluer, toute la population virile de l'année avec ses dieux sur des
bâtons, et les princes déchus dans les sables du Nord, leurs filles
tributaires nous prodiguant les assurances de leur foi, et le Maître
qui dit: j'ai foi dans ma fortune . . .

'Ou bien vous leur contez les choses de la paix: aux pays infestés
de bien-être une odeur de forum et de femmes nubiles, les monnaies
jaunes, timbre pur, maniées sous les palmes, et les peuples en
marche sur de fortes épices—dotations militaires, grands trafics
d'influence à la barbe des fleuves, l'hommage d'un puissant voisin
assis à l'ombre de ses filles et les messages échangés sur des
lamelles d'or, les traités d'amitié et de délimitation, les conventions
de peuple à peuple pour des barrages de rivières, et les tributs
levés dans les pays enthousiasmés! (constructions de citernes, de
granges, de bâtiments pour la cavalerie—les carrelages d'un bleu
vif et les chemins de brique rose—les déploiements d'étoffes à loisir,
les confitures de roses à miel et le poulain qui nous est né dans les
bagages de l'armée—les déploiements d'étoffes à loisir et, dans les
glaces de nos songes, la mer qui rouille les épées, et la descente, un
soir, dans les provinces maritimes, vers nos pays de grand loisir et
vers nos filles

'parfumées, qui nous apaiseront d'un souffle, ces tissus . . .')

—Ainsi parfois nos seuils pressés d'un singulier destin et, sur
les pas précipités du jour, de ce côté du monde, le plus vaste, où le
pouvoir s'exile chaque soir, tout un veuvage de lauriers!

swift upon the seeds of sedition and our helmets sniffed by the fury of the day . . . In the exhausted countries where the ways of life are to be remade, so many families to be composed like cages of whistling birds, you shall see us, the way we act, gatherers of nations under vast shelters, readers aloud of decrees, and twenty peoples under our law speaking all tongues . . .

'And already you know their favourite tale: the needy captains   ix
in immortal paths, the notables crowding to do us obeisance, the whole male population of the year holding aloft its gods on staves, and the princes fallen in the Northern wastes, their daughters tributary swearing fealty to us, and the Master saying: I have faith in my destiny . . .

'Or else you will tell them of the deeds of peace: in countries   x
infested with comfort an odour of forum and of nubile women, the yellow coins of purest ring, fingered under palms, and peoples on the march on strong spices—military endowments, great traffic of influence in the teeth of the rivers, the homage of a powerful neighbour seated in the shadow of his daughters, and messages exchanged on leaves of gold, treaties of amity and of boundary, conventions of people with people for damming of streams, and tribute levied in lands roused to passion! (building of cisterns and of granges and of cavalry barracks—the floors of bright blue and the ways of rose red brick—leisurely unfolding of stuffs, the honey rose jelly and the colt which is born to us among the army gear—the leisurely unfolding of stuffs, and in the mirror of our dreams, the sword-rusting sea, and, one evening, descent into the coast provinces, towards our lands of great ease and towards our

'scented girls, who shall soothe us with a breath, silken   xi
webs . . .')

—In this wise sometimes our threshold trodden by a strange   xii
destiny, and on the hurried steps of day, on this side of the world, the most vast, where power each evening is exiled, all a widowhood of laurels!

Mais au soir, une odeur de violettes et d'argile, aux mains des filles de nos femmes, nous visitait dans nos projets d'établissement et de fortune

et les vents calmes hébergeaient au fond des golfes désertiques.

But at evening an odour of violets and clay in the hands of   xiii
our wives' maidens, haunted us in our thoughts of foundation
and fortune

and the still winds harboured in the depths of the desert-like   xiv
gulfs.

VII

Nous n'habiterons pas toujours ces terres jaunes, notre délice . . .

L'Eté plus vaste que l'Empire suspend aux tables de l'espace plusieurs étages de climats. La terre vaste sur son aire roule à pleins bords sa braise pâle sous les cendres—. Couleur de soufre, de miel, couleur de choses immortelles, toute la terre aux herbes s'allumant aux pailles de l'autre hiver—et de l'éponge verte d'un seul arbre le ciel tire son suc violet.

Un lieu de pierres à mica! Pas une graine pure dans les barbes du vent. Et la lumière comme une huile.—De la fissure des paupières au fil des cimes m'unissant, je sais la pierre tachée d'ouies, les essaims du silence aux ruches de lumière; et mon cœur prend souci d'une famille d'acridiens . . .

Chamelles douces sous la tonte, cousues de mauves cicatrices, que les collines s'acheminent sous les données du ciel agraire—qu'elles cheminent en silence sur les incandescences pâles de la plaine; et s'agenouillent à la fin, dans la fumée des songes, là où les peuples s'abolissent aux poudres mortes de la terre.

Ce sont de grandes lignes calmes qui s'en vont à des bleuissements de vignes improbables. La terre en plus d'un point mûrit les violettes de l'orage; et ces fumées de sable qui s'élèvent au lieu des fleuves morts, comme des pans de siècles en voyage . . .

A voix plus basse pour les morts, à voix plus basse dans le jour. Tant de douceur au cœur de l'homme, se peut-il qu'elle faille à trouver sa mesure? . . . 'Je vous parle, mon âme!—mon âme tout enténébrée d'un parfum de cheval!' Et quelques grands oiseaux de terre, naviguant en Ouest, sont de bons mimes de nos oiseaux de mer.

A l'orient du ciel si pâle, comme un lieu saint scellé des linges de l'aveugle, des nuées calmes se disposent, où tournent les cancers

VII

We shall not dwell forever in these yellow lands, our pleasure . . .   i

   The Summer vaster than the Empire hangs over the tables   ii
of space several terraces of climate. The huge earth rolls on its
surface over-flowing its pale embers under the ashes—Sulphur
colour, honey colour, colour of immortal things, the whole
grassy earth taking light from the straw of last winter—and from
the green sponge of a lone tree the sky draws its violet juices.

   A place glittering with mica! Not a pure grain in the wind's   iii
barbs. And light like oil.—From the crack of my eye to the level of
the hills I join myself, I know the stones gillstained, the swarms
of silence in the hives of light; and my heart gives heed to a
family of locusts . . .

   Like milch-camels, gentle beneath the shears and sewn   iv
with mauve scars, let the hills march forth under the scheme
of the harvest sky—let them march in silence over the pale
incandescence of the plain; and kneel at last, in the smoke of
dreams, there where the peoples annihilate themselves in the
dead powder of earth.

   These are the great quiet lines that disperse in the fading blue   v
of doubtful vines. The earth here and there ripens the violets of
storm; and these sandsmokes that rise over dead river courses,
like the skirts of centuries on their route . . .

   Lower voice for the dead, lower voice by day. Such gentleness   vi
in the heart of man, can it fail to find its measure? . . . 'I speak
to you, my soul!—my soul darkened by the horse smell!' And
several great land birds, voyaging westwards, make good likeness
of our sea birds.

   In the east of so pale a sky, like a holy place sealed by the blind   vii
man's linen, calm clouds arrange themselves, where the cancers

du camphre et de la corne ... Fumées qu'un souffle nous dispute!
la terre tout attente en ses barbes d'insectes, la terre enfante des
merveilles!...

Et à midi, quand l'arbre jujubier fait éclater l'assise des tombeaux,
l'homme clôt ses paupières et rafraîchit sa nuque dans les âges ...
Cavaleries du songe au lieu des poudres mortes, ô routes vaines
qu'échevèle un souffle jusqu'à nous! où trouver, où trouver les
guerriers qui garderont les fleuves dans leurs noces?

Au bruit des grandes eaux en marche sur la terre, tout le sel de
la terre tressaille dans les songes. Et soudain, ha! soudain que nous
veulent ces voix? Levez un peuple de miroirs sur l'ossuaire des fleuves,
qu'ils interjettent appel dans la suite des siècles! Levez des pierres à
ma gloire, levez des pierres au silence, et à la garde de ces lieux les
cavaleries de bronze vert sur de vastes chaussées!...

(L'ombre d'un grand oiseau me passe sur la face.)

of camphor and horn revolve . . . Smoke which a breath of wind claims from us! the earth poised tense in its insect barbs, the earth is brought to bed of wonders! . . .

And at noon, when the jujuba tree breaks the tombstone,   viii man closes his lids and cools his neck in the ages . . . Horse-tramplings of dreams in the place of dead powders, O vain ways a breath sweeps smoking toward us! where find, where find, the warriors who shall watch the streams in their nuptials?

At the sound of great waters on march over the earth, all the   ix salt of the earth shudders in dream. And sudden, ah sudden, what would these voices with us? Levy a wilderness of mirrors on the boneyard of streams, let them appeal in the course of ages! Raise stones to my fame, raise stones to silence; and to guard these places, cavalcades of green bronze on the great causeways! . . .

(The shadow of a great bird falls on my face.)   x

VIII

Lois sur la vente des juments. Lois errantes. Et nous-mêmes.
(Couleur d'hommes.)

Nos compagnons ces hautes trombes en voyage, clepsydres en
marche sur la terre,

et les averses solennelles, d'une substance merveilleuse, tissées de
poudres et d'insectes, qui poursuivaient nos peuples dans les sables
comme l'impôt de capitation.

(A la mesure de nos cœurs fut tant d'absence consommée!)

* * *

Non que l'étape fût stérile: au pas des bêtes sans alliances (nos
chevaux purs aux yeux d'aînés), beaucoup de choses entreprises sur
les ténèbres de l'esprit—beaucoup de choses à loisir sur les frontières
de l'esprit—grandes histoires séleucides au sifflement des frondes et
la terre livrée aux explications . . .

Autre chose: ces ombres—les prévarications du ciel contre la
terre . . .

Cavaliers au travers de telles familles humaines, où les haines
parfois chantaient comme des mésanges, lèverons-nous le fouet sur
les mots hongres du bonheur?—Homme, pèse ton poids calculé en
froment. Un pays-ci n'est point le mien. Que m'a donné le monde que
ce mouvement d'herbes? . . .

* * *

Jusqu'au lieu dit de l'Arbre Sec:
et l'éclair famélique m'assigne ces provinces en Ouest.
Mais au delà sont les plus grands loisirs, et dans un grand
pays d'herbages sans mémoire, l'année sans liens et sans

VIII

Laws concerning the sale of mares. Nomad laws. And ourselves.   i
(Man colour.)

   Our companions these high waterspouts on the march,   ii
clepsydrae travelling over the earth,

   and the solemn rains, of a marvellous substance, woven   iii
of powders and insects, pursuing our folk in the sands like a
headtax.

   (To the scale of our hearts was such vacance completed!)   iv

* * *

   Not that this stage was in vain: to the pace of the beasts   v
akin to none (our pure bred horses with eyes of elders) many
things undertaken on the darkness of the spirit—infinity of
things at leisure on the frontiers of the spirit—great selucid
histories to the whistling of slings and the earth given over to
explanations . . .

   And again: these shadows—the prevarications of the sky   vi
against the earth . . .

   Cavaliers, across such human families, in whom hatreds sang   vii
now and then like crested tits, shall we raise our whip over the
gelded words of happiness?—Man, weigh your weight measured
in wheat. A country here, not mine. What has the world given
me but this swaying of grass? . . .

* * *

   To the place called the Place of the Dry Tree: viii

   and the starved lightning allots me these provinces in the   ix
West.

   But beyond are the greater leisures, and in a great   x

   land of grass without memory, the year without ties or   xi

anniversaires, assaisonnée d'aurores et de feux. (Sacrifice au matin d'un cœur de mouton noir.)

* * *

Chemins du monde, l'un vous suit. Autorité sur tous les signes de la terre.

O Voyageur dans le vent jaune, goût de l'âme! ... et la graine, dis-tu, du cocculus indien possède, qu'on la broie! des vertus enivrantes.

* * *

Un grand principe de violence commandait à nos mœurs.

anniversaries, seasoned with dawns and heavenly fires. (Sacrificed, in the morning, the heart of a black sheep.)

* * *

Roads of the world, we follow you. Authority over all the signs of the earth. xii

O Traveller in the yellow wind, lust of the soul! ... and the seed (so you say) of the Indian cocculus possesses (if you mash it!) intoxicating properties. xiii

* * *

A great principle of violence dictated our fashions. xiv

IX

Depuis un si long temps que nous allions en Ouest, que savions-nous des choses
   périssables? ... et soudain à nos pieds les premières fumées.

—Jeunes femmes! et la nature d'un pays s'en trouve toute parfumée:

* * *

'... Je t'annonce les temps d'une grande chaleur et les veuves criardes sur la dissipation des morts.
   Ceux qui vieillissent dans l'usage et le soin du silence, assis sur les hauteurs, considèrent les sables
   et la célébrité du jour sur les rades foraines;
   mais le plaisir au flanc des femmes se compose, et dans nos corps de femmes il y a comme un ferment de raisin noir, et de répit avec nous-mêmes il n'en est point.

'... Je t'annonce les temps d'une grande faveur et la félicité des feuilles dans nos songes.
   Ceux qui savent les sources sont avec nous dans cet exil; ceux qui savent les sources nous diront-ils au soir
   sous quelles mains pressant la vigne de nos flancs
   nos corps s'emplissent d'une salive? (Et la femme s'est couchée avec l'homme dans l'herbe; elle se lève, met ordre aux lignes de son corps, et le criquet s'envole sur son aile bleue.)

'... Je t'annonce les temps d'une grande chaleur, et pareillement la nuit, sous l'aboiement des chiens, trait son plaisir au flanc des femmes.
   Mais l'Étranger vit sous sa tente, honoré de laitages, de fruits. On lui apporte de l'eau fraîche
   pour y laver sa bouche, son visage et son sexe.

IX

Such a long time now we were making westward, what did we   i
know of those things which are
    perishable? . . . and sudden at our feet the first smoke . . .   ii

    —Young women! and the nature of a land is all scented   iii
therewith:

* * *

    '. . . I foretell you the time of great heat, and the widows crying   iv
over the dissipation of the dead.
    They who grow old in the custom and the care of silence,   v
seated on the heights, contemplate the sands,
    and the lustre of the day over open roadsteads;   vi
    but the pleasure forms itself within the womb, and in our   vii
women's bodies there is as a ferment of black grape, and of
respite with ourselves there is not.

    '. . . I foretell you the time of a great blessing and the felicity   viii
of leaves in our dreams.
    Those who know the springs are with us in this exile; those   ix
who know the springs will they tell us at evening
    beneath what hands pressing the vine of our wombs   x
    our bodies are filled with a sap? (And the woman has lain   xi
down with the man in the grass; she rises, arranges the lines of
her body, and the cricket makes off on blue wing.)

    '. . . I foretell you the time of great heat, and likewise the   xii
night, when the dogs bark, takes its pleasure from the womb of
women.
    But the Stranger dwells in his tent, honoured with gifts of   xiii
dairy produce and fruit. He is offered fresh water
    to wash therewith his mouth, his face and his sex.   xiv

On lui mène à la nuit de grandes femmes bréhaignes (ha! plus nocturnes dans le jour!) Et peut-être aussi de moi tirera-t-il son plaisir. (Je ne sais quelles sont ses façons d'être avec les femmes.)

'. . . Je t'annonce les temps d'une grande faveur et la félicité des sources dans nos songes.

Ouvre ma bouche dans la lumière, ainsi qu'un lieu de miel entre les roches, et si l'on trouve faute en moi, que je sois congédiée! sinon,

que j'aille sous la tente, que j'aille nue, près de la cruche, sous la tente,

et compagnon de l'angle du tombeau, tu me verras longtemps muette sous l'arbre-fille de mes veines . . . Un lit d'instances sous la tente, l'étoile verte dans la cruche, et que ie sois sous ta puissance! nulle servante sous la tente que la cruche d'eau fraîche! (Je sais sortir avant le jour sans éveiller l'étoile verte, le criquet sur le seuil et l'aboiement des chiens de toute la terre.)

Je t'annonce les temps d'une grande faveur et la félicité du soir sur nos paupières périssables . . .

mais pour l'instant encore c'est le jour!'

* * *

—et debout sur la tranche éclatante du jour, au seuil d'un grand pays plus chaste que la mort,

les filles urinaient en écartant la toile peinte de leur robe.

At night he is brought tall barren women (more nocturnal in the day!) And perhaps of me also will he have his pleasure. (I know not what are his ways with women.)   xv

'. . . I foretell you the time of great blessing, and the felicity of springs in our dreams.   xvi

Open my mouth in the light, as a honey store among the rocks, and if fault be found in me, let me be dismissed! otherwise   xvii

may I enter in under the tent, may I enter naked, near the cruse, under the tent,   xviii

and companion of the grave-corner, you shall see me for long time unspeaking under the girl-tree of my veins . . . A bed of entreaties under the tent, the green star in the cruse, and may I be under your dominion! no serving-maid under the tent but the cruse of cool water! (I have ways to depart before day without wakening the green star, the cricket on the threshold and the baying of the dogs of the whole world.)   xix

I foretell you the time of great blessing and the bounty of the evening on our eyelids that endure not . . .   xx

but for the time being it is still day!'   xxi

* * *

—and erect on the shining edge of the day, on the threshold of a great land more chaste than death,   xxii

the girls made water straddling and holding aside the painted cloth of their gowns.   xxiii

X

Fais choix d'un grand chapeau dont on séduit le bord. L'œil recule d'un siècle aux provinces de l'âme. Par la porte de craie vive on voit les choses de la plaine: choses vivantes, ô choses
   excellentes!

des sacrifices de poulains sur des tombes d'enfants, des purifications de veuves dans les roses et des rassemblements d'oiseaux verts dans les cours en l'honneur des vieillards;
   beaucoup de choses sur la terre à entendre et à voir, choses vivantes parmi nous!

des célébrations de fêtes en plein air pour des anniversaires de grands arbres et des cérémonies publiques en l'honneur d'une mare; des dédicaces de pierres noires, parfaitement rondes, des inventions de sources en lieux morts, des consécrations d'étoffes, à bout de perches, aux approches des cols, et des acclamations violentes, sous les murs, pour des mutilations d'adultes au soleil, pour des publications de linges d'épousailles!
   bien d'autres choses encore à hauteur de nos tempes: les pansements de bêtes au faubourgs, les mouvements de foules au devant des tondeurs, des puisatiers et des hongreurs; les spéculations au souffle des moissons et la ventilation d'herbages, à bout de fourches, sur les toits; les constructions d'enceintes de terre cuite et rose, de sècheries de viandes en terrasses, de galeries pour les prêtres, de capitaineries; les cours immenses du vétérinaire; les corvées d'entretien de routes muletières, de chemins en lacets dans les gorges; les fondations d'hospices en lieux vagues; les écritures à l'arrivée des caravanes et les licenciements d'escortes aux quartiers de changeurs; les popularités naissantes sous l'auvent, devant les cuves à fritures; les protestations de titres de créance; les destructions de bêtes albinos, de vers blancs sous la terre, les feux de ronces et d'épines aux lieux souillés de mort, la fabrication d'un beau pain

X

Select a wide hat with the brim seduced. The eye withdraws by   i
a century into the provinces of the soul. Through the gate of
living chalk we see the things of the plain: living things,
   excellent things!   ii

   sacrifice of colts on the tombs of children, purification of   iii
widows among the roses and consignments of green birds in
the courtyards to do honour to the old men;
   many things on the earth to hear and to see, living things   iv
among us!
   celebrations of open air festivals for the name-day of great   v
trees and public rites in honour of a pond; consecration of black
stones perfectly round, discovery of springs in dead places,
dedication of cloths held up on poles, at the gates of the passes,
and loud acclamations under the walls for the mutilation of
adults in the sun, for the publication of the bride-sheets!
   many other things too at the level of our eyes: dressing the   vi
sores of animals in the suburbs, stirring of the crowds toward
sheep-shearers, well-sinkers and horse-gelders; speculations in
the breath of harvests and turning of hay on the roofs, on the
prongs of forks; building of enclosures of rose red terra cotta, of
terraces for meat-drying, of galleries for priests, of quarters for
captains; the vast court of the horse-doctor; the fatigue parties
for upkeep of muleways, of zig-zag roads through the gorges;
foundation of hospices in vacant places; the invoicing at arrival
of caravans, and disbanding of escorts in the quarter of money-
changers; budding popularities under the sheds, in front of
the frying vats; protestation of bills of credit; destruction of
albino animals, of white worms in the soil; fires of bramble and
thorn in places defiled by death, the making of a fine bread of

d'orge et de sésame; ou bien d'épeautre; et la fumée des hommes en
tous lieux . . .

ha! toutes sortes d'hommes dans leurs voies et façons: mangeurs
d'insectes, de fruits d'eau; porteurs d'emplâtres, de richesses!
l'agriculteur et l'adalingue, l'acuponcteur et le saunier; le péager,
le forgeron; marchands de sucre, de cannelle, de coupes à boire en
métal blanc et de lampes de corne; celui qui taille un vêtement de
cuir, des sandales dans le bois et des boutons en forme d'olives:
celui qui donne à la terre ses façons; et l'homme de nul métier:
homme au faucon, homme à la flûte, homme aux abeilles; celui qui
tire son plaisir du timbre de sa voix, celui qui trouve son emploi
dans la contemplation d'une pierre verte; qui fait brûler pour son
plaisir un feu d'écorces sur son toit; qui se fait sur la terre un lit de
feuilles odorantes, qui s'y couche et repose; qui pense à des dessins
de céramiques vertes pour des bassins d'eaux vives; et celui qui a
fait des voyages et songe à repartir; qui a vécu dans un pays de
grandes pluies; qui joue aux dés, aux osselets, au jeu des gobelets;
ou qui a déployé sur le sol ses tables à calcul; celui qui a des vues sur
l'emploi d'une calebasse; celui qui traîne un aigle mort comme un
faix de branchages sur ses pas (et la plume est donnée, non vendue,
pour l'empennage des flèches), celui qui récolte le pollen dans un
vaisseau de bois (et mon plaisir, dit-il, est dans cette couleur jaune);
celui qui mange des beignets, des vers de palmes, des framboises;
celui qui aime le goût de l'estragon; celui qui rêve d'un poivron;
ou bien encore celui qui mâche d'une gomme fossile, qui porte
une conque à son oreille, et celui qui épie le parfum de génie aux
cassures fraîches de la pierre; celui qui pense au corps de femme,
homme libidineux; celui qui voit son âme au reflet d'une lame;
l'homme versé dans les sciences, dans l'onomastique; l'homme en
faveur dans les conseils, celui qui nomme les fontaines, qui fait un
don de sièges sous les arbres, de laines teintes pour les sages; et
fait sceller aux carrefours de très grands bols de bronze pour la
soif; bien mieux, celui qui ne fait rien, tel homme et tel dans ses

barley and sesame; or else of spelt; and the firesmoke of man
everywhere . . .

ha! all conditions of men in their ways and manners; eaters   _{vii}
of insects, of water fruits; those who bear poultices, those who
bear riches; the husbandman, and the young noble horsed; the
healer with needles, and the salter; the toll-gatherer, the smith,
vendors of sugar, of cinnamon, of white metal drinking cups
and of lanthorns; he who fashions a leather tunic, wooden shoes
and olive-shaped buttons; he who dresses a field; and the man
of no trade: the man with the falcon, the man with the flute, the
man with bees; he who takes his delight in the pitch of his voice,
he who makes it his business to contemplate a green stone;
he who burns for his pleasure a thornfire on his roof; he who
makes on the ground his bed of sweet-smelling leaves, lies down
there and rests; he who thinks out designs of green pottery for
fountains; and he who has travelled far and dreams of departing
again; he who has dwelt in a country of great rains; the dicer, the
knuckle-bone player, the juggler; or he who has spread on the
ground his reckoning tablets; he who has his opinions on the
use of a gourd; he who drags a dead eagle like a faggot on his
tracks (and the plumage is given, not sold, for fletching); he who
gathers pollen in a wooden jar (and my delight, says he, is in this
yellow colour); he who eats fritters, the maggots of the palmtree,
or raspberries; he who fancies the flavour of tarragon; he who
dreams of green pepper, or else he who chews fossil gum, who
lifts a conch to his ear, or he who sniffs the odour of genius in
the freshly cracked stone; he who thinks of the flesh of women,
the lustful; he who sees his soul reflected in a sword blade; the
man learned in sciences, in onomastic; the man well thought
of in councils, he who names fountains, he who makes a public
gift of seats in the shady places, of dyed wool for the wise men;
and has great bronze jars, for thirst, planted at the crossways;
better still, he who does nothing, such a one and such in his

façons, et tant d'autres encore! les ramasseurs de cailles dans les plis de terrains, ceux qui récoltent dans les broussailles les œufs tiquetés de vert, ceux qui descendent de cheval pour ramasser des choses, des agates, une pierre bleu pâle que l'on taille à l'entrée des faubourgs (en manière d'étuis, de tabatières et d'agrafes, ou de boules à rouler aux mains des paralytiques); ceux qui peignent en sifflant des coffrets en plein air, l'homme au bâton d'ivoire, l'homme à la chaise de rotin, l'ermite orné de mains de fille et le guerrier licencié qui a planté sa lance sur son seuil pour attacher un singe . . . ha! toutes sortes d'hommes dans leurs voies et façons, et soudain! apparu dans ses vêtements du soir et tranchant à la ronde toutes questions de préséance, le Conteur qui prend place au pied du térébinthe . . .

O généalogiste sur la place! combien d'histoires de familles et de filiations?—et que le mort saisisse le vif, comme il est dit aux tables du légiste, si je n'ai vu toute chose dans son ombre et le mérite de son âge: les entrepôts de livres et d'annales, les magasins de l'astronome et la beauté d'un lieu de sépultures, de très vieux temples sous les palmes, habités d'une mule et de trois poules blanches—et par delà le cirque de mon œil, beaucoup d'actions secrètes en chemin: les campements levés sur des nouvelles qui m'échappent, les effronteries de peuples aux collines et les passages de rivières sur des outres; les cavaliers porteurs de lettres d'alliance, l'embuscade dans les vignes, les entreprises de pillards au fond des gorges et les manœuvres à travers champs pour le rapt d'une femme, les marchandages et les complots, l'accouplement de bêtes en forêt sous les yeux des enfants, et des convalescences de prophètes au fond des bouveries, les conversations muettes de deux hommes sous un arbre . . .

mais par dessus les actions des hommes sur la terre, beaucoup de signes en voyage, beaucoup de graines en voyage, et sous l'azyme du beau temps, dans un grand souffle de la terre, toute la plume des moissons! . . .

manners, and so many others still! those who collect quails in the wrinkled land, those who hunt among the furze for green-speckled eggs, those who dismount to pick things up, agates, a pale blue stone which they cut and fashion at the gates of the suburbs (into cases, tobacco-boxes, brooches, or into balls to be rolled between the hands of the paralysed); those who whistling paint boxes in the open air, the man with the ivory staff, the man with the rattan chair, the hermit with hands like a girl's and the disbanded warrior who has planted his spear at the threshold to tie up a monkey . . . ha! all sorts of men in their ways and fashions, and of a sudden! behold in his evening robes and summarily settling in turn all questions of precedence, the Story-Teller who stations himself at the foot of the turpentine tree . . .

O genealogist upon the market-place! how many chronicles   viii of families and connexions?—and may the dead seize the quick, as is said in the tables of the law, if I have not seen each thing in its own shadow and the virtue of its age: the stores of books and annals, the astronomer's storehouses and the beauty of a place of sepulture, of very old temples under the palmtrees, frequented by a mule and three white hens—and beyond my eye's circuit, many a secret doing on the routes: striking of camps upon tidings which I know not, effronteries of the hill tribes, and passage of rivers on skin-jars; horsemen bearing letters of alliance, the ambush in the vineyard, forays of robbers in the depths of gorges and manœuvres over field to ravish a woman, bargain-driving and plots, coupling of beasts in the forests before the eyes of children, convalescence of prophets in byres, the silent talk of two men under a tree . . .

but over and above the actions of men on the earth, many   ix omens on the way, many seeds on the way, and under unleavened fine weather, in one great breath of the earth, the whole feather of harvest! . . .

jusqu'à l'heure du soir où l'étoile femelle, chose pure et gagée dans les hauteurs du ciel . . .

Terre arable du songe! Qui parle de bâtir?—J'ai vu la terre distribuée en de vastes espaces et ma pensée n'est point distraite du navigateur.

until the hour of evening when the female star, pure and x
pledged in the sky heights . . .

Plough-land of dream! Who talks of building?—I have seen xi
the earth spread out in vast spaces and my thought is not
heedless of the navigator.

CHANSON

Mon cheval arrêté sous l'arbre plein de tourterelles, je siffle un sifflement si pur, qu'il n'est promesses à leurs rives que tiennent tous ces fleuves (Feuilles vivantes au matin sont à l'image de la gloire)...

* * *

Et ce n'est point qu'un homme ne soit triste, mais se levant avant le jour et se tenant avec prudence dans le commerce d'un vieil arbre, appuyé du menton à la dernière étoile, il voit au fond du ciel à jeun de grandes choses pures qui tournent au plaisir...

* * *

Mon cheval arrêté sous l'arbre qui roucoule, je siffle un sifflement plus pur.... Et paix à ceux, s'ils vont mourir, qui n'ont point vu ce jour. Mais de mon frère le poète on a eu des nouvelles. Il a écrit encore une chose très douce. Et quelques-uns en eurent connaissance...

SONG

I have halted my horse by the tree of the doves, I whistle a note   i
so sweet, shall the rivers break faith with their banks? (Living
leaves in the morning fashioned in glory) . . .

* * *

And not that a man be not sad, but arising before day and   ii
biding circumspectly in the communion of an old tree, leaning
his chin on the last fading star, he beholds at the end of the
fasting sky great things and pure that unfold to delight . . .

* * *

I have halted my horse by the dove-moaning tree, I whistle a   iii
note more sweet . . . Peace to the dying who have not seen this
day! But tidings there are of my brother the poet: once more he
has written a song of great sweetness. And some there are who
have knowledge thereof . . .

Anabasis: Commentary

1. St.-John Perse   2. Editions   3. Apropos of Publication
4. *Anabase* to Anabasis   5. Translation

1. ST.-JOHN PERSE

St.-John Perse was the pseudonym of the French diplomat Alexis St. Léger Léger
(1887–1975), of whom Henry Eliot noted: "a French exile, sometime head of the
French Foreign Office; was offered ambassadorship to Washington after the German
occupation, but declined. A bachelor, pro-British; was in USA in 1940" (catalogue
of items given to Eliot House, Harvard). Perse was a friend of Alain-Fournier and
Valery Larbaud (editor of the *Nouvelle Revue Française*), of Léon-Paul Fargue and
André Gide. In 1944 it was proposed that TSE "should join Alexis Léger on his staff
for the season 1945–1946, to promote international cultural relations" (TSE to
Hayward, 1 June 1944). Perse published *Éloges* (1911), *Anabase* (1924), *Exil, suivi
de Poème à l'Étranger, Pluies, Neiges* (1944), *Vents* (1946) and *Amers* (1957). (*Anabase*
was published, in French only, in New York in 1945.) Perse was awarded the Nobel
Prize in 1960.

2. EDITIONS

The publication history of *Anabasis* is complex and the textual revisions between
editions were much more extensive than in any of TSE's other publications.
   The first edition was published in 1930, in Britain only, with a limited edition of
350 signed copies on hand-made paper. Less than a third of the ordinary copies sold
at ten shillings and sixpence, so in 1937 the remaining sheets were cut down and
reissued in a plainer volume at five shillings. A revised text, Gallup's "Second edition
(first American edition)", was published in 1938. A further revision, Gallup's "Third
edition, revised and corrected", was published in the US in 1949, with TSE's "Note to
Revised Edition". It also included a Bibliography (I. The works of St.-John Perse in
French and foreign editions. II. *Anabasis*), and reprinted prefaces by Valery Larbaud,
Hugo von Hofmannsthal and Giuseppe Ungaretti to the Russian, German and Italian
translations respectively. When Gallup's "English edition" of 1959 appeared, the text
had undergone its most thorough revision since publication, with Perse taking a
decisive part, as TSE acknowledged in the "Note to the Third Edition" (1958). It also
had an expanded Bibliography, and the Note by Lucien Fabre (1924) referred to in
TSE's Preface. *Anabasis* has not previously been published in collections of TSE's
writings. He did not make a recording.

3. APROPOS OF PUBLICATION

PREFACE

   I am by no means convinced that a poem like *Anabase* requires a preface at all. It is
better to read such a poem six times, and dispense with a preface. But when a poem is

presented in the form of a translation, people who have never heard of it are naturally inclined to demand some testimonial. So I give mine hereunder.

Anabase is already well known, not only in France, but in other countries of Europe. One of the best Introductions to the poem is that of the late Hugo von Hofmannsthal, which forms the preface to the German translation. There is another by Valery Larbaud, which forms the preface to the Russian translation. And there was an informative note by Lucien Fabre in the *Nouvelles Littéraires*.

For myself, once having had my attention drawn to the poem by a friend whose taste I trusted, there was no need for a preface. I did not need to be told, after one reading, that the word *anabasis* has no particular reference to Xenophon or the journey of the Ten Thousand, no particular reference to Asia *Minor*; and that no map of its migrations could be drawn up. Mr. Perse is using the word *anabasis* in the same literal sense in which Xenophon himself used it. The poem is a series of images of migration, of conquest of vast spaces in Asiatic wastes, of destruction and foundation of cities and civilizations of any races or epochs of the ancient East.

I may, I trust, borrow from Mr. Fabre two notions which may be of use to the English reader. The first is that any obscurity of the poem, on first readings, is due to the suppression of "links in the chain", of explanatory and connecting matter, and not to incoherence, or to the love of cryptogram. The justification of such abbreviation of method is that the sequence of images coincides and concentrates into one intense impression of barbaric civilization. The reader has to allow the images to fall into his memory successively without questioning the reasonableness of each at the moment; so that, at the end, a total effect is produced.

Such selection of a sequence of images and ideas has nothing chaotic about it. There is a logic of the imagination as well as a logic of concepts. People who do not appreciate poetry always find it difficult to distinguish between order and chaos in the arrangement of images; and even those who are capable of appreciating poetry cannot depend upon first impressions. I was not convinced of Mr. Perse's imaginative order until I had read the poem five or six times. And if, as I suggest, such an arrangement of imagery requires just as much "fundamental brainwork" as the arrangement of an argument, it is to be expected that the reader of a poem should take at least as much trouble as a barrister reading an important decision on a complicated case.

I refer to this poem as a poem. It would be convenient if poetry were always verse—either accented, alliterative, or quantitative; but that is not true. Poetry may occur, within a definite limit on one side, at any point along a line of which the formal limits are "verse" and "prose". Without offering any generalized theory about "poetry", "verse" and "prose", I may suggest that a writer, by using, as does Mr. Perse, certain exclusively poetic methods, is sometimes able to write poetry in what is called prose. Another writer can, by reversing the process, write great prose in verse. There are two very simple but insuperable difficulties in any definition of "prose" and "poetry". One is that we have three terms where we need four: we have "verse" and "poetry" on the one side, and only "prose" on the other. The other difficulty follows from the first: that the words imply a valuation in one context which they do not in another. "Poetry" introduces a distinction between good verse and bad verse; but we have no one word to separate bad prose from good prose. As a matter of fact, much bad prose is poetic prose; and only a very small part of bad verse is bad because it is prosaic.

But *Anabase* is poetry. Its sequences, its logic of imagery, are those of poetry and not of prose; and in consequence—at least the two matters are very closely allied—the *declamation*, the system of stresses and pauses, which is partially exhibited by the punctuation and spacing, is that of poetry and not of prose.

The second indication of Mr. Fabre is one which I may borrow for the English reader:

a tentative synopsis of the movement of the poem. It is a scheme which may give the reader a little guidance on his first reading; when he no longer needs it he will forget it. The ten divisions of the poem are headed as follows:

    I. Arrival of the conqueror on the site of the city he is to found.
    II. Marking out of its boundary walls.
    III. Consultation of the augurs.
    IV. Founding of the city.
    V. Longing for new worlds to conquer.
    VI. Plans for establishment and for filling the coffers.
    VII. Decision to undertake fresh expedition.
    VIII. March through desert wastes.
    IX. Arrival at borders of a great land.
    X. Warrior-prince received with honours and celebrations. He rests for a spell but is soon yearning to be on his way again, this time with the navigator.

And I believe that this is as much as I need to say about Perse's *Anabasis.* I believe that this is a piece of writing of the same importance as the later work of James Joyce, as valuable as *Anna Livia Plurabelle*. And this is a high estimate indeed.

I have two words to add, one about the author, the other about the translation. The author of this poem is, even in the most practical sense, an authority on the Far East; he has lived there, as well as in the tropics. As for the translation, it would not be even so satisfactory as it is, if the author had not collaborated with me to such an extent as to be half-translator. He has, I can testify, a sensitive and intimate knowledge of the English language, as well as a mastery of his own.

T. S. ELIOT

1930

(Rossetti to Hall Caine, 1882: "Conception, my boy, *fundamental brain-work*—that is what makes the difference in all art". For TSE on prose poems, a speciality of the French, see headnote to *Hysteria*.) TSE's Preface first appeared in *1930* but is given above in its final form, from *1959* (see Textual History). Because this final edition contained E. M. Hatt's translation of Lucien Fabre's Note, her phrasing of the description of the ten divisions of the poem was adopted also in TSE's Preface. Previous editions had given a different translation, presumably by TSE:

    I. Arrival of the Conqueror at the site of the city which he is about to build.
    II. Tracing the plan of the city.
    III. Consultation of augurs.
    IV. Foundation of the city.
    V. Restlessness towards further explorations and conquests.
    VI. Schemes for foundation and conquest.
    VII. Decision to fare forth.
    VIII. March through the desert.
    IX. Arrival at the threshold of a great new country.
    X. Acclamation, festivities, repose. Yet the urge towards another departure, this time with the mariner.

TSE to Robert Giroux, 31 Mar 1948: "I have just had a letter from Léger asking about the rights of my translation of *Anabasis*. He tells me that you released to him the rights in his poem as the volume had been out of print for some years, but he is not sure whether that includes the right to use my translation or not. I have told him that if he could get another publisher to reprint his poem with my translation I should be quite glad for him to do so. He has now found a publisher who is ready to go ahead with it. So far as I am concerned I have no interest in this translation by itself and have no intention of ever reprinting it amongst my own works. I think I shall not allow it to be used apart from the French text."

NOTE TO REVISED EDITION

Since the first publication, nineteen years ago, of the text of *Anabase* together with my translation, this and other poems of the author have extended his reputation far beyond the bounds of his own country. St.-John Perse is a name known to everyone, I think, who is seriously concerned with contemporary poetry in America. It has therefore seemed high time that the translation should be revised and corrected.

When this translation was made, St.-John Perse was little known outside of France. The translator, perhaps for the reason that he was introducing the poem to the English-speaking public, was then concerned, here and there, less with rendering the exact sense of a phrase, than with coining some phrase in English which might have equivalent value; he may even have taken liberties in the interest of originality, and sometimes interposed his own idiom between author and reader. But (to revert to the first person) I have always refused to publish the translation except in this way, *en regard* with the French text. Its purpose is only to assist the English-speaking reader who wishes to approach the French text. The method of the author, his syntax and his rhythm, are original; his vocabulary includes some unusual words; and the translation may still serve its purpose. But at this stage it was felt that a greater fidelity to the exact meaning, a more literal translation, was what was needed. I have corrected not only my own licences, but several positive errors and mistakes. In this revision I have depended heavily upon the recommendations of the author, whose increasing mastery of English has enabled him to detect faults previously unobserved, and upon the assistance of Mr. John Hayward, to whom I also wish to make acknowledgement.

T. S. ELIOT
1949

NOTE TO THE THIRD EDITION

The alterations to the English text of this edition have been made by the author himself, and tend to make the translation more literal than in previous editions.

T. S. ELIOT
1958

1930 front flap (as also *1937*):

Mr. T. S. Eliot, who has translated this poem from the French, in collaboration with the author, considers the *Anabase* of St.-J. Perse one of the most remarkable poems of this generation. It has already been translated into several other languages. Here, the French text appears side by side with Mr. Eliot's English version, so that readers may judge for themselves of the merit and accuracy of the translation, and of the beauty of the original.

1937 Faber catalogue (initialled by TSE, King's):

This very remarkable and important poem, *Anabase*, was translated from the French by Mr. Eliot and published by us in 1930. Much interest was taken in it by poets; and it has, we believe, made its mark on English poetry, so that it will be an essential document in studying English poetry of the present time. In the hope of introducing it to a wider public, because of its great beauty and originality, we have now reduced the price from 10s. 6d. to 5s.

The front panel of the jacket of *1937* read "ANABASIS | a poem translated by | T. S. ELIOT", with the spine likewise failing to mention Perse, and the rear panel listed "Other books by T. S. Eliot". The front of the *US 1938* jacket was worded the same, causing TSE to write to Marguerite Caetani, 13 Dec 1938: "I had overlooked the omission of the name of Perse on the cover or jacket. It is of course on the title page, but that is not enough. I had not even seen proofs of the book, but sent Harcourt, Brace & Co a revised copy of the original edition, so that I had no knowledge of what the appearance of the book would be. I will mention the matter to Harcourt, Brace in the hope that they will alter the jacket wrapper · · · P.S. Perhaps you had better remove the jacket before presenting the copy to Léger. But I had assumed that Harcourt, Brace & Co would have sent him six author's copies. If this was not done, it must have been an oversight."

The front panel of the *US 1949* jacket read: "ST.-JOHN PERSE | ANABASIS | A translation by | T. S. ELIOT | 'A poem of vast dimensions, impersonal | as the sea journeys of Homer.' | Archibald MacLeish."

Peter du Sautoy to Richard de la Mare, 3 Apr 1958 (Faber archive):

Mr. Eliot does not like the format of the American edition · · · He also does not like the way the jacket is laid out, nor the title page, since they both suggest that only the translation is included. He thinks his name is too prominent on the jacket · · · What Mr. Eliot suggests for the title page is something like this:

ANABASIS
A POEM BY ST.-JOHN PERSE
THE FRENCH TEXT WITH A TRANSLATION BY T. S. ELIOT

US 1949 front flap:

"I believe that this is a piece of writing of the same importance as the later work of James Joyce." T. S. Eliot | ST.-JOHN PERSE | ANABASIS

This is a new, definitive edition of St.-John Perse's famous poem, *Anabasis*, which was first introduced to American readers by T. S. Eliot in 1938. The text has been reset and redesigned, and the book presented in a new and larger format with French and English on facing pages. Mr. Eliot has revised and corrected his translation. The French text, corrected by the author, is now presented in definitive form. Three notes on *Anabasis* by Hugo von Hofmannsthal, Valery Larbaud, and Giuseppe Ungaretti are included, together with a bibliography of St.-John Perse's work.

US 1949 rear panel:

ST.-JOHN PERSE is the pen-name of Alexis Léger. He was born in the Antilles in 1889, served as Permanent Secretary of the French Foreign Office and as Ambassador of France under the Third Republic. A world traveler, he has lived in China and journeyed through the Gobi Desert. His other poems include *Exile*, *Eloges*, *Vents*, and *Amitié du Prince*. | ARCHIBALD MACLEISH: "The poetry of Perse, with its presentness of time, its odor of eternity, its vast image of life like a landscape without trees, is a poetry written not out of action but against it or behind it." | ROGER CAILLOIS: "His work, which fills less than a hundred pages, appears to be one of the vastest. [His poems] continue to astonish the reader by an enigmatic power which belongs only to them." | ALAIN BOSQUET: "St.-John Perse [is] the poet of solitude and of a prophetic gift, one of those who tower above the men and things about which they sing."

1959 jacket material:

> When the text of *Anabasis*, together with the translation by T. S. Eliot, was first published in 1931 [1930], neither the author nor his translator was as well known as they have both since become. The fame of St.-John Perse has spread rapidly in recent years and his reputation as a poet has been enhanced by every subsequent volume that he has published. Not only is his genius now universally acknowledged but his influence is recognized in the work of poets writing in other languages, including Mr. Eliot himself. *Anabasis*, however, remains a landmark in modern French poetry and the demand for a new edition has been insistent. The author, who has become very much at home in the English language, has himself revised the translation for this third edition.
>
> St.-John Perse, as all the world now knows, is the pseudonym of Alexis St. Léger Léger, a brilliant diplomat who, until the fall of France in 1940, was permanent Chief of Staff of the Ministère des Affaires Etrangères.

4. *ANABASE* TO *ANABASIS*

It was through a distant cousin of TSE's, Marguerite Caetani (Princess di Bassiano), that he came into contact with Perse. In 1924 she founded *Commerce*, with Fargue, Larbaud and Paul Valéry as editors, and in Winter 1924 it printed Perse's *Chanson* (later *Chanson du Présomptif*), followed by TSE's *Poème* (later part I of *The Hollow Men*) with Perse's translation opposite.

It was at Caetani's request that TSE translated *Anabase* (see TSE to Stephen Spender, 14 Mar 1935, quoted below, 5. TRANSLATION). He continued to support her in the late 1940s when she began another journal, *Botteghe Oscure*, which he recommended to poets as a place to publish.

TSE's copy of Perse's *Anabase* (*TSE's Anabase*) is dated 1926, in which year the Hogarth Press took over British distribution of *Commerce*. TSE to Marguerite Caetani, 19 May 1926: "about *Anabase*. Circumstances have been *most* adverse and complicated—I have got no farther—and it is unlikely that I can even touch it for a couple of months. In the circumstances, and as I have tried your patience so long, it has occurred to me that my friend F. S. Flint is the man. He is a *brilliant* translator." TSE had published only one book with Faber & Gwyer when he wrote to Geoffrey Faber, 4 Sept 1926: "About Léger. I am afraid that the arrangement in our conversation, and subsequently in conversation between myself and Madame de Bassiano, was that she should pay the author and should pay me for the translation, and the cost of publishing to be borne by the publishers. But this was purely verbal. The book is a small one; the French text is 41 pages not wholly covered, so that it might be as well to include the preface by Valery Larbaud which does not appear in the French edition but was written for the Russian translation. That is 5 pages. But if there is a misunderstanding, let me have an estimate of the cost of printing etc. and I will take the matter up with her and come to an arrangement. I should suggest a small book, almost a pamphlet, like some of the Hogarth Press, and a printing of 500." To Caetani, 27 Sept 1926: "I confess it is more difficult than I thought at first, because the idea (and there decidedly is one) is conveyed by a cumulative succession of images—and one *cannot* simply translate the images. One must find equivalents—that cannot be done bit by bit, but by finding an English *key* to the combination."

The first correspondence between the two poets is a letter from Perse, 15 Oct 1926, inviting TSE to visit him at the Quai d'Orsay. At or just after that brief meeting—as is suggested by TSE's subsequent letter to Perse from London (19 Nov 1926)—they began to come to terms regarding the publication of *Anabasis*.

To Caetani, 18 Jan 1927: "complete translation of *Anabase* enclosed herewith. I have sent another copy to Léger together with thirty or forty notes of passages on which I want his opinion · · · As soon as he answers all my questions it will be a matter of only a few days to repair the translation. I then propose to write a short introduction myself, which I can do because I now like the poem immensely. I only hope that the translation will produce a fraction of the impression which the original has made on me."

He had sent the translation to Perse three days earlier, writing: "je crois que je pourrais écrire une petite préface que présenterait mieux votre poème aux lecteurs anglaises · · · Autre chose: dans ma préface, peux-je dire que St.-J. Perse et St. Léger Léger, l'auteur d'*Anabase* et l'auteur d'*Éloges*, sont identiques, ou voulez-vous garder votre anonymat fragile?" [I think I could write a short preface which would better present your poem to English readers · · · Another thing: in my preface, may I speak of St.-J. Perse and St. Léger Léger, the author of *Anabase* and the author of *Éloges*, as identical, or would you rather guard your fragile anonymity?]

To Caresse Crosby, Editions Narcisse, Paris, 8 Oct 1928: "I am sorry that I can do nothing about *Anabase* · · · We have been waiting for two years only for him to sign the contract and make any suggestions about my translation, which I did not wish to publish until he had approved it · · · I have long given up hope that it can ever be published by anybody!"

To Caetani, 9 Aug 1929: "I am very glad to get Léger's contract and his revision of my translation · · · I shall have to go through Léger's notes very carefully and type out another text and send it to him with explanations wherever I maintain my own version. I am quite aware that from his point of view some of my departures from the exact translation must seem unjustified, but they are often determined by exigencies of rhythm and association which he could hardly be expected to follow. I see however that there are many places where I can fall in with his recommendations." TSE offered to dedicate his translation to Caetani, but she declined (letter to her, 12 Dec). Nor did *Commerce* publish the translation.

In a letter of 2 Sept 1929, Perse granted TSE great latitude "to take liberties with the necessities of rearrangement which any living translation inevitably demands" (tr. Haffenden).

Meanwhile, Edouard Roditi had set about translating the poem. Discovering that TSE had already done so, he approached TSE (who was subsequently to publish Roditi's poem *Trafalgar Square* in *Criterion* Apr 1934). TSE to Roditi, 31 Aug 1929: "Léger has now sent me back my first draft of the poem, with a great many corrections and suggestions, including those which you noticed yourself. So I have rewritten my translation with his alterations in front of me. For this reason I do not think I should accept your kind offer; for I have all I need to ensure approximate accuracy; and I do not want to go further and pilfer from another translator. And perhaps in the end your translation will supersede mine."

To Perse, 2 Sept 1929: "Cher ami, Since your revision of my translation makes evident that you know English much more intimately than I know French, and indeed puts me to shame, I shall write to you henceforward in this language · · · I marvel first at the pains that you have taken, and more at the accuracy of your emendations. You will find that I have used *most* of your suggestions. Where I have not, it has been usually for some reason of rhythm, or for *compensation*: that is to say, trying to supply by a richness of association of the word in English in one place, a richness of the word in French in another place which could not there be conveyed. After all, a translation must be made *globalement*, by loading in one place to compensate for an impoverishment in another place! I shall send you shortly a copy of my revision. If you have any alterations to make in that, and if you can let me have them by the end of this year, I shall use them and shall be glad of them. But if you have not time · · · then the copy you will receive will be printed in the spring · · · I must say that it has been a great pleasure to me to know and to translate your poem, which has indeed, in at least one or two places which I could point out, affected my own subsequent work." (To Vernon Watkins, 8 June 1944, on Watkins's translations of Heine: "this work is a useful exercise to keep your hand in; and you will probably find, as one does with translation, that in doing it you have learned something which will be of future use in your own poetry".)

To Perse, 15 Nov 1929, enclosing galley proofs: "You will observe that I have accepted the great majority of your revisions, that in a few places I have compromised, and only in a few have stuck to my first version. I think I could justify most of these; but if you still find any gross alterations of the sense I hope you will let me know quickly."

Perse was to prove a demanding collaborator, repeatedly failing to reply to letters, but then asking for last-minute revisions. For details of his changes in the successive editions, see Textual History and *Rigolot*.

Hayward's copy of *US 1938* (King's) is inscribed: "to John Hayward Esqre in grateful acknowledgment of his inestimable assistance in correcting and much improving the text of this the second edition of this Translation. 5. iii. 38 T. S. Eliot". Later, TSE would publicly acknowledge his obligation to Hayward "for improvements of phrase and construction" of *Four Quartets* (see headnote, 8. PUBLICATION).

TSE did not give details when he wrote of G. W. Stonier (of the *New Statesman & Nation*): "several years ago he wrote an intelligent review of my translation of *Anabase*, in which he made some useful suggestions of which I have subsequently taken advantage", On a Recent Piece of Criticism in *Purpose* Apr–June (1938).

On 25 Feb 1948, TSE wrote to John D. Barrett declining to translate Perse's *Vents* for a collection of Perse in English. "I would, of course, have liked to be able to do this, but I know from experience that it would be a major undertaking of many months and I should have, incidentally, to discuss interpretations continually with the author in Washington, and this correspondence would further protract the labours."

5. TRANSLATION

To Laurence Binyon, 16 May 1930: "The only attempts at any translation that I have made, suggest to me that it is quite impossible to translate anything."

To Donald Gallup, 11 Oct 1951, discussing the arrangement of his Bibliography: "If my work in translation had been more extensive, I might have pleaded for a separate section, but I think it would be ridiculous and tiresome to make a section for *Anabasis* alone."

Anabasis was the only translation other than prose that TSE ever published, although at a date unknown he also began a translation from Johannes Theodor Kuhlemann (1891–1939); see headnote to *The Dry Salvages*, 3. COMPOSITION. He also considered making a translation from Hugo von Hofmannsthal (whose Preface to *Anabase* was published in *Commerce* in Summer 1929 and reprinted in *US 1949*);

see headnote to *Sweeney Agonistes*, 11. BRITISH PERFORMANCES. To Herbert Read, "Friday" [6 Dec 1929]: "I am glad you like *Anabase*. I think it is a big thing myself—as important as *Anna Livia Plurabelle*—but there *is* a considerable loss in the translation—which I have tried to compensate as far as possible by drawing on the greater resources of our language—but what Léger has done with French is prodigious."

During the Second World War, TSE lent his name to one further translation. To Hayward, 15 Oct 1944: "Dr. Slonomski, has asked me if I will 'do something for his distressed country' · · · revise his translation of some Polish carols". *Five Fantasies on Polish Christmas Carols* with music by Arnold Bax, 1945, included Jan Sliwinski's translation of *God is Born*, "kindly approved by T. S. Eliot".

To Anne Ridler 20 Mar 1946: "André Gide's translations of Shakespeare, for instance, are quite able—that is to say, they sometimes manage to convey about half of the meaning of the original." See letter to Jean Mambrino, 24 July 1952, quoted in headnote to *Landscapes*.

To Mrs. J. J. Hawkes, 9 Oct 1947, in response to a proposal from UNESCO: "it is *most undesirable* that all the classics should be translated in all the languages".

To W. H. Auden, 11 May 1931: "I have read *The Orators* with great interest · · · The second part seems to me very brilliant, though I do not quite get its connexion with the first. My chief objection to it is that it seems to me to have lumps of undigested St. Jean Perse embedded in it. I admire your success with the Perse method, which I should not have believed possible, but I think it still needs a further process of purification. And the third part is apparently perfectly lucid, but I must confess that so far I cannot make head or tail of it."

Proust, *À la recherche du temps perdu: Sodome et Gomorrhe* I (1921): "Un jour pourtant, elles trouvèrent sur mon lit un volume. C'était des poèmes admirables mais obscurs de Saint-Léger Léger. Céleste lut quelques pages et me dit: 'Mais êtes-vous sûr que ce sont des vers, est-ce que ce ne serait pas plutôt des devinettes?'" [One day, however, they found lying on my bed a book. It was a volume of the admirable but obscure poems of Saint-Léger Léger. Céleste read a few pages and said to me: "But are you quite sure that these are poetry, wouldn't they just be riddles?"], Scott Moncrieff tr. VII 346.

TSE to Stephen Spender, 14 Mar 1935: "I am entirely in agreement with you that translations of Hölderlin ought to be made, and also in agreement that it is equally important if only a few people read them · · · As for *Anabase*, I quite agree that it was worth it, even on the assumption that no one read it but you and Wystan [Auden]. I may tell you, however, in confidence, that I was paid to translate it by a friend and admirer of the author, so that Faber and Faber had only the cost of production without having any royalties to worry about." 24 Apr 1936: "as I may have told you, the sales of my translation of *Anabase*, over which I took a good deal of trouble, stopped completely after only some hundreds. I am very glad that I did it, both for my own sake and because it brought the poem to the notice of the few people who could make the most use of it, but it certainly did not pay the firm to do it."

TSE was pressed to contribute to a special issue of *Cahiers de la Pléiade* (Summer/Autumn 1950) in homage to Perse and on 7 Dec 1949 he sent to Jean Paulhan a letter of tribute: "Nearly twenty-five years ago I made the acquaintance of *Éloges* and of *Anabase*, and set myself to translate the latter work into English. I am proud of the fact that my translation of *Anabase*—imperfect as it was, though improved, I think, in later editions—was the first presentation of St.-J. Perse to the English and American public. It appeared with the French text and English translation *en regard*, and will never, I hope, be printed by itself: for its sole purpose was to introduce a new and important poet to a foreign audience, and to facilitate understanding of his work. Certainly, a quarter of a century ago, St.-J. Perse was to be considered a difficult poet. He fitted in to no category, he had no obvious literary ancestry or consanguinity: a great part of the difficulty was that his poem could not be explained in terms of anything but itself. I myself should have a far more imperfect understanding of *Anabase* if I had not set myself to the task of translating it. It was beyond my resources to do it justice: I came to think that not only my command of the French but my command of English was inadequate. But its influence appears in some of the poems which I wrote after completing this translation: influence of the imagery and perhaps of the rhythm. Critics of my later work may find that this influence still persists." (See, for instance, note to *Journey of the Magi* 9–10.)

In the letter to Paulhan, 7 Dec 1949, TSE wrote of Perse: "his influence can be seen in some of the poems I wrote after I finished the translation: he influenced my images and also perhaps my rhythm. Whoever examines my late work will find that this influence perhaps never disappeared", *Honneur à St.-John Perse: Hommage et témoignages littéraires* (1965) 19.

To Perse, 3 Feb 1958: "I think that the first requirement for a translator is to realise that he does not know French as well as he should and the second qualification is that he should realise that he does not know his own language as well as he should. I experienced both these realisations when translating *Anabase*."

TSE on Perse: "The interesting point is that Léger wanted to avoid the (French) Bible, and whenever he spotted the Bible in my translation he wanted me to alter it", to Herbert Read [6 Dec 1929].

Perse on TSE: "Eliot's interest in words was literary and etymological; he learned about words by reading the Oxford dictionary; whereas my own vocabulary comes from my knowledge of many skills and crafts", in conversation with Kathleen Raine, *Southern Review* Jan 1967.

Readings from editions other than *1959* are designated *variant*.

I

I viii **towns on the slopes with powder** (*variant*: **in sugar of coral the diverse quarters of cities on the slopes**): "palaces on slopes · · · sherbet", *Journey of the Magi* 9–10.

I ix **the idea pure as salt**: for Remy de Gourmont's fascination with "l'idée pure", see note to *First Debate between the Body and Soul* 8.

I xv **men from the marches**: "the guards shake dice on the marches", *Coriolan* I. *Difficulties of a Statesman* 24. *Anabase*: "*gens des confins*" [men of the borders].

I xv *variant* **O light folk blown by a breath of wind**: "Carrying | Away the little light dead people", *WLComposite* 175–76. "My life is light, waiting for the death wind", *A Song for Simeon* 4.

I xv **in the little dawn wind**: "blown, like the metal leaves | Before the little dawn wind unresisting", *Little Gidding* II 35 *variant*.

I xix **destiny · · · the seeds of time:** *Macbeth* I iii: "If you can look into the seeds of time, | And say which grain will grow, and which will not".

I xx **god-drunken:** Novalis, on Spinoza: "Ein Gott-betrunkener Mensch" [A God-intoxicated man].

I xxi **drawing to our dockyards eternal keels:** "forever bailing, | Setting and hauling · · · drawing their money, drying sails at dockage", *The Dry Salvages* II 25–28.

II

II v, III x **the same man may burn with desire for a woman and for her daughter · · · the man tainted with gonorrhoea washes his linen in clean water:** "Mrs. Porter | And · · · her daughter | They wash their feet in soda water", *The Waste Land* [III] 199–201 (see note).

III

III i **imposing:** TSE underlined "emphatiques" in *TSE's Anabase*, with "collocation of conversat. ₵ rhetorical".

III iii *variant* **Senectus:** *Anabase*: "*vieillesse*". See note to *Gerontion* 19–20, "juvescence".

III v **And doubt is cast on the reality of things:** to Virginia Woolf, 5 Mar 1933: "In this country, as my friend St. Léger Léger says in his *Anabase*: Doubt is Cast on the Reality of Things." 25 Apr: "Very grateful thanks I proffer for your letter. If I had more such letters it would help me to preserve my sense of the Reality of Things."   **if a man shall cherish his sorrow:** for Pater on those who "*wilfully lived in sadness*", see note to *The Love Song of J. Alfred Prufrock* 13–14. "There is no relief but in grief", *Five-Finger Exercises* I. *Lines to a Persian Cat* 6 (see note).

III viii **the power of signs and visions:** "we would see a sign", *Gerontion* 18 ("Scenters of signs and seeds", *Anabasis*, I xv).

III ix, IV x **the princes, the ministers, the captains · · · the bankers:** "The captains, merchant bankers, eminent men of letters", *East Coker* III 3.

III ix **The saddle of the weakling is burnt:** Bonamy Dobrée to TSE, 24 July 1930, on the translation of "On fait brûler la selle du malingre": "I think your *wilfulness* here and there goes too far (incidentally I don't believe that Perse knows any English worth speaking of). Nothing will persuade me that *Anabasis* does not contain two undeniable *mistakes*. 'They burnt the saddle of the malingerer' (I quote from memory) should be 'They burnt the dung of the weakling' · · · If you don't like dung for *selle*, you could use the similar word stool." TSE to Dobrée, 28 July: "Léger ought to know enough English to distinguish between dung and saddle; but there you may be right · · · I owe you a glass of sherry about *selle*. Léger certainly overlooked that? But why should the stool of the weakling (malingerer) rather than his saddle [be burnt]? Answer me that. If he belonged to a race of horsemen it wd. be more significant to burn his saddle than his stool. Can you cite any authorities for burning the stool of the malingerer? Anyway, it's not so bad as the German translator who turned *Fétus de paille* into 'foetuses made of straw'" (III ii; TSE translates correctly as "bits of straw"). TSE emended "saddle" to "stools" in *US 1938* only, before reverting to "saddle".

III xii **my soul · · · say to the Prince to be still:** "I said to my soul, be still", *East Coker* III 23.

IV

IV v **living waters on the mountains:** "exhausted wells · · · among the mountains", *The Waste Land* [V] 384–85 and for "the fountain of living waters", see note to [V] 384; for "the living Rock", see note to *Airs of Palestine, No. 2.*

IV vii **disembarkation of girls:** Laforgue: "Et comment quelques couples vraiment distingués | Un soir ici ont débarqué . . ." [and how several really refined couples disembarked here one evening . . .], *Cythère* 11–12. See *Goldfish* II, note to title *Embarquement pour Cythère.*

IV viii **ships taller than Ilion:** Marlowe: "Was this the face that launched a thousand ships | And burnt the topless towers of Ilium?" *Doctor Faustus* sc. XIV (see note to *A Proclamation* 7, 19).   **the white peacock:** D. H. Lawrence's first novel was *The White Peacock* (1911). He died the year before *Anabasis* was published.

IV vii *variant* **in our places:** "returned to our places", *Journey of the Magi* 40.

IV viii **the ships · · · having crossed the bar:** Tennyson: "When I have crost the bar", *Crossing the Bar.*

IV ix **deadwater:** OED "dead water, dead-water": "still water". See note to *Little Gidding* II 10–11. *Anabase*: "*point mort*" [dead point].

IV x **vacant lots and rubbish:** *Anabase*: "*ce quartier aux détritus*" [this area of rubbish].   **vacant lots:** see *Preludes* IV 16 and note.

IV xiv **girls' waist cloths hanging at the windows:** "Out of the window perilously spread | Her drying combinations", *The Waste Land* [III] 224–25. The previous eds. had translated "*ses caleçons de filles*" as "camiknickers" (*1930*), "knickerbockers" (*US 1938*) and "drawers" (*US 1949*). (See "the publication of the bride-sheets", X v.)

IV xv **lunation:** OED 1. "The time from one new moon to the next, constituting a lunar month." 2. "The time of full moon." 3. "A menstruation. *rare.*"

V

V i *variant* **an hundred fires in towns wakened by the barking of dogs:** TSE to Dobrée, 28 July 1930: "the *Manchester Guardian* says I have made the towns, not the fires, 'awakened'. Error." Emended in *US 1938* and *US 1949* to "in towns an hundred fires revived by the barking of dogs", and in *1959* to "an hundred fires revived in towns by the barking of dogs". *Anabase*: "*cent feux de villes avivés par l'aboiement des chiens*".

V v–vi **squadrons of stars · · · bivouacs:** for Meredith's "the stars · · · marched, rank on rank, | The army", see note to *Cousin Nancy* 13.

V vii **falling Bielides:** OED: "An Andromede . . . supposed to come from the remains of Biela's comet", with "The Bielid meteors were observed here in considerable numbers", *Science* (1885). (See A. J. Knodel, *PMLA* June 1964.) For "Comets . . . Leonids", see *East Coker* II 13 (and note to II 1–17).

V xii **benighted:** OED 1. "To be overtaken by the darkness of night (before reaching a place of shelter)". *Variants:* "put up for the night" (*1930*), "held up for the night" (*US 1938*). *Anabase*: "*l'étoile s'anuitait*" [the star turns to night]. "Under the twinkle of a fading star ··· dying stars", *The Hollow Men* III 6, IV 3.

V xii–xiii **when the star ··· did we know ··· spears ··· Ablutions:** Blake: "When the stars threw down their spears | And watered heaven with their tears, | Did he smile", *The Tyger* 13–15.

V xv **the woman extends herself from nail to nail:** "Princess Volupine extends | A meagre, blue-nailed, phthisic hand", *Burbank with a Baedeker: Bleistein with a Cigar* 25–26. In *TSE's Anabase*, TSE underlined "*la femme s'étire sur son ongle*" with "de bout" and "du pied".

V xix **there is no more substance of man in him:** John 8: 44: "there is no truth in him".   **winged seeds, like a poet in his thoughts:** Tennyson: "his thoughts were ··· winged with flame ··· like the arrow-seeds ··· wingèd shafts", *The Poet* 10–11, 19, 26.

VI

VI i *variant* **scented girls, who shall soothe us with a breath of silk webs:** "And the silken girls bringing sherbet", *Journey of the Magi* 10. See note to I viii.

VI i–ii **girls ··· silk webs ··· springes for happiness:** OED "springe": "A snare for catching small game", citing Farquhar, *Love and a Bottle*: "And have your ladies no springes to catch 'em in?"   **girls ··· high places ··· springes:** *Hamlet* I iii, OPHELIA: "with all the vows of Heaven". POLONIUS: "Ay, springes to catch woodcocks." (See Textual History for variants including "daughters".)

VI iii **sang ··· like Memnon:** *Lemprière*: "The Ethiopians, over whom Memnon reigned, erected a celebrated statue to the honour of their monarch. This statue had the wonderful property of uttering a melodious sound every day, at sunrising, like that which is heard at the breaking of the string of a harp when it is wound up."

VI vi **shaking an iron tree:** "shaken from the wrath-bearing tree", *Gerontion* 47.

VI viii **this race settled on the slopes:** the three editions *1930–US 1949* read "this folk squatting on the slopes" ("the Jew squats on the window-sill", *Gerontion* 8). *Anabase*: "*cette race établie sur les pentes*" [this race established on the slopes]. See note to IX v.   **swift upon the seeds of sedition:** Francis Bacon quotes John Morton, Lord Chancellor of England and Archbishop of Canterbury: "it is not the blood spilt in the field that will save the blood in the city ··· the true way is, to stop the seeds of sedition and rebellion in their beginning", *Henry VII*.

VI x **peace ··· military endowments ··· treaties of amity and of boundary, conventions of people with people:** "I believe that modern war is chiefly caused by some immorality of competition which is always with us in times of 'peace'; and that until this evil is cured, no leagues or disarmaments or collective security conferences or conventions or treaties will suffice to prevent it", *The Church's Message* (1937).   **cisterns:** see *The Waste Land* [V] 384 and note.   **leaves of gold, treaties of amity and of boundary:** following the Anglo-French treaty of 1514, Henry VIII met Francis I of France in amity in 1520 at the Field of the Cloth of Gold, in what was then the English Pale of Calais.

VI xiii **an odour of violets:** to John Hayward, with diagrams of various states of dress and undress of gentlemen's legs 25 June [1934]: "The radial lines indicate that peculiar emanation or rather effulgence which usually accompanied with the odour of Violets is accustomed to envelop the Limbs and torso of very Holy persons." (OED "odour" 5: "odour of sanctity (Fr. *odeur de sainteté*, 17th c.) ··· a sweet or balsamic odour stated to have been exhaled by the bodies of eminent saints at their death, or on subsequent disinterment ··· reputation for holiness: sometimes used ironically or sarcastically.")

VII

VII iv *variant* **Camels, gentle beneath the shears**: Dobrée to TSE, 24 July 1930: "Chamelles douces sous la tonte ··· I do not think means that the camels didn't mind being clipped: I should say rather: As camels smoothed by the shears, stitched with mauve scars ··· douces being opposed to the shagginess of unclipped camels: clipped camels do look as though they were cousues de mauves cicatrices. I think that the whole paragraph is simply comparing a line of hills to a trail of camels, which finally barrack in the distant mist." TSE to Dobrée, 28 July: "I admit that you know more about camels than I do; but then why did he put she-camels instead of he- or he-and-she camels? You are quite right about the camels and the hills, but I found that out in discussion with Léger." TSE emended "Camels" (*1930*) to "Milch-camels", *US 1938+*.

VII v **sandsmokes**: sole citation in OED ("sand" *n.*²).

VII vii **wind ··· wonders**: "windy spaces ··· wonders", *Gerontion* 16–17.

VII viii, x **the jujuba ··· a great bird**: Carroll: "Beware the Jubjub bird", *The Jabberwocky* in *Through the Looking-Glass* ch. I.

VII ix **Levy a wilderness of mirrors**: "multiply variety | In a wilderness of mirrors", *Gerontion* 64–65. *Anabase*: "*un peuple de miroirs*" (= a people, nation, of mirrors).

VIII

VIII ii **clepsydrae**: OED: "An instrument used by the ancients to measure time by the discharge of water; a water-clock", with Sir Thomas Browne, "They measured the hours not only by..water in glasses called Clepsydræ, but also by sand in glasses called Clepsammia", *Pseudodoxia Epidemica* (*Vulgar Errors*, 1646) V xviii.

VIII iv **vacance**: OED: "*poet. nonce-use.* A rendering of Fr. *absence*", citing this only.

VIII v **the frontiers of the spirit**: on Maritain's *Situation de la poésie*: "he is concerned with the risks to which are exposed those poets who endeavour to cross *les frontières de l'esprit* ··· poetry, if it is not to be a lifeless repetition of forms, must be constantly exploring 'the frontiers of the spirit.' But these frontiers are not like the surveys of geographical explorers, conquered once and for all and settled. The frontiers of the spirit are more like the jungle ··· always ready to encroach and eventually obliterate the cultivated area", *That Poetry is Made with Words* (1939); see note to *East Coker* V 11–18. (To Robert Waller, 19 Oct 1942, alluding to Mallarmé's retort to Degas: "Poetry is made with words not with ideas, though it exploits ideas just as a poet exploits his private experiences and emotions. It isn't that he wants to tell the world about what he feels, but that what he feels is the only thing he has to tell it: he wants to write a poem, and so he uses whatever material he has. A poem is primarily FORM and making words come alive.") **selucid**: OED "Seleucid": "One of the Seleucidæ or members of the dynasty · · · which reigned over Syria from 312 to 65 B.C. and subjected a great part of Western Asia."

VIII viii **To the place called the Place of the Dry Tree:** Luke 23: 33: "to the place, which is called Calvary".

VIII xiii **Indian cocculus · · · intoxicating properties:** OED: "cocculus indicus": "a climbing plant found in Malabar and Ceylon; the berry is a violent poison, and has been used to stupefy fish, and in England to increase the intoxicating power of beer and porter."

IX

IX i **making westward, what:** Wordsworth: *"What, you are stepping westward?"*, *Stepping Westward.*

IX v **old · · · seated on the heights:** Tennyson (first line and title): "Of old sat Freedom on the heights".   **seated:** the three editions *1930–US 1949* read "squatting" (*Anabase:* "assis"). See note to VI viii.

IX xiv **his sex:** Dobrée to TSE, 24 July 1930: "I do not think that sex for *sexe* (meaning cock, prick or tool) is English, though I see from one of the American magazines that it is American. I do not think that in English I can wash my sex any more than I can wash my nationality. What I wash is my parts." TSE to Dobrée, 28 July 1930: "As for *sex*, that was deliberate on my part, an innovation if you like." OED: "sex" 3c: "Genitalia; a penis. *slang*" from 1938.

X

X i **with the brim seduced:** TSE annotated Perse's "séduit" in *TSE's Anabase:* "cf. Latin: se ȶ ducere" (= "to lead aside").   **provinces · · · the things of the plain:** Genesis 19: 29: "the cities of the plain". Proust's *À la recherche du temps perdu: Sodome et Gomorrhe* (1921–22) was published in C. K. Scott Moncrieff's translation as *The Cities of the Plain* (1928), two years before *Anabasis.*

X v **the publication of the bride-sheets!:** showing of blood-stained sheets to the families as proof of consummation.   **the bride-sheets:** OED cites this only. "the bridegroom . . . blood upon the bed", *Ode* ("Tired. | Subterrene") 9–10.

X vi **dressing the sores of animals:** Dobrée, misquoting this translation of "les pansements de bêtes", to TSE, 24 July 1930: "'They dressed the wounds of the animals' should be 'They groomed the animals.' · · · *Panser* is the ordinary word for to groom." TSE to Dobrée, 28 July 1930: "I am quite aware that *panser* means *groom*, but it also means *dress.*" Unchanged in later eds. TSE omits eleven definite articles present in the French sentence (as often elsewhere).   **building of enclosures of rose red:** J. W. Burgon: "A rose-red city—'half as old as Time'!" *Petra* 132 (TSE: "rose red", VI x).   **fatigue parties:** OED "fatigue" 3: "The extra professional duties of a soldier, sometimes allotted to him as punishment for a misdemeanour".

X vi *variant* **ribbon roads:** "And now you live dispersed on ribbon roads", *Choruses from "The Rock"* II 44.

X vii **all conditions of men · · · all sorts of men:** "we humbly beseech thee for all sorts and conditions of men", Bk. of Common Prayer.   **water fruits:** OED's sole citation for this formation, among combinations "denoting vegetable growths that live in water" ("water" 31).   **the smith ··· for fletching:** "the fletchers and javelin-makers and smiths", *Coriolan* II. *Difficulties of a Statesman* 22.   **onomastic:** OED B. 3: "*pl.* The study of the origin and formation of proper names, esp. of persons". On this, its first citation, OED comments: "The *sing.* in quot. 1930 is unusual" (rendering Fr. *l'onomastique*.)   **quails in the wrinkled land:** Tennyson: "The wrinkled sea beneath him crawls", *The Eagle* 4 (see note to *East Coker* I 48–49). Tennyson: "o'er a weary sultry land ··· Sown in a wrinkle of the monstrous hill, | The city sparkles like a grain of salt", *Will* 17–20. (*Anabasis* has "salt" eight times.)

X viii   **palmtrees ··· a mule and three white hens:** "three trees ··· And an old white horse", *Journey of the Magi* 24–25.   **skin-jars:** not in OED. "wine-skins", *Journey of the Magi* 28.   **the ambush in the vineyard:** 1 Kings 22: 18: "Jezebel his wife said unto him ··· I will give thee the vineyard of Naboth ··· Ahab ··· is in the vineyard of Naboth, whither he is gone down to possess it."   **coupling of beasts:** "The time of the coupling of man and woman | And that of beasts", *East Coker* I 44–45 (see note).

SONG

i–iii   **so sweet ··· rivers ··· the morning ··· star ··· the dove-moaning tree ··· more sweet ··· my brother the poet: once more he has written a song of great sweetness:** Tennyson: "(the shepherd sang) ··· star ··· Morning ··· sweet is every sound, | Sweeter thy voice, but every sound is sweet ··· rivulets ··· The moan of doves in immemorial elms", *Come down, O maid, from yonder mountain height.*

ii   **fasting sky:** to Marguerite Caetani, 18 Jan 1927 on his difficulty with Perse's "ciel à jeun": "I have not yet found a way of expressing 'fasting sky' in English; if I don't I shall commit myself to the mistranslation in the footnote." Unchanged; no footnote.

iii   **the poet ··· has written a song of great sweetness ··· And some there are who:** revised in *US 1949* from "has written well", emphasising the allusion to Ecclesiasticus 44: 5–9: "musical tunes, and recited verses ··· There be of them that have left a name behind them ··· And some there be, which have no memorial."

Other Verses

"The best of Denham's verse is not poetry; it is charming verse."
Sir John Denham (1928)

"His early poems show what the poems of a boy of genius ought to
show, immense power of assimilation. Such early poems are not, as
usually supposed, crude attempts to do something beyond the boy's
capacity; they are, in the case of a boy of real promise, more likely
to be quite mature and successful attempts to do something small."
William Blake (1920)

Valerie Eliot specified that TSE's first poem was composed in 1897, "four little verses,
about the sadness of having to start school again every Monday morning" (*Letters 1*
xxiii).

Fireside: A Weekly Magazine

No. 1, 28 Jan 1899:

"Fiction, Gossip, Theatre, Jokes, and all interesting. Edited by T. S.
Eliot. The T. S. Eliot Co., St. Louis" [*title page*].

"Do you subscribe
To 'Fireside'?"

Poet's Corner

I thought I saw a elephant
A-riding on a 'bus
I looked again, and found
Alas! 'Twas only us.

Eliot, S. Thomas.

No. 2, 29 Jan 1899:

[Omitted here: Selections from the Poets I:
Longfellow, first stanza of *The Village Blacksmith*]

Poet's Corner

> I thought I saw a banker's clerk
> A-riding on a 'bus,
> I looked again and saw,
> It was a hippo[po]tamus.
> "If he should stay to tea," thought I,
> *"What would be left for us?"*

Anon.

Poetry

> I thought I saw a brindle bull
> A-running after me
> I looked again, and found
> That it was just a bee.

Editor

No. 3:

Poet's Corner

> I thought I saw an antique ship
> A-sailing on the sea,
> I looked again it was
> Alas! twas nought but me!

No. 4:

Poets' Corner

> I thought I saw a chimpanzee
> A-sitting on a branch,
> I looked again and found
> Behold! it was a pair of pants.

No. 5:

Poet's Corner

> I thought I saw a little bird
> A-sitting on a pan

I looked again, and found
It was a man c[r]ushin' a can

No. 6:

Poet's Corner

I thought I saw a kangaroo,
A-jumping on the ground,
I looked again and lo!
It was a earthern mound!

No. 7:

Poet's Corner

I thought I saw a pair of shoes
A-flinging at my head,
But, lo! behold! I found it was
Some of Mrs. Rogers bread.

Ed—

No. 8:

Poet's Corner

I thought I saw a log fi-ER
A-crackling in the chimney,
I looked again and found
Behold! I said o jiminey.

No. 11:

There was a young lady named Lu,
Who felt so exceedingly blue,
She was her-ad to state
That it was her fate—
And then she began to bu-hu.

— Anon.

Poet's Corner

> Hasty Ned, the Negro Hustler,
> Started out one (1) wintry day
> For to take a bundle quickly
> For which he expected to get good pay.
> (2.
> *be continued.*)

No. 14, 19 Feb 1899:

Poet's Corner

> *The fate of the Naughty Boy*
>
> A Boy who went to bed one night,
> (We all saw him go up)
> The Goblins came and they—
> They just on him did sup!
>
> Paul Palavier, P. L.

Eliot's Floral Magazine: A Journal of Floriculture. St. Louis, Mo. Feb 1899:

Poem.

> Dear little flower, lift up your head,
> One would verily think you were dead.
> Come! do not stay in the ground all year long,
> Come! while the little birds sing you a song.

The catalogue by TSE's brother Henry of materials presented to Eliot House at Harvard includes "12 issues of *Fireside*, a magazine written by TSE aet. 9 or 10", with a note: "4 others were sent to TSE in 1929 by HWE". (Henry's count of 12 comprises 11 copies of *Fireside* and the sole surviving number of the similar *Eliot's Floral Magazine: A Journal of Floriculture.*) Three drawings are kept in the same box.

Soldo 1982a: "At 2635 Locust Street, St. Louis, in January of 1899, Thomas Stearns Eliot undertook his first literary creation · · · a magazine called *Fireside*. Eliot was then living at home and attending Smith Academy in St. Louis. The fall semester was over on 27 January 1899 and during the following three days the ten-year-old Eliot produced the first eight issues of a little home-made magazine · · · Houghton Library, Harvard University, has in its collection of the Eliot Family Papers eleven extant issues of *Fireside*: numbers 1–8, 11, 13 and 14. (There are no duplicate copies.)

The numbers are not bound together. The approximate dimensions are 12.6cm by 10.2cm ··· The writings and drawings are in pencil on low quality paper and total 176 pages." Several of the *Fireside* poems were quoted in *Soldo 1982a*, identifying Lewis Carroll as a source, and reprinted in *Soldo 1983*. Three issues have dedications: "This Magazine (all) is dedicated to My Wife" (No. 3); "Remember, to *my Wife*!" (No. 6); "To my WIFE!" (No. 7). (See Carroll's "A letter from his wife" in note to No. 1.) A page of No. 13 is headed "POETRY", but is then blank. The poems are published in full for the first time here.

TSE to James Laughlin, 26 Jan 1939: "I was very glad to hear that you have met my brother, who is a very nice person. It was charming of him to show you the souvenirs of my nonage, but I feel that there is no particular justification for a facsimile reproduction of the Fireside Magazine at this moment."

No. 1

Title page; 1, 4 **The T. S. Eliot Co.** ··· **a elephant** ··· **'Twas only us:** for the Eliots and elephants, see headnote to *Noctes Binanianæ*, 2. COMPOSITION AND CONTRIBUTORS' PET NAMES.

I thought I saw a elephant: Lewis Carroll: "He thought he saw an Elephant, | That practised on a fife: | He looked again, and found it was | A letter from his wife. | 'At length I realise', he said, | 'The bitterness of Life!'" *Sylvie and Bruno* ch. V (The Gardener's Song).

No. 2

I thought I saw a banker's clerk: "He thought he saw a Banker's Clerk | Descending from the bus: | He looked again, and found it was | A Hippopotamus: | 'If this should stay to dine', he said, | 'There wo'n't be much for us!'" *Sylvie and Bruno* ch. V.

No. 6

I thought I saw a kangaroo ··· **I looked again:** Carroll: "He thought he saw a Kangaroo | That worked a coffee-mill: | He looked again, and found it was | A Vegetable-Pill", *Sylvie and Bruno* ch. VIII (*Soldo 1982a*).

No. 7

Mrs. Rogers bread: referring to a recipe on the previous page, "Cook's Corner: How to make turnip pie."

No. 14

Attribution **Paul Palavier:** Peter Parley was the pen-name of Samuel Griswold Goodrich, successful children's author from 1827. See note to *Landscapes* V. *Cape Ann* 13, "palaver", and headnote.   **P.L.:** perhaps "Poet Laureate"?

TEXTUAL HISTORY

No. 8

2 **in the chimney]** on the hearth *1st reading*

Beneath the poem TSE wrote "that's what I think", before crossing through the whole page.

No. 11

2 **blue**] bleu *Soldo 1983*   *Hasty Ned* 2 **wintry**] winter *Soldo 1983*

No. 14

Title **Boy**] *Boys Soldo 1983*   2 **all**] *not* 1ˢᵗ *reading*   3 **and they—** *not Soldo 1983*   4 **on**] one 1ˢᵗ *reading*

Eliot's Floral Magazine

4 **the**] *written over* I

Dear Charlotte, Hoping you are better

Dear Charlotte,

Hoping you are better,
At least enough to read my letter,
Which I have twisted into rhyme
To amuse you, I have taken time,
To tell you of the happenings,
Swimming, rowing, other things
With which I have the time been killing.
Wednesday morning, weather willing,
We after breakfast took a start,
Four of us, in a two horse cart
Together with a little luncheon,
Including things quite good to munch on,
To climb a mountain, quite a feat,
3000 ft., and in the heat.
To make a lengthy story short,
We did not take the path we ought,
And though we exerted all our powers,
It took us all of three long hours
To reach the top, when, what a view,
Mt. Washington, and Montreal too!
We took one hour down the road,
Then two hours more to our abode.
I suppose now I should desist,

For I am needed to assist
In making a raft.   25
            The family sends
To you their love and complimen's.
I must not close without once more a
Health to you and Theodora.

I am afraid this letter will not please you but I hope you will excuse
your brother

        Tom.

To Charlotte Eliot Smith, Aug [1904], from Oliver's Corner, Province of Quebec (ms, Houghton).

Published in *Letters* (1988). Valerie Eliot: "Third in the family, Charlotte (1874–1926) had married George Lawrence Smith, an architect, in September 1903. She studied at the St Louis and Boston Art Schools, sculpture being her special interest · · · In 1903 TSE's uncle, Christopher Rhodes Eliot, had bought some land over the border in Canada on Lake Memphremagog, as a site for a family camp. In the early years everyone slept under canvas. Her daughter, Theodora, was born on 25 July 1904."

TEXTUAL HISTORY

4 **time,**] time *Letters 1*   5 **happenings,**] happenings *Letters 1*   18 **three**]
~~two~~ three *ms*   20 **Mt.**] Mount *Letters 1*

There's No One Left to Press my Pants

As I was walking down the street
           upon a winter's day
I saw a man outside a bar,
           his aspect was *distrait*;

His ears were flapping in the breeze,
His pants* were baggy at the knees,   * i.e. trousers
He had a baby in his arms
           and thus I heard him sigh: 5
"If whiskey's‡ 15¢ a drink   ‡ American whiskey
           how many can I buy?"

                                                <

Then soon becoming bolder
I tapped him on the shoulder,
         And I said to him: "Look here!
Tell me what's the matter, mister,
10   Has some wretch deceived your sister?
Or can't you find an opener for the beer?"

Then straightway he did turn around
         and I did hear him sigh.
He flipped the ash from his segar*   * cigar
         and to me did reply:

"O there's no one left to press my pants[2]   [2] trousers
15   since Nellie's went away.
Don't let me hear that stupid joke:
         'Does matrimony pay?'
Of my eye she was the apple
When I led her to the chapel,
But the cost of living's risen since our wedding day.
She took the silver-plated spoons,
20   she took the whirling spray,
And all she left me was the kid
         and all the bills to pay.
O there's no one left to mix the drinks,
There's no one left to clean the sinks,
There's no one left to press my pants[3]   [3] see above
         since Nellie's went away!"

Published in *The Everyman Book of Light Verse* ed. Robert Robinson (1984), without TSE's marginal notes.

Valerie's Own Book: fair copy on four pages. Date of composition unknown.

Title] Beneath this, TSE wrote: "Composed about 1910. Still awaiting a [*added*: musical] composer" (but see note to 15).

  1–2 **As I was ··· I saw a man**: "I was lunching one day ··· when I passed some remark to a man", *Pollicle Dogs and Jellicle Cats* 1–2.

  2 *distrait*: OED 2: "Having the attention distracted from what is present; absent-minded. [from mod. F., and usually treated as an alien word ··· with F. fem. *distraite*.]"

  14 **segar**: OED lists the variant spelling from the 18th and 19th centuries.

15 **since Nellie's went away**: Herbert H. Taylor's sentimental song *Since Nellie Went Away* (1905) inspired a Broadway show of 1907 and a novel.

16 **"Does matrimony pay?"**: Corinne Bacon: "It's all like the old question: 'Does matrimony pay?' That depends upon the man (and somewhat upon the woman)", *New York Libraries* Apr 1908.

20 **whirling spray**: OED "whirling" *ppl. a.*: "whirling plant · · · *Desmodium gyrans.*" John Lindley, *The Treasury of Botany* (1866), "Desmodium": "*D. gyrans*, the Moving plant, a native of India · · · The singular rotatory motion of the leaflets of this plant renders it an object of great interest. In the trembling poplar · · · the least breath of wind causes the leaf to whirl · · · The movements are most evident if the plant be in a close hothouse."

21 **And all she left me was the kid**: "What you get married for if you don't want children?" *The Waste Land* [II] 164.

Dearest Mary | *Je suis très affairé*

Dearest Mary
Je suis très affairé
And Bucktooth Maclaggan
An undernourished bagman
And Mrs H (though rich)   5
A dreary kind of bitch
But the Hope of meeting Rodger
The Aphrican artful Dodger
And the magnetic
Sympathetic pathetic aesthetic   10
Quality
Of your own personality
And because Im wishin
To see the Great Politician
Who is Quite Above Suspicion   15
Attract me
                    T.S.E.

Vivien would have made the party brighter
Its a Pity you didnt Invite her
But she wouldnt have Come if you had   20

[*envelope*]

(1.)

Take, postman, take your little skiff
And ply upstream to HAMMERSMIFF,
And rest your oar (nay, but you shall),
By RIVER HOUSE, at UPPER MALL;
5   This letter, when all's said and done,
Is meant for Mrs. HUTCHINSON.

W6

To Mary Hutchinson, a half-cousin of Lytton Strachey, 4 June [1923?] (Texas).

3 **Bucktooth Maclaggan**: art historian Eric MacLagan was knighted for his work at the Ministry of Information during the Great War, and became Director of the Victoria and Albert Museum in 1924. Buck Mulligan is Stephen's friend in Joyce's *Ulysses*.

4 **bagman**: see note to *Macavity: The Railway Cat* 19.

5 **Mrs. H (though rich)**: Violet Mary Hammersley, society hostess whose late husband had been a partner in Cox's Bank.

7 **Rodger | The Aphrican artful**: Roger Fry's *Vision and Design* (1920) included his essays *The Art of the Bushmen* and *Negro Sculpture*.   **Aphrican**: among possible 16th-century spellings, OED lists "Aph-".

14 **the Great Politician**: H. H. Asquith, Prime Minister 1908–16. TSE expressed esteem for him in a letter to his mother, 29 Dec 1918. To Mary Trevelyan, 16 Nov 1942: "Perhaps some day you will tell me what it feels like, or what it ought to feel like, to be a Great Man · · · I was brought up to believe that the most one could possibly achieve was to be a Credit to the Family, though of course one's Grandfather was the Great Man, so there was no hope of reaching that eminence." Again: "Of some great men, one's prevailing impression may be of goodness, or of inspiration, or of wisdom. I think the prevailing impression one received of Valéry was of intelligence", *"Leçon de Valéry"* (1947). To Herbert Read, 24 Feb 1951, after meeting Martin Buber: "One is always hoping to know a Great Man, and in time having afterthoughts, but Buber seems to me pretty close to it." ("Great duties · · · great deeds · · · heroes greater than were e'er of yore!" *To the Class of 1905* 25–30.) See note to title *Difficulties of a Statesman* in *Coriolan*.

14–15 **Great Politician | Who is Quite Above Suspicion**: "Caesar's wife must be above suspicion", trad., based on Plutarch's Life of Julius Caesar.

Envelope 4 **RIVER HOUSE**: next door to Kelmscott House. TSE of Yeats's play *The Shadowy Waters*: "it strikes me—this may be an impertinence on my part—as the western seas descried through the back window of a house in Kensington, an Irish myth for the Kelmscott Press", *Yeats* (1940).   **MALL**: for the vowel sound, see TSE's notes to *Montpelier Row*. Pope rhymed "the Mall" with "ball" in *The Second Satire of the First Book of Horace*. Pronunciation of both "The Mall" and "Pall Mall" has varied.

Aldous Huxley's *Crome Yellow* (1921) ch. XX mentions "Mallarmé's envelopes with their versified addresses".

TSE to Hutchinson, from Princeton, 10 Oct 1948: "I was very much touched by your having preserved that Hammersmiff envelope all this time", with a postscript: "Isn't this a magnificent envelope? But I dare not try any rhyming addresses on the American post-office." The envelope verse was included in *Would the Real Mr. Eliot Please Stand Up?* by Thomas Dozier, *Month* Oct 1972. After this first in the sequence, further versified addresses followed, to different correspondents.

———

O Postman, will you quickly run   (2.)
To house of *COBDEN-SANDERSON*
Minding in measures metrical
The address: *15, UPPER MALL*;
Or row and tie your little skiff
Hard by the *DOVES* at *HAMMERSMIFF*,   5
This house is neatly built of bricks
And stands in *LONDON* at *W.6.*
ENGLAND.

Addressing an envelope to Sally Cobden-Sanderson, from Cambridge, Mass., 28 Oct 1932 (McCue collection).

4 **address**: metrically as recommended in OED, *àd-dress*. See *The Ad-dressing of Cats*.

6 **the DOVES**: the Hammersmith pub gave its name to the Doves Press (1900–16), founded by T. J. Cobden-Sanderson. His son Richard was publisher of the *Criterion* until 1925, and the husband of Sally.

———

(3.)

O Postman! take a little skiff
And ply your oar to HAMMERSMITH;
And let your nearest Port of Call
Be No. 15, UPPER MALL.
5   Demand, before your task is done,
The name of COBDEN-SANDERSON.
The house is plainly built of bricks;
The district, clearly, is

W.6.

Addressing an envelope postmarked S. Kensington, SW7, 7 Oct 1934. The letter, dated the previous day, included the verse *I have teeth, which are False & Quite Beautiful* (see *How to Pick a Possum* in *Noctes Binanianæ*) and was sealed with an impression of the TSE family elephant.

———

(4.)

Perhaps you will have been appal-
led by rhyme of upper mall and call.
For everybody knows that Sal-
ly lives at 15, UPPER MALL;
5   Long may the Thames serenely run
By house of COBDEN-SANDERSON.
Until death leaves me cold & stiff:
I'll praise the town of HAMMERSMITH (W.6.)

Postcard of a window in Winchelsea Church, sent on the following day (8 Oct) also from S. Kensington, bearing no message (Hornbake Library, U. Maryland).

5–6 **Long may the Thames serenely run** · · · · –SON: "Sweet Thames, run softly till I end my song", *The Waste Land* [III] 176.

7–8 **stiff** · · ·**HAMMERSMITH**: recalling the rhyme of "skiff" and "HAMMERSMIFF" on previous envelopes.

———

My good friend Postman, do not falter,   (5.)
But hasten to Sir Arthur Salter,
And then enquire for LESLIE ROWSE,
Who's hidden somewhere in the house—
For having fled from dons and wardens   5
He must be sought in CORNWALL GARDENS,
Among the stucco, stones and bricks
You'll ask for him at SIXTY-SIX.
And now to make my rhyming even,
Observe the district,   10

S.W.7,

You hardly need a lens bi-focal
To see that this address is LOCAL.

Addressing an envelope to A. L. Rowse, 28 Sept 1937 (Exeter U.). Rowse had been elected a Fellow of All Souls in 1925, and later he lectured at Merton. Each of these colleges is headed by a Warden.

  2 **Sir Arthur Salter:** fellow of All Souls and Gladstone Professor of Political Theory, who had been elected MP for Oxford University earlier in 1937.

Good Postman, leave this at the door   (6.)
   of FIFTY GORDON SQUARE to-day:
I want it to arrive before
   The bailey beareth CLIVE BELL away.
W.C.1

Addressing an envelope to Clive Bell, 12 Oct 1937 (Berg). Printed (misdated and mispunctuated) *TLS* 22 June 2007. TSE to Clive Bell 3 Jan 1941 has a postscript: "Knowing limitations of country postmistresses, I think it more prudent to address this letter in the ordinary way, and not try to burst into *vers de circonstance*", but see *O stalwart SUSSEX postman* for a later versified envelope to Bell, 6 Jan 1948.

  4 **The bailey beareth CLIVE BELL away:** "The bailey beareth the bell away; | The lily, the rose, the rose I lay", *The Bridal Morn* (anon, 15th–16th century); see note to *Billy M'Caw: The Remarkable Parrot* 16, "Lily La Rose".

(7.)

    Postman, propel thy feet
    And take this note to greet
    The Mrs. HUTCHINSON
    Who lives in CHARLOTTE STREET.

5   The number's hard to fix:
    But it is SEVENTY-SIX.*
    O Postman, leap and run
    To take this to
           WEST ONE.

    * (A stately pleasure-dome
10   Called "The Policeman's Home").

Addressing an envelope to Mary Hutchinson, 26 Mar 1947 (Texas). The first four lines were quoted in *Time* 6 Mar 1950.

  9 **stately pleasure-dome**: Coleridge: "In Xanadu did Kubla-Khan | A stately pleasure-dome decree", *Kubla Khan* 1–2.

 10 **"The Policeman's Home"**: the painter John Constable lived and died in the house, which no longer stands but appears from photographs to have had a plaque.

———

(8.)

    O stalwart SUSSEX postman, who is
    Delivering the post from LEWES,
    Cycle apace to CHARLTON, *FIRLE*,
    While knitting at your plain and purl,

5   Deliver there to good CLIVE BELL,
    (You know the man, you know him well,
    He plays the virginals and spinet)
    This note—there's almost nothing in it.

Addressing an envelope to Clive Bell, 6 Jan 1948 (Berg). Printed by Bell, with the correct house name, "CHARLESTON", in *March & Tambimuttu eds.* 17.

Are you a-

My dear Humbert,

Are you a-
live and a-
bout, and
if
so, why   5
should we not
have lunch
, one day
before too
long?   10
?

Yours e-
ver

,
T. S. Eliot

To Humbert Wolfe, 20 Nov 1928 (Berg).

Wolfe's *Troy* was published as an Ariel Poem in 1928.

"But there are two types of true bad poet. The first is a lover of words; he has nothing to say that has not already been said, but he thinks that originality consists in expressing the commonplace sentiment in a slightly unusual syntax, metric, and vocabulary. I knew one such poet, a very intelligent and charming man, who made one great discovery: that by placing a comma, not at the end of the line, but at the beginning of the next line, he could achieve a certain appearance of originality. The other type of bad poet is not a virtuoso; he has found a serious purpose; he has a message to convey", *The Social Function of Poetry* (1943), original printed text.

To R. Ellsworth Larsson, 22 May 1928: "there is a tendency in modern verse to make the eye do duty for the ear. That is to say there is always a danger which I have experienced myself of making typographical arrangement a substitute for rhythm. I don't know whether it could be of any use to you, but I have found myself that it is a great assistance to me to correct my verses by reciting them aloud to myself with the accompaniment of a small drum."

To E. Foxall, 3 Feb 1932: "My own experience has been that forcing experimentation has sometimes tended to conceal from myself a poverty of what I had to communicate, and I have destroyed a fair number of my verses for this reason."

Invitation to all Pollicle Dogs & Jellicle Cats

To Tom Faber, Easter 1931 (Valerie Eliot collection):

I Believe that you are to have a Birthday soon, and I think that you will then be Four Years Old (I am not Clever at Arithmetic) but that is a Great Age, so I thought we might send out this

INVITATION
TO ALL POLLICLE DOGS & JELLICLE CATS
TO COME TO THE BIRTHDAY OF
THOMAS FABER

Pollicle Dogs and Jellicle Cats!
Come from your Kennels & Houses & Flats;
Pollicle Dogs & Cats, draw near;
Jellicle Cats & Dogs, Appear;
Come with your Ears & your Whiskers & Tails
Over the Mountains & Valleys of Wales.
This is your ONLY CHANCE THIS YEAR,
Your ONLY CHANCE to—what do you spose?—
Brush Up your Coats and Turn out your Toes,
And come with a Hop & a Skip & a Dance—
Because, for this year, it's your ONLY CHANCE
To come with your Whiskers & Tails & Hair on
To
     Ty Glyn Aeron
         Ciliau Aeron—

Because you are INVITED to Come
With a Flute & a Fife & a Fiddle & Drum,   15
    With a Fiddle, a Fife, & a Drum & a Tabor*
To the Birthday Party of
        THOMAS ERLE FABER!

Oh But P.S. we mustn't send out this Invitation after All, Because, if
ALL the Pollicle Dogs & Jellicle Cats came (and of course they all *would*
come) then all the roads would be blocked up, and what's more, they
would track Muddy Feet into the House, and your Mother wouldn't
Like that at All, and what's More Still, you would have to give them All
a Piece of your Birthday Cake, and there would be so Many that there
wouldn't be any Cake left for *you*, and that would be Dreadful, so we
won't send out this invitation, so no more for the Present from your
Silly Uncle Tom.

* (A Musicle Instrument that makes a Joyful Noise)

The 18th-century nursery rhyme *Boys and Girls Come out to Play*, on which this is
rhythmically based, is itself an invitation. "Boys and girls come out to play | Come
with a whoop and come with a call, | Come with a good will or not at all · · · Up the
ladder and down the wall." TSE's drawing for the jacket of the first edition of *Old
Possum's Book of Practical Cats* featured kittens dancing and climbing a ladder up a
wall; see section title illustration in the present volume.

13 **Ty Glyn Aeron | Ciliau Aeron:** the Fabers' country address in Wales. See
    headnote to *Landscapes* III. *Usk.*

TEXTUAL HISTORY

ts1: original letter on Faber stationery to Tom Faber, Geoffrey Faber's son and TSE's
    godson, Easter [5 April] 1931. Decorated with the drawing of a dancing cat with
    top hat and umbrella. The letter reproduced in facsimile in Bonhams catalogue
    of "Presentation Copies and Letters from T. S. Eliot to the Faber family", 20 Sept
    2005. (ts readings: "your are", 14; "flute", 15 *1ˢᵗ reading.*)

ts2 (Columbia U.): ribbon copy of a different typing on paper of Barnard College,
    with a version of *The Jim Jum Bears* on the verso. Phrasing and lineation differ
    from *ts1*, but this is the version that TSE recorded. Whereas the rest of the poem
    is double spaced, [11–13] are single spaced, suggesting that [12] was initially
    omitted:

Pollicle dogs and Jellicle cats
Come from your houses and kennels and flats
Pollicle dogs and cats appear;
Jellicle cats and dogs draw near;
5   For this is your only chance this year.
Your only chance to—what do you s'pose?
Brush up your coats and turn out your toes
And come with a hop and a skip and a dance,
Because this year, it's your only chance
10   To come with your ears and your whiskers and tails
Over the mountains and valleys of Wales
To come with your tails and your whiskers and hair on
To Ty Glyn Aeron   Ciliau Aeron
To come with a drum and a pipe and a tabor
15   To the birthday party of THOMAS ERLE FABER.

O but stop, just think, if all the pollicles and jellicles came—and they all *would* come—then all the roads of Cardiganshire and Monmouthshire and Glamorganshire would be blocked for miles and miles; and what's more they would track muddy feet into the house and your mother wouldnt like that; and what's more you would have to give them all your birthday cake and there wouldnt be any left for You; so I dont think we will send out this invitation.

TSE made a recording of the poem on an aluminium disc, in New York, probably in 1933. The disc, given to Tom Faber, is now in BL. A section of it was played at the exhibition *In a Bloomsbury Square* (2009) and broadcast by the BBC's *Front Row*, 14 Sept 2009. TSE omits "To" at the beginning of 10, 12, 14.

Cat's Prologue

Be not astonished at this point to see
Creep on the stage a little cat like me.
This pageant is a kind of pantomime
Where anything may come at any time;
And what's a pantomime without a Cat?   5
And I'm no ordinary puss at that.
For I was to a worthy master loyal
Who built St. Michael Paternoster Royal:
I am the Cat who was Dick Whittington's,
And now we'll show you how our story runs.   10

Extra lines for *The Rock*, written in [Apr?] 1934 for Patricia Shaw Page, who played the part of the cat at Sadler's Wells, and spoke to introduce the "Ballet: The legend of DICK WHITTINGTON and his CAT" (*The Rock* 81). This appears to precede the posting of the earliest of the *Practical Cats* poems, *The Naming of Cats*. ("I once understudied Dick Whittington's Cat", *Gus: The Theatre Cat* 32.)

Sadler's Wells programme note: "Dick, miserable as a scullion, is loved by his master's daughter. He ventures his Cat on a ship going to the Barbary coast; the Cat rids the Court of vermin and the king buys it for much gold. Meanwhile, Dick has run away; but Bow Bells bring him back to find fortune and his bride."

8 **Who built St. Michael Paternoster Royal**: as four-times Lord Mayor of London, Richard Whittington gave money in 1409 to rebuild and extend this City church, later rebuilt under the aegis of Christopher Wren. See note to *WLComposite* 421.

TEXTUAL HISTORY

ts1 (Valerie Eliot collection): on Faber stationery, folded in eight, almost certainly typed by TSE (with characteristic run-together, "St.Michael"). With a letter to the actress's mother: "Let me assure you about Patricia's delivery of the verses. I thought she recited them very nicely indeed; and I did try to write verses that would not sound inappropriate when delivered by a child of eleven. I believe that the whole ballet is extremely popular with the audience; and I am sure that it deserves its popularity", 7 June 1934. A carbon, also on Faber stationery, is at Houghton (no variants).

Valerie's Own Book: headed "Lines spoken by the Cat in the little scene in *The Rock*", but without 7–8 (which are shown by lines of dots). A note beneath explains: "Imperfect. Sent me 18/9/61 by Patricia Shaw-Page, who had been the Cat. She hoped I could fill the gap."

4 **time;**] time. *Valerie's Own Book* 5 **pantomime**] Pantomime *Valerie's Own Book* 6 **puss**] Puss *Valerie's Own Book* 2nd *reading* 10 **we'll show**] I'll tell *Valerie's Own Book*

Back & head be full of aches

How very kind of you. The New Yorkers to nourish my mind and the Turtle Soup my body. I had never tasted it before.

> Back & head be full of aches
> Chest be full of croup,
> But Belly see thou have store enough
> Of jolly good turtle soup.

To Hayward (who had sent him Lusty's tinned turtle soup), 24 Oct 1934 (King's). (As an alternative to "Chest" or "Chest be", TSE wrote "or Weasand?" [= gullet].)

Mr. Possum wishes that his name was Tristram Shandy

Mr. Possum wishes that his name was Tristram Shandy,
Or Mahatma Gandhi
Or even Yankee Doodle Dandy
So that he could reply in poetry to the kind invitation of
5   Miss Alison Tandy:
But as it is, this is only verse
Going from worse to worse.
In the first place, January 5th is a Sunday,
NOT a Saturday or a Monday,
10   And Saturday is the Four
Of January, neither less nor more.
FURTHERMORE:
Mr. Possum has inadvisedly said
That alive or sleeping or dead
15   And whether well or poorly
He would go to visit Mr. & Mrs. Morley
As well as Donald Oliver and Susanna Morley
(Though he may regret it sorely)
And their zoo and aviary,
20   Carrying his breviary,
And whether sad or merry,

On the Fourth of January,
And with a spell of the Dry G(r)in
To see the New Year WELL in.
O Dear will Miss Tandy give another party a little later   25
And Mr. Possum would love to come all rolled up in
        gravy and sweet pertater.

P.S. I ADMIRE your Handsome Drawing.

To the five-year-old Alison Tandy [Dec 1935] (BL). (Undated, but 5 Jan 1936 was a Sunday, and the Faber stationery is of the right era.)

  2 **Gandhi**] TSE typed "Ghandi".
 19 **their zoo and aviary:** at Pike's Farm, the Morley family kept farmyard animals and hens. In a comic list of characters expected at a *Criterion* meeting, TSE listed "F. V. Morley, An honest downright farmer" (to Bonamy Dobrée, 20 Apr 1932). See headnote to *Mr. Pugstyles: The Elegant Pig* for TSE's advice to Morley on obtaining a good pig (3 May 1933).
20–21 **breviary ··· merry:** John Crowe Ransom rhymes "merry ··· breviary", *Armageddon* 1, 4.
 26 **Mr. Possum would love to come all rolled up in gravy and sweet pertater:** "A Practical Possum once lived in a Pye, | Surrounded by Gravy and Sweet Pertaters", *A Practical Possum* 1–2.

Many thanks for your letter and card which details

Dear Tom,

        Many thanks for your letter and card which details
        With precision the pleasures of winter in Wales.
        Your snow-man is truly a stout looking yeoman
        Of noble proportions and ample abdomen
        Or abdomen, if you pronounce it like that;   5
        I also admire both his pipe and his hat.
        And I venture to hope you are still feeling perky,
        After such a huge pudding and such a small turkey.
        The subjoined design, although rude and ungainly,
        Will exhibit our Christmas festivities plainly—   10
        I mean me and my friend, the Man in White Spats,
        Both buried in Cheese till you can't see our hats.

And afterwards, see us take our constitutional
Along Piccadilly, and also Constitution Hill.
15 And now as there's danger that I may be froze
From the ends of my fingers to tips of my toes,
I am thinking, dear Thomas, it's time that I close.
So sending my love (or whatever is proper)
To your brother & sister & mommer & popper,
20 Without stopping to think about colons and commas
I will end,

most devotedly yours,

UNCLE THOMAS

For the eight-year-old Tom Faber, dated 25 Dec 1935.

1 **details:** *Fowler:* Pronounce the noun *dee'tale*, the verb *dita'le*. OED now gives the stress on either the second or the first syllable for both noun and verb.

4–5 **abdomen:** *Fowler:* "Pronounce *ab-doughmen*." OED, which gives abb-d'men before ab-doughmen: "L. abdōmen, of unknown etymology; it has been suggested from abd-ĕre to stow away, conceal, cover; and from adeps, adip-em, fat, as if for adipomen. Occurs first in transl. from French. 1. *orig.* Fat deposited round the belly; the fleshy parts of the belly or paunch. *Obs.*"

12 **buried in Cheese:** a week earlier, on 18 Dec, TSE had written to J. D. Aylward: "There cannot be too many kinds of cheese, and variety is as important with cheeses as with anything else. I partook yesterday of the best bit of Wensleydale that I have tasted this year · · · I hope that you will come to lunch or dinner and partake of a little cheese with me. You mention one cheese which is unknown to me, but a part of the reason for living is the discovery of new cheeses. I have visited Poitiers and its environs but I have never before heard of Chabichou. But there are other excellent French cheeses which you do not mention, Pont l'Evêque for instance, which in prime condition is better than an imperfect Brie. And also Bondon, which has its attractions. You mention the Welsh cheeses, which as you say are not too easy to get, but have you also tasted a good

Fressingfield? Double Cottenham I have never tasted. Perhaps it is the rarest of all. There are also the exotic cheeses such as Liptauer and Yet Ost, the delicate Bayerische Beerkase, which as I remember is a delicious shell-pink. I do not like a month to pass without one good feast of Limburger, which requires the accompaniment of quantities of dark Münchener. And beyond them all rises in gloomy and solitary grandeur the majestic Gammel Ost, the Mount Everest of cheeses, in its brilliant colours of bright orange and emerald green, made of reindeer milk and then stored for years under the beds of the Norwegian farm folk. I have only made one ascent of this cheese, which ended in disaster, but I hope to try again with a better equipped expedition."

13 **constitutional:** OED B. "a walk taken for health's sake, or for the benefit of the constitution. (App. this originated at the English Universities.) *colloq.*"

15 **froze:** OED "freeze": for forms of *frozen*, "froze (now *vulgar*)",

16 **the ends of my fingers to tips of my toes:** "With rings on her fingers and bells on her toes, | She shall have music wherever she goes", nursery rhyme. TSE: "And the tips of his ears and his tail and his toes", *A Practical Possum* 61. "From the tips of his ears to the ends of his pedals", *Mr. Pugstyles: The Elegant Pig* 11.

20 **colons:** OED colon¹: "*Anat.* The greater portion of the large intestine .. Formerly, *popularly*, the belly or guts; *to feed or satisfy colon*: to appease hunger."

Now my Idea of Bliss

Now my Idea of Bliss
Were this—
Upon the Whole—
Eternal Chats
About Cats   5
With Major Sidney Woodiwiss
And Mrs. Cattermole.

On an enclosure to the Tandys (BL), alongside a cutting from *The Times*, 28 Jan 1937, exhaustively detailing the Class Winners at the Southern Counties Cat Show. Major E. Sydney Woodiwiss won three prizes and Mrs Cattermole two. TSE underlined the final word of the report, "Siamese", adding "*3 CHEERS*". TSE had sent a draft of *The Naming of Cats* to Tom Faber on 7 Jan, but such names in the *Times* report as Ballochmyle Hot Pot, Gippeswych Uncle Podger and Standish Sinia Ladybou are likely to have caught his eye.

To Polly Tandy, 30 Dec 1937: "Have you seen that remarkable Piece in the Standard about Mr. Woodiwiss the bull-dog breeder? Well it seems Mr. Woodiwiss went to some dog show some years ago and he noticed a 'smell of cats'; so he went upstairs and there was a cat show in progress, and his attention was caught by a short-haired tabby named Champion Xenophon. 'Within a few minutes he was mine'. And that's how Mr. Woodiwiss began to breed cats. You do get yr. 1d. [penny's] worth out of the Evening Standard, and no mistake, every time."

———

Untraced. TSE to Frank Morley and his wife, 19 Feb 1936: "I hope Christina received the poem I sent her, care of Harcourt, Brace, about the goats. I did not keep a copy of it, and I was rather proud of the effort, except the last line, which I think could be improved."

This Lion which I have pourtrayed

Dear Tom,

This Lion which I have pourtrayed Will hardly make you much afraid And he is much more mild because Of what I put between his jaws And he, I hasten to remark Is called the Lion of St Mark: A Saint of whom you have heard tell Who wrote a book that sold quite well And had considerable fame Before the firm of Faber came But not to leave you in the dark The reason why I name St. Mark And in my feeble fashion try on A portrait of his favourite lion (Were I an artist which I ain't) Is that this literary Saint Is so to speak a kind of neighbour Of Thomas of the house of Faber Because the day that bears his name Is most auspiciously the same As that on which for Thomas' sake We all are willing to partake Of something called a birthday-cake. With wishes for your health and cheer And wealth throughout the coming year And closing with a joyful psalm I sign myself your

Uncle Tom

Sent to Tom Faber for his tenth birthday, 25 Apr 1937 (Valerie Eliot collection).

pourtrayed: OED lists the spelling as 16th–19th century. Edward Lear: "the quaintest monsters ever pourtrayed", *Journals of a Landscape Painter in Albania* (1851) 315.   **what I put between his jaws:** a ten shilling note, in the drawing.

Whan Cam Ye Fra the Kirk?
or
THE LASS WHA WRAPT ME IN HER PLAIDIE
or
THE BONNIE BONNIE BRAES OF GLENGOOFIE

A Porpoise Sang
by
Tam o' Elliot
The Skewbald o' Galloway.

Where Castleawray's froonin' peaks
  Reflect upo' Lochaisie,
'Tis there that every grannoch speaks
  Remembrance o' ma Maisie.
There's na a brae fra Inverloch   5
  Tae Caverkeld an' Drumpit,
Fra Cabertoch tae Clandagoch
  That we twa hae na thumpit.

The mavis an' the laverock
  Sang blithely in the marnin';   10
The dew was airly on the brock
  Ere we twa turned tae scornin'.
The skevertary tauld the truth
  That was past a' subornin':
For he sang: "Wale a wale tae youth   15
  Sae airly in the marnin'."

It was the bannocks and the boons
  That toorned ma stomach soorly,
The baps an' the potato scoons
  That made me skimple doorly.   20

Ah mony a guid Talisker
An' mony a Tobermory
I'll need before ma pibroch skirr
Tae sing auld Scotland's glory.

25   An' though I be a lauchin'stock
         Frae Strathstrachern tae Paisley,
         Yet bide ye weel, ma honest Jock,
         Ma honest sonsie bawsent Jock —
         I'll be wi' ye by eicht o'clock
30   O' Sunday evenin' aislie.

Dated by Hayward, 9 Apr 1937.

Lawrance Thompson describes a dinner at the St Botolph Club, Boston, on 15 Nov 1932, at which Robert Frost heard TSE say "that no good poetry had ever been written north of the Scottish border except, perhaps, for one poem, William Dunbar's *Lament for the Makers* with its Latin refrain 'Timor Mortis conturbat me'." Frost asked if an exception might be made for Robert Burns. "No, Eliot thought not." Was he at least a good song-writer? "'One might grant that modest claim', Eliot acknowledged", *Robert Frost: The Years of Triumph* (1971) 402. In 1926, in his seventh Clark Lecture, TSE had referred to the "maudlin provincialism of Burns" (*The Varieties of Metaphysical Poetry* 202). At Harvard in 1933: "Perhaps I have a partiality for small oppressive nationalities like the Scots that makes Arnold's patronising manner irritate me; and certainly I suspect Arnold of helping to fix the wholly mistaken notion of Burns as a singular untutored English dialect poet, instead of as a decadent representative of a great alien tradition", *The Use of Poetry and the Use of Criticism* 106. In 1937, TSE visited Burns's grave.

Although *Was There a Scottish Literature?* (1919) implies that any such Scottish literary tradition had been broken, TSE wrote to Bruce Richmond, Editor of the *TLS*, 14 Aug 1931: "I wonder if you could make any use of a Scot named C. M. Grieve, who under the name of Hugh MacDiarmid has written a good deal of Scottish verse published by Blackwood? His verse · · · seems to me to have a good deal of vigour although I have not the patience myself to take much trouble over dialect poetry." (For "little Jock Elliot" and the Scottish branch of the family, see headnote to *The Marching Song of the Pollicle Dogs*.)

To John Hayward, 12 June 1943: "I don't want to tackle Chaucer or the Scotch poets in a lecture because I have forgotten how to pronounce the former language and have never acquired the other speech." In 1941: "As an example of religious verse on a relatively primitive level · · · I would offer the Christian prayers and incantation found in that remarkable repository, the *Carmina Gadelica* or anthology of Gaelic (Scottish) poetry", *Moot Paper 58*. "I myself have got a good deal of stimulation from Carmichael's *Carmina Gadelica*, a collection of Highland folk poetry", *Ezra Pound* (1946). *Chiari* 9 recalls discussing Scottish clans with TSE in Edinburgh in 1949: "he told me that he thought the Eliots came originally from Scotland, and he had a very extensive knowledge of Scottish history and literature, including its songs and ballads, such as *Bonnie Dundee*, *Sir Patrick Spens* and *The Twa Corbies*."

TSE to Frank Morley, Whit Monday 1944, referring to Morley's wife Christina: "I wish that she could have been present the other day in this corner of Surrey which is Little Scotland, to take part in a discussion as to the precise question whether old Mrs. Stewart of Auchielockie was a Grant of Rossiemucous or a Grant of Monybuigs and to enjoy the season."

Although some of the poem's place names are genuine, such as Tobermory (22) and Paisley (26), most are invented or adapted, such as Castleawray (1, Castlecary?), Inverloch (5, Inverlochy?), Drumpit (6, Drumnadrochit?), Strathstrachern (26, Strachur + Strathearn?), while Cabertoch (7) apparently metamorphoses the Highland Games sport of tossing the caber (Robert Crawford, personal communication, as throughout).

First title **Kirk**: church.

Second title **Plaidie**: Scottish pleated garment. Burns: "My plaidie to the angry airt, | I'd shelter thee", *Oh Wert Thou in the Cauld Blast*.

Third title **The Bonnie Bonnie Braes**: "By yon bonnie banks an' by yon bonnie braes", *The Bonnie Banks o' Loch Lomond*, anon 19th-century song (chorus: "On the bonnie, bonnie banks o' Loch Lomon"). **Glengoofie**: to Enid Faber, 6 Apr 1937: "the universal goofiness of the Highlands". To Geoffrey Faber, 20 Apr 1937: "that goofy country". For "too goofy in thy goofiness", see *Ode to a Roman Coot* 6 (*Noctes Binanianæ*).

Subtitle **A Porpoise Sang**: TSE had recently chosen the poems for *The Image o' God and Other Poems* (1937) by the Scottish miner and poet Joe Corrie, published by the Porpoise Press in Edinburgh (1922–39) in which Faber had a commercial interest. During 1936–37, TSE exchanged several letters with John Dover Wilson and others, on behalf of the Porpoise Press, in an attempt to commission scholarly editions of *The Kingis Quhair*, attributed to James I of Scotland, and of Gavin Douglas's *Aenead*. "I have heard the mermaids singing", *The Love Song of J. Alfred Prufrock* 124.

Attribution **Tam o' Elliot**: Burns, *Tam o' Shanter*. **Elliot**: to his Mother, 7 Feb 1928: "I always have to be tactful with Scotch people, because they think my name is Elliot, and they say you must be Scotch, why do you spell it Eliot. So then I apologise for not being Scotch." (For TSE's fascination with his pedigree, see letters to W. T. T. Elliott, 20, 22 and 28 Mar 1928.) To Virginia Woolf, 17 Apr 1936: "I have interviewed a Scot who wanted to sell a book, because my name was Eliot; and, said he, all we El(l)iots are alike—hot-tempered, obstinate, and dislike to agree with anybody." See headnote to *The Marching Song of the Pollicle Dogs*. **Skewbald**: not Scots, but Old Northern French. OED: "Of animals, esp. horses: Irregularly marked with white and brown or red"; see note to 28, "bawsent".

3 **grannoch**: proper noun only: Loch Grannoch Crags are in Galloway. See note to *East Coker* II 41, "grimpen".

4 **Maisie**: Scott's *Proud Maisie* is sung on her deathbed in *The Heart of Mid-Lothian* ch. XLV.

5 **brae:** OED 1: "The steep bank bounding a river valley." 2: "A steep, a slope, a hill-side."

5, 8 **brae ··· we twa hae:** Burns: "We twa hae run about the braes", *Auld Lang Syne*.

8 **thumpit:** fired (Scots). Burns: "the tither shot he thumpit", *Tam Samson's Elegy* 56.

9 **mavis:** song-thrush (Scots).　　**laverock:** lark (Scots).

11 **brock:** badger (here apparently as in "Brock Hill", a common place name).

13 **skevertary:** not in OED or *A Scots Dialect Dictionary* ed. Alexander Warrack and William Grant (1911). "skiver" (OED: "a workman who pares or splits leather") + "secretary"?

16 **Sae airly in the marnin':** adapted from the shanty *What Shall We Do with the Drunken Sailor*, upon which TSE had drawn in *The Rock* for *When I was a lad what had almost no sense.*

17–20 **It was the bannocks and the boons | That toorned ma stomach soorly, | The baps an' the potato scoons | That made me skimple doorly:** to Enid Faber, 6 Apr 1937: "I am rather exhausted, not so much by the potations ··· as by the baps, bannocks, potato scones, and mutton pies ··· My heart is in the highlands, but I am very glad that my digestive system is back in London ··· I am very unhappy because of my indigestion on account of baps and bannocks etc."　　**bannocks:** home-made bread, usually unleavened, of large size, round or oval.　　**boons:** this pronunciation of "buns" prevails in the north of England, but "buns" is not used in Scotland (see note to 28).

18 **toorned ma stomach:** Burns: "I wonder didna turn thy stomach", *Tam o' Shanter* 162.

19 **scoons:** the village of Scone in Perthshire is pronounced *Skoon* (as the rhyme here demands). The Stone of Scone (or Stone of Destiny) had been used in the coronation ceremonies of Scottish kings, but was taken to Westminster Abbey by Edward I's army.

20 **skimple:** not in OED or *A Scots Dialect Dictionary.*　　**doorly:** OED "dour": "dourly *adv.* with hard sternness, stubbornly, obstinately."

21–22 **guid:** good (Scots).　　**Talisker ··· Tobermory:** single malt whiskies. TSE stayed in Apr 1937 with Neil M. Gunn, author of *Whisky and Scotland* (1935).

23 **pibroch:** bagpipe music, often ceremonial.　　**skirr:** OED "skirl" b: "Of the bagpipe (or its music) ··· to sound shrilly", with Burns: "He screw'd the pipes and gart them skirl", *Tam o' Shanter* 123.

28 **Ma honest sonsie bawsent Jock:** Burns: "His honest, sonsie, baws'nt face", *The Twa Dogs* 31.　　**sonsie:** glossed by Burns as "having sweet, engaging looks; lucky, jolly", *Poems, Chiefly in the Scottish Dialect* (1787). TSE to Mappie Mirrlees (Hope Mirrlees's mother Emily), 31 Dec 1947: "Hope rapped me over the knuckles for referring to the Bishop of Chichester as a sonsie wee bishop ··· Chambers' Scottish Dictionary (a miserable affair) gives me no support, but I find Wright's Dialect Dictionary more helpful. Hope's use of the word is certainly correct, but it is not the only one recognised. Sense 4 is: 'cheerful, pleasing, tractable; sensible' ··· The only weakness is that Wright's Dialect Dictionary does not always make quite clear to what part of the island, or county

of England, Scotland or Wales, a particular use is limited; so that my use of the word may be local to Cumberland or Westmorland, and unknown north of the border." **bawsent:** OED "bausond": "*Obs.* or *dial.* Of animals: Having white spots on a black or bay ground."

TEXTUAL HISTORY

ts1 (King's): on two leaves, dated by Hayward, 9 Apr 1937.

ts2 (Valerie Eliot collection): first three stanzas only, sent to Geoffrey and Enid Faber, postmarked 22 Apr 1937.

Title **BRAES OF**] BRAES O' *ts2*   *Subtitle* **o' Elliot | The Skewbald**] O' Elliott | Skewbald *ts2*   3 **every**] ev'ry *ts2*   12 **turned tae**] toorned to *ts2*   17 **and the boons**] an' the boons, *ts2*   21 **Ah mony**] Och Mony *ts2*   22 **An'**] And *ts2*   23 **before**] befure *ts2*   24 **Tae sing**] To crail *ts2*

Poor Poony now is meek and mild

Dear Alison,
    Poor Poony now is meek and mild,
    And very like a Christian Child.
    She must be peaceable and good:
    She could not Bite me if she would.
    I know it's very hard in youth   5
    To be without a sweetened Tooth,
    And so I send this floral wreath
    In memory of Poony's teeth.
    But Oh! when you would like to gnash
    On Food more firm than Succotash,   10
    And Oh! when you would like to grind
    The tough refract'ry bacon rind,
    And Oh! when you would like to champ
    Some food more firm than porridge damp—
    The sorrow from your face efface   15
    And think upon Poor Possum's case.
    For he is much worse off than you
    In losing teeth: but two by two
    And year by year, they are extracted.
    His agony is more protracted.   20
    And though you now must feed on mushes,

You very soon will have new tushes
(To crack a nut or chicken bone)
Which you can call your very own.
25 But Poor Old Possum has to wait
For something called a Dental Plate
That's not in any way so good
For human nature's daily food
And not so powerful to bite
30 And not so beautiful and white.
I hope this letter will convey
A mite of all I'd like to say
And will express in Microcosm
The sympathy of faithful

35 Possum

To Alison Tandy, 16 Apr 1937 (BL).

1 **Poony:** the two Tandy daughters were known as Poony (Alison, b. 1930) and Poppette (Anthea, b. 1935).

1–2 **meek and mild, | And very like a Christian Child:** Charles Wesley: "Gentle Jesus, meek and mild, | Look upon a little child", *Gentle Jesus* 1–2.

1, 8 **meek ··· teeth:** TSE wrote to E. M. W. Tillyard, 26 Oct 1947, postponing a visit until he felt "more certain of my teeth (I have a premonition that they will fall out the moment I begin to speak in public in French). | Yours very meekly, | T. S. Eliot".

10 **Succotash:** OED: "A dish of North American Indian origin, usually consisting of green maize and beans boiled together."

18–19 **two by two | And year by year, they are extracted:** TSE had the last of his teeth out in 1947.

25–26 **Old Possum ··· Dental Plate:** "He has teeth, which are false and quite beautiful", *How to Pick a Possum* 53.

26–27 **Dental Plate | That's not in any way so good:** to Tillyard, 21 Nov 1947: "What I now advise anybody is, to stick to his natural teeth until the moment when he begins to be sure that he would really be better without them. The substitute is never as good as the original article and the blades are not so sharp."

AMONG the various Middle Classes

AMONG the various Middle Classes
(Who live on treacle and molasses)
A custom has (for want of better)
Been called the Bread & Butter Letter.
But Mrs. Woolf would not rejoice   5
In anything that's so bourgeoise,
So what can poor Old Possum do,
Who's upper-middle through and through?
For centuries and centuries
And under President or King,   10
He's always told the proper lies
And always done the proper thing.
Still growing longer in the tooth,
He sometimes yearns to speak the truth,
And would express his gratitude   15
For conversation, bed and food,
And quiet walks on downs and knolls,
And Sunday morning game of bowls.
Whoever gives him their approval—
He only hopes that Mrs. Woolf'll.   20

To Virginia Woolf, [Oct 1937] (Berg).

Lines 1–8, 19–20 published in Woolf's *Letters VI* (1980). A previous letter, [6 Jan] 1935, had spoken of not being asked to New Year celebrations: "If I had been, I should have brought a bottle of Champagne, and sung one of my songs, viz.: I dont want any Wurzburger" (a popular song by Jean Schwartz).

   4 **Bread & Butter Letter:** OED b: "bread-and-butter letter. Orig. *U.S.*, a letter of thanks for hospitality", from 1901.

   6 **so bourgeoise:** rather than TSE's comic rhyme with "rejoice", *Fowler* "bourgeois" recommends the pronunciation *boor'zhwah*. OED also gives *berj-wa*, and cites Aldous Huxley: "so disgustingly bourgeoise, Pamela" (1930).

15–16 **gratitude | For conversation, bed and food:** KING LEAR: "That you'll vouch-safe me raiment, bed and food", II iv (with "dues of gratitude" later in scene).

  18 **Sunday morning game of bowls:** Virginia Woolf to Angelica Bell, 3 Oct 1937: "Tom was miraculous at bowls".

ts1 (Berg): on verso of a circular letter (addressed to "Mr Elliott"), dated Oct 1937, from the Secretary of the St Stephen's [Church] Bridge Tournament. On the recto TSE has underlined an invitation to the fundraising "American tea", and noted "I am using this in my new play". A typed copy (not by TSE) is at Sussex U.

  2 **(Who]** Who *ts 1st reading* (*perhaps, given the position of the bracket in the margin*)

 10 **President]** *typed over* one or (*perhaps for* one or other) *ts1*

What O! Epitaff

From Pound:

What O! Epigraff
O wot avails the beauteous face,
O wot avails the sceptered line,
The statesman's brain, the artist's grace?
Ole Possum, all were thine.

TSE to Pound, 22 Nov 1937 (Beinecke), as a postscript reply:

O wot avails the noble race,
  O wot the form divine,
The statesman's gift, the artist's grace???
  Ole Possum, all were thine.

The second line originally began "O wot avails".

Landor: "Ah, what avails the sceptred race, | Ah, what the form divine! | What every virtue, every grace! | Rose Aylmer, all were thine!" *Rose Aylmer.*

  3 **The statesman's gift:** Yeats: "We have no gift to set a statesman right", *On Being Asked for a War Poem* 3. Linda Melton, TSE's secretary 1941–46, typed a copy of Pound's lines and the close of TSE's letter to Pound, 19 Dec 1937: "So wot I sez | To ole Ez | Is what the 'ell, | NOEL   NOEL" (Houghton). These are followed by two lines from TSE's letter to Pound 25 Jan 1934:

   I will arise and go NOW, and go to Rappaloo
   Where the ink is mostly Green, and the pencils mostly Blue . . .

  Yeats, *The Lake Isle of Innisfree*: "I will arise and go now, and go to Innisfree".

An *Exhortation*
to Chas. Williams Esqre.

Charles Williams's play *Thomas Cranmer of Canterbury* was produced at the Canterbury Festival, in the Chapter House, in June 1936, the year after *Murder in the Cathedral*. It too was directed by E. Martin Browne and had Robert Speaight in the leading role. On 30 Nov 1937, Williams wrote to TSE: "I enclose a copy of the verses of which I spoke to you. The joyous fact is that it records an actual incident" (Valerie Eliot collection). Enclosed was his verse:

> I am not one of those who squabble for a penny,
> I am as little conceited as any, and always on guard
>   against discontent; praise of others is my second nature.
> But I must say I do think it hard
> at my own play on my own day
> to have an elderlyish woman meet me afterwards
> and look silently at me for a great while—
> and I? I looked back—for minutes—with an inquiring smile.
> Presently she said: "Do you know Mr. Eliot?"
> I said: "Yes".
> More minutes went by; we still gazed—
> I gravely now, partly out of respect to Mr. Eliot,
> partly in my own patience, partly to play up to her.
> Presently she said: "Do you know *Murder in the Cathedral?*"
> I said: "Yes".
> Time slipped into a crack and slept and came back.
> She said: "I think that's a very fine play".
> (No emphasis, no hostility, nothing, a mere fact
>   discovered in a voice.) I said: "yes".
> She looked at me again for some time and then went away.
> That was all. As I say
> against bitterness I am always on guard, but I *do* think it hard.

TSE to Williams, [Dec 1937]:

> Beware, my boy, the aged maid,
>   beware the tongue which is so ven-
> -omous, but be thou not dismayed
>   by the austere paroissienne!
>
> Her taste in poetry is obs-   5
>   -olete, she gives her benison
> only to sentimental daubs
>   of imitation Tennyson.

<

Your verses look like crazy rhomb-
10   -oid shapes to her; for she enjoys
no verse more new than that of Thom-
        -as Eliot, or the nobler Noyes.

She, educated in the pur-
        -lieus of some dim suburban Surrey,
15 admires the nonconformist vir-
        -tues of prophetic John Macmurray.

Of subtle thought like Tom Aqui-
        -nas's she is quite ignorant;
perhaps she is a press propri-
20   -etor's relict or maiden aunt.

Between her mind and yours is fixt
a canyon or abyss or gulf.
Her values are completely mixed,
and she admires Humbert Wolfe.

25 She's probably a Kensitite,
or else of Bishop Barnes's band:
so cease thou not from mental fight,
nor let thy sword sleep in thy hand!

T. S. E.

Carbon copy probably sent to Anne Ridler (her papers, Wade Center, Wheaton College). Later ts copy capitalises the first letter of several lines and omits the hyphens which begin others (Valerie Eliot collection).

1–2 **Beware, my boy, the aged maid, | beware the tongue which:** Carroll: "Beware the Jabberwock, my son, | The jaws that bite, the claws that catch! | Beware the Jubjub bird", *Jabberwocky* 5–7.

4 **paroissienne:** female parishoner. ("Le paroissien" = prayer book.) Spelt "parioissienne" in the carbon among Anne Ridler's papers.

6, 8 **benison** ··· **Tennyson:** Hardy: "The bower we shrined to Tennyson, | Gentlemen, | Is roofwrecked ··· The spider is sole denizen; | Even she who voiced those rhymes is dust", *An Ancient to Ancients* 36–42. TSE rhymes "venison ··· ben'son" in *Bustopher Jones: The Cat About Town* 21.

12 **Noyes:** Alfred Noyes (1880–1958) was best known for ballads such as *The*

Highwayman, but also wrote the historical verse drama *Robin Hood* (1911, rev. 1926). See note to *Mr. Apollinax* 6.

14–15 **dim suburban Surrey · · · nonconformist:** for "dim religious light" see note to *Burnt Norton* III 3.

16 **John Macmurray:** the philosopher was published by Faber for some thirty years from 1932. His most recent book was *The Structure of Religious Experience* (1936).

17–18 **Tom Aqui- | nas:** see note to *Burnt Norton* V 27–28.

20 **maiden aunt:** "Miss Helen Slingsby was my maiden aunt", *Aunt Helen* 1. In the Commentary on *To Walter de la Mare*, see note 5, 7–8 to the second of the Draft Sonnets.

21–22 **fixt | A canyon:** HAMLET: "fixt | His canon 'gainst self-slaughter", I ii.

24 **Humbert Wolfe:** see headnote, above, to *Are you a-*.

25 **Kensitite:** John Kensit (1853–1902) had founded the Protestant Truth Society in 1889.

26 **Bishop Barnes's band:** Ernest Barnes (1874–1953) had been a controversial Bishop of Birmingham since 1924, expressing support for pacifism and eugenics.

27–28 **So cease not · · · in thy hand!:** Blake: "I will not cease from mental fight, | Nor shall my sword sleep in my hand", from *Milton* ("And did those feet") 13–14.

DEAR ALISON, I fear I can-

DEAR ALISON, I fear I can-
not join you on the First of Jan-
uary for your Birthday Part-
y and it nearly breaks my Heart.
Unhappily I have a pre-   5
vious engagement: were I free,
there is no doubt but I would scam-
per gleefully to you at Ham-
pton, singing Yankee Doodle Dand-
y to the family of Tand-   10
y on the afternoon of Sat-
urday the First. Alas, I must
go where I was invited fust,
because that is considered yet
a rigid rule of etiquette.   15
So on that day I have to hurry

to Mr. Morley's house in Surrey—
the reason being, strange but true,
he was born on the same day as you.
20   But still I find it very vex-
ing not to be in Middlesex
at Hampton in the street called High
among the Tandy family.
At least, I'm glad that I shall be
25   with you on Sunday next for tea
and in the Tandy family buzzim,
and sign myself, with love, your

Possum.

To the seven-year-old Alison Tandy, 23 Dec 1937, on *Criterion* notepaper (Valerie Eliot photocopy).

9–11 **Yankee Doodle Dand-| y to the family of Tand- | y:** "Yankee Doodle Dandy ··· Miss Alison Tandy", *Mr. Possum wishes that his name was Tristram Shandy* 3–5 (likewise apologising for absence because of a previous engagement with Morley).

26 **family buzzim:** to Eleanor Hinkley, 26 July 1914: "Here I am, safely out of harm's way, settled in the bosom of the family of the Lutheran Pastor."

Chandos Clerihews

Mr. Philip Mairet
Crossed the Styx in a beret
Remarking to Charon:
"I *must* keep my hair on".

Mr Maurice B. Reckitt
Followed Thomas A. Becket;
But he found the Church so pokey
  That he went to Le Touquet
  To practise his croquet.

Mr. Hilderic Cousens
Ordered oysters by dozens,
And after fifteen Guinnesses
Resembled Epstein's *Genesis*.

Written *c.* 1937. Transcribed in *Valerie's Own Book*, without title, except in the list of Contents at the end of the first exercise book.

The first of these was printed in 1958 by Philip Mairet in *Braybrooke ed.*, where he recalled meetings of the "Chandos Group" (associated with *New English Weekly*), which met fortnightly at the Chandos Restaurant, St. Martin's Lane. "The other most regular members of this circle were Maurice Reckitt, V. A. Demant, Geoffrey Davies, Hilderic Cousens and, later, T. M. Heron · · · T. S. E. once lampooned us all in clerihews." (*Braybrooke* printed "Explaining" *for* "Remarking" and "must" *for* "must", with three punctuation errors.) Inaccurate versions of the first two lines of *Mr. Philip Mairet* and the last two of *Mr. Hilderic Cousens* were printed by Thomas Dozier in *Month* Oct 1972.

For the clerihew form, see notes to *Clerihews* II.

1 1 **Mr. Philip Mairet** (1886–1975): successor to A. R. Orage as editor of *NEW* in 1934 and later dedicatee of *Notes Towards the Definition of Culture*.

2 1 **Maurice B. Reckitt:** Maurice Bennington Reckitt, editor of *Christendom*, 1931–50, and of *Prospect for Christendom* (Faber, 1945), to both of which TSE contributed. Like this verse (not strictly a clerihew), TSE's letters to him emphasise the form of name he preferred. In that of 6 May 1941, "Dear Reckitt, My firm is interested in your suggestion that the series of broadcast talks in which we were recently engaged might be collected into a small book" is emended by hand to read "Dear Reckitt, My firm is interested in Mr. Maurice B. Reckitt's suggestion · · ·" See note on the title *The Love Song of J. Alfred Prufrock* and *Ricks 1988* 2–3.

2 2 **Thomas A. Becket** · · · **Church so pokey:** the 12th-century Archbishop of Canterbury was the subject of *Murder in the Cathedral* (1935).   **Becket:** *Valerie's Own Book* 1ˢᵗ reading: "Beckett".

2 4 **croquet:** for *Alice in Wonderland*, see note to *Mr. Apollinax* 13, 19.

3 1 **Hilderic Cousens:** author of *New Policy for Labour: An Essay on the Relevance of Credit Control* (1921). In *Valerie's Own Book*, TSE wrote "Cousins" (perhaps through confusion with the trade union leader Frank Cousins).

3 2–3 **oysters by dozens, | And after fifteen Guinnesses:** TSE to Virginia Woolf, 5 Mar 1933, from Harvard: "if I · · · were back in England now consuming a dozen of Whitstable Natives and a Pint of Guinness I should be heaps happier". See Carroll's *The Walrus and the Carpenter* on eating oysters by dozens (*Through the Looking-Glass* ch. IV).

3 4 ***Genesis:*** Jacob Epstein's marble sculpture of a heavily pregnant woman, exhibited 1931. Epstein was to make a bust of TSE in 1951.

The authorship of three further clerihews, headed *Memoria Obstetrica*, is unknown.

I

F. V. Morley,
Suddenly took poorly,
Was delivered of a still-born ditty,
In the middle of the Book Committee.

II

Geoffrey Faber
Had a difficult labour:
But being left in the dark,
Brought forth a passable lark.

III

T. S. E., being multiparous,
And confined in a Chapter House,
At last produced something germane—
Without apparent effort or pain.

Carbon in Geoffrey Faber's papers (Faber archive). Half of the Geoffrey Faber verse was originally typed beneath the numeral I (two lines and the first character of the third), before being typed over, with the Morley verse substituted. The "passable lark" of Faber's was probably the sonnet *For F. C. G. L*, addressed to Falconer Larkworthy, dated 1 Feb 1939 (see *McCue and Soden 2014*). Frank Morley left Faber and moved to the US in July 1939, so these verses were probably written between those dates. TSE had published no new poetry since *Burnt Norton* appeared within *1936*. The "something germane" that he finally now produced was *Abschied Zur Bina*, which was received by Hayward on 31 Jan 1939 (in time for his birthday on 2 Feb). This became the German finale to *Noctes Binanianæ*, to which all three men were contributors.

Title **Obstetrica**: see Pound's "obstetric effort" *Sage homme*, quoted in headnote to *The Waste Land*, for his role in "the Caesarean operation" during its "Difficult birth". See *How to Pick a Possum* 39, "upsetrical", and note (*Noctes Binanianæ*).

I 4 **the Book Committee**: a Wednesday afternoon fixture for the directors at Faber (a house of many chapters). To Hayward, 25 Sept 1943: "I always have the *T.L.S.* for Book Committees, but confine myself to the list of recommended books and the crossword, which is insoluble, and therefore helps me through the duller parts of the session."

III 1 **multiparous**: OED: "Bringing forth many young at a birth" (usually of animals), citing "the multiparous Opossums" (1839–47).

III 2 **Chapter House**: from late 1934 until 1937 TSE lodged in the presbytery of Father Cheetham at 9 Grenville Place, Cromwell Road.

The Whale that leapt on Bredon

The Whale that leapt on Bredon
   When roselipt girls were leaping,
Now hangs his tail in Ludlow gaol
   Where whales that sleep are sleeping. — *A Shropshire Lad.*

First of two verse entries in *Whalebones from the Cetacean Anthology*, a typed sheet playing upon Frank Morley as the Whale, so probably dating from the late 1930s (Geoffrey Faber papers, Faber archive). For the entry that ends *Whalebones*, see note to *Ode to a Roman Coot* 43–48.

Heading **Whalebones:** *1ˢᵗ reading*: "Flowers".

  1 **on Bredon:** *A Shropshire Lad* XXI, BREDON HILL: "In summertime on Bredon" (with Housman's note: "Pronounced BREEDON.")

  2–4 **roselipt girls were leaping · · · Where whales that sleep are sleeping:** *A Shropshire Lad* LIV: "By brooks too broad for leaping · · · The rose-lipt girls are sleeping | In fields where roses fade."

  3–4 **hangs his tail in Ludlow gaol · · · are sleeping:** *A Shropshire Lad* IX: "They hang us now in Shrewsbury jail · · · There sleeps in Shrewsbury jail to-night." *A Shropshire Lad* LVIII: "Ned lies long in jail, | And I come home to Ludlow".

Possum now wishes to explain his silence

Possum now wishes to explain his silence
And to apologise (as only right is);
He had an attack of poisoning of some violence,
Followed presently by some days in bed with laryngitis.
Yesterday he had to get up and dress—   5
His voice very thick and his head feeling tetrahedral,
To go and meet the Lord Mayor & Lady Mayoress
At a meeting which had something to do with repairs to
      Southwark Cathedral.
His legs are not yet ready for much strain & stress
And his words continue to come thick and soupy all: 10
These are afflictions tending to depress
Even the most ebullient marsupial.
But he would like to come to tea

One day next week (not a Wednesday)
15   If that can be arranged
                          And to finish off this letter
     Hopes that you are no worse and that Leonard is much better.

To Virginia Woolf, 3 Feb [1938] (Berg).

Published in *New York Times* 31 Jan 1974 (with "Lord Mayoress") and in facsimile in *Other People's Mail* ed. Lola L. Szladits, who tentatively suggested the date 1940, although TSE's laryngitis occurred in 1938.

13–14 tea · · · **Wednesday:** for this rhyme see note to *WLComposite 237–38*.

16–17 **And to finish off this letter** · · · **better:** Swift: "Over and above, that I may have your *Excellencies'* Letter, | With an Order for the *Chaplain* aforesaid; or instead of him a better", *The Humble Petition of Frances Harris* penultimate couplet.

17 **are no worse ... is much better:** attrib. Alfred Austin: "Across the wires the electric message came: | 'He is no better, he is much the same'", *On the Illness of the Prince of Wales, Afterwards Edward VII* (see note to *Amaz'd astronomers did late descry* 3).

Be sure that Possums can't refuse

     Be sure that Possums can't refuse
     A tea with Mrs. Woolf on Tues.
     And eagerly if still alive,
     I'll come to tea with you at five.
5   I'd like to come at half past four,
     But have a business lunch before,
     And feel responsibility
     To do some work before my Tea.
     But please don't let the kettle wait
10   And keep for me a cup and plate,
     And keep the water on the bile,
     A chair, and (as I hope) a Smile.

To Virginia Woolf, probably 1938.

Published by Leonard Woolf in *Beginning Again* (1964) 244, giving no date: "The following is his letter accepting an invitation to tea, new style." The original letter is untraced. A later typed copy headed "From T. S. Eliot" (Valerie Eliot collection) gives the address "The Vestry, St. Stephen's Church, Gloucester Road, S.W.7.", which indicates 1934 onwards (Woolf's Diary for 11 Jan 1935 tells of TSE suggesting fortnightly teas). With the typed copy is a letter (apparently unpublished) from Woolf headed only "52 T[avistock] S[quare] Sunday" asking whether he would "come to tea, finding me alone, on Tuesday week, which is the 8th—at 4.30 sharp? so that we may have time for a gossip". A typed copy of a similar letter from TSE to Woolf apparently dates from Aug 1935, but their other correspondence and her Diary suggest that there was no Tues. 8th before 1938 when they could have had tea together.

1 **Be sure that:** "Whatever you think, be sure that it is what you think; whatever you want, be sure that it is what you want; whatever you feel, be sure that it is what you feel", *Address by T. S. Eliot, '06, to the Class of '33* (1933).

11 **bile:** *boil* pronounced in an 18th-century manner (as in the rhyme "conjoined ... mind", *Long may this Glass endure* 4–5).

Miss Mary Trevelyan

Miss Mary Trevelyan
Is like Godfrey of Bouillon.
For *his* name means *pottage*
And *her* name means *cottage*.
(Remove, if you will,   5
The elegant varnish
Provided by Cornish,
It means "public house under the hill".)

Presentation card (Texas) accompanying—and now pasted into—a copy of *Old Possum's Book of Practical Cats* (1939). Reproduced in *Sackton* 257. Presumably dating from around the time of publication, 5 Oct 1939. A letter of 15 Sept 1942 ends with a list of appointments and:

> I have an uneasy feeling that in November I have to do a talk, chat or reading, I forget which, for
>
>   Miss Trevelyan's
>   Tatterdemallions
>   And sundry rapscallions.

1, 4, 7 **Trevelyan** · · · *cottage* · · · **Cornish:** her Cornish surname derives from *trev*, a homestead + the personal name Elian.

2 **Godfrey of Bouillon:** Godfrey de Bouillon, leader of the First Crusade, 11th-century; hero of Tasso's *Gerusalemme liberata*, tr. Edward Fairfax as *Godfrey of Bouillon* (1600).

2–3 **Bouillon** · · · *pottage*: OED, "bouillon" 1a: "Broth, soup." (Fr. *potage* = soup) "Esau selleth his birthright for a mess of potage", Genesis ch. 25 chapter heading (Geneva Bible, 1560). TSE: "idealism, having sold his mess of pottage for a birth-right, is perhaps beginning to show signs of inanition", *The Relativity of Moral Judgment* (1915).

7 **Cornish:** a rhyme for "varnish" if spoken in a Cornish accent.

Put on your old grey corset

Put on your old grey corset
To drive down to Dorset:

We will hitch up Dobbin to the shay.

We will tarry for a while
5   In the pleasant vyle of Ryle

Before next Lammas Day.

To Polly Tandy, 17 June 1939 (BL).

1–3 **old grey · · · Dobbin:** "The old gray mare, she ain't what she used to be", trad. American song.

4–5 **tarry · · · pleasant vyle:** TSE alluded to 2 Kings 2: 16–19, "into some valley · · · he tarried at Jericho · · · this city is pleasant", in a scrap of verse (Houghton):

> Who tarried in Jericho
> Until their beards did grow?
> Judas Iscariot, Captain Marryat
> And Harriet Martineau

5 **vyle of Ryle:** Ryall, a village in Dorset that looks across Marshwood Vale.

6 **Lammas Day:** (loaf-mass day) 1 Aug.

Lift her up tenderly

Lift her up tenderly,
   Treat her with Care,
Poor Jeanie Kennerley,
   Young and so Fair!
5   Who'll break the news to her?
   Who's going to tell her
What it's like to be in for
   A spell of Rubella?

Typed on a folded leaf below a drawing of an ailing Jean Kennerley in bed, drinking and apparently smoking; on the facing page, a drawing of Old Possum in a hat, pointing to the patient's bed, with "What you *should* envy me is my morning Eno's—says Old Possum." Signed in pencil "To Jean from T. S. Eliot". (For "Eno's", see *A Practical Possum* 39 and note.)

To Hayward, 8 Feb 1940 (King's): "Jean Kennerley has German measles [Rubella]. I never know what to write to Jean, so I did a drawing, with some verses to the tune of the Song of the Shirt (no, it isn't that, but the other one, you know, about the girl who jumped off the Embankment)—Puir Jeanie Kennerley | Young & so fair etc. which apparently worked all right, as she mentioned it to Morley on the telephone."

Thomas Hood was the author of *The Song of the Shirt* and also *The Bridge of Sighs*, with its repeated lines "Take her up tenderly, | Lift her with care; | Fashion'd so slenderly, | Young, and so fair."

Clerihews II

To Hayward, 8 Feb 1940 (King's):

For three days I slept most of the time; and in the short intervals of consciousness read the Psalms (which are very good reading in such a state, being not too closely knit for an addled pate to follow. St. Paul is quite out of the picture) and composed clerihews, another good pass time for the addlepated. I could not do you anything better than

> Mr. John Hayward
> Is froward and wayward.
> I think it's untoward
> To be quite so froward.

But then what can you do with a name like that? FABER, on the other hand, is almost inexhaustible. After you have worked through all the normal rhymes, so to speak (the last of which, so far as my researches have gone, is Lochaber) you start afresh with *macabre, slobber,* and such variants; and after that you work into the adjectival form *Fabrous,* which has considerable possibilities, and I have still to explore the resources of *Galfridius Fabricius.* Faber himself is a-bed with flu, and so is a ready victim. I believe my most pungent was on a bird ~~named~~ Davies, who I believe is active in local government reform in Watford, viz.:

Mr. Geoffrey Davies
Takes an interest in slaveys—
By which I mean, of course,
That he's a second Wilberforce.

(*Galfridius* = Geoffrey (L.), as Galfridius Fontibus, the 12th-century hagiographer Geoffrey of Wells.) OED "slavey" 1: "A male servant or attendant." 2: "A female domestic servant, *esp.* one who is hard-worked".

The mention of St. Paul invokes one of the most famous of clerihews:

> Sir Christopher Wren
> Said, "I am going to dine with some men.
> If anybody calls
> Say I am designing St. Paul's."

(See headnote to *Choruses from "The Rock"*, 4. COMPOSITION.) TSE may have known that the inventor of the Clerihew, E. C. Bentley, was educated at St. Paul's School. Bentley's third and last collection, *Baseless Biography*, had been published in 1939 with pictures by his son Nicolas, who during 1940 was at work on drawings for the illustrated edition of *Practical Cats* (pub. Nov).

2, 4 **froward**: see note to *Airs of Palestine, No. 2* 38.

Clerihews III

Mr. Geoffrey Faber
Likes to brandish his sabre
At Bishops and Rectors
And Minor Directors.

Mr. Geoffrey Faber
Still likes to belabour
The Wassops on Blossoms
And Aerial Possums.

Convalescents

Mr. Geoffrey Faber's
"Farewell of Lochaber" 's
Annoying the neighbours.
(And it's getting much worse
Since he's had a Scotch Nurse).

Convalescence II

Mr. Geoffrey Faber
Likes to chatter and jabber
About what one ought to do
At the Battle of Waterloo.

Mr. Geoffrey Faber
Enjoys the macabre.
To be quite so Fabrous—
Well! *I* think it scabrous.

Five ts pages with pen and ink drawings, sent to Geoffrey Faber, 10 and 11 Feb 1940, the second envelope addressed to "Mr. Geoffrey Faber, | (or else his cadaver)". Pen and ink drawings by TSE.

2 3 **Wassops:** perhaps "wasps", although this is not one of the many forms recorded by OED. Not in *Wright*.

2 4 **Aerial Possums:** Ariel Poems are in the air.

3 2 **Farewell of Lochaber:** *Farewell to Lochaber*, ballad by Allan Ramsay (1686–1758), often sung or set for bagpipes.

4 3–4 **what one ought to do | At the Battle of Waterloo:** Stephen Weir: "a regular military shortfall of fighting the last war", *History's Worst Decisions* (1940) 128. *Life* magazine, 5 Oct 1942: "we are re-fighting the Abyssinian War and re-fighting the last war ⋯ Napoleon ⋯ used young generals against enemy generals who ⋯ were always fighting the last war". Carola Oman's *Britain against Napoleon* was published by Faber in 1942.

5 1–2 **Faber ⋯ macabre:** *Fowler* recommends the pronunciation *macaber*, and OED "macabre" 1. *danse macabre* gives among anglicised forms "dance macaber", with citation from Longfellow.

When icicles hang by the wall

When icicles hang by the wall,
  And Tom the typist blows his nail,
O then comes in the sweet o' the year
  With the stirrup pump in the frozen pail.

From a letter to Hayward, 3 Jan 1941 (King's). Published in *Smart* 161.

Love's Labour's Lost V ii:

  When icicles hang by the wall,
   And Dick the shepherd blows his nail,
  And Tom bears logs into the hall,
   And milk comes frozen home in pail ⋯

The Winter's Tale IV ii:

  When daffodils begin to peer,
   With heigh! the doxy over the dale,
  Why, then comes in the sweet o' the year;
   For the red blood reigns in the winter's pale.

An old man sat baldheaded, 'twas Christmas in Bombay

From the same letter to Hayward, 3 Jan 1941:

··· The hostess was cheered by a cable from her son the Brigadier, who had leave to spend Christmas with his wife in Cairo. Which reminds me not very relevantly of the old jingle

> An old man sat baldheaded, 'twas Christmas in Bombay:
> He had a gang of coolies to keep the flies away.
> He wished he was in Greenland, where flies are frozen stiff.
> Someone said "Happy Christmas!" and he up and hit him: Biff.

We have no flies.

The sage will refrain from sitting in with Archbishops

To Hayward, 8 Feb 1941 (ts, King's):

Whereupon he cast his turban to the ground, sprinkled his head with dust, and plucking at his beard, recited the following couplet:

> The sage will refrain from sitting in with Archbishops:
> They deal from the bottom of the pack.

Oh dae ye ken the turdie lads

To Hayward [12 Feb 1941] (King's), telling him that *The Dry Salvages* would appear in *NEW* in ten days' time:

This, however, need not be regarded as the final version ··· and I shall be grateful for further comments. Whereupon the old minstrel, bending his grey locks over the harp, and striking the strings with rheumatic fingers, burst into the following rude but stirring ballad of the old time:

Oh dae ye ken the turdie lads
    Betwixt the Goble an' the Tay,
Wha spear the lachsen fish a' nicht
    An' hunt the horned stag a' day?

Oh weel I ken the turdie lads   5
    Betwixt the Goble an' the Tay:
They'll nae mair spear the fish a' nicht
    Or hunt the horned stag a' day.

Oh wae is me on Knockiemuir
    And sair my hert on Kinkiebrae;   10
And a' for a' the turdie lads
    Wha speer nae mair the licht o' day.

Oh Muckieburn to Goble rins
    An' Goble rins intae the Tay—
They're rid wi' bluid o' turdie lads   15
    Wha speer nae mair the licht o' day.

Yr faithful TP

---

1 **O dae ye ken**: "D'ye ken John Peel with his coat so gay?", traditional North Country song.   **turdie lads**: Robert Fergusson: "strappin dames and sturdy lads", *Hallowfair* 7 (Robert Crawford, as throughout, personal communication).

3, 7 **spear · · · spear**: (*as also* "speer", 12, 16): = ask, inquire, request (Scots, usually *speir*).   **lachsen**: = salmon (Germ.), for which the Tay is famous.

6 **Goble**: "goble" in ts.

9 **Knockiemuir**: Loch Knockie is near Loch Lomond, whereas the other names are invented. "I rode to the Knockie Muir to see that view of Loch Lomond", *The Reminiscences of Charlotte, Lady Wake* (1909) 63.

13–14 **Oh Muckieburn to Goble rins | An' Goble rins intae the Tay**: Burns: "Now Sark rins o'er the Solway sands, | An' Tweed rins to the ocean", *Such a Parcel of Rogues in a Nation* 5–6.

16 **Wha speer nae mair the licht o' day**: *Cymbeline* IV ii: "Fear no more the heat o'th'Sun" (see note to *Five-Finger Exercises* II. *Lines to a Yorkshire Terrier* 4–5, 10–12).

after 16 **TP**: Tom Possum.

Speaking Piece, or Plum for Reciters

To Hayward, 2 Apr 1943 (King's):

During train journeys, to occupy my mind restfully, I have been starting to compose a special SPEAKING PIECE, or Plum for Reciters, to be available free of charge. It begins something like this:

> I love to stroll
> By sleepy sedges where soft sewage seepeth,
> Or breakers roll
> On beaches where the piping pee-wit peepeth.
> 5   I like my tea
> In that high style at which the kipper kippeth,
> Not such as be
> The nursery nuisance where the nipper nippeth
> Or spurious crea-
> 10   M of Devon where the towny trippeth. . . .

Tennyson: "Sadly the far kine loweth: the glimmering water outfloweth · · · The ancient poetess singeth, that Hesperus all things bringeth", *Leonine Elegiacs* X 13.

6–8 **the kipper kippeth** · · · **the nipper nippeth:** OED "kip" *v.*² *slang*: "To go to bed, sleep", from 1889, with C. Rook, *Hooligan Nights* (1899): "that's where me and my muvver kipped when I was a nipper."   **nipper:** OED b. *slang*: "A boy, a lad · · · the smallest or youngest of a family", from 1847 (*Dombey and Son*).

His note is harsh and adenoid

> His note is harsh and adenoid,
> His manners are not nice:
> O cuckoo! shall I call thee boid?
> Or jist a wandering v'ice?

And it is also the vacuum cleaner which is apt to begin just outside the door as I settle down for composition.

To Hayward, 30 Apr 1943 (King's).

3–5 **O cuckoo ⋯ wandering v'ice:** Wordsworth: "O Cuckoo! shall I call thee Bird | Or but a wandering Voice?", *To the Cuckoo* 3–4. Two similarly famous lines prompted another such verse in a letter to Mary Trevelyan, 6 Aug 1943:

> I hope that you will be enjoying a carefree holiday and amongst the haunts of
>
>> The boast of heraldry, the pomp of power
>> And all that beauty, all that wealth e'er gave,
>> Forget awhile the sombre street of Gower . . .
>
> Yours etc.

where Gray's *Elegy Written in a Country Church Yard* 33–34 became the first two lines. (Gower Street is in Bloomsbury.)

Wee Dolly Sayers

> Wee Dolly Sayers
> Wouldn't say her prayers.
> Take her by the hind leg
> And throw her down stairs.

To Mary Trevelyan, 11 Mar 1944 (Houghton), asking the identity of "the original on which the following Mother Goose is based". The Mother Goose rhyme runs: "Goosey, goosey, gander, | Whither dost thou wander? | Upstairs and downstairs | And in my lady's chamber. | | There I met an old man | Who wouldn't say his prayers; | I took him by the left leg, | And threw him down the stairs." TSE uses "the following Mother Goose" to mean "nursery rhyme".

To John Hayward, 2 Apr 1943, on C. S. Lewis: "He irritates me in somewhat the same way that, on a lower plane, Dorothy Sayers does: a kind of cock-sureness, as if they were the first people who had ever discovered Theology, and were the accredited interpreters of it to the ignorant public." 12 Apr: "I fear he is going the way of Dorothy Sayers and taking the Church under his wing."

TSE respectfully discussed with Dorothy L. Sayers the religious dramas she wrote for the Canterbury Festival and others. She went on to translate Dante for Penguin Classics (*Hell*, 1949; *Purgatory*, 1955; *Paradise*, completed by Barbara Reynolds, 1962).

1 **Dolly:** to Eric Fenn, 24 Feb 1941: "I am rather puzzled by not seeing Dotty Sayers billed in the *Radio Times* this week. Has the whole series been pushed off the air ⋯?" The seven broadcasts included TSE's *Towards a Christian Britain* (1941) and Sayers's *The Religions behind the Nation*. At TSE's suggestion, they were collected as *The Church Looks Ahead* (1941).

Mr Maurice Bowra

Mr Maurice Bowra
Gets sourer and sourer,
Having been in a hurry
To succeed Gilbert Murray
5   And is now (poor soul) at the bottom:
I.e. Warden of Wadham.

Inscribed beneath the greeting "H. Hope Mirrlees | from T. S. Eliot | Christmas 1944" on the front free endpaper of a copy of *Sophoclean Tragedy* by C. M. Bowra (1944) (Bodleian). John Sparrow (Warden of All Souls, 1952–77) pencilled a box around "And" (5), with the suggestion "? He".

This squib is perhaps in reply to one of the "witty and scurrilous poems about his friends" which Hayward reported (to Frank Morley, May 1941) that Bowra was writing. TSE to Hayward, 23 June 1944: "Maurice Bowra is no doubt enjoying himself wire-pulling: was there ever a more vulgar little fat Head of a House than he?"

"C. M. Bowra on Eliot's American education—he had read a lot but didn't really understand anything—a very stupid man, slow", Edmund Wilson, *The Forties* (1983) 151. Valerie Eliot consulted Bowra about classical references when publishing the drafts of *The Waste Land*.

The sudden unexpected gift

Response to the gift in 1946 of a plastic cigarette-case from Stephen Spender. Accompanying the gift was a rhyme (typed entirely in capitals) on notepaper headed "ORGANISATION DES NATIONS UNIES | POUR L'EDUCATION, LA SCIENCE & LA CULTURE" and "Please address all correspondence to The Executive Secretary":

TO THE MASTER OF RUSSELL SQUARE

When those aged eagle eyes which look
Through human flesh as through a book,
Swivel an instant from the page
To ignite the luminous image
With the match that lights his smoke—
Then let the case be transparent
And let the cigarettes, apparent
To his X-ray vision, lie
As clear as rhyme and image to his eye.
To Tom with love from Stephen August 21 1946.

TSE replied:

A L'ORGANISATEUR DES NATIONS UNIES
POUR L'EDUCATION, LA SCIENCE ET LA CULTURE

The sudden unexpected gift
  Is more precious in the eyes
  Than the ordinary prize
Of slow approach or movement swift.
  While the cigarette is whiffed   5
  And the tapping finger plies
  Here upon the table lies
The fair transparency. I lift
  The eyelids of the aging owl
  At twenty minutes to eleven   10
  Wednesday evening (summer time)
To salute the younger fowl
  With this feeble halting rhyme
  The kind, the Admirable Stephen.

Published in *The Oxford Book of Letters* ed. Frank Kermode and Anita Kermode (1995).

There are two typescripts (without variants). *ts1* (Northwestern U.): copy of Spender's poem followed by Eliot's. *ts2* (Valerie Eliot collection): later copy of TSE's poem only, with "TSE" at foot in Valerie Eliot's hand; together with a photocopy of Spender's letter.

The gift followed a row over Roy Campbell's remarks about "MacSpaunday" in *Talking Bronco*, which neither TSE nor Geoffrey Faber had recognised as referring to MacNeice, Spender, Auden and Day Lewis. TSE had written to Geoffrey Faber, 3 July 1946: "Campbell is not one of *my* authors · · · When he turned up with these new poems, I only thought of him as one of our authors, whose book we should publish if we possibly could. I gave a good deal of time to the book, and corresponded with Campbell over a long period, and gradually removed all the references to individuals that I could identify." Twenty years before, TSE had been spontaneously enthusiastic about Campbell's poem *Tristan da Cunha*, writing to the *New Statesman* on 15 Oct 1927 to praise it (see *McCue 2014d*). To Campbell, 23 Jan 1946, about *Talking Bronco*: "May I say that reading the book through together for the first time in proof, I think it is a very good piece of work and the satire in it seems to me the best verse satire of our time." 14 Mar 1946: "I do not at all like asterisks and much prefer an invented name. The trouble about asterisks is first that they are a very strong invitation to the reader to stop and guess the name and second that they break the verse. If you know the name, the verse flows easily, if you don't, it is a ruined line, so if you don't mind we will stick to the vaguer Spaunday."

1 **The sudden unexpected gift**: "the unexpected guest", *The Waste Land* [III] 230.

14 **the Admirable Stephen**: the Admirable Crichton was renowned for his exploits in Europe. See note to *VERSES To Honour and Magnify Sir Geoffrey Faber Kt.* 2.

Clerihews IV

Unsigned postcard to Hope Mirrlees, 21 Aug 1946 (U. Maryland):

Before accepting this startling statement I should wish to investigate the political sympathies of yr. C. of P. and M.

> Graham of Claverhouse
> Was not inclined to favour Mouse:
> This is scandal and a
> Bit of Whig propaganda.

But are they sure of the HOUSE? I cling to CLAVERS or CLAVERUS. *Scott* writes it *CLAVER'SE*.

(The significance of "C. of P. and M." is unknown.)

1] John Graham of Claverhouse, 1st Viscount Dundee (1649?–1689), was among the leaders of the first Jacobite rising, in which he lost his life.

2 **Mouse**: Latin *mus* would rhyme with *Claverus*.

4 **Whig propaganda**: Walter Scott: "tremble, false Whigs, in the midst o' your glee, | Ye ha' no seen the last o' my bonnet and me", *Bonnie Dundee*. (For *Bonnie Dundee* see headnote to *Whan cam ye fra the Kirk?* and note to *Little Gidding* III 33–38.) In a letter to Hayward, 12 May 1944, TSE regretted the omission of Scott's poem from an anthology. In Anglicised form, TSE included it in *A Personal Anthology* (1947) for the BBC.

I don't want to see no Shakespeare or Napoleon

> I don't want to see no Shakespeare or Napoleon,
> I don't want to see no Lincoln or George Washington.
> I paid mah money in advance
> So kindly perpetrate a trance:
> I want to see Jac Johnson fo' to ask him fo' mah tin.

5

Beneath: "Old lyric" (in TSE's hand); with (in another hand): "Dashed off in about two minutes by T. S. Eliot at Faber ♂ Faber Book Committee Meeting after a plea for a spiritualist MS by Richard de la Mare 12 March 1952."

1–2] "I shall not want Honour in Heaven | For I shall meet Sir Philip Sidney . . . Coriolanus", *A Cooking Egg* 9–11.

5 **Jac Johnson:** Jack Johnson (1878–1946) was the first black heavyweight world champion.   **mah tin:** my money.

Richards & Roberts were two merry men

Richards & Roberts were two merry men,
They shinned up the Alps like a 3 legged hen.

Prompted by the mountaineering exploits of I. A. Richards and Michael Roberts, this couplet was sent to Pound, 7 Apr 1936. It was published in Janet Adam Smith's *Tom Possum and the Roberts Family* in *Olney ed.* (with "three-legged" and no comma after "men").

Again making use of the 18th-century nursery rhyme

Robin and Richard were two pretty men
They lay in bed till the clock struck ten

TSE wrote an impromptu quatrain concerning the two Lords Chancellor Simon and Simmonds, which was recorded by Mary Trevelyan in 1952, in her memoir *The Pope of Russell Square*, to which the present editors have not been granted access.

Your cablegram arrived too late

Your cablegram arrived too late
And insufficiently addressed
So you confuse my modest muse
Who none the less cannot refuse
Compliance with your kind request   5
To greet *The Harvard Advocate*.

Telegram to the editor of the *Harvard Advocate* on the occasion of the magazine's move to a new home. Printed in George H. Watson's *Mother Advocate Removes from Bow to South Street* in *Harvard Crimson* 20 May 1957, from which this text is taken (and newly lineated).

He who in ceaseless labours took delight

He who in ceaseless labours took delight,
And scarcely ate or slept, by day or night:
Let this obedient engine as it mows
Teach him with Grace to enjoy well-earned repose.

Printed on the menu card for the dinner in W. J. Crawley's honour, 1 June 1961, and engraved upon a plate for the lawnmower that was his retirement present. Published in *The Times* 5 Apr 1969; *TLS* 20 July 2007. (When the printed card from which the plate was engraved was sold at Bloomsbury Book Auctions, 6 Sept 1990, the catalogue erroneously claimed it was for "Mr Lister, the Faber & Faber caretaker".)

Monteith: "when W. J. Crawley, our elderly sales director—almost incredibly hard-working, often maddeningly obstinate, nearly always lovable—finally retired, he was presented by the board with a new and rather grand lawn-mower: a devoted gardener, he had particularly asked for it. At lunch, when the purchase was announced, I asked Eliot if he would compose a suitable short verse which could be engraved on a brass plate and be attached to the mower. The following week he produced it." TSE to W. H. Auden, 22 Oct 1942: "our Sales Manager, Mr. Crawley · · · a very sapient person".

The plate on the lawnmower and the menu card for the retirement dinner, 1 June 1961 (*Gallup* E2m), have no variants. Because the menu card breaks the last line, *Monteith* printed it as though it were two ("enjoy | Well-earned repose.") TSE's transcription in *Valerie's Own Book* is headed *W. J. C.* but has no other variants.

4 **Teach him · · · to enjoy well-earned repose:** "Teach us to sit still", *Ash-Wednesday* I 39. **Grace:** Crawley's wife.

Dearest Mr. Groucho Marx

Dearest Mr. Groucho Marx,
I'm sending a request
I'd like a signed picture
You'll know which one is best
5   My esteemed Mr. Marx,
I am your biggest fan
So please do not disappoint me
That would be completely underhand
With respect, Mr. Marx,
10   Your humour has me on the floor

I'm not that known for laughing
But your comedy I adore
So Julius—that's your real name—
Please make my day, month, year,
By sending me a photograph   15
And I will give a cheer.
Oh brother of Chicolini
Sibling of silent Harpist
Please use a fountain-pen to sign
(If a pencil, use the sharpest)   20
To put you next to Paul Valéry,
You'll be snuggled up to Yeats
I'd like you as Rufus T. Firefly
Or perhaps on roller-skates
Forgive me this lengthy piece   25
For several months I have been grappling
So if you don't send me a signed photo
I shall switch my allegiance to Chaplin.

TSE wrote to Groucho Marx in 1961, requesting a photograph. Disappointed with the picture he received, he asked for one in character, which he had framed for his office. After a correspondence, TSE and Valerie Eliot entertained Groucho and his third wife to dinner in 1964, their only meeting. See *The Groucho Letters* (1967).

13 **Julius:** Groucho disliked his given name, Julius.

17 **Chicolini:** the character played by Chico Marx in *Duck Soup* (1933).

18 **silent Harpist:** Harpo Marx played a mute in the Marx Brothers films.

21–22 **Valéry, Yeats:** these poets, as well as other friends and Groucho with a cigar, can be seen in photographs of TSE's office.

23 **Rufus T. Firefly:** the character played by Groucho in *Duck Soup*.

24 **roller-skates:** Groucho, Chico and Harpo Marx roller-skate through a department store to escape a criminal in *The Big Store* (1941). The roller-skating figures of Mr. Eliot and the Man in White Spats appear in a drawing by TSE on the back of the jacket of the original unillustrated edition of *Old Possum's Book of Practical Cats*.

28 **Chaplin:** "Charlie Chaplin is not English, or American, but a universal figure, feeding the idealism of hungry millions in Czecho-Slovakia and Peru", *The Romantic Englishman, the Comic Spirit, and the Function of Criticism* (1921). For "Charles, the Chaplain", see letter to Conrad Aiken, 10 Jan 1916, in "Improper Rhymes".

NOCTES
BINANIANÆ

Certain Voluntary and Satyrical
Verses and Compliments as were lately
Exchang'd between some
of the Choicest Wits of the Age

LONDON

*Collected with the greatest care
and now printed without
castration after the most correct copies*

MCMXXXIX

Noctes Binanianæ

1. Title   2. Composition and Contributors' Pet Names
3. Printing   4. After Distribution

1. TITLE

Noctes Binanianæ, printed privately in an edition of 25 copies in summer 1939, contains verses by TSE, John Hayward, Geoffrey Faber and another director of Faber & Faber, Frank Morley. These four dined regularly, with occasional guests, at Hayward's London flat at 22 Bina Gardens in Kensington (a short walk from TSE's home at the time).

The volume was named after *Noctes Ambrosianæ*, a popular series of 71 imaginary conversations in Ambrose's Tavern in Edinburgh, which were devised by J. G. Lockhart and written largely by John Wilson. Published first in *Blackwood's Magazine* 1822–35, they were subsequently collected. (OED "ambrosial" 1: "Immortal, divine · · · *orig.* in the Greek mythology: Belonging to or worthy of the gods, as their food, anointing oil · · · etc." Lockhart and Wilson's title itself recalled Aulus Gellius' commonplace book *Noctes Atticæ* [*Attic Nights*]).

The title page alludes to the kind seen in volumes collected by Hayward as an editor of Rochester, such as *The Canting Academy · · · with several new Catches and Songs, compos'd by the Choicest Wits of the Age* (1673) or *Poems on Affairs of State from the time of Oliver Cromwell, to the abdication of K. James the Second. Written by the greatest wits of the age. Viz. Duke of Buckingham, Earl of Rochester, Lord Bu——st, Sir John Denham, Andrew Marvell, Esq; Mr. Milton, Mr. Dryden, Mr. Sprat, Mr. Waller, Mr. Ayloffe, &c. With some miscellany poems by the same: most whereof never before printed. Now carefully examined with the originals, and published without any castration* (1697). OED "castrate" 4: "To mutilate (a book, etc.) by removing a sheet or portion of it; *esp.* to remove obscene or objectionable passages from; to expurgate", with Boswell on Johnson: "Talking of Rochester's Poems, he said, he had given them to Mr. Steevens to castrate for the edition of the poets."

In proof, the blocks of type were eccentrically arranged, and the date on the title page read "MDCXXXIX".

2. COMPOSITION AND CONTRIBUTORS' PET NAMES

Manuscript note by Hayward:

> The following poetical effusions were composed for the most part in the summer and autumn of the year 1937. The pieces in French, Latin and German belong to the latter part of the following year. The authors were Mr. Geoffrey Faber, Chairman of the publishing house of Faber & Faber Ltd., Mr. T. S. Eliot and Mr. F. V. Morley, partners in the same, & Mr. John Hayward, their friend. The pieces, now printed, circulated among the authors in MS. for many months, until, through the kind offices of Mr. MacKnight Kauffer, the artist, Mr. Eric Gregory, a genial and generous printer, undertook to see them through the press at his own charge. The edition of 25 copies was distributed as follows:

Copies 1–6.	John Hayward, who prepared the copy for the printer.
7.	E. MacKnight Kauffer.
8.	Anne Ridler, who typed the fair copy.
9–12.	T. S. Eliot
13–16.	Geoffrey Faber
17–20.	F. V. Morley
21–22.	Eric Gregory
23–25.	Reserved for the files of the Printers, Lund Humphries, Ltd.

Helen Gardner: "After Eliot's return from his visit to America of 1932–3, a group of friends, all directors of Faber and Faber, began to meet regularly at Bina Gardens. The host, John Hayward, was nicknamed Tarantula, being at the centre of the web and having, as all his friends were aware, considerable power of stinging; Eliot was the Elephant, presumably because he 'never forgot', though he retained his old nickname of Possum; Faber was the Coot, presumably because of his baldness; and Frank Morley, for reasons I cannot guess at, was the Whale or Leviathan", *Composition FQ* 7. Morley had been on a whaling expedition as an observer, and was joint author with J. S. Hodgson of *Whaling North and South* (1926).

TSE to Bonamy Dobrée, 29 July 1927: "I am afraid that I cannot accept your Identification with either the Ibex or the Ape. My family tradition is that we are descended from the White Elephant; not the Siamese, but the Indian White Elephant. 'Eliot' is merely a corruption of 'Elephant'." (Referring to the corruption—perhaps an urban myth?—of the Infanta of Castile into the Elephant and Castle. TSE had signed another letter to Dobrée earlier that day: "I Remain your obliged obt. servt. | T. S. Eliot | or Elephant ↄ Castle.")

An elephant's head appears on the bookplate TSE used from his Harvard days until at least 1922, and he used an elephant seal on a letter to Mrs. I. A. Richards, 15 Nov 1935. In his childhood he may have read of the Indian elephant that "In captivity he is very docile and gentle, but sometimes, when provoked, will take a very ample revenge. Of this propensity many anecdotes are told", J. G. Wood, *The Boy's Own Book of Natural History* [1893].

For the friends' continuing poetic exchanges, see note to *Lines Addressed to Geoffrey Faber Esquire*. TSE to Hayward, 13 Dec [1938]: "I fear that there is to be another explosion of poetry. I have received a neatly typed copy of some couplets addressed by the Whale to the Tarantula, but I don't propose to intervene (in either *persona*) at the moment." With this he enclosed Morley's couplets, *The Mark of the Spider is 666* (King's). Early in the war, Hayward sent Geoffrey Faber *A Gratulatory Epistle*, beginning "Airborne, courageous COOT" (McCue collection). Morley moved to Connecticut in 1939.

The present edition reprints TSE's contributions to the 1939 volume (*Gallup* B34), with poems by others to which he (nominally) responded. The item numbers follow A. S. G. Edwards's *T. S. Eliot and Friends: "Noctes Binanianae"* (1939) in *Book Collector* Winter 2009 (which lists the then whereabouts of printed copies).

[1]   *How to Pick a Possum*
[2]   [*"An Answer to the Foregoing Poem" by Geoffrey Faber*]
[3]   *The O'Possum Strikes Back*
[4]   *The Whale and the Elephant: A Fable*
[10] *Ode to a Roman Coot*

[13] ["Nobody knows how I feel about you" by Geoffrey Faber]
[14] Three Sonnets
[16] Vers pour la Foulque
[17] Translation into English of "Verses for the Coot"
[20] Abschied zur Bina

Five other items by Faber, two by Hayward and three by Morley are not reprinted in the present edition, although their positions in the volume are marked within the sequence.

3. PRINTING

Hayward's "Copy of Verses by T. S. Eliot sent to me in September, 1937" in the vol. *Miscellaneous Essays and Addresses* which he had bound up contains: *How to Pick a Possum*, *Geoffrey Faber's Sonnet* [*An Answer to the Foregoing Poem*], *The O'Possum Strikes Back*, *Ode to a Roman Coot*, *Three Sonnets*, *Vers pour la Foulque*, *Translation: "Verses for the Coot"*, *Festschriftgeschenck* [*Abschied zur Bina*] and two postcards.

King's also has Hayward's bound tss:

> *The Whale and the Elephant*
> [*Fable XIV* – Morley, two copies]
> [*Expostulatory Epistle of a Coot* – Faber]
> [*A Refutation* – Morley]
> [*Thoughts of a Briton on his Country's Subjugation to America* – Faber]
> [*A Fig for a Foolish One or Faber in a Firkin* – Hayward]
> [*Portion of a Soliloquy* – Faber]
> [*Nobody knows how I feel about you* – Faber]
> [*Tarantula tarantulae* – Faber]
> [*Album Leaflet No. 2* (*Revised Edition*) – Faber]

A letter from Hayward to Morley, 15 Nov 1937 (King's), gave a preliminary list of contents, and TSE added notes as to the whereabouts of the typescripts. Hayward ended: "Could you compare this list with your own and with those of your co-director? When agreement is reached on the canon, Dick [de la Mare] can go ahead with his plan to preserve these rare effusions—not for an age, but for all time!" (Jonson: "He was not of an age, but for all time", *To the memory of my beloved, The Author Mr. William Shakespeare*, prefaced to the First Folio, 1623.)

The title of the volume appears first in a letter from TSE to Hayward, 31 Mar 1937, before a trip to Scotland: "On the eve of my departure for the Northern Kingdom, I employ a short respite to pen these hasty lines by way of valedictory. From the frequentation of my society, and my abundant conversation (it afflicts me to think how often I must have wearied you with my dilatations on this and other topicks) (O noctes Binanianae!!) you will be fully acquainted with my abhorrence of the uncouth manners, the barbarous repasts, and the heady liquours of our northern neighbours." To Hayward, 19 Nov [1937], concerning a title for the volume:

> Your suggestion is admirable in itself but I wonder ... I mean ... perhaps there is enough Vapulation of the Coot in the text, and I should like the Title to suggest collaboration between the Coot and others ... Besides, the possum should not be too forward ... perhaps some such title as originally proposed by me:

NOCTES BINANIANAE

Wherein are contained such Voluntary & Satyrical Compliments and Verses as
were lately Exchang'd between some of the *Choicest [in margin:* Younger]
Wits and *Most Profound Deipnosophists* of the AGE

(Ornament or Emblem of a Coot,
or other Absurd Bird, or Figure
in which is tapester'd an Elephant,
upon whose back capers a Whale, upon
whose head a Coot with wings extended,
holding in his mouth a *stockfish*, and
above all a *Vesperal Spider* suspended,
which spinneth his Web about all.)

Imprinted for Rchd. de la Mare, His Maiestie's Printer, dwellinge
in Paules Churchyard, at the South west doore of *Saint Paules*
Church, and are there to be had.

But am I mixing the periods. Anyway, what about the capital point?

OED "Deipnosophist": "A master of the art of dining: taken from the title of the Greek
work of Athenæus, in which a number of learned men are represented as dining
together and discussing subjects which range from the dishes before them to literary
criticism and miscellaneous topics of every description." See *Deipnosophistic*, a verse
sent to Bonamy Dobrée, 29 Sept [1927], in "Improper Rhymes". For the "*Vesperal
Spider* suspended", see *Translation into English of "Verses for the Coot"* and "What will
the spider do, | Suspend its operations . . .?" *Gerontion* 65–66. From 1564, books
from the printing office of Richard Jones were to be had at his shop "at the South-
west door of St. Paul's church". Printers used similar imprints for two centuries.
TSE's letter suggested, alternatively: "Frognal's Helicon? A Paradise of . . ." (Geoffrey
Faber lived in Frognal, a district of Hampstead in the London Borough of Camden;
see note to *Ode to a Roman Coot* 9. *A Paradise of Dainty Devices* was published in 1576,
England's Helicon in 1600 and Hayward's *Love's Helicon* in 1940.)

Hayward thanked Anne Bradby (later Ridler) for typing out *Noctes Binanianæ*, 1
May 1939 (BL). He wrote to Morley on 14 Aug 1939 to say that "the treasurable little
booklets" had arrived, and copies were in the post "under separate cover".

4. AFTER DISTRIBUTION

TSE to Henry Eliot, 14 Oct 1939: "Dear Me! I am somewhat embarrassed by having
this pamphlet taken so seriously: it is merely the last flicker of expiring civilisation, a
commemoration of the elegant pastimes of gentlemen and scholars. The verses were
not, of course, composed with a view to publication; but after the accumulation of a
year or two, Hayward arranged with a nice man named Gregory, who has a printing
business, to have a few copies printed, as a *Festschrift* for Faber's birthday, and in
commemoration of pleasant evenings that are past. The company is dispersed.
What else is there to say about the verses? They naturally contain a number of
private allusions, of little interest or value to posterity. But the name of Madame de
Margerie, wife of the First Secretary of the French Embassy, should be kept green."

How to Pick a Possum

To Geoffrey Faber Esqre.

When the flowering nettle's in blossom
    And spring is about in the air,
How delightful to meet the O'Possum
    With fragments of hay in his hair.

When the bullocks have horns (and they toss 'em)   5
    And summer is seen on the lea,
How delightful to meet the O'Possum
    As he swings from a neighbouring tree.

At home, he appears in a mitre
    And a cope, or a cape and a cowl.   10
Although he's not known as a fighter
    He has a most terrible growl.

On some days he's duller or brighter,
    He abominates pencil and ink;
Yet he bangs on an ancient typewriter   15
    Without ever stopping to think.

He's inclined to frequent railway stations
    Where he studies the maps on the wall;
He is skilful at solitaire patience,
    And never reads poetry at all.   20

From April to middle-December
    He is apt to occur in the parks,
For which reason it's well to remember
    His peculiar distinguishing marks:

His habits are strictly arboreal,   25
    Affording protection from cows;
And in spring he affects such sartorial
    Display as the fashion allows.

          <

When he walks, he is quite perpendicular
30   Although rather weak in the knees;
His diet's extremely particular,
             For he eats almost nothing but cheese.

He's a nose which in summer is pinky,
             And in winter a beautiful blue;
35   He has hair, which is not at all kinky—
             Which I would not say, were it not true.

He has ears, which are almost symmetrical,
             And of use when the wind is behind;
And a mouth, which is rather upsetrical
40   And not always easy to find.

At the sound of a sudden sub-pœna
             He withdraws in alarm to his lair—
Very much like the spotted hyæna
             When pursued by the cinnamon bear.

45   In the summer, when flowers are blooming,
             His voice is compelling and gruff
And can not be confused with the booming
             Of the bittern, or cry of the chough.

In the winter, when fields are forsaken,
50   He develops a saturnine laugh,
Which prevents him from being mistaken
             For the hyperborean giraffe.

He has teeth, which are false and quite beautiful,
             And a wig, with an elegant queue;
55   And desires to convey his most dutiful
             Respects to your family and you.

3 **How delightful to meet the O'Possum**: "How delightful to meet Mr. Hodgson!" *Five-Finger Exercises* IV. *Lines to Ralph Hodgson Esqre.* 1.   **O'Possum:** "The nickname by which the author was known to his friends", Hayward marginalium, copy 1.

5 **bullocks have horns (and they toss 'em)**: "horns that toss and toss", *The Burnt Dancer* 35 (see note).

6, 8 **And summer is seen on the lea ··· tree:** Tennyson: "the tree ··· As the pimpernel dozed on the lea", *Maud* I xxii.

8 **he swings from a neighbouring tree:** J. G. Wood: "The Opossum uses its tail for climbing and swinging from branch to branch", *The Boy's Own Book of Natural History* [1893]. "Swing up into the apple-tree", *New Hampshire* 1, 12.

19 **He is skilful at solitaire patience:** asked by Auden why he liked playing patience, TSE replied: "Because it's the nearest thing to being dead" (*Spender* 240). To Lady Richmond, 11 June 1949. "I ··· have played several games of SPYDER. I was beginning to think that it requires mental abilities much superior to my own, but I got out the last game by cheating only once, so I hope that I may become more proficient".

22 **He is apt:** "apt" as a variant for "inclined" also at *The Ad-dressing of Cats* 27.

25 **arboreal:** "jaguar ··· arboreal ··· feline", *Whispers of Immortality* 25–27. *Old Possum's Book of Practical Cats* was published in Oct 1939, two months after the printing of *Noctes*.

27–28 **And in spring he affects such sartorial | Display as the fashion allows:** *Humouresque* 15–16:

> "The snappiest fashion since last spring's,
> "The newest style, on Earth, I swear."

32 **For he eats almost nothing but cheese:** "nothing less is required than the formation of a Society for the Preservation of Ancient Cheeses", *Stilton Cheese* (1935). To Geoffrey Hutchinson, 1 Jan 1936: "I have made enquiries at my club and I am informed by one of the stewards that we do actually obtain our Cheshire cheeses from you. As this is the only depository I have for cheese there is therefore no point in my ordering another, and I have only to continue to eat as much of your cheese as possible. I wish indeed that I had the knowledge to be able to write such a fine article as that about Stilton which you read in *The Times*." *Kenner 1972* 441, quoting TSE at the Garrick Club: "'That is a rather fine Red Cheshire ... which you might enjoy.' It was accepted: the decision was not enquired into, nor the intonation of *you* assessed."

35 **hair, which is not at all kinky:** OED "kinky" 1 includes "Sambo the blubber-lipped .. the kinky-haired" (1865).

38 **when the wind is behind:** "Laissons nos culs se ventiler", *Vers pour la Foulque* 35.

39 **And a mouth, which is rather upsetrical:** Pope: "And Douglas lend his soft, obstetric hand", *The Dunciad* (1742) IV 394.

44 **cinnamon bear:** OED: "a cinnamon-coloured variety of the common black bear of North America", with 1829: "The Cinnamon Bear of the Fur Traders is considered by the Indians to be an accidental variety of this species." J. G. Wood: "On account of this change of colour of the fur, the juvenile Musquaw has been considered as a separate species ... under the name of Yellow, or Cinnamon Bear", *Wood's Animal Kingdom Illustrated* (1870).

47–48 **the booming | Of the bittern:** Goldsmith: "dismally hollow as the booming of the bittern", *An History of the Earth, and Animated Nature*, "Birds of the Crane Kind" ch. VI.

49 **In the winter, when fields are forsaken:** Carroll: "In winter, when the fields are white", *Through the Looking-Glass* ch. VI, "Humpty Dumpty".

50 **develops a saturnine laugh:** to Hayward, 19 June 1940: "Yours saturninely but affectionately, TP."

52 **hyperborean:** OED: "Of, pertaining to, or characterizing the extreme north of the earth, or (colloq. or humorously) of a particular country". TSE to Anne Ridler, 12 April 1943: "Alison Kate, with red hair too, sounds very Scotch, though I did not know that there was anything hyperborean on either side of the family." Pronounced here with stress on the penultimate syllable.

53 **He has teeth, which are false and quite beautiful:** to Pound, 17 Feb 1938: "I expect to get some nice teeth before long." ("To get yourself some teeth", *The Waste Land* [II] 144; see note.) To McKnight Kauffer, 4 Oct: "I have to go into a nursing home for three nights, to have my teeth out · · · in ten days time I shall be learning to chew again; but I gather from my dentist that I shall be better looking with new teeth of the right size. Plastic teeth, of course." See *Poor Poony now is meek and mild*: "two by two | And year by year, they are extracted · · · Poor Old Possum has to wait | For something called a Dental Plate", *Poor Poony now is meek and mild* 18–26. "Smiles at the world through a set of false teeth", *In the Department Store* 2.

54 **wig · · · queue:** OED 2: "a pig-tail", with Goldsmith: "The largeness of the doctor's wig arises from the same pride as the smallness of the beau's queue", *An History of the Earth, and Animated Nature*, "Quadrupeds" ch. V.

Geoffrey Faber then wrote:

An Answer to the Foregoing Poem

Arboreal though the natural habitat
    Of Possums may have been in far-off times,
    And apt though Possums are to play with rhymes
Recalling feats a human acrobat
Might envy, what a Possum is best at
Is not the swinging creeper Tarzan climbs
    Nor yet the chimney-pot that poor old Grimes
Got stuck in—No Sir! *certainly* not that.
Ancestral memory reaches farther back,
    When water was the stuff he wallowed in,
Reminding Possum when and how to tack,
    To jibe the boom and wag the tiller-fin.
That is what Possum's godson hopes to see,
In Regent's Park, next Sunday, before tea.

13 **Possum's godson:** "A master ~~Richard~~ Tom Faber, a promising youth", Hayward marginalium, copy 1.

The O'Possum Strikes Back

At a point between Edgware and Morden,
    At a place between Wapping and Kew,
Dwells a very hardworking churchwarden
    With at least six men's business to do.
His name is not Spender or Auden,   5
    And his pleasures are simple and few:
An occasional abuse of Burgundian booze,
An occasional cruise on the Serps (or the Ouse)
    And a view of the gnu at the Zoo.

Here and there between Wessex and Mercia,   10
    Here and there between Orkney and Kent,
Strays a wholly preposterous burser,
    And before he is there he has went.
And I even suspect that his spouse is
    Unaware how his time has been spent: 15
An occasional tea with a casual spinster
At Stranraer, Kidwelly, or else Kidderminster,
An occasional spree on the banks of the Dee,
An occasional fling among heather (or ling)
    Where he points his proboscis at innocent grouses—   20
Or a revel at Burton-on-Trent.

But what among worst things still worse is,
    And again among worse things is worser,
I must mention the sybilline verses
    Of this more than surrealist burser.   25
Not content with the bursing of burses
And picking his tenantry's purses
(The technical skill of his verses
    Is such, I acknowledge, as I respect,
    Whether Latin or in Yorkshire dialect)   30
He over the mill throws his bonnet,
And produces a frivolous sonnet
    To one who, when considering how his life is spent,
    Regards Montrachet as his native element,
    And does not often repent.   35

Title **The O'Possum Strikes Back**] Sapper [H. C. McNeile]: *Bulldog Drummond Strikes Back* (US, 1933).

1 **Edgware and Morden:** north and south ends of the London Underground Northern Line.

2 **Wapping and Kew:** east and west London.

3 **churchwarden:** "An office held by the author at St. Stephen's Church, Gloucester rd. S.W.7.", Hayward marginalium, copy 1.

4 **With at least six men's business to do:** the tss have a footnote:

> E.G. presuming poets to be taken down, Sir,
> Or morning coffee with our Mrs. Trouncer.

TSE's workload was the subject of an elaborate office joke when the Faber & Faber Secretary, C. W. Stewart, sent him a cutting advertising "Eliot's Club, 28 Charing Cross Road" and wrote requiring a full account of his moonlighting. TSE retaliated ("7th July, 1936: 1.30 a.m. of the 8th"), writing to Geoffrey Faber: "a man is entitled to be judged by his peers: in the firm of Faber & Faber that is hardly possible for me; but the person who comes nearest to being a peer is surely a Chairman · · · The suggestion is made that it is improper for me to be connected in a business way with a Dance Club · · · It is added that I 'can scarcely bring the necessary freshness of mind to a Board Meeting, if my nights are spent . . .' etc. I should like to bring your attention to another possible point of view which is ignored. If the Directors of Faber & Faber Ltd. suppose that it is improper for me to be associated with Eliot's Club, what do they suppose the members of Eliot's Club think of my being associated with Faber & Faber? Which is the more sordidly corrupt activity—dancing or publishing? · · · I would point out that my emoluments from the publishing house of Faber are not only ridiculously inadequate in consideration of the burden or responsibility that I bear, but are only just sufficient to enable me to dress modestly and to entertain the innumerable bores at whom I should be able to snap my fingers were I not connected with a publishing house. In a dance club, if any individual fails to behave properly, you chuck him out; in a publishing house, you take him out to lunch." (TSE's now estranged wife Vivien joined Eliot's Club in the same year; see *Seymour-Jones* 550.)

5 **His name is not Spender or Auden:** "Mr. W. H. Auden & Mr. Stephen Spender, young poets protected by the author", Hayward marginalium, copy 1. TSE, jacket copy for *Stephen Spender's "Poems"* (1933):

> Like W. H. Auden, who has already been recognised for a writer of great significance and originality, Stephen Spender comes from Oxford, and he is of almost the same generation as Auden.
>
> If Auden is the satirist of this poetical renascence Spender is its lyric poet.

7 **occasional abuse of Burgundian booze:** "Mr. E. was a great lover of fine Burgundy", Hayward marginalium, copy 1.

8 **Serps:** the Serpentine, in Hyde Park, where miniature yachts are sailed. TSE writes in the role of godfather to Faber's son, Tom.

12 **preposterous burser:** "Mr. F. was Estates Bursar of All Souls Coll: in Oxford", Hayward marginalium, copy 1. Misspelling presumably deliberate (correctly spelt in *Ode to a Roman Coot* 24).

14 **his spouse:** "one Enid", Hayward marginalium, copy 1.

18–31 **spree on the banks of the Dee · · · the mill:** Isaac Bickerstaffe: "There was a jolly miller once, | Lived on the river Dee."

21 **a revel at Burton-on-Trent:** "A fleer at the brewing interests of Mr. F's family", Hayward marginalium, copy 1. Housman: "dancing · · · Say, for what were hop-yards meant, | Or why was Burton built on Trent?" *A Shropshire Lad* LXII 15–18.

24 **sybilline verses:** Coleridge (title): *Sibylline Leaves* (1817).

33 **when considering how his life is spent:** Milton: "When I consider how my light is spent", *Sonnet* [*On his Blindness*] 1.

34 **Montrachet:** region that produces the finest Chardonnay.

The Whale and the Elephant: A Fable

To the learned and ingenious Dr. Morley

The *Elephant* at forty-nine
Cannot be caught with *hook* and *line*,
Especially when it leads into
The Precincts of the *Hamburg Zoo.*
The *Whale*, at nearly thirty-eight,   5
Has less grey matter in his pate.
The *Elephant*, of beasts alive,
Is quite the most *Conservative;*
(Of beasts Conservative, the most
Have perish'd, like the *Morning Post*).   10
While other creatures change and roam,
He lingers in his *jungle* home,
In vegetarian flatulence.
Slow in attack, *strong* in defence,
The *Whale*, of more *Mercurial* mind,   15
Is driven about by *tide* and *wind:*
A mammal with no nobler wish
Than live like fish among the fish:
A Monster who escap'd the *Flood,*
With watery *diluted* Blood,   20
And, sacrificing *hoof* to *fin,*
Perpetuates pre-diluvial Sin.
Yet ah! might *Whales* perhaps repent?

And leave their fluid Element?
25   Prepare the higher life to meet,
And stand at last on *legs* and *feet*?
With *fatted calves* we'd welcome 'em
Into the New Jerusalem.

TSE to Geoffrey Faber [1 Oct ?] 1937 enclosing *ts1*, which lacks 9–10: "There is some question whether the enclosed Poem, the manuscript of which has just been discovered in the British Museum, is correctly attributed to the late Mr. GAY; and it is therefore sent to the chief living authority on that Author, for the benefit of his opinion. One reason why the attribution has been doubted, is that the identity of the Gentleman to whom the Poem is addressed, is completely obscure. Had there been such a Person among the Poet's acquaintance, we might expect to have heard of him before." Geoffrey Faber's 700-page edition of Gay's *Poetical Works* had appeared in 1926 and was "marked not only by erudition and industry but also, even when dealing with such matters as punctuation and spelling, by an instinctive sureness which reflects his innate sympathy with Gay's work and temperament" (*Oxford Dictionary of National Biography*).

To Hayward, 1 Oct 1937: "Here is a very curious item on which you must prove your scholarship. The manuscript of the enclosed poem was recently found inserted in a copy of the first edition of *A Tale of a Tub* in the British Museum. It was immediately submitted to Mr. G. C. Faber, the recognised authority on the works of Mr. GAY. Mr. Faber has pronounced against its ascription to that poet—I think myself, with some over-confidence in his own knowledge, for he writes: 'Had GAY had any friend or correspondent of that name, I should certainly know of his existence'. However, I am now authorised to submit it to the recognised authority on the works of the late DEAN of ST. PATRICK'S [Jonathan Swift], in the hope that you will be able to assign it to that author. If you deny the authorship, a curious situation arises: can it be that there was another Poet, a luminary obviously equal in magnitude to these two giants, whose other works and even whose name have completely disappeared? The suggestion is absurd. I await your pronouncement with vast curiosity."

To Geoffrey Faber, 2 Oct 1937:

> I am writing in haste to prevent you from spending any more time over the problem which, as it now appears, I presented prematurely. I hope that you have not begun to write your full report, questioning, if not wholly disproving, the ascription to Mr. GAY. Because meanwhile a new copy of the Poem has turned up in the British Museum, this time entitled simply 'A Fable'. It was found by a research student from Nigeria, between the leaves of Vol. III of *The Complete Works of Harold J. Laski*. It is identical in dedication and in every other respect, including paper and ink, except that after the lines

> > The *Elephant*, of beasts alive,
> > Is quite the most *Conservative*,

> we have a couplet which does not occur in the first version, viz.:

> > (Of *beasts conservative*, the most
> > Have perish'd, like *The Morning Post*);

> Which appears to give us an approximate date for the Poem. Doesn't it? or does it not?

Title **The Whale and the Elephant: A Fable**: Gay's octosyllabic Fables all concern animals, and include *Fable X. The Elephant and the Bookseller.*

Dedication **Dr. Morley**: to Henry Eliot, 19 Oct 1929: "I got into the firm a very able American named Morley, a brother of Christopher Morley, to supply a business sense which I felt was wanting; who shares my room with me, and whom, fortunately, I find sympathetic. He was a Rhodes Scholar from Baltimore, and was and is still the London representative of the Century Company. While congenial to everybody, he supplies an element of push and initiative, as well as of caution, which was very much needed in this rather close correct Oxford atmosphere of Faber & Faber."

"Mr. Morley has the art of interrupting himself, and seldom has an author succeeded in cramming so many irrelevancies into so few pages", *F. V. Morley's "My One Contribution to Chess"* (1947), jacket copy by TSE. Morley had invented a way to play with more than 64 squares.

1 The *Elephant* at forty-nine: "Mr. E., at this time, aged 49", Hayward marginalium, copy 1.

2 **Cannot be caught with *hook* and *line***: Job 41: 1, of the whale: "Canst thou draw out leviathan with an hook?"

5 The *Whale*: "Mr. M[orley]", Hayward marginalium, copy 1.

7–8 alive · · · *Conservative*: W. S. Gilbert: "How Nature always does contrive | That every boy and every gal, | That's born into the world alive, | Is either a little Liberal, | Or else a little Conservative!", *Iolanthe* act II. (For a little Socialist, Harold Laski, see TSE to Geoffrey Faber, 2 Oct 1937, quoted above.)

10 *Morning Post*: "A famous newsheet later incorporated with ye 'Daily Telegraph'", Hayward marginalium, copy 1. Before this take-over in 1937, the *Morning Post* had become notorious for anti-Semitism, its editor having written the introduction to *The Cause of World Unrest* ("The Protocols of the Elders of Zion") in 1920.

15–16 *Mercurial* mind · · · *tide* and *wind*: for TSE's tilting at the *London Mercury* and *Land and Water*, see the list of journals in the headnote to *Airs of Palestine, No. 2.* He never wrote for either, but first wrote for *Time and Tide* in 1935.

20 **With watery *diluted* Blood**: J. G. Wood: "the object of breathing is to oxygenize the blood · · · The most natural way to supply this want in the whale would be to give it much more lungs · · · But if this were the case, the animal would be seriously inconvenienced by such an amount of air, which would make it too buoyant · · · But there must be a reservoir somewhere, and, therefore, instead of a reservoir of air to arterialize the blood, there is a reservoir of blood already arterialized", *The Boy's Own Book of Natural History*. See first two notes to *The Hippopotamus* for "mud · · · blood" and for the behemoth.

23–24 **repent? | And leave their fluid Element**: Marlowe: "That Faustus may repent and save his soul! · · · O soul be changed to into little water-drops, | And fall into the ocean", *Dr. Faustus* sc. XVI (with "repent" a dozen times in the play).

27 *fatted calves* · · · **welcome**: Luke 15: 20: "his father · · · fell on his neck, and kissed him · · · bring hither the fatted calf".

Not included in the present edition: *For Doctor Thomas Eliot* and *Fable XIV: The Whale, the Elephant, the Coot, and the Spider* both by Frank Morley, *Expostulary Epistle of a Coot to a Self-Styled Whale and a Soi-Disant Elephant* by Geoffrey Faber, *A Refutation: To the Lethargic Doctor and the Ingenious Master Freyburg* by Frank Morley, and *Thoughts of a Briton on his Country's Subjugation to America* by Geoffrey Faber.

Ode to a Roman Coot
By the author of
"The Fantasy of Fonthill: or Betjeman's Folly"
and
"John Foster's Aunt."

My head aches, and a drowsy numbness pains
My sense, as though of White Horse I had drunk,
Or else had fuddled my too sensitive brains
With Menninger, or some equivalent bunk.
'Tis not through envy of thy happy lot
But being too goofy in thy goofiness,
That thou, light-headed zany of the trees,
In some melodious plot
Of Frognal, or of villas numberless,
Sing'st of cetaceans in pot-bellied ease.

For most, I know, thou lov'st retired ground.
Thee, with uncertain and tumultuous feet,
Quite trustworthy observers oft have seen
Crossing the stripling High near Oriel Street,
Distraught, or in a deep somnambular swound,
Or idly strumming on a mandoline,
With hair dishevelled and with throat unbound,
Turning thy steps to greet
(By some instinctive act centripetal)
The line of festal drunks in All Souls' Hall.

Thou wast not born for death, immortal Coot!
No dwindling populations tread thee down.
No transitory Wardens give the boot
To Oxford's biding bursar, bird and clown.

Thee have we seen at dawn on Hampstead Heath,   25
Forever panting and in cotton pants,
Forever biting upon rubber fruit,
Forever singing, although short of breath,
The self-same song, from Galloway to Hants,
The song of England's transatlantic doom: 30
The same that oft-times hath
Charmed the loud roisterers in the common room
And mazed th'attendants in the Turkish Bath.

Yet, William, we receive but what we give;
And in our life alone does Nature live: 35
And what must be his life who can confuse
The Whale and Elephant, two divers species?
And overlooking all the obvious clues,
Conclusions draw, most libellous and vicious?
And in one breath abuse   40
Cetacean coothlessness and elephantine beauty?
Such nature can be nothing else than cooty.
Look homeward, angel! not so far as France;
Look neither to the jungle where the dance
Of Kala Nag is hid from human eyes,   45
Nor seek thou to surprise
The horrid whale who lies
Curl'd on the Bottome of the monstrous world.

The parody of Keats's *Ode to a Nightingale* is closest to the original in 1–10 and 21–22.

Title **Roman Coot**: for Geoffrey Faber (the Coot) as the Roman censor Fabricius, see note to *Lines Addressed to Geoffrey Faber* 13.

Note on the Author] This appeared first in one of the typescripts for *Old Possum's Book of Practical Cats*, see Textual History of *Mungojerrie and Rumpelteazer*. **Betjeman's Folly**: "A choice wit of the period, a lover of architectural fantasy", Hayward marginalium against "Betjeman", copy 1. John Betjeman worked for the *Architectural Review* 1930–35, then as editor of the Shell Guides, and probably visited William Beckford's Gothick abbey in Wiltshire with John Piper. **John Foster's Aunt**: "A pseudo-aunt, housekeeper in the Temple of that famous figure Mr. Foster", Hayward marginalium against "John Foster". TSE makes play with Dickens's magazine *Once a Week* in a spoof report to Geoffrey and Enid Faber, 12 Feb 1939, headed "THE AUTOLYCAN INTELLIGENCER | Once a Week | For Private Circulation Only | edited by | John Foster's Aunt".

The pseudonym "Autolycus" headed the gossip column which John Hayward contributed to the *Sunday Times* (in *The Winter's Tale* IV ii, Autolycus speaks of himself as "a snapper-up of unconsidered trifles"). John Foster also figures in "SPOTLIGHT ON 22, BINA GARDENS: THROWN BY JOHN FOSTER" (1938), for which see note to *Sweeney Erect* 40.

1–10] Keats, *Ode to a Nightingale* 1–10.

> My heart aches, and a drowsy numbness pains
> My sense, as though of hemlock I had drunk,
> Or emptied some dull opiate to the drains
> One minute past, and Lethe-wards had sunk:
> 'Tis not through envy of thy happy lot,
> But being too happy in thine happiness—
> That thou, light-winged Dryad of the trees,
> In some melodious plot
> Of beechen green, and shadows numberless,
> Singest of summer in full-throated ease.

2 **White Horse**: "A whisky whose vile flavour could be recognized by a man blind-fold", Hayward marginalium, copy 1.

4 **Menninger**: Harcourt Brace published *Man Against Himself* by the American psychiatrist Karl Menninger in 1938. TSE's spelling is here emended. Hayward put an asterisk beside "Meninger" but without a note, copy 1.

6 **goofy ··· goofiness**: see note to the third title of *Whan Cam ye fra the Kirk*.

9 **Frognal**: "In the North of London, the seat of Mr. F.", Hayward marginalium, copy 1. Hayward contributed *Frognal: A Pindarick Ode* to the volume.

9 *variant* **loonies numberless**: Geoffrey Faber's ts has a side-note: "Can the Poet be thinking of Mr. Unwin? See Kelly's Guide to Hampstead." *Sex and Culture* (1934) by the social anthropologist J. D. Unwin was regarded by Aldous Huxley as "a work of the highest importance". TSE met Unwin in 1936.

11–12 **For most, I know, thou lov'st retired ground. | Thee**: Arnold, *The Scholar-Gipsy* 71–72.

12 **tumultuous feet**: Yeats: "hiding their tossing manes and their tumultuous feet", *Michael Robartes bids his Beloved be at Peace* 12.

14 **Crossing the stripling High near Oriel Street**: Arnold: "Crossing the stripling Thames at Bab-lock-hithe", *The Scholar-Gipsy* 74. "In Oxford, where Mr. F. passed his week-ends", Hayward marginalium, copy 1.

16 **idly strumming on a mandoline**: "The pleasant whining of a mandoline", *The Waste Land* [III] 261.

19 **centripetal**: with stress on second syllable.

20 **The line of festal drunks in All Souls' Hall**: Arnold: "The line of festal light in Christ-Church hall", *The Scholar-Gipsy* 129.

21–24, 29–33] Keats, *Ode to a Nightingale* 61–64:

> Thou wast not born for death, immortal Bird!
> No hungry generations tread thee down;
> The voice I hear this passing night was heard
> In ancient days by emperor and clown:

> Perhaps the self-same song that found a path
> Through the sad heart of Ruth, when, sick for home
> She stood in tears amid the alien corn;
> The same that oft-times hath
> Charmed magic casements, opening on the foam
> Of perilous seas, in faery lands forlorn.

26–28] Keats: *Ode on a Grecian Urn* 24, 26–27: "For ever piping songs for ever new · · · For ever warm and still to be enjoyed, | For ever panting, and for ever young."

29 **Hants**: Hampshire.

30 **The song of England's transatlantic doom**: Geoffrey Faber's poem *Thoughts of a Briton on his Country's Subjugation to America* appears immediately before this in *Noctes*.

32 **the common room**: All Souls, having no undergraduates, has only a (Senior) Common Room; other colleges have a Junior Common Room too.

33 **Turkish Bath**: "Mr. F. was much addicted to this luxury", Hayward marginalium, copy 1. TSE to John Hayward, 20 Feb 1943:

> The brotherless Eumenides
> Freeze in such Turkish baths as these.

Marvell: "The brotherless *Heliades* | Melt in such Amber Tears as these", *The Nymph Complaining for the death of her Faun* 99–100 (John Haffenden, personal communication). For the Eumenides, see headnote to *Sweeney Agonistes*.

34 **William**: the tss have a side-note: "At this point the unknown poet himself seems to have become fuddled, and imagined that he was addressing the late Wm. Wordsworth."

34–35 **we receive · · · Nature live**: Coleridge: "O Lady! we receive but what we give, | And in our life alone does nature live", *Dejection* 47–48.

43 **not so far as France**: Arnold: "the French coast · · · the cliffs of England", *Dover Beach* 3–4.

43–48 **Look homeward, angel! · · · The horrid whale who lies | Curl'd on the Bottome of the monstrous world**: *Lycidas* 157–67:

> Where thou perhaps under the whelming tide
> Visit'st the bottom of the monstrous world · · ·
> Look homeward angel now, and melt with ruth.
> And, O ye dolphins, waft the hapless youth.
>   Weep no more, woeful shepherds weep no more,
> For Lycidas your sorrow is not dead,
> Sunk though he be beneath the watery floor.

(See note to *Mr. Apollinax* 11–15 for TSE and the submarine world.) The final parodic entry in TSE's *Whalebones from the Cetacean Anthology* (?1937; see "Other Verses") reads "Are thy bones hurried where the horrid Whale | Visit'st the Bottome of the monstrous world?—MILTON." Phyllis Bottome (whose name was stressed on the second syllable) had submitted a manuscript about Ezra Pound to TSE for the *Criterion* in 1936, and her book *The Mortal Storm* was published by Faber in 1937.

44–45 the dance | Of Kala Nag is hid from human eyes: in Kipling's tale *Toomai of the Elephants* in *The Jungle Book*, the old elephant Kala Nag takes the boy Toomai to watch the elephants dance, as no human has before.

_____

Not included in the present edition: *A Fig for a Foolish One or Faber in a Firkin* by John Hayward and *Fragment of a Soliloquy* by Geoffrey Faber.

_____

The next contribution, by Geoffrey Faber, was again directed towards TSE:

By Special Request

Nobody knows how I feel about you

(As sung by Layton and Johnstone.)

Nobody knows how I feel about you
Everybody knows what you've done to me.
It seems only yesterday the skies were so blue
And now to-day life's just a stormy sea.
Yesterday my heart was so full of poetry,
And now there ain't nothin' for me to say or to do.
Everybody knows what you've done to me,
Nobody knows how I feel about you.

I'm glad that I ain't an elephant in the Zoo.
I guess you'd hand me up a sawdust bun.
I'm glad I ain't a whale to be harpooned by you.
I'm glad I ain't got your ideas of fun.
You'se the sort that likes to get folks on the run,
You'se the sort that gives the last twist to the screw
But how could you do the things that you've done,
When I hadn't done nothin' to you?

Somewhere up above, if the good book's true,
Somebody's gwine to wipe away the tears.
Honey, that ain't just what's coming to you.
You'se gwine to pay up some of your arrears.
Maybe when I'm climbin' up the golden stairs,
You'll be down below an' you'll be feelin' blue,
An' I wouldn't be surprised if a tinglin' in you ears
Told you what the angels thought about you.

Hayward's proof corrections were not followed (see end of *Noctes Binanianæ* section for Textual History). They were presumably intended to make the poem more "barbaric" to suit TSE's rejoinder. Turner Layton and Clarence "Tandy" Johnstone were a popular duo of the 1920s and 1930s.

Three Sonnets

To Geoffrey Cust Faber Esqre., as a reply to a ballad entitled
"Nobody knows how I feel about you."

GEOFFREY! who once did walk the earth like Jove,
    Who on his brow and shoulders once did drape
    The *Victor's* laurels and the prophet's *Cape*,
Ruling the world below, the sky above;

With monsters of the sea and jungle strove,   5
    Triumphant, as a God in human shape
    Sustained by juice of juniper and grape,
Respected by the Trade in Bath and Hove,

Now takes to crooning like a Harlem coon,
    A blackface Ruth amid the alien corn   10
    Upon the cob; and in degenerate verse

Which still declines from bad to worse and worse
    Like Lucifer he falls: from dewy morn
    To noon: still falling through the afternoon.

CUST! whose loud martial oaths did once proclaim
    Thee the most virile of the Brownlow clan,
    Captain or Colonel—but more than man,
Gallant protector of th'oppressèd dame,

A spotless knight without reproach or blame   5
    In Cheapside, Lothbury or Barbican,
    How can you do it? Answer now: how can
You be so lost to dignity and shame

As caper to the rhythm known as "swing,"
    And dance to the lubricious saxophone,   10
    And sway your hips to the barbaric drum?

                <

Can such things be? O death where is thy sting,
  When drunken Muses on the banjo strum,
  And pipe to negro ditties of no tone?

FABER! of thy great exploits 'twas not least,
  That thou ofttimes didst twist the mighty tail
  (Alone thou didst it) of the basking whale
And tamed with words the elephantine beast,

5   And (what were minor trophies for thy feast)
  Slew the wild albatross, the penguin pale,
  And the white liddell hart in coat of mail,
And the sly cat of Bina Gardens fleec'd;

Great hunter! whose past glories we dissect,
10   To what decay'd estate art thou now come,
  Ensiren'd by the Cotton Club bassoon,

Enchanted by the Broadway dialect,
  And, masticating Wrigley's pepsin gum,
  Expectoratest in the loud spittoon.

Title **Three Sonnets**: many of Geoffrey Faber's own poems, including one in *Noctes*, were sonnets.

[I]

1 **GEOFFREY! who**: Milton: "Fairfax, whose name in arms through Europe rings", sonnet, *On the Lord General Fairfax*. (Wordsworth took up the exclamatory opening in "Milton! thou shouldst be living at this hour: | England hath need of thee", *Sonnet*.)

3 **The *Victor's* laurels and the prophet's *Cape***: "Mr. Victor Gollancz & Mr. Jonathan Cape, two famous publishers of London", Hayward marginalium, copy 1. Geoffrey Faber joined the council of the Publishers' Association in 1934 (Treasurer, 1937; President, 1939).

8 **the Trade**: OED 6a: "*spec.* the publishers and booksellers".   **Bath and Hove**: genteel retirement towns.

9 **crooning like a Harlem coon**: ragtime "coon songs" were named after *All Coons Look Alike to Me* (1890) by the black performer Ernest Hogan, about a "dusky maiden" torn between two handsome men.

10 **Ruth amid the alien corn**: Keats: "Through the sad heart of Ruth, when, sick for home, | She stood in tears amid the alien corn", *Ode to a Nightingale* 66–67.

12 **worse and worse:** see note to "Wux and Wux" in letter to Bonamy Dobrée, 10 May 1927, in "Improper Rhymes".

13–14 **Like Lucifer he falls: from dewy morn | To noon:** *Henry VIII* III ii: "And when he falls, he falls like Lucifer." *Paradise Lost* I 742–43: "from Morn | To Noon he fell, from Noon to dewy Eve".

[II]

1 *variant* **soldier's oaths:** *As You Like It* II vii: "Then a soldier, | Full of strange oaths".

1–2 **Cust · · · Brownlow:** Faber was descended from Sir Richard Cust (1680–1734), who married Anne, elder daughter of Sir William Brownlow, MP. The Brownlow barony, in Lincolnshire, was created in 1776 for Sir Brownlow Cust.

3 **more than man:** LADY MACBETH: "When you durst do it, then you were a man; | And, to be more than what you were, you would | Be so much more than man" (I vii).

3–6 **Captain or Colonel · · · protector · · · knight · · · Barbican:** Milton: "Captain or colonel, or knight in arms · · · him within protect", Sonnet VIII. *When the assault was intended to the City* (TSE's Cheapside and Lothbury are streets in the City of London, and the Barbican was a fortified area in the City in Roman times). **Colonel:** trisyllabic until late in the 17th century ("coronelle").

4 **Gallant protector of the oppressed dame:** the marriage of Geoffrey and Enid Faber contrasted with that of Geraint and the oppressed Enid in Tennyson's *Idylls of the King*.

5 **A spotless knight without reproach or blame:** "chevalier sans peur et sans reproche", 16th-century description of Pierre Bayard. Chaucer: "He was a verray parfit gentil knight", *The Canterbury Tales* Prologue 72.

5–6 **without reproach or blame | In Cheapside:** Middleton (title): *A Chaste Maid in Cheapside.* **Cheapside, Lothbury:** for Wordsworth, see note to *Mr. Pugstyles* 26–28.

9–14 **caper to the rhythm · · · ditties of no tone:** TSE took the opposite tack in his facetious letter to Geoffrey Faber, 7–8 July 1936 (see note to *The O'Possum Strikes Back* 4): "I may find myself tempted to devote the whole of my attention to the legitimate entertainment industry, providing innocent and rhythmical pleasure for people's bodies, instead of conniving at providing so much trash for their minds."

9 **"swing":** Duke Ellington's *It Don't Mean a Thing (if it ain't got that swing)* had been a hit in 1932.

9–10 **As caper to the rhythm known as "swing," | And dance to the lubricious saxophone:** *Richard III* I i, RICHARD: "He capers nimbly in a lady's chamber, | To the lascivious pleasing of a lute."

12 **Can such things be:** MACBETH: "Can such things be | And overcome us like a summer's cloud?" (III iv). **O death where is thy sting:** 1 Corinthians 15: 55.

13 **drunken Muses:** Pope: "Is there a Parson, much be-mus'd in Beer, | A maudlin Poetess, a rhyming Peer", *An Epistle to Dr. Arbuthnot* 15–16 (for a previous use by TSE, see note to *WLComposite* 286, 291).

14 **And pipe to negro ditties of no tone:** Keats: "Not to the sensual ear · · · Pipe to the spirit ditties of no tone", *Ode on a Grecian Urn* 13–14. TSE: "Here's a negro (teeth and smile) | Has a dance that's quite worthwhile", *The smoke that gathers blue and sinks* 20–21.

[III]

3 **Alone thou didst it:** CORIOLANUS V vi: "like an eagle in a dove-cote, I | Flutter'd your Volscians in Corioles. | Alone I did it."

6 **the wild albatross, the penguin pale:** "The 'Albatross' & 'Penguin' cheapjack books", Hayward marginalium, copy 1. (Albatross Books were the first mass-market paperbacks.)

7 **the white liddell hart:** "Capt. Liddell Hart, a military historian", Hayward marginalium, copy 1. TSE: "The white hart behind a white well", *Landscapes* III. *Usk* 3.

8 **sly cat of Bina Gardens:** "Mr. H. then residing in Bina gardens S.W.5", Hayward marginalium, copy 1.

9 **Great hunter:** Genesis 10: 9: "Even as Nimrod the mighty hunter before the Lord". Faber enjoyed shooting and fishing on his Welsh estate.

9 **glories** (*variant:* **grandeur**): Poe: "To the glory that was Greece | And the grandeur that was Rome", *To Helen*.

9–10 **we dissect, | To:** Wordsworth: "we murder to dissect", *The Tables Turned* 23.

10 **decay'd estate:** 1 Maccabees 3: 43: "Let us restore the decayed estate of our people".

11 **Cotton Club:** "A famed negro club in New York City", Hayward marginalium, copy 1.   **bassoon:** a jazz rarity at this period.

11–14 **bassoon · · · loud spittoon:** Coleridge: "The Wedding-Guest now beat his breast, | For he heard the loud bassoon", *The Rime of the Ancient Mariner* I 31–32.

13 **Wrigley's pepsin gum:** chewing gum sold as a digestive aid.

14 **Expectoratest in the loud spittoon:** *Fowler* (1926): expectorate "seems to be now the established American for *spit* · · · an object-lesson on the vanity of genteelism. The mealy-mouthed American must be by this time harder put to it with *expectorate* than the mealy-mouthed Englishman with *spit*; his genteelism has outgrown its gentility & become itself the plain rude word for the rude thing."

———

Not included in the present edition: *Frognal: A Pindarick Ode* by John Hayward.

Vers pour la Foulque

Feuillet d'Album

Allons nous promener, si tu veux.
Nous allons diriger nos pas
Du côté de chez Bina:
Cherchons le numéro vingt-deux.

N'as-tu pas vu, que c'est grotesque,   5
Ce paysage aux plates-bandes ternes?
C'est un pays de balivernes!
Il n'est pas lieu moins pittoresque.

Le facteur même grince des dents
Et prend un aspect plus farouche   10
En passant par ce quartier louche—
Un faubourg des moins alléchants.

C'est un pays de bambochades,
Où par des portiques de Willett
Des boniches insolentes vous guettent   15
En attendant vos sérénades.

Peu de vivant qui se remue—
Un terrain vague et désolé:
On voit des chats avariés,
Et même parfois une ancienne grue.   20

Mais derrière une vaste fenêtre
Où s'étale un vase de nénuphars,
Ecoute! des chuchotements épars
Et des rires fous. C'est lui! l'être

Immonde! c'est la Tarentule   25
Aux yeux multiples, au vénin sur,
Qui nous fait, d'un regard impur,
Un geste que le strabisme annule.

Allons nous promener, si tu veux;
Nous allons filer droit jusqu'à   30

Ces chétifs jardins de Bina:
Cherchons le numéro vingt-deux.

Nous allons nous donner la peine
De nous soulager—et sonner;
Laissons nos culs se ventiler
En attendant la *Madeleine*.

35

This appears to be the only one of the poems from *Noctes Binanianæ* that TSE contemplated printing in a different context. On 3 Dec 1945 he wrote to Pierre Leyris, who was preparing a volume of French translations of TSE's earlier poems: "I think the best title would probably be *La Terre Gaste*, précédé de quelques poèmes anciens [*The Waste Land* preceded by some old poems]. Only if you put in the French poem that John Hayward had [*Vers pour la Foulque* from *Noctes Binanianæ*], that dates from 1938 and therefore *ancient* hardly applies. But that is I think, the only one of the French poems which I would like to have included. I do not think that the others [from *Poems* (1920)] are good enough to take their place in such a small selection as this. You are quite at liberty to use that poem only I cannot provide you with a copy of it at the moment as the only copy I have is buried somewhere in a box of books, but I daresay Hayward would be very glad to type out a copy for you. It would need a few notes for which I could supply the material."

1 **Allons nous promener, si tu veux**: "Let us go then, you and I", *The Love Song of J. Alfred Prufrock* 1.

4 **numéro vingt-deux**: "The residence of Mr. H.", Hayward marginalium, copy 1.

12 **faubourg**: to Hayward, 6 Sept 1939, on the blackout: "The darkness is rather pleasant in districts that you know like the palm of your hand, but terrifying in unfamiliar faubourgs."

14 **Willett**: "Wm. Willett (temp. XIX cent) creator of 'Pont St. Dutch' ⱥ 'Etruscan Tudor'", Hayward marginalium, copy 1. The architect built Bina Gardens in 1884–86. "Pont Street Dutch" was John Betjeman's description of the style of London's late Victorian brick mansion blocks. "Etruscan Tudor" was Hayward's own term, as when he wrote to William Empson on 26 Mar 1939: "I made up my mind to leave my Etruscan-Tudor bed-sitting room in Earl's Court after the Munich Crisis".

36 **la *Madeleine***: "One Magdalene, a rude skivvy at No. 22. Afterwards in a Convent but was removed", Hayward marginalium, copy 1.

Translation into English of
"Verses for the Coot"
Album Leaflet

Let us proceed to make a walk, if you give your consentment. We are going to aim our steps of the direction of Bina's. Let us search the No. 22. Hast thou not seen, that this landscape with the tarnished herbaceous borders is queer? It is a land of trash. Nothing could be less picturesque. Even the Postman grinds his teeth and barbarises his face when he traverses this ambiguous quarter, which is one of the less attractive working-class districts. It is a land of bad and low jokes! in which, from the porticoes of Willett, rude skivvies keep an eye on you, hoping that you will pay court to them. There is very little life about! It is a waste and desolate piece of ground. One observes damaged cats, and even now and then a retired great coarse woman. But, behind a huge window where a vase of water-lilies shows off itself: listen! there are rare whispers and lunatic laughter. It is it. It is the disgusting creature. It is the vesperal spider with complex eyes and deadly poison, who, with an immodest look, makes to us a gesture which is cancelled by his strabismus. Let us proceed to make a walk, if you give your consentment. We are going to file off to these paltry gardens of Bina. Let us search the No. 22.

The rest is untranslate-able

Hayward's attribution confirms that the translation is by TSE. Both poem and translation echo and parody many elements of TSE's own poems.

water-lilies · · · whispers and lunatic laughter: "Whispers and small laughter between leaves · · · the waters", *Marina* 20–21 (and see note). ***The rest is untranslate-able***: [We are going to take the trouble to relieve ourselves—and to ring the bell; let our arses fart as we wait for Magdalene.] For TSE, "Perhaps best omitted", see Textual History 33–36.

Hayward to Anne Ridler, 20 Mar 1945, of his translation of *Mon Faust* (*Horizon* May 1945): "The Valéry was, I should add, commissioned by the old boy himself who wrote to me when the posts between France & England were restored to say—don't laugh!—'Je n'oublierai jamais Bina gardens'! I ought to record this memorable fantasy in my copy of *Noctes Binanianæ*" (BL).

———

Not included in the present edition: *Poema Latina* and *Album Leaflet No. 2*, both by Geoffrey Faber.

Abschied zur Bina

Im schönen Binagarten
    Wo die Lorbeeren blühen,
Sang der Kuckuck im Frühling
    Mit Stimme knapp und kühn.

5   Im schönen Binagarten,
    In der frechen Jugendzeit,
Einst trafen sich Gesellen
    Für Heiterkeit bereit.

Zu Nummer zweiundzwanzig
10   Da kamen allerlei
Bedeutende Personen:
    Ach, weh! das ist vorbei.

Verschiedene Arten Leute —
    Sie kamen gern besuchen
15   Die alte schlaue Spinne
    Zum Thee, mit Schnapps und Kuchen.

Feinschmecker manchmal kamen
    Zum Essen und zum Trinken —
Bei Leberwurst und Butterbrot
20   Und Aquavit und Schinken.

Da trafen sich beisammen
    Politiker und Richter
Und Diplomat und Advokat
    Und Schauspieler und Dichter.

25   Der stolze Ritter Meiklejohn
    War oftmals abgespannt;
Macdonald von den Inseln
    Davon war nicht verbannt.

>

Es kam der alte Kauffer
    Der Spiegeleier ass,   30
Der jung' Holländer Betjeman
    Der liebte Witz und Spass.

Und traurig wie ein Witwen-Vogel
    Blass mit Leid und Schmerz,
Kam manchmal Richard Jannings   35
    Der macht' uns immer Scherz.

Mit leichter Unterhaltung
    Und komischem Gedicht,
Und mit Gelache und Gesang
    Bis helles Morgenlicht,   40

Man hatte nie Langweile,
    War immer froh darein,
Mit Schnupftabak und Zigarett,
    Kaffee und Burgundwein.

War alles ganz behaglich,   45
    Grossartig und bequem;
Mit kolossaler Freundlichkeit
    War's allzu angenehm.

    *   *   *   *

Die höheren Herrschaften,
    Sie machten gern Besuch: 50
Damen mit seidenen Strümpfen
    Und köstlichem Geruch;

Die elegantsten Damen,
    Sie kamen alle gern:
Die Schlanksten und die Schönsten   55
    Vom innern Mayfairkern.

Da kamen Herzoginnen,
    Korrekt und wohlgesinnt;
Da kamen manchmal andere
    Die anonymer sind.   60

    <

Und kam die fromme Jenny
Die gut verwaltet sich;
Und kamen auch Dorinda
Und Janni Kennerlich.

65   Die nette Kodringburger,
Die schöne Kamerun —
Und wegen Regenwetter,
Sie trugen Gummischuhen.

*   *   *   *

Zu Nummer zweiundzwanzig
70   Im schönen Binagarten,
Zuströmt nicht mehr Adel,
Gibt's nichts mehr zu erwarten;

Im schönen Binagarten,
Der Kuckuck singt nicht mehr;
75   Da sieht man nur Kobolde
Die kriechen ab und her.

Im schönen Binagarten
Der Sommer ist vorbei.
Ich irre langsam und allein,
80   Mir bricht das Herz entzwei.

Hayward to Anne Ridler, 16 Aug 1944: "I must, alas, discountenance, once again, the pleasing legend · · · that I hold court, or whatever the word is, to the Great ȸ Good and Beautiful ȸ Intelligent of the five continents. I can't conceive how this popular fallacy arose, unless it is that my sedentary life ȸ consequently relatively rare appearances in public places lead people to suppose that I'm incessantly closeted with visitors! The legend is played up, you may recall, in the Master's German verses in *Noctes Binanianæ*" (BL).

Rupert Hart-Davis to George Lyttelton, 15 July 1961: "T. S. E. and I are supposed (separately) to record something for a twenty-minute radio programme on the Library *in German* · · · T. S. E. said he could read out a sentence or two, and then his pronunciation went haywire and sounded like bad French", *The Lyttelton–Hart-Davis Letters* VI (1984).

Title **Abschied zur Bina**: [Farewell to Bina]. "Mr. H. removed from Bina Gardens in Nov. 1938", Hayward marginalium, copy 1.   *variant* **Geburtstag**: Hayward, who received the poem on 31 Jan 1939, turned 34 on 2 Feb. For another poem for Hayward's birthday, probably by Geoffrey Faber (and now in the Faber archive), see Jim McCue and Oliver Soden, *N&Q* Mar 2014.

25 **Ritter Meiklejohn:** "Sir Roderick Meiklejohn, formerly Chief Civil Service Commissioner", Hayward marginalium, copy 1.

27 **Macdonald von den Inseln:** "A great bore", Hayward marginalium, copy 1. Hugh Macdonald worked at the Royal Courts of Justice. Hayward to TSE, [27 Feb 1938]: "I shall postpone Hugh Macdonald ('Macdonald of the Pisles' in his own country) until next week". Frederick Etchells and Macdonald were the publishers of the editions of Dryden's *Of Dramatic Poesy* (1928) and Johnson's *"London" and "The Vanity of Human Wishes"* (1930), each with a contribution by TSE.

29 **Kauffer:** "A celebrated artist", Hayward marginalium, copy 1.

35 **Richard Jannings:** "Mr. Jennings, a notable man of sorrows and a great wit", Hayward marginalium, copy 1. TSE to John Betjeman, 18 Sept 1939: "I have been having a correspondence with Jennings · · · to quote the words of the Master [Conan Doyle] · · · in the whole history of Gloom, 'Never have I risen to such a height, and never have I been so hard pressed by an opponent'." A leader-writer at the *Daily Mirror* and a famously fastidious book collector, Jennings was the recipient of no. 11 of *Noctes* (Sotheby's, 13 July 1966). In 1933 TSE briefly shared a flat with Jennings, C. H. B. Kitchin and Ken Ritchie.

61 **Jenny:** "Mme. Roland de Margerie" Hayward marginalium, copy 1. Jenny Fabre-Luce was the wife of the diplomat Roland de Margerie and was an admirer of Rilke. See headnote to the volume: 4. AFTER DISTRIBUTION.

63 **Dorinda:** "Mrs John Maxse", Hayward marginalium, copy 1. (*Née* Dorinda Thorne.)

64 **Janni Kennerlich:** "Mrs. Morley Kennerly", Hayward marginalium, copy 1.

65 **Die nette Kodringburger:** "Mrs John Codrington", Hayward marginalium, copy 1.

66 **Die schöne Kamerun:** "Mrs. Alan Cameron better remembered as Elizabeth Bowen, a renowned writer", Hayward marginalium, copy 1.

75 **Kobolde:** [goblins]. "Two High-Church curates now residing at No. 22", Hayward marginalium, copy 1.

Farewell to Bina
A translation (for the present edition) by Rodney Dennis

In lovely Bina Gardens
Where the laurel blooms,
The cuckoo sang in springtime
With voice brief and bold.

In lovely Bina Gardens,   5
In the fresh time of youth,
Once the comrades used to meet
All composed for fun.   <

To number twenty-two
   All sorts came,   10
People of importance:
   Alas! That's all gone by.

Various types of people—
   They loved to pay a visit
To the clever old spider   15
   For tea and Schnapps and cakes.

Sometimes gourmets came
   To eat and to drink—
Liverwurst and bread and butter
   And aquavit and ham.   20

And there met together
   Judge and politician,
Diplomat and advocate,
   Actor and poet.

Proud knight Meiklejohn   25
   Was often at his ease;
Macdonald from the Island
   Was also not unwelcome.

Old Kauffer used to come
   And eat fried eggs.   30
The young Dutchman Betjeman
   Who liked jokes and fun.

And sad as a widow bird,
   Pale with pain and sorrow,
Richard Jennings used to come   35
   And always told us jokes.

With light conversation
   And with amusing poems,
With songs and with laughter
   Till the bright light of day.   40

One was never bored,
   Was always happy there
With cigarettes and snuff,
   Burgundy and coffee.

Everything was pleasant,   45
   Comfortable and great;
With colossal kindness
   It was just too nice.

*   *   *   *

Gentlemen of rank
   Liked to pay a visit,   50
Ladies with silk stockings
   And expensive scent;

The elegant ladies
   All loved to come:
The thinnest and the fairest   55
   From Mayfair's inner core.

And duchesses arrived,
   Proper and well-intended,
And other people came
   Who were anonymous.   60

And pious Jenny came,
   Who nicely herself comported;
And Dorinda came as well
   And Janni Kennerlich.

Cute Kodringburger,   65
   Lovely Kamerun—
The day being rainy
   They wore rubber boots.

*   *   *   *

To number twenty-two
   In lovely Bina Gardens   70
The nobility stream no longer;
   There's nothing left to see;

In lovely Bina Gardens,
   No longer sings the cuckoo;
You only see goblins   75
   Creeping here and there.

In lovely Bina Gardens
   Summer now is past.
I wander slowly and alone,
   My heart has broke in two.   80

Noctes Binanianæ: Textual History

Text: Hayward's copy, no. 1 (King's), has been compared with copy no. 12 (thanks to the generosity of Rick Gekoski). Copy no. 1 has attributions and explanatory annotations by Hayward in ink, and his pencilled emendations to *Abschied zur Bina*.

Hayward's sheaf (King's): mixed ribbon and carbon copies in the Hayward Bequest, bound in two volumes, H2 (TSE poems and Geoffrey Faber's sonnet) and V8A. *How to Pick a Possum*, Geoffrey Faber's sonnet and *The O'Possum Strikes Back* are copies typed by Hayward; the rest were typed by TSE.

Proofs. *Edwards* suggests that each of the contributors probably had a proof, to be returned to and co-ordinated by Hayward.

Texas proof (Texas): first proof from Hayward's library, with emendations throughout, including some by Hayward. Sold Sotheby's, 12 July 1966.

BL proof (BL): second proof from Hayward's library, with a single emendation by TSE to *Abschied zur Bina*. Sold Sotheby's, 12 July 1966.

Bodleian proof (Bodleian): second proof without emendations. Sold Sotheby's, 11 July 1967.

revise proof (King's): a copy of the printed volume with "Revise proof" pencilled on the front cover, and emendations made, after printing, by Hayward. (None was adopted.) A printed slip, "CORRIGENDA FULICALIA" [= "of the Coot", Geoffrey Faber], bears two corrections for poems not by TSE and not included in this edition.

Titles were typeset in italics in proof, but changed to small capitals for the final printing. Other headings were also changed, with italics for roman type and vice versa.

How to Pick a Possum

ts1 (BL): verse letter to Alison Tandy, 12 Sept 1937.

ts2 (Faber archive): revision on two leaves (the first on *Criterion* headed notepaper), sent to Geoffrey Faber, dated in another hand "Sept 13 1937".

Hayward's sheaf (King's): Hayward has typed at head "Copy of Verses by T. S. Eliot sent to me in September, 1937". A carbon, with no variants, is among the Tandy papers (BL).

An earlier version of the final stanza appeared in TSE's letter to Bonamy Dobrée, 11 July 1934 (following the first five lines of *Pollicle Dogs and Jellicle Cats*, below added asterisks):

> I have teeth, which are False and quite Beautiful,
> And a Wigg with an Elegant Queue;

> And in closing I send my most dutiful
> Respects to your Lady and You.

These lines appeared again at the end of a letter to Sally Cobden-Sanderson, 6 Oct 1934 (with "Consort &" *for* "Lady and", and with "& Quite ··· Closing ··· Most Dutifull").

Dedication] *not ts1*   **To**] *to ts2*

   3, *as also* 7 **the O'Possum**] Uncle Possum *ts1, ts2*

   6 **summer is seen**] summer's about *ts1, ts2*

   9 **appears**] is drest *ts1, ts2*

   14 **abominates**] objects to both *ts1, ts2*

   17 **He's inclined**] He is apt *ts1*

   24 **peculiar**] important *ts1, ts2*

   25–28] *not ts1* ‖ *following last line as a* P.S. (*probably through oversight*) *Hayward's sheaf*

   27] But he likes to afford such sartorial *ts2*

   29–32] *not ts1, ts2*

   33 **He's**] VIZ. *ts1*

   35 **not at all**] straight and not *ts1, ts2*

   36 **would not**] wouldn't *ts1, ts2*   **were it not**] but that it's *ts1, ts2*

   39 **rather**] small and *ts1, ts2*

   40 **always**] very *ts1, ts2*

   42 **withdraws in alarm**] will quickly retire *ts1* ‖ will shyly retire *ts2*

   44 **When pursued by**] Imitating *ts1, ts2*

   45–48] *after* 52 *ts1*

   46 **compelling**] uncertain *ts1, ts2*

   47] Which distinguishes it from the booming *ts1, ts2*   **can not**] cannot *Hayward's sheaf, Texas proof* 1st *reading*

   48 **or cry of the**] the raven or *ts1* ‖ the raven, or *ts2*

   50 **saturnine**] casual *ts1, ts2*

   54 **wig**] wigg *ts1, ts2*

   55 **desires to convey**] asks me to send *ts1* ‖ he asks to convey *ts2*

   56 **family**] fambly *ts1, ts2*

after 56] (Signed) | THE MAN IN WHITE SPATS. *ts1 only*

[*An Answer to the Foregoing Poem by Geoffrey Faber*]

ms1 (Faber archive): fair copy retained by Geoffrey Faber, with, at foot: "Addressed to the Rev. Uncle Possum by his unworthy coadjutator, Father Faber (who, alas!, will be unable to be present.) Sept. 15th 1937" (Faber archive).

Hayward's sheaf (King's): Hayward has typed at head "Copy of Geoffrey Faber's Sonnet, sent to me by T. S. Eliot."

6 **creeper**] *ms1, Hayward in revise proof* ‖ creepers *Noctes*

9 ^ 10] *line space ms1*

The O'Possum Strikes Back

ts1: ribbon copy sent to Geoffrey Faber (Faber archive).

Hayward's sheaf (King's): Hayward has typed at head "Copy of Verses by T. S. Eliot sent to me by the author. Sept. 1937".

Title ^ 1 **Dedication**] To Geoffrey Faber Esqre. *Hayward's sheaf only*

4] *tss have a footnote:*

> E.G. presuming poets to be taken down, Sir,
> Or morning coffee with our Mrs. Trouncer.

26 **burses**] bursers *Texas proof 1ˢᵗ reading*

The Whale and the Elephant: A Fable

ts1 (Faber archive): carbon of an early version, sent to Geoffrey Faber, probably on 1 Oct 1937. Subscribed "Anon."

Hayward's sheaf (King's): ribbon copy of a retitled version, sent to Hayward also probably on 1 Oct 1937.

Title] AN EPISTLE *ts1* ‖ THE WHALE AND THE ELEPHANT: *A FABLE Hayward's sheaf*

Dedication] To the *Learned* and *Ingenious* DR. MORLEY. *ts1, Hayward's sheaf* ‖ *all italic with lower case "l" and "i" Noctes*

1 **at**] of *ts1*

5 **at**] of *ts1*

9–10] *not tss (see notes)*

12 *jungle* **home,**] jungle home *ts1*

16] Is driv'n about by Tide and Wind; *ts1* ‖ Is driven about by *tide* and *wind*; *Hayward's sheaf 1ˢᵗ reading*

23 **might *Whales* perhaps**] might even *Whales ts1*

26] And stand at last upon their feet? *ts1*   ***feet**?] feet Texas proof 1ˢᵗ reading* ‖ *feet? Texas proof*

27 **'em**] them *ts1*

Ode to a Roman Coot

ts1 (Faber archive): single leaf from Geoffrey Faber's collection, with typed sidenotes at 9 and 34 (see notes).

Hayward's sheaf (King's): carbon of *ts1* before the addition of the sidenote at 9. Otherwise as *ts1*.

Author description] *not tss*

4 **Menninger**] *this ed.* ‖ Meninger *previous texts (see note)*

5 **happy lot**] goofy lot, *tss*

7 **light-headed zany**] light-hearted songster *tss*

8, *as also* 10] *indented tss*

9 **Frognal**] Golders Green *tss*   **or of villas**] and loonies *tss*

18, *as also* 20] *indented tss*

18 **Turning**] Tuning *tss*

19 **(By]** By *tss*   **centripetal)]** centripetal *tss*

22 **populations**] generations *tss*

27] *before 25 tss*

29 **from Galloway to Hants,**] in Galloway or Hants— *tss*

31, *as also* 33] *indented tss*   **oft-times**] often *tss*

32 **Charmed the loud**] Charm'd noisy *tss*

33 **th'attendants**] the attendant *tss*   **Bath**] bath *tss*

34 **William,**] William! *tss*   **give;]** give *tss*

35 **Nature live:**] nature live. *tss* ‖ nature live: *Texas proof*

41 **coothlessness**] couthlessness *tss*

42 ^ 43] *new page so line spacing indeterminate Noctes*

43 **angel! not so far as France;**] Angel! between Hants and France: *tss*

44 **to**] toward *tss*

47 **whale**] Whale *tss*

48 **Curl'd on the Bottome**] Close to the bottom *tss*

[Nobody knows how I feel about you by Geoffrey Faber]

ts1 (Faber archive): Geoffrey Faber's retained carbon.

2, *as also* 7 **you've**] you *ts1 final reading*

4, *as also* 6 **And**] An' *Hayward in revise proof*

12 **ideas**] idea *ts1*

13 **get**] git *ts1 final reading*

19 **coming**] comin' *ts1 final reading, Hayward in revise proof*

20 **some of**] *del ts1, Hayward in revise proof*

23 **you**] your *ts1, Hayward in revise proof*

Three Sonnets

ts1 (Faber archive): ribbon copy, attributed *"Anon."* at foot; first carbon, sent to Hayward (King's); second carbon, sent to Frank Morley (Berg). The sonnets are numbered with roman numerals (as, for convenience, below).

Dedication] To G. C. Faber Esqre., of *Oakhill ts1*

[I]

1 **did**] didst *ts1 1ˢᵗ reading*

4 **Ruling**] Who ruled *ts1*

9 **Harlem**] Haarlem *ts1*

11, *as also* 14] *no indent ts1*

12 **declines**] proceeds *ts1*

14] To noon; and keeps on all the afternoon. *ts1*

[II]

1 **martial**] soldier's *ts1*

2 **Thee the**] The *Texas proof 1ˢᵗ reading*

5 **spotless**] virtuous *ts1*

11, *as also* 14] *no indent ts1*

11 **the barbaric**] tapping of the *ts1*

12 **sting,**] sting? *ts1*

14 **And**] Or *ts1*   **negro**] negroid *ts1*   **tone?**] tone. *ts1*

[III]

1 **FABER!**] FABER!!! *ts1*   **'twas not least,**] not the least *ts1*

2] Was, that thou oftentimes didst twist the tail *ts1*

3 **basking whale**] active whale, *ts1*

5 **trophies for**] glories of *ts1*

9 **glories**] grandeur *ts1*

11, *as also* 14] *no indent ts1*

12 **Enchanted**] Corrupted *ts1*

13 **And,**] Now *ts1*

14 **Expectoratest**] Expectorating *ts1*   **spittoon.**] spittoon! *Texas proof emendation*

Vers pour la Foulque

ts1 (Faber archive): ribbon copy, with ms corrections of a version of the first eight stanzas.

Hayward's sheaf (King's): ribbon copy, with ms corrections, of all nine stanzas; together with uncorrected carbon. Alternate lines indented.

Subtitle] not *ts1* ‖ *Feuillet d'album. à Laurent Tailhade, le maitre Hayward's sheaf 1*[st] *reading*

5] Tu vois bien, que c'est bien grotesque *tss* (*with terminal comma Texas proof*)

6 **ternes?**] ternes; *tss*

8] Et point n'est lieu moins pittoresque. *Hayward's sheaf 1*[st] *reading* ‖ Point n'est endroit moins pittoresque. *Hayward's sheaf 2*[nd] *reading*

9 **grince**] se grince *ts1, Texas proof 1*[st] *reading*   **des**] les *tss, Texas proof 1*[st] *reading*

12] Tu vois, ce n'est alléchant. *ts1*

13 **pays**] quartier *Hayward's sheaf*   **bambochades,**] bambochades! *tss*

16 **En attendant**] Solicitant *Hayward's sheaf*

17] Peu d'êtres vivants qui se remuent. *Hayward's sheaf*

18] Ce n'est pas un endroit des plus gais— *ts1*

21 **derrière une**] dans le cadre d'une *Hayward's sheaf*

22 **Où s'étale un vase de**] Et derrière des *Hayward's sheaf*   **un**] une *ts1 1*[st] *reading*

24 **l'être**] c'est l'etre *Hayward's sheaf 1*[st] *reading* ‖ C'est l'être *Hayward's sheaf 2*[nd] *reading*

25-29] *typed as three lines instead of four Hayward's sheaf 1*[st] *reading, all del*

30 **filer droit jusqu'à**] diriger nos pas *ts1* ‖ marcher droit jusqu' à *Hayward's sheaf*

31] Vers les jardins de chez Bina; *ts1*

32 **chétifs**] chetifs *Hayward's sheaf, Texas proof*

33-36] *not ts1* ‖ *bracketed by TSE in pencil with the comment "Perhaps best omitted." Hayward's sheaf*

34] De chier sur le seuil. Sonnez! *Hayward's sheaf* [To crap on the doorstep. Ring the bell!]

Translation into English of "Verses for the Coot"

ts1 (Faber archive): ribbon copy of the variant text (which misspells "syphilitic" with *-ll-*) given below; a carbon of this sent to Hayward (King's) has TSE's pencilled emendation from "squint" to "strabismus".

Let us proceed to make a walk, if you give your consentment. We are going to aim our steps in the direction of Bina's garden. Let us search No. 22. You notice beyond doubt, that this landscape with the tarnished herbaceous borders is queer enough. It is a land of trash. Nothing could be less Picturesque. Even the Post-man grinds his teeth and barbarises his face when he traverses this squinting quarter, which is one of the less attractive sub-urbs. It is a quarter of bad and low jokes! in which, from Willett porticoes, rude skivvies keep an eye on you, hoping that you will pay court to them. There is very little life about! it is a waste and desolate piece of ground. One observes syphilitic cats, and even now and then a superannuated prostitute. But, in the frame of a huge window and behind some water-lilies: listen! there are rare whispers and lunatic laughter. It is it. It is the disgusting creature. It is the vesperal spider with complex eyes and deadly poison, who, with an immodest look, makes to us a gesture which is cancelled by his ~~squint~~ strabismus. Let us proceed to take a walk, if you give your consentment. We are going to walk straight at these picayune gardens of Bina. Let us search No. 22.

Abschied zur Bina

Hayward's sheaf (King's): dated on receipt by Hayward "31 Jan 1939". A carbon sent to Geoffrey Faber (Faber archive) has the same inked emendations by TSE, but not those in pencil to 71 and 75.

PS and *PPS*: typed Faber postcards from TSE each with four lines (29–33 and 33–36). Respectively headed "P.S." and "P.P.S.", both cards are postmarked 3 Feb 1939 (King's). An undated letter to Hayward follows in the bound volume "Essays, Addresses and Verses":

> I thought of putting in a stanza something like this:
>
> > Der Walfisch spielte frevelhaft
> > (Ein Prosenschwergewichter)
> > Poetisch quakt' de Wasserhuhn —
> > Der Elefant sprach schlichter.
>
> But on the whole perhaps it breaks the frame to introduce the fauna for the sake of the canon. I have no copy of the text. You will give me your opinion.
>
> [The whale played wickedly | (A prose heavywieght) | The coot croaked poetic-ally— | The elephant spoke more plainly.]

ts2 (Houghton): sent to Henry Eliot, 7 Feb 1939: "I may also have to send you a copy of some poems privately printed, 'As were lately exchang'd between several of the choicest wits' to which I contributed—the printing was an afterthought. I enclose for your amusement a copy of one of mine, written in relation to one of the wits, John Hayward, having lately moved from Bina Gardens Kensington to Chelsea."

The text follows that of *Noctes* as emended by Hayward in copy no. 1, although some of his emendations, judged inessential, have been undone, and some other corrections of spelling, agreement and orthography have been introduced.

Title] FESTSCHRIFTGESCHENCK | Zum Geburtstag Jonny Heywald | 2 Februar, 1939 *Hayward's sheaf* ‖ Abschied von Binagarten *ts2* (*"von" underlined with "Changed to* zur." *in Henry Eliot's hand*)

3 der] Der *Hayward's sheaf 1ˢᵗ reading*

5 schönen] Schönen *Hayward's sheaf 1ˢᵗ reading*　　Binagarten,] Binagarten *Hayward's sheaf 1ˢᵗ reading, ts2*

6 **In der frechen**] Im frecher *Hayward's sheaf* ‖ In der frecher *ts2*

7 **trafen sich**] *Hayward in copy no. 1* ‖ troffen die *Hayward's sheaf* ‖ troffen sich *ts2, Noctes*　　**Gesellen**] die Gesellen *Hayward's sheaf*

9 **Zu**] *this ed.* ‖ Zum *tss, Noctes* ‖ Nach *Hayward in copy no. 1*　　**zweiundzwanzig**] zweiund zwanzig *Hayward's sheaf*

13 **Arten Leute—**] *Hayward in copy no. 1* ‖ Arte Leute, *tss* ‖ Arte Leuten— *Noctes*

17–20] *not Hayward's sheaf*

17, *as also* 59 **manchmal**] *Hayward in copy no. 1* ‖ manchmals *tss, Noctes*

19 **Bei**] *Hayward in copy no. 1* ‖ Beim *ts2, Noctes*

21 **trafen sich**] *Hayward in copy no. 1* ‖ troffen sich *tss, Noctes*

22 **Richter**] Richter, *Hayward's sheaf*

23 **Advokat**] Advocat *Hayward's sheaf 1ˢᵗ reading*

24 **Schauspieler**] Schauspierler *Texas proof 1ˢᵗ reading*

27 **den**] *Hayward in copy no. 1* ‖ der *tss, Noctes*

28 **nicht**] nivht *Hayward's sheaf 1ˢᵗ reading*

29–32] *supplied by PPS* ‖ *not Hayward's sheaf*

30 **ass,**] ass; *ts2*

31 **Betjeman**] Betjemann *PS* ‖ Betjeman, *ts2*

33–36] *supplied by PPS* ‖ *not Hayward's sheaf*

33 **Witwen-Vogel**] *this ed.* ‖ Witwe-Vogel, *PPS, ts2* ‖ Witwen Vogel *Hayward in copy no. 1*

35 **manchmal**] *Hayward in copy no. 1* ‖ jemals *ts2, Noctes*

39 **Gelache**] Gelächter *Hayward in copy no. 1*

40] Bis zum hellen Morgenlicht, *Hayward in copy no. 1*　　**helles**] *this ed.* ‖ helle *tss, Noctes*

41 **Langweile,**] Langweile *Hayward's sheaf*

43 **Zigarett**] *this ed.* ‖ Zigarrett *tss, Noctes*

45–48] *not Hayward's sheaf*

49 **höheren**] *Hayward in copy no. 1* ‖ höhere *tss, Noctes*

51 **seidenen**] *tss* ‖ siedene *Texas proof 1ˢᵗ reading, BL and Bodleian proofs* ‖ seidene *TSE in BL proof, Hayward in copy no. 1* ‖ siedenen *Texas proof, Noctes*　　**Strümpfen**] *Hayward in copy no. 1* ‖ Strumpfen *tss, Noctes*

52 **Geruch;**] Geruch. *Hayward's sheaf*

53 **elegantsten**] *Hayward in copy no. 1* ‖ elegantste *tss, Noctes*

54 **gern:**] gern, *Hayward's sheaf*

55 **Schlanksten**] *Hayward in copy no. 1* ‖ Schlankste *tss, Noctes*   **Schönsten**] *Hayward in copy no. 1* ‖ Schönste *tss, Noctes*

58 **Korrekt**] *Hayward in copy no. 1* ‖ Korret *Hayward's sheaf 1st reading* ‖ Korrect *Hayward's sheaf 2nd reading, ts2, Noctes*

60 **anonymer**] *Hayward in copy no. 1* ‖ anonyme *tss, Noctes*

61 **Jenny**] Jenny, *Hayward's sheaf*

62 **verwaltet**] aufführte *Hayward's sheaf*

66 **Kamerun—**] Kamerun: *Hayward's sheaf*

67 **Regenwetter,**] Regenwetter *tss*

68 **Sie trugen**] Trugen sie *Hayward in copy no. 1*

69 **Zu**] *this ed.* ‖ Zum *tss, Noctes* ‖ Nach *Hayward in copy no. 1*

71 **Zuströmt nicht mehr Adel**] *this ed.* ‖ Kommen die Adel jetzt nicht mehr— *Hayward's sheaf 1st reading* ‖ Kommen die Adel nimmer mehr— *Hayward's sheaf 2nd reading* ‖ Zuströmen kein mehr Adel, *ts2*

74 **mehr;**] mehr: *Hayward's sheaf*

75] *indent ts2 (error)*   **Da sieht man nur**] schwarzgekleidete *Hayward's sheaf 2nd reading*   **Kobolde**] *Hayward in copy no. 1* ‖ Prelaten *Hayward's sheaf 1st reading* ‖ Kobolden, *Hayward's sheaf 2nd reading* ‖ Kobolden *ts2, Noctes*

76 **kriechen**] gehen *Hayward's sheaf*   **her**] her; *Hayward's sheaf*

78 **vorbei.**] vorbei; *Hayward's sheaf*

79 **allein,**] allein— *Hayward's sheaf* ‖ allein *ts2*

80 **Mir**] Und *tss 1st reading*   **das**] mein *Hayward's sheaf*

Improper Rhymes

"In attempting to be amusing he sometimes has recourse, as other men than harried playwrights have been known to do, to the lowest bawdiness, which leaves us less with a sense of repugnance for the man who could write it than with a sense of pity for the man who could think of nothing better." *Thomas Heywood* (1931)

"The only disinfectant which makes either blasphemy or obscenity sufferable is the sense of humour: the indecent that is funny may be the legitimate source of innocent merriment, while the absence of humour reveals it as purely disgusting." *After Strange Gods*

In 1904, the *Smith Academy Record* published TSE's *A Fable for Feasters*, a burlesque, in the Regency manner, on monastery life ("And flogged his mates 'till they grew good and friarly"). Also in 1904, in Gloucester, Massachusetts, TSE's mother Charlotte Eliot engaged an old mariner to teach her two sons to sail. The following summer, when TSE was sixteen, his school magazine printed two of his stories. *A Tale of a Whale* (1905) tells how the "Parallel Opipedon" (= "O pipe down") became becalmed off Tanzatatapoo Island, where "the captain was pacing the quarter-deck, fanning himself. The watch were amusing themselves holystoning the deck, while the rest of the crew were eating ice-cream in the fore chains". Harpooning a whale, and shipwreck, follow. *The Man Who Was King* (1905) tells of a sea-dog shipwrecked on the island of Matahiva, where he finds "a little mob of men beating bhghons (a sort of cross between tin pan and gong) and chanting monotonously". Instead of being eaten by the natives, he is made king, and enjoys a life of "fishing, bathing, feasting, and getting drunk on wine made of the madu-nut", before setting out again, for Tahiti. "Not long after the captain was there, the French got hold of it and built a post there. They educated the natives to wear clothes on Sunday and go to church, so that now they are quite civilized and uninteresting."

The year after TSE's death, Bonamy Dobrée set the Bolo and Columbo verses within "an elaborated joke, nurtured through years ··· about some primitive people called the Bolovians, who wore bowler hats, and had square wheels to their chariots. This invention he apparently began to toy with when he was at Harvard, there figuring King Bolo and his Queen. He did not tell me much about those characters—though he sent me a drawing of them—but I was given portions of a Bolovian Epic (not always very decorous) and something about their religion. This latter was in part an amiable satire on the way people, anthropologists especially, talk about the religion of others" (*Dobrée*).

Among suggestions as to the name Bolo, two of the most plausible are those of *Southam* and *Crawford*. Southam (in his notes to *A Cooking Egg* 28): "King Shamba Bolongongo (known today as Shyaam aMbul aNgoong) (died *c.* 1628), ruler of the Kuba tribes, legendary for the number of widows and children he left". Southam adds that Eliot could have come across his name in *Notes ethnographiques* (1911) by Emil Torday, who had presented a wooden figure of Bolo to the British Museum.

(TSE might also have seen a fetish figure in Bolobo, Upper Congo, illustrated and described in *Folk-Lore* Sept 1909. See note to title of *The Waste Land* I: *The Burial of the Dead*.) Alternatively, *Crawford* 83: "His name, as Eliot knew from fine art classes, meant 'ground for gilding'", citing TSE's notes on Edward Waldo Forbes's Harvard course Fine Arts 20b (see note to *Mr. Eliot's Sunday Morning Service* 10, "gesso ground"). TSE to Conrad Aiken, 19 July 1914, had featured a table, BLESS and BLAST, imitating the lists in Wyndham Lewis's *Blast* 1 (June). BLESS began with Columbo and Bolo and included the Chaplain. BLAST included the Bosun, the Cook and Prof. Dr. Krapp.

Lewis to Pound [Jan 1915]: "Eliot has sent me Bullshit ⁊ the Ballad for Big Louise [*The Triumph of Bullshit* and *Ballade pour la grosse Lulu*]. They are excellent bits of scholarly ribaldry. I am longing to print them in *Blast*; but stick to my naif determination to have no 'Words ending in -Uck, -Unt, and -Ugger'", *Pound/Lewis* ed. Timothy Materer (1985). (These particular words do not appear in either of the poems, for which see "Uncollected Poems".) TSE to Pound, 2 Feb [1915]:

> I have corresponded with Lewis, but his puritanical principles seem to bar my way to Publicity. I fear that King Bolo and his Big Black Kween will never burst into print. I understand that Priapism, Narcissism etc. are not approved of, and even so innocent a rhyme as
>
> > ... pulled her stockings off
> > With a frightful cry of "Hauptbahnhof!!"
>
> is considered decadent.

("central station", German.) Pound to Harriet Monroe, 28 June 1915: "If you think he lacks vigour merely because he happens to have portrayed Mr Prufrock the unvigorous, vous vous trompez. His poem of Christopher Columbus is vigorous, and male, not to say coarse. I think however he may produce something both modest and virile before the end of the chapter."

The printing and censorship of books later became a professional concern for TSE. To Leonard Woolf, 18 Mar 1932: "We had to have a directors' meeting of over three quarters of an hour a couple of days ago to deal with fuck and bugger in a book of verse."

TSE to James Joyce, 21 May 1921:

> I am delighted to hear that even a limited and very expensive edition [of *Ulysses*] is to appear. Has it been properly circularised in England? If not, I might supply a few names. I wish that Miss Beach would bring out a limited edition of my epic ballad on the life of Christopher Columbus and his friend King Bolo, but
>
> > Bolo's big black bastard queen
> > Was *so* obscene
> > She shocked the folk of Golder's Green.

Pound to TSE [28? Jan 1922]: "You can forward the Bolo to Joyce if you think it wont unhinge his somewhat sabbatarian mind. On the hole he might be saved the shock, shaved the sock."

Pound to TSE, 29 Aug 1922: "your admirer [John Peale] Bishop thinks of collecting Bawdy Ballads, of War and Peace. (the real folk litterchure), including 'She Was Pore but she wuz honest' and others that ought n't be left longer to the incertitude of verbal tradition."

TSE'S proposals for an "OPEN WIRELESS VAUDEVILLE", sent to Dobrée on 30 Dec 1929 (*Letters 4*), included: "*T. S. Eliot* | The Bellowing Baritone | With Bolovian Ballads | 'The Blue Baboon'."

To Clive Bell, 3 Jan 1941: "I may even take in hand the long neglected task of putting in order the epical ballad on the life of Chris Columbo (the famous Portuguese navigator) and his friends King Bolo and his Big Black Queen."

To Dobrée, 6 Aug 1941, signing off: "So meanwhile, as the Bolovians used to say (for their happy island has now disappeared): 'wux-ho!'"

On the verso of an undated wedding announcement card sent to Aiken in 1957: "I am, I may tell you, intensely happy, except for the fact that Valerie wants to learn about King Bolo. That's your fault. So far, I have withstood all her appeals to me to burst into Bolovian song." Valerie Eliot, *TLS* 17 Feb 1984: "It is not true, as William Baker asserts (Letters, February 10), that T. S. Eliot was still writing his 'King Bolo' limericks 'in the late 1950s'. Almost all were written during his Harvard days and none later than 1916." When TSE was asked by Donald Hall, "Do you write anything now in the vein of *Old Possum's Book of Practical Cats* or *King Bolo*?" he replied: "Those things do come from time to time ··· Oh, yes, one wants to keep one's hand in you know, in every type of poem, serious and frivolous and proper and improper. One doesn't want to lose one's skill", *Paris Review* (1959).

Valerie Eliot to Aiken, 23 Nov 1964, acknowledging a copy of *A Seizure of Limericks* (1964): "Tom was so pleased to receive your limericks and we laugh over them together." In an obituary for *Life*, 15 Jan 1965, Aiken wrote: "I'm the official custodian of his King Bolo poems, which are all quatrains or octets about an imaginary monarch and his queen, but he neglected to send the bulk of them to me."

Given first here are the verses that figure within letters (to Aiken, Pound and Dobrée, respectively) and some context to make clear what kind of writing this is. Second, *The Columbiad* partly published in *March Hare* (being from the Notebook) and now supplemented with other "stanxos" and "stanzos" from *Valerie's Own Book* and elsewhere. Third, miscellaneous ribald rhymes. Some verses that were recycled have here been printed only once. A sense of the changes involved is given by comparing the verses sent to Bonamy Dobrée as *The Catalogue of Ships* (15 Aug 1927) and *Deipnosophistic* (29 Sept 1927) with *The Columbiad* st. 19 and st. 43.

In Letters to Conrad Aiken

To Aiken, 19 July 1914:

I've written some *stuff*—about fifty lines, but I find it shamefully laboured, and am belabouring it more. If I can improve it at all I will send it you. [On 25 July he sent *O little voices of the throats of men* and *The Love Song of St Sebastian*.] If you write me Poste Restante I shall get it; and if you are in the country (or just off for the country) you must of course leave my luggage out of consideration. It is *not* essential to me. If you are not in the country or going to the country you might wait a few days, and I will send you an address. Meanwhile I will send you this to go to sleep on:

> Now while Columbo and his men
> Were drinking ice cream soda
> In burst King Bolo's big black queen
> That famous old breech l[oader].
> Just then they rang the bell for lunch
> And served up—Fried Hyenas;
> And Columbo said "Will you take tail?
> Or just a bit of p[enis]?"

The bracketed portions we owe to the restorations of the editor, Prof. Dr. Hasenpfeffer (Halle), with the assistance of his two inseparable friends, Dr. Hans Frigger (the celebrated poet) and Herr Schnitzel (aus Wien). How much we owe to the hardwon intuition of this truly great scholar! The editor also justly observes: "There seems to be a *double entendre* about the last two lines, but the fine flavour of the jest has not survived the centuries".—Yet we hope that such genius as his may penetrate even this enigma. Was it really the custom to drink ice-cream soda just before lunch? Prof. Dr. Hasenpfeffer insists that it was. Prof. Dr. Krapp (Jena) believes that the phrase is euphemistic, and that they were really drinking—SEIDLIDZ POWDER. See Krapp: STREITSCHRIFT GEGEN HASENPFEFFER I.xvii §367, also Hasenpfeffer: POLEMISCHES GEGEN KRAPP I–II. 368ff. 490ff.

————

To Aiken, 30 Sept [1914]:

My war poem, for the $100 prize, entitled

UP BOYS AND AT 'EM!

Adapted to the tune of *C. Columbo lived in Spain* and within the compass of the average male or female voice:

> *Now* while our heroes were at sea
> They pass'd a German warship.
> The captain pac'd the quarterdeck
> Parading in his corset.
> What ho! they cry'd, we'll sink your ship!
> And so they up and sink'd her.
> But the cabin boy was sav'd alive
> And bugger'd, in the sphincter.

The poem was declined by several musical publishers on the ground that it paid too great a tribute to the charms of German youth to be acceptable to the English public. I acknowledg'd the force of the objection, but replied that it was only to be regarded as a punitive measure, and to show the readiness and devotion to duty of the British seaman.

Title **Up Boys and at 'Em!**: although Wellington denied the attribution to him, *Up Guards and at them!* became current after Waterloo. Kipling: "'Ye-es. Same old catchwords—same old training. "Shoulder to shoulder"—"up, boys, and at 'em!"'" *The Outsider* (1900).

we'll sink your ship!: more than a dozen warships, enemy and allied, were lost in the first two months of the Great War.

———

To Aiken, 10 Jan 1916:

I owe you many apologies, but I have been most frightfully busy. The news is that I am to be at Highgate School, near town, next term, that I am starting to rewrite my thesis, that my wife has been very ill, that I have been taken up with the worries of finance and Vivien's health, that my friend Jean Verdenal has been killed, that nothing has been seen of [Martin] Armstrong, who is now a captain in Kitchener's army, that compulsion is coming in, that my putative publisher will probably be conscripted, that we are very blue about the war, that living is going up, and that

> King Bolo's big black bassturd kween
> That airy fairy hairy un
> She led the dance on Golder's green
> With Cardinal Bessarion.

I am *keen* about rhymes in –een:

> King Bolo's big black bassturd kween
> Her taste was kalm ❧ klassic
> And as for anything obscene
> She said it made her ass sick.

As for literature, have you seen our Katholick Anthology? (Elk. Matthews). It has not done very well, in spite of the name of Yeats. I have written nothing lately, too much absorbed by practical worries. Your idea of a kwaterly is very attractive but

> King Bolo's big black bassturd kween
> Was awf'ly sweet ❧ pure
> She interrupted prayers one day
> With a shout of Pig's Manure.

But I repeat that

> K. B. b. b. b. k.
> Was awfly sweet ❧ pure
> She said "I don't know what you mean!"
> When the chaplain* whistled to her

* Charles, the Chaplain.

But about the P[oetry] *Journal*, you see I would be thrown out of *Poetry* if I wrote for that, and *Poetry pays*—which is everything to me.

That airy fairy hairy un: "She was a beau-ti-ful Bul-ga-ri-an, | Oh! Such a light and fair-y air-y 'un", from *The Maid of Phillipopolis* (*Popular College Songs* ed. Lockwood Honoré, 1891, 30–31) (*Schuchard* 235).

Cardinal Bessarion: Roman Cardinal of Greek origin who contributed to the 15th-century revival of letters.

Elk. Matthews: the publisher Elkin Mathews.

Charles, the Chaplain: beginning in Feb 1914, Charlie Chaplin had made some fifty short films in two years. "Charlie Chaplin is not English, or American, but a universal figure, feeding the idealism of hungry millions in Czecho-Slovakia and Peru", *The Romantic Englishman, the Comic Spirit, and the Function of Criticism* (1921). "The egregious merit of Chaplin is that he has escaped in his own way from the realism of the cinema and invented a *rhythm*", *Dramatis Personæ* (1923). For TSE photographed with "Charlie Chaplin moustache" by E. McKnight Kauffer, see *Letters 4* following 410. For Groucho Marx and Charlie Chaplin, see *Dearest Mr. Groucho Marx* 28.

In Letters to Ezra Pound

To Pound, 31 Oct 1917:

I have been invited by female VANDERVELDE to contribute to a reading of pOETS: big wigs, OSWALD and EDITH Shitwell, Graves (query, George?) Nichols, and OTHERS. Shall I oblige them with our old friend COLUMBO? or Bolo, since famous?

> One day Columbo went below
> To see the ship's physician:
> "It's this way, doc" he said said he
> I just cant stop a-pissin' . . .

or

> King Bolo's big black kukquheen
> Was fresh as ocean breezes.
> She burst aboard Columbo's ship
> With a cry of gentle Jesus.

Vandervelde · · · a reading: almost certainly the invitation from Sibyl Colefax to read at her house in Onslow Square on 12 Dec 1917. See note to *A Cooking Egg* 14, Sir Alfred Mond, and headnote to *The Hippopotamus.*

gentle Jesus: Charles Wesley: "Gentle Jesus, meek and mild" (hymn).

———

To Pound, 30 Aug 1922:

99% of the people who "appreciate" what one writes are undisguis-able shits and that's that. Your notes, epistolary, telegraphic, etc. are cordially appreciated and after I have corrected the spelling will in due

time appear and in due time be paid for. With most grateful thanks
yours always sincerely, faithfully. I received a letter from your friend
Watson most amiable in tone

> For below a voice did answer, sweet in its youthful tone,
> The sea-dog with difficulty descended, for he had a manly bone.
>   (From *The Fall of Admiral Barry*).

offering $150 for the "Waste Land" · · ·

More presently.

> King Bolo's big black basstart kuwheen,
>   That plastic & elastic one,
> Would frisk it on the village green,
>   Enjoying her fantastikon.

T.

The Fall of Admiral Barry: Rear-Admiral Edward B. Barry became commander of the
US Pacific fleet, 2nd Division in 1899. His flagship, the *West Virginia*, docked in
Manila Harbour, in 1909. After 45 years' service he was forced to resign in 1911
after an alleged liaison with a cabin boy.

plastic & elastic: elastic deformation returns to its original shape, plastic defor-
mation to its deformed shape.

fantastikon: OED "fantastico": "*Obs.* An absurd and irrational person." *Romeo
and Juliet* II iv: "The pox of such antique lisping affecting fantasticoes [*Q1*;
phantacies *F*] · · · a very good whore".

––––––––

TSE sent Pound more of this ballad on 22 Oct 1922:

> "In old Manila harbour, the Yankee wardogs lay,
> "The stars & stripes streamed overhead, & the band began to play;
> "The band struck up the strains of the old Salvation Rag,
> And from the ~~quarter~~ mizzentop there flew REAR ADMIRAL
>   BARRY'S flag."

Oser 24: "Though Mrs. Eliot doesn't identify the author of *The Fall of Admiral Barry*
in her edition of her husband's letters, Donald Gallup, who did the research on the
ballad for Mrs. Eliot, finds 'justification for saying that the verses are Eliot's' (Donald
Gallup, conversation with the author, September 15, 1993). Marie Borroff has since

pointed out to me that Eliot's chief source was Tennyson's *The Revenge*." Tennyson: "At Flores in the Azores Sir Richard Grenville lay, | And a pinnace, like a fluttered bird, came flying from far away", *The Revenge: A Ballad of the Fleet* 1–2.

Yankee wardogs: among the Tandy papers (BL) is a version of Major Innes Randolph's *Good Ol' Rebel Soldier* ("I'm a reconstructed rebel") with a note at foot: "Typed by TSE in Room 510 at Broadcasting House, 24 June 1938". The last verse reads: "I hate the Yankee Nation | And everything they do; | I hate the Declaration | Of Independence too. | I hate the Yankee eagle | With all his scream and fuss: | BUT the lyin' theivin' Yankee— | I hate him WUSS AND WUSS." See headnote to *The Dry Salvages*, 2. "THE RIVER IS WITHIN US, THE SEA IS ALL ABOUT US".

————

TSE to Pound, 3 Sept 1923, during the gestation of *Sweeney Agonistes* (see headnote there, 2. ARISTOPHANES):

have mapt out Aristophanic comedy, but must devote study to phallic songs, also agons.

> King Bolo's big black basstart queen
>   Was awfly bright & cheerful;
> Well fitted for a monarch's bride
>   But she wasnt always keerful.
> Ah yes King Bolo's big black queen
>   Was not above suspicion;
> We wish that such was not the case—
>   But whats the use of wishin?

>   The dancers on the village green
>   They breathed light tales of Bolo's queen

> The ladies of King Bolo's court
>   They gossiped with each other
> They said "King Bolo's big black queen
>   Will soon become a mother"
> They said "an embryonic prince
>   Is hidden in her tumbo;
> His prick is long his balls are strong
>   And his name is Boloumbo".

Basstart is the feminine form of bassturd. Brock is a bassturd.

King Bolo's · · · queen | Was not above suspicion: "Caesar's wife must be above suspicion" (trad., based on Plutarch's Life of Julius Caesar).

Brock: OED 1: "A badger: a name, in later times, associated especially with the epithet *stinking*." 2: "A stinking or dirty fellow; one who is given to 'dirty tricks', a 'skunk'." TSE reviewed Arthur Clutton-Brock's *The Ultimate Belief* in *International Journal of Ethics* Oct 1916, and in this letter to Pound he writes of "your friend Clutton Brock, who is the dirtiest shit with the worst mind in London".

———

To Pound, Holy Innocents' Day [28 Dec] 1934:

Podesta whats this rumour about me bain COARSE you know better than that Podesta mirthful I am truthful I am drunken I am and when I get with those Harvard professors hilarious I sometimes may be but no never Coarse thats just your joke or somebody gettin a rise out of You: That said Columbo was a Joke / But I call it crude & coarse / Such conversation I have heard / From the lips of Maltese whores etc. etc. so heres yours for better breaks,

TP

Podesta: local governor or official in Italy, where Pound was then resident.

———

To Pound, 17 Jan 1935:

ROAR Podesta ROAR, like any efficient druid, shanachie or scop:
And if you hear anyone else talking, tell him from me that I wish him
    to stop.
ROAR Podesta ROAR, the only original Anglo-American wop.

Let us celebrate the Podesta's merits:
they say his prick has steel springs in it like a tape-measure,
So that it can be adjusted to fit any size or shape of cunt,
    thus giving the maximum of pleasure,
Thus solving completely various problems of work and of leisure.

shanachie: OED "sennachie": "In Ireland and the Scottish Highlands: One professionally occupied in the study and transmission of traditional history, genealogy, and legend". **scop:** OED: "An Old English poet or minstrel."

In Letters to Bonamy Dobrée

Having served on the Palestine front during the Great War, Dobrée met TSE in 1924. Two years later, despite discouragement from TSE (letter 11 Aug 1926), he accepted a post as professor in Cairo, where he remained until 1929 (*Dobrée*).

To Dobrée, 10 May 1927, introducing the primitive inhabitants of Bolovia:

> A notoriously lazy race. They had two Gods, named respectively Wux and Wux. They observed that the carving of Idols out of ebony was hard work; therefore they carved only one Idol. In the Forenoon, they worshipped it as Wux, from the front; in the Afternoon, they worshipped it from Behind as Wux. (Hence the Black Bottom). Those who worshipped in front were called Modernists; those who worshipped from behind were called Fundamentalists.

named respectively Wux and Wux: "WUSS AND WUSS" (worse and worse); see note to letter to Pound, 30 Aug 1922.
Black Bottom: Ma Rainey (1886–1939), "the mother of the blues", recorded *Black Bottom* in 1927.

———

To Dobrée, 22 June 1927:

> Since I Last Wrote I have much more Information about the theology of primitive Bolovians (a race of comic Neogroes wearing bowler Hats—why did they wear bowler Hats—that I will Tell you—because their Monarch wore a Top hat (they were divided into monophysites, duophysites, hecastophysites and heterophysites. (Also I have

discovered the text and tune of their National Anthem, which I have learned to Sing.)

To Dobrée, 26 July [1927]:

It appears that an unpublished poem by Miss Elizabeth Barrett has been discovered in Salamanca, suppressed from publication by her husband the flagitious Robt. Browning, which throws new light on the God Wux. The first verse (or stanzo) runs as follows:

> What was he doing, the Great God Wux?
>> Down in the weeds by the river?
> Splashing and paddling with feet of a dux
> And washing his sox with a packet of lux
> And smashing the vegetable matter that mux
>> About on the face of the river?

It is known that Wux was always depicted with duck feet (the images have perished, as the island of Bolovia sank into the sea in the year 1500, doubtless as a protest against the Renaissance, including Pater, Bernhard Berenson, Vernon Lee and Middleton Murry). But as Miss Barrett says "feet of a dux" it may be inferred that she inclined to the Duophysite or alternatively to the Duotheistic party. Four feet means two Gods. This is a serious check to my own opinions, which were that Wux or Wuxes were two Persons and one Substance, or alternatively two Substances and one Person.

What was he doing ⋯ the river?: Elizabeth Barrett Browning, *A Musical Instrument* (in *Oxf Bk of English Verse*):
> What was he doing, the great god Pan,
>> Down in the reeds by the river?
> Spreading ruin and scattering ban,
> Splashing and paddling with hoofs of a goat,
> And breaking the golden lilies afloat
>> With the dragon-fly on the river.

lux: a brand of soap powder.

Pater, Bernhard Berenson, Vernon Lee: see note to *WLComposite* 285: "Symonds—Walter Pater—Vernon Lee". Berenson had anglicised his first name to Bernard in 1914.

To Dobrée, 7 Aug [1927]:

You should now, I think, be prepared to accept the first stanzos of the Boloviad. You must not be impatient, as this great poem—only to be compared to the Odyssey and the Chansong de Roland—moves slowly. The first Stanxo is as follows (in my forthcoming edition there will be 36 pages of commentary to make this stanzo more intelligible):

> NOW Chris Columbo lived in Spain—
>   Where Doctors are not many:
> The only Doctor in his town
>   Was a Bastard Jew (named Benny).
> To Benny then Columbo went—
>   With countenance so Placid:
> And Benny filled Columbo's Prick
>   With Muriatic Acid.

You may say that this exordium—magnificent as it is—has nothing to do with Bolovia and the Bolovians. But wait. You must first work through the Catalogue of Ships, the Inventory of Sailors, the Voyage etc. before we bring C. Columbo (Able Seaman) to the western Land of Bolovia. So no more for the Present. Yours etc.

T. S. E.

The next Stanxo starts—

> Columbo and his Caravels
>   They set sail from GenOHa,
> Queen Isabella was aboard!—
>   That famous Spanish HO-AH . . .

Muriatic Acid: household cleaner.

Caravels: OED 1: "A kind of ship: variously applied at different times, and in relation to different countries", with Thomas Fuller, 1642: "The King of Spain .. sent a Caravall of adviso to the West Indies."

To Dobrée, Monday [15 Aug 1927]:

I will treat your Convalescence with literary-historical instead of Philosophico-theological matters, and introduce

THE CATALOGUE OF SHIPS

> The Flagship of Columbo's Fleet
>   Was call'd THE VIRGIN MARY;
> An able vessel fully mann'd
>   By Seamen brown & hairy.
> The other Ships came on behind—
>   The HOLY GHOST and JESUS;
> Well stock'd, to sail o'er perilous seas,
>   With Ham and Cheddar Cheeses.

THE CATALOGUE OF SHIPMATES

> The Cook who serv'd them Pork & Beans
>   Was known as Careless Cora;
> A Dame of Pure Australian Blood—
>   (With a tincture of Angora).
> She wore a Jumper short and red,
>   Which closely did her shape fit;
> And the hair that Lay along her Back
>   Was Yellow (like ripe ape-shit).

Catalogue of Shipmates to be continued through 25 stanzoes.

What, you will say, has all this to do with Bolovia? Patience. It took Chris. Columbo 3 months to reach Bolovia; can you not wait a fortnight?

Catalogue of Ships: as in *Iliad* bk II.

Flagship of Columbo's Fleet | Was call'd THE VIRGIN MARY: Columbus sailed on the *Santa María* and Spanish ships long continued to bear religious names (Donald Sommerville, personal communication).

Angora: OED "Angostura" has M. E. Braddon: "Propped up with sherry and Angostura bitters."

the hair that Lay along her Back | Was Yellow (like ripe ape-shit): Rossetti: "Her hair that lay along her back | Was yellow like ripe corn", *The Blessed Damozel* 11–12.

To Dobrée, [17 Aug 1927]:

I am like the Antient Mariner: Intuition (in the Murravian Sense) impels me to fix from time to time One Person with my Eye, and compel him to listen to Bolovian affairs; many are passed over, but One is chosen, and you are among the chosen to pass on the Gospel:

> The Wedding Guest Here Beat his Breast
> For He Heard the Loud Wuxoon.

··· I have some more Surprises for You about the Crew: including the Boatswain (Bill so-called of Barcelona) and especially the Chaplain (the Reverend Philip Skinner, known familiarly as "Prick" Skinner), he who converted the Bolovians to Hard-Shell Baptism; the Cook (Mrs. Cora Bumpus) and the Cabin-Boy (Orlando (fam. Orlo) K. Putnam).

Murravian: John Middleton Murry's *Towards a Synthesis* in the *Criterion* of June 1927 distinguished intelligence from intuition ("the faculty of apprehending a whole as a whole, and not as the sum of its parts"), and was much discussed in subsequent issues.

The Wedding Guest ··· Wuxoon: Coleridge: "The Wedding-Guest here beat his breast, | For he heard the loud bassoon", *The Rime of the Ancient Mariner* I 31–32.

To Dobrée, [Sept 1927?]:

Dear Bungamy:

The Stanxo suppressed on Friday (out of respect to Mr. Felsinger as a Loyal Son of the Stars & Stripes, and the General Pudicity of Sectarians such as Harold) is as follows:

It is called

AMERICA DISCOVER'D

> NOW when they'd been 4 months at Sea
> Columbo Slapped his Breaches.
> Let someone go Aloft, Said He;
> I'm *Sure* that I Smell Bitches!
> Just then the LOOKOUT man exclaim'd:
> He's spoken like an Oracle!
> I see a Big Black KING & QUEEN
> Approaching in a Coracle!

Of Columbo's sense of Smell, there will be more evidence Later. But you will agree that it was Tactful of me not to Recite this Stanzo in the presence of Mr. Felsinger.

Before acknowledging this Stanzo, await my EPISTLE DEDIC-ATORY to Maister Bomany Dobrée, Tutor in Culture to the Egyptians, Ethiopians and Nubians, and Envoy Extraordinary to the Court of Prester John; and my EPISTLE EXPIATORY to Maister Herbert Read.

————

To Dobrée, [Sept? 1927], *Letters 3* 666–67:

Dear Bungamy: Re C. C.'s Sense of Smell we have the Following:

> One Day Columbo & His Men
>   They Took & Went Ashore.
> Columbo Sniffed the Banyan Trees
>   And Mutter'd: *I* Smell Whore!
> And when they'd Taken Twenty Steps
>   Into the Cubian Jungle,
> They Met King Bolo's BIG BLACK QUEEN
>   A-scratching of her Bung Hole.

The foregoing is Private and Confidential.
Yours etc.
T. S. E.

Our Next Instalment will be a Description of the Columbian Sport of: Fucking the Tortoise.

THINGS YOU OUGHT TO KNOW:

What is a Wuxuar?
What is a Cuxative?

————

To Dobrée, 29 Sept [1927]:

Dear Buggamy:

I have this day of St. Michael sent you a Wire. I have No doubt that meanwhile you have thought of me as what the Bolovians, in their simple, terse and classical tongue call a "Horse's Arse" · · · My reference above to Bolovian terminology recalls a Stanxo which you may not know, viz:

DEIPNOSOPHISTIC

Now while Columbo & his Crew
   Were drinking (Scotch & Soda),
In Burst King Bolo's Big Black Queen
   (That Famous Old Breech-loader).
Just then the COOK produced the Lunch—
   A Dish of Fried Hyeneas;
And Columbo said: "Will you take Tail?
   Or just a bit of Penis?"

With reference to the Hyena, I should be very much obliged, if, on your next Excursion to the land of Prester John, you would look into the matter, and tell me, What the Hell has the Hyena to laugh at?

Also, about the famous Blue Bottom'd Babboon: Is he *really* the Aristocrat of the Simian World?

I shall shortly begin agin again my instruction in Bolovian Theology. Meanwhile I warn you against one Heresy. Certain authorities (e.g. Schnitzel aus Wien, Holzapfel aus Marburg) think that the Bolovians were the Tenth (lost) Tribe of Israel. This is based on a Corrupt Stanzo, i.e.

Now while King Bolo & his Queen
   Were feasting at the Passover,
In Burst Columbo & His Men—
   In fact Tea-Kettle-Arse-Over.

Now I maintain that this Stanzo is Corrupt (but how lovely it must have been before it was corrupted!) and that it should read

Now the Jewboys of Columbo's Fleet
   Were feasting at the Passover:
King Bolo & His Big Black Queen
   Rolled in Tea-kettle-arse-over . . . .

I have written a Monograph to shew that the true Bolovian rhyme is Simple and pure; and whenever we find elaborate rhymes (e.g.

Stockings Off and Hauptbahnhof) we are confronted with a spurious XVII Century addition (Concettismo) · · · Please do not address me as Thomarse.

DEIPNOSOPHISTIC: see headnote to *Noctes Binanianæ*, 3. PRINTING.

begin agin again: the nursery rhyme *Michael Finigan* ends each verse with "begin again", and does so indefinitely (Donald Sommerville, personal communication).

Schnitzel aus Wien: Viennese schnitzel.

Holzapfel: Rudolf Maria Holzapfel, Austrian psychologist.

Tea-kettle-arse-over: OED "tea-kettle": "Phr. *ass* (= arse) *over tea-kettle*, head over heels (cf. *arse over tip*), *U.S. slang*". OED "half-seas over" 1: "Halfway across the sea". 2: "Half-drunk" (*humorous*)", from 1700.

———

To Dobrée, "This Day of St. Gumbolumbo" [? Oct 1927]:

Dear Buggamy,

On due Reflexion, I consider that you are probably by this time in a fit State to resist influenza, and receive the true Doctrine of the Bolovian Quarternion. In other words, WUX. But before I Impart the Dogma of WUX, it is As Well that you should know something of the Proper pronunciation of the word WUX.

First, the W. You will understand that WUX is correctly transliterated, but that the transliteration is quite inadequate to the pronunciation, which is Almost impossible for European Lips. The W, then, is half way between the WH as pronounced in the Gateshead & Newcastle district (sc. as in WHORE in Gateshead) and the HW of Danish (not the corrupt Danish of Jutland and West Friesland, which are affected by High and Low Dutch respectifly, but the Pure Danish of East Friesland) as in *hwilken*. An accurate transliteration would be like this [WH *typed over* HW] but Printers say this is impossible.

Second, the U. The U is very long, and might be rendered OOUHOUHUH. There is a slight, a very slight, Caesura in the middle of the U, which is expressed, in Pure Bolovian, by a slight Belch, but no European can render this, so do not try.

Third, the X. This is a combination of the Greek Ksi and the German *schch*. If you attentively Cough and Sniff at the same time you will get nearer to it.

That is enough for one lesson. You will now realise that the Bolovian tongue is extreamly Subtile, impossible to the European Mouth. You have heard of the Zulu Click, a sound that no Caucasian can make? Well, the Zulu Click is nothing to the Bolovian Fart, by which in that language the most subtle distinctions are rendered. Even our analytic terminology is hopelessly inadequate. Fracastoro, and Cuntarella, in the XVI and XVII centuries respectively, went a little way with their distinctions between the Fart Proper, the Fart Improper, the Farticle, the Gaspop, the Pusspurr and the Butterbreath, but the Bolovian distinctions are comparatively Legion.

At any rate, you should in a week's time, with an Hour's devotions a day, be able to pronounce WUX as well as you ever will.

Yr. Brother in Wux

T. S. E.

Gumbolumbo: OED "gumbo", *U.S.* "[Negro patois; 'from the Angolan *kingombo*']". 1: "a. A colloquial name for the okra plant · · · b. A soup thickened with · · · this plant." 3: "A patois spoken by Blacks and Creoles".

the Proper pronunciation of the word WUX: Paul Elmer More described the Hindu *Om* as "made up of three corresponding elements, O being a diphthong composed of the vowels A and U. Now they say the first letter, A, because of its Attachment to all other letters and because it is the first among them, is no other than Vaiçvanara · · · But the fourth, they say, is not a letter at all, but the whole syllable *Om*, the incommunicable · · ·" *The Great Refusal* 136–37.

Quarternion: OED 5: "Consisting of four persons, things, or parts", with first citation from *Purgatorio* XXXIII: "The trinal now, and now the virgin band | Quaternion their sweet psalmody began" (tr. Cary).

sc.: *scilicet* (= namely, L.)

the Fart Proper, the Fart Improper: *As You Like It* V iv. TOUCHSTONE: "this is called the Retort Courteous · · · this is called the Quip Modest · · · this is called the Reply Churlish · · · And so to the Lie Circumstantial and the Lie Direct." Touchstone's distinctions are a parody of manuals of courtly rhetoric.

In *John Ford* (1932), TSE quoted Ford's "They are the silent griefs which cut the heart-strings; | Let me die smiling" (*The Broken Heart* V iii). On 10 Nov 1936, he wrote to Theodore Spenser: "I can only say, in the words of JHON [?JOHN] FOORDE who put it so pithily in his play *The Broken Wind*—

> It is the silent farts that wet the pantseat!
> Let me die smiling . . .

———

To Dobrée, 12 Nov 1927:

Dear Buggamy · · · I am very busy writing a Poem about a Sole. That is, it is about a Channel Swimmer who has a Sole as a mascot; you see it is allegorical, and everything can be taken in an allegorical, analogical, anagogical, and a bolovian sense. So it is giving me much trouble. There is also a Dove that comes in, but I dont understand how

> The Dove dove down an oyster Dive
> As the Diver dove from Dover . . .

Then the sole

> was solely sole
> Or solely sold as sole at Dover . . .

you get the drift of it, but it is Difficult. When he reaches the other side

> "He's saved his sole whole!" Cry'd the Priest;
> Whose Sole? OUR Sole! the folk replied . . .
> His balls are Bald! the people Bawled . . .
>
> This Sole, which had been Dover bred,
> Was shortly cooked with chips in Greece . . .

It is very difficult to put all this together; it is called How we Brought the Dover Sole to Calais · · ·

> ever yrs.
> T. S.

The Sole—

> Although it hung about the Plaice
> 'Twas solely sold as Sole at Dover . . .

Or solely sold as sole: TSE typed "sold solely" and transposed them. *Ash-Wednesday* V 8: "Against the Word the unstilled world still whirled".

How we Brought the Dover Sole to Calais: Browning, *How They Brought the Good News from Ghent to Aix*. TSE to F. S. Flint, also 12 Nov 1927: "I am at present engaged on a poem about a Channel Swimmer which I will send when completed. It is called 'How we Brought the Good Sole from Dover to Calais'."

To Dobrée, [22 Nov?] 1927 (*Letters 2*, 720):

DO YOU KNOW

that King Bolo's Big Black Queen was called the CHOCOLATE CLEOPATRA?

DO YOU KNOW

that this is due to her words when she first glimps'd C. Columbo,

viz.:

> Give me my Crown, put on my Robes, I have
> Immortal Longings in Me.

DO YOU KNOW
    that

> One day Columbo & the Queen
>   They fell into a Quarrel.
> Columbo shew'd his Disrespect
>   By Farting in a Barrel.
> The Queen she call'd him Horse's Arse—
>   And Blueballed Spanish Loafer:
> They arbitrated the Affair
>   Upon the Cabin Sofa.

DONT FORGET
To Sport your Bowler among the heathen Tarbouches.

That "Bowler" is derived partly from "Bolo". Why is it called (in France) "melon". Because the Melons of Bolovia were perfectly Sperical, and the Hat was moulded upon half a Melon. Why was it called Bowler? For one reason, because the Bolovian game of Bowls was played in the ripe melon season.

[22 Nov?] 1927: TSE typed "Saint Clelia's Day" but probably intended "St. Cecilia's Day". (St. Clelia's feast day is 13 July, but she was canonised only in 1989.)

CHOCOLATE CLEOPATRA: for *The Chocolate Soldier* see *Goldfish* I 10 and notes. The name hovers between different syllable-counts.   CLEOPATRA · · · Give me my Crown: *Antony and Cleopatra* V ii. CLEOPATRA: "Give me my robe, put on my crown; I have | Immortal longings in me."

One day · · · Upon the Cabin Sofa: TSE repeats the first four lines when writing to Hayward, [24 Aug] 1940, about Hayward's anthology *Love's Helicon* (1940): "True, there are aspects of Love which, I dare say, fall outside the terms of reference. Such as: *A Little Bit of What you Fancy always Does you Good*. Or the topic of 'Lovers' Quarrels', e.g. · · ·"

Quarrel · · · Barrel · · · Tarbouches: Lewis Carroll: "Tweedledum and Tweedledee · · · Just then flew down a monstrous crow, | As black as a tar-barrel; | Which frightened both the heroes so, | They quite forgot their quarrel", *Through the Looking-Glass* ch. IV.   **Tarbouches:** OED "tarboosh", "a cap of cloth or felt (almost always red) with a tassel". From the Arabic, tarbush, "so called in Egypt".

———

Undated greeting to Dobrée:

11 Century   J. Wesley

> "'Tis WUX that makes the world go round,
> And sets the balls a-rolling;
> WUX fills with ecstacy our soul,
> Our soul in whole consoling".

This was explained, 24 Jan 1928: "The tune is 11th century, the words were adapted by J. Wesley from the original and literal translation. The tune has also been used for *Auld Lang Syne*, *Of All the Fish that Swim the Sea* etc. There is no relation between Wuxianity and Islam." (For "the *X. Society*"—*The Idea of a Christian Society*—see *Four Quartets* headnote, 5. THE WAR.)

———

To Dobrée, [early Feb? 1928]:

QUESTIONS TO ANSWER: What makes the World go Round? Why did they wear Bowler Hats? Why did their Chariots have square Wheels? · · · Morley is reformed and now always wears a Bowler or a Melon · · · It is well to remember that

> King Bolo's Big Black Bastard Queen
> Was very seldom Sober—
> Between October and July
> And then until October;
> Ah Yes King Bolos Big Black Queen

Was call'd a Heavy Drinker;
But still she always kept Afloat
And Nobody could Sink her.

very seldom Sober— | **Between October and July** | **And then until October:** "I'm drunk today and I'm seldom sober", *Carrickfergus* (trad. Irish song). Burns: "frae November till October ··· thou was na sober", *Tam O'Shanter* (Donald Sommerville, personal communicastion).

The Columbiad

Following publication of Bolovian verses in *Letters* (1988), stanxos 6, 41 and 44 were published in *The Faber Book of Blue Verse* (1990). Stanxos 1–16 and 49 were published in *March Hare* (1996).

Title **The Columbiad**: used by TSE in *Valerie's Own Book*, where a dozen stanzos are transcribed in the first exercise book and two in the second. The title, which TSE may have had in mind for half a century, had previously been used for several earnest long poems about American history, of which the best known was Joel Barlow's *The Columbiad* (1807).

This editorial composite begins with sixteen stanxos (st. 3 and 9 having only four lines each) from leaves among Ezra Pound's papers in the Beinecke Library, Yale. They were published in *March Hare* because they appear on leaves excised from the Notebook, and the same order is retained here. The final stanxo in *March Hare*, followed by its "Flourishes" and "Exeunt", here becomes the last of *The Columbiad* (st. 49).

St. 17–48 are from various sources. St. 17 and 18 appear on a torn leaf, with *ms frag* of *Portrait of a Lady* (III 31–41) on the verso. (Not being excised from the Notebook, this leaf was not available to the editor of *March Hare*.)

Six leaves from a small notebook, with one edge perforated, are also in the Beinecke, accompanied by an envelope postmarked 11 Jan 1915, on which Pound pencilled the soubriquet "Chançons ithyphallique". These leaves provide st. 19–38. The order is uncertain and of little consequence, but they are here designated *A–F*, with contents as follows (noting verso and recto):

$A(r)$	st. 19 and 20
$A(v)$	st. 21 and 22
$B(r)$	st. 23 and 24
$B(v)$	st. 25 and 26
$C(r)$	st. 27 and 28
$C(v)$	st. 29 (preceded by four lines similar to last four of st. 8)
$D(r)$	st. 30 and 31

$D(v)$ st. 32 and 33

$E(r)$ st. 34 and 35
$E(v)$ st. 36 (preceded by a version of st. 27)

$F(r)$ st. 37 (followed by the first four lines of st. 28)
$F(v)$ st. 38

(Of these, *A* is torn in two, which explains the reference in *March Hare* 321 to "seven leaves".)

The remaining stanxos of *The Columbiad* are from later sources, though the date of composition is unknown:

st. 39 from TSE to Howard Morris, 24 Oct 1929.

st. 40 and 41 from TSE to Theodore Spencer, 1 Dec 1932, which also contains st. 36 (ts, Pusey Library, Harvard).

st. 42–47 from *Valerie's Own Book*. (The first four lines of st. 42 were sent to Dobrée, 7 Aug [1927]; the last four are a version of another stanxo sent to him [22 Nov?] 1927. For a version of st. 43 sent to Aiken at the end of TSE's life, see note below.)

st. 48 from an undated ms fragment, written out in prose by TSE and subscribed "Rippling Rimes". The ms was sold by House of Books, Oct 1978 (untraced; photocopy in a private collection).

Valerie's Own Book also contains versions of stanxos 6 (twice), 18, 20, 23, 41 and a version of *America Discover'd* (which TSE had sent to Bonamy Dobrée, [Sept 1927?]). For the full contents and grouping, see headnote to the Textual History, 6. *VALERIE'S OWN BOOK*. A typed "Check List of the More Authentic Columbovian Stanzos" (Valerie Eliot collection), probably from the early 1960s, lists a score of those which comprise *The Columbiad*, with two of those sent to Dobrée, [Sept 1927?], plus opening lines of some others: "The sailors of Columbo's fleet | Were called 'The Rectum Rammers'"; "'Avast, my men!' Columbo cried, | 'Regard the placid waters'"; and "Columbo and his merry men | Enjoyed a game of rugger". A "Select Bibliography" explains that "The classical work on Bolovian customs is Lipschitz: *Grundlinien der Bolo'shen Sittenlehre*, 3 Bänder, Pforzheim, 1873", and lists also "Trautwein: *Streitschrift gegen Holzapfel* and Holzapfel: *Polemisch gegen Trautwein*, both Pforzheim also, 1912 and 1913."

On 3 Dec 1959, Alie Rehnquist of *Bonnier Litterära Magasin*, Stockholm, wrote to John Hayward enclosing "a small piece of light-verse purporting to be written by Mr Eliot", beginning "Old king Bolo's big black queen | who's bum was big as a soup tureen".

A. David Moody wrote that in autumn 1988, together with the leaves at the Beinecke, he saw "a small black hard-covered notebook, containing a fair copy of the full King Bolo or Colombo epic, written in a very neat small hand, together with a considerable number of other similar verses. I should think that it was this fair copy, rather than the miscellaneous drafts and fragments, which EP [Pound] referred to as 'his earlier EPOS on King Bolo.' In 1994 Donald Gallup told me the notebook was no longer in the Beinecke Pound archive", *Ezra Pound: Poet* I: *The Young Genius* (2007) 471.

The present composite text of *The Columbiad* is given without variants, but examples can be seen by comparing st. 30 with st. 46, and comparing st. 19–20 with the versions later sent to Bonamy Dobrée (15 Aug 1927), shown above (and in *Letters 3*).

The Columbiad

Let a tucket be sounded on the hautboys. Enter the king and queen.

Columbo he lived over in Spain (st. 1)
Where doctors are not many
The only doctor in his town
Was a bastard jew named Benny
To Benny then Columbo went
With countenance so placid
And Benny filled Columbo's prick
With Muriatic Acid.

One day the king & queen of Spain (st. 2)
They gave a royal banquet
Columbo having passed away
Was brought in on a blanket
The queen she took an oyster fork
And pricked Columbo's navel
Columbo hoisted up his ass
And shat upon the table.

Columbo and his merry men (st. 3)
They set sail from Genoa
Queen Isabella was aboard
That famous Spanish whore.

Columbo and his mariners (st. 4)
They were a merry chorus
One Sunday evening after tea
They went to storm a whore house.

As they were scrambling up the steps
Molto vivace >   Twas then Columbo his got
A great big whore from the seventh story window
She floored him with a pisspot.

(st. 5)   ~~The cabin boy they had aboard~~
~~His name was Orlandino~~
~~A child of upright character~~
~~But his language was obscene-o.~~
~~"Fuck Spiders" was his chief remark~~
~~In accents mild and dulcet —~~
~~They asked him what there was for lunch~~
~~And he simply answered "Bullshit."~~

(st. 6)   King Bolo's swarthy bodyguard
Were called the Jersey Lilies
A bold and hardy set of blacks
Undaunted by syphilis.
They wore the national uniform
Of a garland of verbenas
And a pair of great big hairy balls
And a big black knotty penis.

(st. 7)   King Bolo's swarthy bodyguard
They numbered three and thirty
An innocent and playful lot
But most disgusting dirty.

st. 5 **"Fuck Spiders" was his chief remark**: "syphilitic spider", *He said: this universe is very clever* 6 (see note).

st. 6 **swarthy · · · hardy**: the two versions in *Valerie's Own Book* both read "royal · · · bestial". The first of them was published in *The Faber Book of Blue Verse*. **Jersey Lilies**: Lillie Langtry, actress and mistress of Edward VII, was known as Jersey Lily (having been born on the island). **bold**: *March Hare* read "wild" in error. **Undaunted by syphilis**: Henry Ware Eliot (TSE's father) to Thomas Lamb Eliot (TSE's uncle), 7 Mar 1914: "I hope that a cure for Syphilis will never be discovered. It is God's punishment for nastiness. Take it away and there will be more nastiness, and it will be necessary to emasculate our children to keep them clean." **hairy balls**: *Valerie's Own Book* 79 reads "testacles".

And Bolo lay down in the shade
His royal breast uncovering
They mounted in a banyan tree
And shat upon their sovereign.

One day Columbo and his men   (st. 8)
They took and went ashore
Columbo sniffed around the air
And muttered "I smell whore"
And ere they'd taken twenty steps
Among the Cuban jungles
They found King Bolo ⊄ his queen
A-sitting on their bungholes.

She put the gunner to the bad   (st.9)
The first mate, cook, and bo'sun,
But when she saw Columbos balls
She jumped into the ocean—

One Sunday morning out at sea   (st. 10)
The vessel passed Gibraltar
Columbo sat upon the poop
A-reading in the psalter.

st. 7 **And Bolo lay:** *March Hare* reads "King Bolo lay", but just as "lay" was written over "sat", so "And" was written over "King". **They mounted in a banyan tree | And shat upon their sovereign:** Swift: the Yahoos "leaped up into the Tree, from whence they began to discharge their Excrements on my Head", *Gulliver's Travels* bk. IV, ch. I. TSE: "*Under the* · · · *banyan*", *Sweeney Agonistes: Fragment of an Agon* 63.

st. 8 **bungholes:** recurrent in Urquhart's Rabelais. TSE on Tudor translations: "If comparison could be made at all, I should single out, after the Bible, Florio's *Montaigne*, Holland's translation of another work of Plutarch, the *Moralia*, and Sir Thomas Urquhart's *Rabelais*, *The Tudor Translators* (1929).

st. 9 **She put the gunner to the bad:** (emending *March Hare*). *Partridge* "bad, go to the": "To be ruined; become depraved · · · From ca. 1860". *Chambers* "bad: have someone to the bad": "[1900s] to put someone at a disadvantage".

st. 10 **poop:** OED n^1: "The aftermost part of a ship" (for Shakespeare's usage, see note to *The Waste Land* [III] 279). OED n^2 2: "*slang* (orig. children's). An act of breaking wind or of defecation; faeces." *Partridge* dates this, as a verb, "(? late) C.19–20".

The bosuns wife came up on deck
With a bucket full of cowshit
Columbo grabbed her round the neck
And raped her on the bowsprit.

(st. 11)

Now when they were three weeks at sea
Columbo he grew rooty
He took his cock in both his hands
And swore it was a beauty.
The cabin boy appeared on deck
And scampered up the mast-o
Columbo grasped him by the balls
And buggered him in the ass-o.

(st. 12)

One day Columbo and the queen
They fell into a quarrel
Columbo showed his disrespect
By farting in a barrel.
The queen she called him horse's ass
And "dirty Spanish loafer"
They terminated the affair
By fucking on the sofa.

(st. 13)

Before another day had passed
Columbo he fell sick-o
He filled the pump with argyrol
And rammed it up his prick-o.
And when they touched Cadiz he cried
(And let down both his anchors):
"We'll see if there's a doctor here
Can cure the whistling chancres."

st. 13 **argyrol**: antiseptic introduced in the US 1901 and used particularly to treat gonorrhea.   **Cadiz · · · chancres**: Byron on escaping cannibalism on board: "he saved himself · · · his saving clause, | Was a small present made to him at Cadiz, | By general subscription of the ladies", *Don Juan* II lxxxi. The voyages of Christopher Columbus, two of which set out from Cadiz, are believed to have brought syphilis to Europe in the 1490s.   **whistling**: OED "whistle" 11: "To smell unpleasantly or strongly. *slang. rare*", citing only Auden and Isherwood, *The Dog Beneath the Skin* II v: "Cor! I don't 'alf whistle!" (Perhaps the derivation also of "Now whistleprick! Columbo cried".)

Columbo and his merry men   (st. 14)
They went to storm a castle
A bullet came along the road
And up Columbo's asshole.
Columbo grew so angry then
He nearly shit his breeches.
"Come on my merry men," he cried
"We'll kill the sons of bitches."

"Avast my men" Columbo cried   (st. 15)
In accents mild and dulcet
"The cargo that we have aboard
Is forty tons of bullshit."
The merry men set up a cheer
On hearing this reparty.
And the band struck up "The Whore House Ball"
In accents deep and farty.

On Sunday morning after prayers   (st. 16)
They took their recreation
The crew assembled on the deck
And practiced masturbation.
Columbo being full of rum
He fell down in a stupor.
They turned his asshole S.S.W.
~~And he cried "I'll die a pooper!"~~

st. 15 **In accents mild**: Carroll: "*His accents mild took up the tale*", *Through the Looking-Glass* ch. VIII, the White Knight's song.   **The Whore House Ball**: "And come to the Whore House Ball!", refrain of *Ballade pour la grosse Lulu*. "at the undertakers' ball", *Opera* 17. "*Jellicles come to the Jellicle Ball* · · · saving themselves to be right | For the Jellicle Moon and the Jellicle Ball", *The Song of the Jellicles* 4, 35–36.

st. 16 **practiced masturbation**: to Hayward, 2 Apr 1936: "I presume that your reference to the organ is an allusion to that Gilbertian character, Master Bates, who practised every evening upon that intrument."   **die a pooper**: more usually, a pauper. Martin Tupper: "we count him happy who did not die a pauper", *The Crock of Gold* ch. I. Variant readings of the last line were "And he let a noble pooper" and "And he fired off a pooper."

(st. 17)

Among the heroes of the fleet
Was a pimp named Buck McManus
Who had the entertaining trick
Of whistling through his anus.

(st. 18)

One day King Bolo from the shore
Began to cheer and chortle.
He cried "I see Columbo's ass
A shitting through a porthole."
His big black queen set up a shout
And all his swarthy vassals
And the band struck up the national hymn
Of "Hairy Balls and Ass-Holes".

(st. 19)

The flagship of Columbo's Fleet
Was named the "Virgin Mary"
An able vessel fully manned
With sailors short and hairy.
The other ships came on behind
The "Holy Ghost" and "Jesus"
And people on the shore remarked
An odour as of cheeses.

(st. 20)

The cook who served them pork and beans
Was known as Careless Cora.
A dame of pure Australian blood
With a tincture of Angora.
She wore a sweater short and red
Which closely did her shape fit
And the hair that lay along her back
Was yellow like ripe ape shit.

(st. 21)

One day the king ⱴ queen of Spain
They gave a royal dinner
To Chris Columbo of Genoa
That famous old prickskinner.
They sat around the groaning board
On cushions, (trimmed with tassels)
ⱴ the queen served up a steaming dish
Of buttered-hot-apes'-assholes.

One day the chaplain came aboard (st. 22)
With a bunch of big verbenas.
Columbo sat upon the hatch
A rubbing of his penis.
The bosuns wife sat on the rail
A eating jam and crackers.
The mate was in the bathtub and
The cook was in the backhouse.

Columbo thought that he would take (st. 23)
A safeguard and precaution.
So to a medium he went
For telling of his fortune.
The medium was so very wise
It really was a miracle.
She ~~gaze~~ went into a trance and cried
"I see your balls are spherical."

The cabin boy they had aboard (st. 24)
His name was Orlandino,
A child of manners most refined
Though his language was obscene-o.
~~His prick was 13 inches long~~
~~And wound around with marlin.~~
Columbo sketched his character
When he called him "Whorehouse Darling."

st. 22 **The bosuns wife** · · · **bathtub:** "The queen was in the parlour, | Eating bread and honey, | The maid was in the garden", *Sing a song of sixpence*, nursery rhyme, with many obscene variations (Richard Luckett, personal communication). **backhouse:** *U.S.* a privy (Webster 1847). The rhyme "crackers · · · backhouse" may exploit the propensity to reduce the suffix as in malt-house (where OED gives both pronunciations). Similarly with "bitters · · · shit-house", st. 30.

st. 23 **The medium was so very wise** · · · **She:** "Madame Sosostris, famous clairvoyante · · · Is known to be the wisest woman in Europe", *The Waste Land* [I] 43–45.

(st. 25)

One day Columbo slapped his thigh
And said "I feel like frigging!"
He chased the chaplain round the deck
And up among the rigging.
The chaplain he that good old man
Had no one to protect him.
Columbo grasped him by the balls
And buggered him (in the rectum).

(st. 26)

Now whistleprick! Columbo cried
Regard the tranquil waters:
The sea is calm, the sea is still,
Lets go and fuck a tortoise.
The beast was caught, the beast was fucked,
And christened (name of Jumbo);
And the merry men set up a cheer
For their captain, bold Columbo.

(st. 27)

King Bolo and his big black queen
Those two prodigious bastards,
They swarmed aboard Columbo's ship
In a rattling fire of assturds—
They sat around upon the deck
On cushions trimmed with tassels
And the first word that the monarch spake
Was "Let us talk of assholes".

(st. 28)

The hottest sailor in the fleet
Was Bill from Barcelona.
For coons his passion was so marked
That they called him Desdemona.

st. 27 **swarmed aboard · · · In a rattling fire of assturds**: "With a frightful burst of fireworks the Chinks they swarmed aboard", *Growltiger's Last Stand* 42. This stanxo's "swarmed" is an emendation of "came", which is the reading of the version on leaf $E(v)$.

st. 27–28 **And the first word that the monarch spake | Was "Let us talk of assholes". | | The hottest sailor in the fleet**: Lewis Carroll: "To talk of many things: | Of shoes—and ships—and sealing wax— | Of cabbages—and kings— | And why the sea is boiling hot", *The Walrus and the Carpenter*.

Though coarsened by experience
His soul was not embittered.
He looked the whole world in the face—
A fucked up blueballed shittard.

Now when the KING and QUEEN of Spain   (st. 29)
Were filling up their glasses
In burst Columbo ⊄ his crew
Of brawny horses asses.
He introduced the queen all round
To all his royal navy
And punctuated his address
By spitting in the gravy.

Now bugger my ear! the bosun said   (st. 30)
Now where does all my rum go?
My reason leads me to suspect
That great big bitch Columbo.
Columbo sat upon the hatch
Consuming orange bitters
He took the bosun by the drawers
And rammed him down the shit-house.

King Bolo's big black bastard queen   (st. 31)
She was extremely lecherous.
She kissed the chaplain on the ear
In fashion most impetuous.
The chaplain he that good old man
Was reading out of Pascal.
He skipped so quickly round the mast
He buggered himself (in the asshole).

st. 28 **He looked the whole world in the face**: Longfellow: "He looks the whole world
in the face", *The Village Blacksmith* 11.   **shittard**: (shit hard?) Urquhart's
Rabelais I xiii: "Shittard, | Squitard, | Crackard, | Turdous" etc.

(st. 32)

One day King Bolo's big black queen
That pestilential bastard
She rolled aboard Columbo's ship
In a state not drunk, but plastered.
The chaplain he that good old man
That shy old whorehouse rascal
He slipped his prick inside her drawers
And buggered her (in the asshole).

(st. 33)

Now while Columbo and his men
Were shaking dice for roubles
In burst King Bolo and his queen
With a frantic cry of "Blueballs!"
They rolled around beneath the trees
And lunched on ham sandwiches
And Columbo cried "Produce the rum
For these epoch-making bitches."

(st. 34)

One day Columbo came aboard
With a bunch of big bananas
He took the chaplain by the drawers
And shoved one up his anus.
The chaplain he that good old man
Was reading in a missal
He dropped the book upon the deck
And cried out loudly "Kisshole".

(st. 35)

One time Columbo when at sea
Grew very constipated
For forty nights and forty days
It was ~~just~~ as I have stated.
Then to the Virgin he did pray
Before his faithful vassals
"Give me a hundred shits apiece
From 100,000 assholes."

st. 34 **"Kisshole":** *kissel* (rhyming with "missal"), a sweet dish made of fruit juice mixed with sugar and water.

st. 35 **For forty nights and forty days:** of Lent. G. H. Smyttan and F. Pott: "Forty days and forty nights | Thou wast fasting in the wild, | Forty days and forty nights | Tempted, and yet undefiled" (hymn).

The queen said just to pass the time (st. 36)
I will ask you a conundrum.
And the question which I will propose
Is "what's Chinese for cundrum?"
That, said Columbo, is a joke
But it seems to me so coarse
Such conversations I have heard
From the lips of Spanish whores.

Two eunuchs from the sultans court (st. 37)
Were very curious figures.
Some Chinese pimps from Hoangho
The rest were jews and niggers.
They also had among the crew
Ten brawny Irish muckers.
And to keep them going on the trip
Some Portuguese cocksuckers.

Now fry my balls! Columbo cried (st. 38)
I feel as strong as Sandow
Let someone quickly go and fetch
My passionboy Orlando.

st. 36 **conundrum** · · · **"what's Chinese for cundrum?":** Browning: *"What's the Latin name for 'parsley'? | What's the Greek name for Swine's Snout?",* *Soliloquy of the Spanish Cloister,* 15–16 (with its dirty book, "scrofulous French novel", 57). **conundrum** · · · **cundrum:** *Chambers Slang Dictionary* "cum" has "cum drum . . . (also . . . cundrum) [1930s+] a condom with a reservoir for semen." OED "cond, cund" 2. "To conduct (a ship): to direct the helmsman how to steer" with *Smith's Seaman's Grammar* (1692): "To *Cond* or *Cun*, is to direct or guide, and *to cun a Ship* is to direct the Person at the Helm". For "confected by the cunning French · · · female stench" see note to *WLComposite* **268–69.**

st. 37 **niggers:** for six lines of uncertain authorship, including "We had two niggers to carry our grips", see TSE to Frank Morley, 2 June 1933. **muckers:** "a coarse, rough person", *Cent. Dict.* (1890). OED includes, from 1897, Kipling, *Captains Courageous* (a pertinent title): "Don't I know the look on men's faces when they think me a—a 'mucker', as they call it out here?" *Partridge:* "A friend, mate, pal: Army" since *ca.* 1917".

st. 38 **Sandow:** Eugen Sandow (1867–1925), father of modern bodybuilding.

(st. 39)

The Boatswain was a man of mark
Well known as Worthless Walter.
He found the Chaplain fast asleep
Perusing of the psalter.
He took him swiftly by the pants
And buggered him on the alter;
And the Mate said, (with a knowing look),
"I've seen that done in Malta".

(st. 40)

'Twas Christmas at the Spanish Court!
They dined on roast flamingo.
Columbo gave a Awful belch
That broke a stained-glass window.
The King at that was so perturbed
He nearly was struck dumb (oh!)
But the Queen exclaimed, with perfect tact,
"You son of a bitch, Columbo!"

(st. 41)

'Twas Christmas on the Spanish Main,
The wind it up and blew hard;
The vessel gave an awful lurch
And heeled 'way down to leeward.
The Chaplain was so very scared
His breeches he manured;
And Columbo slid along the deck
And raped the smoke-room steward.

(st. 42)

Columbo and his caravels
They set sail from Genoa.
Queen Isabella was aboard—
That famous Spanish whore.
Before they'd been three hours at sea
They fell into a quarrel,
And Columbo showed his disrespect
By farting in a barrel.

---

st. 39 **The Boatswain was a man of mark**: sent by TSE to his Milton Academy and
Harvard contemporary Howard Morris, 24 Oct 1929, with the first four lines of
st. 30.

Now while King Bolo and his Queen   (st. 43)
Were feasting at the Passover
Columbo and his Merry Men
Rolled in teakettle-arse-over.
They all sat round his festive board
And dined on fried hyaenas;
And the King said: "Have a piece of tail
With a juicy bit of penis".

The Ladies of King Bolo's Court   (st. 44)
Were called "the Broadway Benders",
And likewise called "The Fore and Aft"
Or else "The Double Enders".
Columbo took a single look
And hitched up his suspenders.
"Come on, my merry men" said he:
"*These* look like old offenders."

King Bolo crowned his Big Black Queen   (st. 45)
As Queen of Love and Beauty.
"For", said he, "who is there on our isle
At once so sweet and sooty?
At once so fresh and fruity?
At once so rough and rooty?

st. 43 **Passover:** *Particulars of the lively behaviour of King Bolo at the celebration of the Passover* (ms, Huntington; title from envelope). Postscript of a letter to Aiken, 21 Nov 1963: "Do you remember what happened when the Columbian crew were feasting at the Passover? If not, I will rehearse it to you."   **And dined on fried hyaenas:** "I also like to dine on becaficas", second of the epigraphs to *The Sacred Wood* (unattributed there; Byron, *Beppo* 337).

st. 44 **Benders:** *Historical Dictionary of American Slang* ed. J. E. Lighter (1994–): "7. *Homosex.* a male homosexual who habitually assumes the passive role in anal copulation" (but first citation 1971).   **The Double Enders:** Edna St. Vincent Millay: "My candle burns at both ends; | It will not last the night; | But oh, my foes, and oh, my friends— | It gives a lovely light", *First Fig* in *Poetry* June 1918. For "*double entendre*", see letter to Aiken 19 July 1914, quoted above.   **suspenders:** OED 4a: "straps passing over the shoulders to hold up the trousers. *Chiefly U.S.*" (as opposed to 4b: "A device attached to the top of a stocking").

Let's celebrate the day!" he cried,
"With a game of water polo!"
And bestial blacks set up a shout
For their Monarch, Good King Bolo.

(st. 46)   "Now buggar my ear!" the bo'sun cried,
"Now *where* does all my rum go?
"My reason leads me to suspect
That bastard, Chris Columbo".
Columbo sat upon the poop
Perusing Titus Livius;
But ~~the~~ he took that bo'sun by the ears
And rammed his head down the privy-house.

(st. 47)   King Bolo's big black Cousin Hugh
Was called the family failure:
His ~~pot~~ bum was large and black and round –
But he had no genitalia!
And yet he was so full of fun
That nothing could deject him;
And the children, for a bed-time treat,
Would buggar him in the rectum.

(st. 48)   King Bolo's big black bastard Kween
(That practickle Bacchante)
Was always tidy fore and aft
Although her clo'es were scanty
And when the monarch ⊄ his men
Went out to throw the discus
The Kween sat by to rince her Kwunt
And comb her belly whiskus.

(st. 49)   Now when Columbo and his ships
Regained the Spanish shores
The Spanish ladies swarmed aboard
By twos ⊄ threes ⊄ fours.

st. 48 **Bacchante**: OED: "A priestess or female votary of Bacchus", from 1797: "She capered with the intoxication of a Bacchante". **rince her Kwunt**: for "They wash their cunts in soda water", see note to *The Waste Land* [III] 199–201.

Columbo first took off his bags
And then his shirt and drawers
He spun his balls around his head
And cried "Hooray for whores!"

Flourish. Skirmishes and alarums. Cries without. Exeunt the king and queen severally.

st. 49 **bags**: OED 16: "Clothes that hang loosely about the wearer; (*colloq.*) trousers. *pl.*" from 1853. *Partridge*: "A low variant, from ca.1860 but ob., is *bum-bags*". (The line is corrected from *March Hare.*)

Fragments

1.   There was a jolly tinker came across the sea
      With his four and twenty inches hanging to his knee
Chorus   With his long-pronged hongpronged
      Underhanded babyfetcher
        Hanging to his knee.

2.   It was a sunny summer day the tinker was in heat
      With his eight and forty inches hanging to his feet—

13.   O tinker dear tinker I am in love with you
      O tinker jolly tinker will half a dollar do?

24.   O daughter dear daughter I think you are a fool
      To run against a man with a john like a mule.

25.   O mother dear mother I thought that I was able
      But he ripped up my belly from my cunt to my navel.

41.   With his whanger in his hand he walked through the hall
      "By God" said the cook "he's a gona fuck us all."

50.   With his whanger in his hand he walked through the hall
      "By God" said the cook "he's a gone and fucked us all."

Published in *March Hare*. Verso of the last leaf of *Suite Clownesque*, which is dated Oct 1910 at the foot. The comic numbering of the *Fragments* is TSE's, alluding to the many traditional variations.

four and twenty · · · **the hall** · · · **"he's gona fuck us all"** · · · **the hall** · · · **"he's gone and fucked us all"**: *The Ball of Kirriemuir* (trad.): "Four and twenty virgins | Came down from Inverness · · · They fucked them on the balcony; | They fucked them in the hall. | *God save us*, said the porter, *but* | *They've come to fuck us all*", text from *The Faber Book of Blue Verse* 293 (see *Ricks 1992*).

Balls to you said Mrs. Sonnenschien

Balls to you said Mrs. Sonnenschien. God strike you where youre sittin
And as for this here house of yours, it isn't fit to shit in.

Published in *March Hare* from recto of the leaf with *ms frag* of *Portrait of a Lady* (III 31–41) on verso. The leaf (Beinecke) is headed, in pencil, *Fragments from the Ballad of Harmony Court*, but only these lines are also in pencil. Two other fragments, in ink and in a more spiky hand, are incorporated as st. 17 and 18 in *The Columbiad*.

Harmony Court: written and composed by F. Allsopp & C. Yorke (1904).

Balls to you said Mrs. Sonnenschien: "Balls to Mr Finkelstein, Finkelstein, Finkelstein | Balls to Mr Finkelstein, dirty old man" (trad. blue verse).

Mrs. Sonnenschien · · · **house**: "Sonnenschien" in ms, but referring to the publisher W. S. Stallybrass of the publishing house Swan Sonnenschein. Born Sonnenschein, Stallybrass had taken his mother's maiden name (TSE to Richard Aldington, 12 Feb 1926).

it isn't fit to shit in: "He wasn't fit to shovel shit, | The dirty rotten bugger", *The Good Ship Venus* (trad. blue verse).

There was a young lady named Ransome

There was a young lady named Ransome
Who surrendered 5 times in a hansom,
    When she said to her swain
    He must do it again
He replied: "My name's Simpson, not Samson".

To Frank Morley, from Harvard, "St. Stephen Protomartyr [26 Dec] 1932".

TSE had written to Morley, 20 Dec 1932: "I have an undeserved reputation for limericks which I must live down", but less than a week later, enclosing this, he admitted "I know several good Limericks now."

There was a young girl of Siberia

There was a young girl of Siberia
Who had such a tempting posterior
That the Lapps and the Finns
Kept inventing new sins
As the recognised types were too stereo–.

Published in *The Faber Book of Blue Verse* from ms in *Valerie's Own Book*. Date of composition unknown. C. L. Sulzberger recalled TSE at Harvard in 1933: "Timid and withdrawn as Eliot was in class, he had a talent for banging the piano and singing a huge number of limericks, some of which I suspect he had written himself", *A Long Row of Candles* (1969) 4 (James Loucks, personal communication).

COME, Glorious Rabbitt, how long wilt thou slumber

COME, Glorious Rabbitt, how long wilt thou slumber,
    lying supine or prone in luxurious lair.
Shaking the sleep from besotted eyes, spring a sur-
    prise, do something to make 'em all stare,
Sturdy of hoof and long in the toof, Thunderer, grasp
    hard the bastards by the short hair.
Not once, or twice, shalt thou bugger 'em, in our
    rough island story,
But again and again and again and again, leaving
    their arseholes all gory;
And when I say, again and again, I mean repeatedly, I
    mean continually, I mean in fact many times,
Chaunting a one-way song in mellifluous proses and
    rugged tempestuous lines I mean rhymes.
Lord of a hundred battles, a cauliflower ear and 1000
    hardwon scars,
Proclaim aloud to the morning that a r s e spells arse.

Enclosed with letter to Pound, 7 Jan 1934.

Rabbitt: to Pound, 5 Apr 1933: "Rabbitt my Babbitt". 29 Nov 1934: "a big man like Brer Rabbitt can spit whar he please".

how long wilt thou slumber: Proverbs 6: 9–10: "How long wilt thou sleep, O sluggard? · · · slumber".

Shaking the sleep from besotted eyes: Milton: "Methinks I see in my mind a noble and puissant Nation rousing herself like a strong man after sleep, and shaking her invincible locks", *Areopagitica* (1644) 34.

Thunderer: OED 2: "*fig.* A resistless warrior; a powerful declaimer or orator, an utterer of violent invective or the like; *spec.* as a sobriquet of the London *Times* newspaper." (Pinned to the poem was a press cutting with a photograph of the newspaper proprietor Lord Rothermere.) Pope: "E'er Pallas issued from the Thund'rer's head, | Dulnes o'er all possess'd her antient right", *The Dunciad* (1728) I 8–9.

our rough island story · · · gory: Tennyson: "Not once or twice in our rough island-story, | The path of duty was the way to glory", *Ode on the Death of the Duke of Wellington* 201–202, 209–10. See note to *Defence of the Islands* [18]. To Pound, 12 Feb [1935]: "Not once, nor 2ce, in our rough island story, the Possum's Stink has saved the land of Hope & Glory."

one-way song: Faber published *One-Way Song*, Wyndham Lewis's "considerable poem of two thousand lines", in Nov 1933. TSE wrote a Foreword to Methuen's new edition in 1960.

a r s e spells arse: as opposed to "ass" in *The Columbiad*.

That bird wych in the dark time of the yeerë

To John Hayward, 26 Oct 1936, on Emile B. d'Erlanger's translation into French of *Murder in the Cathedral*:

> its first impression is to make me feel like that morose bird, the scritch-owl, in the words of Thomas Chatterton (the something boy who perisht in his pride), to wit (to who):

> That bird wych in the dark time of the yeerë
> Sitteth in dudgeon[1] on the aspen bouwe
> And cryeth *arsehole arsehole* lhoude and cleerë . . .

(1) The word does not occur in this sense until 1573.

Published in *Smart* 101.

Chatterton · · · pride: Wordsworth: "Chatterton, the marvellous Boy, | The sleepless Soul that perished in his pride", *Resolution and Independence* 43–44.

this sense: OED 2: "A feeling of anger, resentment or offence", first cited from G. Harvey, *Letter-book* (1573).

Kierkegaard and Rilke shouting in the lava

Kierkegaard and Rilke shouting in the lava
   And Lorca semaphoring "expropriate the owners";
Who shall dilate with a lingering loofa
   The focus of the foetus or the onus of the anus?
Not my angry Madonnas, with fists like bananas
   And pharmacopeas of gushing mucous
      Or O my lovely boy, with eyes like gopher's,
      The albacore sorrow, and an icicle in his penis.

The foregoing is merely a selection from my *Imitations of the Poets*, to be published with facsimile marginal annotations by Old Possum.

To John Hayward, 5 Aug 1944.

Pope's *Imitations of English Poets* include a Chaucerian fabliau, ending "Better · · · Then trust on Mon, whose yerde can *talke.*" For an imitation by TSE of contemporary poetry, sent to Hayward, 27 Jan 1937, see *A Proclamation* in "Uncollected Poems": "You know my aversion to Modernism in all forms, and especially in Poetry; and you know that Movements like Surrealism are things that I cannot make Head or Tail of."

1] against this line, TSE wrote "why?", perhaps because of the shortening of "lavatory", not to "lav" (OED from 1913) but to the unrecorded "lava".

3 **dilate:** underlined by TSE with "do you mean *delate* or *delete*? Use a dictionary."

4–8 **anus · · · O my lovely boy · · · icicle in his penis:** "emotions that turn out *isiculous* · · · stick it up your ass", *The Triumph of Bullshit* 15–16. Shakespeare sonnet 126: "O thou, my lovely boy, who in thy power | Dost hold Time's fickle glass, his sickle, hour". For "icicle", see note below to the limerick *The Blameless Sister of Publicola.*

6 **pharmacopeas:** underlined by TSE with "cornucopias, I think".

7 **gopher's:** emended by TSE to "a gopher's".

8 **albacore · · · penis:** "Then he knew that he had been a fish | With slippery white belly held tight in his own fingers", *The Death of Saint Narcissus* 24–25.

The Blameless Sister of Publicola

I know a nice girl named Valeria
Who has a delicious posterior
And beautiful thighs
Where her true lover lies
While his penis explores her interior.

Valerie's Own Book: fair copy, one page, dated "16. ix. 59".

Coriolanus V iii, VOLUMNIA: "Do you know this lady?" CORIOLANUS: "The noble sister of Publicola; | The moon of Rome: chaste as the icicle | That's curdied by the frost, from purest snow, | And hangs on Dian's Temple: dear Valeria!"

Textual History

"I shall certainly delete nothing from my collected poems. As Pilate, and after him Robert Browning, said, 'what I have written I have written'. It is all part of the progress." To Henry Eliot, 1 Jan 1936

1. Scope 2. Notation 3. Key to Editions
4. Proofs and Association Copies
5. The *March Hare* Notebook and Accompanying Leaves
6. *Valerie's Own Book* 7. On Composition and Manuscripts

1. SCOPE

The Textual History provides information about the writing of the poems and their history in print. Although considerations of scale mean it cannot claim to be comprehensive, notably with regard to punctuation, it attends closely to drafts and early printings of each poem. It includes a selection of mis-writings or mis-typings which may indicate readings that were momentarily considered. For instance, in a typescript of *Burbank with a Baedeker: Bleistein with a Cigar* the "D" of "Descending" in the second line is typed over "A". This is recorded because it suggests that "Ascending" (or some other word) may have been in TSE's mind. The mis-typing "phthsic" for "phthisic" is retained as indicating that a word was not entirely familiar to TSE. Not recorded, however, is TSE's typing "Sg" before correcting to "Stares". Other errors are recorded in acknowledgement of their having appeared in previous editions, sometimes for many years. In other cases, although individual variants are trivial, the pattern of them offers evidence about the relation between drafts, the reliability of an edition, or the likelihood that an intervening draft has been lost.

The Commentary to each poem lists its transmission through the principal editions. To these witnesses the Textual History adds drafts, proofs and printings which encompass a series of poems (such as *Landscapes*, *Four Quartets* or "Occasional Verses"), listed at the head of each section of the Textual History, and those which relate to a particular poem, given beneath its title.

Drafts are generally listed and numbered in order of composition, but in some exceptionally complex cases such as *The Waste Land*, manuscripts are grouped before typescripts. Typescripts that are cognate—that is ribbon and carbon, or first and second carbons—are designated *ts1a* and *ts1b* but when the readings of each are identical, they are given simply as *ts1*. (The designations of drafts of *Ash-Wednesday* include the relevant Part number: *tsIa*, *tsIIa* etc.) Collective drafts or copies are designated by names indicating their history or location, such as *Hayward's ts sheaf* for John Hayward's collection of typescripts of *Practical Cats*, or *ts Chamb* for the typescript of *The Rock* in the Lord Chamberlain's Papers. Lines drafted on a manuscript or typescript but not part of its principal text are sometimes designated by a separate abbreviation such as *msAdd* of *Gerontion* or *ms3* of *The Waste Land*. When constituents of a draft are now physically separated this is specified in the description, but the whole draft is given a single designation. Most of *ms1* of *Portrait of a Lady*, for instance, is in the Berg Collection, New York Public Library, but another part is the Beinecke Library at Yale.

TSE's texts are characterised by experimentation and overlappings of all kinds. Just as he returned again and again to particular passages in other writers, adapting them to his new purposes, so he returned to materials of his own, excerpting, adapting and recombining. Boundaries and categories were not fixed, because what he wrote for or learnt from one kind of writing often appeared in others, but he consistently divided his poems between those that were part of his Collected Poems and those that were not, and then into periods most of which coincide with the sections in that volume and in the present edition. The order, groupings and whereabouts of drafts also help to structure this history.

The earliest significant collection of TSE's poems in draft is the *March Hare* Notebook with its accompanying leaves, from which some poems were first collected in three books published in his lifetime: *Prufrock and Other Observations*, *Poems* (1919) and *Ara Vos Prec* (with its equivalent, *US 1920*). The contents of the Notebook, published as *Inventions of the March Hare* (1996), are tabulated at the head of the Textual History of *Prufrock and Other Observations*.

After 1920, the next period is represented by *The Waste Land* and its associated miscellaneous poems, the drafts of all of which were sent—like the *March Hare* Notebook—to John Quinn in 1922. The drafts of the Parts of the poem are listed in the Textual History, and *WLComposite* provides a reading text. The story of the associated miscellaneous poems and their relations to *The Waste Land* is given in an inventory within the headnote to the Commentary on the poem, 1. COMPOSITION.

One of these miscellaneous poems, *Song* ("The golden foot I may not kiss or clutch"), was largely re-used in *The wind sprang up at four o'clock*. In this form, along with *Eyes that last I saw in tears*, it became part of the writing and publishing of *The Hollow Men*. The various combinations of publication are tabulated at the head of the Commentary on *The Hollow Men*. Likewise, *Ash-Wednesday* was the final product of experiments with several combinations, and these are tabulated at the head of its Commentary. The bibliography of *Four Quartets* is complicated by the first of them, *Burnt Norton*, having appeared as a section within *1936*.

The Textual History of the poems in Vol. I, as also of *Old Possum's Book of Practical Cats* and *Anabasis*, is given here. Textual details of "Other Verses", *Noctes Binanianæ* and "Improper Rhymes" are briefly given within those sections.

2. NOTATION

Each entry in the Textual History has a lemma which begins with the line number or numbers, or a descriptive term such as *Title* or *Epigraph*. Ordinarily, the line number is in roman type. In the few cases where more than one text of a poem is printed, the line numbering of the secondary text is given in bold, as for instance *WLComposite* **25** or *The Cultivation of Christmas Trees* **25** (for the earliest full draft of that poem, given in the Textual History). When passages not amounting to a full draft are printed within the Textual History, they have their own numbering in square brackets: for instance, the two draft stanzas between lines 8 and 9 in *A Cooking Egg*, within which "I wanted Peace here on earth," is line [5]. This is the case also with *Prufrock's Pervigilium* and with some draft passages of *Little Gidding*. The full reference to a variant might for instance be *The Cultivation of Christmas Trees* **10–11** *ts6* [3]. Here, the bold numerals indicate that the readings are variants not of the published text but of the earliest full draft, and [3] indicates that in place of lines **10–11**, *ts6* has a variant passage of which this is the third line. In the Commentary, references are abbreviated to the easiest unmistakable form, such as "16 *variant*".

The lemma's line reference is followed by the lemma reading: the word or words (and if necessary the punctuation) of which variants are being noted. The lemma ends with a square bracket:

> 114 **prince; no doubt,**]

Where no lemma reading is given before the square bracket, the reference is to the whole of the specified element: II 20] *bracketed by Pound ts2* means the whole line is bracketed, while

> I 7] And all the disturbing things that are left unsaid *ms1 1ˢᵗ reading*

means that this was the first reading of the whole line in *ms1*. (The superscript forms "*1ˢᵗ reading*", "*2ⁿᵈ alt*" are used to distinguish readings from "*1st ed.*", "*2nd draft*" etc.)

Readings and proposed readings are given in roman type, while other annotations, intended as comments, whether or not by TSE, are given in italics between quotation marks. For instance,

> 337] *with "Keep" ts3*

indicates that "Keep" was TSE's reminder to himself and is not a variant. Proposed readings by others are attributed:

> [2] **change**] change, *Hayward ts3*

Likewise comments:

> II 80, 81] *transposed with "?" Hayward ts10b*

The symbol ‖ is used to separate different readings within the collations:

> 24 **sleep and feed**] feed and sleep *1919* ‖ sleep and eat *AraVP*

In cases where the lemma began as one reading among others before becoming established, its history too is spelt out:

> 8 **Where the**] *ms1 1ˢᵗ and final reading* ‖ Where *ms1 2ⁿᵈ reading*

If only a *1ˢᵗ reading* is specified, it was superseded by the lemma reading. If a *2ⁿᵈ reading* is specified but not a *1ˢᵗ reading*, the first was as the lemma. If a *1ˢᵗ reading* and a *3ʳᵈ reading* are given but not a *2ⁿᵈ reading*, the second was as the lemma.

Where a *1ˢᵗ reading* was not deleted, an added alternative is described as *alt*. Where the first reading was deleted and more than one replacement was added, these are *2ⁿᵈ reading alts*. Where John Hayward commented on the typescripts of *Four Quartets*, he did not delete words, so his suggested revisions are each technically *alt*, but this is not specified.

Where readings are the same in consecutive versions, the notation is abbreviated.

> **started;**] started: *ts3–ts5*

means that the reading is "started:" in the three typescripts *ts3, ts4, ts5*.

Where one or more of the intermediate drafts does not include the passage, a swung-dash is used:

> **small**] little *ts2~ts9*

means that the reading is "little" consistently from *ts2* to *ts9*, although in at least one of these typescripts the passage in question does not appear.

A plus sign after an abbreviation (*ts4*+ or *1925*+) means "and in derived texts". However, not all editions after a given date do necessarily derive from the one text, and there are anomalies such as continuing discrepancies in American editions, so exceptions may be listed, but "+" signals a firmly established text. In poem headnotes, "+" indicates that the poem itself continued to appear in collected editions.

Typed and manuscript revisions are not distinguished, and the collation does not generally specify *how* a revision was effected (for instance by deletion or transposition). The collation is a record not of all the marks on the paper, but of the resulting readings, which may combine type with manuscript, as well as combining words or punctuation marks that were not revised with others that have additions or deletions and with transpositions and material altogether new. For instance,

> 23] I've kept a decent house for twenty years, she says *ts1 2nd reading*

does not specify that the second reading was formed by the deletion of three words at the head of the original typed line ("Sergeant, I said,") with the words "I've ··· years" retained and "she says" then added in manuscript.

Many of TSE's manuscripts lack titles. Generally, his typescripts have a centred title, in capitals, with a full stop. The titles are rarely underlined. Publishers' house styles then determined their capitalisation and italicisation. Variations are not recorded here except in the case of The *"Boston Evening Transcript"*, which has appeared with several combinations of quotation marks and roman and italic type (and where the style of the present edition departs from that of *1963*, which was in error). TSE's epigraphs were usually centred and printed in italics, but this too varied according to house styles. Their presentation is not recorded other than in exceptional cases such as *The Hollow Men*, where the pagination is involved, and *Marina*, where the short prose extract from Seneca has consistently been set as two lines of verse. Full stops after titles (in drafts) and after the attributions of epigraphs are not noted.

Within the Textual History, titles and epigraphs have been standardised in roman type within the collations, to make them distinct from editorial matter:

> two] two of the *ts1*, *printings prior to US 1920*

avoids the confusion of

> *two] two of the ts1, printings prior to US 1920*

Different journals, editions and publishers have different conventions for the use of capitals, italics and quotation marks in the presentation of poetry. Mostly such differences are of only minor significance, and they are not systematically collated, but the practice of some of the more important volumes is specified in 3. KEY TO EDITIONS. "¶" is used to indicate a new paragraph. When typing, TSE usually omitted the space after "Mr.", which is not noted. Changes from capitals to small capitals or from "&" to "and" are not noted. "^" is used to indicate the point at which the adduced material was deleted or added:

> IV 10 ^ 11] And *del*

> III 12 ^ 13] Seen from the depths of a New York street, *added then del*

The Bodleian Library's manuscript classmarks "MS Eng. misc c." and "MS Eng. misc d." are abbreviated to "c." and "d." in references such as "c. 624 fols 107–108".

3. KEY TO EDITIONS

Cath Anth: *Catholic Anthology 1914–1915* [ed. Ezra Pound] (Elkin Mathews, 1915).

1917: *Prufrock and Other Observations* (The Egoist Ltd, 1917).

1919: *Poems* (The Hogarth Press, 1919).

AraVP: *Ara Vos Prec* (The Ovid Press, 1920).

US 1920: *Poems* (Alfred A. Knopf, 1920). The new editions of 1927 and 1929, each entirely reset, are as *US 1920* except where noted.

Boni: *The Waste Land* (Boni & Liveright, 1922). To Marianne Moore, 23 Mar 1934: "What a very kind thought of you to get me a copy of the original edition of *The Waste Land* . . . not being a collector of first editions, I have almost none of the earlier editions of my own work. I admit, however, that the first thing I do when I receive a second-hand bookseller's catalogue, is to look for my own name, and usually find '*Daniel Deronda*, two volumes, uncut'."

Hogarth: *The Waste Land* (The Hogarth Press, 1923).

1925: *Poems 1909–1925* (Faber & Gwyer, 1925). Published on 23 Nov, a month before the firm moved to Russell Square (28 Dec); memoirs of Ethel Swan (Faber archive). A limited edition was printed separately but is textually identical except where noted, as are the impressions 1926, 1928 and 1930 (which is the first under the imprint of Faber & Faber). Each poem, like each section of *The Waste Land*, opens with a word or words in capitals and small capitals.

1932: resetting of *1925*, apparently following the text of the first impression. (Text as *1925* except where noted.) The aim was to produce an American edition that would end the demand for unauthorised printings of *US 1920* and of *Boni* (letter to Henry Eliot, 3 Sept 1931). A printing in May 1932 was probably for this purpose, but appears to have been withdrawn because the paper was inferior. The sheets were cut down and issued in the Faber Library. A replacement printing in September, on large paper and with the errors in *Portrait of a Lady* II 7 corrected, was used for the American edition. Another in November was used for a second American impression and for a large-format "Sixth Impression" (actually the seventh) for Faber.

Rock: *The Rock: A Pageant Play Written for Performance at Sadler's Wells Theatre 28 May – 9 June 1934 on behalf of the Forty-Five Churches Fund of the Diocese of London. Book of Words by T. S. Eliot* (Faber, 1934). Published 31 May 1934. American edition (*US Rock*) published 23 Aug 1934.

1936: *Collected Poems 1909–1935* (Faber, 1936). Set from a copy of *1932* with corrections (*Conversation Galante* 16, *The Waste Land* [V] 428). The text remained the same through the eighteen impressions to 1961 except where noted. Physically modelled on *1932*, being the same size, with untrimmed pages, *1936* had much better typography, and more lines per page (which meant that for the first time since *AraVP*, the eleven stanzas of *A Cooking Egg* did not run on to a third page, so avoiding a two-page spread with no title). A paperback was first issued in 1958 (*1958 pbk*) between the 16th and 17th hardback impressions (1957 and 1959), but this was omitted from the list of impressions. The physical format of the book was slightly reduced beginning with its 13th impression (1949). Faber catalogue Spring 1936:

It is a chronic malady that Mr. Eliot's poems are dissipated through numerous emaciated tomes, and that some have not yet been clothed with the respectability of cloth bindings. *Poems 1909–1925* is the *only* collection so far; but, as the title would suggest, this does not include Mr. Eliot's verse subsequent to 1925, or any of his experiments in dramatic form. To our occasional nagging, Mr. Eliot has invariably replied that if he did not have to read so many manuscripts he would have more time for writing poetry. To which our reply has always been that after all we make it possible for him to keep body and soul together, and he ought to take the rough with the smooth. He has also observed that he was not ready; that the *Poems 1909–1925* summed up one phase, and that no further collection could be made until another phase had been more clearly defined.

What is, however, certain, is: this volume contains in the first part all the poems in the previous volume, and in the second everything written subsequently that Mr. Eliot wishes to preserve—including *Sweeney Agonistes* and the *Choruses from The Rock*—with the exception of *Murder in the Cathedral* and certain nonsense verses which will in due course have a proper book to themselves (see page 69 [announcing *Mr. Eliot's Book of Pollicle Dogs and Jellicle Cats As Recited to Him by the Man in White Spats*]). Here, then, in definitive form and in a convenient volume, is Mr. Eliot's poetical work for a period of 25 years. *Demy 8vo. 7s. 6d.*

US 1936: *Collected Poems 1909–1935* (Harcourt, Brace & Co., 1936). Set from proofs of *1936* which contained errors not in the final Faber text (TSE to Donald Brace, 22 May 1936).

Sesame: *The Waste Land and Other Poems* (Faber, 1940; frequently reprinted with the same title after the "Sesame" series was discontinued). Text as *1936* except where noted. "This *Sesame* volume consists of a selection of poems from *Collected Poems*, made by Anne Ridler with the author's consent, and designed to constitute an introduction to Mr. Eliot's poetical work", *Books by T. S. Eliot* flyer, c. 1948. All lifetime and some later impressions have bold numerals before the poems, either on the section-title page or above the text itself: **1**. *The Love Song of J. Alfred Prufrock* **2**. *Preludes* **3**. *Gerontion* **4**. *Sweeney Among the Nightingales* **5**. *The Waste Land* **6**. *Ash-Wednesday* **7**. *Journey of the Magi* **8**. *Marina* **9**. *Landscapes* [I–III] **10**. *Two Choruses from "The Rock"* [I, X]. In early printings the contents page is headed "*From* COLLECTED POEMS (1909–1935)", and although the contents appear not all to have been set directly from this, the text is as *1936* except where noted. In 1998, also under the title *The Waste Land and Other Poems*, Frank Kermode edited for Penguin in the US a different selection likewise ending with *The Waste Land*, with a very inaccurate text in which, for instance, a version of *The Love Song of J. Alfred Prufrock* 96–98 appears again in place of 107–110.

Later Poems: *Later Poems 1925–1935* (1941). Complementing *Poems 1909–1925*: the two books together contain the whole of *1936*. Contents: *Ash-Wednesday, Journey of the Magi, A Song for Simeon, Animula, Marina, Sweeney Agonistes, Coriolan, Eyes that last I saw in tears, The wind sprang up at four o'clock, Five-Finger Exercises, Landscapes, Lines for an Old Man, Choruses from "The Rock", Burnt Norton*. Text follows *1936* except where noted. A bound proof (McCue collection) is titled *Poems 1925–1935*. TSE to his secretary, Miss Sheldon, 10 Feb 1941: "I cannot think of any better title for the new volume in the Faber library than the one suggested—'Later Poems'. It at least leaves open the possibility of a third volume to be called 'Last Poems' and perhaps a fourth volume of 'Posthumous Poems'."

US 1943: *Four Quartets* (NY, 1943). For the destruction of most of the defective first impression, see *Gallup*.

1944: *Four Quartets* (Faber, 1944), following the separate pamphlet publications of *East Coker (EC)*, *Burnt Norton (BN)*, *The Dry Salvages (DS)* and *Little Gidding (LG)*.

Guild: *Selected Poems* (Guild Books, Vienna, 1946). Selection differs from the later *Penguin / Sel Poems*. Geoffrey Faber to Allen Lane of Penguin, 13 May 1947:

> After the war Eliot himself prepared for Austrian publication, through Guild Books, an edition of his *Selected Poems* ⋯ The only differences between the *Selected Poems* and the present edition of the *Collected Poems* are as follows:
>> Omitted from the *Selected Poems [Guild]*:—
> In the section called "Prufrock": two short passages, *Hysteria* (which is prose) and *Conversation Galante* (which I think he regarded as not up to the level of the others).
> In "Poems 1920":—"Four short poems in French".
> The four "Ariel Poems"; namely *Journey of the Magi, A Song for Simeon, Animula* and *Marina*.
> The so-called "Minor Poems"; namely *Eyes that last I saw in tears, The wind sprang up at four o'clock, Five-Finger Exercises, Landscapes* and *Lines for an Old Man*.

Poèmes: *Poèmes 1910–1930* tr. Pierre Leyris and others, with notes by John Hayward (Éditions du Seuil, Paris, [1947]). *Gallup* D87. For Hayward's notes, see "Hayward, John" in Bibliography of the present edition. *Gallup 1970* 36: "The poems are dated on the basis of information supplied by T. S. Eliot." For the possibility of including *Vers pour la Foulque*, see headnote to that poem in *Noctes Binanianæ*.

Penguin / Sel Poems: *Selected Poems* (Penguin, 1948, then Faber, 1954); this designation is used when the texts are identical. "A selection by the Author", according to the redesigned cover of the 1951 reprint of *Penguin*. Contents: *The Love Song of J. Alfred Prufrock, Portrait of a Lady, Preludes, Rhapsody on a Windy Night, Gerontion, Burbank with a Baedeker: Bleistein with a Cigar, Sweeney Erect, A Cooking Egg, The Hippopotamus, Whispers of Immortality, Mr. Eliot's Sunday Morning Service, Sweeney Among the Nightingales, The Waste Land, The Hollow Men, Ash-Wednesday, Journey of the Magi, A Song for Simeon, Animula, Marina, Choruses from "The Rock"* (I–III, VII, IX, X). Text follows *1936* except where noted.

To C. Day Lewis, 27 July 1944, on anthologies: "I should like to be able to say 'I am willing to be represented by this poem (or group of poems) for (say) five years; but by that time I may cease to consider your selection representative, so that if you wish to keep the book in print you must ask my permission again'."

Sel Poems 1954: *Selected Poems* (Faber, 1954). Text follows *Penguin* except where noted (probably being set from the 2nd imp.).

Sel Poems pbk: *Selected Poems* (1961). First Faber paperback edition. Text follows *Sel Poems 1954* except where noted.

Undergrad. Poems: *The Undergraduate Poems* [Harvard, 1949]. Reprinted, without authorisation, from *Harvard Advocate* Nov 1948.

Poems Written in Early Youth (Stockholm, 1950). Ed. John Hayward. Twelve copies only.

Poems Written in Early Youth (1967). Ed. John Hayward, with a Note by Valerie Eliot.

US 1952: The Complete Poems and Plays (NY, 1952). Poems do not each begin on a new page. No part-title pages divide the chronological sections, and this affects the positioning of titles and epigraphs (this not being noted in the Textual History).

Mardersteig: limited editions of *Four Quartets* and *The Waste Land* printed by Giovanni Mardersteig at the Officina Bodoni, Verona, respectively in 1960 and 1962. Of *The Waste Land*, TSE wrote: "I think it may be taken that the recent limited edition is the standard text. I have made one or two corrections in the notes in that edition, and Mr. Mardersteig, the publisher of that limited edition, suggested corrections in the quotations from Dante based on a more authentic text than the one I had used before", *Woodward* 264. Problems became apparent later, however: see Textual History.

1963: Collected Poems 1909–1962 (Faber, 1963). Incorporating poems later than 1936: the last three Quartets; *The Cultivation of Christmas Trees* (added to the Ariel Poems); and the five "Occasional Verses".

US 1963: Collected Poems 1909–1962 (Harcourt Brace, 1963).

1969: Complete Poems and Plays (Faber, 1969).

WLFacs: The Waste Land: A Facsimile and Transcript of the Original Drafts including the Annotations of Ezra Pound ed. Valerie Eliot (Faber, 1971).

1974: Second edition of *1963*, reset.

Composition FQ: The Composition of "Four Quartets" by Helen Gardner (Faber, 1978).

March Hare: Inventions of the March Hare ed. Christopher Ricks (Faber, 1996).

Recent copies of the British *Collected Poems 1909–1962* and *Selected Poems*, and of the American *Collected Poems 1909–1962*, have also been consulted.

For editions, proofs and copies of *Old Possum's Book of Practical Cats*, see Textual History headnote for that volume.

4. PROOFS AND ASSOCIATION COPIES

The following proofs and association copies have been collated. The text of each is that of the published edition except where noted. Proofs are listed first, followed by published copies.

1932 proof (Joseph Baillargeon collection): bound proof (small format), with brown paper wrapper marked "Mr. Eliot" and, in his hand, "Corrected TSE 9. iv. 32". (Apparently the copy sold at Sotheby's, 18 Dec 1980.)

1936 proof (King's): bound proof, with TSE's emendations beginning at *The Waste Land*.

Hayward's 1936 proof (King's): bound proof with corrections and annotations by Hayward. Selected annotations are recorded in the Textual History.

1944 proof (photocopy, Faber archive): unbound page proofs of *Four Quartets*, dated by printer 26 May 1944 and marked "Corrected TSE 2. 6. 44". Original sold at Bloomsbury Book Auctions, 6 Sept 1990.

US 1952 proof (U. Maryland): bound proof, uncorrected.

Sel Poems 1954 proof (photocopy, Faber archive): unbound page proofs corrected by TSE. Original sold Bloomsbury Book Auctions 6 Sept 1990.

1963 proof (McCue collection): bound proof, uncorrected.

Curtis's 1936: Geoffrey Curtis's copy with emendations and an addition by TSE. Another hand has erroneously pencilled "Proof copy" on the front endpaper. Dated 25 x 38, probably by Curtis. None of the emendations was made in the 2nd impression of 1937. (Christie's, 23 Nov 2009.)

Hayward's 1925 (King's): John Hayward's copy, with the respective poems dated by TSE. On the front free endpaper TSE wrote: "2 Jan 1943. The pencilled dates after each poem in this copy of *Poems 1909–25* are, at the date above, notes written in my own hand. These are the dates for the respective poems, to the best of my knowledge and belief. I do not guarantee their accuracy; and it is possible that they may subsequently be altered by some other hand either in order to correct them, or mischievously to falsify the record. T. S. Eliot."

Hodgson's 1932 (Beinecke): Ralph Hodgson's copy, inscribed by TSE on 5 Apr 1932.

Isaacs's US 1920 (McCue collection): Professor J. Isaacs's copy with notes on dates and places of composition pencilled by him on contents page and at the foot of some poems. Isaacs was a literary scholar, film critic and occasional contributor to the *Criterion*.

Morley's US 1920 (King's): Frank Morley's copy, formerly TSE's. With emendations and notes on dates and places of composition pencilled in by TSE. Some dates (not noted here) are demonstrably inaccurate, because later than first publication. However, on the front pastedown is written "T. S. Eliot", which appears to be an early ownership (rather than a presentation) signature, and other annotations appear to be of the same period. The deletion of full stops at the end of each epigraph (and at the end of "THE END.") gives the impression that it may have been marked up for a future edition. Morley left Faber to work in America in 1939, so it is possible that this copy was a parting gift from TSE.

Quinn's AraVP (Beinecke): presentation copy to John Quinn, in which TSE has written out *La Figlia Che Piange*. Quinn to TSE 25 May 1921: "I should have written to you months ago to thank you for writing that poem in the vellum copy of Rodker's edition of your poems."

[*Quinn's Boni & Liveright* (untraced): John Quinn's copy of *Boni*, sold at the Anderson Galleries, NY, Nov 1923, described in the sale catalogue as "Editorial copy".]

Rodker's 1917 (Texas): copy of *Prufrock and Other Observations* used by John Rodker when typesetting *AraVP*. On the half-title page, TSE has written: "I have no doubt that this is the copy Rodker used. The two quotations, from Lucian ↄ Virgil, are certainly in my hand. With cordial wishes, to Frederic Prokosch, T. S. Eliot 15. v. 33". The supplied quotations are the epigraphs to *Mr. Apollinax* and *La Figlia Che Piange*.

Thayer's AraVP (Houghton): Lucy Thayer's copy of *AraVP*, annotated by TSE. Some of the annotations have been erased.

TSE's 1949 (Valerie Eliot collection): *1936* 13th imp., lightly annotated by TSE.

VE's 1951 (Valerie Eliot collection): *1936* 14th imp. (1951), annotated by Valerie Eliot, probably beginning while she worked as TSE's secretary. Alongside "jew" in *Burbank with a Baedeker: Bleistein with a Cigar*, she wrote "cap". Alongside *The*

Waste Land [III] 277–78 ("Weialala leia | Wallala leialala") she wrote "Wagner | *Götterdämmerung* | Read Wagner's text". The last three words may have been an instruction to herself, or may indicate that this copy was to be consulted when checking future editions and that the lines were to conform to Wagner's published text. If the latter, it indicates that TSE was prepared to change his wording where it was in error, as in his Note to "C.i.f." in *The Waste Land* [III] 211.

Virginia program (U. Virginia): see headnote to the Textual History of *Gerontion*.

Washington copy 1954 (Washington U., St. Louis): copy of *1936* 15th imp. (1954) marked up by TSE and Faber's production editor David Bland, with TSE's note on the front free endpaper: "This copy to be used in preparing next edition. Return to T.S.E." See also *ts Occasional Verses* (which was sold with this volume). Although the dates on the title page are emended from "1909–1935" to "1909–1962", his earliest emendations appear to be those such as the accents in the epigraph to *The Love Song of J. Alfred Prufrock* made in pencil which were adopted by *1936* 17th imp. in 1959 (here abbreviated to *CP 1959*). Next come the emendations in black ink, which were adopted in *1936* 18th imp. in 1961 (here *CP 1961*). Later emendations are in pencil, blue ballpoint and pencil again. In the Contents, TSE added dates in ballpoint to the four Ariel Poems of *1936* (also inserting "*The Cultivation of Christmas Trees—1954*"); to *Triumphal March* (though this date, 1931, was not printed); and to the section heading "*Choruses from 'The Rock'*". Still in ballpoint, he added the section heading "*Four Quartets*", the names of the last three Quartets and the dates of all four; the section heading "Occasional Poems" and the titles and dates: "*Defense of the Islands—1940*" (spelt so), "*A Note on War Poetry—1942*", "*To the Indians who died in Africa—1943*" and "*A Dedication—1959–1962*". Between the last two he then added "*To Walter de la Mare—1948*". In pencil he changed "Occasional Poems" to "Occasional Verses" (with a chevron beneath and "notes first", these then deleted). In blue ink he later deleted the dates of these poems. In pencil, beneath "Minor Poems", he changed the title of *Lines to a Duck in a Park* to *Lines to a Duck in the Park*, before going on to re-number the pages from *The Cultivation of Christmas Trees* through to *A Dedication*. In addition he re-numbered the pages in the book itself, pencilling new numbers beginning on the half-title "Unfinished Poems" through to the blank verso after *Choruses from "The Rock"*. (These numbers were eventually rendered incorrect by the addition of an extra flyleaf, so that the title page was counted as [5] rather than [3]. A note in red crayon in an unknown hand accordingly cautions: "Reader to check the page nos—will be two on from here.")

At a late stage, four typed slips were pasted into the Notes on the Waste Land (over Notes to 63, 64, 411 and 427), attempting to rectify the quotations from Dante. On the first three TSE has written in blue ink "Cf. etc as before", and on the last "V. etc. as before". The quotation in Note 427 adopts the wording recommended by Giovanni Mardersteig when he sent his proofs to Faber on 27 June 1961 (see Textual History of the Notes on the Waste Land).

Although the "new edition" was originally to be called *Collected Poems 1909–1960*, the latest emendations are probably later than 19 Apr 1962. TSE wrote on that day to Alan Clodd accepting that he had been wrong about "C.i.f." in the Notes on the Waste Land. The typed list of TSE's books prepared for the verso of the section-title page and now accompanying *Washington copy 1954* is dated 1 Mar 1963.

TSE's emendations were first adopted in 1959 in the 17th imp. of *1936* (here *CP 1959*); in 1961 in the 18th imp. of *1936* (here *CP 1961*); and in *1963*:

Prufrock and Other Observations epigraph rewritten (black ink and then pencil, adopted *CP 1959*; new errors *CP 1961, 1963*)

The Love Song of J. Alfred Prufrock emendations to epigraph (two in pencil, adopted *CP 1959*; five in black ink, adopted *CP 1961*; further emended *1963*)

The Love Song of J. Alfred Prufrock, instruction to change square brackets to round brackets throughout (later pencil, adopted *1963*)

Portrait of a Lady III 25 ^ 26 line space added (ballpoint, adopted *1963*)

Preludes I 12 ^ 13 and II 5 ^ 6 line spaces added (both later pencil, adopted *1963*)

The "Boston Evening Transcript" 7 (later pencil, adopted *1963*)

Mr. Apollinax epigraph (later pencil)

Gerontion 8 (ballpoint, adopted *1963*)

Gerontion 28 (different ballpoint not used elsewhere in the vol, adopted *CP 1959*)

Burbank with a Baedeker: Bleistein with a Cigar 23 (ballpoint, adopted *1963*)

The Waste Land [I] 37 (black ink, adopted *CP 1961*)

The Waste Land [I] 74, [II] 85 and [III] 173 (all pencil, adopted *CP 1961*)

The Waste Land [V] 376 ^ 377 (pencil and ballpoint, adopted *CP 1961*)

Notes on the Waste Land 63 (black ink, adopted *CP 1961*; however this correction was later obscured by a typed slip with blue ink, the text of which was adopted by *1963*, but which did not include an accent on *si*)

Notes on the Waste Land 64 (typed slip with blue ink, adopted *1963*)

Notes on the Waste Land 92 (pencil adopted *CP 1959*, and later pencil, adopted *1963*)

Notes on the Waste Land 210 (blue ink, adopted *1963*)

Notes on the Waste Land 218 (pencil, adopted *CP 1959*; ballpoint, adopted *1963* and blue ink, adopted *1963* but with new misspelling *1963*)

Notes on the Waste Land 357 (blue ink, confirmed in pencil, adopted *CP 1959*)

Notes on the Waste Land 411 (typed slip with blue ink emending Dante, partially adopted *1963*; ballpoint, adopted *1963*)

Notes on the Waste Land 427 (typed slip with blue ink, adopted *1963*)

Ash-Wednesday V 8 (pencil and ballpoint, adopted *CP 1961*)

Journey of the Magi 22 and 24 (later pencil, adopted *1963*)

Sweeney Agonistes: Fragment of an Agon 97 speaker name (pencil, adopted *CP 1959*)

Five-Finger Exercises V. *Lines for Cuscuscaraway and Mirza Murad Ali Beg* 2 noting broken type (pencil)

Landscapes V. *Cape Ann* 12 ^ 13] *line space* (pencil, adopted *1963*)

Lines for an Old Man 13 ^ 14] *line space* (pencil, adopted *1963*)

Other instructions written by David Bland in the volume concern the taking in of *The Cultivation of Christmas Trees* and *Four Quartets* (the pages of *Burnt Norton* being paperclipped together in accordance with his note: "Here take in *The Four Quartets* (set from file copy herewith, and page as rough dummy herewith)".

5. THE *MARCH HARE* NOTEBOOK AND ACCOMPANYING LEAVES

Apart from juvenilia and the doggerel letter *Dear Charlotte,* | *Hoping you are better* ("Other Verses"), the earliest poetic manuscripts by TSE to survive are those in the *March Hare* Notebook and its accompanying leaves. They comprise

1) one of the seven poems printed in the *Harvard Advocate*: *Humouresque* ("Uncollected Poems")

2) seven of the twelve poems in *Prufrock and Other Observations*, plus *Prufrock's Pervigilium*, a 32-line addition to *The Love Song of J. Alfred Prufrock* (see Textual History, after 69)

3) eleven poems from *Ara Vos Prec* and *Poems* (1920), one of which, *Ode* ("Tired. | Subterrene"), was published only in *Ara Vos Prec* and never collected

4) thirty-five poems published in *Inventions of the March Hare* (1996), which in the present edition appear in "Uncollected Poems".

In order of publication in their respective volumes, the poems are:

Notebook	Laid-in Leaves	Loose Leaves
Prufrock and Other Observations		
The Love Song of J. Alfred Prufrock	*Preludes* (IV)	*Rhapsody on a Windy Night*
Portrait of a Lady		*Mr. Apollinax*
Preludes (I–III)		
Morning at the Window		
Conversation Galante		
Ara Vos Prec / *Poems* (1920)		(Ordered as in *Poems* (1920) and later editions)
		Gerontion
		Burbank with a Baedeker: Bleistein with a Cigar
		Sweeney Erect
		A Cooking Egg
		Mélange Adultère de Tout
		Lune de Miel
		Dans le Restaurant
		Whispers of Immortality
		Mr. Eliot's Sunday Morning Service
		Sweeney Among the Nightingales
		Ode ("Tired. | Subterrene") *Ara Vos Prec* only)

Notebook	Laid-in Leaves	Loose Leaves

Poems Written in Early Youth
Humouresque (Published
  in *Harvard Advocate*
  then privately printed in
  Undergraduate Poems)		

Inventions of the March Hare		
Convictions (*Curtain Raiser*)	*Easter: Sensations of* *April* II	*Introspection*
First Caprice in North Cambridge	*Paysage Triste*	*To Helen*
Fourth Caprice in Montparnasse	*In the Department Store*	*The Burnt Dancer*

Second Caprice in North
  Cambridge
	The Little Passion: From
	  "*An Agony in the Garret*"
		First Debate between the Body
		  and Soul

Interlude in London		*Bacchus and Ariadne: 2nd*
		  Debate between the Body
		  and Soul

Opera		*The smoke that gathers blue and* *sinks*
Silence		*He said: this universe is very* *clever*
Mandarins		*Inside the gloom*
Easter: Sensations of April I		*Oh little voices of the throats* *of men*
Goldfish (*Essence of Summer* *Magazines*)		*The Love Song of St. Sebastian*
Suite Clownesque		*Do I know how I feel? Do I know* *what I think?*
[*Prufrock's Pervigilium*]		*Hidden under the heron's wing*
Entretien dans un parc		*O lord, have patience*
Interlude: in a Bar		*Airs of Palestine, No. 2*
Afternoon		*Petit Epître*
Suppressed Complex		*Tristan Corbière*
		The Engine

plus copies by TSE of two of
  the *Rondels pour après* from
  Tristan Corbière's *Les Amours*
  jaunes, written on versos
  of unnumbered leaves and
  upside-down in relation to
  the front of the volume (see
  headnote to *Tristan Corbière*)
	plus two further *Rondels*
	  by Corbière (see
	  headnote to *Tristan*
	  Corbière)
		plus typescript of *Autour d'une*
		  Traduction d'Euripide (1916),
		  an unpublished review in
		  French

Between 1968 and 1996, leaves excised from the Notebook came to light among the
Ezra Pound papers (Beinecke). In the catalogue of an exhibition in honour of Pound,
Donald Gallup explained that "On various occasions, over many years, Ezra Pound
expressed his admiration for a series of vigorously scatological poems that Eliot had
begun while at Harvard, dealing with two redoubtable characters, King Bolo and his
Queen", and that when TSE sold the Notebook to Quinn, "he took the precaution
of excising those leaves containing parts of the Bolo series. He seems to have given
them, along with scraps of other versions ⋯ to Pound" (*Gallup 1976*, item 69). For
these, see "Improper Rhymes".

The quarter-leather Notebook was bought by TSE in Gloucester, Massachusetts, and in Gallup's judgment TSE used it "beginning after January and before April 1910" (although TSE's own account puts it slightly earlier). Blue ink, black ink and pencil were used, the blue ink preceding the black. A detailed bibliographical description appeared in *Gallup 1968*:

> Originally it must have contained 72 leaves of ruled white paper, of which 12 have been excised, 10 leaving traces of stubs. Eight leaves contain manuscript on rectos only, two on versos only, 22 on both rectos and versos, and 28 are blank. The leaves or pages actually written upon (with the exception of the last two) are numbered from 1 to 52, possibly by T. S. Eliot at a later date.

(As in *March Hare*, the numbering, 1–52, is followed in the present edition.) A manuscript endpaper to the Notebook with the title INVENTIONS | OF THE | MARCH HARE was reproduced as the half-title page of the edition of 1996. For TSE's description of the Notebook, its sale to John Quinn along with the gift of the drafts of *The Waste Land*, and the story of their disappearance and rediscovery, see headnote to *The Waste Land*, 11. THE FATE OF THE DRAFTS.

6. *VALERIE'S OWN BOOK*

Two exercise books entitled "VALERIE'S OWN BOOK | OF POEMS BY T. S. ELIOT" (Valerie Eliot collection), the second of which is priced in pencil, "4/-". TSE copied into them for his wife a wide range of his poetry, in blue ink, on rectos only except for *The Blameless Sister of Publicola* (on 148), a substitute stanzo of *The Columbiad* (on 92), and occasional notes and corrections. Variations of the ink and interruptions in, for instance, *East Coker* suggest that some rectos too were left blank and filled in later. The exercise books perhaps date from the late 1950s, although *Cat's Prologue* was transcribed after 18 Sept 1961. For convenience, the pages of both books are here allotted consecutive page numbers, including blank versos.

Vol I

1:	"VALERIE'S OWN BOOK | OF POEMS BY T. S. ELIOT"
3–17:	*The Love Song of J. Alfred Prufrock*
19:	*Chandos Clerihews*
21–23:	*How the Tall Girl and I Play Together*
25–73:	*The Waste Land*
75:	*Columbiad: 2 stanzos*
	"Columbo thought that he would take" (st. 23)
	"Columbo and his caravels" (st. 42)
77:	*A Dedication* [*A Dedication to my Wife*]
79:	*Landscapes*: I. *New Hampshire*
81:	*Columbiad: 2 stanzos*
	"'Twas Christmas on the Spanish main" (st. 41)
	"King Bolo's royal body guard" (st. 6)
83:	*Landscapes*: II. *Virginia*
85:	III. *Usk*
87:	IV. *Rannoch, by Glencoe*
89:	*Sleeping together includes a little waking*
91:	[*Landscapes:*] V. *Cape Ann*

93: *Grizabella: The Glamour Cat*
94–95: *Columbiad: 2 stanzos*
    "The Ladies of King Bolo's Court" (st. 44)
    "King Bolo's Royal Body Guard" (st. 6, *here struck out*)
    "Now while King Bolo and his Queen" (st. 43)
97–99: *How the Tall Girl's Breasts Are*
101–107: *Of the Awefull Battle of the Pekes and the Pollicles*
109–15: *East Coker* (I & II)
117–21: *Journey of the Magi*
123–25: *Animula*
127: *There was a young girl of Siberia*
    Columbiad: 1 stanzo
    "'Twas Christmas on the Spanish main" (st. 41)
129–43: *East Coker* continued (II–V)
145: *Stanzos*
    "One day King Bolo, from the beach" (st. 18)
    "King Bolo crowned his Big Black Queen" (st. 45)
147: *2 stanzos*
    "The cook who served them pork and beans" (st. 20)
    "Now when they'd been three months at sea" (a version of
    America Discover'd, sent to Bonamy Dobrée, [Sept 1927?])
149: *East Coker* continued (V completed)
150: *The Blameless Sister of Publicola*
151 and rear paste-down: Contents of Vol. I

Vol. II

front paste-down: "VALERIE'S OWN BOOK | OF POEMS BY T. S. ELIOT | VOL. II"

153–55: *Of Cows: A Poem* [*A Country Walk*]
155: *Columbiad: A Stanzo*
    "'Now buggar my ear!' the bo'sun cried" (st. 46)
157: *Eyes that last I saw in tears*
159–63: *Whispers of Immortality*
165: *The wind sprang up at four o'clock*
166–69: *For the Indian Soldiers who died in Africa*
171: *W. J. C.* [*He who in ceaseless labours took delight*]
173–77: *Preludes*
179: *A stanzo*
    "King Bolo's big black cousin Hugh" (st. 47)
180–85: *The Marching Song of the Pollicle Dogs*
187: *Lines spoken by the Cat in the little scene in "The Rock"*
    [*Cat's Prologue*]
188–91: *There's No One Left to Press my Pants*
193: *Dedication II*
195: *Lines to the Editor of the Westminster Gazette*
197–99: *Defence of the Islands*
201–205: *Montpelier Row*
207–11: *A Song for Simeon*
213–41: *Little Gidding*
242–end: blank

7. ON COMPOSITION AND MANUSCRIPTS

TSE to William Spens, 4 May 1931: "I am a person who destroys nothing and loses everything."

To Harry Crosby, 8 Sept 1927, responding to an offer to buy the drafts of *The Love Song of J. Alfred Prufrock* or *La Figlia Che Piange*: "I am sorry to have to tell you that I gave away the manuscripts of those two poems some years ago. And of recent years I never have any manuscripts for the reason that I compose on the typewriter and the nearest approach to a manuscript I ever have is the first draft with pencil corrections."

To Godfrey Childe, 18 Feb 1936: "I never have anything of interest in the way of manuscripts. I work on my verse from a few rough indecipherable notes, followed by a succession of typed versions, and all my prose I produce at once on the typewriter ⋯ I am not even sure that I like the idea of selling manuscript, unless in this case it is going to be of some personal use to yourself."

Sending some manuscript notes towards *Murder in the Cathedral* to Childe, 26 Feb 1936:

> My practice is to start a passage with a few pencilled pages, and then when I get going I usually continue it on the typewriter, so that I should never have a complete pencilled manuscript of any poem of any length, and I never have any ink manuscripts at all, unless I prepare them especially. In sending you these specimen pages there are two points I want to make.
>
> i. The amount of my manuscript of any sort in existence is very small. The manuscript of some of my early poems, and the typescript of *The Waste Land* with corrections by myself and Ezra Pound belonged to the late John Quinn of New York. Since his death both these are untraceable, and I should think it was as likely as not that they had been destroyed. The typescript-manuscripts of *Anabasis* and *The Rock* are in the possession of the Bodleian Library. There are two short poems in ink in the possession of some unknown stockbroker. Besides these, the 14 pages of *Murder in the Cathedral* are practically all that exists. I mention this point in order to justify placing a rather higher value on my manuscript than I otherwise should, especially as I have been told that occasionally letters of mine of no importance have been sold at auctions.
>
> ii. If we should agree about the price I do not want to accept any money myself for the manuscript, as I don't like the idea of selling manuscript unless one is in a state of destitution. I should therefore ask the purchaser to make out the cheque in another name for a charitable purpose which I have in mind.

To C. D. Abbott, 15 Dec 1936: "I have your letter of November 27th, and should be glad to help the Lockwood Memorial Library if I had any manuscripts which could be of any use to you. Unfortunately all my manuscripts up to the last two years have been disposed of in one way or another. I say 'manuscripts', but in recent years it would be truer to say that I never make any manuscripts. My method of composition of verse is to put down a few scraps at a time in illegible notes in pencil and develop them by successive drafts on the typewriter, and I am in the habit of consigning these to the wastepaper basket."

TSE to Henry Eliot, 30 Dec 1936: "As for manuscripts, I do all my prose stuff straight onto the typewriter, so there is never anything of that; and as for verse, I usually make a few rough notes and then draft and redraft on the machine. Sometimes I start with a pencil and then when I have got going work straight on with the typewriter. I gave two mixed manuscripts of this kind, *Anabasis* and *The Rock*, to the Bodleian." To John Hayward, 25 Sept 1940 (autograph): "A full description of Belvedere [Hotel] society · · · must await the flow of the machine."

To Christopher Lee, 25 Apr 1957: "I thank you for your enquiry of the 24th April but can not say honestly that I now have any MSS. of my own poems. In the first place, it is only occasionally that I set down bits of the first draft of a poem in pencil and these first drafts usually get destroyed. I am entirely dependent on the typewriter and do most of my composition on that machine. I do not possess any drafts of my works. There are some, I think, in the Houghton Library at Harvard University; there are one or two in the Bodleian Library at Oxford, and a few in the Library of Magdalene College, Cambridge. Practically nothing has remained in my possession after the publication of any work."

Paris Review interview (1959): "As a rule, with me an unfinished thing is a thing that might as well be rubbed out. It's better, if there's something good in it that I might make use of elsewhere, to leave it at the back of my mind than on paper in a drawer. If I leave it in a drawer it remains the same thing but if it's in the memory it becomes transformed into something else."

Prufrock and Other Observations

VOLUME VARIANTS

Seven of the twelve poems in *Prufrock and Other Observations* are found in the *March Hare* Notebook and its accompanying leaves. The Notebook also contains *Prufrock's Pervigilium*, a 32-line addition to *The Love Song of J. Alfred Prufrock* (printed Textual History, after 69), which TSE suppressed, on the advice, he later said, of Conrad Aiken.

Section-title page] *The exact form of this crystallised over a long period, though its constituents appear on the front free endpaper of the March Hare Notebook, which, with TSE's signature in blue ink and the rest in black ink, has:*

COMPLETE POEMS OF

T. S. Eliot

FOR
JEAN VERDENAL
1889–1915,
MORT AUX DARDANELLES

. . . TU SE' OMBRE ED OMBRA VEDI.

. . . PUOI, LA QUANTITATE
COMPRENDER DEL AMOR CH' A TE MI SCALDA,
QUANDO DISMENTO NOSTRA VANITATE
TRATTANDO L'OMBRE COME COSA SALDA.
PURG. XXI.

Having only one group of poems, *1917* has no section-title page. In *AraVP* the section-title page introducing the second half of the book read simply "*PRUFROCK.*" There was no equivalent in *US 1920*, where the *Prufrock* poems follow straight after *Sweeney Among the Nightingales*. The section-title page in *1925* expanded the title to "PRUFROCK | AND OTHER OBSERVATIONS | 1917" and added the dedication and the epigraph, although without the attribution and not in final form. The combined dedication and full, corrected epigraph appeared first in *US 1952* (with the first poem beginning—with its own epigraph—immediately beneath). The combined dedication and full, corrected epigraph and attribution first appeared in Britain in *Sel Poems 1954*.

Dedication] *not AraVP* ‖ TO | JEAN VERDENAL | 1889–1915 *1917, US 1920* ‖ For Jean Verdenal, 1889–1915. | mort aux Dardanelles. *1925* ‖ *the same without the full stops 1932+* (The preposition was changed in *1925* because the volume itself was dedicated "TO | HENRY WARE ELIOT | 1843–1919", as was *1932*.)   **1889–1915**] *correctly* 1890–1915 (*see Commentary*)

Volume epigraph] *not 1917, US 1920, Sesame* ‖ *before the post-1917 poems (beginning* with "*Geronition*") *at front of volume, AraVP* ‖ on "*Prufrock and Other Observations*" *section-title 1925+. Capital first letter for each full line in all editions prior to Sel Poems 1954 and in imps. of 1936 prior to pbk (1958).* To R. W. Chapman, 7 Sept 1948: "I must some day seize the opportunity of a new impression to clear up several slips in this volume. You do not mention what I discovered for myself—a quotation from Dante which accompanies the dedication to Jean Verdenal is also incorrect. In this case the error was not pure ignorance but quoting from memory." The epigraph was retyped, presumably by TSE, on the proof of *Sel Poems 1954*, with the final line beginning slightly to the left, as in the Temple edition of Dante, being the first line of a tercet. *Sel Poems 1954* did not observe this, though it did print the words correctly for the first time. Other errors appeared in *1936 pbk* (1958) and *1936* 17th imp. (1959) and 18th imp. (1961). Noting that the quotation was "incorrectly given", TSE typed the four lines on an undated leaf now in Valerie Eliot's collection. Marking up *Washington copy 1954*, he wrote out the epigraph in black ink, beginning with two extra words, then apparently added a further word before those, in pencil (and underlined each line). Unfortunately, *1963* printed the epigraph with each line centred, as did *1974* and the resetting in 2002 of both *Collected Poems* and *Sel Poems*.

[1] **Or puoi la**] *US 1952, Sel Poems 1954, Washington copy 1954 2nd emendation, 1936 17th imp. (1959), 1963+* ‖ Or puoi, la *AraVP* ‖ la *1925, 1936 prior to 17th imp.* ‖ puoi la *Washington copy 1954 1st emendation, 1936 18th imp. (1961)*

[2] **comprender**] *AraVP, US 1952, Sel Poems 1954, Washington copy 1954, 1936 17th imp. (1959)+* ‖ Puote veder *1925, 1936 prior to 17th imp., Guild, Penguin (see Commentary)* **dell'amor**] *AraVP, US 1952, Sel Poems 1954, Washington copy 1954 emendation, 1936 17th imp. (1959)+* ‖ del amor *1925, 1936 prior to 17th imp.* **ch'a**] *AraVP, US 1952, Sel Poems 1954, Washington copy 1954 emendation, 1936 17th imp. (1959)+* ‖ che a *1925, 1936 prior to 17th imp., Guild, Penguin*

[3] **vanitate,**] *Sel Poems 1954, Washington copy 1954 emendation, 1963+* ‖ vanitate *printings prior to 1936, 1936 (all imps.)*

Acknowledgement] Certain of these poems appeared first in *Poetry* and *Others 1917, verso of dedication* ‖ *not AraVP, 1925+*‖ Certain of these poems first appeared in *Poetry, Blast, Others, The Little Review,* and *Art and Letters. US 1920, recto before* "*Table of Contents*"

The Love Song of J. Alfred Prufrock

Published in *Poetry* June 1915; then *Cath Anth, 1917+*.

ms1 (Berg): Notebook 28–31. Undated, but appearing between *Suite Clownesque* IV, which is dated Oct 1910, and *Entretien dans un parc*, dated Feb 1911. Includes, after 69, *Prufrock's Pervigilium*, an additional passage first published in *March Hare*. In that transcription, *Prufrock's Pervigilium* was longer by six lines, because it was taken as including 73–74 ("I should have been a pair of ragged claws | Scuttling across the floors of silent seas.") and the four deleted lines 74^75 from *ms1*. The present edition treats those four lines as a separate variant, owing something to *Prufrock's Pervigilium* [29–32], which had perhaps already been deleted.

ts1 (U. Maryland): four leaves of "Falcon Bond" typing paper, with text closely following *ms1*. Typed for Conrad Aiken on a Blickensderfer italic typewriter with a very uncertain left margin. (Only indents that appear intentional are recorded.) Pencilled at the head is the address of a friend of Aiken's: "c/o M. D. Armstrong | 37 Great Ormond Street | WC". Facsimile of first leaf in *Modern Literature* auction catalogue of Sotheby Parke Bernet, NY, 31 Oct 1972. *Rainey* 198 assigns this and *ts2* to July 1914. For Aiken's attempts to place the poem with British publishers, see volume headnote. For other typescript and manuscript poems owned by Aiken, see headnotes to *Oh little voices of the throats of men*, *The Love Song of St. Sebastian*, *Afternoon* and *The Little Passion: From "An Agony in the Garret"*.

ts2 (U. Chicago): ribbon copy on six leaves of typing paper, sent to *Poetry*, Chicago. Facsimile in *Famous Verse Manuscripts: Facsimiles of Original Manuscripts as submitted to "Poetry"* (Modern Poetry Association, 1954). *Rainey* 198 assigns this and *ts1* to July 1914. Several layers of emendation cannot be distinguished with certainty. Neat emendations in black ink (commas added at 4, 113 and 130, colon at 49 and asterisks 74^75) are almost certainly authorial, since TSE signed his name in ink (over an erasure) at the foot of the poem. The punctuation at the end of many other lines is in pencil and may be authorial but appears more likely to be editorial. Although the evidence is unclear, *ts2* apparently shows TSE removing some of the line-end punctuation present in *ms1*, and submitting poems to *Poetry* with very light pointing, only to have the editors add line-end punctuation of their own, in which TSE generally acquiesced in subsequent printings. Numerous final readings are accordingly shown as "(*not by TSE?*)". Each page of *ts2* has at foot, circled, an editorial line count, including spaces. At the head of first page is a calculation with the initials of Harriet Monroe and Henry B. Fuller, "28) 165/168 lines (6 pps HM HBF". This may have been added once a galley proof had been set, for the line count of 165 includes not only line spaces but turned lines. The magazine's page was 28 lines deep, which over six pages gave available space of 168 lines. When printed, the poem occupied pages 130–35. TSE's typing occasionally strays over the left margin, but this was marked editorially for alignment. Where a line space is called for, the editor put a partial rule with "sp". TSE repeatedly fails to leave a space after typed commas. The indents and insettings of TSE's typing are recorded below, but not those of the editors.

Valerie's Own Book: fair copy (eight pages).

Title] **Prufrock** *AraVP contents*   **Love Song**] Love-Song *ts1*

Subtitle] (Prufrock among the Women). *ms1*

Running headline] Love Song of J. A. Prufrock *Cath Anth* ‖ The Love Song of Prufrock *1917* ‖ *not AraVP+*

Epigraph] *not ts1* ‖ *roman in ts2 but braced by editor with "It. 8-pt". Apostrophes and accents added by hand to ts2, except that the apostrophe in the last line is typed. Each line begins with a capital in ts2 and in print until corrected by TSE in Washington copy 1954 (black ink, with which he also corrected* credesse *to* credessi*) and thence in 1936 18th imp. (1961). The capitals continued to appear in Sel Poems for many years and were copied in Valerie's Own Book. Insetting of the second and third lines of the terza rima not observed in ts2 (although this had equivalent line space [3 ^ 4]) or in printings prior to this edition or in Valerie's Own Book.*

[1–6] *not ms1 1ˢᵗ reading* ‖

> "Sovegna vos al temps de mon dolor"—
> Poi s'ascose nel foco che gli affina.

ms add, squeezed between title and first line, with arrow from left margin

[1] **credessi**] *ts2, Poetry, Cath Anth, Washington copy 1954 emendation (black ink), 1936 18th imp. (1961)+* ‖ credesse *printings 1917–59*

[3] **più**] *ts2, Sel Poems 1954 (accent added by TSE in proof), Washington copy 1954 emendation (pencil), 1936 17th imp. (1959)+* ‖ piú *Poetry, Cath Anth* ‖ piu *1917, AraVP, US 1920, 1925, 1936 imps. prior to 1959*

[3 ^ 4] *line space ts2*

[4] **per ciò che**] *Sel Poems 1954 (so emended by TSE in proof), 1963+* ‖ perchiocche *ts2 1ˢᵗ reading* ‖ perciocchè *ts2 2ⁿᵈ reading, Poetry, Cath Anth* ‖ perciocche *1917, AraVP, US 1920, 1925, 1936*

[5] **tornò**] *Poetry, Cath Anth, Sel Poems 1954 (accent added by TSE in proof), Washington copy 1954 emendation (accent added in pencil), 1936 17th imp. (1959)+* ‖ torno *1917, AraVP, US 1920, 1925, 1936 imps. prior to 1959*   **alcun**] alcum *Poetry (corrected by TSE in copy at University College, Oxford)*

[6] ^ 1] *four asterisks ts2 (del by ed.)*

1 **Let**] . . . Let *ms1*   **I,**] *ts2 2ⁿᵈ reading (not by TSE?)+* ‖ I *ms1, ts2 1ˢᵗ reading*

3 **Like**] —Like *ms1 1ˢᵗ reading*   **etherised**] *ms1, tss, 1925+* ‖ etherized *printings prior to 1925*   **table;**] table— *ms1 1ˢᵗ reading* ‖ table *ms1 2ⁿᵈ reading*. (The punctuation at the beginning and end of the line which *March Hare* erroneously records as # consists of dashes struck through by TSE to delete.)

4 **streets,**] *ts2 2ⁿᵈ reading (comma in ink, presumably by TSE as at 130)* ‖ streets *ms1, ts2 1ˢᵗ reading*

6 **one-night**] one night *March Hare (TSE's pen did not leave the paper)*   **hotels**] hotels, *ts1*

7 **sawdust**] saw-dust *ts1*   **oyster-shells**] oyster shells *ms1, ts1*

8 **follow**] join *ms1*   **like**] tlike *ts1 1st reading (as if about to type "tedious"?)*

10 **question . . .**] *Poetry, Cath Anth, 1925 ltd ed. and later imps., 1932+* ‖ question.
ts1 ‖ question. . . . *1917, AraVP, US 1920, 1925 1st imp.*

10 ^ 11] *line space ms1, tss, Poetry, Cath Anth* ‖ *new page so line spacing indeterminate
1917* ‖ *no line space AraVP+, Valerie's Own Book*

11 **Oh,**] Oh *ms1, ts1, ts2 1st reading*   **ask, "What**] *ts2 2nd reading (not by TSE?)+* ‖
ask "what *ms1* ‖ ask:"What *(run together) ts1* ‖ ask"what *(run together) ts2 1st
reading*

12 ^ 13] *new page so line spacing indeterminate Cath Anth, 1932, Valerie's Own Book*

14, as also 36 **Michelangelo**] Michaelangelo *ts1*

14 ^ 15] *new page so line spacing indeterminate 1925* ‖ *no line space 1932 proof, with
"wider space" TSE*

15 **window-panes,**] *ts1, 1917+* ‖ window panes *ms1, ts2 1st reading* ‖ window panes,
ts2 2nd reading (not by TSE?), Poetry, Cath Anth

16 **muzzle**] back *ts1*   **window-panes,**] *ts1, 1917, AraVP, 1963+* ‖ window panes
ms1, ts2 1st reading ‖ window panes, *ts2 2nd reading (not by TSE?), Poetry, Cath
Anth* ‖ window-panes *US 1920 and printings prior to 1963, Valerie's Own Book 2nd
reading*

17 **evening,**] *ts2 2nd reading (not by TSE?)+* ‖ evening *ms1, ts2 1st reading*

18 **drains,**] *ts2 2nd reading (not by TSE?)+* ‖ drains; *ts1* ‖ drains *ms1, ts2 1st reading,
Valerie's Own Book*

19 **soot**] spot *Poetry, Cath Anth*. The error was caused by faint typing. In a copy
of *Poetry* now at University Coll., Oxford, TSE wrote: "damn! *soot*" (*Macbeth*
V i: "Out damned spot"). He corrected the error in the copy of *Cath Anth* he
sent to his mother (Houghton).   **chimneys,**] *ts2 2nd reading (not by TSE?)+* ‖
chimneys; *ms1* ‖ chimneys *ts2 1st reading*

20 **leap,**] *ms1, ts1, ts2 2nd reading (not by TSE?)+* ‖ leap *ts2 1st reading*

21 **And**] And, *ts1*   **night,**] *ts2 2nd reading (not by TSE?)+* ‖ night *ms1, ts1, ts2 1st
reading*

22 ^ 23] *new page so line spacing indeterminate ts2, AraVP, 1936 (not US 1936), US
1963*

24 **street**] street, *ts2 2nd reading (not by TSE?), printings prior to 1936, US 1936, US
1952*. The comma was probably an editorial addition in *Poetry*, but was adopted
by TSE. In *1932* it was under-inked so the compositor of *1936* overlooked it and
it was lost from British editions. The compositor of *US 1936* included it, so the
American text diverged until it was brought to conform with the British for *US
1963*. TSE tacitly accepted the line both with and without a comma, so the last
lifetime text, with no comma, is followed in the present edition.

25 **window-panes;**] *1917, 1925+* ‖ window panes; *ms1, ts2 2nd reading (not by TSE?),
Poetry, Cath Anth, US 1920* ‖ window-panee; *ts1 1st reading* ‖ window panes *ts2
1st reading*

26] *excessive spacing above and below line, with braces indicating that this was
inadvertent ts1*   **time**] time, *ts1*

30 **plate;**] *1917*+ ‖ plate: *ms1, tss, Poetry, Cath Anth*

32 **indecisions,**] *ts1, ts2 2ⁿᵈ reading (not by TSE?)*+ ‖ indecisions *ms1, ts2 1ˢᵗ reading*

33 **revisions,**] *ts2 2ⁿᵈ reading (not by TSE?)*+ ‖ revisions *ms1, ts1, ts2 1ˢᵗ reading*

34 **Before**] Between *ms1 1ˢᵗ reading, ts1*

34 ^ 35] *new page so line spacing indeterminate ms1*

38 **wonder, "Do I dare?" and, "Do I dare?"**] *1917*+ ‖ wonder "Do I dare?" and "Do I dare?" *ms1* ‖ wonder: Do I dare? and Do I dare? *ts1* ‖ wonder "do I dare?" and "do I dare?" *ts2 1ˢᵗ reading* ‖ wonder, "Do I dare?" and, "Do I dare?"— *ts2 2ⁿᵈ reading (not by TSE?), Poetry, Cath Anth*

39 **descend**] *the* s *obscured by an ink blot ts1*   stair,] *ts2 2ⁿᵈ reading (not by TSE?)*+ ‖ stair *ms1, ts2 1ˢᵗ reading* ‖ stsir *ts1*

40 **a**] my *ts1*   hair—] *ts2 2ⁿᵈ reading (not by TSE?)*+ ‖ hair *ms1, ts1, ts2 1ˢᵗ reading*

41 *as also* 44, 64, 82] *square not round brackets in printings 1936–61. In Washington copy 1954 TSE wrote "to printer: parentheses, not brackets, throughout". Both 1936 and US 1936 had substituted square for round brackets in this poem, and they were followed by* Sesame, Penguin *and* Sel Poems 1954. *Round brackets were reinstated in 1963 and US 1963.*

41 **say:**] say *ms1*   **"How**] *ts2 2ⁿᵈ reading (not by TSE?)*+ ‖ How *ts1* ‖ "how *ts2 1ˢᵗ reading*   **growing**] getting *ts1 1ˢᵗ reading*   **thin!"**)] thin! *ts1 1ˢᵗ reading* ‖ thin!) *ts 2ⁿᵈ reading*

41 ^ 42] *excessive line space ts1 1ˢᵗ reading*

42 **chin,**] chin *ms1, ts2*

43 **and**] ɑ *Valerie's Own Book*

44 **say:**] say *ms1*   **"But how**] "How *ts1* ‖ "but how *ts2*   **thin!"**)] thin") *ms1* ‖ thon"! *ts1 1ˢᵗ reading* ‖ thin"!) *ts 2ⁿᵈ reading*

45 **dare**] dare . . *ms1*

47–48] *one line ts1*

47 **minute**] moment *ts2 1ˢᵗ reading (with* minute *typed over)*

48 **reverse.**] reverse . . . *ms1*

48 ^ 49] *two-line space ts1*

49–52] *first word ("For") on its own line and underlined (as though introducing a performance), with other lines inset (then new page 52 ^ 53) ms1*

49 **them all already, known**] *ms1, ts2, 1917*+ ‖ them already, known *Poetry, Cath Anth (TSE added* all *in the copy he sent to his mother, now Houghton)*   **all—**] *1936 and later British printings, US 1963 and later US printings* ‖ all *ms1, ts1, ts2 1ˢᵗ reading* ‖ all: *ts2 2ⁿᵈ reading, printings prior to 1936 (colon changed to a dash by TSE in a copy of Poetry at University Coll., Oxford)* ‖ all:— *US 1936, US 1952 (probably misreading an attempt on the US 1936 proof to replicate a change from colon to dash made by TSE on the British proof)*

50 **Have**] I have *ts1*   **the evenings, mornings, afternoons,**] *ts1, ts2 3ʳᵈ reading (not by TSE?)*+ ‖ the evenings, mornings, afternoons *ms1* ‖ them all *ts2 1ˢᵗ reading* ‖ the evenings mornings afternoons *ts2 2ⁿᵈ reading*

51 **spoons;**] spoons, *ts1*

53 **Beneath**] Among *ms1, ts1*

54] *no indent ts1* ‖ *double indent ts2, Poetry, Cath Anth*

54 ^ 55] *no line space ts1 (but indenting of 55 may indicate new paragraph)*

55] *no indent ms1, ts2 1ˢᵗ reading, 1917+* ‖ *indent ts1, ts2 2ⁿᵈ reading (editorial), Poetry, Cath Anth, Penguin, 1963 (not 1963 proof, US 1963)* **eyes already, known**] eyes, I have known *ms1, ts1* **all—**] *ts2 2ⁿᵈ reading (not by TSE?)+* ‖ all *ms1, ts2 1ˢᵗ reading* ‖ all, *ts1*

56 **fix**] fit *Cath Anth* **in**] like *ts2 1ˢᵗ reading* **phrase,**] *1917+* ‖ phrase *ms1, ts1 1ˢᵗ reading* ‖ phrase; *ts1 2ⁿᵈ reading* ‖ phrase. *ts2, Poetry, Cath Anth*

57 **formulated,**] *ts2 2ⁿᵈ reading (not by TSE?)+* ‖ formulated *ms1 (uncertain), ts1, ts2 1ˢᵗ reading* **pin,**] *ts2 2ⁿᵈ reading (not by TSE?)+* ‖ pin *ms1 (uncertain), ts1 1ˢᵗ reading, ts2 1ˢᵗ reading* ‖ pin— *ts1 2ⁿᵈ reading*

58 **wriggling**] squirming *ms1 1ˢᵗ reading* **wall,**] *ts2 2ⁿᵈ reading (not by TSE?)+* ‖ wall *ms1, ts1 1ˢᵗ reading, ts2 1ˢᵗ reading* ‖ wall— *ts1 2ⁿᵈ reading*

59 **begin**] begin? *ms1, ts1*

60 **To**] —To *ms1* **butt-ends**] butt ends *ms1, ts1* **days and ways?**] ways and days? *AraVP*

61] *no indent ts1* ‖ *double indent ms1, ts2* ‖ *single indent Poetry, Cath Anth* **And**] But *ms1, ts1*

62 **the arms already,**] the arms, I have *ms1* ‖ them all, I have *ts1* **all—**] *ts2 2ⁿᵈ reading (not by TSE?)+* ‖ all *ms1, ts1, ts2 1ˢᵗ reading*

63 **braceleted**] braceleted, *ms1*

64 **But**] But, *ms1* **lamplight,**] lamp light *ts1* **hair!)**] hair) *ms1, Valerie's Own Book* ‖ hair). *ts1*

65–66] *no insetting 1917+* ‖ *inset to align with 61 ts2, Poetry, Cath Anth* ‖

        —Is it the skin, or perfume from a dress
        That makes me so digress?—

ms1 (second line indented so)

65] Is it the skin or perfume on a dress *ts1 with* the *changed to* white

67 **table,**] cushion, *ms1 2ⁿᵈ reading* ‖ cushion *ts1* **wrap**] wh *Valerie's Own Book 1ˢᵗ reading (uncertain)* **shawl.**] shawl— *ts1*

68] *no indent ts1* **presume?**] presume? ... *ms1, ts1 2ⁿᵈ reading*

69] *single indent ms1, 1917+* ‖ *no indent ts1* ‖ *double indent ts2, Poetry, Cath Anth* **begin?**] begin? ... *ms1* ‖ presume? ... *ts1, where line is then del*

Prufrock's Pervigilium

after 69] *line space and row of dots, then new page and title* PRUFROCK'S PERVIGILIUM *(over illegible erasure) with subtitle* (Testimony of J. A. Prufrock) *(first word uncertain) erased ms1* ‖ *several lines of space and new leaf ts1* ‖ *three asterisks del by editor with "Row of dots" ts2* ‖ *six dots Poetry, Cath Anth* ‖ *four asterisks 1917, AraVP* ‖ *eight dots US 1920* ‖ *five dots 1925+* ‖ *series of dashes Valerie's Own Book. The rows of dots here and elsewhere in* The Love Song of J. Alfred Prufrock *followed house style at* Poetry. *Divisions by asterisks and dots are used in several of the 1920 Poems, for instance*

A Cooking Egg at a place where two stanzas were deleted. TSE uses a row of dots when quoting three stanzas of *The Weeper* in *A Note on Richard Crashaw* (1928), indicating that lines are omitted.

70–72]   *ms1 has these 32 lines, all of them del except* [1–3], *and with a line space after* [32]:

> Shall I say, I have gone at dusk through narrow streets
>> And seen the smoke which rises from the pipes
>> Of lonely men in shirtsleeves, leaning out of windows.
> And when the evening woke and stared into its blindness
> I heard the children whimpering in corners   [5]
> Where women took the air, standing in entries—
> Women, spilling out of corsets, stood in entries
>> Where the draughty gas-jet flickered
>> And the oil cloth curled up stairs.
>
> And when the evening fought itself awake   [10]
> And the world was peeling oranges and reading evening papers
> And boys were smoking cigarettes, drifted helplessly together
>> In the fan of light spread out by the drug store on the corner
>> Then I have gone at night through narrow streets,
>> Where evil houses leaning all together   [15]
> Pointed a ribald finger at me in the darkness
>> Whispering all together, chuckled at me in the darkness.
>
> And when the midnight turned and writhed in fever
> I tossed the blankets back, to watch the darkness
> Crawling among the papers on the table   [20]
> It leapt to the floor and made a sudden hiss
> And darted stealthily across the wall
> Flattened itself upon the ceiling overhead
> Stretched out its tentacles, prepared to leap
>
> And when the dawn at length had realized itself   [25]
> And turned with a sense of nausea, to see what it had stirred:
> The eyes and feet of men—
> I fumbled to the window to experience the world
> And to hear my Madness singing, sitting on the kerbstone
> [A blind old drunken man who sings and mutters,   [30]
> With broken boot heels stained in many gutters]
> And as he sang the world began to fall apart . . .

[1] **gone**] walked *1st reading*

[13] **drug store**] drugstore *March Hare (error)*

[14] **narrow**] vacant *1st reading*

[15] **all together**] altogether *1st reading*

[17 ^ 18] *new page so line spacing indeterminate*

[30–31] *alignment shows square brackets were not a later addition*

Published text resumes

70 **Shall I say,**] Shall I say: *ts1*   **dusk**] night *ts1*   **streets**] *ts2 1st reading,*
    1917+ ‖ streets, *ts2 2nd reading (not by TSE?), Poetry, Cath Anth*

71 **watched**] seen *ms1, ts1*

72 **shirt-sleeves**] shirtsleeves *ms1, ts2, Poetry, Cath Anth, AraVP* ‖ shirt sleeves *Valerie's Own Book*   **windows? . . .**] *ts2 2ⁿᵈ reading (not by TSE?)*+‖ windows . . . *ts1, ts2 1ˢᵗ reading* ‖ windows? *Valerie's Own Book*

72 ^ 73] *two-line space ts1* ‖ *new page so line spacing indeterminate Penguin, Valerie's Own Book*

73 **I**] *ms1, ts2 2ⁿᵈ reading (not by TSE?)*+ ‖ . . . I *ts2 1ˢᵗ reading*

74] *slight indent ts2 (aligning with first word of 73 after the ellipsis)*   **across**] along *ts1*   **seas.**] seas . . . *ms1*

74 ^ 75] *two blank lines then new page with four lines, del*:

      —I have seen the darkness creep along the wall
      I have heard my Madness chatter before day
      I have seen the world roll up into a ball
      Then suddenly dissolve and fall away.

ms1 with "P.T.O.", then blank verso before poem resumes below a flourish ‖ *two-line space ts1* ‖ *three asterisks added in ink (probably TSE) but del by editor with "Row of dots" ts2* ‖ *six dots Poetry, Cath Anth* ‖ *four asterisks 1917* ‖ *three asterisks, AraVP* ‖ *eight dots US 1920* ‖ *five dots 1925*+ ‖ *series of dashes Valerie's Own Book*

76 **Smoothed**] Soothed *ts1*   **fingers,**] *ts2 2ⁿᵈ reading (not by TSE?)*+ ‖ fingers; *ms1, ts1 (where last letter is inked over indecipherable character)* ‖ fingers *ts2 1ˢᵗ reading*

77 **malingers,**] malingerd *ts1 1ˢᵗ reading* ‖ malingers *ts1*

78 **here beside**] here between *ms1* ‖ stretched between *ms1 alt added, ts1*

79 **Should**] *ts2 2ⁿᵈ reading (not by TSE?)*+ ‖ —Should *ms1, ts2 1ˢᵗ reading* ‖ Shouls *ts1 1ˢᵗ reading*   **tea and**] so many *ms1, ts1*   **ices,**] *ts2 2ⁿᵈ reading (not by TSE?)*+ ‖ ices *ms1, ts1, ts2 1ˢᵗ reading*

81 **prayed,**] prayed; *ms1*

82 **head (grown slightly bald)**] head, grown slightly bald, *ts1*   **platter,**] *ms1, ts1 2ⁿᵈ reading, ts2 2ⁿᵈ reading (not by TSE?)*+ ‖ platger *ts1 1ˢᵗ reading* ‖ platter *ts2 1ˢᵗ reading*

83 **prophet—**] prophet, *ts1*   **here's**] that's *ms1*   **matter;**] matter: *ms1*

84 **flicker,**] *ts2 2ⁿᵈ reading (not by TSE?)*+ ‖ flicker *ms1, ts2 1ˢᵗ reading*

85 **I have seen**] I seen *ms1 1ˢᵗ reading (given as* seen *in March Hare in error)*   **Footman**] FOOTMAN *ms1*   **coat,**] coat *ts1*   **snicker,**] snicker— *ms1*

86] *no indent ts1, 1917*+ ‖ *double indent ms1, ts2, Poetry, Cath Anth*   **And in short,**] And—in short— *ts1*

86 ^ 87] *two-line space Valerie's Own Book*

88 **cups**] toast *ts1*

90 **while,**] while *ms1, tss, Poetry, Cath Anth*

91 **smile,**] *ts2 2ⁿᵈ reading (not by TSE?)*+ ‖ smile *ms1, ts1, ts2 1ˢᵗ reading*

92 **To**] Or *ts1*

93 **roll**] have rolled *ts1*   **towards**] *Cath Anth, 1963 proof, 1963* ‖ toward

ms1, tss, printings prior to 1963, some later printings, Valerie's Own Book (see Commentary) **question,**] question— *ms1, ts1*

94 **say:**] say *ms1* ‖ have said: *ts1* "I] I *ts1* **dead,**] *ts1, ts2 2nd reading (not by TSE?)*+ ‖ dead *ms1, ts2 1st reading*

95 **all"—**] all;" *ms1* ‖ all, *ts1*

96 **If**] —If *ms1* **one,**] *ms1, ts2 2nd reading (not by TSE?)*+ ‖ one *ts2 1st reading* **head,**] *ts2 2nd reading (not by TSE?)*+ ‖ head *ms1, ts2 1st reading* ‖ heqd, *ts1*

97] *no indent ts1* **say:**] say, *ms1* "That] This *ts1 over uncertain reading* **meant**] meant, *ms1, ts1, Valerie's Own Book* **all.**] *ms1, 1936*+ ‖ all; *ts1, ts2 2nd reading (not by TSE?), printings prior to 1936* ‖ all, *ts2 1st reading, AraVP, Valerie's Own Book*

98] *single indent 1917*+ ‖ *no indent ts1* ‖ *double indent ms1, ts2, Poetry, Cath Anth* **That**] This *ts1* **all."**] all. *ts1* ‖ all". *ms1, ts2*

98 ^ 99] *two-line space Valerie's Own Book*

99 **been**] *not ts2 1st reading* **all,**] *ms1, ts1, ts2 2nd reading (not by TSE?)*+ ‖ all *ts2 1st reading*

100 **while,**] *ts2 2nd reading* ‖ while *ms1, ts2 1st reading* ‖ ehile *ts1*

101 **streets,**] *ts1, ts2 2nd reading (not by TSE?)*+ ‖ streets *ms1, ts2 1st reading*

102 **after the teacups, after**] and the tea-cups, and *ts1* **floor—**] floor, *ms1, ts1*

103 **more?—**] *ts2 2nd reading (not by TSE?)*+ ‖ more *ms1, ts2 1st reading* ‖ more— *ts1*

104 **It**] —It *ms1*

104 ^ 105] Perhaps it will make you wonder and smile: *ms1 (originally ending with a comma?), ts1 (without punctuation)*

105 **magic lantern**] magic-lantern *ts1* **a screen:**] a screen *ts1* ‖ the floor *Valerie's Own Book 1st reading (the words then underlined before deletion)* ‖ a screen; *Valerie's Own Book*

107 **one,**] *ts2 2nd reading (not by TSE?)*+ ‖ one *ts1, ts2 1st reading* **pillow**] pillow, *ms1 (probable reading, not recorded in March Hare)* **shawl,**] *ts2 2nd reading (not by TSE?)*+ ‖ shawl *ms1, ts1 2nd reading, ts2 1st reading* ‖ shawm *ts1 1st reading*

108–10] *ts1:*

> Should say: This is not what I meant, at all,
> This is not it, at all.

108–109] *two lines 1917*+ ‖ *one line ms1, tss, Poetry, Cath Anth*

108 **say:**] say *ms1*

109 **it at all,**] it, at all; *ms1*

110] *double indent ms1, ts2, Poetry, Cath Anth* **all."**] all". *ms1, ts2, Valerie's Own Book*

110 ^ 111] *five dots 1925*+‖ *two-line space ms1, ts1* ‖ *four asterisks ts2, 1917* ‖ *six dots Poetry, Cath Anth* ‖ *three asterisks, AraVP* ‖ *eight dots US 1920* ‖ *series of dashes Valerie's Own Book.*

111 **Prince**] *not ms1* **was**] am *ms1* **be;**] *Poetry*+ ‖ be. *ms1* ‖ be, *ts2*

112 **attendant**] attendent *ts2* **lord,**] lord— *ms1*

113 **two,**] two *ts2 1ˢᵗ reading*

114 **prince; no doubt,**] *1917*+ ‖ prince; withal, *ts1* ‖ prince—withal, *ts2 1ˢᵗ reading* ‖
   prince: withal, *ms1, ts2 2ⁿᵈ reading* (*not by TSE?*), *Poetry, Cath Anth*   **tool,**]
   tool; *ms1, ts1*

116 **meticulous;**] meticulous, *ms1, ts1*

118 **indeed, almost**] indeed, appear *ms1, ts1*   **ridiculous—**] ridiculous; *ms1*

119] *indented ms1*   **Fool**] fool *ts1*

119 ^ 120] *two-line space US 1952, Valerie's Own Book*

120 ^ 121] *accidental line space ts1*

121 **shall**] will *ms1 2ⁿᵈ reading* (*before reverting to* shall)   **bottoms**] bottom
   AraVP   **trousers**] *1917*+ ‖ trowsers *ms1, tss, Poetry, Cath Anth* (see
   Commentary)

121 ^ 122] *two-line space Valerie's Own Book*

122] *no indent ts2 1ˢᵗ reading, 1917*+ ‖ *indent ms1, ts2 2ⁿᵈ reading* (*editorial*), *Poetry,
   Cath Anth, Penguin, 1963* (*not 1963 proof, US 1963*) ‖ *indent indeterminate
   ts1*   **dare to**] dare *1974* (*often reprinted*)

123 **shall**] will *ms1*   **wear**] *over illegible mistyping ts1*   **trousers,**] *1917*+ ‖
   trowsers, *ms1, ts2, Poetry, Cath Anth* ‖ trowsers *ts1*

124 **each.**] each, *ms1*

124 ^ 125] *new leaf so line spacing indeterminate ts2* ‖ *no line space Poetry* (*but in copy
   now at University Coll., Oxford, TSE added caret marks with "space"*), *Cath Anth,
   1932 proof, with "space wider" TSE* ‖ *two-line space Valerie's Own Book*

125 ^ 126] *two-line space Valerie's Own Book*

126 **waves**] *tss, 1917*+ ‖ waves, *ms1, Poetry, Cath Anth*

128 ^ 129] *two-line space Valerie's Own Book*

130 **sea-girls**] *1917*+ ‖ seamaids *ms1, ts2 1ˢᵗ reading* ‖ mermaids *ts1* ‖ seagirls *ts2 2ⁿᵈ*
   reading, Poetry, Cath Anth   **brown**] *ts1, ts2 1ˢᵗ reading, Cath Anth*+ ‖ brown,
   ms1, ts2 2ⁿᵈ reading (*comma inked by TSE*), *Poetry*

131 **Till**] Til *ts1 1ˢᵗ reading*   **us**] up *ms1 1ˢᵗ reading* (*error*)

after 131] *Flourish and then "July–August 1911" ms1* ‖ *five pairs of asterisks then, in
   manuscript,* T. S. Eliot *ts2 1ˢᵗ reading* ‖ *asterisks del with "Row of dots"* (*editor*) *ts2
   2ⁿᵈ reading* ‖ *six dots then author's name Poetry* ‖ *six dots Cath Anth*

Portrait of a Lady

Published in *Others* Sept 1915, then *Cath Anth* (London, Nov 1915), *Others Anth* (NY,
Mar 1916; following *Others* except where specified) and *The New Poetry: An Anthology*
ed. Harriet Monroe and Alice Corbin Henderson (NY, Feb 1917), then *1917, AraVP, US
1920*+. An edition of the poem separately in 40 copies was printed by Marlborough
College Press in 1941.

ms1 (Berg): Notebook 22–23, 41–45; pencil and black ink. An additional excised
   leaf (Beinecke) supplies draft of I 37–40, plus two additional lines and the

succeeding epigraph (from Laforgue). Also in pencil and black ink, this leaf has on the verso *The Columbiad* st. 6 and 7.

ms frag (Beinecke): verso of a torn leaf with pencil first draft of III 31–41. The recto has *The Columbiad* st. 17 and 18 and *Fragments from the Ballad of Harmony Court* (see *Balls to you said Mrs. Sonnenschein*). Not being excised from Notebook, this leaf was not available to the editor of *March Hare*.

ts Smart Set (untraced): Ezra Pound to H. L. Mencken, co-editor of *The Smart Set* (NY), 3 Oct 1914: "I enclose a poem by the last intelligent man I've found—a young American, T. S. Eliot · · · I think him worth watching—mind 'not primitive.' His 'Lady' is very nicely drawn."

ts Pound (untraced): TSE to Ezra Pound, 2 Feb 1915: "I enclose a copy of the Lady". Pound appears to have sent this ts to Wyndham Lewis for *Blast*, some time before July 1915, writing: "I think that this thing of Eliot's would probably be more advantageous than anything of Rodker's admitting that it is a bit archaic · · · if you want to use this Portrait you'll have to get his permission. = or I will have to." This may also have been the ts sent to *Others*, where the poem was published.

TSE inscribed I 29–33 (ending with a full-stop) in a copy of *Journey of the Magi* for Edwin Sly (illustrated in Quill & Brush catalogue of the Thomas Shelton collection, 2002, item 43).

Epigraph] *Others*+ ‖ I have caught an everlasting cold:—The White Devil. *ms1 (where the published epigraph heads Part II)* ‖ *no epigraph New Poetry*   [1] **Thou**] "Thou *Others*   **committed—**] committed—" *Others* ‖ committed *Cath Anth*   [2] **Fornication**] "Fornication *Others*   [3] **dead.**] dead." *Others*

I

Numeral] *not ms1*

I 1 **smoke and fog**] fog and smoke *ms1*

I 3 **With**] With an *ms1 (written over [illegible])*   **have saved**] designed *ms1 1st reading*   **you";**] you" *ms1, Others*

I 4 **room,**] room *ms1, Others*

I 5 **overhead,**] overhead *ms1, Others* ‖ overhead: *New Poetry*

I 6 **tomb**] *Others, New Poetry, 1917+* ‖ tomb— *ms1* ‖ tomb, *Cath Anth, TSE's emendation in Morley's US 1920*

I 7] And all the disturbing things that are left unsaid *ms1 1st reading*

I 7 ^ 8] *no line space 1917+ (where 8 is the last line on the page in 1917)* ‖ *line space ms1, Others, Cath Anth, New Poetry*

I 9 **Transmit**] *rewritten (probably to clarify the word, although March Hare suggests over another word, perhaps* Translate*) ms1*   **Preludes**] Preludes *ms1*   **finger-tips**] *Others, AraVP, US 1920, 1936+* ‖ finger tips *ms1* ‖ finger-|tips *broken across line Cath Anth, Others Anth, 1917, 1925, 1932*

I 11 **friends**] friends— *New Poetry* ‖ friends, *TSE's emendation in Morley's US 1920*

I 13 **room."**] room" *ms1*

I 14 **—And**] And *ms1 2nd reading, Cath Anth*

I 15 **regrets**] *ms1, Others, 1917+* ‖ regrets, *Cath Anth, New Poetry, TSE's emendation in Morley's US 1920*

I 16 **Through**] Through ~~mod~~ *ms1*

I 18] **And begins.** *1917+* ‖ And begins— *ms1 1st reading* ‖ And then begins— *ms1 2nd reading* ‖ And begins *Others* ‖ And begins: *Cath Anth, New Poetry*

I 18 ^ 19] *no line space ms1, Others Anth, New Poetry, 1925+* ‖ *new page so line spacing indeterminate Others, US 1920, US 1936* ‖ *line space Cath Anth, 1917, AraVP, US 1963*

I 19 **friends,**] friends *ms1* ‖ friends; *New Poetry*

I 21 **odds**] ways *ms1 1st reading*   **ends,**] *1917+* ‖ ends *ms1, Others, Cath Anth* ‖ ends— *New Poetry*

I 22–23] *square not round brackets in printings 1936–61*

I 22] (Indeed I am not social—you knew it? ah, I knew you were not blind! *ms1 1st reading* ‖ (For indeed I do not love it—you knew? you were not blind! *ms1 2nd reading*

I 24 **To**] —To *ms1*   **these qualities,**] those qualities *ms1, recording (1955)*

I 24 ^ 25] So rare and strange and so unvalued too *ms1*

I 26 **lives.**] lives *ms1* ‖ lives: *New Poetry*

I 27 **you—**] you! *ms1*

I 28 **life,**] life— *ms1*   **what**] *ms1 1st and final reading+* ‖ quel *ms1 2nd reading*

I 28 ^ 29] *line space ms1, Cath Anth, New Poetry, 1936+* ‖ *four-line space Others* ‖ *no line space 1917 (where 29 is last on page), AraVP, US 1920, 1925* ‖ *new page so line spacing indeterminate 1932*

I 31 **cracked**] our *ms1 1st reading* ‖ shrill *ms1 2nd reading*   **cornets**] cornetts *ms1 1st reading* ‖ cornets, *Cath Anth, New Poetry*

I 32 **a**] an *ms1 1st reading*   **dull**] *ms1 final reading+* ‖ droll *ms1 1st reading (uncertain)* ‖ strong *ms1 2nd reading* ‖ rude *ms1 3rd reading*

I 33 **Absurdly hammering**] Hammering *ms1 1st reading*   **own,**] own *ms1* ‖ own— *New Poetry*

I 34 **monotone**] monotone . . *ms1*

I 35 **note."**] note". *ms1, Others, AraVP, Penguin*

I 36 **—Let**] Let *Cath Anth, New Poetry*

I 37–41] *inset March Hare (new page begins at 38 in ms1)*

I 37 **monuments,**] *Others, Cath Anth, New Poetry, 1925+* ‖ monuments *ms1, 1917, AraVP, US 1920 (comma added by TSE in Morley's US 1920)*

I 38 **events,**] events *ms1*

I 39 **clocks.**] clocks; *New Poetry* ‖ clocks *March Hare (error in transcription of ms1)*

I 40 **for half an hour**] down for a time *ms1 1st reading (omitted in error by March Hare)*   **bocks.**] bocks *ms* *after* I 40] *ms1 (from Laforgue, Locutions des Pierrots* XVI 1–2, 9–10):

> And pay our reckoning and go home again
> They are lighting up the lamps, and it begins to rain.
>
> III
>
> Je ne suis qu'un viveur lunaire   [3]
> Qui fait des ronds dans les bassins
>
> — — — — — — — — —
>
> ~~Devenez un legendaire~~   [5]
> ~~Au seuil des siècles charlatans!~~ . . . Pierrots.

Numeral] *TSE wrote* III *despite the position between* I *and* II.

[1] **And**] Then *1ˢᵗ reading*

[3] **lunaire**] Lunaire *March Hare (error in transcription of ms1)*

II

Numeral] Part II *with epigraph*: "Thou hast committed—" | "Fornication—but that was in another country | And besides, the wench is dead": Jew of Malta *ms1*

II 1 **bloom**] bloom, *TSE's emendation in Morley's US 1920*

II 3 **one**] them *AraVP*   **she talks.**] we talk *ms1 2ⁿᵈ reading*

II 4 **Ah,**] Ah *Others, New Poetry*

II 5 **life**] Life *ms1*   **who**] should *US 1920, 1925, 1936 proof*   **hands";**] hands;" *ms1, AraVP* ‖ hands;—" *Others* ‖ hands—" *New Poetry*

II 6 **(Slowly**] Slowly *ms1*   **stalks)**] stalks— *ms1 1ˢᵗ reading* ‖ stalk— *2ⁿᵈ reading* ‖ stalks); *New Poetry*

II 7 **"You**] You *AraVP (error)*   **it · · · it**] if · · · if *1932 (overlooked by TSE in 1932 proof; corrected in a new printing for the US, Sept 1932. See headnote to Textual History,* 3. KEY TO EDITIONS)   **flow,**] flow *ms1, AraVP*

II 8 **And**] "And *ms1*   **no remorse**] no remorse, *New Poetry* ‖ no more remorse *1969, 1974 (each corrected in later printings)*

II 9 **And**] "And *ms1*   **cannot see."**] does not see"— *ms1*

II 10 **course,**] course *ms1*

II 11 ^ 12] *no line space printings prior to 1936, 1963 proof* ‖ *new page so line spacing indeterminate 1936, US 1963* ‖ *new page with* II 12 *erroneously indented 1963* ‖ *line space with* II 12 *erroneously indented 1969, some printings of Sel Poems later than 1963*

II 13 **Spring,**] spring— *ms1* ‖ spring, *New Poetry*

II 15 ^ 16] *with line spaces before and after these lines, ms1*:

> Oh, spare these reminiscences!
> How you prolong the pose!
> These emotional concupiscences
> Tinctured attar of rose.
>   (The need for self-expression   [5]
>   Will pardon this digression).

II 17] **broken**] cracked *ms1*

II 18–28] *opening quotation marks start each line, with closing quotation marks at end of* 27 *reopening at* 28 *ms1*

II 19 **feelings**] feeling *ms1*　　　**feel,**] feel . . . *ms1*

II 21 **You**] "You *Cath Anth*

II 23 **can say**] will think *ms1*　　　**at · · · failed.**] 'At · · · failed.' *New Poetry*

II 23 ^ 24] *line space ms1, Cath Anth, 1917, AraVP, US 1920* ‖ *new page so line spacing indeterminate Others, Others Anth, 1925, 1932, US 1936* ‖ *no line space New Poetry, 1936+*

II 24 **But**] "But *Cath Anth*　　　**friend,**] friend *ms1*

II 25 **can**] have *ms1* 1ˢᵗ *reading*

II 26 **Only**] —Only *ms1*

II 28 **I**] "I *Cath Anth, New Poetry*　　　**friends . . ."**] friends"— *ms1*

II 29 **I**] —I *ms1*　　　**hat: how**] hat. How *ms1*

II 30 ^ 31] *line space ms1, Others, New Poetry, AraVP* ‖ *no line space Cath Anth, 1925+* ‖ *new page so line spacing indeterminate 1917, US 1920*

II 33 **remark**] remark. *1969* (*error, corrected in later printings*)

II 36 **confessed.**] confessed:— *ms1*

II 37 **countenance,**] countenance— *ms1*

II 38 **self-possessed**] self-possessed. *ms1* ‖ self-possessed, *TSE's emendation in Morley's US 1920*

II 39 **street piano**] *ms1 and texts prior to 1963* ‖ street-piano *1963+*　　　**tired**] tired, *New Poetry, TSE's emendation in Morley's US 1920.*

II 40 **song**] song, *Cath Anth, New Poetry*

II 41 **garden**] garden— *ms1*

II 42 **desired.**] desired— *ms1*

III

III 1 **down; returning**] down, recurring *ms1* ‖ down. Returning *New Poetry*　　　**before**] before, *Cath Anth, New Poetry, TSE's emendation in Morley's US 1920*

III 2 **ease**] ease— *ms1* ‖ ease, *Cath Anth, New Poetry, TSE's emendation in Morley's US 1920*

III 3 **door**] door, *Cath Anth*

III 4 ^ 5] *no line space 1932+* ‖ *line space ms1 and printings prior to 1925* ‖ *new page so line spacing indeterminate 1925*

III 5 **"And so**] "So *ms1*

III 6–8] *opening quotation marks start each line ms1*

III 7 **You**] Indeed, you *ms1*　　　**back,**] back *ms1*

III 9 **bric-à-brac**] bric-a-brac *ms1, Others, Cath Anth, New Poetry*

III 11 **second;**] second— *ms1*

III 12 ^ 13] *no line space ms1, printings prior to US 1920, 1936+* ‖ *line space 1925* ‖ *new page so line spacing indeterminate US 1920, 1932.* It may be that during the setting of *1925* from *US 1920*, the compositor noticed that several speeches by the lady begin after a line space, and assumed that one was intended here. But when *1936* was set from *1932*, where the spacing was again indeterminate, the new compositor took the opposite decision.

III 14–15] *opening quotation marks start each line ms1*

III 14 (**But**] —(And *ms1*   **ends!)**] ends!)— *ms1*

III 15 ^ 16] *line space AraVP*

III 16 **turning**] turning, *ms1*

III 18 **gutters; we**] gutters. We *ms1*

III 19–24] *opening quotation marks start each line ms1*

III 19 **friends,**] friends— *ms1*

III 22–24] *inset ms1*

III 24 **late.**] late." *ms1*

III 24 ^ 25] *line space AraVP*

III 25] *not ms1 1st reading*

III 25 ^ 26] *line space ms1, printings prior to 1936, US 1936, US 1952, added by TSE in Washington copy 1954, 1963+ ‖ no line space 1936 (where 25 is the first line on the page) and subsequent printings until 1963*

III 26 **I must**] I . . . must *ms1*

III 27 **To find**] For my *ms1*   . . . **dance,**] —dance *ms1*

III 28 **Like**] Dance like *ms1*

III 29 **Cry**] Whistle *ms1 1st reading*   **ape.**] ape; *ms1*

III 30 **trance—**] trance. *Cath Anth* ‖ trance . . . *New Poetry*

III 30 ^ 31] *line space ms1, Others, Cath Anth, 1936+ ‖ new page so line spacing indeterminate New Poetry, 1917, AraVP, 1932 ‖ no line space US 1920, 1925.* The compositor of *US 1920* may have been misled by the setting of *1917*, but anyway had to set this final page tight to prevent III 40 (the final line of the poem) appearing alone on a new page. The *US 1920* setting itself became an erroneous precedent for *1925* (where III 30 began a new page, so a line space immediately following would have been ungainly). The spacing was again indeterminate in *1932*, so the reintroduction of a line space in *1936* may have come about by chance or through revision.

III 31 **Well! and**] Well. And *ms frag*   **afternoon,**] afternoon *ms frag*

III 32–36 *and* 38–41] *inset ms frag*

III 32 **smoky**] sombre *ms frag*   **rose;**] rose *ms frag*

III 33 **die**] die, *ms frag, ms1*

III 34 **above**] across *ms frag, ms1*   **housetops;**] *US 1920+* ‖ housetops— *ms1 frag* ‖ house-tops *ms1* ‖ house tops; *Others, Cath Anth, New Poetry* ‖ house-|tops; *(turned line) 1917* ‖ house-tops; *AraVP*

III 35] *not ms frag 1st reading*   **Doubtful,**] Doubtful *ms1*   **for**] *1925+* ‖ for quite *ms frag, ms1, printings prior to 1925, US 1927, US 1929*

III 36 **feel**] suppose, *ms frag* ‖ feel, *ms1, Cath Anth*   **or**] nor *ms1*   **if I**] what to
 ms frag   **understand**] understand, *Cath Anth*

III 37 **Or whether**] Whether *ms frag 1ˢᵗ reading* ‖ And whether *ms frag 2ⁿᵈ
 reading*   **foolish,**] ~~silly~~ *ms frag 1ˢᵗ reading* ‖ puerile *ms frag 3ʳᵈ reading* ‖ futile
 ms frag final reading   **soon . . .**] soon *ms frag* ‖ soon, *ms1*

III 38 **Would**] —Would *ms1*   **advantage,**] advantage *ms frag (perhaps with a dash
 afterwards), ms1*   **all?**] all *ms frag*

III 39 **This**] (This *ms1*   **with**] "with *ms frag (uncertain 1ˢᵗ reading, not erased
 but presumably superseded by the quotation mark before "dying" which is more
 evident)*   **fall"**] fall," *TSE's emendation in Morley's US 1920*

III 40 **dying—**] dying—) *ms1*

Preludes

Published *Blast* 2, July 1915 (on the two pages before the heading "Poems | by |
T. S. Eliot", beneath which appears the single poem *Rhapsody on a Windy Night*),
then *1917+*. Repr., after publication of *1917*, in *Others Anthology* (*1917*), which TSE
reviewed in *Observations* (1918). *Others Anth* follows *Blast* except where noted.

ms1 (Berg): Notebook 15–17, plus leaf laid in (supplying IV); black ink and pencil.

Valerie's Own Book: fair copy (three pages).

Title] *Four Preludes* recording label of 78 rpm disc issued by the London Transcription
 Service (10PH 8166). The same title was used in a BBC broadcast, May 1942.

Numerals] not *ms1* ‖ arabic numerals *Others Anth*

I

Title] Prelude in Dorchester | (Houses) *ms1 1ˢᵗ reading* ‖ Prelude in Roxbury |
 (Houses) *ms1 2ⁿᵈ reading*

I 1, 5 **winter · · · gusty**] *ringed and linked ms1*

I 2 **smell**] smells *Others Anth*   **passageways**] passage ways *ms1, Blast*

I 3 **o'clock**] o clock *ms1*

I 4 **burnt-out**] *ms1, Others Anth, 1917+* ‖ burnt out *Blast* ‖ Burn-out *AraVP*

I 7 **about**] around *ms1*   **your**] our *Others Anth*   **feet**] feet, *ms1*

I 8 **lots;**] lots. *ms1*

I 10 **chimney-pots,**] chimney pots *ms1*

I 12 **cab-horse**] cab horse *ms1* ‖ cabhorse *Valerie's Own Book*

I 12 ^ 13] *line space ms1, added by TSE in Washington copy 1954, 1963+* ‖ *no line space
 printings prior to 1963*

I 13 **of the**] up of *ms1*   **lamps.**] lamps! *ms1, Blast*

II

Title] Prelude in Roxbury *ms1*

II 3 **sawdust-trampled**] sawdust trampled *ms1*

II 4 **all**] *not ms1*   **feet that**] feet | that *ms1* (*stepped down on to new line*)

II 5 ^ 6] *line space ms1, 1917, US 1920, added by TSE in Washington copy 1954, 1963+* ‖
  *no lines space Blast, 1932 and subsequent printings prior to 1963, Valerie's Own
  Book (where* II 5 *is the first line of a page*) ‖ *half-line space AraVP* ‖ *new page so line
  spacing indeterminate 1925*

II 6 **the**] all *ms1 1ˢᵗ reading*   **masquerades**] *last two letters apparently written over
  -i- (for "masquerading"?)*

II 7 **resumes,**] resumes *ms1*

II 7 ^ 8] *half-line space AraVP*

II 9 ^ 10] ~~(Such indeterminacies!)~~ *ms1 with first word written over* These *and second
  word doubtful (perhaps* ~~indelicacies!~~*). (This collation corrects March Hare.)*

II 10 **rooms.**] rooms . . . *ms1*

III

Title] (Morgendämmerung) | Prelude in Roxbury *ms1 only*

Epigraph] "Son âme | de petite putain": | Bubu. (*stepped down on three lines*) *ms1 only*

III 1 **bed,**] bed *ms1*

III 2 **waited;**] waited *ms1*

III 2 ^ 3] You flung an arm above your head *ms1*

III 3 **revealing**] *final "g" not penned Valerie's Own Book*

III 4 **The**] A *ms1 1ˢᵗ reading*

III 5 **Of**] *ms1 alt, Blast+* ‖ From *ms1 1ˢᵗ reading*   **constituted;**] constituted: *ms1*

III 6 ^ 7] *line space ms1*

III 7 **all**] *not Blast*

III 8 **shutters,**] *printings prior to 1936, 1974+* ‖ shutters *ms1, printings 1936–69, US
  1963 and later US printings, Valerie's Own Book. Sesame and Sel Poems were not
  brought to conform with 1974 for many years*

III 9 **gutters,**] gutters *ms1*

III 12 **along**] upon *ms1*

III 13 **curled**] dropped *ms1 1ˢᵗ reading*   **hair,**] hair *ms1*

IV

Title] Abenddämmerung *ms1 only*

IV 2 **block,**] block *ms1*

IV 3 **Or trampled**] *ms1 final reading+* ‖ Trampled *ms1 1ˢᵗ reading* ‖ ~~And~~ trampled *ms1
  2ⁿᵈ reading*   **insistent**] ~~the~~ insistent *ms1*

IV 4 **At**] Of *1ˢᵗ and final reading ms1* ‖ And *ms1 alt*   **four and five and six**] seven
  and of six *ms1 1ˢᵗ reading*   **o'clock;**] o'clock: *ms1*

IV 5 **And**] —And *ms1*   **stuffing**] *ms1 alt, Blast*+ ‖ cramming *ms1 1ˢᵗ reading*   **pipes,**] pipes *Blast*

IV 6 **newspapers,**] newspapers— *ms1*

IV 7 **Assured**] S *ms1 1ˢᵗ reading*   **certain**] ~~un~~certain *ms1*   **certainties,**] certainties: *ms1*

IV 9 ^ 10] *no line space Blast*

IV 10 **moved**] wrought *ms1*   **fancies that are**] *ms1 alt and final reading* ‖ various fancies, *ms1 1ˢᵗ reading*

IV 11 **and cling:**] which cling— *ms1 1ˢᵗ reading* ‖ and cling— *ms1 alt and final reading* ‖ and cling; *Valerie's Own Book (perhaps a colon smudged)*

IV 12 **gentle**] *ms1, 1917*+ ‖ gentle, *Blast, Others Anth, TSE's emendation in Morley's US 1920 (see McCue 2012, Proposal 18)*

IV 13 ^ 14] *no line space Blast*

IV 14 **Wipe**] —Wipe *ms1*   **laugh;**] laugh. *ms1*

IV 16 **lots.**] lots *ms1*

after 16] *ms1, line space and*

> —And we are moved into these strange opinions
> By four-o'clock-in-the-morning thoughts.

Rhapsody on a Windy Night

Published *Blast* 2, July 1915, then *1917*+. Repr., after publication of *1917*, in *Others Anthology* (1917). *Blast* prints the poem as a single passage without line spaces or indents. It has opening quotation marks at the beginning of each quoted line (thirty-five lines in all); this succession ends at 76, but without closing quotation marks. *Others Anth*, which follows *Blast* except where noted, tidies this up by enclosing the final two lines within the quoted passage, providing closing quotation marks at the end.

ms1 (Berg): leaf of lightweight wove typing paper accompanying Notebook. Pencil. Very faint, especially as to punctuation. Re-examination has led to correction of some readings in *March Hare*. There are short pencil rules 12 ^ 13, 32 ^ 33, 45 ^ 46.

Title **on**] of *Blast, AraVP contents page*

1 **o'clock.**] o'clock *ms1* ‖ o'clock, *Blast*

3 **synthesis,**] synthesis *ms1, AraVP*

4 **Whispering**] And all the *ms1 1ˢᵗ reading*   **incantations**] incantations, *TSE's emendation in Morley's US 1920*

5 **Dissolve**] Disolve *US 1920 (corrected by TSE in Morley's US 1920)*   **of memory**] *Others Anth, US 1920*+ ‖ of the memory *ms1, Blast, 1917, AraVP (see McCue 2012, Proposal 11)*

6 **relations,**] relations *ms1, US 1936, US 1952* ‖ relations. *TSE's emendation in Morley's US 1920*

7] —Its divisions, | Definite precisions (*two lines*) *ms1*   **precisions.**] *1963+* ‖ precisions *ms1* ‖ precisions, *printings prior to 1963 (see McCue 2012, Proposal 20)*

9 **drum,**] drum *ms1*

11 **Midnight**] The nig *ms1 1ˢᵗ reading* ‖ The midnight *March Hare (error in transcription of ms1 1ˢᵗ reading)*   **the**] my *ms1 1ˢᵗ reading*

11, 12 **memory | As**] *marks resembling brackets added by TSE in Morley's US 1920 perhaps to transpose lines:* memory) | (As

13 *as also* 33, 46 **Half-past**] *1917+* ‖ Half past *ms1, Blast*

13 **one,**] one *ms1* ‖ one. *AraVP*

14 *as also* 16 **street-lamp**] *ms1, 1925+* ‖ street lamp *printings prior to 1925*   **sputtered,**] sputtered *ms1*

15] **The street-lamp**] *1925+* ‖ The " " (*ditto marks*) *ms1* ‖ The street lamp *printings prior to 1925*   **muttered,**] muttered *ms1*

16 **said,**] said *ms1* ‖ said: *Others Anth*   **Regard**] regard *ms1*

17–22] *opening quotation marks start each line ms1 (except 18 which is a later add.), Blast*

17 **toward**] towards *1969*   **in the light of the door**] on the corner *ms1 1ˢᵗ reading*

18] *not ms1 1ˢᵗ reading*   **grin.**] grin *ms1*

19 **border**] corner *ms1 1ˢᵗ reading*

20 **torn**] torn, *ms1*   **sand,**] sand *ms1*

21 **you see**] *not ms1 1ˢᵗ reading*

22 ^ 23] *line space ms1, 1917, AraVP, 1932+* ‖ *no line space Blast* ‖ *new page so line spacing indeterminate US 1920, 1925*

24 **twisted**] *brackets added (for reconsideration) ms1*   **things;**] things *ms1*

25 **A**] —A *ms1*

26 **smooth,**] smooth *ms1, AraVP*   **polished**] polished, *TSE's emendation in Morley's US 1920*

28 **skeleton,**] skeleton *ms1*

29] *not AraVP*   **Stiff**] Hard *ms1 1ˢᵗ reading*   **white.**] white *ms1*

30 **yard,**] yard *ms1, Blast*

31 **that**] which *ms1*   **strength**] *ms1 alt added, Blast+* ‖ force *ms1 1ˢᵗ reading*   **left**] left, *TSE's emendation in Morley's US 1920*

32 **snap.**] snap *ms1*

33 **two,**] two *ms1*

34 **The**] A *ms1*   **street-lamp**] street lamp *ms1, printings prior to US 1920*   **said,**] said *ms1* ‖ said: *Others Anth*

35 **"Remark**] Remark *1932 proof, with quotation mark added TSE*   **which**] *ms1 1ˢᵗ and final reading, Blast+* ‖ that *ms1 2ⁿᵈ reading*   **itself**] himself *ms1 1ˢᵗ reading*   **gutter,**] gutter *ms1*

36 **its**] his *ms1 1ˢᵗ reading*

37 **rancid**] *not ms1 1ˢᵗ reading*   **butter."**] butter *ms1*

37 ^ 38] *line space ms1*

38 **the child**] *US 1920+* ‖ a child *ms1, Blast, 1917, AraVP*   **automatic,**] automatic *ms1*

39 **was**] *ms1 1ˢᵗ reading unclear, perhaps* he (*March Hare*) *or* I   **quay.**] *1917+* ‖ quai *ms1, Others Anth* ‖ quai. *Blast* ‖ quay, *1969*

40 **that**] the *ms1, Others Anth*   **child's eye.**] eye ~~oft~~ *ms1 1ˢᵗ reading*

42 **shutters,**] shutters *ms1*

43 **pool,**] pool *ms1*

44 **An old crab**] A crab green and *ms1 1ˢᵗ reading*   **barnacles**] a barnacle *ms1.*   **back,**] back *ms1*

45 **Gripped**] S *ms1 1ˢᵗ reading (for "Seized"?)*   **which I held him.**] I held him *ms1*

46 **three,**] three *ms1*

47 **lamp sputtered,**] lamps sputtered *ms1*

48 **dark.**] dark *ms1*

48 ^ 49] *line space 1917 (to avoid an ungainly line space after the first line on the following page), US 1920* ‖ *no line space ms1, AraVP, 1925 (probably to avoid a short page), 1936+*

49 **The**] A *ms1*   **hummed:**] hummed *ms1*

50 **moon,**] moon *ms1*

51 **La**] "La *ms1*   **rancune,**] rancune *ms1*

52 **feeble**] watery *ms1 1ˢᵗ reading*   **eye,**] eye *ms1*

53 **into corners.**] from the corners of a face *ms1 1ˢᵗ reading*

54] *not ms1 1ˢᵗ reading* ‖ She touches the hair of the grass. *ms1 2ⁿᵈ reading* ‖ She smooths the hair of the grass. *ms1 final reading*   **smooths**] *ms1, Others Anth, US 1920+* ‖ smoothes *Blast, 1917, AraVP*

55] *not ms1 1ˢᵗ reading* ‖ The moon has lost her memory! *ms1 2ⁿᵈ reading, with* feeble *above* moon

56] Wrinkles the hideous scars of a washed-out pox *with* small *above* pox *ms1 1ˢᵗ reading (with "hideous" doubtful)* ‖ A washed out smallpox cracks her face *ms1 2ⁿᵈ reading*

57 **rose,**] rose *ms1* ‖ rose; *March Hare (error in transcription of ms1)*

58 **eau de Cologne,**] *1925+* ‖ old cologne *ms1* ‖ old cologne. *Blast* ‖ old Cologne, *1917, AraVP, US 1920 (see Commentary)*

59 **She is**] All *ms1*

60] Oblivious of the sentiments *ms1 1ˢᵗ reading* ‖ Unconscious of remembered *ms1 2ⁿᵈ reading* ‖ With all the old nocturnal smells *ms1 final reading. (This collation corrects March Hare.)*

61 **brain."**] *1925+* ‖ face *ms1 1ˢᵗ reading* ‖ brain *ms1 2ⁿᵈ reading* ‖ brain. *printings prior to 1925 (with quotation consequently continuing to 68)*

62 **The**] *ms1 final reading+* ‖ Always the *ms1 1ˢᵗ reading* ‖ Still the *ms1 2ⁿᵈ reading* ‖ And still the *ms1 3ʳᵈ reading (TSE deleted* the *at the same time as* Always *but inadvertently?)*

63 **sunless**] withered *ms1 1ˢᵗ reading*

64 **crevices,**] corners *ms1 1ˢᵗ reading* ‖ crevices *ms1 2ⁿᵈ reading*

65 **chestnuts**] *del ms1*   **in**] on *ms1*   **streets,**] streets *ms1* ‖ street, *Blast*

66 **shuttered**] darkened *ms1 1ˢᵗ reading*   **rooms,**] rooms *ms1, Sel Poems 1954* (*corrected long after*)

67] **cigarettes in**] cigarette smoke bl *ms1 1ˢᵗ reading* (*perhaps for "blue" or "blown"?*) ‖ cigarette smoke of *March Hare* (*error in transcription of ms1 1ˢᵗ reading*)

68 **bars.**] bars . . . *ms1* ‖ bars." *printings prior to 1925*

69 **lamp**] last lamp *ms1*   **said,**] *Blast, 1917, US 1920+* ‖ said *ms1, AraVP* ‖ said: *Others Anth*

70] Four o'clock *ms1*

71 **the**] your *ms1 1ˢᵗ reading*   **door.**] door *ms1*

73 **the**] thè *AraVP*   **key,**] key *ms1, AraVP*

74 **little**] not *ms1 1ˢᵗ reading*   **stair.**] stair *ms1* ‖ stair, *printings prior to 1936* (*see McCue 2012, Proposal 10*)

76 **open;**] *Blast, 1917, US 1920+* ‖ open *ms1* ‖ open: *AraVP*   **tooth-brush**] toothbrush *ms1, Blast*   **wall,**] wall *ms1*

77 **Put**] "Put *Others Anth*   **your shoes at the door,**] the toys in the drawer, *ms1 1ˢᵗ reading*. (*This collation corrects March Hare.*)   **life."**] life. *Others Anth*

78 **The**] —The *ms1* ‖ "The *Others Anth*   **knife.**] knife." *Others Anth*

Morning at the Window

Published in *Poetry* Sept 1916, then *1917+*.

ms1 (Berg): Notebook 51; black ink.

ts1 (U. Chicago): ribbon copy, with no indents. After the publication of *The Love Song of J. Alfred Prufrock* in *Poetry*, Pound made two further submissions of poems by TSE. (For the second submission, see headnote to *The "Boston Evening Transcript"*.) This poem was one of the five, each on a separate leaf, that constituted the third submission, sent 29 May 1916: "Here are five poems by Eliot. I am sending off the mss. of his book to the publisher by the same post so there wont be unlimited time for printing these. (I should think three months.)" Four poems were printed in Sept 1916, and ribbon copies of these survive, with pencil numbers in corresponding order, at the head of each, possibly in TSE's hand: (1) *Conversation Galante*; (2) *La Figlia Che Piange*; (4) *Mr. Apollinax*; (5) *Morning at the Window*. Along with them is a violet carbon (apparently from the same typewriter) of the other poem, numbered (3), *The Death of Saint Narcissus*. Together with this is a galley proof of this poem alone (see headnote to it in Commentary). At the head of *Conversation Galante*, Harriet Monroe's assistant Henry B. Fuller has pencilled "The first 3 are unusual H. B. F.", beside which is a note of reminder about the deadline Pound had set: "Only three months time from June 15".

ts Virginia (U. Virginia): later typing not by TSE but endorsed in his late hand (together with typings of *Eyes that last I saw in tears* and *The wind sprang up at four o'clock* and poems by Conrad Aiken). As these have no independent authority, they are not collated here. See also tss of *The "Boston Evening Transcript"*.

1 *as also* 5] *indent added ts1 (not by TSE?)* ‖ *indent Poetry*

1 **in**] ~~at~~ *ts1 1ˢᵗ reading*   **basement**] basements *ts1 1ˢᵗ reading (deletion of "s" not by TSE?)*   **kitchens,**] *ts1 2ⁿᵈ reading (not by TSE?)*+ ‖ kitchens *ms1, ts1 1ˢᵗ reading, AraVP*

4 **Sprouting**] Hanging *ms1, ts1 2ⁿᵈ reading, Poetry* ‖ Handing *ts1 1ˢᵗ reading*

6 **street,**] *ts1 2ⁿᵈ reading (not by TSE?)*+ ‖ street *ms1, ts1 1ˢᵗ reading*

7 **passer-by**] passerby *ts1, Poetry* ‖ *no clear hyphen but words linked ms1*

8 **An**] And *ms1 1ˢᵗ reading (error)*

The *"Boston Evening Transcript"*

Published in *Poetry* Oct 1915, then *Cath Anth*, then *1917*+.

After *The Love Song of J. Alfred Prufrock* appeared in *Poetry*, Pound submitted two further batches of TSE's poems. The first, sent in July or Aug 1915, comprised four items. *The "Boston Evening Transcript"*, *Aunt Helen* and *Cousin Nancy* were published in the magazine under the heading "Three Poems" in Oct 1915, but no typescripts survive. Although Donald Gallup, John Hayward and Valerie Eliot believed that the fourth item was *The Death of Saint Narcissus*, this was part of the third submission (see headnote above to *Morning at the Window*). The fourth item may instead have been *Hysteria* (see headnote to *The Death of Saint Narcissus* in Commentary).

Texas and U. Virginia each have a ts of the poem signed by TSE on "13.iv.61". The Texas copy was signed again on "2.i.62" for William Turner Levy. Although *Sackton* (F1) claims that TSE was "making a gift of an early typescript", the watermark is not among those listed in *Rainey*, and neither ts was made by TSE. Not collated here.

Title **The "Boston Evening Transcript"**] *1936 Contents, 1963 Contents, 1974+ poem heading and Contents* ‖ The Boston Evening Transcript *printings prior to US 1920, 1936, 1963, 1969* ‖ The Boston Evening *Transcript US 1920* ‖ The *Boston Evening Transcript 1925, US 1936+. The masthead title of the paper was* Boston Evening Transcript. (*This summary standardises all-capital titles to upper and lower case; italic to roman, and quotation marks from single to double. Where the general style was to italicise titles and a distinction was made by the occasional use of roman, this summary reverses the two.*)

1 *as also* 5, 9] *title all roman Cath Anth*

3 **street,**] street *Cath Anth*

4 **some**] some, *Cath Anth*

6 **steps**] stairs *AraVP*

7 **nod**] say *Cath Anth*   **La Rochefoucauld,**] *Washington copy 1954 emendation, 1963+* ‖ Rochefoucauld *Cath Anth* ‖ Rochefoucauld, *printings other than Cath Anth prior to 1963 (see Commentary)*

8 **time**] Time *Poetry, Cath Anth*   **street,**] street. *1925 (broken comma?)* ‖ street *1925 ltd edn. and 2nd imp. (1926).* The comma was restored in *1925 3rd imp.* (1928), though not present or marked in the printer's proof (McCue collection) and despite a Faber memo to the printer, 22 June 1928, specifying that corrections "are confined to the title page and to the matter on the reverse of the title page".

Aunt Helen

Published in *Poetry* Oct 1915, then *Cath Anth*, then *1917+*. No drafts known (see headnote to The *"Boston Evening Transcript"*).

Title] Miss Helen Slingsby *Cath Anth*

  1 **aunt,**] aunt *Cath Anth*

  2 **square**] square, *TSE's emendation in Morley's US 1920*

  6 **feet—**] feet: *Cath Anth*

 10 **mantelpiece,**] mantel- | piece *(broken across line) Cath Anth, 1925*

 11 **dining-table**] *1917+* ‖ dining table *Poetry, Cath Anth*

 12 **housemaid**] house-maid *AraVP*   **knees—**] knees *Cath Anth*

Cousin Nancy

Published in *Poetry* Oct 1915, reprinted in the *New York Times Book Review* 17 Oct 1915, "at random from the current number of *Poetry*", and without attribution, as an example of vers libre; then *1917+*. No known drafts (see headnote to The *"Boston Evening Transcript"*), and no published variants.

Mr. Apollinax

Published in *Poetry* Sept 1916, then *1917+*.

ms1 (Berg) = A in *March Hare*: leaf of laid Excelsior typing paper accompanying Notebook. Pencil. First draft.

ms2 (Berg) = B in *March Hare*: leaf of blind-ruled laid paper accompanying Notebook. Fair copy in black ink. Paper and writing match The *Engine ms2*. With a rule at head, as though separating this from previous writing.

ts1 (U. Chicago): ribbon copy sent to *Poetry* (see headnote to *Morning at the Window*).

Title] not mss ‖ Mr Appolinax *AraVP* (*error; correct in Contents*) ‖ Mr. Appollinax *US 1927, US 1929* (*correct in Contents of both*)

Epigraph] *Rodker's 1917* (*added by TSE*), *AraVP* (*as one line*), *1932*+ ‖ *not mss, ts1, Poetry, 1917, US 1920, 1925, 1932 proof, but added in the last by TSE. In Washington copy 1954, TSE wrote beside the Greek "106–11?"* παραδοξολογίας] παραδοξογίας *AraVP, corrected by TSE in copies for Edgar Jepson, 5 Feb 1920 and John Quinn, 23 Sept 1920* (*both Beinecke*) *and Emily Hale, 5 Sept 1923* (*Gekoski*). εὐμήχανος] εὐμή- | χανος *Rodker's 1917* (*hyphenated across the line-end*) LUCIAN] *1936*+ ‖ *not Rodker's 1917, AraVP, 1932*

Both mss use superscript for Mr *and* Mrs. *The stops after* Mr *and* Mrs *in 1, 6, 13 and 21 in ts1 appear to be editorial additions.*

1] *indent added editorially ts1* ‖ *indent Poetry* **Mr. Apollinax**] Mr Apollonax *ms1* ‖ Mr Apollinax *ms2*

2] *not ms1 1ˢᵗ reading* **among**] *across mss*

3 **I**] We *ms1 1ˢᵗ reading* **birch-trees,**] *1917*+ ‖ birch trees *ms1, ts1 1ˢᵗ reading* ‖ birch trees, *ms2, ts1 2ⁿᵈ reading* (*not by TSE?*), *Poetry*

4 **Priapus**] Priapus, terra cotta *ms1 1ˢᵗ reading* (*comma not del*)

5 **the swing**] a swing *ms1 1ˢᵗ reading*

6 **In**] At *ms1* **Phlaccus,**] Phlaccus, again *ms1 1ˢᵗ reading* **Cheetah's**] Cheetah's, *ts1 2ⁿᵈ reading* (*not by TSE?*)

7] *not Poetry* (*see Commentary*) **fœtus**] foetus *mss, ts1 1ˢᵗ reading, Guild* ‖ fetus *ts1 2ⁿᵈ reading* (*not by TSE?*)

8–9] *ms1 1ˢᵗ reading:*

> His laughter was submarine and profound
> Without sound
> Like the old man of the seas

ms1 2ⁿᵈ reading:

> And his laughter was submarine and profound   [1]
> He sometimes laughed   [2]
> Without sound   [3]
> Like the old man of the seas   [4]

with the lines braced and numbered apparently so as to run [2], [3], [4], [1], *and finally* [2], [3], [1], [4]

[1] **And**] *not March Hare* (*error*)

8 **profound**] profound: *ms2*

9 **sea's**] seas *ms1, ms2 2ⁿᵈ reading*

9 ^ 10] Under a rock in the green silence *ms1 del*

10 **islands**] islands, *ts1 2ⁿᵈ reading* (*not by TSE?*), *although Poetry has no comma*

11–12] *as one line mss, ts1, Poetry* **Where**] While *ms1 1ˢᵗ reading not del* **worried**] the desperate *ms1 1ˢᵗ reading* ‖ the worried *ms1* **down**] by *ms1 alt del* ‖ down under the surf *last three words added then del ms1*

12 ^ 13] You must listen under the surf *ms1 add del*

12 ^ 13] *line space 1963*+ (*apparently moved here from* 13 ^ 14 *for the sense: see McCue 2012, Proposal 12*) ‖ *no line space prior to 1963*

13 **I**] And I *ms1 1st reading*   **Mr. Apollinax**] Mʳ Apollonax *mss, ts1 1st reading*   **under**] un *1925 3rd & 4th imps.* (*1928, 1930, error*)   **chair**] *mss, ts1 1st reading, US 1920+* ‖ chair, *ts1 2nd reading* (*not by TSE?*), *Poetry, 1917, AraVP* ‖ chair. *US 1952* (*see McCue 2012, Proposal 15*)

13 ^ 14] *no line space prior to 1932, 1963+* ‖ *new page so line spacing indeterminate 1932* ‖ *line space 1936, US 1952*

14 **grinning**] grinning inanely *ms1*

15 ^ 16] *no line space in printed texts, although 1917 is indeterminate because of a new page* ‖ *line space mss, ts1*

16 **centaurs'**] *ms2, ts1 2nd reading, Poetry, 1917, AraVP* ‖ centaur's *ms1, ts1 1st reading, US 1920+* (*see Commentary*)   **hard**] soft *ms1, ms2 1st reading*

18–20] *ms1*:

> "He is a charming man."—"But his pointed ears—he must be unbalanced."
> —"There was something he said which I might have challenged".

(*the first and third dashes being additions*), *with* What did he mean? *added between these two lines, then ringed to move above 18, and with* ~~But~~ And after all, what does he mean? *also added between the lines*

18 **man**"—**"But**] *1917+* ‖ man"—"but *ms2, ts1 1st reading* ‖ man", "but *ts1 2nd reading* (*possibly not by TSE?*) ‖ man", "But *Poetry*   **after all**] *ts1 2nd reading* (*possibly not by TSE?*)+ ‖ ~~after his~~ *ms2 1st reading* ‖ after all, *ms2, ts1 1st reading*   **mean?**"—] mean?" *ms2, ts1, Poetry*

19 **ears ... He**] *US 1920+* ‖ ears—he *mss, ts1, Poetry* ‖ ears ... he *1917, AraVP*   **unbalanced."—**] *1963+* ‖ unbalanced". *ms1* ‖ unbalanced", *ms2, ts1, Poetry* ‖ unbalanced,"— *printings 1917–61*

20 **"There**] —"There *ms1 2nd reading*   **that**] which *mss, ts1, Poetry*

22 **a slice of lemon,**] lemon in the cup, *ms1 1st reading*   **bitten**] bitter *1936 proof* (*corrected in Hayward's 1936 proof*)

Hysteria

Published *Cath Anth*, then *1917+*. Line-ends vary between editions since this prose poem is set across different measures. The arrangement of *1917* is given here because it has no line-end hyphenations, whereas *1963* has the presumably fortuitous "teeth only acci-dental". For TSE on verse and prose as different systems of punctuation, see headnote in Commentary.

No known drafts.

saying: "If] saying: "if *Cath Anth*   **stopped,**] stopped *Cath Anth*

Conversation Galante

Published in *Poetry* Sept 1916, then *1917+*.

ms1 (Berg): Notebook 1; blue ink.

ts1 (U. Chicago): ribbon copy sent to *Poetry* (see headnote to *Morning at the Window*). Assigned to May 1916 by *Rainey* 198.

Title] Short Romance *ms1 1st reading*

1 **Our**] *ts1 2nd reading* (*not by TSE?*)+ ‖ our *ms1, ts1 1st reading*

2 **Or**] —Or *ms1 2nd reading*

3 **Prester**] *ms1 1st reading del then rewritten* ‖ simply *ms1 alt del*   **balloon**] balloon, *ms1 1st reading* ‖ balloon— *ts1 2nd reading*

6 **then:**] then; *AraVP*   **How**] *ms1, ts1 2nd reading* (*not by TSE?*)+ ‖ how *ts1 1st reading*

7 **Someone**] *ts1 2nd reading* (*not by TSE?*), *Poetry, 1925+* ‖ someone *ms1, ts1 1st reading* ‖ Some one *1917, AraVP, US 1920*

8 **nocturne,**] *ts1 2nd reading* (*not by TSE?*)+ ‖ nocturne *ms1* ‖ noctourne, *ts1 1st reading*

9 **moonshine;**] moonshine: *ms1* ‖ ~~moonlight~~ *ts1 1st reading*   **which**] that *ms1 1st reading*

10 **forth**] out *ms1*   **own**] *not US 1920* (*but added in Morley's copy*), *1925, 1932 proof, but added in the last by TSE*

12] *no indent ts1, Poetry*   **inane."**] *1917+* ‖ inane". *ts1 1st reading* ‖ inane. *ts1 2nd reading* (*not by TSE?*), *Poetry*

13 **madam**] *ts1 2nd reading* (*not TSE?*)+ ‖ madame *ms1, ts1 1st reading*   **humorist,**] *1917+* ‖ humourist, *ms1* ‖ humourist *ts1 1st reading* ‖ humorist *ts1 2nd reading* (*not by TSE?*), *Poetry*

15 **twist!**] twist!— *ms1*

16 **air**] *ms1, ts1, 1917, 1936+* ‖ aid *US 1920* (*corrected by TSE in Morley and Virginia Woolf's copies*), *1925, 1932*

17 **confute—"**] confute. *ts1 1st reading*

18 **Are**] *ts1 2nd reading* (*not by TSE?*)+ ‖ are *ms1, ts1 1st reading*

La Figlia Che Piange

Published in *Poetry* Sept 1916, then *1917+*. Reprinted in *An Anthology of Modern Verse*, ed. AM [Algernon Methuen] (1921) with extended epigraph.

For five words which Valerie Eliot suggested might have been an outline for *La Figlia Che Piange*, see *The Death of the Duchess* Textual History.

ts Aiken (untraced): Conrad Aiken twice claimed to have had a copy which he was unable to persuade editors in London to print (*March & Tambimuttu ed.* and *Ezra Pound Perspectives: Essays in Honour of His Eightieth Birthday* ed. Noel Stock, 1965).

ts1 (U. Chicago): ribbon copy sent to *Poetry* (see headnote to *Morning at the Window*). Assigned to May 1916 by *Rainey* 198.

ms Quinn (Beinecke): fair copy by TSE on the last page of *Quinn's AraVP*, where it is signed by TSE, with a wax seal.

Title **Che Piange**] che piange *ms Quinn* ‖ Che Pianga *US 1920 Contents* (*corrected by TSE in Morley and Virginia Woolf's copies*)

Epigraph] *Rodker's 1917* (*added by TSE*), *AraVP*+ ‖ *not ts1, Poetry, 1917* ‖ *O quam te memorem virgo . . . O dea certe! Methuen Anthology*

1 **stair**—] *ts1 final reading* (*not by TSE?*)+ ‖ stair *ts1 1ˢᵗ reading* ‖ stair, *ts1 2ⁿᵈ reading* (*not by TSE?*)

2 **urn**—] *ts1 final reading* (*not by TSE?*)+ ‖ urn *ts1 1ˢᵗ reading* ‖ urn, *ts1 2ⁿᵈ reading* (*not by TSE?*)

3 **Weave, weave**] Weave, weave, weave *ts1, Poetry*   **hair**—] *ts1 2ⁿᵈ reading* (*not by TSE?*)+ ‖ hair *ts1 1ˢᵗ reading*

4 **surprise**—] *ts1 2ⁿᵈ reading* (*not by TSE?*), *Poetry, 1917, US 1920*+ ‖ surprise *ts1 1ˢᵗ reading, AraVP*

6 **eyes:**] *ts1 2ⁿᵈ reading* (*not by TSE?*)+ ‖ eyes *ts1 1ˢᵗ reading* ‖ eyes; *Methuen Anthology*

7 **weave, weave**] weave, weave, *ms Quinn*

8 **leave,**] *ts1 2ⁿᵈ reading* (*not by TSE?*)+ ‖ leave *ts1 1ˢᵗ reading*

9 **grieve,**] *ts1 2ⁿᵈ reading* (*not by TSE?*)+ ‖ grieve *ts1 1ˢᵗ reading*

11 **bruised,**] *ts1 2ⁿᵈ reading* (*not by TSE?*)+ ‖ bruised *ts1 1ˢᵗ reading*

14 **deft,**] *ts1 2ⁿᵈ reading* (*not by TSE?*), *Poetry, 1917, US 1920*+ ‖ deft *ts1 1ˢᵗ reading* ‖ deft. *AraVP*

15 **understand,**] *ts1 2ⁿᵈ reading* (*not by TSE?*)+ ‖ understand *ts1 1ˢᵗ reading*

18 **days,**] *1917*+ ‖ days *ts1 1ˢᵗ reading* ‖ days— *ts1 2ⁿᵈ reading* (*not by TSE?*), *Poetry*

20 **flowers.**] *1917*+ ‖ flowers *ts1 1ˢᵗ reading* ‖ flowers— *ts1 2ⁿᵈ reading* (*not by TSE?*), *Poetry*

22 **lost**] a lost *Poetry*

Poems (1920)

The poetry volumes published by TSE in Britain and America in 1920 have slightly different contents, with *AraVP* including *Ode* ("Tired. | Subterrene") but not *Hysteria*, whereas *US 1920* has *Hysteria* but not *Ode*. Both volumes print all the new poems in front of those from *Prufrock*, but they are differently ordered and there is no evidence as to why. Seven of the poems had appeared in a Hogarth Press pamphlet, *Poems* (1919).

In the table below, a chevron indicates a printing of a quatrain poem with alternate lines indented. The order of original appearance of seven of the poems in journals is given—as 1st to 7th—in square brackets. The poem entitled *Le Spectateur* in *1919* and *AraVP* is listed by its final title, *Le Directeur*.

Poems (1919)	Ara Vos Prec	Poems (1920)
Sweeney Among the Nightingales [2nd]	Gerontion	Gerontion
The Hippopotamus [1st]	>Burbank with a Baedeker: Bleistein with a Cigar [>6th]	>Burbank with a Baedeker: Bleistein with a Cigar
Mr. Eliot's Sunday Morning Service [4th]	>Sweeney Among the Nightingales	>Sweeney Erect
Whispers of Immortality [3rd]	>Sweeney Erect [>7th]	>A Cooking Egg
Le Directeur	>Mr. Eliot's Sunday Morning Service	Le Directeur
Mélange Adultère de Tout	>Whispers of Immortality	Mélange Adultère de Tout
Lune de Miel	>The Hippopotamus	Lune de Miel
	>A Cooking Egg [5th]	The Hippopotamus
	Lune de Miel	Dans le Restaurant
	Dans le Restaurant	Whispers of Immortality
	Le Directeur	Mr. Eliot's Sunday Morning Service
	Mélange Adultère de Tout	Sweeney Among the Nightingales
	Ode ("Tired. | Subterrene")	
	followed by:	followed by:
	Prufrock and Other Observations excluding Hysteria	Prufrock and Other Observations including Hysteria

Printing and binding of the Hogarth Press *Poems* (1919) varies between copies. *Gallup*: "The first ones printed have two misprints on page [13] ··· which were corrected in later copies" (see Textual History of *Lune de Miel*). TSE to Donald Friede, 22 Sept 1930: "I am ashamed to be unable to enlighten you at the moment on my bibliography, as I don't collect my own first editions or anybody else's. And I have no copy of that Hogarth Press edition in question [*1919*]. I can only tell you this, that the first copies bound and those which I saw were bound in the wallpaper, described by Fry. I think that there were seven short poems in the volume, and I am sure that THE HIPPOPOTOMOS was in the first edition. To the best of my knowledge and belief only one edition was printed by the Hogarth Press, but it is quite possible that later copies of the same edition were bound in a different paper. I seem to remember that objections were raised by some purchaser to the wallpaper cover, which might account for it. The whole edition has been out of print for over six years, I believe."

In *Ara Vos Prec*, the seven quatrain poems, all in English, appear first, followed by the four French poems. In *US 1920*, *The Hippopotamus* appears amid the French poems. Three quatrain poems with indents appear before the French group, and three without indents appear after it. Whereas the basic rhyme scheme of the other quatrain poems is ABCB, *The Hippopotamus*—which TSE originally entitled *Vers anglais*—follows the ABAB of Gautier's *L'Hippopotame* (see Commentary).

Because it was used in the setting of *1925*, the arrangement of the poems in *US 1920* has been followed ever since. The order is the same, but with the poems in French omitted, in *Penguin* and *Sel Poems 1954*. There, however, the shape of *Whispers of Immortality* and *Mr. Eliot's Sunday Morning Service* was especially distorted for many years by the indenting of the first line of the second and subsequent stanzas, except those immediately following the subdivision marked by a row of dots (see "This Edition", 5. SPACING AND PUNCTUATION in Vol. I).

The loose leaves that accompany the *March Hare* Notebook include all the poems in *AraVP* and *Poems* (1920) except *Le Directeur* and *The Hippopotamus*. See headnote to Textual History, 5. THE *MARCH HARE NOTEBOOK* AND ACCOMPANYING LEAVES.

Section-title page] *1925*+, variously using capitals, italics, comma, dash and brackets

Gerontion

Published in *AraVP*, *US 1920+*.

ts1 (Berg) = *A* in *March Hare*: two leaves of lightweight typing paper accompanying Notebook. Ribbon copy with title emended in pencil.

ts2 (Berg) = *B* in *March Hare*: two leaves of lightweight typing paper accompanying Notebook. Violet carbon of a revised version with pencil suggestions by Pound. Paper and typing match those of *Burbank with a Baedeker: Bleistein with a Cigar ts1* and *Sweeney Erect ts1*.

msAdd: pencil draft of 69–73 on verso of second leaf of *ts2*.

ms Cunard (Texas): copy by Nancy Cunard on four pages of her commonplace book, with her note "July 1919. T. S. Eliot" at foot. Presumably a copy of either *ts1* or *ts2*, as it follows their early reading of 69–73; *ts2* is the more likely, since Cunard does not follow the line space 46 ^ 47 in *ts1*. As this ms has no independent authority, variants are not recorded below. Cunard's papers also contain a ts copy of the text as published in what she calls *Ara vos Prek*.

ts3 (U. Virginia): two leaves of lightweight typing paper. Carbon of a new typing adopting some of Pound's suggestions from *ts2* (see 70); sent to Rodker in summer 1919. With printer's marks and apparent page divisions "5 | 6 | 7" changed to "7 | 8 | 9", although these do not correspond to the pagination of *AraVP* (or *US 1920*); see *Burbank with a Baedeker: Bleistein with a Cigar ts3*.

Virginia program (U. Virginia): hybrid text printed for a McGregor Room Seminar at the university led by Willard Thorp, 21 Mar 1947. *Marshall* describes this text and the marks TSE made some time between 1947 and 1952. TSE did not always comment on variants in this programme.

Title] Gerousia *ts1 1ˢᵗ reading*

Epigraph **were**] were, *ts3*, *AraVP*

Unadopted second epigraph] *ts1 only, with first line stepped down from epigraph above*:

Come il mi corpo stea

Nel mondo su, nulla scienza porto.

1 **Here I am, an**] *ringed and del Pound ts2*   **month,**] month *ts3*, *AraVP*, *Virginia program*

2 **Being read to by · · · b · · ·**] *underlined with "Being" ringed by Pound with "? to by" ts2. Also, on four lines, "b — b — b | B d ⊲ bb | consonants, | ⊲ two prepositions" Pound ts2*

3–14] *with "don't know whether | vide letter" Pound ts2*

4 **rain**] rain, *ts1* (*erroneously given as ts2 in March Hare*)

7 **house,**] *ts2* (*not noted in March Hare*), *US 1920+* ‖ house *ts1*, *ts3*, *AraVP*

8 **Jew**] *Washington copy 1954 emendation, 1963* ‖ jew *tss, printings prior to 1963*   **window-sill**] *1963, 1974+* ‖ window sill *tss, printings prior to 1963, US*

1963, 1969   **owner**] *ringed by Pound with "vs the 'my' denouement of 'rented' rather delayed" ts2*

14 ^ 15] *line space tss, AraVP, US 1920, 1925* ‖ *new page so line spacing indeterminate 1932* ‖ *no line space 1936+*

15–16] *inset AraVP*

17 **wonders.**] wonders, *Penguin*   **sign!"**] *1932+* ‖ sign". *(punctuation marks superimposed) ts3* ‖ sign." *AraVP* ‖ sign": *ts1, ts2, US 1920* ‖ sign"! *1925*

20 ^ 21] *line space US 1920+* ‖ *no line space tss, AraVP*

25 ^ 26] *no line space prior to 1925, Penguin, Sel Poems 1954, 1969* ‖ *line space 1925 (probably to avoid a widow), 1932, US 1936 and subsequent US eds.* ‖ *new page so line spacing indeterminate 1936, 1963 and many subsequent British eds.*

26 **Hakagawa**] *underlined, with "? the gentleman's name ends [1st reading: means] in affix meaning* river *⅋ wd. be taken for some Tiber or Garonne by anyone knowing as much Jap as I do" Pound ts2* ‖ Hakagama *ts3, AraVP*

28] *added ts3*   **Fräulein**] *1925, Sesame, US 1936, Guild, Penguin, US 1952, US 1963* ‖ Fraülein *tss, AraVP, 1932, 1936 but corrected 17th and 18th imps. (1959, 1961) and in Washington copy 1954 (probably by TSE, although in a blue ballpoint he did not use elsewhere in the volume)* ‖ Fraulein *US 1920, 1932 proof, with erroneous emendation "ü" by TSE.*

29] *last two words on new line with indent US 1936, US 1952, US 1963 (error)*

30 **the**] *bracketed Pound ts2*

33 **Think now**] *ringed by Pound ts2*

34 **History**] Nature *ts1 1st reading*   **has many**] *bracketed Pound ts2*

35 **issues,**] *US 1920+* ‖ issues; *tss, AraVP, Virginia program*   **deceives**] deceived *Pound ts2, with arrow to move it between* whispering *and* ambitions

36 **by**] with *ts1 1st reading*   **Think now**] *del Pound ts2*

37 **She**] *del Pound ts2*   **gives**] gives, *Pound ts2*   **distracted**] *ts2 (with comma added by Pound), US 1920+* ‖ distracted, *ts1, ts3, AraVP, Virginia program*

38 **gives with such**] *with first and third words bracketed Pound ts2*

39 **Gives**] *bracketed and underlined by Pound with "stet" ts2*

40 **if**] is *1963 (corrected 4th imp., 1968), US 1963 (later corrected).* To Gallup, 1 Oct 1963, of this error: "If you notice any more errors in my *Collected Poems* other than that one on page 30 [of *US 1963*], which · · · does, I am sorry to say, occur in both editions [British and American], do let me know."

44 **Neither fear nor courage**] How courage *ts1 1st reading*

46 ^ 47] *no line space US 1920+* ‖ *line space ts1, ts3, AraVP* ‖ *new leaf so line spacing indeterminate ts2*

51 **purposelessly**] purposelessly, *TSE's emendation in Morley's US 1920*

53 **devils.**] devils. It is commonly said *with last four words del ts1*

53 ^ 54] *new page so line spacing indeterminate 1936* ‖ *line space Penguin (error)*

54] *indent Penguin (error)*

55 **near**] in *ts1*

57 **need**] *ts1, ts2, US 1920+, endorsed by TSE in Virginia program* ‖ want *ts3, AraVP*   it] it, *TSE's emendation in Morley's US 1920*

60 **use**] lose *ts3 1ˢᵗ reading*   **them**] *1936+* ‖ it *tss, printings prior to 1936, emended by TSE to* them *in Virginia program*

60 ^ 61] *two-line space ts1* ‖ *new page so line spacing indeterminate AraVP, 1932*

62 **profit**] *AraVP, US 1920, 1932+* ‖ profit, *1925, US 1920 2nd printing (1927), 1932 proof with comma del TSE. To P. M. Jack, 19 Jan 1927:* "You are quite right about the comma. It is one of the misprints that I had noted. I think that you would find that it is not in the previous editions."   **of their**] ~~when the~~ *ts3 1ˢᵗ reading (error, anticipating the reading in 63)*

66 **operations, will**] operations? Will *TSE's emendation in Morley's US 1920*

67 **Mrs.**] Mrs *tss, AraVP, Penguin*   **Cammel**] *ts1, ts2, US 1920+* ‖ Cammell *ts3, AraVP*

69–73] *ts1, ts2:*

> In fractured atoms. We have saved a shilling against oblivion
> Even oblivious.

with line space before 74

69 **In fractured atoms.**] *not msAdd*

70 **running**] driven *msAdd 1ˢᵗ reading*   **on**] *US 1920+ (endorsed by TSE in Virginia program)* ‖ by *msAdd, ts3, AraVP*   **Horn.**] *1963, 1969, 1974* ‖ horn, *msAdd 1ˢᵗ reading* ‖ Horn, *msAdd, ts3, printings prior to 1963.* The comma remained in reprints of *Sel Poems* for some years after *1963*, was then changed to a full stop, but was reintroduced long after in Britain in *Sel Poems* and *Coll Poems.* (*Moody 305* lists the stop as "probably authorial".)

71 **Gulf claims,**] *US 1920+* ‖ gulf claims *msAdd, ts3, AraVP*

72 **man**] *US 1920+ (endorsed by TSE's deletion of comma in Virginia program)* ‖ man, *msAdd, ts3, AraVP*   **by**] *msAdd 1ˢᵗ reading, US 1920+ (endorsed by TSE in Virginia program)* ‖ on *msAdd, ts3, AraVP*   **Trades**] trades *msAdd*

73] To a sleepy corner. Twitching with rheumatism *msAdd*   **a**] a a *US 1920 corrected in 2nd and 3rd printings (1927, 1929) and by TSE in Morley's US 1920*

73 ^ 74] *no line space ts3, AraVP, Penguin (corrected long after)*

74 **the**] an old man's *ts1, ts2*

Burbank with a Baedeker: Bleistein with a Cigar

Published in *Art & Letters* Summer 1919, where this and *Sweeney Erect* were editorially numbered I and II. Then *AraVP, US 1920+*.

ts1 (Berg) = A in *March Hare*: leaf of lightweight typing paper accompanying Notebook. Ribbon copy with comments by Pound. At top left, Pound wrote "Dyptich", corrected to "Diptych". No indents except 2–5, indented a single space.

ts2 (Berg) = B in *March Hare*: leaf of lightweight typing paper accompanying Notebook. Violet carbon of a later version. Even-numbered lines indented.

ts3 (U. Virginia): violet carbon sent to Rodker for *AraVP.* Marked in unknown hand with page division for printer "8 / 9" changed to "10 / 11", although these do not correspond to the pagination of *AraVP* (or *US 1920*); see *Gerontion ts3.* With even-numbered lines indented.

Three typescripts appear to have been used as setting copy. The epigraph and 31 suggest that the second printing, *AraVP*, was not set from *A&L*. The epigraph and 7 suggest that *US 1920* was not set from either of the first two printings.

Title] Bleistein with a Cigar *ts1* ‖ Burbank *AraVP contents*

Epigraph] **Tra-la-la-la-la-la-laire**] *no hyphens ts1* (*with* TRA), *ts3, AraVP* **est;**] est *ts1* **caetera**] *US 1920*+ ‖ Caetera *ts1* ‖ cætera *A&L, AraVP* **stopped, the**] stopped the *tss, AraVP* ‖ stopped—the *A&L* **there, how**] there—how *A&L* ‖ there How *ts1, ts3, AraVP* ‖ there how *ts2* **its**] it's *ts1, ts3, AraVP* **and**] & *AraVP* **goats**] Goats *ts1, ts3, AraVP* **and**] & *AraVP* **monkeys,**] monkeys! *ts1* **too!**] too *ts1* **countess**] Countess *ts1, ts3, A&L, AraVP* **came**] passed *ts3 1ˢᵗ reading* **and so**] & so *AraVP*

2] And Triton blew his wrinkled shell. *ts1, where Pound bracketed the line with "if you 'hotel' this rhythm shd. be weighted a bit, I *think*"* **Descending**] A *ts3 1ˢᵗ reading, typed over*

3 **arrived,**] arrived; *ts1*

4 **fell.**] fell: *Pound ts1*

6 **seaward with**] slowly like *ts1*

7 **Slowly**] Seaward *ts1* **God**] god *ts1, ts3, A&L, AraVP*

8 ^ 9] *double rule with "OK. from here anyhow" Pound ts1*

13 **way:**] way; *ts3*

20 **candle end**] candle-end *Pound ts1*

21] *"punctuation?" Pound ts1* **Declines**] Burns *ts3 1ˢᵗ reading, typed over*

23 **Jew**] *Washington copy 1954 emendation, 1963+* ‖ jew *tss, printings prior to 1963* **lot.**] lot, *Guild*

26 **phthisic**] phthsic *ts3 1ˢᵗ reading, typed over*

27 **lights,**] lights; *ts1*

29 **Klein.**] *Pound marked the full stop and twice put a comma with "?" ts1* **wings**] *ts2*+ ‖ mane, *ts1, changed to* wings *by Pound*

29–30 **Who · · · claws?**] *enclosed in quotation marks by Pound, who repeated them in margin with "for clarity?" ts1*

31 **Thought**] —Thought *ts3, AraVP*

Sweeney Erect

Published in *Art and Letters* Summer 1919, *AraVP*, *US 1920+*.

ts1 (Berg) = *A* in *March Hare*: leaf of lightweight typing paper accompanying Note-book. Ribbon copy, without indents.

ts2 (Berg) = *B* in *March Hare*: leaf of lightweight typing paper accompanying Note-book. Violet carbon with even-numbered lines indented.

Title] Sweeny erect *AraVP*

Epigraph] not *ts1* ‖ *Voici ton cierge,* | *C'est deux livres qu'il a coute* ... *ts2* (*each line centred*)   [1] **me,**] me *AraVP*   [2] **and**] & *AraVP*   [3] **and**] & *AraVP*   **me**] me, *US 1920, 1925, 1932*   [4] **Look, look,**] Look, Look, *AraVP*

  5 **Aeolus**] *tss, US 1920+* ‖ Æolus *A&L, AraVP*

  8 **with**] the *ts1 1ˢᵗ reading*

10 **Polypheme).**] *1936+* ‖ Polypheme) *tss, A&L* ‖ Polypheme); *AraVP* ‖ Polypheme), *US 1920, 1925*

11 **orang-outang**] Orang-outang *ts1*

15 **teeth:**] teeth; *ts2, A&L, AraVP*

16 **sickle motion**] sickle-motion *ts1*

17 **Jackknifes**] Jack-knifes *A&L*

18 **out**] *A&L, US 1920+* ‖ down *tss, AraVP*   **hip**] hip, *TSE's emendation in Morley's US 1920*

20 **pillow slip**] pillow-slip *ts1*

21 **full length**] full-length *tss, A&L, AraVP*   **shave**] shave, *ts1, TSE's emendation in Morley's US 1920*

23 **temperament**] temperament, *TSE's emendation in Morley's US 1920*

26 **said**] says *tss, A&L, AraVP*   **Emerson**] *ts1, US 1920+* ‖ Emerson, *ts2, A&L, AraVP, TSE's emendation in Morley's US 1920*

28 **sun.)**] *1925+, TSE's emendation in Morley's 1920* ‖ sun). *tss, printings prior to 1925*

29 **leg**] leg, *TSE's emendation in Morley's US 1920*

30 **subsides.**] subsides; *tss, A&L, AraVP*

34 **disgraced,**] disgraced; *ts2, A&L, AraVP*

36 **And deprecate**] Deprecate *tss, A&L, AraVP*   **of**] oft *Guild*   **taste**] taste, *TSE's emendation in Morley's US 1920*

41 **Doris,**] Doris *tss, A&L, AraVP*   **bath,**] bath *tss, A&L, AraVP*

A Cooking Egg

Published in *Coterie* May Day 1919, *AraVP*, *US 1920+*.

ts1 exists in two versions:

> *ts1a* (Berg) = *A* in *March Hare*: leaf of lightweight typing paper accompanying Notebook. With comments by Pound. No indents except inadvertently at 1, 2, 6, and 33.

> *ts1b* (Berg) = *B* in *March Hare*: leaf of lightweight typing paper accompanying Notebook. Carbon of *ts1a* with final line missing, supplied in margin in pencil by TSE.

Coterie prints without indents.

Title] *not ts1* ‖ oking Egg *1963 proof*

Epigraph] *not ts1, Coterie*   **beues . . .**] beues. *Sel Poems 1954 (and later hardback imps.)* ‖ beues *Sel Poems 1961 pbk (corrected long after)*

  3 *of the*] *printings prior to 1963* ‖ *Of The ts1a 2ⁿᵈ reading* ‖ *of 1963+ (see McCue 2012, Proposal 7).*

  5 **Daguerreotypes**] Daguerrotypes *ts1, AraVP*   **silhouettes,**] silhouettes *ts1*

  6 **great great aunts**] great-great-aunts *Coterie*

  8 ^ 9] *ts1*:

> When Pipit's slipper once fell off
> It interfered with my repose;
> My self-control was somewhat strained
> Because her stockings had white toes.

> I wanted Peace here on earth,   [5]
> While I was still strong and young;
> And Peace was to have been extended
> From the tip of Pipit's tongue.

> *ts1a with [1–4] ringed, [7–8] bracketed, and both stanzas then del by Pound, ts1b with both stanzas then del in blue crayon, apparently by TSE*

>> [3] *marked "X" at beginning and end of line by Pound with "used before" ts1a*   **strained**] shaken *ts1b 2ⁿᵈ reading*

>> [4] **stockings had white toes**] *ringed by Pound with a swooping line to the end of* [1] *ts1a*

>> [5] **Peace**] Pipit *ts1a 2ⁿᵈ reading*

  8 ^ 9] *three asterisks AraVP, six dots US 1920.* This division in the printed poem (like that between the sixth and seventh stanzas) coincides with the omission of the stanzas deleted in draft, but the similar divisions between the fourth and fifth stanzas of *Whispers of Immortality* and *Mr. Eliot's Sunday Morning Service* do not correspond to known deletions.

9 *as also* 13 **Heaven**] heaven *ts1* ‖ Heaven, *Coterie, TSE's emendation in Morley's US 1920*

9–12] *with "le preux Bayard mirrour of Chivalry & Coriolanus. Cola da Rienzi", Pound ts1a*

10 **Sidney**] Sidney, *ts1*

12] *bracketed Pound ts1a*   **that**] my *ts, with* ? that *Pound ts1a* ‖ his *Coterie*

16 **five per cent.**] *1925+* ‖ Five Per Cent *ts1* ‖ five per cent *Coterie, AraVP, US 1920*

17 **Society**] Conversation *ts1* ‖ Company *ts1b 2ⁿᵈ reading*   **Heaven,**] heaven *ts1* ‖ Heaven *AraVP*

18 **Lucretia**] For I *ts1 1ˢᵗ reading (typed over)* ‖ Lucrezia *ts1, Coterie*   **Bride;**] bride: *ts1*

20 **Pipit's experience**] those which Pipit *ts1* ‖ Pipit's memory *Coterie*

21 **Heaven:**] heaven: *ts1*

22 **will**] shall *Coterie*

23 **Trances;**] Trances: *ts1*

24 **de**] de' *ts1, Coterie, AraVP*   **me.**] *1932 2nd imp. (for the US, Sept 1932), 1936+* ‖ me *ts1* ‖ me . . . *printings prior to 1932* ‖ me . *1932 proof, 1932*

24 ^ 25] *ts1:*

> To the communion of the Lord,
> With bread and wine the tables drest;
> I hope the potables will be
> Such as my stomach can digest.

with fourth line underlined by Pound with diagonal strokes at corners ts1a (matching 25)

24 ^ 25] *five dots 1925* ‖ *line space Coterie* ‖ *three asterisks AraVP* ‖ *six dots US 1920*

25] *underlined by Pound with diagonal strokes at corners ts1a (matching 24 ^ 25 [4])*

27 **creeping**] feeding *ts1*

28 **From**] In *ts1*   **Green;**] Green. *ts1*

28 ^ 29] *new page so line spacing indeterminate 1932*

29 ^ 30] *no line space ts1*

30] *no indent AraVP*   **Alps.**] Alps; *ts1*

31–33] *inset (equally) AraVP*

32–33] *"other matter intruded on the purely religious", glossing "other matter" as "the 'modern' or joltographic" Pound ts1a*

33] *line end with asterisk, indicating footnote (for American readers):* * i.e. an endemic teashop, found in all parts of London. The Initials signify: Aerated Bread Company, Limited. *US 1920*

Le Directeur

Published in *Little Review* July 1917, then *1919+*.

Title] LE SPECTATEUR *1919, AraVP*
   1 **Tamise**] Tamise! *printings prior to 1925*
   2 **près**] pres *US 1920*
   4] *not AraVP*
  11 **Bras dessus bras dessous**] Bras-dessus bras-dessous *1919, AraVP*

Mélange Adultère de Tout

Published in *Little Review* July 1917, then *1919+*.

ts1 (Berg): leaf of lightweight paper accompanying Notebook. Carbon without accents.

Title] Mélange adultère de tout *ts1* (*with no accents*), *LR* (*with no accents on cover contents list*), *US 1920* ‖ *all capitals, no accents 1919, AraVP, US 1920 3rd printing* (*1929*) ‖ *all capitals with accents 1925* ‖ *all capitals with second accent only 1932* (*because the first accent had been badly printed in 1925*)
   1 **Amérique**] Amerique *LR, US 1920, 1925*
   4 **à**] á *LR, US 1920*
   5 **conférencier**] conferencier *LR, US 1920*
   6 **banquier,**] banquier; *1919, AraVP*
   7] *enclosed in brackets 1919, AraVP*
   9 **noir**] noire *1919*
  14 **tra là là**] tra la la *printings prior to 1925*
  15 **jusqu'à Omaha.**] jusque à Omaha; *1919, AraVP* ‖ jusqu' à Omaha. *1963* ‖ jusqu' a Omaha. *1974*
  16 **célébrai**] *1925+* ‖ celebrai *LR, US 1920* ‖ célebrai *1919, AraVP*
  17 **une**] un *AraVP*   **d'Afrique**] *LR, US 1920+* ‖ d'Afrique, *1919, AraVP*
  18 **Vêtu**] Vetu *LR*
  20 **côtes**] cotes *US 1920 3rd printing* (*1929*)   **brûlantes**] brulantes *1919, AraVP, US 1920 3rd printing* (*1929*)

Lune de Miel

Published in *Little Review* July 1917, then *1919+*.

ts1 (Berg): leaf of lightweight paper accompanying Notebook. Carbon copy, without accents.

Omega (private collection): single printed leaf, with a woodcut by Roger Fry on verso. From the type of *1919* and with text of early copies.

1 **Pays-Bas**] Pay-Bas *1974+* (*error*)   à] á *AraVP*   **Terre Haute**] Terre-Haute *1919*

3 **A l'aise**] Deux epoux *ts1*   **punaises;**] poux. *ts1*

4 **aestivale,**] *LR, US 1920+* ‖ aestival, *1919 early copies* ‖ estivale, *1919 later copies* ‖ estivale *AraVP*

5 **écartant**] écartent *1974+* (*error*)

7 **relève le drap**] rélève le draps *1919*

8 **Moins d'une**] Pas meme une *ts1*   **Saint Apollinaire**] St Apollinaire *ts1* ‖ Saint-Apollinaire *1919* ‖ Sainte Apollinaire *AraVP*

9 **En**] *1925+* ‖ In *ts1, printings prior to 1925*   **Classe,**] Classe' *LR*

10 **chapitaux**] capitaux *1919 early copies*   **tournoie**] tourbillonne *ts1*

12 **de Padoue à**] a Padoue et *ts1*

13 **Où**] *AraVP, 1936, US 1952, 1963* ‖ Ou *ts1, LR, 1919, US 1920, 1925, US 1963* ‖ On *1936 proof*   **se**] l'on *ts1*   **trouve**] *ts1, 1936+* ‖ trouvent *printings prior to 1936*   **la**] *1936+* ‖ le *ts1, printings prior to 1936, 1936 proof* (*see Commentary*)   **cher**] chere *ts1 1st reading*

14 **aux**] a ses *ts1*   **rédige**] *1919, AraVP, 1925+* ‖ redige *LR, US 1920*

16 **Saint**] St *ts1* ‖ Sainte *AraVP*

18 **écroulantes la forme précise**] ècroulantes la forme precise *LR, US 1920*

The Hippopotamus

Published in *Little Review* July 1917, then *1919+*. *The Little Review Anthology*, ed. Margaret Anderson (1953) as *LR*.

ts1 (Beinecke): leaf of lightweight typing paper. Ribbon copy with Pound's pencilled annotations. Described by Gallup in *Yale Univ Gazette* Jan 1976.

AraVP indents even-numbered lines.

Title] Vers anglais *ts1*

"US" epigraph] not ts1, LR, 1932 (*including copies for the US*), 1936 and subsequent British editions ‖

> Similiter et omnes revereantur Diaconos, ut mandatum Jesu Christi; et Episcopum, ut Jesum Christum, existentem filium Patris; Presbyteros autem, ut concilium Dei et conjunctionem [Conjunctionem *AraVP*] Apostolorum. Sine his Ecclesia non vocatur; de quibus suadeo vos sic habeo.
>
> S. Ignatii ad [Ad *1919, 1936*] Trallianos.

1919, AraVP, US 1920, 1925, US 1936 and subsequent US editions, where this precedes the "British" epigraph

"British" epigraph] 1919, *AraVP and subsequent British and American editions* ‖ not ts1, LR

1 **broad-backed**] broad backed *LR, AraVP*

2 **in**] on *AraVP*

3 **us**] us, *1919, TSE's emendation in Morley's US 1920*

4 **He**] Yet he *ts1 with first word boxed and "X" by Pound, LR*

5 **Flesh and blood**] Flesh-and-blood *ts1, printings prior to 1925*

7 **While**] *boxed Pound ts1* ‖ But *1919*   **fail**] err *ts1 1st reading* (*error, anticipating the reading in* 9) ‖ fail, *1919, TSE's emendation in Morley's US 1920*

8 **based upon**] founded on *1919*

10 **ends,**] ends; *1919*

11 **While**] *ts1, boxed by Pound*

13 *as also* 25 **'potamus**] potamus *ts1, LR, 1919, AraVP*

14 **mango-tree**] mango tree *1919, AraVP*

16 **Church**] Church, *1919*

18 **Betrays**] Is raised *ts1 1st reading* ‖ betrays *ts1 2nd reading with capital added*   **odd,**] odd; *1919*

19 **rejoice**] the Church *ts1 1st reading*

22 **passed**] past *ts1, LR, 1919, AraVP*

23 **mysterious way—**] mysterious-way *AraVP*

24 **sleep and feed**] feed and sleep *1919* ‖ sleep and eat *AraVP*

27 **round him**] came to *ts1*

28 **God,**] God *AraVP*

29 **Lamb**] lamb *1919*   **clean**] clean, *1919*

30 **enfold,**] enfold; *1919*

32 **gold.**] gold; *1919*

Dans le Restaurant

Published in *Little Review* Sept 1918, then *AraVP*, *US 1920+*.

ts1 (Berg): leaf of lightweight typing paper accompanying Notebook. Carbon copy with comments and changes by Pound. Some accents added in ms by TSE and Pound, but all missing in 2, 6, 11, 15, 16, 22–24, 27–30.

LR deeply insets 3–5 and 8–19, with 15 and 20 ("Mais alors · · · Mais alors") aligned halfway across the page. *AraVP* insets 8–19 only slightly, and does not indent 20 quite so much as 15.

Title **Restaurant**] restaurant *ts1*, *LR*

1   **garçon**] garcon *ts1*, *US 1920*, *1925*

2   **doigts**] doights *1932 proof, corrected TSE*

3   **fera**] sera *ts1*, *corrected by Pound*

4   **soleil,**] soleil *AraVP*

7   **te**] *ts1*, *US 1920+* ‖ t'en *LR*, *AraVP*   **ne bave pas**] ne pas baver *ts1*, *with "de ne pas | ne baves pas | Je t'en pris, au moins | ne bave pas" by Pound*

8   **trempés**] toutes trempés *ts1 1ˢᵗ reading* ‖ toutes trempées *ts1 2ⁿᵈ reading* ‖ touts trempés *ts1 final reading* ‖ tout trempés *LR*, *AraVP*

11 **Elle**] *printings prior to 1925, US 1936, US 1952* ‖ Ellé *1925+ (error).* The enduring misprint probably derives from an instruction to add the acute accent to the first letter of the following word, which was missing in *US 1920*, from which *1925* was set (see *McCue 2012a*).   **était**] etait *ts1*, *US 1920*   **primevères**] primaveres *ts1* ‖ primavères *US 1920*

12 **taches**] tâches *ts1*, *printings prior to 1925*

14] *1936+* ‖ Elle avait une odeur fraiche qui m'etait inconnue, | Et j'eprouvais un instant de puissance et de delire". *ts1* ‖ Elle avait une odeur fraîche qui m'était inconnue,—" *LR (with* fraiche), *AraVP* ‖ J'éprouvais un instant de puissance et de délire. *US 1920*, *1925*

15] *half page indent ts1*, *AraVP* ‖ *single indent LR*, *1932+* ‖ *triple indent US 1920*, *1925*   **lubrique, à cet âge . . .**] lubrique— *LR*, *AraVP*

15 ^ 16] *line space LR*, *AraVP*

16] *indented (to range with* 17–19) *printings prior to 1932* ‖ *no indent 1932+*

17] *bracketed Pound ts1*   **peloter,**] peloter, amicalement *ts1* ‖ péloter, *LR*, *AraVP*

18 **quittée**] quitté *LR*   **mi-chemin.**] mi-chemin; *ts1*, *LR*, *AraVP*

19 **dommage."**] dommage. *ts1 1ˢᵗ reading (the added punctuation may be French »)*

19 ^ 20] *line space ts1*

20] *half page indent ts1*, *AraVP* ‖ *triple indent US 1920*, *1925 (aligned with* 15) *1932 (deeper than* 15)   **vautour!**] *1936+ (with the "o" marked for possible deletion and "?" Curtis's 1936)* ‖ vautour. *LR*, *AraVP* ‖ vautur! *ts1*, *US 1920*, *1925*

21 **te]** *ringed by Pound ts1*   **du]** *Pound ts1, LR+* ‖ de ton *ts1 1ˢᵗ reading*

22 **crâne.]** crane, *ts1* ‖ crâne, *LR, AraVP*

23 **De quel]** *Pound ts1, LR+* ‖ Quel *ts1 1ˢᵗ reading*   **payes-tu]** as-tu a *ts1* ‖ te paye *Pound ts1* ‖ paies-tu *AraVP*

25 **Phlébas,]** Phlébas *ts1 1ˢᵗ reading*   **Phénicien]** Phenician *LR*   **pendant]** *LR+* ‖ etait *ts1* ‖ ~~fut~~ pendant *Pound ts1*

26 **Oubliait]** Oubliant *ts1* ‖ Oubliat *Pound ts1*   **les cris]** *ts1 1ˢᵗ reading, LR, US 1920+* ‖ le cris *ts1 2ⁿᵈ reading (error)* ‖ le cri *AraVP*   **des mouettes]** de muettes *ts1 1ˢᵗ reading*   **la houle]** l'ecume *ts1 1ˢᵗ reading, changed to final reading by both Pound and TSE*

28 **très]** tres *US 1920, 1925*

30 **pénible;]** *1925+* ‖ penible, *ts1* ‖ penible. *LR* ‖ pénible. *AraVP* ‖ penible; *US 1920*

Whispers of Immortality

Published in *Little Review* Sept 1918, then *1919+*.

Eight tss (Berg): eight leaves of lightweight typing paper accompanying Notebook. *March Hare* prints the five typings in full.

	March Hare	This ed.
First typing:	A	*ts1a*
	B	*ts1b*
Second typing	C	*ts2*
Third typing	D	*ts3a*
	E	*ts3b*
Fourth typing	F	*ts4*
Fifth typing	G	*ts5a*
	H	*ts5b*

ts1a: ribbon copy, heavily annotated by Pound. At the foot TSE wrote: "Do you think this is worth doing anything to? It is very scrappy. I feel that it ought to be remodelled, if at all, entirely in the third person. Also the first two lines of the fifth verse wont do, they are conscious, and exhibit a feeble reversion to the Laforgue manner. Minor: breastless and lipless." Pound suggested titles: *Night Thoughts on immorality* or *Night thoughts on Gautier*, and on the verso he summarised the stanzas, one below the other: "Webster | " | Done | Gautier | " | f | g | h", the last three braced with "general statement & conclusion no pipit". Also: "Predelections maccabres | or the maccabre predilections". Against the third stanza he wrote: "a | b | transition". Other jottings by Pound are illegibly deleted.

ts1b: carbon annotated by Pound.

ts2: ribbon copy of another typing.

ts3a: ribbon copy with part numbers, I at head and II before "Grishkin is nice . . ." Some annotation by Pound.

ts3b: carbon on which Pound has written "A." beside 11–12 and "B." beside the last stanza. These are explained in a page by him typed on paper headed "5. Holland Place Chambers, Kensington, W.":

> "SODOMY!" said the Duchess, approaching the Ormolu clock.
>
> If at A. you shift to "my" i.e. *your* "experience" you would conceivably reach Grishkin's Dunlap tyre boozum by the line of greatest directness.
>
> If at B. you should then leap from the bloody, boozy and Barzeelyan Jag-U-ARRRR to the Abstracter entities who would not have resisted either the boozom or the "smell of baked meats", you could thence entauthenexelaunai to the earlier terminer
> But I must crawl, etc. metaphysics warm.
> having in the lines precedent used your extant rhyme in "charm", applying same to either boozum, odour, or enticement of the toutensemble
>
> om [*pencilled false start, before typing resumes*]
>
> Omitting fourth stanza of present Nth. variant.
> wash the whole with virol and leave in hypo.
>
> At any rate, I think this would bring us nearer the desired epithalamium of force, clearness and bewtie.   EP

ts4: ribbon copy.

ts5a: ribbon copy, with some annotation by Pound.

ts5b: carbon.

Valerie's Own Book: fair copy (three pages), with two-line spaces between stanzas.

On the basis of differences in the paper, *Rainey* 198 assigns *ts1–ts4* to 1917, and *ts5* to 1918.

AraVP indents even-numbered lines. *1963* erroneously ranged the first page of this poem (1–24) to the left margin (*US 1963* set all the poems this way).

Title] *not ts1, ts4*; TRY THIS ON YOUR PIANO | WHISPERS OF IMMORTALITY *ts3*

  1 **much**] pre *alt by Pound ts1a*   **death**] death; *ts1, ts2* ‖ death, *ts3*

  2 **And saw**] He saw *ts1, ts2* ‖ and saw *Pound ts1a* ‖ who saw *Pound ts2* ‖ Seeing *ts3* ‖ ~~who~~ he saw *Pound ts5a*

  3 **And**] The *Pound ts1a* ‖ "? The" *Pound ts2* ‖ ~~or while~~ *Pound ts5a*   **under ground**] underground *1919*

  4 **backward**] "image ? | backward | up " [*ditto signifying upward*] | Looked Toward [*six or so illegible words, del*]" *Pound ts1a, all del*   **lipless**] "canine?" *by TSE with* "dachshund" *by Pound ts1a* ‖ ringed with "canine" *by TSE ts1b*

  5 **balls**] eyes *ts2 1st reading* (*error*)

  6 **the eyes**] "the" *underlined Pound ts1a* ‖ "? their" *Pound ts5a*

  7 **limbs**] *bracketed Pound, with* "?" *ts1a*

Third stanza, with variants listed below each version:

   ts1:

> I think John Donne was such another
> With passions chiselled out of stone;   10
> He found no substitute for death
> But toothed the sweetness of the bone.

with "a | b | transition" Pound ts1a (perhaps referring to rhyming and to the position of 11 after his deletions)

   9 **I think**] *ringed Pound ts1a*

   10, 12] *del Pound ts1a*

   11 **He**] *ringed Pound with* who *ts1a*   **death**] *sense ts1a 2nd reading, ts1b 2nd*
     reading

   12 **toothed**] *underlined Pound ts1a*

   ts2:

> I think John Donne was such another
> Who cracked the marrow now and then.   10
> Our sighs pursue th' elusive shade
> But these w[e]re really serious men.

   9] **I**] Who *1st reading (error)*

   9–10] *with "clutched ?" in margin by TSE*

   10] *ringed Pound with* who found no substitute for *sense*

   11–12] *del Pound*

   ts3, ts4:

> Donne, I suppose, was such another
> Pursuing sense within the sense   10
> To seize and clutch and penetrate.
> Expert beyond experience

   10] *with "Or do you prefer the original line? This one however more coherent—in fact it is the whole idea" ts3b;* Who found no substitute for sense *Pound ts3a*

   11 **penetrate.**] penetrate: *ts4*

   12] Expert beyond my experience *Pound ts3b (see description of ts3b for Pound's comment);* This passes my experience. *ts4*

ts5 is as the published text, with variants as follows:

   10 **sense,**] *1936+* ‖ sense *ts5, LR, 1919, AraVP* ‖ sense; *US 1920, 1925, 1936 proof*

   11 **penetrate;**] *1936+* ‖ penetrate, *ts5, LR, 1919, AraVP, US 1920, 1925, 1936 proof*

   12 **experience,**] *US 1920+* ‖ experience *ts5, LR, 1919, AraVP*

10–12] *TSE to Bonamy Dobrée 17 Nov 1930:* "It's ALL wrong; please read COMMA after sense, SEMI-COLON after penetrate; and COMMA after experience. That's better" *(Tate ed. 85).*

13–16] *not ts1, ts2, ts4* ‖ *with "too many possessives?" by TSE and stanza then del apparently first by EP then by TSE ts3b*

13 **marrow**] marrow, *ts3*

16 ^ 17] *no dots ts1–ts4* ‖ *five asterisks ts5* ‖ *four asterisks LR, 1919, AraVP* ‖ *eight dots US 1920* ‖ *five dots 1925+* ‖ *five "x"s Valerie's Own Book*

17 **Grishkin**] Grisk *1ˢᵗ reading Valerie's Own Book (error)*　　　　**nice:**] nice; *ts1-ts3, LR, 1919, AraVP*

19 **Uncorseted,**] *comma altered to semi-colon then back to comma, apparently by Pound ts1a*

20] *caret mark beneath line added ts1a*　　　　**bliss.**] bliss; *Pound ts3a*

21–28] *not ts1, ts2*

21–24] *not ts3, ts4* ‖ *typed in margin as alt to 25–28 ts5a and ts5b with "alternative" added in each, then del from ts5b. (Alternative stanzas became successive stanzas.)*

21/25] *comparing the alt stanzas, Pound del Brazilian in 25 then wrote "but stet the sleek couched" ts5a. At the foot of the leaf TSE jotted "sleek ⊕ spotted / sinuous / sleek couched sinuous / couched detensive" (last word presumably for "defensive")*

22 **Compels**] Can charm *ts5 1ˢᵗ reading*　　　　**marmoset**] marmoset, *2ⁿᵈ reading ts5a*

23 **With subtle**] Distilling *ts5 1ˢᵗ reading*

24 **Grishkin**] And Grishkin *ts5*　　　　**maisonnette;**] *1936+* ‖ maisonette. *ts5, Valerie's Own Book* ‖ maisonette: *LR, 1919, AraVP* ‖ maisonette; *US 1920, 1925, US 1936, US 1952, some post-1969 imps. of Sel Poems, Valerie's Own Book 1ˢᵗ reading.* OED has "maisonette. Also maisonnette", remarking "The correct spelling with *-nn-* is rarely found."

25 **Brazilian**] *ts3–ts5, US 1920+* ‖ and sinuous *LR, 1919, AraVP*

26 **not**] not, *ts3*　　　　**its**] his *ts3, ts5 1ˢᵗ reading, LR, 1919, AraVP*　　　　**arboreal**] aboreal *1963, US 1963, 1969 (error, corrected in reprints of 1969 and in 1974 but persisting in US editions. See McCue 2012 Proposal 3).*　　　　**gloom**] gloom, *ts3*

27 **so**] the *ts3* ‖ the *ringed by Pound with so ts3a*　　　　**rank a**] strong rank *ts3*

28 **As**] Of *ts3* ‖ Of *ringed by Pound with as ts3a*　　　　**drawing-room**] drawing room *ts3*

Eighth stanza:

　　ts1, ts2, ts4:

> And some abstracter entities
> Have not disused a certain charm.　　　　　　　　30
> But I must crawl between dry ribs
> To keep my metaphysics warm.

29–32] *bracketed by Pound with 30 and 32 additionally bracketed by him ts1a*

29 **And**] *ringed by Pound ts1a*　　　　**And some**] There are *ts4*

30 **disused**] *ringed by Pound with "??? otherwise O.K." ts1a*

30] Preserve a sacerdotal charm, *ts2* ‖ Which still maintain a certain charm. *ts4*

29–30] *del Pound with* The sons of god ~~might~~ may feel this charm *ts2*

ts3:

> But Donne and Webster passed beyond
> The text-book rudiments of lust,
> And crawled at last between dry ribs,
> Having their Ethics of the Dust.

       30

29–32] *bracketed with* If abs ents [= abstracter entities] | would fall | for this charm | Our Webster Donne [*the names ringed*] | Tribe | run [*uncertain*] crawl | betw ribs, *and, at foot, if and two illegible words by Pound ts3a* ‖ Tho entities | I must to keep | metam warm *Pound ts3b.*

30 **lust**] *with "Should I avoid using the word twice?" ts3b*

ts5 is as the published text, with variants as follows:

29–30] *"And" and "the" bracketed Pound ts5a, with "If | might" and, below, "abstracter" (perhaps for "If even abstracter entities | Might circumambulate her charm")*

29 **the Abstract Entities**] *ts5, US 1920+* ‖ abstracter entities *LR, 1919, AraVP*

30 **charm;**] charm: *ts5*

31 **crawls**] *Pound ts5a, LR+* ‖ crawl *ts5*

32 **our**] *ts5, US 1920+* ‖ its *Pound ts5a, LR, 1919, AraVP*

Additional stanzas:

ts1:

> As long as Pipit is alive
> One can be mischievous and brave;
> But where there is no more misbehaviour
> I would like my bones flung into her grave.

forming the final stanza of a six-stanza poem, with Pound having ringed the first line, ringed where and joined it to "??", and ringed and del the whole stanza with "why" ts1a.

ts2:

> Our sighs pursue the vanishd shade
> And breathe a sanctified amen,
> And yet the Sons of God descend
> To entertain the wives of men.
>
> And when the Female Soul departs
> The Sons of Men turn up their eyes,
> The Sons of God embrace the Grave—
> The Sons of God are very wise.

       [5]

forming the final stanzas of a seven-stanza poem, above which TSE wrote: "I think it had better stop here".

[1] **vanishd**] *the* d *typed over* e

[3] **descend**] *"? tense" and "when did you last | fear the converse | or | what angel hath cuckwoled thee" by Pound (alluding to "And when did you last see your father?", a popular catchphrase after the title of W. F. Yeames's Victorian painting).*

Further jottings by Pound: "or did Jahveh | ? The Sacred Ghost | did not disdain |

copulationion in carnal form | —et les anges, | le diodem | de son" (perhaps recalling Villon: "Je ne suis, bien considéré, | Fils d'ange portant diadème" [I'm not, duly considered, the son of an angel wearing a diadem] Le Grand Testament XXXVIII.)

Mr. Eliot's Sunday Morning Service

Published in *Little Review* Sept 1918, then *1919+*.

ts1 (Berg): leaf of lightweight typing paper accompanying Notebook. Ribbon copy annotated by Pound.

Epigraph] *not ts1 1ˢᵗ reading, then added above title*   **Look, look,**] Look look *ts1* ‖ "Look, look *printings prior to US 1920*   **master,**] master *ts1*   **two**] two of the *ts1, printings prior to US 1920*   **caterpillars.**] *ts1, US 1920+* ‖ caterpillars." *LR, 1919* ‖ caterpillars". *AraVP*   Attribution] *1936+* ‖ *not ts1* ‖ *capitals and small capitals US 1920, 1925, US 1952*   **The Jew**] *1932+* ‖ Jew *printings prior to 1932*

AraVP indents even-numbered lines.

1–4] *bracketed Pound ts1*

5 **Word,**] *ts1, printings prior to US 1920* ‖ Word. *US 1920+* (*see McCue 2012, Proposal 8*).

6 τὸ ἔν,] *ts1, US 1920* ‖ το εν *LR, AraVP* ‖ τὸ ἔν *1919* ‖ τὸ ἔν, *US 1920 2nd and 3rd printings (1927, 1929), 1925+ (corrected long after). In printing ts1, March Hare mistranscribes the third character.* Faber director Peter du Sautoy agreed with a correspondent in 1965 that the breathing then in print should be changed, but it was not. *Schmidt 1982a restores the original breathing, but changes the punctuation to a semi-colon.*

7] And after many [*illegible*] months *ts1 alt del*   **mensual**] menstrual *ts1 1ˢᵗ reading ringed and emended by Pound*

8 **enervate**] the ~~eastrate~~ *ts1 1ˢᵗ reading, with* enervate *supplied and ringed by Pound after "o.k."*

9–16] *braced Pound ts1*

11 **Baptized**] *US 1920+* ‖ Baptised *ts1, printings prior to US 1920 (see McCue 2012 Proposal 17)*

12 **browned**] browned. *1974*

16 **Father**] father *AraVP*

16 ^ 17] *three asterisks ts1* ‖ *four asterisks printings prior to US 1920* ‖ *six dots US 1920*

18 **penitence;**] penitence, *ts1. Pound braced the word here and in 21 and linked them*

20 **pence.**] *ts1, US 1920+* ‖ pence, *printings prior to US 1920.* (*Moody 307 suggested removing the full-stop but did not mention that there had previously been a comma which made the sequence follow conventional grammar.*)

21–28] *braced by Pound with "lacking syntactic symplycyty"*

21] And through the gates of penitence *ts1 1ˢᵗ reading* ‖ And through the penitential gates *ts1 2ⁿᵈ reading. Above the line Pound wrote* ~~ports of~~ p. *Deleting the first two typed words he wrote* Under *and* "Qy. Penetrate?" (*probably because of* "penetrate" *in* Whispers of Immortality 11)

23 **Where**] To where *ts1, with first word del Pound*   **souls**] soils *1925, 1932 proof, corrected by TSE*

24 **dim.**] *1919* ‖ dim.* [*footnote:* *Vide Henry Vaughan the Silurist, from whom the author seems to have borrowed this line.] *ts1* ‖ dim, *LR*

25–28] *ts1 1ˢᵗ reading*:

> Salmon stretched red along the wall
> Sweet peas invite to intervene
> The hairy bellies of the bees
> Blest office of the epicene

with 26 underlined by Pound with "?" *The stanza then struck through probably by TSE* ‖ *ts1 2ⁿᵈ reading*:

> Along the garden wall the bees
> With hairy bellies ~~go~~ pass between
> the staminate ⊲ pistilate
> Blest . . .

27 **pistillate,**] *1936, Sel Poems, 1963+* ‖ pistilate: *printings prior to US 1920* ‖ pistilate, *US 1920, 1925, 1936 proof, US 1936, US 1952*

29–30] *braced Pound ts1*

30 **the water**] *not Sel Poems 1954, Sel Poems 1961 pbk* (*later corrected*). The omission was pointed out by David Curry and acknowledged by TSE, 21 June 1962.

32 **polymath**] *underlined and divided* "poly | math", *with* "μαθαιος or μανθανο?" [*for* μάταιος, μανθανω] *Pound ts1* (*see Commentary*)

Sweeney Among the Nightingales

Published in *Little Review* Sept 1918, then *1919+*.

ts1 (Berg): leaf of lightweight typing paper accompanying Notebook. Carbon emended by TSE and Pound.

ts2 (Berg): leaf of lightweight typing paper accompanying Notebook. Carbon emended by TSE and Pound.

ts3 (Cornell, Wyndham Lewis collection (4612), Box 51 Folder 25): violet carbon with annotation by Wyndham Lewis. He probably did the typing (letter-spacing the title and leaving spaces in "coffee- cup", "window- sill" and "some one").

AraVP indents even-numbered lines.

Title] *letter spaced, originally with only first word having a capital, although* among *was emended to* Among *ts3* ‖ Sweeny among the Nightingales *AraVP contents*

Epigraph] *not ts1 1ˢᵗ reading, ts2 1ˢᵗ reading, ts3*   ὤμοι,] ὤμοι *ts1, ts2*   πέπληγμαι] πεπλήγμαι *ts1* ‖ πεπληγμαι *ts2* ‖ πέπγηλμαι *LR*   καιρίαν πληγὴν ἔσω] ἐν πλευροῖς εἴσω *ts1* ‖ *ἐν πλευροις εἴσω ts2*   καιρίαν] χαιρίαν *Sel Poems 1954 proof (corrected in unknown hand with "chi, not kappa")*   πληγὴν] *πγηλὴν LR, AraVP (corrected by TSE in Edgar Jepson's AraVP, autographed 5 Feb 1920, and in John Quinn's copy, autographed 23 Sept 1920; both Yale)*   ἔσω.] ἔσω *LR, AraVP, Sesame, Sel Poems 1954, Sel Poems 1961 (later corrected)*

Second epigraph (1919 and AraVP only)] Why should I speak of the nightingale? The night- / ingale sings of adulterate wrong. 1919 ‖ WHY SHOULD I SPEAK OF THE NIGHTINGALE? THE | NIGHTINGALE SINGS OF ADULTEROUS WRONG. *AraVP (the only epigraph in the volume set in small caps), corrected by TSE in Quinn's copy to* ADULTERATE

4 **giraffe.**] giraffe, *ts1*

6 **westward toward**] *Pound underlined* ward · · · ward *with "X" ts1* ‖ westward to *LR, 1919, AraVP*

8 **hornèd**] *1936+, emendation by TSE in Thayer's AraVP* ‖ horned *printings prior to 1936, Faber Bk Mod V*   **gate.**] gate; *ts1*

12 **sit**] rest *alt added and del by Pound ts1 (see 18)*   **knees**] knees; *ts3* ‖ knees, *TSE's emendation in Morley's US 1920*

13 **pulls**] *del and restored ts1 (see 16)*   **cloth**] cloth, *ts3, TSE's emendation in Morley's US 1920*

14–15] *one line ts3, with division added by Lewis*

15 **Reorganised**] Reorganized *ts3, LR, 1919, US 1920, US 1952*   **floor**] floor, *TSE's emendation in Morley's US 1920*

16 **draws**] pulls *ts1 1ˢᵗ reading*

18 **Sprawls**] Sits *ts1 1ˢᵗ reading, ringed by Pound and linked to* sit *in 12, with* Lops *(Pound) and* Stands *(TSE) alts. (OED "lop", v.² 2a and 2b.)*

19 ^ 20] *line space ts3, with arrow to cancel it by Lewis*

20 **Bananas**] *ts1, ts2 with comma added by Pound, ts3, US 1920+* ‖ Bananas, *LR, 1919, AraVP*   **grapes;**] grapes, *ts1*

21] The animalcule in brown *alt ts2*   **silent**] ?~~tacit~~ *alt by Pound ts2*   **silent vertebrate**] individual *ts1, with "economic unit" Pound*   **in brown**] *ts1, ts2 1ˢᵗ reading, US 1920+* ‖ contracts *ts2 2ⁿᵈ reading* ‖ exhales *ts2 3ʳᵈ reading, LR, 1919, AraVP*

22 **Contracts**] Hovers *ts2 alt*

23 **Rachel**] Rachel, *ts3*   née] *US 1920+* ‖ nee *ts1 with* née *by Pound in margin (uncertain, with illegible word scrawled over or perhaps del), ts2* ‖ née *ts3 (the accent added by Lewis) LR, 1919, AraVP*

26 **suspect,**] suspect; *ts1*

29 **reappears**] reappears, *ts2 1ˢᵗ reading*

30 **in,**] in *ts3, with comma added by Lewis*

31 **wistaria**] wisteria *ts1, ts2*

33 **someone**] some one *ts3*

38–40] *typing not showing at head of lines, probably because of a fold in the carbon paper, ts3. Supplied in pencil:* Wh (38), And (39). *The final line begins with the half-word* -in *but* To sta- *has not been supplied*

38 **aloud**] *AraVP, 1963* ‖ aloud, *tss, LR, US 1920, 1925, printings prior to 1963, some printings afterwards of Sesame, Sel Poems and 1963.* (*Moody* 307 advocated restoration of the comma.)

39 **their**] the *ts3*   **siftings**] *Pound ts2, LR+* ‖ droppings *tss, enclosed between slashes by Pound ts1, US 1920 (emended in Morley's US 1920)*

The Waste Land

This Textual History includes readings from the four original editions and subsequent lifetime editions as well as *1969* and *1974* (which were supervised by Valerie Eliot), with occasional reference to subsequent editions. It also gives the readings of "the drafts": the manuscripts and typescripts of the poem as seen in *The Waste Land: A Facsimile and Transcript* (*WLFacs*) plus the two leaves of "Fresca couplets" *ms1924* in the Bodleian Library (following note to 298 below). Also included are the readings of three other pre-publication typescripts not by TSE, and two autograph copies made by him late in life. Reference is made to the "miscellaneous poems" found with the drafts (which are printed among the "Uncollected Poems"), when specific lines of *The Waste Land* are indebted to them.

1. THE DRAFTS

The earliest extant drafts consist of both manuscripts and typescripts in the Berg Collection, reproduced in *WLFacs*. The manuscripts are:

ms1 (*WLFacs* 36/37): pencil draft, probably written in Margate, of [III] 259–65 = 422–28 ("O City, City"; given in *WLComposite* but omitted from *ts3* before being reinstated in the published poem) and, below a rule, of 334–47 ("London, the swarming life"; lines adopted in *ts3*, which are given in *WLComposite*, but were deleted by Pound in *ts3a* and *ts3b*). Apparently from the same pad as *ms2* and the leaf used for *Elegy* and, on the verso, *Dirge ms1* (*WLFacs* 116–19), although not torn out at the same moment (see headnote to Commentary, 1. COMPOSITION). Assigned to Nov 1921 by *Rainey* 200–201.

ms2 (*WLFacs* 48–53): pencil draft, probably written in Margate, of [III] 266–311 = 429–74 ("The river sweats"; given in *WLComposite*). Three pages on two leaves (recto, recto, verso). "First draft" (Valerie Eliot). The last page has a sum, upside down:

$$
\begin{array}{r}
76 \\
97 \\
\underline{113} \\
286
\end{array}
$$

Valerie Eliot suggests (*WLFacs* 53) that these figures refer to the number of lines in Parts I (after the deletion of 1–50), II and V. The date of the sum is unknown, but it might relate, for instance, to TSE's dilemma over whether to divide the poem for serial publication (see Commentary headnote, 3. THE *DIAL* AND THE *CRITERION*).

At the same time as these two leaves, TSE tore from his pad the leaf he used for *Elegy* and, on the verso, *Dirge ms1* (*WLFacs* 116–19). Assigned to Nov 1921 by *Rainey* 200–201.

ms3 (*WLFacs* 24/25): pencil draft of the published opening of Part III ("The river's tent") written upside down on verso of first leaf of *ts3a* and collated among the variant readings to [III] 173–182. Written to replace the Fresca passage of seventy lines which Pound deleted from *ts3a*. The bracketed line "(Sweet Thames etc)" and the curtailed line "By the waters" suggest that the allusions to Spenser and Psalm 137 were already understood, although there is no earlier documentary record of them. If TSE was remembering correctly when he wrote to J. M. Aguirre on 23 Nov 1958 that the line "By the waters of Leman I sat down and wept" was "probably written at Lausanne", then a previous draft may have disappeared.

ms4 (*WLFacs* 28/29): pencil draft of seventeen lines ("From which, a Venus Anadyomene") on a single leaf, for insertion in Part III (285^286) but subsequently omitted. Written on Pound's quad-ruled paper, evidently before Pound's deletion in *ts3a* of the passage into which these lines were to have been inserted. Assigned to Nov–Dec 1921 by *Rainey* 200–201, but more probably dating from Jan 1922 in Paris. Being subsequent to *ts3*, these lines are not used for *WLComposite* but appear within the variant readings.

ms5 (*WLFacs* 54–61): ink fair copy of the original, long Part IV, 475–567 ("The sailor, attentive to the chart", given in its entirety in *WLComposite* as Part IV). "The writing suggests that Eliot may have been copying from an unpreserved draft" (Valerie Eliot). The four quad-ruled leaves are matched by *ms4*, but the neat hand is not. Both paper and hand, however, are matched by *Dirge ms2*, the fair copy (*WLFacs* 120–21). Assigned to Nov–Dec 1921 by *Rainey* 200–201, but more probably dating from Jan 1922 in Paris.

ms6 (*WLFacs* 70–81): untitled pencil draft of the whole of Part V, 568–678 (given in its entirety in *WLComposite*). On six quad-ruled leaves, matching *ms4* and *ms5*, numbered upper right. Head of first leaf endorsed by Pound "OK" and "OK from here on I think." "First draft" (Valerie Eliot). Assigned to Nov–Dec 1921 by *Rainey* 200–201.

The typescripts were made on three typewriters. The first, used to type Parts I and II (each with the head title "He Do the Police in Different Voices"), was in poor condition by the time Henry Eliot visited his brother in 1921, so when Henry left on 20 Aug, he substituted his own machine along with a gift of money (see Vivien Eliot's letter to him, 23 Aug). This second typewriter, used to type Part III, was a Corona which TSE wore out in the service of the *Criterion* in two years (TSE to Richard Cobden-Sanderson, 22 Aug 1923). The third typewriter, used to type Parts IV and V, was probably Pound's, as Valerie Eliot suggested (*WLFacs* 63, 83). Magnification in the facsimile differs according to the size of leaf, as is especially evident from the typescripts of Parts IV and V.

ts title (*WLFacs* 2/3): ribbon copy from second typewriter on a single leaf of Verona Linen, formerly folded in half, with holes from having been twice pinned. Paper and typing match those of *ts3a*, with which this leaf appears to have been folded, although *ts3a* has no pin-holes. The crease does not match those of *ts1*, *ts2a* or *ts2b*. Assigned to Jan 1922 by *Rainey* 200–201.

ts1 (*WLFacs* 4–9): first known typescript of Part I. First typewriter. Ribbon copy, annotated by Pound and TSE. Three leaves of British Bond paper, formerly folded in half, with holes from having been twice pinned. "Probably a first draft", *Gallup 1968*. Assigned to Feb–May 1921 by *Rainey* 200–201. Given in *WLComposite* for 1–130.

ts2: first known typescript of Part II. First typewriter. Assigned to Feb–May 1921 by *Rainey* 35. Two versions on British Bond paper:

ts2a (*WLFacs* 10–15): ribbon copy. Three leaves, formerly folded in quarters, with holes from having been twice pinned. "Probably a fair copy", *Gallup 1968*. Annotated by Vivien Eliot, Pound and TSE. Vivien Eliot was apparently the first to comment, writing on the verso of the last leaf: "Make any of these alterations—or *none* if you prefer. Send me back this copy & let me have it". This suggests that it was sent to her by post, probably from Margate. TSE copied some of her notes onto the carbon (*ts2b*), before Pound annotated the ribbon copy. Given in *WLComposite* for 131–228.

ts2b (*WLFacs* 16–21): blue carbon, annotated by TSE. Three leaves, formerly folded in half, with holes from having been twice pinned.

ts3: first known typescript of Part III, with much of the published text absent. Second typewriter. Assigned to Nov 1921 by *Rainey* 200–201. Two versions on Verona Linen paper:

ts3a (*WLFacs* 22/23, 26/27, 30–35): ribbon copy on five leaves, formerly folded in half. Annotated by Vivien Eliot, Pound and TSE. Given in *WLComposite* for 229–421. Vivien Eliot's marginal suggestion "Our" (231) is in the same pencil as her closing comments on *ts2a*, and the resemblance suggests that she read Parts II and III on the same occasion (these being the only parts that she marked). Her annotations are written lightly in pencil, and often of uncertain intention. TSE's sharp pencil deletion of "room" at 360 is quite different from Pound's blunt pencil and bold marks at 245–46, 374–384 which are similar to marks and deletions at 244, 270–73, 282, 284, 326, 335–43. These suggest that several of TSE's emendations were prompted by Pound's deletions. When ringing a word or phrase, TSE characteristically began by underlining it before looping around; Pound began at top left and usually formed something more like a box.

ts3b (*WLFacs* 38–47): blue carbon on five leaves, formerly folded in half. Annotated by Pound in pencil and ink prior to his annotation of the ribbon copy, *ts3a*. Grover Smith noted that this order of marking is borne out by Pound's comment on the fourth page of *ts3a*, "vide other copy". At some stage Pound incorporated into *ts3b* the third page only of *ts3a* (without removing the cognate page of *ts3b*), so forming a six-page working draft, which he renumbered 1–6. The cognate third pages, showing 317–56, are both heavily annotated. (*WLFacs* 30/31, 42/43)

Although *Gallup 1968* described *ts3* as "probably a first draft", TSE had written a previous draft of Part III, in manuscript, at Margate (see Commentary headnote, 1. COMPOSITION).

ts4 (*WLFacs* 62–69): violet typing of the long first draft of Part IV (475–567), derived from *ms5* and annotated by Pound. Assigned to Jan 1922 by *Rainey* 200–201. Four leaves, formerly folded in quarters, of India paper of the kind Pound used when writing to James Sibley Watson 4 Jan 1923. Both this and *ts5* were probably typed on Pound's typewriter. Although Valerie Eliot states that this was "typed with the violet ribbon used by Pound", the colour was probably from a carbon sheet not a ribbon, as suggested by a letter and article sent to Watson by Pound on 4 Mar 1922: the letter is typed in black, but he encloses a violet carbon (double-spaced) of his review of *The New Therapy* by Louis Berman, "knocked off ··· during the morning", the top copy of which was sent to *New Age* (Berg). Like Pound's article, *ts4* is double spaced. On the verso of the last leaf is a note in TSE's hand:

> 1. Sunburn ⊰ salusta lotion
> 1. Smallest pot skinfood O.
>
> -------------------------------------
>
> 62 Ch.[amps] Elysees

which confirms a connection with Paris.

ts5 (*WLFacs* 82–89): violet typing of Part V, derived from *ms6* and annotated by Pound. Typed on the same machine as *ts4*, likewise with double spacing, but on a different paper: two halves of a cut sheet of double foolscap (*WLFacs* 82/83 and 88/89) and fols. 1 and 3 of another sheet, folded (*WLFacs* 84/85 and 86/87). "In violet ink on the double foolscap used by Pound, it may have been typed by him, or by Eliot when he visited his friend in Paris on his way home from Lausanne, where this section was written" (Valerie Eliot). Kenner pointed out that Pound's "mannerism of hitting the space-bar twice is nowhere visible" (*Litz ed.* 42). On the other hand, TSE typed page numbers (from "2") in all the other typescripts. Assigned to Jan 1922 by *Rainey* 200–201.

All of these drafts were sent by TSE to Quinn on 21 Sept 1922. The posting label has Quinn's stamp of receipt dated 13 Jan 1923. Other materials sent to Quinn in the same sheaf as *The Waste Land* appear in the present edition among the "Uncollected Poems".

WLComposite is made up of seven groups of lines:

1–130	from *ts1*
131–228	from *ts2a*
229–421	from *ts3a*
422–428	from *ms1*
429–474	from *ms2*
475–567	from *ms5*
568–678	from *ms6*

2. NON-AUTHORIAL TYPESCRIPTS

None of the drafts listed so far gives a fair copy of the entire poem. No collation of the earliest extant witnesses to the poem as an organised and edited whole has hitherto been published. Although not by TSE himself, the typescripts made for John Quinn in New York at the end of July 1922 (*Q*) and for James Sibley Watson in Paris in August (*T* and *W*) are copies following two distinct typescripts by TSE, both of which are now lost.

As well as being the first to show the entire poem essentially as it was published, the typescripts made for Quinn and for Watson are the first to show numerous words and phrases in their final form. *Q* is also the earliest with line numbers. These typescripts also contain the *last* appearance of other words and phrases, for they were not to occur in any of the subsequent witnesses, as the poem finally reached print. The phrase "Ionian white and gold" ([III] 265), for instance, had read "Corinthian white and gold" in a manuscript (*ms1*) but not in TSE's known typescripts. "Corinthian" is also the reading in *T* and *W*, but all printed texts have "Ionian". Both how "Corinthian" came to appear in *T* and *W* and how "Ionian" came to be printed are unknown.

These three typescripts, *Q*, *T* and *W*, differ in small ways not only from the drafts and from any of the published texts but from each other. Even the two copies made for Watson—one at first glance a carbon of the other—turn out to be different. The Quinn copy (*Q*) is not consistently closer to the published texts than the Watson copies (*T*/*W*), but nor are the Watson copies consistently closer than the Quinn, which suggests that just as TSE sometimes worked on more than one copy of a Part of the poem in the draft stage, he continued to do so during the first half of 1922. At [I] 8, the draft (*ts1*) reads "Summer surprised us, coming over the Königssee". The first appearance of "Starnbergersee", the reading in all editions, is in *T*/*W*. Yet *Q*, which was typed by a professional stenographer who made only a very small number of slips, reads "Stainberger". The typist of *T*/*W*, by contrast, does not appear to have been a professional, and a less than perfect grasp of English is suggested by "corps" (for "corpse", [I] 71, in *T*); "Onguent" (for "Unguent", [II] 88); "remenber" ([II] 122 and 124); "voilet" (for "violet", [III] 220); "madoline" ([III] 261) and "canée" (for "canoe" [III] 295). Yet the unusual word "Starnbergersee" is correct in *T*/*W*. Perhaps the typist was more familiar with German, or possibly the copy followed by *T*/*W* was typed, whereas in the source for *Q* it was an unclear manuscript emendation, which would accord with TSE's letter to Quinn, 19 July 1922: "I had wished to type it out fair, but I did not wish to delay it any longer. This will do for him to get on with, and I shall rush forward the notes to go at the end."

Other variants, too, tend to suggest that the source typescript for *Q* was not the most current when TSE sent it. For instance, the nightingale's "Jug Jug" ([II] 103) was not enclosed in quotation marks in the draft or in *Q*, but appeared as "'Jugjug'" in *T*/*W* and as "'Jug Jug'" in printed editions. Likewise, "I think we met first in rats' alley" ([II] 115) in *ts2* was unchanged in *Q*, though revised in *T*/*W* to the text of printed editions: "I think we are in rats' alley". The spelling "fuoco" ([V] 427) seen in *ms5* and *ts6* had not yet been revised in *Q* to "foco", but it was in *T*/*W* and in print. In *T*/*W*, the Sanskrit "Damyata" appears as "*Demyata*" in two places, fourteen lines apart ([V] 418, 432), making it likely that this spelling appeared in the typescript being copied, although it does not occur in any surviving draft or printed text.

Q (Houghton): fair copy, (second?) carbon on 19 leaves (plus title leaf) of Cambrai Bond. Folded in thirds and sent by John Quinn's office to Jeanne Robert Foster on 31 July 1922 (envelope preserved with "Elliot copy to JR The Waste Land" vertically on the front). "Made in the office of John Quinn from typescript sent to him by Eliot" (Houghton library card). The Greek in the epigraph on the title-page is in black ink, as is the envelope. Quinn detailed his negotiations with Liveright, receipt of the poem, the stenographic copying of it, disappointment on reading it, and recommendation that as a book it would benefit from some additional poems in a 14-page letter to TSE of 28 July–1 Aug, for which see *Egleston ed.* He wrote that he had had the poem copied, and was having both

TSE's typing and the copy delivered to Liveright on 1 Aug. On 31 July he sent this copy, *Q*, to Jeanne Robert Foster who took it to be the original (no accompanying letter has been traced).

After a misunderstanding in March over money (see headnote to *The Waste Land*, 4. THE *DIAL* AND THE *CRITERION*), TSE's negotiations with Scofield Thayer of the *Dial* had foundered, yet the journal's principals remained keen to publish the poem. At the end of July, as impresario to both TSE and the *Dial*, Pound wrote to TSE on behalf of Thayer (the editor) and James Sibley Watson (the president). TSE replied on 28 July: "I will let you have a copy of *The Waste Land* for confidential use as soon as I can make one. Of the two available copies, one has gone to Quinn to present to Liveright on completion of the contract, and the other is the only one I possess. I infer from your remarks that Watson is at present in Paris. I have no objection to either his or Thayer's seeing the manuscript."

Here, the term "the manuscript" may have referred to the fresh copy he was promising. On the other hand, a working draft would serve to maintain the interest of the *Dial*, and two letters from Watson to Thayer (12 and 16 Aug) suggest that by "the manuscript" TSE may instead have meant a copy that Pound still had in hand from his final sieving in January. A fortnight later, TSE did send the promised new typescript to Paris, but such was Watson's hurry to despatch a copy to Thayer (then in Germany) that *T/W* may have been made in the interim from the January text. This might help to explain not only why Watson had had time to read the poem three times (as he wrote on 16 Aug) before sending it on, but why the source for *T/W* read "the walls | Of Magnus Martyr stood and stand and hold", following the manuscript reading, which was superseded in *Q* and all printings by "the walls | Of Magnus Martyr hold ([III] 263–64).

T/W: two versions of a 19-page typing made probably in Aug 1922 for Watson in Paris on a French typewriter (typed grave accent at **130**). Both *T* and *W* are collated below, with the abbreviation "*T/W*" being used for variants on pages which are cognate. Faced with these two copies and a secondary carbon of *W* to correct, Watson thoroughly corrected the ribbon copy, *T*, to send to Thayer, but in *W* made only three corrections (on the first three pages), while in the secondary carbon he made none. Most of the leaves of *W* are carbons from *T*, but some leaves, and parts of leaves, are not cognate. Perhaps because the carbon paper slipped at the foot of the first leaf, [I] 19–24 were typed twice, with single spacing in *T* but double spacing in *W*. The third leaves ([I] 50–76) are not cognate, these lines having been typed twice, with "I had not thought death had undone so many." ([I] 63) being omitted from *T* and supplied by hand. On the seventh leaf of each, the final "Good night" of Part II has been typed in error as its own line, but then on *W* it has been typed also in its correct place at the end of the previous line (without any deletion). The typist also had difficulty with the Rhine-maidens' song. The two lines first appear at the foot of the eleventh leaf of each, with a first attempt at the line "Weialala leia" ([III] 277) being scratched out on both *T* and *W* and separately retyped over the top, the new alignment on *W* being wrong. At the song's reappearance, the second line has been wrongly typed (copying the first), but only *T* has been corrected, by hand.

T (*Dial*/Thayer papers, Beinecke): ribbon copy, variously on paper watermarked Boar's Head English Bond, Typewriting Parchment (second leaf) and note-paper of the Hotel Meurice, 228 Rue de Rivoli (seventh leaf). Double-spaced on a distinctive typewriter, with lower parts of characters not printing properly (especially in early leaves). Typed commas often appear as full stops. This typescript omits five lines at the start of Part III (caused by an eye-skip). On the first page, the last six lines ([I] 19–24) are single-spaced. Since the typing on each of these pages ends significantly short of the foot, the typist may have been copying another typescript page-for-page (for which, in *Q*, see textual note to [V] 345 = 591, 592 on the counting of lines).

W (Watson papers, Berg): carbon on 19 leaves of lightweight wove typing paper, accompanied by a secondary carbon (formerly pinned to *W* and similarly folded in three).

3. RELATION OF *Q* AND *T/W* TO THE PRINTED POEM

Since the source of *T/W* may have been either earlier or later than *Q*, it is hard to know whether *Q* or *T/W* should come first in a full collation of these typescripts, though it is clear that neither is the direct source of the other. Also unknown is their relationship to the setting copy for each of the four original printings.

On 25 June, TSE wrote to Quinn that he would send "as quickly as possible a copy of the poem merely for your own interest, and I shall send you later the complete typescript with the notes, in the form to be handed to the publisher". In the event, on 19 July he sent only a typescript such as would "do for him to get on with" (the source typescript for *Q*), implying that a fair copy was still to come, and added that he would "rush forward the notes to go at the end". In his long serial letter of 28 July–1 Aug (NYPL), Quinn wrote "I daresay you'll send the notes direct to Liveright." No typescript of the Notes is known, but since TSE must have sent one to New York and there is no further mention of them in the Quinn papers, he almost certainly did send it direct to the publisher in August for setting. Having told Quinn that he wanted to type a fair copy of the poem, and given the importance he attached to "the punctuation and the spacing" in what was then planned as the poem's American debut, it is likely that he took the opportunity to send a fresh typescript of the entire poem.

A fair copy sent direct to Liveright would have incorporated revisions which TSE had made since sending the source typescript for *Q* and would explain some of the textual differences between the Liveright edition and *Q*, including the absence of the line Vivien Eliot wanted excised, "The ivory men make company between us" ([II] 137a). The addition of the Notes almost certainly required a text with line-numbering, and this too gives an indication that the typescript that was the source for *Q* was not Liveright's setting copy. For although *Q* is the earliest text with line numbers, they do not quite match those printed in Liveright's edition, which counts

> From doors of mudcracked houses
> If there were water

as the single line [V] 345. TSE could not have written notes to the poem such as "Cf. Part III, l. 204" without giving line numbers, so the line numbering in the edition probably derives from such a typescript sent to Liveright but now lost. Neither the *Dial* nor the *Criterion* printing has line numbering, for they have no Notes. When the Hogarth Press edition was set in 1923, the Notes certainly and the text almost certainly derived from the Boni & Liveright edition, yet the poem has no line numbering.

The relation of *T/W* to the printed editions is also distant and enigmatic. In these typescripts, the poem is without a title, and is set apart from the printed texts by variants such as "a pack of cards" (for "a wicked pack of cards", [I] 46), "laquenaria" (for "laquearia", [II] 92) and "reforms" (for "reforms and bursts", [V] 372). However, as well as preparing the American book and journal publications of the poem, TSE was arranging its appearance in the first issue of the *Criterion* in October. During July or August, he therefore sent a typescript to the printer, Richard Cobden-Sanderson, and this evidently overlapped with the source typescript for *T/W*. Of the four original printings, only the *Criterion* shares with *T/W* "in the sunlight" (for "in sunlight", [I] 10), "The chair" (for "The Chair", [II] 77), "Wherefrom" (for "From which", [II] 80), "she says · · · she says" (for "she said · · · she said", [II] 158–59) and "Upper Thames Street" (for "Lower Thames Street", [III] 260). Like *T/W* but unlike *Q* and unlike the other original printings, the *Criterion* text has no epigraph.

4. PRINTINGS

The order of publication of the earliest printings of *The Waste Land* was probably: *Criterion* (Oct 1922 issue), *Dial* (Nov 1922 issue), Boni & Liveright (15 Dec 1922), Boni & Liveright 2nd imp. (early 1923), Hogarth Press (12 Sept 1923).

TSE had the chance to bring the details of the British and American texts into line, since he had proofs from both Boni & Liveright (on 15 Sept he wrote to Pound "Liveright's proof is excellent") and from the *Criterion* (letters of 27 Sept and 3 Oct). His preferences, however, were not completely settled, and many small differences remained. To Gilbert Seldes of the *Dial*, 12 Nov 1922: "Liveright's proof was on the whole very good indeed and I have no doubt that the appearance in *The Dial* will be equally good · · · Nov. no. just received. Poem admirably printed." As well as confirming that TSE read proofs for *Boni* (as for *Criterion* and *Hogarth*), this indicates that he did not read any for *Dial*, which was apparently set either from the TSE's ts or from proofs of *Boni*. No proofs of *Boni* or *Criterion* have been traced. The John Peale Bishop papers at Princeton contain a gathering from the setting of the *Dial* of Nov 1922 which includes *The Waste Land*, but it has no variants and is unlikely to be a proof.

The first British trade printing of the poem was in *1925*, Faber & Gwyer's first poetry book. Other printings collated here: *1932*, *1936 proof* (King's), *1936* (and later impressions), *Sesame*, *Guild*, *Penguin* / *Sel Poems 1954*, *US 1952*, *Mardersteig* (*1962*) (all these, from *Guild*, as *1936* except where noted), *1963*, *US 1963*, *1969*, *1974* (all as *1963* except where noted), and "Text of the First Edition" in *WLFacs* (*1971B*) (which is as *Boni* except where noted). A marked proof of *Mardersteig* kept by David Bland of Faber has also been collated (Susan Shaw collection). *Sel Poems pbk* (*1961*) is a reprint of *Sel Poems 1954* with [III] 263 corrected.

5. THE "FRESCA COUPLETS"

ms1924 (Bodleian): the "Fresca couplets" relating to the original opening of Part III (c. 624 fols 107–108). Two leaves (similar to but slightly larger than *The Death of Saint Narcissus ms2*), one side blind-ruled (lines impressed but no ink).

In typescript, Part III originally opened with seventy lines of pastiche in couplets, 229–98, beginning with the awakening of Fresca. Valerie Eliot noted (*WLFacs* 127) that "Vivien Eliot contributed an article, *Letters of the Moment* II, over the initials FM" to the *Criterion* of April 1924, and that it contained a run of couplets reminiscent of these about Fresca. Valerie Eliot reproduced F. M.'s couplets in full, and in a footnote on another page (*WLFacs* 23) she mentioned "Vivien Eliot's use of an earlier draft", although she did not identify this as the two leaves among the papers Vivien had bequeathed to the Bodleian Library in 1947.

More than thirty-five years were to pass between Valerie Eliot's mention of this pencilled manuscript by TSE and its publication by John Haffenden in *PN Review* May–June 2007:

> Eliot told his patron John Quinn on 21 September 1922, "I have gathered together all of the manuscripts in existence"—by way of preparing to post the lot to Quinn in the USA. He must have missed out these pages, for they somehow ended up in Vivien's hands; maybe he had sent them to her from his sanatorium in Lausanne, so they became mislaid among her papers and were not included in the bundle.

These manuscript leaves, Haffenden wrote, "enable us to establish a simple stemma: these two hitherto unexamined autograph sheets represent a prior state of the typescript of 'The Fire Sermon' ··· and also of the version that Vivien incorporated".

There was, however, a problem. The typescript, *ts3*, was made by TSE on TSE's new machine in London before he left for Lausanne (where he wrote out parts IV and V of the poem by hand for want of a typewriter). In this typescript, an arrow and an asterisk mark the place where the additional couplets of *ms4* (beginning "From which a Venus Anadyomene") are to be inserted. These couplets, which begin with the answering asterisk, were hastily written in Paris on Pound's distinctive quad-ruled paper (*WLFacs* 28–29). In it, the first three words of the line "But Fresca rules even more distinguished spheres" were the outcome of four stages of drafting, and clearly did not derive from the manuscript in the Bodleian which has, without hesitation: "But Fresca rules even more exalted spheres". The finished line cannot have preceded the drafting that produces it, and this and other details show that the Bodleian manuscript must be later than *ms4*, which is itself later than *ts3*.

Fortunately, there is an explanation. Among the jumble of drafts preserved from the brief period in 1924–25 when, with TSE's help, Vivien Eliot was writing for the *Criterion*, many are written on the same distinctive paper as this manuscript of the "Fresca couplets", which is blind-ruled on one side only. TSE used this paper when helping to draft part of *Letters of the Moment* I (1924), and Vivien Eliot used it for two manuscript stories. Although TSE had used similar paper for the fair copies of both *The Engine* and *The Death of Narcissus* (1915–16), it is unlike any of the papers used for the drafts of *The Waste Land* itself (and there are no marks by Pound). Apart from a quite separate collection of correspondence from a decade or so later at the back, there is no reason to suppose that anything in the bound volume of Vivien Eliot's papers belongs other than to 1924–25. If this applies also to the Fresca leaves, then this manuscript was not written until after publication of *The Waste Land* and is not "a prior state of the typescript of *The Fire Sermon*". On the contrary, its very considerable differences of wording and arrangement from the typescript suggest that TSE's letter to Quinn was accurate and that having sent all the drafts, TSE no longer had sight of the couplets when he wrote this manuscript in 1924 and had to reconstruct or reimagine the scene from memory. As he told Donald Hall: "As a rule, with me an unfinished thing is a thing that might as well be rubbed out. It's better, if there's something good in it that I might make use of elsewhere, to leave it at the back of my mind than on paper in a drawer. If I leave it in a drawer it remains the same thing but if it's in the memory it becomes transformed into something else", *Paris Review*, Interview (1959). Accordingly *ms1924* is part memory and part re-imagining.

TSE would not have written the scene again for his own use elsewhere. Valerie Eliot quoted his Introduction to Pound's *Selected Poems* (1928): "Pound once induced me to destroy what I thought an excellent set of couplets; for, said he, 'Pope has done this so well that you cannot do it better; and if you mean this as a burlesque, you had better suppress it, for you cannot parody Pope unless you can write better verse than Pope—and you can't.'" The lesson sank in, and TSE repeated it (see note to 229–300). However, he often wrote prompts for his wife to work up into sketches, as is the case with *Letters of the Moment* II, which was compiled from numerous fragments of writing in her exercise books and scrapbook. One of Vivien Eliot's exercise books (d. 936/3) contains a pencilled first draft of the *Letter*, headed "March 1924" and "For Criterion of April 15th". The recto and verso of the first leaf sketch out the first two paragraphs, after which Vivien leaves a space and writes simply "Verses", where the "Fresca couplets" were to appear in the next surviving draft, a typescript probably made by Vivien Eliot. TSE did not write the verses in this cramped space, although he did make a short and deleted addition that suggests a very different direction which the scene might have taken: "Ah yes, Fresca, but w^d you have the courage to stick a hypodermic ~~morph.~~ cocaine needle into yrself—w^d you take a risk *once*—as the go^s did every day?" (see *McCue 2016*). The next stages of composition were a typescript (*tsLM1*), in which the verses appear, somewhat modified, followed by a typescript apparently made by TSE, and certainly marked up for the printer by him.

In the collation below, TSE's manuscript draft, *ms1924*, appears separately, after the Fresca section of the typescript of Part III which Pound deleted (following 298). There is also a collation of the typescripts and the final text published by "F. M." in *Letters of the Moment* II.

6. OTHER WITNESSES

WLLetter (Houghton): TSE to Pound [26? Jan 1922] suggesting emendations to the poem. Published *Hudson Review* Spring 1950 and in *Letters of Ezra Pound*; tentatively dated [24? Jan 1922] by Valerie Eliot in *Letters* (1988), but evidently in part a response to Pound's letter of that day. Pound annotated *WLLetter* and apparently returned it to TSE, as an enclosure with his own further letter of [28? Jan 1922], which answers TSE's remaining points. Printed in Commentary headnote, 1. COMPOSITION.

Clarabut's Criterion (U. Delaware): C. E. R. Clarabut's copy of *Criterion* Oct 1922, signed by TSE and with three corrections.

Hogarth proof (Berg, bought from Bertram Rota, 5 Feb 1974): proof, trimmed after correction close to the block of text (TSE's emendation to "were suggested" in the first of the Notes has been shaved) and bound in black and white dappled boards. A single gathering (pages 25–32, giving [V] 419–33 and Notes as far as 276, ending at "why they") has author's corrections and has been folded, presumably for posting, which suggests that this is not the entire author's proof but an amalgam of corrected and uncorrected gatherings. Additionally, pages 6 and 7 are blank, so [I] 17–68 are missing. As *Hogarth* except where noted.

Valerie's Own Book: fair copy on 25 pages with two-line spaces in many places where other texts have only a single line space. Only those of special interest are listed below.

ms1960 (Texas): autograph copy on 24 pages (including title-page) made to raise funds for the London Library, of which TSE was President. Two pages are illustrated in *An Exhibition of Manuscripts and First Editions of T. S. Eliot* (Texas HRC, June 1961). Rupert Hart-Davis to George Lyttelton, 27 Feb 1960: "T.S.E. has been laboriously copying out *The Waste Land* in Morocco, and yesterday I got a postcard from him, beginning: Oh Chairman, my Chairman, The fearful task is done!" (*The Lyttelton–Hart-Davis Letters* V, 1983). (Whitman: "O Captain! my Captain! our fearful trip is done", *O Captain! My Captain!* In 1944, according to *Gallup 1985*, TSE "called this poem a low point for Whitman but, unfortunately, of the correct size and shape for makers of anthologies".) Hart-Davis to Lyttelton, 26 June 1960: "When the T.S.E. manuscript was knocked down for £2800, the audience clapped and cheered and the old boy beamed modestly."

7. A TYPESCRIPT NOT COLLATED

Not included in the collation below is an amateurish fair copy typescript on foolscap (without watermark) from the library of John Hayward (King's). Decades after publication, TSE endorsed the first leaf: "An early typing [*add*: by myself] of this poem T. S. Eliot". On a flyleaf, he added: "This typescript certainly antedates the first publication of the poem, and may be the copy used by the printers of *The Criterion* of Oct. 1922". A pencilled note declares "This is not so. The text disproves it. J. H." In a letter to Daniel H. Woodward, 16 Aug 1963 (before the discovery of the drafts now in the Berg collection), Hayward wrote: "I would infer that it was the penultimate copy from an earlier draft before the copy text was finally typed out." Almost certainly this typescript is not by TSE and dates from after the poem's publication.

In 1930, Albert Boni, formerly of Boni & Liveright, printed *The Waste Land* in an anthology of *Prize Poems 1913–1929* (ed. Charles A. Wagner, with an introduction by Mark Van Doren). TSE's poem was included without his authorisation but headed "*The Dial* | *1922* | *T. S. ELIOT* | The Waste Land". The poem was eligible for inclusion because TSE had been awarded the *Dial* prize in 1922, which is a prima facie reason for supposing that the anthology would follow the *Dial* text; wherever the *Dial* text is distinctive, it is followed by *Prize Poems*, not least in printing "If there were only water amongst the rock" as both [V] 335 and [V] 338.

The setting in *Prize Poems* was careless, however, and introduced many new idiosyncrasies, almost all of which are shared by the King's typescript (which in turn has many of its own, including the omission of ten lines, so that *Prize Poems* cannot have been copied from this typescript). The King's typescript matches *Prize*

Poems in reading "Shakesperian Rag" ([II] 128), "With my hair down so . . ." (adding ellipsis, [II] 133), "thinking of poor Albert" (for "think of poor Albert" [II] 147), and "fortnight dead" (omitting "a", [IV] 312). Like *Prize Poems*, it capitalises "Zu" ([I] 32), "King" ([II] 99), "Lidless" ([II] 138) and "Leia" ([III] 277 and 290). Like *Prize Poems*, it runs on at what are manifestly breaks in the poem where the other texts leave line spaces, after [I] 18, [II] 138, [III] 248 and [V] 330. In *Prize Poems*, [V] 358 is the last line on a page, so the line space is invisible, and in the King's typescript the line space is lost. Perhaps the most misleading error in *Prize Poems* is the setting of [III] 306—"la la"—as a centred line in small capitals, in precisely the same style as the titles of the Parts of the poem (which it does not number). It occurs on the same page as "DEATH BY WATER" and "WHAT THE THUNDER SAID" and appears to have exactly the same status, and is even indexed by the volume as a title. For whatever reason (and unfortunately for bibliographical clarity) this error is *not* replicated by the King's typescript, but its omission of the line altogether may be telling.

If, as these details suggest, the King's typescript is a copy from *Prize Poems*, the mystery about it becomes a question of why anyone should type out the poem after publication, let alone from such an unreliable source.

Although Hayward left no record of how it came into his hands, practically all of his collection of TSE's papers came as gifts from the author, and it is hard to imagine how else he could have acquired what would, by the 1940s, have been a very expensive document had it been sold. The absence of word spacing in "Mrs.Equitone", "Mrs.Porter" and "Mr.Eugenides" is characteristic of TSE's typing, but whereas he usually left two or more spaces between sentences, the typist here left one or none. Nor are the dashes typed as TSE typed them. Some of the errors are of a kind that he could hardly have made, most strikingly the running on of Part II, without title, immediately after the last line of Part I. A secretary, such as TSE occasionally employed privately, would be unlikely to type "Bestwos" for "Bestows", or to produce such an uneven, chaotic typescript as this. If, however, it was once among his papers, there is another person who might have been the typist: Vivien Eliot.

As her papers show, during 1924–25, TSE not only helped her with her writing, but proposed—even assigned—things for her to write (see above 5. THE "FRESCA COUPLETS"). He wrote simple French words on widely spaced lines, apparently for her to begin sentences. Also, she made a French translation of *Preludes* III (see *McCue 2016*). It appears, both from his interventions and from her descriptions of her own boredom and anxiety, that he was finding things to distract her when she was often not well enough to leave their flat. Asking her to type for him may have been another such activity. In early summer 1930, he received a copy of *Prize Poems* from the publisher. On 13 May, he wrote to his brother: "I knew nothing what ever of this until receiving the book · · · So far as I am concerned the poem has simply been lifted from me for Boni's profit." He asked Henry to "get a copy of the book in New York if you can" and to consult a lawyer. The action taken by Henry was, in the end, "ineffectual" (TSE to Henry, 28 July 1931), and this breach of copyright was outdone by publication of a new edition of *The Waste Land* later that year by Liveright—the second following the lapsing in 1927 of his right to publish. TSE considered "bringing out in New York a new edition of 'collected poems', so as merely to kill the sale · · · This would be the only economical way to act. I had not wanted to bring out another collected edition for some time" (to Henry, 3 Sept 1931).

Although this is only speculation, it is at least possible that the King's typescript is a copy made by Vivien from *Prize Poems*. Unlike those made for Quinn and Watson, this typescript is far removed from the story of the transmission of *The Waste Land*.

8. METHOD OF TEXTUAL DESCRIPTION

For the original printings, this collation follows the presumed order of typesetting: *Boni, Dial, Criterion, Hogarth*. Of these, *Boni* was preferred by TSE as setting copy for *1925*. Variants found in the post-publication mss *Valerie's Own Book* and *ms1960* are listed at the end of collations, as these are presumed to have had no influence on printed texts, though they may be said to represent the latest evidence of TSE's engagement with the poem.

In his account of the editing of *WLFacs*, Donald Gallup writes: "Determining whether Eliot or Pound had been responsible for a particular cancellation was difficult, even with the manuscript before us. Fortunately, Pound had used a softer pencil and his slashes tended to be more emphatic than Eliot's, but there were instances where distinguishing between the two was just not possible" (*Gallup 1998* 283–84). A few marks have been re-attributed, mainly to Pound or Vivien Eliot, but the attribution in *WLFacs* is also recorded. Marks were made in pencil, crayon and ink, but neither all the pencil nor all the ink marks were made on the same occasion, and it is rarely possible to establish priority. In a few cases, an expository account of an aspect of the text's history is given with the relevant lines.

Where a reading appears in both the published text and *WLComposite*, the lemma uses the form of the published text, giving the *WLComposite* line number in bold:

> [I] 62 = **116 flowed**] flow *ts1*   **over London Bridge**] under London Bridge
> Hogarth

In this instance, the published text in all editions is "flowed", but the earliest known reading is "flow", which is therefore the reading of *WLComposite*. "over London Bridge" is the text in all drafts and editions except the Hogarth Press edition.

Where a reading in *WLComposite* has no equivalent in the published text, the lemma uses the *WLComposite* form, with the line number in bold:

> **288 From**] For *ts3* 1ˢᵗ *reading*

Proposed readings by others are attributed:

> **277 Or**] Now *Pound ts3a*

Likewise comments:

> **379 Perhaps**] *ringed with "Perhaps be dammed" Pound ts3b*

The order in which witnesses are listed is: *ts1, ts2a, ts2b (or combined as ts2), ms1, ms2, ts3a, ts3b (or combined as ts3), ms3, ms4, ms5 ts4, ms6, ts5, WLLetter, Q, T, W (or combined as T/W), Boni, Boni later impressions, Dial, Criterion, Hogarth proof, Hogarth, 1925, 1932, 1936 proof, 1936, US 1936, Sesame, Guild, Penguin, Sel Poems 1954, Sel Poems pbk (1961), Washington copy 1954, 1936 17th imp. (1959), 1936 18th imp. (1961), Mardersteig, 1963, US 1963, 1969, 1974, Valerie's Own Book, ms1960, 1971B, other posthumous printings.*

Because *Boni* is taken to be the earliest setting of the poem in type, *Boni+* indicates all printed editions.

Section-title page] 1925+

Poem title] *on section-title page only* 1936+ ‖ *on top sheet only, ts title, Q* ‖ *not T/W* ‖ *on title-page only Boni* ‖ *above poem only Dial, Criterion* ‖ *on section-title page and above poem Hogarth, 1925*

Unadopted epigraph **The horror! the horror!**] The horror! the Horror! *ts1* 1st *reading* *Attribution.* CONRAD.] *ts1 addition* (*ink, imitation of type*). The epigraph from Conrad was then dropped in favour of Petronius, TSE writing to Pound, 12 Mar 1922:

> I have substituted for the J. Conrad the following, or something like it:
> Nam Sibyllam quidam Cumis ego ipse meis oculis vidi, in ampulla pendere, et ubi pueri dicerent, "Σιβύλλαμ, τι θέλεις;" respondebat illa, "ἀποθανεῖν θέλω."

Epigraph] *on section-title page* 1925+ ‖ *not T/W, Criterion* ‖ *on title-page Q, Boni, Hogarth* ‖ *above poem Dial* (*all italic*)

Epigraph Quotation marks] *around entire epigraph Q, Boni,* 1925, 1936 *2nd imp.* (1937)+ ‖ *quotation mark at start of epigraph only* 1936 ‖ *no quotation marks Dial, Hogarth,* 1971B ‖ *quotation mark at close of epigraph only Valerie's Own Book* (*error*)

Epigraph **Nam**] 1936+, 1971B ‖ NAM *Q, Boni, Hogarth,* 1925 ‖ Nam *Dial* **dicerent:**] dicerent, *Hogarth* **Σίβνλλα**] Σίβνλλα, *Hogarth* ‖ Σιβνλλα *Faber Bk Mod* V **θέλεις**] θελεις *Q* **illa:**] illa; *Q* ‖ illa, *Hogarth* **ἀποθανεῖν**] ἀπο θανεῖν *Dial* (TSE to Richard Aldington, 15 Nov 1922: "I do not know how the *Dial* separated the prefix of 'Apothanein'; I spelt it out carefully enough for them.") *Attribution*] PETRONIUS · SATIRICON *added Mardersteig*

Dedication] *centred beneath epigraph* 1932+ ‖ *not prior to* 1925 ‖ *stepped, lower right of section-title page* 1925 ‖ *first line all capitals Mardersteig* **fabbro.**] fabbro *Penguin, Sel Poems* 1954 (*corrected long after*), *Mardersteig*

Parts] *each starting new page in drafts, Q, T/W, Boni, Hogarth,* 1925+ ‖ *run on Dial, Criterion, Sesame, US* 1952

Numerals, italic face] *not Q, T/W, Dial* ‖ *roman face Boni, Hogarth,* 1925, *Faber Bk Mod V, Sesame, Penguin, US* 1952, 1969 (*some later printings of Sel Poems have italic numerals except for roman* I)

Line numbering] *not drafts, T/W, Dial, Criterion, Hogarth,* 1936 *proof, Mardersteig* ‖ *every ten lines Q, Boni,* 1925+. Lines are here counted as in most editions, including *Boni* and 1963, with

> From doors of mudcracked houses
> If there were water

as the single line [V] 345. See collation. (For other part-lines, see note below to [II] 117–28.)

I. *THE BURIAL OF THE DEAD*

The only draft of this Part I is *ts1* (ribbon copy only, *WLFacs* 4–9), which is given in *WLComposite*. The published poem begins at [I] 1 = 55.

Unadopted heading **HE DO THE POLICE IN DIFFERENT VOICES: Part I**] *ts1.* Kenner in *Litz ed.* 38: "This comprehensive heading is misaligned with the rest of the page, which suggests a second, probably later, insertion of paper into machine. At the head of Part II, however, the Dickens title sits on the page as though it had been meant to be there from the start · · · he did not write or type it on any of the extant copies of Parts III, IV, and V."

1–54] *ts1 only, whole page finally deleted by TSE*

7–8] *ringed with* Meet me in the shadow of the watermelon Vine | Eva Iva Uva Emmaline *del, and* [Tease. Squeeze lovin & wooin | Say Kid what're y' doin'

19–34] *small marginal ink marks at beginning and end of this passage, perhaps for new paragraphs*

20] *accidentally indented ts1*

23] I've kept a decent house for twenty years, she says *ts1 2nd reading*

27 **on account]** off *ts1 2nd reading*

33 **good laugh,]** couple of laughs (?) *ts1 2nd reading (ink, del pencil)* ‖ good laugh *ts1 3rd reading (pencil) with all then del*

34 **was always a good sport").]** *ts1 1st reading (the quotation marks being a manuscript addition)* ‖ was always a real good (?) sport"). *ts1 2nd reading* ‖ always treated me white. *ts1 3rd reading*

41–42 I thought · · · peevish.] *del ts1*

41 **who I am?]** me? *ts1 2nd reading*

45 **We]** Us *ts1 2nd reading*   **Joe Leahy]** Heinie Krutzsch *ts1 2nd reading* ‖ Gus Krutzsch *ts1 3rd reading*

46 **Found it shut.]** *del ts1*

Published poem begins. Also ts1.

Row of four asterisks at head of leaf ts1

[I] 1 = 55] *indent 1963 (not 1963 proof, US 1963)*   **April]** *two-line drop capital and capitals Boni, Criterion, Hogarth* ‖ *capital and small capitals 1925* ‖ *three-line drop capital and capitals Mardersteig*   **cruellest]** cruelest *Dial*

[I] 4 **spring]** Spring *W 2nd reading*

[I] 6 = 60 **in]** *with Valerie's Own Book*   **forgetful]** *ringed Pound ts1*

[I] 8 = 62 **Starnbergersee]** *T/W, Boni, Dial, Criterion, 1925+* ‖ Königssee *ts1* ‖ Stainberger *Q* ‖ Starnbergersee, *Hogarth*

[I] 9 **rain;]** rain: *T*   **stopped]** *(or perhaps* stepped*) over malformed characters ms1960*   **colonnade,]** Colonnade *T* ‖ colonnade *W*

[I] 10 = 64] *accidentally indented ts1*   **sunlight]** the sunlight *T/W, Criterion, Sel Poems 1954, Sel Poems pbk (1961, later corrected)*

[I] 11 = 65 **and talked for]** talking *ts1*

[I] 12] *italic Dial*

[I] 13 **archduke's,]** *printings prior to 1932, US 1952, Library of Congress recording notes 1949* ‖ arch-|duke's, *(breaking across line) 1932, US 1936* ‖ arch-duke's, *1936+, Valerie's Own Book, ms1960. TSE deleted the hyphen in 1936 proof*

[I] 14] *typed both in its proper place and in the line space* 13 ^ 14 *T/W (the lower line del Watson in T)* **cousin's,**] cousin's *T/W* **sled,**] sled. *T (twice)*

[I] 15 **said, Marie**] said, "Marie *Criterion*

[I] 16 **tight.**] tight." *Criterion*

[I] 17 = 71 **there you feel free.**] *ringed Pound ts1*

[I] 18 ^ 19 = 72 ^ 73] *line space Boni, Criterion, Hogarth, 1932+* || *row of four asterisks between line spaces ts1* || *new page so line spacing indeterminate Dial, 1925* || *no line space 1932 proof, with "space" TSE*

[I] 19–24] *reduced line spacing T*

[I] 21 **only**] only, *T*

[I] 22 **sun beats**] sunbeats *T 1ˢᵗ reading, W*

[I] 23 **relief,**] relief *T*

[I] 26–30] *see The Death of Saint Narcissus 1–6*

[I] 26 **rock),**] rock) *T 1ˢᵗ reading, W, Dial* || rock). *1936 proof (which was not corrected)*

[I] 27 = 81 **And**] ~~And~~ *ts1* **something**] some thing *T/W, Criterion*

[I] 29 **meet**] greet *ms1960 1ˢᵗ reading* **you;**] you *Mardersteig*

[I] 30 **handful**] handfull *T/W*

[I] 30 ^ 31 = 84 ^ 85] *line space Boni, Criterion, 1925* || *row of four asterisks between line spaces ts1* || *two-line space Q, Dial* || *no line space T/W, 1932 (to fit 31–34 onto page), 1936+* || *half-line space Hogarth*

[I] 31–41 = 85–95] *ringed to move before* [I] 19 = 73 *ts1*

[I] 31–34 = 85–88] *reduced line spacing Q, T/W, Boni* inset] *ts1, Boni+* || *not inset Q, T/W, Dial, Criterion* italic] *Boni, Dial, 1925+, ms1960* || *roman ts1, Q, T/W, Criterion, Hogarth, Valerie's Own Book.* (Variations solely between roman and italic within these four lines are not noted below.)

[I] 31 = 85 *Frisch weht der Wind*] ~~Mein~~ *ts1 1ˢᵗ reading (not inset)* || Frisch schwebt der Wind *ts1 2ⁿᵈ reading* || Frisgh weht des Wind *T 1ˢᵗ reading, W*

[I] 32 *zu,*] zu *1936, Sesame (with full stop added long after), 1963, 1969* || zu. *Penguin, Mardersteig, 1971B*

[I] 33 = 87 *Irisch*] Irisch' *ts1* || irisch *Penguin, Sel Poems 1954 (changed to capital "I" long after), Valerie's Own Book* || irish *Valerie's Own Book 1ˢᵗ reading.* (Although German does not capitalise the word—so that the reading current in *Sel Poems* from 1948 until at least 1970 and found in *Valerie's Own Book* has its claim— the capitalised form appeared in all of the first four printings and is found in *ms1960.*) *Kind,*] Kind. *T/W* || *Kind 1969*

[I] 34 ^ 35 = 88 ^ 89] *line space Boni, Dial, Criterion, 1925* || *no line space ts1, Q, T/W, 1936+* || *half-line space Hogarth* || *new page so line spacing indeterminate 1932.* In *ts1*, the four lines of German follow a row of asterisks and there is no line space before the English resumes.

[I] 35–36 = 89–90] *with two question marks, one deleted, zigzag mark and "Marianne" (with what may be "V" crossed through the middle) Pound ts1*

[I] 35 **hyacinths**] Hyacinths *1974*

[I] 36 = 90 "They] They *Dial, Criterion, Valerie's Own Book*　　**girl."] girl". *ts1, T/W,*
Valerie's Own Book

[I] 37 = 91 —**Yet**] Yet *T/W, Criterion* ‖ —Yet, *Valerie's Own Book*　　**we**] I *ms1960*
1ˢᵗ reading　　**hyacinth**] *ts1, Q, Dial, Mardersteig, Washington copy 1954*
emendation, 1936 18th imp. (1961), 1963+, Valerie's Own Book ‖ Hyacinth *T/W,*
Boni, Criterion, Hogarth, 1925, Faber Bk Mod V, 1936 to 17th imp. (1959), Sesame,
Penguin (these emended long after), Library of Congress recording notes 1949,
ms1960

[I] 38 **arms**] arm *T/W*

[I] 38–39 = 92–93 **I could not | Speak**] *underlined Pound ts1*

[I] 41 ^ 42 = 96 ^ 97] *line space ts1, Q, T/W, Criterion* ‖ *no line space Dial, 1925+, Valerie's*
Own Book, ms1960 ‖ *new page so line spacing indeterminate Boni, Hogarth.* (TSE to
P. M. Jack, 19 Jan 1927: "there ought to be a double space to isolate the quotation
line 42 like the quotation above." This presumably means a line of space before
and after, since the quoted lines 31–34, also from *Tristan und Isolde*, are isolated
by single, not double line spaces. Other than *Criterion*, no printing has isolated
the line in this way until the present ed.)

[I] 42 = 95 ^ 96] *ms addition ts1*　　**Oed'**] *1936, Sesame, Guild, 1963+* ‖ Öd' *ts1, Dial,*
Penguin, Sel Poems 1954 (later emended to Oed') ‖ Od' *Q, T/W, Boni, Criterion,*
Hogarth ‖ Od' *1925, Faber Bk Mod V, 1971B*

[I] 42 ^ 43] *line space Q, T/W, Boni, Criterion, 1932, Faber Bk Mod V, Sesame, Penguin,*
1969, 1974+ ‖ *no line space Dial, Hogarth* ‖ *new page so line spacing indeterminate*
1925, ms1960 ‖ *two-line space 1936, 1963 (to avoid widow on the next page)*

[I] 43 = 96 **clairvoyante,**] clairvoyant, *ts1 1ˢᵗ reading* ‖ clairvoyante *T/W*

[I] 46 **wicked**] *not T/W*　　**Here,**] "Here," *Criterion*

[I] 47 **Is**] "Is *Criterion*　　**Phoenician**] Phoenicien *T/W* ‖ Phœnician *Criterion,*
Valerie's Own Book　　**Sailor**] sailor *Valerie's Own Book, ms1960*

[I] 48 = 101] *del Pound ts1*　　**eyes. Look!)**] eyes. See! *WLFacs 122–23*

[I] 49 = 102 **Lady**] lady *T/W*

[I] 50 = 103 **situations.**] situations, *ts1, Valerie's Own Book*

[I] 51 = 104 **man with three staves,**] *ringed with King fishing ts1 alt del* ‖ fisher King
ts1 further alt　　**Wheel,**] wheel, *T, ms1960 1ˢᵗ reading* ‖ Wheel *Mardersteig*

[I] 52 **one-eyed**] *not T/W*

[I] 54 = 107 **I do not find**] I look in vain *ts1, ringed for del Pound*

[I] 55 = 108 **The Hanged**] For the Hanged *ts1* ‖ The hanged *T 1ˢᵗ reading*

[I] 56 ^ 57 = 110] (I John saw these things, and heard them). *ts1, del Pound*

[I] 59 **careful**] careful, *Valerie's Own Book*　　**these days.**] in these days." *Criterion*

[I] 59 ^ 60 = 113 ^ 114] *two-line space ts1, Q* ‖ *new page so line spacing indeterminate*
US 1963

[I] 60 = 114] *braced, with slash through comma (to start new line?) Pound ts1*　　**Unreal**]
Terrible *ts1 1ˢᵗ reading*　　**City,**] City, I have sometimes seen and see *ts1 (with*
first letter over lower-case c) ‖ City. *Valerie's Own Book*

[I] 61 = 115 **a**] your *ts1, ringed Pound*　　**dawn,**] dawn *ts1*

[I] 62 = 116 **flowed**] flow *ts1*   **over London Bridge**] under London Bridge *Hogarth*

[I] 63 = 117] *not T 1ˢᵗ reading, added by Watson*

[I] 64 = 118] *with "J.J." (boxed) by Pound ts1 (for James Joyce see Commentary)*   **Sighs**] Signs *Q*   **exhaled,**] *Q, T/W, Boni+* ‖ expired, *ts1 1ˢᵗ reading* ‖ exhaled *ts1 2ⁿᵈ reading* ‖ expired. *ts1 3ʳᵈ reading* ‖ exhaled. *ts1 final reading*

[I] 65 = 119 **And**] and *W*   **man**] one *ts1 1ˢᵗ reading*   **fixed**] *ts1 final reading+* ‖ kept *ts1 1ˢᵗ reading* ‖ held *ts1 2ⁿᵈ reading*   **eyes**] iyes *T*

[I] 67–68 = 121–22] *braced and del, with "Blake. Too ~~old~~ often used" Pound ts1*

[I] 67 = 121 **Saint**] St *ms1960 1ˢᵗ reading*   **hours**] time, *ts1*

[I] 69 = 123 **I saw**] saw *Valerie's Own Book 1ˢᵗ reading*   **crying:**] crying *T/W, Hogarth, Mardersteig*   **"Stetson!**] *over-running onto new line and indented almost to the right margin Hogarth* ‖ "Stetson"! *Valerie's Own Book 1ˢᵗ reading*

[I] 70–76] *no quotation marks at heads of lines Dial, Criterion*

[I] 70–71 = 124–25] *ts1 1ˢᵗ reading*:

> That corpse you buried last year in the garden,
> Has it begun to sprout yet? Will it bloom this year?"

(erased and typed over)

[I] 72 = 126 **sprout?**] sprout yet? *ts1 2ⁿᵈ reading*

[I] 74 = 128 **O**] *Washington copy 1954 emendation, 1936 18th imp. (1961), 1963+* ‖ Oh *ts1, Q, T/W, all printings prior to 1961, later printings of Sel Poems (emended long after), Valerie's Own Book, ms1960. David Bland's proof of the Mardersteig edition has "Oh" with the "h" struck through in an unknown hand, but the printed volume has "Oh". A memo from Bland to Faber's printers, MacLehose, 19 July 1961, requested the same change in Collected Poems and this was done in time for the final impression of 1936 (in 1961) and in 1963. (See Commentary.)*   **friend**] foe *ts1 1ˢᵗ reading*

[I] 76 = 130] *all but first word italic ts1, Dial, Criterion*   **lecteur!**] *Boni+* ‖ lecteur, *ts1* ‖ lecteur, *Q, T/W* ‖ lecteur, *Criterion*   **semblable,—**] semblable; *Valerie's Own Book*

II. *A GAME OF CHESS*

The only draft of Part II is *ts2* (ribbon copy and carbon, *WLFacs* 10–21), which is given in *WLComposite*.

Unadopted heading **HE DO THE POLICE IN DIFFERENT VOICES: Part II**] *ts2 only*

Title **A Game of Chess**] *ts2+* ‖ IN THE CAGE *ts2 1ˢᵗ reading*

[II] 77 *as also first lines of succeeding Parts*] *two-line drop capital and capitals for first word Boni, Hogarth, 1925, Mardersteig*

[II] 77 = 131] *indent 1963 (not 1963 proof, US 1963)*   **Chair**] chair *T/W, Criterion*   **throne,**] throne *ts2, Q, T/W, Dial, Criterion*

[II] 77–102 = 131–57] *"Dont see what you had in mind here" Vivien Eliot ts2a*

[II] 77–79 = 131–33] *with "3 lines too tum-pum at a stretch" Pound ts2a*

[II] 78 = 132 **glass**] swinging glass *ts2*

[II] 79 = 133 **Held up**] Held i *T/W 1ˢᵗ reading* ‖ Sustained *WLLetter*   **fruited**] *WLLetter, Q, T/W, Boni+* ‖ golden *ts2*

[II] 80 = 134 **From which**] *ts2, Q, Boni, Dial+* ‖Wherefrom *WLLetter (with "OK" Pound), T/W, Criterion*   **a**] *Q, T/W, Boni+* ‖ one *ts2, ringed with "X" and "'one' wee red mouse" Pound ts2a.* In the copy of *WLFacs* she sent to I. A. Richards, Valerie Eliot emended "X" in the transcription to "α" and subsequent printings of *WLFacs* have given this as "a".   **golden**] *Q, T/W, Boni+* ‖ tender *ts2*

[II] 81 **behind**] beneath *Valerie's Own Book*

[II] 82 = 136 **Doubled**] Doubli *ts2 1ˢᵗ reading*   **sevenbranched**] *Q, Boni, Dial, 1925+* ‖ seven-branched *ts2, T/W, Criterion, Hogarth*

[II] 83 = 137 **as**] ~~where~~ as *ts2*

[II] 84 = 138 **it,**] ~~it;~~ it, *ts2 (deleted punctuation uncertain)*

[II] 85 = 139 **profusion.**] *Washington copy 1954 emendation, Mardersteig, 1936 18th imp. (1961), 1963, US 1963, 1969, 1974* ‖ profusion; *ts2, Q, T/W, printings to 1959, Sel Poems, Valerie's Own Book, ms1960.* Although after many printings *Sel Poems* adopted the full stop, both it and *Collected Poems* reverted to the semi-colon in 2002.

[II] 87 = 141 **Unstoppered,**] Unstoppered *T/W*   **perfumes,**] *Boni, Hogarth+* ‖ perfumes *ts2, Q, T/W, Dial, Criterion*

[II] 89 = 143 **the sense**] the sense the sense *T 1ˢᵗ reading, W*

[II] 90 = 144 **ascended**] *Q, T/W, Boni+* ‖ ascended, *ts2*

[II] 91 = 145] *marked apparently to move to before* 150 *Pound ts2a* ‖ Fattening the candle flames, which were prolonged, *ts2* ‖ Fattening the prolonged candle flames, *Pound ts2a, Q, T/W, Boni+*   **candle-flames**] candle flames *ts2*

[II] 92 = 146 **Flung**] *Pound in ts2a, Q, T/W, Boni+* ‖ And flung *ts2*   **laquearia**] *Boni+* ‖ laquenaria *ts2, Q, T/W*

[II] 94 = 148] *Q, T/W, Boni+* ‖ Upon the hearth huge sea-wood fed with copper *ts2, with first three words ringed Pound ts2a*

[II] 95 ^ 96 = 149 ^ 150] *chevrons, hatchings and "Space" Pound ts2a*

150–53 *and* 151–53] *braced Pound ts2a*

150–53] *braced with "1921" Pound ts2a*

[II] 96 = 150] *marked with angle bracket at each end Pound ts2a*   **carvèd**] *ts2a (accent added in ink), Boni, Dial, Criterion, 1925+* ‖ carved *ts2, Q, T/W* ‖ coloured *Hogarth* ‖ carven *TSE in presentation copies of Hogarth including that sent to his mother (Houghton)*   **swam.**] *Q, T/W, Boni+* ‖ swam; *ts2*

[II] 97 ^ 98 = 152] *not Q, T/W, Boni+* ‖ In pigment, but so lively, you had thought *ts2, with last six words del and last three ringed by Pound with "had. is the weakest point" ts2a*

[II] 98 = 153 **As though a**] *Q, T/W, Boni+*‖ A *ts2*   **scene**] *Q, T/W, Boni+* ‖ scene, *ts2, Valerie's Own Book*

[II] 100 = 155 **forced;**] *Q, T/W, Boni, Dial, Criterion, 1925+* ‖ forced, *ts2* ‖ forc'd; *Hogarth*   **there**] ~~still~~ there *ts2*

[II] 101 = 156 **inviolable**] *ringed, with zigzag and "too penty" Pound ts2a*   **voice**] *Boni, Dial, 1925+* ‖ voice, *ts2, Q, T/W, Criterion, Hogarth*

[II] 102 = **157 cried, and still the world pursues,**] *Q, T/W, Boni, Dial, 1925, 1936+* ‖ cried (and still the world pursues) *ts2* ‖ cried (and still the world pursues), *Criterion* ‖ cries (and still the world pursues), *Hogarth proof* ‖ cries (and still the world pursues) *Hogarth* ‖ cries, and still the world pursues, *TSE's unadopted emendation (from* cried,) *in 1936 proof (see McCue 2012, Proposal 16).*

[II] 103 = **158 "Jug Jug"**] *Boni+* ‖ Jug Jug, *ts2* ‖ Jug Jug *Q* ‖ "Jugjug" *T/W*   **to dirty ears.**] *Q, T/W, Boni+* ‖ into the dirty ear of death; *ts2 1ˢᵗ reading* ‖ into the dirty ear of lust; *ts2a 2ⁿᵈ reading (last word ink, in imitation of type, and then ringed by Pound)* ‖ into dirty ear *Pound ts2a*

[II] 104 = **159**] *Q, T/W, Boni+* ‖ And other tales, from the old stumps and bloody ends of time *ts2, braced with first five words del Pound ts2a*

[II] 105 = **160 walls;**] walls, *ts2* ‖ wells; *T/W*   **staring**] *Q, T/W, Boni+* ‖ where staring *ts2 with first word del Pound ts2a*

[II] 106–116 = **161–71**] *"WONDERFUL" Vivien Eliot ts2a*

[II] 106 = **161**] *T/W, Boni+* ‖ Leaned out, and hushed the room and closed it in *ts2 with the three words* and · · · and · · · in *del Pound ts2a* ‖ Leaned, staring, hushing the room enclosed *Q*

[II] 107 = **162**] *WLLetter (with "OK" Pound), Boni, 1925+* ‖ There were footsteps on the stair, *ts2 with first word ringed by Pound and del, and his "Re this point" and "Il cherchait des sentiments pour les accommoder a son vocabulaire" ts2a* ‖ Footsteps shuffled on the stair, *Q, Dial, Criterion, Hogarth* ‖ Footsteps shuffled on the stairs. *T/W*

[II] 108–38 **Under the firelight · · · upon the door**] in the copy of *Boni* given by TSE to Vivien Eliot (dated "January 10ᵗʰ 1923"; Berg), this passage is scored, probably by her.

[II] 108–10 = **163–65**] *see The Death of the Duchess II 20–22:*

> Under the brush her hair
> Spread out in little fiery points of will
> Glowed into words, then was suddenly still.

[II] 109 = **164 fiery**] little fiery *ts2, with* little *del Pound ts2a*   **points**] points of will, *ts2 with last two words ringed and del, with "dogmatic deduction but wobbly as well." Pound ts2a*

[II] 111–14 = **166–69**] *braced with "photography?" Pound ts2a* ‖ *the four lines inset, with 113 further indented 1974*

[II] 112–14 = **167–69**] *quotation marks at heads of lines ts2, Boni, 1925, 1936, 1963, Valerie's Own Book* ‖ *no quotation marks Dial, Criterion, Hogarth, 1974+, some reprints of Sel Poems and 1969* ‖ *quotation marks at head of 114 only T/W*

[II] 112 = **167 never speak.**] *ts2, Boni, British printings 1925–70, US 1932, US 1952, US 1963, Valerie's Own Book, ms1960* ‖ never speak? *Dial, Criterion, Hogarth, 3rd and 4th printings of Boni (1928, 1930), Mardersteig, 1971B, 1974+ (see Commentary)*

[II] 113 = **168**] *no indent ts2, printings prior to 1925, Valerie's Own Book, ms1960* ‖ *indent 1925+.* The compositor of *1925* could not fit the last word, "What?" onto the line, so set it as a line of its own. In order to justify the preceding words, an initial indent and very wide word spaces were introduced. Ever since, the line has been indented as though a new act of speech (although no closing quotation marks have ever been added at the end of [II] 112). Probably, the lady continues speaking (see Textual History [II] 131), so, as in the drafts and earliest printings, the line should not be indented.　　**What?**] ~~Think.~~ What? *ts2*

[II] 115 = **170　are in**] *T/W, Boni*+ ‖ met first in *ts2, Q*　　**rats'**] rat's *Hogarth*　　**alley**] *Q, T/W, Boni*+ ‖ alley, *ts2*

[II] 117–28] the arrangement on the page of the later part of the dialogue was progressively changed from the way it appeared in the earliest typescript (*WLFacs* 10–13, *WLComposite* 174–82), which preceded the writing of 120. The next extant typescript, though not made by TSE, is *Q*:

"What is that noise?"　　　　　　　　　　　　　　117
　　　　　　　The wind under the door.
"What is that noise now? What is the wind doing?"
　　　　　　　Nothing again nothing.　　　　　　120
　　　　　　　　　　"Do
"You know nothing? Do you see nothing? Do you remember
"Nothing?"
　　　　　　I remember
The hyacinth garden. Those are pearls that were his eyes.　　125
"Are you alive, or not? Is there nothing in your head?"
　　　　　　　　　　　　But

O O O O that Shakespeherian Rag—

The reading of *Boni* was numerically the same, but three words were omitted at the start of 125, and the narrow page caused 119, 122 and 126 to overrun, making the visual pattern very different and the number of lines hard to ascertain:

"What is that noise?"　　　　　　　　　　　　　117
　　　　　　　The wind under the door.
"What is that noise now? What is the
　　wind doing?"
　　　　　　　Nothing again nothing.　　　　　120
　　　　　　　　　　　"Do　　　　　　　　121
"You know nothing? Do you see nothing?
　　Do you remember　　　　　　　　　122
"Nothing?"
　　　　　　I remember
Those are pearls that were his eyes.　　　　　125
"Are you alive or not? Is there nothing
　　in your head?"
　　　　　　　　　　　But

O O O O that Shakespeherian Rag—

The arrangement differed again in the *Dial* printing, notably with "The wind under the door" (118) and "Nothing again nothing" (120) each ranged to the right margin. In the *Criterion* and *Hogarth* settings, "The wind under the door" was stepped from "What is that noise?" and "Nothing again nothing" was indented to align with it. The setting of *1925* was different again, and other variations have followed (with, for instance, *Penguin* and *1963* indenting 111, 115, 117 because they follow line spaces).

　　The arrangement of this passage in the present edition is based on a reading of the lines as comprising not only words spoken (given by TSE always in quotation marks) and words thought (or hummed in the case of the "Shakespeherian Rag"), but also two parenthetical intercalations describing the scene. This offers for the first time a consistent rationale for the indentings, rather than treating them as deliberately irrational.

In *ts2*, the only extant typing by TSE, the indenting of "I remember" (124), "But" (127) and "The hot water at ten" (135) is very different in each case, because they step down from 123, 126 and 134 respectively (which establishes their correct alignment). These part-lines are unspoken thoughts, in response to the spoken part-lines that precede them. In *ts2*, also, "The wind under the door" (118) appears to be a part-line stepped down from 117. However, the indenting in printed texts of "Nothing again nothing" (120, which does not appear in *ts2*) cannot be explained as stepping down, because it is not positioned after the end of the previous line. The alignment of "'Do" (121) is also uncertain: the line originates as an emendation by Pound in *ts2a* (*WLFacs* 13); in *Q* and *T/W* it is stepped down from 120, but in *1936* and *1963* it is more deeply indented, and in *Dial* it is ranged to the right margin.

So it is more satisfactory to construe both 118 and 120 less as unspoken reactions to the words spoken than as intercalations, to be centred on the page in the manner of stage directions or a *mise-en-scène*.

> "What is that noise?"
> 　　　　　[The wind under the door.]
> "What is that noise now? What is the wind doing?"
> 　　　　　[Nothing again nothing.]　　　　　　　　　　　　　　120
> 　　　　　　　　　　　　"Do
> "You know nothing? Do you see nothing? Do you remember
> "Nothing?"
> 　　　　I remember
> Those are pearls that were his eyes.　　　　　　　　　　　125

This suggests that "'Do" (121) is a part-line, but stepped down not from 120, but from 119: "'What is that noise now? What is the wind doing?'", so that although interrupted by "Nothing again nothing", the whole line, all spoken by a single voice, consists of

> "What is that noise now? What is the wind doing? Do

In *Boni* (shown second in this note), 119 was a turned line, so 121 could not be shown as stepped (*1925*, likewise). TSE could not have written notes to the poem such as "Cf. Part III, l. 204" without giving line numbers, so the numbering first printed in *Boni* presumably derives from him. Apparently he had no practical option but to number each of these part-lines separately (but see [V] 345).

[II]　117 = 172 **"What is that noise?**"] "What-is-that-noise?" *altered to* "Whatisthatnoise?" *Pound ts2a (after adding hyphens, he indicated that the words should be run together)*

[II] 117 ^ 118 = 172 ^ 173] *line space ts2*

[II] 118] *centred 1936, 1963+ ‖ stepped from end of 117 Q, Criterion, Hogarth, Sesame ‖ ranged to right margin Dial, Boni ‖ deep indent T/W, 1925, Penguin, Valerie's Own Book, ms1960*

[II] 118 = 173] *with "Beddoes" Pound ts2a*

[II] 118 ^ 119 = 173 ^ 174] *line space ts2*

[II] 119 **doing?"**] doing? *Hogarth*

[II] 120–39 = 175–94] *"Yes & wonderful wonderful" Vivien Eliot ts2a*

[II] 120–22 = 175–77] *ts2:*

> Carrying
> Away the little light dead people.
>
> "Do you know nothing? Do you see nothing? Do you remember

with little *ringed with "Blot on Scutcheon" Pound in ts2a. In the line of space, deeply indented, "Do was added in ink, in imitation of type (compare* lust *158), intending that the first word of the next question be brought back as a single-word line from* 177 *(where it is deleted in ink) so as to read "Do | You know ..." (the published reading). The transposition was apparently misunderstood as an insertion into* 177 *and the added "Do was therefore lightly bracketed with "?" in another hand, perhaps Vivien Eliot's. In subsequent texts* Carrying | Away the little light dead people *is replaced by one quite different line:*

> Nothing again nothing.
> "Do
> "You know nothing? Do you see nothing? Do you remember

[II] 120 = 175] *centred this edition* ‖ *aligned with 118 = 173 Q, T/W, Criterion, Hogarth, 1936+* ‖ *indented more ts2, Valerie's Own Book* ‖ *indented less Boni* ‖ *ranged to right margin Dial*

[II] 120 ^ 121] *new page so line spacing indeterminate Criterion*

[II] 121] *stepped from end of 119 1936, 1963* ‖ *very deep indent Q, T/W, Criterion, Boni, Hogarth, 1925, Sesame, Penguin, US 1952, 1974+, Valerie's Own Book* ‖ *ranged right Dial*

[II] 122 **"You**] You *Dial, Criterion, 1974+*

[II] 123 **"Nothing?"**] Nothing?" *Dial, Criterion*

[II] 123 ^ 124 = 178 ^ 179] *no line space Q, T/W, printings prior to 1925, ms1960, Valerie's Own Book* ‖ *new page so line spacing indeterminate 1925* ‖ *line space ts2, 1932+*

[II] 124] *stepped from end of 123 Q, T/W, Criterion, Dial, Hogarth, Valerie's Own Book, ms1960* ‖ *indent Boni, 1925+*

[II] 125 = 180] The hyacinth garden. Those are pearls that were his eyes, yes! *ts2, with* yes! *ringed and del Pound with "Penelope J.J." in ts2a (see Commentary)* ‖ The hyacinth garden. Those are pearls that were his eyes. *Q* ‖ Those are pearls that were his eyes. *T/W, Dial, Criterion (all beginning after an indent equivalent to the space occupied by the omitted words); Boni, 1925+ (all ranged left); Hogarth (ranged right)*

[II] 125 ^ 126 = 180 ^ 181] *line space ts2*

[II] 126 = 181] *with "photo" Pound ts2a*

[II] 126 ^ 127 = 181 ^ 182] *line space ts2*

[II] 127] *stepped from end of 126 this edition* ‖ *very deep indent (beyond 121) Criterion* ‖ *ranged right Q, T/W, Dial, Boni, Hogarth, 1925, Sesame* ‖ *indented below 121 1936+*

[II] 127] *not 1936 proof but added TSE and ticked*

[II] 128 **Rag—**] Rag *T 1st reading, W, Criterion*

[II] 128 ^ 129] *line space Criterion*

[II] 129 = 184 **elegant**] elegant— *ts2*

[II] 130 = 185 **intelligent**] intelligent— *ts2*

[II] 130 ^ 131] *line space Dial, Criterion, Hogarth* ‖ *new page so line spacing indeterminate Boni* ‖ *no line space Hogarth proof, 1925+*

[II] 131 do?] *Dial, Criterion, 1974+, Valerie's Own Book* ‖ do?" *Boni, Hogarth, 1925, 1936, 1963, 1969 (error, see Commentary).* Kristian Smidt wrote to ask about the quotation mark which was long printed at the end of this line, but TSE looked by mistake at [II] 134, and replied, 31 Oct 1958: "The quotation mark at the end of 'What shall I do' is correct." He continued, referring to [II] 135–38: "The remaining lines are thought, but left unspoken by the man to whom the lady is speaking." On 23 Dec after a further inquiry from Smidt, he corrected his initial misidentification: "the first quotation mark [131] should certainly be deleted, and I hope that this correction can be made in all future printings of the book." It was not. A Faber memo from Valerie Eliot, 21 Oct 1969, asked for its deletion. Her memo added that the quotation marks at the beginnings of 132–34 should be deleted as misleading because "it is one person talking throughout", but see Commentary [I] 69–76 for this convention, observed in all texts from 1923 to the end of TSE's life.

[II] 132–34] *no quotation marks at heads of lines Dial, Criterion, 1974+ (see Commentary)*

[II] 133 = 188 **"With**] With *Hogarth, Guild*

[II] 134 ^ 135 = 189 ^ 190] *line space ts2*

[II] 135] *stepped or ranged right (indeterminate) Boni, 1925* ‖ *ranged to right margin Dial*

[II] 135 = 190 **hot water**] hot water bottle *Vivien Eliot with "!" ts2a*

[II] 136–38 = 192–94] *see The Death of the Duchess II 45–49:*

> And if it rains, the closed carriage at four.
> We should play a game of chess
> The ivory men make company between us
> We should play a game of chess
> Pressing lidless eyes and waiting for a knock upon the door.

[II] 136 = 191 **a closed car**] WLLetter *(the proposed new reading, although the first word is underlined to emphasise that it has changed, and is capitalised because of its position in the letter)* with "OK" *Pound, Q, Boni* ‖ the closed carriage *ts2 with last two words ringed by Pound with "Why this <u>between</u> 1922 & Lil" and "(1880)" ts2a* ‖ the closed car *T/W*

[II] 137 = 192 **chess,**] *Q, T/W, Boni+* ‖ chess: *ts2* ‖ chess *ms1960*

[II] 137a = 193 **(The ivory men make company between us**)] *Valerie's Own Book (with footnote: "Line omitted from published text, at Vivien's insistence"), ms1960* ‖ The ivory men make company between us *ts2, Q, added TSE in the margin of Curtis 1936 (ending with comma)* ‖ *line space T/W* ‖ *not Boni+*

[II] 138 **a**] the *TSE's 1933 recording*

[II] 138 ^ 139 = 194 ^ 195] *two-line space Q, 1936 (to avoid widow), 1963+* ‖ *five-line* space ts2 ‖ *single line space T/W, printings prior to 1936, Faber Bk Mod V, Sesame, Penguin.* Both *Sel Poems* and *Collected Poems* reverted to a single space in 2002.

[II] 139 = **195 got demobbed, I said**—] coming back out of the Transport Corps *ts2, all del and last two words ringed with "?" by Vivien Eliot, who then wrote* demobbed *(see Commentary), above which TSE wrote* ~~Discharge out of the army~~ *with "??" ts2a*   **said**—] said, *Q, T/W, Dial, Criterion*

[II] 140 = **196 didn't**] said *ts2 1ˢᵗ reading (typed over)* ‖ didnt *Q*

[II] 141 = **197,** *as also* 152, 165, 168, 169 = **208, 221, 224, 225**] *full capitals ts2, Q, T/W, Valerie's Own Book, ms1960*   ITS] *without apostrophe Q, T/W, Boni, Dial, Hogarth proof, 1925, 1936, Sesame (later emended), 1963, Valerie's Own Book* ‖ *with apostrophe ts2, Criterion, Hogarth, Penguin, Mardersteig, ms1960, 1971B*   TIME] *without full stop T/W (except 152, 165), Boni, Dial, 1925+* ‖ *with full stop ts2, Q (except 168, 169), Criterion*

[II] 141 = **197**] *with "perhaps better not so soon. Cld you put this later." Vivien Eliot ts2a, del* ‖ *with "Later?" TSE ts2b*

[II] 142–64 = **198–220**] *no quotation marks Q, T/W, Boni+.* (See *WLComposite* for their occurrence in *ts2.* It may have been while typing *ts2* that TSE realised the advantages of not specifying where speech begins and ends, for he allowed quotation marks to lapse and did not use them in *222–23*.)

[II] 142 **smart.**] smart, *ms1960*

[II] 143 = **199 what**] with *ts2 1ˢᵗ reading (uncertain, typed over)*   **done**] *T/W, Boni+* ‖ did *ts2, Q*

[II] 144 = **200 I**] he *(or perhaps* be) *ts2 1ˢᵗ reading*   **there.**] there, *Valerie's Own Book*

[II] 145] *not Valerie's Own Book 1ˢᵗ reading (copying error)*   **set,**] set. *Q, T/W*

[II] 147 = **203 can't**] can *ts2*   **said,**] said; *T/W 1ˢᵗ reading*

[II] 148 **time,**] time. *Hogarth*

[II] 149 = **205 don't**] *ts2, T/W, Dial+, 1971B* ‖ dont *Q, Boni*   **there's others will, I said.**] *Boni+* ‖ there's many another will". *ts2 with* s many another *(including last letter of* there's) *marked at corners in pencil by Pound then ringed in ink probably also by Pound ts2a* ‖ theres many another will. *Q* ‖ there's others will. *T/W*

[II] 150 = **206 Oh is there,**] *T/W, Boni, Dial, Hogarth, 1925+* ‖ "Other women", *ts2, bracketed Pound ts2a* ‖ Is there, *Q* ‖ Hoh, is there, *Criterion*   **Something o'**] *Q+* ‖ Something of *ts2, with* Somethink o' *Vivien Eliot and TSE's response "I want to avoid trying show pronunciation by spelling" ts2a*

[II] 151 = **207 give**] gave *ts2*

[II] 153 = **209 If you don't like it you can get on with it,**] *Vivien Eliot in margin of ts2a, added by TSE in margin of ts2b (both without apostrophe), Q, T/W, Boni+* ‖ "No, ma'am, you needn't look old-fashioned at me", *ts2, with first seven words del by Viven in ts2a but only the second word—*ma'am—*del by TSE in ts2b*   **said.**] *1932+, 1971B* ‖ said, *ts2, Boni, Dial, Criterion, Hogarth* ‖ said *1925, 1932 proof with full stop added TSE*

[II] 154 = **210 can't**] *ts2, Boni+* ‖ cant *Q, T 1ˢᵗ reading, W*

[II] 155 = **211 won't**] *ts2, Dial+, 1971B* ‖ wont *Q, T/W, Boni*   **telling.**] telling, *ms1960*

[II] 157 = **213 (And**] —(And *ts2*

[II] 158 = 214 **can't**] cant *Q*   **said**] says *T/W, Criterion*   **pulling**] putting on *ts2*

[II] 159 = 215 **It's**] Its *Q, T/W*   **them**] that *ts2*   **pills**] *Q, T/W, Boni+* ‖ medicine *ts2* ‖ ~~stuff~~ pills *Vivien Eliot ts2a*   **to**] *Vivien Eliot ts2a, Q, T/W, Boni+* ‖ in order to *ts2*   **off, she said.**] *Q, T/W, Boni+* ‖ off". *(quotation marks and full stop superimposed) ts2* ‖ off, she says. *T/W, Criterion*

[II] 161 = 217 **all right**] *Dial, Criterion, 1925+* ‖ allright *ts2* ‖ alright *Q, T/W, Boni, Hogarth (see Commentary)*

[II] 162 = 218 **are**] are *T/W, US 1952, ms1960*

[II] 163 = 219 **Well,**] Well *ts2, Q, T/W, Dial*   **won't**] *ts2, Dial+, 1971B* ‖ wont *Q, T/W, Boni*   **said,**] *Q, T/W, Boni, Dial, Hogarth+* ‖ said. *ts2, Criterion, ms1960*

[II] 164 = 220 **What you get married for if you don't want children?** *Q, T/W, Boni+ (without apostrophe in Q, T/W, Boni)* ‖ "You want to keep him at home, I suppose". *ts2* ‖ What you get married for if you dont want to have children *Vivien Eliot ts2a, with last word perhaps changed to* chillren ‖ What you get married for if you don't want to have children— *TSE ts2b 2nd reading*

[II] 165 = 221 TIME] *with terminal full stop ts2, Q, T/W*

[II] 166 = 222 **Well,**] Well *ts2, Q, T/W, Dial*   **home**] at home *T/W*

[II] 167–72 = 223–28 *line spacing reduced and irregular T/W*

[II] 167 = 223 **asked**] ask *Vivien Eliot ts2a*

[II] 167 ^ 168 *as also* 169 ^ 170] *half-line space ms1960*

[II] 168, 169 = 224, 225 TIME] *with terminal full stop ts2*

[II] 170 = 226 **Goonight Bill. Goonight Lou. Goonight May. Goonight.**] *Q, Boni, Dial, Hogarth+ (in Valerie's Own Book TSE began a "d" in the first word but changed it to "n")* ‖ Good night, Bill. Good night, Lou. Good night, George. Good night. *ts2, with the four "d"s crossed out (probably by Vivien Eliot)* ‖ Good night then, Bill. Good night Lou. Good night May. Good night. *T/W* ‖ Goonight, Bill. Goonight, Lou. Goonight, May. Goonight. *Criterion*

[II] 171 = 227 **Goonight. Goonight.**] *Boni, Dial, Hogarth+* ‖ Good night. Good night. *ts2, del Vivien Eliot ts2a* ‖ Gooonight. Gooonight. *Q* ‖ Good night, good Night. *T/W* ‖ Goonight, goonight. *Criterion*

[II] 172 = 228 *last two words over-running onto new line, with capital "G" in T/W, and with* good night *typed again at the end of 228 in W. (T therefore ends* "sweet ladies, good night, | Good night." *and W ends* "sweet ladies, good night, good night | Good night.") ‖ *last two words run together, probably accidentally, in Valerie's Own Book.*

after 228] *"Splendid last lines" Vivien Eliot ts2a*

III. *THE FIRE SERMON*

The manuscript of Part III, which TSE reported composing in Margate in Oct–Nov 1921, is largely missing, having been superseded by his typing of *ts3*, which is given in *WLComposite* for 229–421. The manuscript leaf *ms1* (*WLFacs* 36/37), on the lower half of which appears a very rough draft of 334–47 ("London, the swarming life"), is a survival from that visit to Margate and is therefore earlier than *ts3*. However, in *WLComposite* it has been judged better to follow the long typescript, rather than interrupt this continuous text and alternate between different archaeological layers.

The leaf *ms1* was probably retained because the lines on the upper half, "O City, City, I have heard ᴐ hear", given here for 422–28, did not find a place in the typescript (although they were reinstated in the published text). After these lines, *WLComposite* follows *ms2* for 429–74 ("The river sweats", "'Trams and dusty trees.'" and "On Margate Sands."), through to the end of Part III, "burning".

229–421	*ts3a* (*WLFacs* 22/23, 26/27, 30–35)
422–428	*ms1* (*WLFacs* 36/37)
429–474	*ms2* (*WLFacs* 48–53)

Both *ts3a* and *ts3b* are annotated by Pound. Also recorded below are *ms3*, "The river's tent is broken and the last fingers of leaf", which was drafted after *ts3* as a replacement when Pound deleted the opening of Part III; and *ms4* (intended as an interpolation, 285 ^ 286).

The headnote to this Textual History, 5. THE "FRESCA COUPLETS", explains how TSE re-imagined the original opening of Part III as a contribution to *Letters of the Moment* II (1924) by "F. M."; see *ms1924* after 298 below.

229–98] *not Q, T/W, Boni+*

229–30 the ··· the] *underlined with* "?" *Pound ts3a, after which he del* 230

231 The] *ringed in pencil with* <u>Our</u> *by Vivien Eliot (although printed in red in WLFacs, signifying that it is by Pound) ts3a, with* <u>Our</u> *del by Pound*

232–69] *del, apparently preserving* 245–46, *Pound ts3a*

234 Brings] Bring *ts3a* 1ˢᵗ *reading, ts3b*

240 needful] *second syllable ringed with* "?" *Pound ts3b*

243–69] *"Too loose [with zigzag] rhyme drags it out to diffuseness [zigzag]" and "trick of Pope etc not to let couple[t] diffuse 'em" Pound ts3b*

244 page of Gibbon] *ts3, del ts3a (perhaps by Pound, although not red in WLFacs)* ‖ the Daily Mirror *ts3a* 2ⁿᵈ *reading*

245–46] *final word and the couplet with its eye-rhyme both braced Pound ts3a*

268 cunning] *ts3, del ts3a (perhaps by Pound, although not red in WLFacs)* ‖ artful *ts3a* 2ⁿᵈ *reading*

269 hearty] *not ts3* 1ˢᵗ *reading (the next two words typed and erased, with the three words typed over)*

270–73] *braced ts3a (probably by Pound, although not red in WLFacs)*

271 lowly] *del Pound ts3a*

274–91] *pen strokes through by Pound ts3a probably to del*

277 Or] Now *Pound ts3a*

282–83] *ringed to move before* 286 *ts3a*

282 Women grown] *ts3, with* grown *del ts3a (probably by Pound, although not red in WLFacs)* ‖ But women *ts3a* 2ⁿᵈ *reading*

284–85] *ringed ts3a*

284 baptised in] *ts3, del ts3a (perhaps by Pound, although not red in WLFacs)* ‖
born upon *ts3a 2ⁿᵈ reading (perhaps* borne upon)

285 ^ 286] *insertion, ms4:*

> From which, a Venus Anadyomene
> She stept ashore to a more varied scene,
> Propelled by Lady Katzegg's guiding hand
> She knew the wealth and fashion of the land,
> Among the fame and beauty of the stage   [5]
> She passed, the wonder of our little age;
> She gave the turf her intellectual patronage.
> She dominates no less distinguished spheres,
> Minerva in a crowd of boxing peers.
> Aeneas' mother, with an altered face,   [10]
> Appeared once in an unexpected place:
> He recognised the goddess by her supernatural grace
> The sweating rabble in the cinema
> Can recognise a goddess or a star.
> And hushed silence worships from afar.   [15]
> Thus art ennobles even wealth and birth,
> And breeding raises prostrate art from earth.

[8] She dominates] *2ⁿᵈ reading (preceding the writing of the rest of the line)* ‖
She reigns *1ˢᵗ reading* ‖ She governs *3ʳᵈ reading* ‖ But F.[resca] rules
final reading   **no less]** even more *2ⁿᵈ reading*

[8–9] *ringed and joined to* [16–17]

[10–12] *final reading (at foot of leaf):*

> To Aeneas, in an unfamiliar place,
> Appeared his mother, with an altered face,
> He knew the goddess by her smooth celestial pace.

[11] Appeared once] Approached him *2ⁿᵈ reading*   **unexpected]**
unfamiliar *2ⁿᵈ reading*

[12] recognised] knew *2ⁿᵈ reading*   **goddess by her supernatural grace]**
divinity's celestial pace *2ⁿᵈ reading* ‖ goddess by her smooth celestial
pace. *3ʳᵈ reading*

[13] The sweating rabble] So the close millions *2ⁿᵈ reading* ‖ So the pact
thousands, *3ʳᵈ reading* ‖ So the close rabble *final reading*

[14] Can recognise] Know *2ⁿᵈ reading* ‖ Sees on the screen *3ʳᵈ reading* ‖
Identify *4ᵗʰ reading*

[15] And hushed silence worships] In reverent silence worships *2ⁿᵈ &
3ʳᵈ readings* ‖ In silent rapture worship *final reading*   **worships]**
worships ~~heaven~~ *2ⁿᵈ reading*

WLComposite text resumes

288–91] *braced and struck through Pound ts3a probably to del* ‖ *struck through
with zigzags Pound ts3b*

288 From] For *1ˢᵗ reading ts3*

292] *brace and double rule at end Pound ts3b*

294 **cautious**] *ringed, with "surely as you are writing of London this adj. is tauto."*
Pound ts3a

297–300] *struck through Pound ts3a probably to del*

298 **salonnière**] *accent added ts3a but not ts3b*

The "Fresca couplets" of 1924

ms1924: twenty-seven lines, in TSE's hand, now bound among Vivien Eliot's
papers, along with typescripts of a contribution by "F. M." to the *Criterion*
Apr 1924, *Letters of the Moment* II.

tsLM1: first typescript (Bodleian c. 624 fol. 35; with carbon, identically emended
by Vivien, fol. 41).

tsLM2: second typescript; the printer's copy (c. 624 fol. 31).

The typescripts were made on different machines. *tsLM1* was typed with a violet
ribbon and has a large face; *tsLM2* was typed with a black ribbon and has a
small face. Correspondence and other tss among Vivien Eliot's papers suggest
that the first was used mostly by Vivien, the second mostly by TSE. The second
readings in *tsLM1* are identical in both ribbon and carbon copies, precisely
following *tsLM2*, from which they were almost certainly taken. Also collated
here are:

LM: *Letters of the Moment* II (1924), published text

Haffenden: transcripts of *ms1924* and *LM* in *PN Review* May–June 2007

When the rude entrance of the Tarquin, day
Flutters the doves that round her bosom play
The amorous Fresca stretches yawns ⅋ gapes
Aroused from dreams of love ⅋ pleasant rapes
Draped in translucent silks   [5]

While the deft Chloe round her chamber trips
And holds the foaming chocolate to her lips
The quill lies ready at her fingertips
She reads ⅋ talks ⅋ pens a letter while she sips
Im very well my dear ⅋ how are you   [10]
I have another book by Giraudoux
My dear I missed you last night at the play
Were you not there? or did you slip away?
Or were you in the seats of cheaper price?
Dorilant sat with me, and I looked nice.   [15]
I told him you were there but I dont think he heard.
Her hands caress the eggs well rounded dome
While her mind labours till the phrases come
But see where Fresca in her salon sits
Surrounded by a cloud of lesser wits,   [20]
Talking of art and of aesthetic laws.   *[new leaf]*
Her little senate whispers its applause.   <<

> But Fresca rules even more exalted spheres
> Minerva in a crowd of boxing peers
> And the close rabble in the cinema   [25]
> Acclaim the social goddess ⊲ the star—
> Wide mouthed, in charmèd rapture worship from afar.

[1] When the embraces of the lusty day *tsLM1 1ˢᵗ reading (emended by Vivien to match tsLM2 1ˢᵗ reading)* ‖ When sniffing Chloe brings the toast and tea *tsLM2 1ˢᵗ reading* ‖ When sniffing Chloe, with the toast and tea, *tsLM2 (emended by Vivien), LM*   **rude entrance**] high summons *ms1924 1ˢᵗ reading* ‖ bold entrance *ms1924 2ⁿᵈ reading*   **Tarquin, day**] Tarquin *ms1924 1ˢᵗ reading* ‖ amorous day *ms1924 alt*

[2] Flutter the doves that round her bosom play, *tsLM1 1ˢᵗ reading (emended by Vivien to match tsLM2)* ‖ Drags back the curtains to disclose the day, *tsLM2, LM* ‖ Disturbs the d *ms1924 1ˢᵗ reading*

[3] **amorous**] ardent *tsLM1 1ˢᵗ reading*   **stretches**] stretches, *tssLM, LM*

[4] **Aroused**] Roused *ms1924 1ˢᵗ reading*   ⊲ **pleasant rapes**] in curious shapes. *tssLM, LM* ‖ in various shapes. *Haffenden (ms1924)*

[5] *not tssLM, LM*   **silks**] silk *Haffenden (ms1924)*

[6–7] *tsLM1*:

> She holds the foaming chocolate to her lips,
> While the deft Chloe round the chamber trips.

with While the *changed to* While her *by Vivien, then all del* ‖ *not tsLM2, LM*

[8] **And holds**] She holds *ms1924 1ˢᵗ reading*   **lies ready**] already *ms1924 1ˢᵗ reading* ‖ is *ms1924 2ⁿᵈ reading (uncertain)*   **fingertips**] finger tips; *tssLM, LM*

[9] **reads** ⊲ **talks** ⊲] drinks, and *tssLM, LM*   **letter**] little *Haffenden (ms1924)*   **sips**] sips: *tssLM, LM* ‖ sips. *Haffenden (ms1924)*

[10] **Im**] "I'm *tssLM, LM* ‖ I'm *Haffenden (ms1924)*   **well my dear** ⊲ **how are you**] well, my dear, and how are you? *tssLM, LM*

[11–16] *quotation marks recur at head of each line tssLM*

[11] **Giraudoux**] Giraudoux. *tssLM, LM*

[12] **dear**] dear, *LM*   **play**] Play; *tssLM, LM*

[13] **or did you slip away?**] ou vous vous etes sauvee? *tsLM1 1ˢᵗ reading (emended by Vivien to match tsLM2)*   **or**] Or *tssLM, LM*

[15] **Dorilant**] Hanover *tsLM1 1ˢᵗ reading (emended by Vivien to match tsLM2)* ‖ Si *ms1924 1ˢᵗ reading*   **nice.**] nice: *Haffenden (ms1924)*

[15 ^ 16] "Once settled in my box, he never stirred— *tssLM and (without quotation marks) LM*

[16] *not ms1924 1ˢᵗ reading but added vertically in margin*   **there**] there, *tssLM, LM*   **heard.**] heard" ... *tssLM* ‖ heard. ...." *LM*

[16 ^ 17] *line space tssLM, LM*

[17] **eggs**] egg's *tssLM, LM, Haffenden (ms1924)*   **well rounded**] well-rounded *LM*   **dome**] dome; *tssLM, LM*; dome: *Haffenden (LM)*

[18] *misaligned, so perhaps left blank originally and supplied later. The*

double spaces [5^6] *and* [22^23] *may have been left for the same purpose.* **While**] As *tssLM, LM* **come**] come. *tssLM, LM*

[18^19] *line space tssLM, LM, Haffenden (ms1924)*

[19] **see**] see, *tsLM1, LM* **salon sits**] boudoir sits, *tssLM, L of M*

[20] **cloud of lesser**] court of sparkish *tssLM, LM* **wits,**] wits: *tssLM, LM* ‖ wits *Haffenden (ms1924)*

[21–22] *tssLM, LM:*

> Her practised eye directs its conscious darts
> At the small tyrants of the several Arts . . .

[21–27] *not tssLM, LM*

[21] **Talking**] Speaking *ms1924 1st reading*

[22] *new leaf begins ms1924*

[23] **spheres**] sh *ms1924 1st reading (false start)*

[26] **the social**] a social *ms1924 1st reading*

[27] **charmèd**] charmed *Haffenden (ms1924)* **afar.**] afar *Haffenden (ms1924)*

Published poem resumes

The dozen lines which begin the published text of Part III ("The river's tent is broken") were not present in *ts3* but were hastily sketched to replace the seventy lines 229–98 (*ms3*). Written upside down on the verso of the first page of *ts3a*, they are not included in *WLComposite* but variants in *ms3* from the published text of [III] 173–82 are listed below.

[III] 173] *indent 1963 (not 1963 proof, US 1963)* **river's**] *Q, T/W, Boni+* ‖ rivers *ms3* **broken; the**] *Washington copy 1954 emendation, Mardersteig, 1936 18th imp. (1961), 1963, 1969* ‖ broken ⊄ the *ms3* ‖ broken: the *Q, printings prior to 1961, Valerie's Own Book, ms1960*

[III] 175 **departed.**] departed *ms3*

[III] 176–79] *not T/W (eye-skip)*

[III] 176] (Sweet Thames etc). *ms3*

[III] 177 **papers,**] papers *ms3*

[III] 178 **Silk handkerchiefs,**] Newspapers, *ms3 written over two letters which WLFacs gives as* Ca *(perhaps for "Cardboard"?) but which might be* Co

[III] 179 **The nymphs are departed.**] *stepped (probably for lack of space) ms3* ‖ *new line but with double indent (aligning with other turns) Hogarth proof*

[III] 180 **And**] (And *ms3* **City**] *ms3, 1963+* ‖ city *Q, T/W, printings prior to 1963, Valerie's Own Book, ms1960* **directors;**] *Q, T/W, Boni, Dial, 1925, 1936, 1963* ‖ directors) *ms3* ‖ directors, *Criterion, Hogarth, Sel Poems 1954 (emended long after)* ‖ directors— *Sesame (emended long after), Mardersteig*

[III] 181 **have**] *WLLetter (where it is underlined, not for italics but to emphasise the change from previous reading), Q, T/W, Boni+* ‖ and *ms3*

[III] 182] By the waters *ms3, which ends here*

[III] 183 **song,**] song; *Criterion* || song. *T/W, Valerie's Own Book, ms1960*

[III] 185 = 299 **in a cold blast**] from time to time *ts3*

[III] 186 ^ 187] *line space ts3, printings prior to 1932, 1963+* || *new page so line spacing indeterminate 1932* || *no line space Faber Bk Mod V, 1936 and printings prior to 1963, US 1952, ms1960* || *in Valerie's Own Book TSE began to write 187 immediately below 186, on the last line of the page, but crossed it out and then left a second line of space at the head of the new page.*

[III] 187–202 = 301–16] *braced (to end of page) with "O.K." and "STET" Pound ts3a* || *marginal rule, zigzag and "(Echt)" Pound ts3b*

[III] 187 **vegetation**] vegetation, *Criterion*

[III] 188 **bank**] bank, *Criterion*

[III] 190 = 304 **gashouse**] gashouse, *ts3* || gas-house, *Criterion* || gashouse. *3rd and 4th printings of Boni (1928, 1930)*

[III] 192 **him.**] him; *Criterion*

[III] 193 = 307 **damp ground**] damp ground, *ts3* || dampg round *Mardersteig (correct in proof)*

[III] 194 = 308 **garret,**] garret *ms1960*

[III] 197 = 311 **shall**] *underlined with "?" Pound ts3b*

[III] 198 ^ 199] *line space Criterion* || *new page so line spacing indeterminate 1963*

[III] 200 **daughter**] daughter, *Criterion*

[III] 201 **water**] water, *Criterion*

[III] 202 = 316] *roman type ts3, Q, T/W, Criterion, Hogarth*   **Et O**] *Et, o Mardersteig, 1971B, 2002 resetting of Collected Poems and Sel Poems (not Sesame)*   **d'enfants,**] *d'enfants Mardersteig, Valerie's Own Book*

[III] 202 ^ 203 = 316 ^ 317] *new leaf so line spacing indeterminate ts3* || *two-line space 1925 (to avoid widow), Valerie's Own Book* || *half-line space 1936* || *no line space Sesame (to avoid widow), Mardersteig*

[III] 203–204 = 317–18] Twit twit twit twit twit twit twit twit | Tereu tereu *ts3 (where the eventual* [III] *203–204 had been 329–30 until del by Pound)*

[III] 203 **Twit twit twit**] Twit, twit, twit, *Criterion*

[III] 204] Jug jug jug ug jug jug *Boni*

[III] 205 = 319 **forc'd.**] forced *T/W* || forced, *Criterion*

[III] 205 ^ 206] *line space Sesame, Mardersteig*

[III] 206 = 320 **Tereu**] Ter *ts3* || Terreu *T/W (corrected and underlined Watson in T)*

[III] 206 ^ 207] *two-line space 1925 (to avoid widow), Valerie's Own Book* || *new page so line spacing indeterminate 1932* || *no line space Faber Bk Mod V* || *half-line space 1936*

[III] 207–11 = 321–25] *marginal and oblique rules with "vocative ?" Pound ts3b*

[III] 207 = 321 **City**] *Boni, Dial, Hogarth, 1925+* || City, I have seen and see *ts3, with all but first word bracketed by Pound ts3a and ringed by him ts3b* || City, *Q, T/W, Criterion* || city *Valerie's Own Book*

[III] 208 = 322 **a**] your *ts3, ringed Pound ts3a and ringed for del Pound ts3b*

[III] 209 = 323 **Mr.**] Mr *Hogarth*   **merchant**] merchant, *ts3, Criterion*

[III] 210 = 324 **Unshaven**] Unshavan *ts3 1ˢᵗ reading* ‖ *last two letters underlined, with "-en or -ed" Pound ts3a*   **currants**] currents *Q*

[III] 211 = 325 **C.i.f.**] *Q, Boni, 1925+* ‖ (C.i,f. *ts3* ‖ C. I. F. *T/W* ‖ C. i. f. *Dial, Hogarth* ‖ C.I.F. *Criterion*   **sight,**] sight), *ts3*

[III] 212 = 326 **Asked me**] Who asked me, *ts3*   **demotic**] abominable *ts3, ringed with "?" and* his vile demotic *alt ts3a* (his vile *and* demotic *may have been intended as alts by TSE, but a slash which appears between them was probably added by Pound, who deleted* his vile *and who in ts3b replaced* abominable *with* demotic)   **French**] French, *ts3*

[III] 213 = 327 **Hotel**] Hotel, *ts3, Criterion*

[III] 214 = 328 **Followed by**] And perhaps *ts3, with second word underlined twice with "dam per'apsez" by Pound in ts3a, and the same word braced with "?" by Pound in ts3b (see Commentary)*

[III] 214 ^ 215] *new page so line spacing indeterminate Hogarth, 1925, US 1936* ‖ *half-line space 1936* ‖ *no line space 1932 proof (but added TSE), Guild* ‖ *two-line space Valerie's Own Book*

WLComposite gives the earliest reading of ts3, including twenty deleted lines:

329–48] *del Pound ts3a and ts3b* ‖ *not Q, T/W, Boni+*

334–47] *divided by marginal short rules after 336, 339 and 343 as if into terza rima ms1*

334–37] *del with "B—ˡˡ—s" Pound ts3a* [*bollocks*] ‖ *braced with five chevrons above Pound ts3b*

334 **life you kill and breed,**] creatures that you breed *ms1 1ˢᵗ reading* ‖ life you kill ⊄ breed ⊄ feed *ms1 2ⁿᵈ reading* ‖ life you kill ⊄ breed ⊄ Daily feed *ms1 3ʳᵈ reading* ‖ life you kill ⊄ breed [⊄] *ms1 final reading*

335] *del (probably by Pound, although not red in WLFacs) ts3a*   **Huddled**] Among half stunned *ms1 1ˢᵗ reading* ‖ Striving half stunned *ms1 2ⁿᵈ reading* ‖ Scampering half stunned *ms1 3ʳᵈ reading* ‖ Huddled, dazed *ms1 4ᵗʰ reading* ‖ Huddled, stunned *ms1 final reading*   **between**] beneath *ms1 1ˢᵗ reading*   **the concrete and the sky,**] a heavy sky *ms1 1ˢᵗ reading* ‖ the concrete and the sky *ms1*

336 **Responsive**] *ms1 1ˢᵗ and 4ᵗʰ readings, ts3* ‖ Quickly responsive *ms1 2ⁿᵈ reading* ‖ Responsive solely *ms1 3ʳᵈ reading*   **need,**] need *ms1*

337] *with "Keep" ts3a (TSE, perhaps referring to deletion by Pound of 334–37)*   **its formal**] *ms1, ts3* ‖ their chords of *ms1 1ˢᵗ reading (first word uncertain, perhaps* the) ‖ their formal *ms1 2ⁿᵈ reading*   **destiny,**] destiny; *ms1 (the punctuation apparently del)*

338] *del (probably by Pound, although not red in WLFacs) ts3a*   **neither how to**] little what they *ms1 1ˢᵗ reading*   **nor how to**] ⊄ much less what they *ms1 1ˢᵗ reading*

339 **But**] *not ms1 1ˢᵗ reading* ‖ *del (by Pound, or perhaps by TSE as indicated in WLFacs) ts3a*   **in**] chiefly in *ms1 1ˢᵗ reading* ‖ only in *ts3a 2ⁿᵈ reading, with*

only *del* (*probably by Pound, although not red in WLFacs*)   **awareness**] *del*
(*probably by Pound, although not red in WLFacs*) *ts3a* ‖ transformations *ts3a*
2ⁿᵈ reading   **observing**] observant *ts3a 2ⁿᵈ reading*   **eye**.] eye; *ms1*

340] *not ms1, ts3 2ⁿᵈ reading*

341] *del in pencil* (*probably by Pound, although not red in WLFacs*) *with "Palmer
Cox's brownies" in ink by Pound ts3a*   **Phantasmal**] Spectral *ms1 1ˢᵗ
reading*   **gnomes, burrowing**] goblins tunnelling *ms1 1ˢᵗ reading*

342 **minds, aberrant**] brains, unbalanced *ms1 1ˢᵗ reading*   **normal**] natural
ms1

343] *del* (*probably Pound, although not red in WLFacs*) *ts3a*   **London,**] London!
ms1   **people**] population *braced alt* (*over a false start*) *ms1*

344 **motions**] movements *ms1 1ˢᵗ reading* ‖ jerky motions *ms1 2ⁿᵈ
reading*   **pavement**] *ms1, ts3* ‖ huddled *ms1 1ˢᵗ reading* ‖ poor cheap *ms1
2ⁿᵈ reading* ‖ tarnished *ms1 3ʳᵈ reading*

345–47] *with light marginal marks probably by Vivien Eliot ts3a*

345 **cryptogram**] *ms1, ts3* ‖ painful, ideal meaning *ms1 1ˢᵗ reading* ‖ cryptograms
ms1 2ⁿᵈ reading   **may be curled**] *ms1, ts3* ‖ they spell *ms1 1ˢᵗ reading* ‖ is
curled *ms1 2ⁿᵈ reading*

346] *sequence of revisions uncertain*: Doubtfully into these faint perceptions of
the noise *ms1 1ˢᵗ reading* ‖ Indistinctly / Vaguely into these faint perceptions
of the noise *ms1 alts* ‖ Vaguely into these faint perceptions of the noise
ms1 2ⁿᵈ reading ‖ Within this penumbral consciousness of the noise *ms1
2ⁿᵈ reading alt* (*with* consciousness *written over* s *and* faint *added as alt to*
penumbral) ‖ Within [faint *undeleted*] these faint perceptions of the noise
ms1 final reading

346 **these**] the (*probably Pound, although not red in WLFacs*) *ts3a*   **noise**]
noise, *ts3a 2ⁿᵈ reading*

348] *with uncertain pencil mark ts3b*   **Ademantus**] Glaucon *ts3a 2ⁿᵈ reading*

Published poem resumes

[III] 215–56 = 349–416] *draft* (*ts3*) *in quatrains separated by line spaces.* (*The ms
quatrains later entitled* Elegy *are likewise separated by line spaces. See Commentary
headnote,* 1. COMPOSITION.)

[III] 215–18 = 349–52] *three marginal zigzags Pound ts3b*

[III] 215 = 349 **violet hour, when**] *Q, T/W, Boni+* ‖ violet hour, the hour when *ts3 with
first two words ringed Pound ts3b*   **back**] back and hand *ts3 with last two words
ringed Pound ts3b*

[III] 216 = 350 **upward**] upwards *Hogarth*   **when**] *not ts3*   **engine**] *ringed
Pound ts3b*   **waits**] waits— *ts3* ‖ waits, *ms1960*

[III] 217 = 351 **throbbing waiting,**] *Boni, Hogarth+* ‖ throbbing waiting at a stand—
ts3, with first, second and last words each underlined Pound ts3b ‖ throbbing
waiting *Q, T/W, Dial* ‖ throbbing, waiting, *Criterion*

[III] 217 ˄ 218 = 352] *not Q, T/W, Boni+* ‖ To spring to pleasure through the horn or
ivory gates, *ts3. In ts3a Pound del the line, and in ts3b he braced it with* spring

underlined twice and "Taxi spring ??", then del To spring *and transposed* the horn or ivory (*to read* the ivory or horn). See Commentary.

[III] 218 = 353 **I Tiresias**] I, Tiresias *Criterion, Hogarth* **blind,**] blind *Hogarth* **lives,**] lines *T/W 1ˢᵗ reading* ‖ lives *T/W*

[III] 221 = 356] *two zigzags Pound ts3b* **sea,**] sea *T/W*

[III] 222–30 = 357–72] *with "VERSE not interesting enough as verse to warrant so much of it" Pound ts3b. Having annotated this passage in ts3b, Pound wrote "vide other copy" in ts3a*

[III] 222–23 = 357–60] *braced with "qui dira les gaffers de la rime"* [*oh who will tell of the gaffs of rhyme*] *Pound ts3b* (*Fr. gaffeur = blunderer*)

[III] 222 = 357–58] *one line Q, T/W, Boni+* ‖

> The typist home at teatime, who begins
> To clear ~~her broken breakfast~~ away her broken breakfast, lights

ts3, with begins *del,* To clear *changed to* clears, *and* broken *ringed and braced all by Pound ts3b* **teatime**] tea time *T/W* ‖ tea-time *Dial*

[III] 223 = 359 **food**] squalid food *ts3* **in tins.**] in tins, *ts3, del Pound ts3b*

[III] 223 ^ 224 = 360] *not Q, T/W, Boni+* ‖ Prepares the room and sets the room to rights. *ts3, with* Prepares the room *and* sets the room to rights *each underlined* (*for comparison*) *by Pound ts3b, and* room *changed to* toast *by TSE ts3a*

[III] 225 = 362 **touched by**] meet *ts3* **sun's last rays**] *each word underlined by Pound ts3b*

[III] 226 = 363 **On the divan are piled** (**at**] And on the divan piled,(at *ts3* (*first word typed over* O *and with space missing*) ‖ And piled on the divan, (at *Pound ts3b with "inversions not warranted by any real exegience of metre"* **bed)**] Q, *T/W, Boni+* ‖ bed, *ts3 1ˢᵗ reading* (*typed over*) ‖ bed), *ts3*

[III] 227 = 364 **Stockings**] Are stockings *ts3* **slippers,**] dirty *ts3* **and stays.**] *del Pound ts3b*

365–68] *not Q, T/W, Boni+*

365 **bright**] *ringed Pound ts3b*

365–66 **sprawls** ··· **nerveless torpor**] *words underlined* (sprawls, nerveless, torpor) *and numbered "1", "2", "3" by Pound ts3b*

366 **window seat;**] *bracketed with "?" and "mix up of the couplet & gris̱hkin not good—" Pound ts3b*

368 **purchased in Oxford Street.**] *del with "not in that lodging house" Pound ts3b*

[III] 228 = 369 **I Tiresias,**] I Teresias, *Q* ‖ I, Tiresias, *Criterion, Hogarth* **dugs**] dugs, *ts3, Criterion*

[III] 229 = 370 **rest—**] Q, *Boni, Dial, Hogarth+* ‖ rest, *ts3* ‖ rest; *T/W, Criterion*

[III] 229 ^ 230 = 371] *not Q, T/W, Boni+* ‖ *square bracket added after line Pound ts3a* ‖ *line del Pound ts3b* **bugs**] *underlined with three-sided glyph* (*similar to* ⊓) *and "Too easy" Pound ts3b*

373–80] *not Q, T/W, Boni+*

373 **A youth of twentyone]** *del Pound ts3b*

373, 374–76] *braced Pound ts3a*

374–76] *ringed with* One of those simple loiterers *underlined and "Personal" Pound ts3b*

374 **One of those]** *ringed Pound ts3a*   **simple loiterers]** *ringed Vivien Eliot ts3a, with other faint underlining by her in this stanza*

376 **almost any hour of night or]** *underlined, perhaps ringed, Vivien Eliot ts3a (shown as deletion in WLFacs)*

377] *del Pound ts3b*

379 **Perhaps]** *ringed with* "Perhaps be da̲mmed" *Pound ts3b*

380] *wavy underline with "?" (probably by Vivien Eliot although WLFacs prints in red as Pound's), the question mark then del (probably by TSE, although red in WLFacs) ts3a ‖ line del Pound ts3b*   **associate]** *del Pound ts3a prompting* mingles *(for* mingle*) ts3a 2nd reading*

381–84] *stanza at first lightly struck through by Vivien Eliot in ts3a, then doubly braced by Pound, who deleted* will stare *(381), extending the deletion to all four lines. In ts3b 381 Pound heavily ringed* will *and also ringed* will stare *with a loop to the start of 382. He added a heavy arrow pointing downwards at the end of 381 and deleted* Boldly about *at the start of 382. He also ringed with a casual air, and* Grandly *383, 384. (His ring around "will" may be an objection to the tense. His loop conjoins "stare | Boldly" and the arrow probably points to the repetitive "bold stare" / "stare", 386, 389. His ringing of "with a casual air" and "Grandly" probably refers to the repetitive "stare | Boldly" / "air, | Grandly".)*   **will stare]** *with* stare *typed over* sit ts3 ‖ arrives, Q, T/W, Boni+*

382–84] *not Q, T/W, Boni+*

[III] 231 = 381 **He,]** He is *Pound ts3b (*He's *WLFacs)*   **the young man carbuncular]** *with two ticks Pound ts3a*

385–88] *ringed (possibly by Vivien Eliot, although WLFacs indicates TSE), with arrow by TSE to move before 377 ts3a ‖ del with "alternate nights" Pound ts3b*

[III] 232 = 385–86] *one line Q, T/W, Boni+ ‖* Perhaps a cheap house agent's clerk, who flits | Daily, from flat to flat, with one bold stare; *ts3 with first word del in ts3a (probably by Pound, although not red in WLFacs) prompting 2nd reading* Or else *‖ first three words del Pound ts3b*   **house agent's]** house-agent's *Dial*

389–92] *del Pound ts3b ‖ not Q, T/W, Boni+*

390 **and that's that!]** *ringed Pound ts3b*

392 **cigarette]** cigarr *(mistyping) ts3 1st reading*

[III] 236 = 394 **tired,]** tired; *ts3*

[III] 237 = 395 **caresses]** caresses, *ts3*

[III] 238 **if]** though *Valerie's Own Book*

[III] 239 = 397 **decided]** e *ts3 1st reading (typed over)*

[III] 240 **defence**] defense *Valerie's Own Book*

[III] 242 **indifference.**] indifference *Criterion*

[III] 243–46 = 401–404] *"Echt" Pound ts3b*

[III] 243 = 401 (**And**] And *ts3 1ˢᵗ reading* (*apparently, since the bracket is to the left of the margin; see* 404) **I Tiresias**] I, Tiresias, *Criterion* **foresuffered**] foretol *ts3 1ˢᵗ reading* (*typed over*)

[III] 244 = 402] *ringed* (*perhaps by Vivien Eliot, although WLFacs indicates TSE*) *ts3a* **this**] the *Valerie's Own Book* **bed;**] bed, *ts3*

[III] 245 = 403 **below**] *Q, Boni, Dial, Hogarth*+ ‖ beneath *ts3, Criterion* ‖ neath *T/W*

[III] 246 = 404 **dead.)**] *Boni, Dial, Hogarth*+ ‖ dead. *ts3 1ˢᵗ reading with bracket added ts3a* (*see* 401) ‖ dead). *Q, T/W* ‖ dead); *Criterion*

[III] 247 = 405 **Bestows**] —Bestows *ts3* **patronising**] patronizing *Dial, Hogarth*

[III] 248 = 406 **unlit . . .**] unlit; *ts3* ‖ unlit . . *1925* (*1st trade imp. only: three stops in ltd. edn. and in 2nd and 3rd imps.*) ‖ unlit . . . . *Valerie's Own Book*

[III] 248 ^ 249 = 407–408] *ts3:*

> And at the corner where the stable is,
> Delays only to urinate, and spit.

followed by line space, braced and del with "probaly over the mark" Pound ts3b

[III] 251 = 411 **Her brain allows**] Across her brain *ts3, with* her *typed over* th **to**] may *ts3, ringed and del with "make up yr. mind you Tiresias if you know know damm well or else you dont." Pound ts3b* (*WLFacs has "damn" in error*) **pass:**] pass; *Q* ‖ pass *T 1ˢᵗ reading, W*

[III] 252 = 412 **now**] now, *Criterion* **done: and I'm**] done, and I am *ts3* ‖ done,— and I'm *Pound ts3a but with his dots to stet the reading* done, and **over."**] *Boni*+ ‖over". *ts3, Q* ‖ over. *T/W*

[III] 253 **folly**] folly, *Valerie's Own Book*

[III] 254 = 414 **Paces**] She moves *ts3* ‖ Then moves *Pound ts3a, ts3b* **her**] the *Criterion*

[III] 255 = 415 **smoothes**] *ts3, Q, T/W, Boni, Dial, Hogarth, 1925, 1936, Penguin, 1963, 1969, Valerie's Own Book, ms1960* ‖ smooths *Criterion, 3rd and 4th printings of Boni* (*1928, 1930*), *Sel Poems 1954, 1974*+

[III] 256 ^ 257 = 416 ^ 417] *sixteen-line space ts3*

[III] 257 **waters"**] waters," *Criterion*

[III] 258 = 418 **up Queen Victoria Street.**] *ts3a 2ⁿᵈ reading* (*with terminal comma*), *Q, T/W, Boni*+ (*with* ub *in Hogarth proof*) ‖ and up theghastly hill of Cannon Street, *ts3 1ˢᵗ reading, with* theghastly hill of *del Pound ts3b*

[III] 258 ^ 259 = 419–21] *ts3, del Pound ts3a* (*pencil and ink*) *and ts3b* ‖ not *Q, T/W, Boni*+ **by**] my *Pound ts3a*

[III] 259 = 422 **City city,**] *Q, Boni, Hogarth proof, 1925*+ (*In 1936 proof TSE emended to* City City, *but this was not implemented in 1936.*) ‖ City, City, *ms1, Criterion* ‖ City City, *T/W, Dial, Hogarth, ms1960* **can sometimes hear**] *Q, T/W, Boni*+ ‖ have heard ⊄ hear *ms1*

[III] 260, 261 = 424, 423] *transposed so ms1*

[III] 260 = 424 **Beside**] Outside *ms1 1ˢᵗ reading*   **Lower**] lower *ms1* ‖ Upper *T/W, Criterion*

[III] 261 = 423 a] the *ms1 1ˢᵗ reading*

[III] 262 = 425] *with arrow to move before* 424 *ms1*   **a chatter**] chatter *Criterion*   **from within**] in the bar *ms1 1ˢᵗ reading*

[III] 263 = 426] *arrow to move before* 425, *the arrow then del ms1*   **fishmen**] fishermen *Penguin 2nd and 3rd imps.* (1951, 1952), *Sel Poems 1954 (later corrected), 1974 (later corrected). See Commentary.*   **at noon: where the walls**] Q, T, *Boni+* ‖ ⊄ loafe ⊄ spit at noon *ms1 1ˢᵗ reading* ‖ at noon, where the walls *ms1 2ⁿᵈ reading* ‖ at noon time, ~~out~~ there the walls *ms1 3ʳᵈ reading* ‖ at noon time, there the walls *T 1ˢᵗ reading, W*

[III] 264 = 427 **hold**] Q, *Boni+* ‖ stood, ⊄ stand, ⊄ hold *ms1* ‖ stood and stand and hold *T/W*

[III] 265 = 428 **Inexplicable**] *ms1 final reading+* ‖ Their joyful *ms1 1ˢᵗ reading* ‖ Inviolable *ms1 2ⁿᵈ reading*   **splendour**] music *braced alt del ms1*   **Ionian**] Q, *Boni+* ‖ Corinthian *ms1, T/W*   **gold.**] Q, *T/W, Boni+* ‖ gold *followed by what may have been part of a word, del ms1*

WLComposite gives the first coherent reading from ms2 for the rest of Part III:

[III] 266–91 = 429–54] *inset 1925+* ‖ *not inset ms2 (uncertain),* Q, *T/W, printings prior to 1925*

[III] 267 = 430 **Oil**] oil *ms2 1ˢᵗ reading*

[III] 270–72 = 433–35] Red sails swing wide | to leeward | On the heavy spar. *ms2 1ˢᵗ reading* ‖ Red sails wide | to leeward | Swing on the heavy spar. *ms2*   **spar.**] spar *Mardersteig*

[III] 273–74 = 436–37 **The barges wash | Drifting logs**] The barges wash, | ~~Like~~ As drifting logs, *ms2* ‖ Drifting logs | The barges wash *WLLetter* ‖ The barges wash, Drifting logs, *T/W (one line). See Commentary.*   **wash**] wash, *Dial, Criterion*

[III] 275 = 438 **Down**] Past *ms2 1ˢᵗ reading*

[III] 277–78 = 440–41] *no indent ms2*

[III] 277 ^ 278 = 440 ^ 441] O O hin hein heinh weihauhhh *added to ms2, emended to* O O hin hein heinh ooahauhhh *then del*

[III] 278 = 441] *second word or both del ms2*

[III] 278 ^ 279 = 441 ^ 442] *line space ms2, Criterion, 1936+, 1971B* ‖ *no line space* Q, *Boni, Dial, Hogarth, 1925, Faber Bk Mod V, Sesame* ‖ *new page so line spacing indeterminate T/W, 1969. (For the setting in 1936 see 279 ^ 280.)*

[III] 279 = 442 **Leicester**] Leicester. *ms2*

[III] 279 ^ 280] *half-line of space and new page 1932* ‖ *line space 1936 proof, where TSE indicated that the space should move up one line* (278 ^ 279).

[III] 280 = 443 **oars**] oars. *ms2*

[III] 281 = 444 **stern**] barge *ms2 1ˢᵗ reading*

[III] 282 = 445 **A gilded shell**] Q, *Boni+* ‖ Of gilded shells, *ms2 1ˢᵗ reading (not WLFacs)* ‖ ~~As~~ a gilded shell, *ms2 2ⁿᵈ reading* ‖ A gilded Shell *T 1ˢᵗ reading, W*

[III] 283 = **446** **gold**] gold. *ms2*

[III] 284 = **447** **brisk**] slow *ms2 1ˢᵗ reading*

[III] 286 = **449** **Southwest**] *Boni, Hogarth+* ‖ South west *ms2, Q, T/W* ‖ South-west *Dial, Criterion*

[III] 288 = **451** **bells**] bells. *ms2*

[III] 289 = **452** **White**] There are still white *ms2 1ˢᵗ reading*   **towers**] towers. *ms2 2ⁿᵈ reading*

[III] 289 ^ 290 = **452 ^ 453**] *line space ms2* ‖ *new page so line spacing indeterminate Boni⁄*

[III] 290–91 = **453–54**] *indent Q, T/W, Boni+*

[III] 290 = **453** **leia**] lalalala *ms2 1ˢᵗ reading*

[III] 291 = **454** **Wallala leialala**] Weialala. *ms2 1ˢᵗ reading* ‖ Weialala leia *T 1ˢᵗ reading, W*

[III] 291 ^ 292 = **454 ^ 455**] *line space Q, Dial, Criterion, Hogarth, 1936+* ‖ *new leaf so line spacing indeterminate ms2* ‖ *no line space T/W* ‖ *no line space but leaded Boni* ‖ *two-line space 1925, Valerie's Own Book*

[III] 292–311 = **455–74** *not inset*] *Q, T/W, printings prior to 1925* ‖ *layout indeterminate ms2* ‖ *inset to 295 where a new page begins 1925* ‖ *all inset 1932+* ‖ *inset, but less so than 266–91 Mardersteig.* (After the double indent of 290–91, both *1925* and *1932* return to the alignment of the inset lines above, and not to the margin as in previous printings; *1925* returns to the margin at the start of the next page, but *1932* and later settings continue the insetting to the end of Part III. *Moody* 308 approves the insetting of 292–306—which he considers part of the Thames-daughters' song—but proposes a return to the margin for 307–11.)

[III] 292–99 = **455–62**] *ms2 has two drafts, the 1ˢᵗ draft of eleven lines, the 2ⁿᵈ draft corresponding to the eight published lines, beside which Pound wrote "O.K. echt".*

> "Highbury bore me. Highbury's children
> Played under green trees and in the dusty Park.
> We were humble people ⊄ conservative
> As neither the rich nor the working class know.
> My father had a small business, somewhere in the city   [5]
> A small business, an anxious business, providing only
> The house in Highbury, and three weeks at Shanklin.
> Highbury bore me. Richmond ⊄ Kew
> Undid me. At Kew we had tea.
> At Richmond on the river, at last I raised my knees   [10]
> Stretched on the floor of a perilous canoe.

ms2 1ˢᵗ draft, del by TSE but with Pound's "Type │ out │ this │ anyhow" (bracketed) and "= O.K."

[3] **We**] Mine *2ⁿᵈ reading*

[6] **anxious**] *uncertain*   **providing**] whi provided *1ˢᵗ reading*

[7] **Shanklin**] Bognor *2ⁿᵈ reading*

[9] **At Kew we had tea.**] *del*

[10] **At Richmond on the river, at last**] Near Richmond on the river, at last *2ⁿᵈ reading, then del*   **I raised my knees**] *ringed to move below* [11]

[11] **Stretched on**] On *2ⁿᵈ reading*

[III] 292] "**Trams**] Trams *Hogarth proof* || "Trains *Collected Poems (2002), Sel Poems (2002) (optical scanning error, later corrected)*

[III] 293] *last line of verso* (18) *Hogarth proof* || *first line of recto* (19) *Hogarth*

[III] 294 = 457 **By**] Beyond *ms2 2nd draft 1st reading*

[III] 295 = 458 **Supine**] Stretched *ms2 2nd draft* **narrow**] perilous *ms2 2nd draft, with slashes added around the word* **canoe."**] *Boni+* || canoe". *ms2 2nd draft, Q*

[III] 295 ^ 296] *new page so line spacing indeterminate 1925* || *no line space 1932 proof (added TSE)*

[III] 296 = 459 **"My**] My *T/W, ms1960* **are**] were *ms2 2nd draft 1st reading*

461 **promised**] offere *ms2 2nd draft 1st reading* **'a new start.'**] *originally with double quotation marks, emended by TSE ms2 2nd draft (because this is speech within quoted speech)* || 'a new start'. *Q, T/W, Sesame, Penguin, Mardersteig, 1971B*

[III] 299 = 462 **comment.**] outcry: *ms2 2nd draft 1st reading* || comment: *ms2 2nd draft 2nd reading* **What**] what *ms2 2nd draft* **should**] shd *ms2 2nd draft* **I**] I *(italicised by underlining) ms2 2nd draft* **resent?"**] resent? *Hogarth proof* || resent" *Hogarth (probably a proof correction error)*

[III] 299 ^ 300 = 462 ^ 463] *new page so line spacing indeterminate ms2, Q, 1932* || *no line space T 1st reading, W* || *no line space Boni* || *half-line space 1936* || *two-line space Valerie's Own Book, ms1960*

[III] 300–303 = 463–66] *ms2 1st draft:*

> "I was to be grateful. On Margate sands
> There were many others. I can connect
> Nothing with nothing. He had
> I still feel the pressure of dirty hand

with loop around I can connect | Nothing with nothing. *and finally all del*

[III] 300 **"On**] On *ms1960* **Sands.**] Sands, *Criterion*

[III] 303 = 466 **fingernails**] finger nails *ms2* || finger-nails *Dial, Criterion*

[III] 304 = 467 **humble**] are plain *ms2 1st reading* **people**] people, *ms2*

[III] 305 = 468 **Nothing."**] nothing". *ms2 1st reading* || Nothing". *ms2 2nd reading, Q, T/W*

[III] 305 ^ 306 = 468 ^ 469] *no line space Q, Boni+* || *line space ms2, T/W, Dial* || *no line space but leaded 1971B*

[III] 306 = 469 **la la**] la la *ms2, T/W*

[III] 306 ^ 307 = 469 ^ 470] *new page so line spacing indeterminate Criterion* || *no line space Mardersteig (overlooking the line space at the foot of page in Sesame, used as setting copy)*

[III] 307 = 470 **came**] came. *ms2*

[III] 308 = 471 **Burning burning burning burning**] *without extra word spacing T/W, Boni, Dial, Criterion, Hogarth, 1932+, Valerie's Own Book, WLFacs, 1971B* || Burning, burning, burning burning *1925 (the two commas removed in 2nd imp., but without extra word spacing)*. To P. M. Jack, 19 Jan 1927: "there are two commas to be deleted and I intended the four 'burnings' to be printed with double spacing between each."

[III] 309 = 472 **Thou**] thou *ms2, Valerie's Own Book 1st reading*

[III] 310 = 473 **Thou**] thou *ms2, Hogarth*

[III] 310 ^ 311] *no line space but leaded 1971B*

IV. *DEATH BY WATER*

The two drafts of Part IV are *ms5* (*WLFacs* 54–61), which is given in *WLComposite*, and *ts4* (*WLFacs* 62–69). On *ms5* Pound wrote "Bad—but cant attack until I get typescript", after which TSE typed *ts4*. The published poem resumes at [IV] 312 = 557.

475–86] *braced twice Pound ts4*

475 **The**] *repeated after a false start ts4* **attentive to the chart or to the sheets.**] *del Pound ts4*

476] *del Pound who additionally del* against *ts4*

477 **Retains,**] Retains., *ts4* ‖ *moved to end of line by Pound ts4* **even**] *del Pound ts4*

478 **clean, and**] *del Pound ts4*

479 **Even the**] *del Pound ts4* **ruffian who**] *del Pound ts4*

480 **backstreet**] *del Pound ts4* **to**] thence to *Pound ts4*

482 **comic**] *del Pound ts4* **gonorrhea**] gonnohrha *ts4 1st reading*

483 **From**] Yet from *ts4* **and snow, as they**] *del Pound ts4*

484 **Are, he is, with**] *del Pound ts4* **endured,"**] endured", *ts4*

485] *del Pound ts4*

486 ^ 487] *no asterisks, four-line space ts4*

487 **"Kingfisher weather**] Kingfisher weather *ts4 del Pound*

488] *del Pound ts4*

489 **and laid our course**] *del Pound ts4*

490 **to the eastern banks.**] *del Pound ts4*

491 **upon**] on *Pound ts4* **phosphorescent**] *del Pound ts4*

492] *del Pound ts4*

493–94] *del Pound ts4*

495–524] *left margin accidentally ragged (ts4 2nd leaf)*

495–96] *del Pound ts4*

496 **wrong.**] wrong, *ts4*

497 **A water cask was opened**] *ms5* ‖ Opened a water-cask *Pound transposition ts4* **water cask**] *ms5* ‖ watercask *WLFacs transcription of ms5* ‖ water-cask *ts4*

498 **Another brackish.**] *del Pound ts4* **Then the main gaffjaws**] The the main gaff jaws *del Pound ts4*

499–500 *del Pound with first and last words also individually del ts4*

501 **And then the**] The *Pound ts4* **garboard-strake**] garboard strake *ts4*

502 **baked**] *del Pound ts4* **only a putrid**] *del Pound ts4*

503 **one cut his hand.**] *del Pound ts4*

504–505] *del Pound ts4*

505 **Was over**] T̶o̶o̶k̶ l̶o̶ *ms5 1ˢᵗ reading* **over time**] overtime *ts4* **justified**] justified, *ts4*

506 **Extenuated thus:**] *del Pound ts4*

507 **eat—**] eat, *ts4*

508 **"For**] For *ts4*

509 **"From**] From *del Pound ts4* **every biscuit,**] *del Pound ts4* **there's**] theres *ts4*

510 **injurious**] *del Pound ts4*

510–11 **So ··· the ship.**] *del Pound ts4*

511 **windward,"**] windward", *ts4*

512] *del Pound ts4* **among**] amongst *ms5 2ⁿᵈ reading, ts4*

513 **coffin,**] ci *ts4 1ˢᵗ reading* ‖ coffin *ts4 2ⁿᵈ reading*

514 **"With**] With *ts4* **Hell**] hell *ts4*

515 **"This**] This *ts4* **windward."**] windward". *ts4*

516 **So the crew moaned;**] So the crew moaned, *ts4 1ˢᵗ reading* ‖ So the crew moaned. *ts4 2ⁿᵈ reading then del Pound* **voices**] woices *ts4* (voices *WLFacs*)

516–17 **the sea ··· moon,**] *del Pound ts4*

518–19] *del Pound ts4*

520 **at last. The**] at last, the *ts4 del Pound* **northern**] *ms5 1ˢᵗ reading, ts4 del Pound* ‖ eastern *ms5 2ⁿᵈ reading* **banks**] seas *ms5 1ˢᵗ reading, ts4 del Pound*

521 **Had**] *del Pound ts4*

523 **home,**] home *ts4* **dollars,**] dollars *ts4*

525–32] *del Pound ts4*

527 **us**] me *WLFacs transcription of ms5* (*corrected in the copy Valerie Eliot sent to I. A. Richards, now Magdalene, and in later printings*)

530 **stars**] stars. *ts4*

533] *five chevrons through line and five after by Pound ts4*

534–37] *del Pound ts4*

534 **islands**] islands, *ts4*

535 **ate slept drank**] *perhaps with extra word spacing (for punctuation) ms5*

539 **us.**] us," (*quotation marks and comma superimposed*) *ts4*

539–41 **One night ··· white hair.**] *del Pound ts4*

540 **cross-trees**] cross trees *ts4*

541 **women**] women w̶i̶t̶h̶ w̶ *ms5 1ˢᵗ reading* ‖ women w̶i̶t̶h̶ w̶h̶i̶t̶e̶ h̶a̶i̶r̶ *ts4 1ˢᵗ reading*

542 *three-sided glyph* ⊓ *Pound in ts4.* (Perhaps half of a transposition mark, drawing attention to the awkwardness of "white hair ··· who".)

543–46] *del Pound ts4*

546 **dream.**] dream, *ts4*

546 ^ 547] *line space ts4* ‖ *new leaf so line spacing indeterminate ms5*

547 **—Something**] Something *ts4*

551 **A wall, a barrier,**] ~~Toward which we~~ *ms5 1ˢᵗ reading*   **towards**] *last letter apparently a second thought ms5*

552–54] *del Pound ts4*

552 **there's**] theres *ts4*

553 **chance.**] chance, *ts4*

554 **Where's**] Wheres *ts4*   **here's**] heres *ts4*

555] *not ts4, which has a two-line space*

556 **Another**] Another *ts4*

557 ^ 558] *no asterisks, three-line space ts4*

Published poem resumes

[IV] 312 = 558 **Phoenician**] Phœnician *Criterion*

[IV] 313 = 559 **deep sea**] deep-sea *ms5, Criterion* ‖ sea *Penguin 2nd and 3rd imps.* (*1951, 1952*)   **swell**] swell, *Criterion*

[IV] 315 *as also* 319] *ranged right Dial, Hogarth*

[IV] 317 **stages**] stage *T 1ˢᵗ reading, W*

[IV] 318 ^ 319] *line space Criterion*

[IV] 319 = 565 **Jew**] Jew, *ms5, ts4, Criterion*

V. WHAT THE THUNDER SAID

The two drafts of Part V are *ms6* (*WLFacs* 70–81), which is given in *WLComposite*, and *ts5* (*WLFacs* 82–89).

Part title] *not ms6* ‖ *repeated on succeeding line, where it is more deeply indented T/W*   **said**] Said *Valerie's Own Book, ms1960 1ˢᵗ reading*

above [V] 322 = 568] *"OK" (green crayon) then "OK from here on I think" Pound ms6*

[V] 322 = 568] *see After the turning of the inspired days 6–7:* "After the judges and the advocates and wardens | And the torchlight red on sweaty faces".

[V] 322] *indent 1963 (not 1963 proof, US 1963)*   **faces**] faces, *ts5*

[V] 323 = 569 **gardens**] gardens, *ts5 with last letter and comma ringed by Pound*

[V] 324 = 570 **places**] places, *ts5*

[V] 325 = 571 **crying**] crying, *ts5*

[V] 326 = 572 **Prison**] Gardens *ms6 1ˢᵗ reading* ‖ Prisons *ms6 2ⁿᵈ reading*   **palace**] palaces *ms6 1ˢᵗ reading* ‖ Palace *T 1ˢᵗ reading, W* ‖ place *1971B (later corrected)*   **reverberation**] Reverberation *T 1ˢᵗ reading, W*

[V] 327 = 573 **over**] ~~of~~ *ms6 1ˢᵗ reading*   **distant**] the *ms6 1ˢᵗ reading*   **mountains**] mountains; *ts5*

[V] 328 = 574 **He who was**] He was *ts5, with* who *added Pound*   **dead**] dead, *ms6, ts5*

[V] 333 = 579 **above**] ahead *ms6 1ˢᵗ reading*

[V] 335] If there were only water amongst the rock *Dial (eye-skip to* [V] 338)   **and drink**] or think *T 1ˢᵗ reading, W (eye-skip to* [V] 336)

[V] 336 = 582 **Amongst**] Among *ms6 1ˢᵗ reading*

[V] 337 = 583 **Sweat**] The sweat *ms6, ts5 ringed Pound*   **feet**] the feet *ms6, ts7 ringed Pound*   **are in the sand**] cannot stop *ms6 1ˢᵗ reading*

[V] 338 = 584 **amongst**] *2ⁿᵈ & final readings ms6, ts5+* ‖ among *1ˢᵗ & 3ʳᵈ readings ms6*

[V] 338 ^ 339] *line space 1936 proof, removed by TSE*

[V] 339 = 585 **mountain**] mount in *Boni later copies, Boni 2nd imp. (1923), (corrected 3rd and 4th printings, 1928, 1930)* ‖ mountian *1932 proof, corrected TSE.* (TSE to Elizabeth Manwaring, 21 Jan 1936: "if you found the word 'mountain' spelt without an 'a' it must be a misprint. I am glad that they did not put a 'g' on the end as well.")   **of**] with *ms6 1ˢᵗ reading*   **carious**] rotten *ms6 2ⁿᵈ reading* ‖ *not Hogarth proof*

[V] 340 = 586 **nor lie nor**] or lie or *ts5 1ˢᵗ reading, emended Pound*

[V] 341 = 587 **in**] ~~among~~ *ts5 1ˢᵗ reading* ‖ on *1932 proof, corrected TSE*   **mountains**] *last letter boxed Pound ts5*

[V] 342 = 588] But red sullen faces sneer and snarl *Guild (eye-skip to* [V] 344)   **without**] and no *ms6*

[V] 343 = 589 **the**] these *ms6*

[V] 344 ^ 345 = 590 ^ 591] *new page so line spacing indeterminate Q, T/W* ‖ *line space Criterion, Valerie's Own Book*

[V] 345 = 591, 592

  no medial line space] *Boni, Dial, Hogarth+* ‖ *medial line space ms6, ts5, Criterion, Valerie's Own Book, ms1960* ‖ *new leaf so line spacing indeterminate Q, T/W*

  overhanging step] *Criterion, 1925, 1936, 1963* ‖ *new line, inset ms6* ‖ *stepped ts5, Q, T/W, Dial* ‖ *overhanging step with second part ranged right Boni, Valerie's Own Book, ms1960* ‖ *stepped with second part reaching right margin Hogarth*

  numbered as one line] *Boni, 1936, 1963* ‖ *unnumbered ms6, ts5, T/W, Dial, Criterion Hogarth, Valerie's Own Book, ms1960* ‖ *numbered as two lines Q, 1925, US 1952, US 1963, some later British printings.* The words "From doors · · · water" have been counted in some printings as one line, in some as two. Neither adjudication can be definitive. The present edition counts them as one so as to conform to the line numbering of most of the important lifetime editions, including the first, *Boni*, and the last, *1963*. In addition, TSE counted only one line when numbering by hand the ts of Menasce's French translation. Of the four original settings, only *Boni* had line numbering, and it counted one line here (unlike similar dubieties at 314–15 and 422–23). Unfortunately, *1925* and *The Faber Book of Modern Verse* attempted to count two here while maintaining the same total number of lines in the poem, with the result that too many lines appear between the marginal numbers 350 and 360. After that, *1936* and *1963* reverted to counting one stepped line. For some reason, *US 1952* made the same mistake as *1925*, again with an extra line between 350 and 360. This was rectified in *US 1963* not by counting one stepped line here, but by adjusting the marginal numbering from here on, adding one to the total, and adjusting the numbering in the Notes from 401 onwards (but neglecting the Notes to 357, 360 and 366–76). British and American line-counts then differed until the counting of an extra line was adopted by Faber in 2002 when resetting *Collected Poems 1909–1962* and *Selected Poems*, although the original numbering remained in reprints of *Sesame*.

"From doors of mudcracked houses" is the last line of the first leaf of the manuscript (*ms6*), with a line of space beneath. The first fourteen lines on the second leaf, beginning "If there were water", are evenly inset. In the typescript (*ts5*), "If there were water" is stepped down from the end of "From doors of mudcracked houses", although with a line space between them. The subsequent lines are not inset. The nineteen-page typescript from Quinn's office (*Q*) also has such a step. Although not used as setting copy for the poem, *Q* (like *T/W*) may here preserve the pagination of the lost typing by TSE in July 1922, with indeterminate line spacing because "If there were water" begins a new leaf. *Boni* and *Dial* have no line space (and nor have *Hogarth, 1925* and *1936* which derive from *Boni*) but a line space is present in *Criterion*. TSE left a line space in both *Valerie's Own Book* and *ms1960* when copying out the poem, over-riding the reading of the late impression of *1936* from which he was copying (see also the spelling of "aetherial", [V] 415 = 661).

[V] 346–58 = 593–605] *not inset ts5, T/W, Dial, Criterion, Hogarth.* (In *ms6* this desert description is inset, apparently to match "The river sweats": *WLFacs* 48–49, 72–73.)

[V] 347 = 594 **rock**] no rock *T/W*

[V] 353 = 600 **cicada**] cicada, and *ms6*

[V] 354 = 601 **And dry**] The dry *ms6 1ˢᵗ reading* ‖ Dry *ms6*

[V] 355 = 602 **a**] *not ms6 1ˢᵗ reading*

[V] 356 = 603 **hermit-thrush**] hermit thrush *ms6, ts5, ms1960*   **sings**] *not ms6 1ˢᵗ reading*   **pine trees**] *ts5, Q, Boni* ‖ pines *ms6 1ˢᵗ reading* ‖ pinetrees *ms6, Valerie's Own Book* ‖ pine tree *T/W* ‖ pine-trees *Criterion*

[V] 357 = 604] Drip-drop   drop   drop   drop *ms6 1ˢᵗ reading* ‖ Drip-drop drip-drop   drop   drop   drop *ms6* (*both with extra word spacing*)

[V] 358 = 605 **there**] here *ms6 1ˢᵗ reading*

[V] 359 = 606 **who**] that *ms6*   **always**] *not ms6 1ˢᵗ reading*   **beside**] besides *ms6 1ˢᵗ reading*

[V] 360 = 607 **count,**] count *Hogarth*   **there**] it *ts5 alt by Pound bracketed by TSE*   **are**] *ts5 bracketed alt, Q, T/W, Boni+* ‖ is *ms6, ts5*

[V] 362 = 609 **one**] *not ms6 1ˢᵗ reading*   **walking**] walking ~~there~~ *ms6 2ⁿᵈ reading*

[V] 363 **wrapt**] wrapped *Hogarth*

[V] 364 = 611 **or a**] or *ms6 1ˢᵗ reading*

[V] 365 **—But**] But *Criterion*

[V] 365 ^ 366 = 612 ^ 613] *new page so line spacing indeterminate Boni, 1971B* ‖ *no line space Hogarth proof, where* 366 *is last line of page* 22 *(moved to page* 23 *in Hogarth)* ‖ *no line space but typed rule apparently as substitute T/W* ‖ *two-line space Valerie's Own Book, ms1960*

[V] 366–76 **What is that sound · · · Unreal**] *in the copy of Boni given by TSE to Vivien, this passage is scored, probably by her.*

[V] 366 **the air**] the air, *Criterion* ‖ air *Valerie's Own Book*

[V] 369 = 616 **endless**] Polish *ms6 1ˢᵗ reading* ‖ perished *ms6 2ⁿᵈ reading* **plains,**] plains. *ts5 1ˢᵗ reading* ‖ plain, *T/W*

[V] 370 = 617 **by**] with *ms6* ‖ iby *ts5 emended by Pound to* in by *and then to* by **the flat horizon only**] a flat horizon, only. *ms6*

[V] 370 ^ 371 = 617 ^ 618] *new leaf so line spacing indeterminate Q, T/W* ‖ *line space Criterion.* (If *Q* and *T/W* preserve the pagination of TSE's lost typing of July 1922, the typesetter of *Criterion* may have inserted a line space where the ts leaf ended. See [V] 345 = **591, 592**.)

[V] 372 = 619 **and bursts**] *ms6 alt, ts5, Q, Boni*+ ‖ and breaks *ms6* ‖ *not T/W*

[V] 373 = 620 **Falling**] Tumbling *ms6 1ˢᵗ reading*

[V] 374 = 621 **Jerusalem Athens**] Jerusalem, Athens, *ms6*

[V] 375 = 622 **Vienna London**] Vienna, London. Unreal *ms6 1ˢᵗ reading* ‖ Vienna, London. *ms6*

[V] 376 = 623] *not ms6 1ˢᵗ reading*

[V] 376 ^ 377 = 623 ^ 624] *no line space 1936, where* [V] 377 *is last on page, Guild, Penguin, Sel Poems 1954 (corrected long after)* ‖ *two-line space Valerie's Own Book, ms1960.* Clarabut's *Criterion* contains a note dated 18 Nov 1942: "He states there is, correctly, a space here after 'unreal'; in the collected edition this has been omitted, but he is still hoping to have it put right in the future—conversation with C. E. R. Clarabut". In *Washington copy 1954* TSE wrote "<" (pencil) and "space" (ballpoint) following which, in 1961, the final impression of *1936* was emended by reducing the leading of line spaces above to allow more space here. The space was consistently present in American eds.

[V] 377] *indent US 1952, 1963 (not 1963 proof, US 1963)*

[V] 377–78 = 623–24] see *So through the evening, through the violet air* 13–16.

[V] 379 = 625 **faces**] faces, *ms6, ts5* **light**] ai̶r̶ *ms6 1ˢᵗ reading* ‖ light, *ms6*

[V] 381–84 = 627–30] see *So through the evening, through the violet air* 19–22.

[V] 381 = 627 **And crawled head**] A man crawled *ms6 1ˢᵗ reading* ‖ A form crawled *ms6, ts5 1ˢᵗ reading*

[V] 383 = 629 **Tolling**] Telling *Criterion (corrected TSE in Clarabut's Criterion)* **bells**] bell *T/W* **hours**] hours. *ms6*

[V] 384 = 630 **wells.**] wells *T 1ˢᵗ reading, W, US 1963*

[V] 384 ^ 385 = 630 ^ 631] *line space, then*:

> The infant hydrocephalous, who sat
> By a bridge end, by a dried up water course
> And fiddled (with a knot tied in one string)
>
> We come

ms6 (with By *emended to* At) *all del, end of leaf*

[V] 387 = **633 chapel**] chapel, *ms6*

[V] 388 = **634 home.**] home, *ms6, ts5, Q, T/W, Dial, Hogarth* ‖ home *Criterion*

[V] 389 = **635 It has**] There are *ms6 1ˢᵗ reading*   **door swings,**] door's swing; *ms6 1ˢᵗ reading (perhaps* doors swing; *as given in WLFacs)*

[V] 391 = **637 Only**] Only, *ms6 2ⁿᵈ reading.* The comma, subsequently rescinded, would have indicated that the sense was not OED "only" A. 1. "nothing more or else than", but B. 1b. "with the exception that". Three lines prior to this, "only the wind's home" could be either A., "home of the wind *and nothing else*" or B., *"with the exception that* the wind is at home". (An example of A. is *"Only the wind moves | Over empty fields"*, *Choruses from "The Rock"* I 99–100. An example of B. is *"Only | There is shadow"*, *The Waste Land* [I] 25–26. See also *Ash-Wednesday* II 22–23: "the wind only for only | The wind".)   **cock**] black cock *ms6, ts5 with* black *boxed by Pound*   **rooftree**] roof treee *ts5 1ˢᵗ reading* (roof trees *WLFacs in error*) ‖ roof tree *ts5 2ⁿᵈ reading* ‖ roof-tree *Dial, Criterion, Hogarth*

[V] 392 = **638** *extra word spacing* ("Co co   rico   co co   rico")] *Q, Boni, Dial, 1925, Faber Bk Mod V, 1936 (very slight)* ‖ *some extra spacing and extra capital* ("Co co rico   Co co rico") *ms6* ‖ *no extra spacing ts5, Criterion, Hogarth, Sesame, Penguin, Mardersteig, 1963, 1969, 1971B*

[V] 393 = **639 lightning. Then**] lightning, then *ms6*

[V] 394 = **640 rain**] rain . . . *ms6*

[V] 394 ^ 395 = **640 ^ 641**] *new leaf so line spacing indeterminate Q* ‖ *no line space Boni*

[V] 396 = **642 Waited**] Writhed *ms6 1ˢᵗ reading*   **rain**] ~~the~~ rain *ms6 (the second word perhaps over a previous uncertain word)*

[V] 398 = **644 silence.**] silence". *ts5 (quotation marks and full stop superimposed with quotation marks del)*

[V] 399 = **645 Then**] The *T 1ˢᵗ reading, W*

[V] 400 = **646**] *indent ts5*

[V] 400 *as also* 417 = **646, 663 DA**] DA *ms6, ts5, Q, T/W, Criterion*

[V] 401 *as also* 411, 418 = **647, 657, 664**] *typewriter tab space between first and second words ts5, Q, T/W*

[V] 401 = **647 Datta:**] *Q, Boni, Dial, 1925+* ‖ DATTA. ~~well then~~ *ms6 (with a blot over the last two words, where WLFacs suggests* we brother *as a "very doubtful reading")* ‖ Datta: *(roman colon) ts5, T/W, Criterion, Hogarth, Mardersteig, 1971B*   **what**] What *Q, T/W, Criterion*

[V] 402 = **648 blood shaking**] my friend, beating in *ms6 1ˢᵗ reading* ‖ my blood shaking ~~within~~ *ms6*   **heart**] heart, *ms6, ts5*

[V] 404 = **650 can never**] cannot *ms6 1ˢᵗ reading*   **retract**] retract— *ms6*

[V] 405 = **651 existed**] existed, *ms6, ts5*

[V] 406 = **652 obituaries**] obituary. *ms6 1ˢᵗ reading* ‖ obituaries. *ms6*

[V] 407 = **653 Or**] Nor *ms6*   **memories**] *ms6 final reading+* ‖ that which *ms6 1ˢᵗ reading* ‖ those treasures *ms6 2ⁿᵈ reading*   **draped by**] *ms6 final reading+* ‖ will busy *ms6 1ˢᵗ reading* ‖ over which creeps *ms6 2ⁿᵈ reading* ‖ shrouded by *ms6 3ʳᵈ reading*   **the beneficent**] *ms6 final reading* ‖ beneficent *ms6 1ˢᵗ reading* ‖

the beneficent / kindly / industrious *ms6 2ⁿᵈ reading alts*   **spider**] spiders *ms6*
1ˢᵗ reading

[V] 408 = 654 **Or**] Nor *ms6*   **under seals broken**] in documents eaten *ms6 1ˢᵗ*
reading

[V] 409 = 655 **rooms**] rooms. *ms6, ts5*

[V] 410 = 656 **DA**] DA. *ms6* ‖ DA *ts5, Q, T/W, Criterion*

[V] 411 = 657 ***Dayadhvam:***] Dayadhvam. *ms6* ‖ *Dayadhvam: (roman colon) ts5, T/W,*
Criterion, Hogarth, Mardersteig, 1971B ‖ Dayadhvam: *Hogarth proof*   **I**] ~~friend,~~
~~my friend~~ I *ms6*

[V] 412 = 658 **once**] once, *Valerie's Own Book*

[V] 413 = 659 **prison**] prison, *ms6*

[V] 414 = 660] *not T/W (eye-skip)*   **confirms**] has built *ms6 1ˢᵗ reading*   **prison**]
prison. *ms6*

[V] 415 = 661 **aethereal**] *1925+* ‖ aetherial *ms6, ts5, Q, T/W, Boni, Dial, Hogarth,*
Valerie's Own Book, ms1960 ‖ æthereal *Criterion*   **rumours**] murmurs *ms6 1ˢᵗ*
reading

[V] 416 = 662] Repair the *ms6 1ˢᵗ reading* ‖ Repair for a moment a broken Coriolanus,
ms6 2ⁿᵈ reading ‖ Restore for a moment a broken Coriolanus, *ms6 3ʳᵈ reading* ‖
Revive the spirits of a broken Coriolanus, *ms6 4ᵗʰ reading* ‖ Revive for a moment
a broken Coriolanus, *ms6 final reading*   **Coriolanus**] Coriolanus. *ts5, Valerie's*
Own Book

[V] 418 = 664 ***Damyata:***] Damyata. ~~the wind was fair, and~~ *ms6* ‖ *Damyata: (roman*
colon) ts5, Q, Criterion, Hogarth, Mardersteig, 1971B ‖ Demyata: *T/W (see also* [V]
432) ‖ Damyata. *ms1960*   **The**] the *ms6*

[V] 419 = 665 **oar**] wheel. *ms6 1ˢᵗ reading* ‖ rudder. *ms6 2ⁿᵈ reading* ‖ oar. *ms6 final*
reading, Criterion

[V] 420 = 666 **calm,**] calm; *Criterion*   **your heart would have**] and your heart *ms6*
1ˢᵗ reading

[V] 421 = 667 **obedient**] responsive *ms6 1ˢᵗ reading*

[V] 422 = 668 **hands**] hands. I left without you *ms6 1ˢᵗ reading* ‖ You over on the shore
ms6 2ⁿᵈ reading ‖ There I leave you *ms6 final reading*

[V] 422 ^ 423 = 668 ^ 669] *no line space ms6, Faber Bk Mod V* ‖ *new page so line spacing*
indeterminate Q, T/W ‖ *two-line space 1974*

[V] 423 = 669] *indented beyond end of previous line but not ranged right 1936+* ‖ *ms6*
beginning at left margin ‖ *indented to align with end of previous line ts5 (this indent*
is equivalent to the space occupied by the words deleted in ms6), Q ‖ *ranged right*
T/W, Hogarth, 1925, Faber Bk Mod V ‖ *indented to align with end of previous line*
and also ranged right Dial   **I sat upon the shore**] ~~Clasping empty hands~~ I sit
upon the shore *ms6 1ˢᵗ reading* ‖ ~~Clasping empty hands~~ I sat upon a shore *ms6*
2ⁿᵈ reading.

[V] 424 = 670 **the arid plain**] the desolate sunset *ms6 1ˢᵗ reading* ‖ a desolate sunset
ms6 2ⁿᵈ reading

[V] 425 = 671 **Shall**] Which now at last *ms6 1ˢᵗ reading* ‖ Can *ms6 2ⁿᵈ reading*   **set**]
see *Criterion (corrected TSE in Clarabut's Criterion)*   **my**] the *ms6 1ˢᵗ*

reading   **lands**] kingdom *ms6 1ˢᵗ reading* ‖ lands *ms6 2ⁿᵈ reading* ‖ own lands *ms6 3ʳᵈ reading* ‖ land *ms6 final reading*

[V] 425 ^ 426 = 671 ^ 672] *line space ts5, T/W, Boni, Dial, Hogarth* ‖ *new page, although almost half the previous page is blank ms6* ‖ *new page so line spacing indeterminate Criterion* ‖ *no line space 1925+, Valerie's Own Book, ms1960*

[V] 426 = 672 **falling down falling down falling down**] falling down, falling down, falling down *ts5* ‖ falling down falling down *T/W*

[V] 426 ^ 427] *new page so line spacing indeterminate Boni, 1969* ‖ *no line space Hogarth, 1925+*

[V] 427–29 = 673–75] *all roman ms6, ts5, Q, T/W, Criterion*

[V] 427 = 673 *foco*] *Boni, Dial, Hogarth+* ‖ fuoco *ms6, ts5, Q* ‖ foco *T/W, Criterion*   *gli*] *li Mardersteig*   *affina*] affina. *ms6*. For changes in this line see Mardersteig's letter of 27 June 1961, quoted in the Textual History of the "Notes on The Waste Land" 427.

[V] 428 = 674] Why then Ile fit you. Hieronimo's mad againe. *ms6 1ˢᵗ reading*   *uti*] *1936+, emendation by TSE in Clarabut's Criterion* ‖ ceu *ms6, ts5, Q, T/W* ‖ *ceu printings prior to 1936, Faber Bk Mod V* ‖ *cen Hogarth proof, emended to ceu by TSE. See Commentary.*

[V] 429 = 675 *Prince*] prince *ms6*   *à*] *Boni, Dial, Hogarth, 1925+* ‖ de *ms6, ts5, Q, T (with à added by Watson as alt with "?"), Criterion* ‖ *á Hogarth proof, corrected TSE*   *tour abolie*] Tour Abolie *T 1ˢᵗ reading, W*

[V] 429 ^ 430 = 675 ^ 676] *line space Hogarth*

[V] 430 = 676 **shored against**] *ms6 alt, ts5+* ‖ spelt into *ms6*   **ruins**] ruins. *ms6*

[V] 431 = 676 ^ 677] *not ms6 1ˢᵗ reading (but added when 674 was emended)*   **then**] the *T/W (with "?" T)*   **Hieronymo's**] Hieronimo's *ms6*

[V] 432, 433] *italic Dial*

[V] 432 = 677 **Datta. Dayadhvam.**] Datta, dayadhvam, *ms6 1ˢᵗ reading* ‖ Datta. Dayadhvam, *ms6 2ⁿᵈ reading*   **Damyata.**] damyata. *ms6* ‖ Demyata. *T/W (see* [V] 418)

[V] 432 ^ 433] *no line space 1925+*

[V] 433 = 678] *widely word-spaced ms6, ts5, Q, T/W, printings prior to 1936, Faber Bk Mod V, US 1936 and later US eds., Valerie's Own Book, ms1960* ‖ *little or no extra word spacing Criterion, 1936+*   **Shantih   shantih   shantih**] Shantih   shantih   shantih. *ms6* ‖ Shantih , shantih , shantih . *WLLetter* ‖ Shantih   Shantih   Shantih *T/W*

[V] 432–33] For readers without Sanskrit, the effect of the last two lines (the first of three words, the second of one word thrice) depends partly upon their spacing. *Boni, Dial, Criterion, Hogarth* all have a line space between the two lines, and all indent the last. Each word in 432 has a full stop, but 433 has no stops. Instead, the words of 433 should be widely spaced (compare 392 and 308). The effect is clear in *Dial* (though it italicises these two lines without apparent authority). But the three other primary texts follow the convention of double spacing after a full stop (as TSE did himself when typing). As a result, in *Hogarth* the double spacing of 433 is the same as that of 432, changing the visual effect. *Boni* too has double spaces after stops, but maintains a distinction by triple-spacing 433

(*1925* follows this). *Criterion* is least satisfactory, because it has double spaces as usual after the stops, but has ordinary word-spaces in 433, making this final line actually tighter than the line before. TSE's two late fair copies, *Valerie's Own Book* and *ms1960* give:

Datta. Dayadhvam. Damyata.

Shantih   shantih   shantih

Notes on the Waste Land

Line numbers are emended to match those of the poem in the present edition, with variants from previous editions listed (see Textual Note to [V] 345 = 591, 592).

As early as 1928, when the American first edition of the poem was reset, it was realised that TSE had been inconsistent about the italicising of titles, and uniformity was imposed. Yet *1963* still had both "Inferno" and "*Inferno*". In the present edition, as in *Sesame* and *US 1963*, titles are italicised throughout, always with a comma before book, canto, act, scene and line numbers. *Sesame* also italicised the names of books of the Bible in the Notes to 20 and 23, but TSE followed standard practice so roman type is preferred here, and no comma is introduced before chapter numbers. Variants from earlier editions are not listed. TSE sometimes wrote "l." before line numbers but sometimes did not, even in consecutive notes. This is easily mistaken for and was sometimes set as "I.", and for consistency within his Notes and with the practice elsewhere in the present edition, "l." has been silently omitted. Many printings have italicised colons and semi-colons following italicised titles. These are silently emended to roman type. TSE's use of both "V." (L. *vide* = see) and "Cf." (L. *confer* = compare) is retained.

Verse quotations are all inset and aligned with one another, following *Sesame*, *US 1952* and *US 1963*. (The failure of other editions to do so was a legacy of the excessive type size on a narrow measure in *Boni*, where the Notes first appeared.) As elsewhere, Dante's words and *terza rima* indents are made to conform to the text of the Temple Classics.

TSE was inconsistent about quotation marks. Some but not all of the extracts from other writers in the Notes are enclosed within quotation marks, even when inset. Within these, speech is sometimes indicated by further quotation marks. In some cases, quotation marks recur at the opening of each line (see Commentary to [I] 69–76 on this convention), although this was not the practice of the Temple Classics Dante.

When the final lifetime edition (*1963*) was in preparation, TSE marked up a copy of *1936* 15th imp. (1954), although this impression was not the most recent. In this copy, *Washington copy 1954*, typed slips are pasted over each of the inset quotations from Dante except that in the Note to 293. The lines on the slips apparently follow the *Mardersteig* (1962) both verbally and in the deletion of enclosing quotation marks. The only quotation marks on the slips are in the Note to 427, which quotes four lines of *Purgatorio*. The first line begins with opening quotation marks, and the third has closing quotation marks before its final full stop, denoting that these three lines are spoken by Arnaut (from a passage italicised in the Temple edition). Both *Mardersteig* and the typed slip eliminate the quotation marks at the start of the second and third of these lines.

TSE evidently intended to bring order to the thicket of quotation marks in his Notes. Yet his emendations in *Washington copy 1954* were not systematic. Despite the simplified treatment of Arnaut's lines, recurring quotation marks remained in the speech of la Pia (in the Note that was not retyped, to 293); and a contrary mistake was made in the Note to 411, where *all* quotation marks were removed from the *Inferno* passage even though these lines too are spoken (by Ugolino). Both enclosing and recurring quotation marks also remained around passages from other authors.

The text of *1963* appears to have been set with reference to *Washington copy 1954* but without following it consistently. For instance, it follows TSE's marks in correcting the lineation and a spelling mistake in the quotation from the *Aeneid* (92; corrected also in *Mardersteig*). But in the first line of the passage from Ovid (218), the compositor of *1963* not only followed TSE's instruction to move the quotation mark from the beginning of the line to its proper place before "maior" (where Jove begins speaking), but changed the spelling to "major". (*Mardersteig* has the quotation mark incorrectly at the head of the line.) If TSE had used the latest impression of *1936* for his corrections, no change would have been necessary here, for the position of the quotation mark had been rectified in the 17th impression (1959). The quotations from Dante fared badly too in *1963*, which followed the slips pasted into *Washington copy 1954* when it removed the enclosing quotation marks from the Notes to 63 and 64, but failed to do so for the Notes to 411 and 427.

The quotation marks in the Notes are therefore unsatisfactory: first, in editions before *1963*; second, in *Washington copy 1954*; and third, in *1963*. The present edition aims to fulfil TSE's impulse to remove unnecessary enclosing quotation marks around inset verse extracts. However, recurring quotation marks at the beginning of successive lines, though not consistently employed, are characteristic of the poem itself (for instance at [I] 35-36 and [I] 69-76). So in the Notes, the present edition chooses to retain them, even if they do not represent speech, as in the quotation from Baudelaire (60). It also retains the quotation marks enclosing Flamineo's words from *The White Devil* (407), where TSE's quotation begins with an ellipsis. Variants in the use of quotation marks are not listed, except in the Note to 218. The Penguin *Selected Poems* generally put full stops after, rather than before, closing quotation marks, and was followed in this by Faber's *Selected Poems* of 1954; later Faber impressions reverted to the previous punctuation, and instances are not listed.

Among the other emendations made by TSE in *Washington copy 1954* were three verbal changes in the Note to 427 which were proposed by Giovanni Mardersteig, in the "Ara vos prec" passage quoted from the *Purgatorio*. Sending proofs of his limited edition to Faber on 27 June 1961, Mardersteig wrote: "*Purgatorio* XXVI, 148-51—All editions of the last forty years which I have consulted (including that of the Società Dantesca and the Italian edition of *The Waste Land* translated by Mario Praz) agree as to the spelling of the Provençal words, but differ from that of the English edition · · · To me it seems that it would be better in our edition to conform with standard practice." The text he proposed and printed in the Notes reads:

> "Ara vos prec, per aquella valor
> que vos condus al som de l'escalina,
> sovenha vos a temps de ma dolor."
> Poi s'ascose nel foco che li affina.

That is, as Mardersteig wrote in the margin of the proofs: "*condus* for *guida*", "*sovenha* for *sovenga*" (although TSE had the accepted spelling, *sovegna*), and "*li* for *gli*". Returning the proofs, David Bland wrote that TSE had asked that this be checked because "his edition, that of the Società Dantesca Italiana, gives 'guida' and you have altered it to 'condus' · · · Mr Eliot is quite prepared to agree with you if you are sure of your reading" (Faber archive). The changes to this Note were adopted in the limited edition and in *1963*. For consistency, Mardersteig also changed the quotation in the poem itself at [V] 427, but this was not done in *1963*. The change to "sovenha" was also unfortunate, because TSE had quoted "Sovegna vos" again in *Ash-Wednesday* IV. Subsequent editions and reprints have treated these three verbal changes inconsistently, with "condus" usually remaining, while "sovenha" and "li" have usually been rejected. In a memo of 21 Oct 1969 Valerie Eliot asked that "guida" be reinstated (Faber archive). In the present edition, the words of the Temple Classics edition, long cherished by TSE, have been restored.

Collated:

Boni proof (Princeton): stamped "THE PLIMPTON PRESS | DATE AUG 26 1922 GALS. PP. | AUTHOR'S PROOFS | CONTAINING PROOFREADER'S MARKS | PLEASE RETURN", and marked in unknown hand. Four galley proofs (headed respectively ZB 15, UP 18, XE 12 and UP 59) cut into fourteen pieces, intended to correspond to final pages. The first three galleys signed off, perhaps by a printer's reader, "PL/ LH". Half-title leaf (fol. 1) with "Here it is. I have added some notes of my own along the margin—as a result of my researches—" The numbering of the lines was more often wrong than right, but without pattern. Some corrections not marked by the reader were made before *Boni* was printed.

Boni

2nd, 3rd and 4th printings of Boni (1923; then, under the imprint Horace Liveright, 1928, 1930)

1971B

Hogarth proof

Hogarth

1925

1932

1936

Sesame

Penguin

US 1952

Sel Poems 1954

Washington copy 1954

US 1963

Title **Notes on the Waste Land**] *1936, Penguin, 1963+* || NOTES *Boni, Hogarth, 1925* || NOTES ON THE WASTE LAND *Sesame* || NOTES ON *THE WASTE LAND Sel Poems 1954* || NOTES ON "THE WASTE LAND" *US 1952, US 1963+*

Author's headnote **of the poem**] *not Hogarth proof, added TSE*   **Ritual**] *with inverted "t" Hogarth proof, corrected TSE*   **(Cambridge)**] *1925+* || (Oxford) *Boni proof, emended, probably later, to correct reading* || (Macmillan) *Boni, Hogarth* || Cambridge Univ. Press *TSE's emendation in copies of Hogarth including that sent to his mother (Houghton)*   **Adonis, Attis, Osiris**] *1936+* || Atthis Adonis Osiris *Boni, Hogarth, 1925*

Part numbers and titles] *full capitals Boni, 1925* ‖ *full capitals ranged left Hogarth* ‖ *small capitals 1932+*

I. THE BURIAL OF THE DEAD

20 **II, i**] 2: 7 *1971B (emended to 2: 1 in later printings)*

23] *not Hogarth* **XII, v**] 12: 5 *1971B*

42 **Id.**] *not Boni proof*

46 **people",**] *1936+* ‖ people," *printings prior to 1936, US 1936, US 1952* **Man with Three Staves**] man with Three Staves *Hogarth*

60] *quotation inset Sesame, US 1952, US 1963* ‖ *ranged left other printings* **rêves**] *1925+* ‖ rêves *Boni, Hogarth* **"Où**] Oú *Hogarth* ‖ Ou *1974* **passant."**] passant. *Hogarth*

63] *Washington copy 1954 has a typed slip over the original note, which is del in blue ink. Third line of quotation on new page 1932 and thence incorrectly indented 1936+ (except Sesame) as also Washington copy 1954 (slip)* **si**] *Temple, emendation in TSE's 1949 and Washington copy 1954 (black ink), 1936 18th imp. (1961), Mardersteig* ‖ si *printings prior to 1936 18th imp. (1961), 1963+* **avrei mai**] *printings prior to Mardersteig, all US eds* ‖ averei *Mardersteig, Washington copy 1954 (slip), 1963, 1969, 1974 (later corrected)* **creduto**] *printings, Washington copy 1954 (slip)* ‖ creduto, *Temple*

64] *Washington copy 1954 has a typed slip over the original note, which is del in pencil. Second and third lines of quotation indented Temple, Sesame, Washington copy 1954 (slip)* ‖ *not indented other printings* 25–27] 2v–27 *Hogarth* **ascoltare**] ascolatre *1969 (later corrected)* **pianto,**] *Temple, printings prior to 1963 (except Mardersteig), US 1963+* ‖ piante *Washington copy 1954 (slip), 1963, 1969, 1974* ‖ pianto *Mardersteig, reprints of 1974+* **ma'**] *Temple, printings prior to 1963 (except Hogarth), US 1963+* ‖ ma *Hogarth* ‖ mai *Mardersteig, Washington copy 1954 (slip), 1963, 1969, 1974 (later reverting)* **sospiri,**] *Temple, printings prior to 1963, US 1963+* ‖ sospiri *Mardersteig, Washington copy 1954 (slip), 1963+*

II. A GAME OF CHESS

92] *first line of quotation not indented Sesame* ‖ *quotation set as prose (first line ending* incensi,*) Hogarth proof, 1925, US 1936* ‖ *prose (first line ending* noctem*) 1936, Penguin, Sel Poems 1954, US 1963* ‖ *prose (first line ending* et*) Guild* ‖ *prose (first line ending* flammis*) US 1952* ‖ *TSE wrote "begin 2nd line" after* aureis *in Washington copy 1954* **dependent**] *printings prior to 1936, TSE emendation Washington copy 1954 (pencil), 1936 final two imps. (1959, 1961), 1963+* ‖ dependant *1936, Guild, Penguin, Sel Poems 1954 (corrected long after)*

99 **Ovid,**] Ovid. *Hogarth*

100 **III,**] III *Hogarth, Boni* **204.**] 207. *Boni proof*

115 **III,**] III *Hogarth, Boni* **195.**] 196. *Boni proof*

118] *Note misnumbered as* 119 *Boni proof*

125] *Note omitted Hogarth* ‖ *Note misnumbered as* 126 *Boni+, emended Hayward in his proof of 1936* **39,**] 37, *Boni, 1925+, emended by Hayward in his proof of 1936*

137] *Note misnumbered as* 138 *all eds except Hogarth, emended Hayward in his proof of 1936* ‖ *misnumbered as* 126 *Hogarth* (*presumably following Boni numbering of previous Note*)

137 ^ 176] *no section title 1936 proof*

III. THE FIRE SERMON

Part number **III.**] III.. *Hogarth*

192] *no full stop after Note number Hogarth*

196, 197] *Notes misnumbered and transposed Boni* (*Boni proof has notes in correct order but numbered 197, 198*), *Hogarth* (*Hogarth proof has inverted full stop after "197"*), *1925*

196 **Mistress.**] *printings prior to 1936 11th imp.*, *Penguin, Sel Poems 1954, US 1963, 1974+* ‖ *Mistress 1936 11th–18th imps.* (1947–61; *broken type*), *1963*

197] *quotation not inset Boni, 1925   no quotation marks Hogarth*   **Actaeon**] Actaon *Hogarth proof* ‖ Actæon *Hogarth*

199 **taken:**] *1925+* ‖ taken; *Boni, Hogarth*

202 **Parsifal.**] *Parsifal.. Hogarth*

210 **cost insurance and freight**] *TSE emendation Washington copy 1954* (*blue ink*), *1963+* ‖ carriage and insurance free *printings prior to 1963*   **Lading, etc.,**] Lading etc. *printings prior to 1932, US 1936, US 1952*

218 **"character",**] "character," *Boni, Hogarth, 1925   . . .* **Cum**] *Boni, Hogarth, 1925, Washington copy 1954* (*pencil*), *1936 final two imps.* (1959, 1961), *1963+* ‖ "... Cum *1936, Sesame, Penguin, Mardersteig* (*erroneously supplying the quotation mark which belongs before* maior. *Corrected long after in Sel Poems*)   **"maior**] *Washington copy 1954* (*blue ink*), *1936 17th and 18th imps.* (1959, 1961), *1974+* ‖ 'maior *Boni proof* ‖ maior *Boni* (*type correction error*), *Hogarth, 1925, 1936, Penguin, Sel Poems 1954* (*corrected long after*), *US 1963 and later US printings* ‖ "major *1963, 1969* (*later corrected*)   **Quam**] *Washington copy 1954* (*ballpoint*), *1963+* ‖ Quam, *printings prior to 1963*   **plagae",**] *1936+* ‖ plagae," *Boni, Hogarth, 1925*   **iocosa**] jocosa *Hogarth*   **Iovis**] Jovis *Guild* ‖ lovis *Penguin, 1954 Sel Poems* (*corrected long after*), *1969* (*later corrected*)   **suique**] suiqve *Hogarth proof*   **Iudicis**] ludicis *1969, 1974* (*later corrected*)   **lumina**] lumine *Hogarth*   **omnipotens**] omipotens *Boni proof*   **poenamque**] poeamque *Boni proof*

221 **as exact**] so exact *Hogarth, despite being emended by TSE to* as exact *in Hogarth proof*   **longshore**] long-|shore *Boni*

264 *as also* 307, 309 St.] St *Penguin* (*only*)

264 **The**] Toe *Hogarth proof, corrected TSE*   **Churches**] *1974+* ‖ Churches: *printings prior to 1974* (*with swash "C" in Hogarth proof, emended TSE*) ‖ Churches: *Hogarth, Sel Poems 1954, US 1963+*   **(P.**] P. *Boni proof*   **Son,**] *1925+* ‖ Son *Boni, Hogarth*

266 **Thames-daughters**] *Hogarth, 1925+* ‖ Thames-|daughters *Boni*   **line 292 to 305**] line 292 to 306 *all eds, emended Hayward in his copy of 1936*   **Götterdämmerung**] Götterdämmerung (*initial letter italicised*) *Hogarth proof emended TSE* ‖ Götterdämmerung *Hogarth*   **Rhine-daughters**] *1936+* ‖ Rhinedaughters *Boni, Hogarth* ‖ Rhine-|daughters *1925, 1932*

279] *Note misnumbered as* 276 *Hogarth* **Elizabeth,**] *Elizabeth Boni, Hogarth, 1925,*
1936 (corrected 2nd imp 1937) **Queen)**] *1963+* ‖ queen) *printings prior to*
1963, US 1963+ **with Lord**] with the Lord *Froude's text*

293] *second line of quotation indented Temple, Sesame only* **"Ricorditi**] "ricorditi
Temple ‖ Ricorditi *Hogarth proof* **"Siena**] Siena *Hogarth* **Maremma."**]
Maremma: *Temple* ‖ Maremma. *Hogarth proof*

307 **"to Carthage then**] to Carthage *Hogarth proof*

308 **Translations**] Translation *all eds (TSE's error)* **Occident**] *1925+* ‖ occident
Boni, Hogarth

308 ^ 309] IV. DEATH BY WATER *1936, US 1936.* Not present in these Notes in previous
editions or in *1936 proof*, this section heading was erroneously added because
of the misnumbering of the note beneath (which properly relates to Part III). In
his copy of *1936* Hayward corrected the line number and deleted the heading,
and TSE did likewise in *Curtis's 1936.* Corrected *1936* 3rd imp. (1939)+.

309] *Note correctly numbered 1936 3rd imp.* (1939)+, *Sesame* ‖ *misnumbered as* 312
Boni, Hogarth, 1925, 1936 1st and 2nd imps.

V. WHAT THE THUNDER SAID

Section Note **Emmaus,**] Emmaus. *Hogarth proof* **eastern Europe**] Eastern Europe
Hogarth proof

356] *Note misnumbered as* 357 *Boni+* **hermit-thrush**] hermit-thrust *1925 (1st imp.*
only: see note below to 428). **Province**] *US 1952, TSE emendation Washington*
copy 1954, Sel Poems 1954 (TSE emendation in proof), 1936 final two imps.
(1959, 1961), 1963+ ‖ County *preceding eds, impressions of 1936 prior to 1959*
(see note) **(Handbook**] Handbook *Hogarth proof* **unequalled**] unequaled
Boni, Hogarth proof

359] *Note misnumbered as* 360 *Boni+* **recorded**] *TSE emendation in Curtis's 1936* ‖
related *Boni+*

366–76 **Schon ist halb Europa**] Schonn ist n lb Euroba (*bad setting and inking*)
Hogarth proof **heiligen**] *1936+* ‖ heiligem *Hesse (error), Boni, Hogarth, 1925,*
US 1952 **Ueber**] Über *Hesse* ‖ Veber *1936 proof* **Bürger**] Büger *Sel Poems*
1954, corrected by TSE in Hayward's copy with "a bad coquille" (corrected in Sel
Poems long after) **sie mit**] *printings prior to 1925, 1932+* ‖ si mit *1925, 1932*
proof, corrected TSE **Tränen**] Taänen *Hogarth proof*

401 **dayadhvam,**] *printings prior to 1925, 1932+* ‖ dayadhvam *1925, 1932 proof,*
corrected TSE **sympathise**] sympathize *Hogarth, Mardersteig* **meaning**
of the] not *Hogarth* **5, 2**] 5, 1 *Boni+ (TSE's error, due to misleading running*
head in Deussen, as William Harmon notes PMLA May 1976).

407 **remarry ^ Ere**] *line space Boni*

411] *Dante quotation del in pencil and typed, without quotation marks, on pasted in slip*
Washington copy 1954. The lines are, however, spoken by Ugolino, and quotation
marks remain in all editions except Mardersteig, which has none. Second line of
Dante quotation indented Temple, Sesame ‖ *indented by only the width of the*
quotation marks Boni ‖ *no indent Hogarth, 1925+ (misreading Boni).* **sentii**]
Temple, printings prior to 1963, US 1963+ ‖ senti *Washington copy 1954 slip,*

1963, 1974 (later corrected) ‖ senti' *Mardersteig, 1980s and 1990s printings of Sesame*   **all'orribile]** l'orribile *(bad inking) Hogarth proof.* Returning Mardersteig's proofs on 19 July 1961, David Bland of Faber wrote that TSE thought the reading should be "a l'orrible" (correctly "a l'orribile"), but it was not changed (Faber archive).   **p. 306]** *TSE emendation Washington copy 1954, 1963+* ‖ p. 346 *printings prior to 1963.* In TSE's own copy of Bradley the passage appears on 346, but in later editions it appears on 306.   **to myself]** to my self *1963+ (later corrected)*

427] *Washington copy 1954* has, pasted over the original Note, a typed slip del in pencil. The terza rima pattern, with second and third lines indented and first and fourth aligned, was clear only in *Mardersteig.* On the typed slip, TSE left a line of space after the third line but this was not adopted in print.   **prec,]** *Temple, printings prior to 1936, Sesame, Mardersteig* ‖ prec *1936+*   **guida]** *Temple, printings prior to Mardersteig* ‖ condus *Mardersteig, Washington copy 1954 typed slip, 1963, 1969, 1974 (later reverting to* guida*), US 1963+*   **sovegna]** *Temple, printings prior to Mardersteig, US 1963+* ‖ sovenha *Mardersteig, Washington copy 1954 slip, 1963, 1969, 1974 (later reverting to* sovegna*), some imps. of Sel Poems after 1970 (later reverting)*   **gli]** *Temple, printings prior to Mardersteig, US 1963+* ‖ li *Mardersteig, Washington copy 1954 slip, 1963, 1969, 1974 (later reverting to* gli*)*

428 ***Pervigilium]*** *Perviglium 1925 (1st imp. only).* TSE to P. M. Jack, 19 Jan 1927: "Besides the misprint of 'pervigilium', the word 'thrush' on the previous page is printed as 'thrust'."

429 **Gérard]** Gerard *previous eds.*

433 **our equivalent to]** *1932+* ‖ a feeble translation of the content of *Boni, Hogarth, 1925, 1932 proof, with final text substituted TSE*   **word.]** word *Hogarth proof*

The Hollow Men

Parts I–IV were published in various combinations in *Commerce*, *Chapbook*, the *Criterion* and the *Dial* during the winter of 1924–25; Part V first appeared in *1925*. See headnote to the Commentary.

ts1 (Texas): ribbon copy of Part I. Illustrated in *An Exhibition of Manuscripts and First Editions of T. S. Eliot* (Texas, 1961). On verso, Rayner Heppenstall has written: "A typescript of Eliot's, given by him to Ottoline Morrell, and by her to me— about 1922. R. J. H." (There is, however, no other evidence of when she acquired it or gave it away.) According to *Bush* 96, TSE had typed "We are the hollow men" during Nov 1924, deciding then to place it first in a sequence taking its title from the first line, before sending it to Ottoline Morrell on 30 Nov. *Bush* 253 adds that it was accompanied by a typescript of *Eyes that last I saw in tears*. In his letter to Morrell, TSE wrote: "I am pleased that you like the poems", referring to the appearance in that month's *Chapbook* of *Doris's Dream Songs* [I–III]. The first of these was *Eyes that last I saw in tears*, so the manuscript of that poem now in Texas was probably enclosed with TSE's letter or sent to Morrell soon afterwards, but there is no evidence that he sent her a typescript.

Perhaps at first uncertain of the number and order of the elements of the poem, TSE ranged the words "*A penny for the Old Guy*" to the right, leaving ambiguous their relation to the main text. He was to do the same, before introducing part numbers, with "*Usk*" and "*Cape Ann*" and with "*The hand of the LORD was upon me,* | *e vo significando*" (*Ash-Wednesday* II).

ms1 (Perse archive): fair copy of Part I sent to *Commerce*. Signed and dated Nov. 1924, and with "Punctuation must *not* be altered TSE" at head. Another hand has written "Italiques" at the head, presumably instructing the printer that the poem (apart from the epigraph) be set in italics. (The French, on the recto, was set in roman, with the English facing in italics.) A facsimile of this ms and of the translation by Perse (in his hand), appeared in *Lettres atlantiques: Saint-John Perse, T. S. Eliot, Allen Tate 1926–1970* ed. Carol Rigolot (2006). As *Commerce* except where noted.

ms2 (King's): early pencil draft of Part III (39–51) on verso of *ts1* of *Eyes that last I saw in tears* and *The wind sprang up at four o'clock* (see description in "Minor Poems" Textual History).

ts2 (King's): foolscap leaf with Part III (headed "iii"), later endorsed: "Early typescript of Part III of The Hollow Men. T. S. Eliot [*footnote*: cf. The Hollow Land by Wm Morris The Broken Men by R. Kipling. T. S. E.]"

ts3 (Beinecke, Thayer/*Dial* papers): fair copy typescript of Parts I, II, IV, sent to Thayer of the *Dial*, 6 Jan 1925. Blue ribbon on airmail paper. Editorially marked up for the printer on three numbered leaves (1, 2, 5) of what were originally five. The eventual Part IV is headed "V", but with "III" substituted by the editor. Text as *Dial* except where noted. TSE had written to Marguerite Caetani on 5 Dec 1924 offering the gift of "MS copies of five new short poems" written out "in *long hand*". A month later, on 6 Jan 1925, he sent *ts3* to Thayer, explaining: "I may be able to send you some prose in a few months and meanwhile here are the poems you have heard of and possibly a few more. The ones marked 'A' have appeared in Harold Monro's *Chapbook*; the ones marked 'B' will have appeared in the January *Criterion* before you receive this letter; the one marked 'C' is to appear in *Commerce*, a French review. There is at least another one in the series which is not yet written. If the fact of publication here is no obstacle I should be glad to see them in *The Dial*." Accordingly, the top leaf (Part I) is marked "C", and the second leaf (Part II) and last leaf (the final Part IV) are marked "B". Since it is most improbable that "*This is the way the world ends . . .*"—concluding Part V—could ever have been placed anywhere but last, it was presumably the other one in the series which TSE had it in mind to write. *Eyes that last I saw in tears*, being about to appear in the *Criterion* as well as having appeared already in *Chapbook*, was probably not submitted to the *Dial* as well, so it is likely that the five submissions to the *Dial* were:

leaf 1. (marked "C") Part I
leaf 2. (marked "B") Part II
leaf 3. (marked "A") *The wind sprang up at four o'clock* (submitted as III, omitted)
leaf 4. (marked "A") Part III (submitted as IV, omitted)
leaf 5. (marked "B") Part IV (submitted as V, pub. as III)

Thayer acknowledged receipt on 10 Feb 1925, without mentioning the intention to omit two of them: "I have just got back to town and found your kind letter and the poems awaiting me here. I was just in time to find a place for them in our March number, which should appear in about ten days now. Of course I am very happy to have the poems, on which I congratulate you."

The change of "twylight" to "twilight" (II 20, IV 14) was editorial. The British spelling "colour" was preserved.

Dial proof (Beinecke): unmarked single leaf galley proof of I, II, IV (the last being numbered III, as editorially marked up in *ts3*). No variants from *Dial*.

Section-title page] 1925+. In 1925, the titles of *The Waste Land* and *The Hollow Men* each appeared on section-title pages and again above their respective poems. In 1936 and 1963+ this was the case only for *The Hollow Men*, where a title above the poem remains necessary because this, uniquely, has a first epigraph beneath its title on the section-title page and a second epigraph beneath the same title on the first page of the poem. In *US 1952*, where there is no section-title page, the poem is headed by *title | first epigraph | rule | title | second epigraph*.

Title **The Hollow Men**] *not ms1* ‖ *added in pencil ts1* ‖ Poème *Commerce contents page (where the author is given as "T.-S. Eliot") and section-title page; with "(Poème inédit)" at foot of text*

First epigraph] *centred below date on section-title page 1936+* ‖ *towards foot of section-title page, ranged right 1925*

Second epigraph] *centred Best Poems of 1925, 1936+* ‖ *ranged right ts1, ts3, Commerce, Dial, 1925, 1932, US 1936, US 1952* **Guy**] Guy. *ts1, Dial*

I

Numeral I] *added in pencil ts1* ‖ *above epigraph but del ts3*

I 1–18] *all italic Commerce (editorial style)*

I 10 **dry**] *ts1 final reading*+ ‖ damp *ts1 1st reading* ‖ dark *ts1 2nd reading*

I 12 **motion;**] pr *ms1 1st reading (uncertain)* ‖ motion *Best Poems of 1925*

I 14 **Kingdom**] *Commerce, 1925*+ ‖ kingdom *ts1, ts3, Dial, Best Poems of 1925*

I 15 ^ 16] *ts1 1st reading*:

> Waters of tenderness
> Sealed springs of devotion.

II

II 15 **coat**] skin *1936 proof (error, anticipating next word) corrected by TSE, US 1936*

II 20, *as also* IV 14 **twilight**] twylight *ts3, editorially changed to* twilight

II 21] *Criterion, Dial* ‖ *not 1925+.*
In printings of the whole of *The Hollow Men* in TSE's books since *1925*, this part has ended with II 20:

> In the twilight kingdom

making it the only part not to conclude with a full stop. (When I. M. Parsons included *The Hollow Men* in *The Progress of Poetry*, 1936, a full stop was supplied following "kingdom".) The anomaly confirms that Part II should end as it had done in the *Criterion* and *Dial*:

> With eyes I dare not meet in dreams.

This omission from *1925* was probably accidental (see *McCue 2012*, Proposal 6). The line does not figure in TSE's recordings.

III

III 2 **cactus**] the cactus *ms2, ts2 1st reading*

III 3 **images**] images are raised *ts2 1st reading*

III 6 **Under**] Behind *ms2 1st reading*

III 6 ^ 7] I *ts2 1st reading (mistyping)* ‖ *no line space Sel Poems 1954 (though* III 7 *is indented. Corrected long after)*

III 9] *not ms2 1st reading*   **Waking**] Walking *1936 proof (corrected by TSE)*

IV

Numeral IV] V *ts3, editorially changed to* III ‖ III *Dial*

IV 5 **kingdoms**] *Criterion, Dial, 1925, 1932*+ ‖ kingdoms. *1925 2nd–4th imps. (1926–30), 1932 proof (allowed to stand by TSE).* The whole standing line of Linotype in *1925* must have been reset to add the stop, but why this was done is unknown. Since TSE did not delete the stop in *1932 proof*, his preference remains unknown. See *McCue 2012* Proposal 13.

IV 5 ^ 6] *new page so line spacing indeterminate 1969*

IV 9 **Gathered**] Cathered *1963 (corrected 4th imp., 1968)*   **river**] *Criterion, Dial,*

1925, 1932+ ‖ river. *1925 2nd–4th imps. (1926–30), 1932 proof (allowed to stand by TSE). See* IV *5.*

IV 14 ^ 15] *line space Criterion, Dial* ‖ *no line space 1925+ (apparently to fit* IV *onto the page in 1925)*

V

V 10, 16, 24] *equally indented 1925* ‖ *ranged to right margin 1936, Penguin,* US *1952,* US *1963, 1969. 1963 ranges 16 and 24 but insufficiently indents 10*

Ash-Wednesday

Chronology of publication:

Part II appeared as *Salutation* in *Saturday Review of Literature* (NY) 10 Dec 1927 and *Criterion* Jan 1928. Reprinted in *Twentieth-Century Poetry* ed. John Drinkwater, Henry Seidel Canby and William Rose Benét (Boston, 1929), with text as *Criterion* except where noted.

Part I appeared (entirely in italics) in *Commerce* (Paris) Spring 1928, with facing translation by Jean de Menasce. (Since TSE did not post the translation until 22 May, the journal probably appeared in midsummer or later.) Reprinted in Walter de la Mare's *Desert Islands* (Apr 1930) 272–73, without title and as a note to words of de la Mare's own (from 71): "*The self within hovers over the envied ashes:*"

Part III appeared (entirely in italics) in *Commerce* Autumn 1929, attributed to "T. S. Eliott", with facing translation by Jean de Menasce.

Parts IV, V and VI were not separately published.

Parts I and II were included in *The Faber Book of Modern Verse* (1936) with text as in *1936*.

A projected limited edition of the complete poem in quarto format, to be printed at the Curwen Press, reached second proof stage before being cancelled. Glenn Horowitz's catalogue 22 (1990), to which Robert Giroux and Donald Gallup were advisers, notes: "It was initially planned to issue *Ash-Wednesday* in a large format on expensive paper and the publishers went so far as to have a handful of these proof copies printed before changing their plans. In the end, and in spite of the expense incurred, it was decided that the poem was too short to warrant such an elaborate presentation, so they had it reset in a small format. A number of the proof copies, in varying stages of production, were preserved by Richard de la Mare." Curwen then printed the signed limited octavo edition published jointly by Faber and the Fountain Press, New York, in April 1930. Trade editions followed from Faber (later in April), and Putnam, New York (September), each with pagination different from the limited ed. In 1933 Faber reset the poem, with different pagination again, for a second trade edition (*1933*). TSE to Donald Brace, 17 Dec 1935, of the poems to be added to *1925* for the forthcoming *Collected Poems 1909–1935*: "I think that *Ash Wednesday* was copyrighted by Putnams in America. At any rate they set it up. But they took it over from a queer bird named Adams who had bought some limited edition press and found he could not make it a success." In the collation below, *1930 ltd ed.*, *US 1930* and *1933* are as *1930* except where noted.

msI (King's): draft of Part I 1–39 (excluding 40–41), on four leaves torn from a pocketbook and headed "All Aboard for Natchez Cairo and St. Louis", with "*Perch'io non spero*" ranged right beneath. Written with propelling pencil, occasionally causing a secondary impression in the paper.

tsIa (Houghton): carbon of Part I; apparently sent to TSE's mother, with pencilled note at head: "to be published by Marguerite de Bassiano in *Commerce*". (Both the angle and the position of a note at the head of *A Song for Simeon tsIb* show that the two notes were pencilled at the same time.) The groups of lines are separated by two-line spaces. (This Houghton folder also contains a carbon by an unknown typist, headed "printed in *Commerce*, Spring, 1928". The carbon follows the printed text.)

tsIb (untraced): Part I, sent to *Commerce* 19 Mar 1928. On 4 Apr TSE wrote again to Marguerite Caetani about I 40–41: "At the beginning of each of the last two lines please alter the words 'be with' to 'pray for'. One might as well stick to the exact quotation."

tsIc (untraced): *Bush* (1983) and *Schuchard* (1999) mention a further typescript of Part I at Texas which is no longer to be found. Describing it as earlier than *tsAW* (below), *Bush* 260 specifies: "in the Ottoline Morrell Collection · · · now attached to an envelope Eliot addressed to Morrell that is postmarked 3(1?) May 1928, but appears to have been taken from a letter of 2 October 1928". The typescript described by *Schuchard* 246–47 was later than *tsIa* and had been "temporarily retitled 'BALLATA: ALL ABOARD FOR NATCHEZ, CAIRO AND SAINT LOUIS.' with 'Perch'io no spero' as the epigraph. Eliot subsequently crossed out the title and epigraph of this typescript and printed the new title 'PERCH' IO NON SPERO . . .' This draft, which was sent to Jean de Menasce for translation into French, bears the blue-pencil holograph of the editor or the printer, 'Commerce 13 ital' and is the English text as printed opposite the French translation in *Commerce*." (No such typescript is mentioned in *Sackton*, the 1975 catalogue of the Texas TSE collection, or in online finding aids.)

tsId (untraced): Theresa Whistler's *The Imagination of the Heart: The Life of Walter de la Mare* (1993) 401 claims that TSE sent a draft of Part I to de la Mare.

tsII (Beinecke): untitled, undated draft of Part II on two leaves sent to William Force Stead. With "Early version of poem sent me by T. S. Eliot WFS" at head.

tsAW (King's): foolscap carbon (in blue) of a draft in five parts, but including much of VI (see below: Part title to VI), sent to Leonard and Virginia Woolf in Oct 1928. Each Part has numeral and title, and begins a new leaf. Leonard Woolf to A. N. L. Munby, Librarian of King's, 10 Dec 1966, offering for sale the typescript and a copy of *1930*: "he hoped that we and Mary Hutchinson would come one evening and criticise it · · · On the first of the five pages of typescript he has written in ink [actually pencil]: 'No need to acknowledge this. We look forward to meeting you on the tenth. T.' We went after dinner on the 17th (not the 10th) and Mrs Hutchinson and McKnight Kauffer were also there. We each in turn criticised the poem. When *Ash Wednesday* was published, Eliot sent us a copy with the following inscription in it: 'For Virginia & Leonard Woolf from T S Eliot. I hope this is better than the first version.' There are considerable differences between the typescript and the published version." William Plomer remembered Leonard Woolf telling this story, about TSE asking them to "assemble and make their opinions known to him. Whatever Mary Hutchinson and Kauffer said he dismissed as of no interest, but when it was Virginia's turn she said she thought too many lines ended with a present participle. 'That's a *good* criticism, Virginia', he said." (*Composition FQ* 5 described this exchange as concerning *East Coker*, but in the library's copy of *Composition FQ* at King's, A. David Moody corrects this to "the occasion, in October 1928, when TSE had the Woolfs, Mary Hutchinson and McKnight Kauffer advise him on a draft of *Ash-Wednesday*". Virginia Woolf to Roger Fry, 16 Oct 1928: "He has written some new poems, religious I am afraid, and is in doubt about his soul as a writer." (Other correspondence with Leonard Woolf about this draft is at Sussex U.)

tsIIIa (Bonn U.): Part III (as *Som de l'escalina*), double-spaced, on two leaves, sent to E. R. Curtius on 2 Aug 1929, inscribed "If you like this I shall be happy, if not, I shall not be disappointed. It will appear in *Commerce* I believe in December. Most cordial wishes T. S. Eliot 2. 8. 29."

tsIIIb (Balliol, Oxford): ribbon copy of Part III (as *Som de l'escalina*), sent to *Commerce* for publication, single-spaced, on a single leaf. With "*Commerce*" and "*B.14*" pencilled at head and "*eu 13 ital.*" pencilled at foot, probably in the hand of Jean de Menasce, whose translation appeared on the facing page in *Commerce*, and many of whose papers are now at Balliol.

Scripps (Scripps College): Part II on single printed leaf torn from *Criterion* Jan 1928, with title *TAN M'ABELIS* added by Vivien Eliot, and with three pairs of lines braced. Of these six lines, three were omitted from the final text.

4to trial page (Texas Christian U., Fort Worth): sheet folded to form four pages. The first page has I 1–20 and the page number 9. Apparently a preliminary trial for *4to 1st proof*. It includes extra punctuation at the end of most lines, matching that of *4to 1st proof* except that a full stop at the end of 15 became a comma in *4to proof*. Also, a "ct" ligature in "actual" (18) was reset using separate letters in *4to proof*. The punctuation is not recorded here.

4to 1st proof (Faber archive): author's marked proof for quarto edition on four folded sheets of hand-made paper. No title, with printed pagination 1–13, followed by three blank pages. No dedication. First page with "*To Printer: Note punctuation. Corrected T.S.E. 30/10/29*" added at head. The printer has supplied stops, question marks and exclamation marks (and occasionally proposed them in the margin, with "qy"). The proof shows TSE deleting almost a hundred of these, mostly from the ends of lines. These are not individually recorded below, although changes from one punctuation mark, already present, to another are recorded. TSE also asked for more space between sentences, writing "to printer:—much more space" after "skull." (II 4) and at each subsequent instance writing "more space" (not noted below). (The *Saturday Review* setting of II, which he may have had to hand, has particularly wide spaces between sentences.) Gallup's uncorrected copy of this proof is at Beinecke and another uncorrected copy, at Texas Christian U., Fort Worth, is laid in a dummy binding. A typescript collation of *4to trial page* and *4to 1st proof* was compiled by Robert Beare and sent to TSE on 9 Apr 1955 (King's).

4to 2nd proof (Princeton): corrected proof, on hand-made paper, with title-page title in black letter and imprints of Faber & Faber and The Fountain Press, NY. Colophon present, but no dedication. Printed at the Curwen Press. The author's corrections in the previous proof were imperfectly followed. Another *4to 2nd proof*, unbound and without title page, was sold in 1981 by Waterfields of Oxford and then by Gekoski of London, but is untraced. It was described by

Gekoski as having "Ash-Wednesday | by | T. S. Eliot" in his hand at the head of the first page, and "eight corrections by him in the text, mostly of punctuation".

1933 proof (untraced): proof of the second edition, "Corrected TSE 14. X. 33", from the library of Richard de la Mare, sold in 1981 by Waterfields to a private US customer. "Corrections pencilled in the text in the author's hand, mostly concerned with its spacing, demonstrating his care over the presentation of his poems on the page: e.g. he notes, pp.18–19, 'I should prefer it if p.18 could be spaced so as to bring the first "Lord, I am not worthy" onto the top of p.19'."

tsBBC (Texas): secretarial ts on nine leaves prepared for TSE's broadcast of 29 Sept 1951. An additional title-leaf, signed by the producer, Terence Tiller, gives details of the rehearsal and recording times and dates. Corrections in red and a small number in black (these possibly by TSE) were probably made before recording, but other notes in red give timings of different passages. Not collated, but see textual note to III 6.

Each Part begins a new page in the quarto proofs, in *1930* and in subsequent book printings except *Sesame* and *US 1952* Part titles were replaced by roman numerals in the quarto proofs and *1930*, and since *1936* these have been italicised. Since *1936*, the contents list in the *Collected Poems* has specified, beneath the title *Ash-Wednesday*, the number and first line of each: ("*I. Because I do not hope to turn again*", etc.), whereas the Parts of *The Hollow Men* are not listed. The contents of *Penguin* / *Sel Poems* and *US 1952* list only the main title, giving the poem the same weight as *The Hollow Men*.

In different editions, the line spacing of *Ash-Wednesday*, perhaps more than any other poem, has been repeatedly altered to accommodate the text to varying depths of page and to avoid isolating lines. In the spacious pages of the planned quarto edition, the poem would have been freed from such constraints in all but a single instance, so that TSE's spacing instructions to the printer on *4to 1st proof* are the best guide to what ideally he wanted—and the proliferation of his instructions demonstrates their importance. With the one exception, then, and despite some conflicting later instructions and practices, the spacing of those corrected proofs is followed in the present edition for the first time. The exception is Part V, which proved in the planned edition to be one line too long to fit on two quarto pages, and was therefore set without a line space before the last line. Visually, this was acceptable, since the penultimate line—"Of drouth, spitting from the mouth the withered apple-seed"—was slightly too long for the page width, so that "seed" had to be turned. The effect was to combine the turn with the line space, and leave the final line, the deeply indented "O my people", isolated in the same way as the repeated "O my people, what have I done unto thee" (10, 28). The full line space was restored in *1930* and is retained here as in all other editions.

Section-title page] *1936+*

Title] *on leaf preceding poem and with only numeral above first line 1930* ‖ *on section-title page (with date) and with only numeral above first line 1936+* ‖ *above poem (with date) but separated from it by a long rule US 1952.* (Only *Ash-Wednesday* and *Choruses from "The Rock"* begin with a numeral alone above the poem in *1936*

and *1963+.*)   **Ash-Wednesday]** *1930+* ‖ Ash Wednesday *US 1952 Contents.*
(Although the title is hyphenated on the title page, spine of both the book and
the jacket and the front flap in *1930*, it appears as ASH | WEDNESDAY on the
front board, and as ASH | WEDNES | DAY on the front panel of the jacket.)

*Part numbers] large italic (matching The Waste Land but larger than The Hollow Men)
1936, 1963 ‖ text-size roman 4to proofs, 1930, Later Poems, Penguin (matching The
Hollow Men but smaller than The Waste Land), Sel Poems (matching The Hollow Men
but smaller than The Waste Land ‖ large roman 1933, 1969, some later printings of
Sel Poems and 1963 ‖ roman small capitals Sesame, Faber Bk Mod V (neither of
which contains The Hollow Men)*

I

Part title **I]** *1930+* ‖ All Aboard for ~~Cair~~ Natchez Cairo and St. Louis *msI (as* Part
I *was probably the second to be composed, these words are unlikely ever to have
been intended as a comprehensive title)* ‖ *Perch'io non spero msI* ‖ PERCH' IO
NON SPERO *tsIa* ‖ PERCH'IO NON SPERO. *tsAW* ‖ PERCH' IO NON SPERO . . .
Commerce

Epigraph] not *tsAW+*‖ *Perch'io non spero ms1 (ranged right)* ‖ di tornar piu mai |
ballatetta, in Toscana . . . *tsIa (deeply inset)*

I 5] (Why should I emulate these things *msI*   **strive to strive]** wish to strive
tsIa   **such]** those *tsIa*

I 6 **(Why]** Why *msI*   **agèd]** aged *msI, tsIa, tsAW*   **its wings?)]** his wings) *msI* ‖
his wings?) *tsAW*

I 7 **mourn]** mourn or why rejoice in pain *msI 2ⁿᵈ reading*

I 8 **vanished]** ringed *msI*   **the usual]** an alien *msI*

I 8 ^ 9] *new leaf msI*

I 10 **infirm]** shallow *msI*   **the]** a *msI*

I 12, 14, 16] *perhaps written first (flow of words, weight of pencil), leaving gaps for* 13
and 15 *msI*

I 12 **know I shall not]** do not think to *msI*

I 13 **The one]** The only *msI* ‖ The *tsIa*   **veritable]** real ⋈ *msI*

I 15] That trees will flower, that wells will flow again *msI*   **again]** again. *4to trial
page* ‖ again, *4to proof 1ˢᵗ reading*

I 15 ^ 16] *no line space Desert Islands*

I 17 **and only]** *not msI*

I 18 **actual is actual only]** fixed is fixed *msI* ‖ actual only *4to trial page (with "ct"
ligature)* ‖ *4to 1ˢᵗ proof 1ˢᵗ reading*

I 19 **And only]** And *msI* ‖ And actual only *tsIa*

I 20 **and]** *not msI*

I 21 **I]** And I *msI*   **blessèd]** not *msI* ‖ blessed *tsIa, Commerce, tsAW, Desert
Islands.*   **face]** face, renounce the voice; *msI*

I 22] *not msI*

I 23 ^ 24] *no line space tsIa, 4to 1st proof, 1930 ltd ed., US 1930, 1936+* ‖ *line space Commerce, tsAW, Faber Bk Mod V* ‖ *new page so line spacing indeterminate 1930*

I 24–25] *not msI*

I 25 ^ 26] *line space 4to proofs* ‖ *new page so line spacing indeterminate 1936, 1963, US 1963* ‖ *no line space Sesame (to avoid isolated line at head of page). TSE endorsed the space in response to a proof query about Later Poems (Faber archive, RdlM 80)*

I 26 **And**] I *msI*   **mercy**] some mercy *msI*

I 27] And to forget *msI*

I 28 **matters that with myself I**] difficulties we *msI*

I 29] Explain, *msI*

I 31 **answer**] answer: *msI*

I 32 **For**] From *msI*   **not to**] ⊄ will not *msI*

I 33 **May**] Let *msI 1st reading*   **judgement**] judgment *msI, tsIa, Commerce, tsAW*

I 33 ^ 34] *new leaf, then* And may the opinion of the world refrain *then line space msI*

I 34 **these**] the *msI, tsIa*   **no**] now no *msI*

I 35] *not msI*

I 36] So that the world is now small *msI 1st reading* ‖ And the air now small ⊄ dry; *msI 2nd reading*

I 37 **will**] will. *msI* ‖ will: *tsIa*

I 38] *not msI*

I 40–41] *not msI*

I 39 ^ 40] *new page so line spacing indeterminate tsIa*

I 40 **death**] death. *tsIa*

I 40 ^ 41] Holy Mary Mother of God *tsIa*

I 41 **now**] sinners now *tsIa, Commerce (in a copy inscribed to Jeanie McPherrin, 2 May 1935,* sinners *is circled in pencil, possibly in TSE's hand; a pencilled sum of his appears on the title page)*   **death.**] death . . . . T. S. ELIOT. *Desert Islands*

II

Part title **II**] *1930+* ‖ *not tsII* ‖ SALUTATION *Sat Rev, Criterion* ‖ II. JAUSEN LO JORN. *tsAW* ‖ TAN M'ABELIS *added by Vivien Eliot, who has deleted the printed title, byline and epigraph, Scripps*

Epigraph] *not 1930+* ‖ *The hand of the LORD was upon me, | e vo significando. tsII* ‖ The Hand of the Lord Was Upon Me:—*e vo significando. Sat Rev* ‖ *e vo significando Criterion, Twentieth Cent Poetry (with a stop)*

II 1 **Lady**] LADY *Criterion, Library of Congress recording text 1949 (following US 1936, which capitalises the opening of many poems and of each part of The Waste Land and Ash-Wednesday)*

II 1 *as also 48* **juniper-tree**] *1930+* ‖ juniper tree *tsII, Sat Rev, Criterion, tsAW*

II 3 **my legs my heart my liver**] my legs, my heart, my liver *Sat Rev* ‖ my legs, my heart my liver, *4to 1st proof with commas del by TSE*

II 5 **Shall**] Can *Criterion*   **shall**] *1930*+ ‖ Shall *tsII*, *Sat Rev*, *4to 1st proof 1ˢᵗ reading* ‖ Can *Criterion*

II 10 **honours**] honors *Sat Rev*   **meditation,**] meditation *tsAW*

II 11 **brightness. And**] brightness, and *tsII*

II 14 ^ 15] *two-line space at foot of page Later Poems*

II 15 **guts**] guts, *Sat Rev*   **eyes**] eyes, *Sat Rev*   **indigestible**] indigestable *Criterion (corrected Twentieth Cent Poetry)*

II 19 **life**] breath *tsII*

II 21 **And**] —And *tsII*, *tsAW* ‖ ———And *Criterion*

II 24 ^ 25] *two-line space tsII* ‖ *single line space Criterion, 4to 2nd proof, 1930, 1936*+ ‖ *no line space 4to 1st proof with chevron and "double space" by TSE, 1936 proof 1ˢᵗ reading, Library of Congress recording text* ‖ *new page so line spacing indeterminate 1933.* The page depth of both *Criterion* and *1930* made impracticable the two-line space that TSE intended.

II 25-47] *inset Sat Rev, Twentieth Cent Poetry, Library of Congress recording text*

II 28-29] *braced by Vivien Eliot in Scripps*

II 29 ^ 30] Spattered and worshipped *tsII, Sat Rev, Criterion, tsAW. This line and the next braced by Vivien Eliot in Scripps*

II 30 **life-giving**] life giving *tsII*

II 32 ^ 33] With worm-eaten petals *tsAW* ‖ With worm eaten petals *tsII, Sat Rev, Criterion*

II 45 ^ 46] *tsII, Sat Rev, Criterion, tsAW*:

  For the end of remembering
  End of forgetting

braced by Vivien Eliot in Scripps

II 47 **ends.**] ends *tsII, tsAW, Twentieth Cent Poetry*

II 47 ^ 48] *two-line space tsII, 1963* ‖ *new page so line spacing indeterminate 1930, US 1936, Later Poems* ‖ *no line space Library of Congress recording text*

II 48 **shining**] shining. *tsII, Sat Rev, Criterion*

II 49 **other,**] *1930*+ ‖ other. *tsII, Sat Rev, Criterion, tsAW*

II 50 **sand,**] *1930*+ ‖ sand. *tsII, Sat Rev, Criterion, tsAW*

II 50 ^ 51] *line space Sat Rev*

II 54 **Matters**] *1930*+ ‖ Matter *tsII, Sat Rev, Criterion, tsAW, 4to 1st proof 1ˢᵗ reading with printer's query "s" endorsed by TSE*

III

Part title **III**] *1930*+ ‖ SOM DE L'ESCALINA. *tsAW, tsIIIa, tsIIIb, Commerce*

III 3, 4] *transposed tsAW, tsIIIa, tsIIIb, Commerce*

III 3 **The same**] My own *tsAW, tsIIIa 1ˢᵗ reading*

III 4 **Under**] Beneath *tsAW, tsIIIa*   **in**] of *tsAW, tsIIIa*

III 6 **and of**] and *tsBBC 1ˢᵗ reading*. The missing "of" was inserted after the initial recording (in the hand noting the duration of each part as delivered). Beneath the caret mark is repeated underlining with "NOT on recording!!" III 1–6 (where the leaf ends) with "Do again".

III 6 ^ 7 *as also* 11 ^ 12] *two-line space 1933 (to avoid widow)*

III 9 **dark,**] dark *tsAW, ts Curtis, tsIIIb, Commerce*

III 10 **Damp**] Harsh *tsAW, tsIIIa 1ˢᵗ reading*   **jaggèd,**] *1930+* ‖ jagged, *tsAW, tsIIIa* ‖ jaggéd, *Commerce* ‖ jaggè *US 1930*. (Over the "e" in *tsIIIb* is superimposed an apostrophe.)

III 11 **agèd**] *1930+* ‖ giant *tsAW, tsIIIa, tsIIIb, Commerce*

III 13 **fig's**] figs's *1974*

III 19 **stair,**] stair. *Guild*

III 21 ^ 22] *no line space 4to 1st proof but with chevron and "double space" by TSE* ‖ *single line space 4to 2nd proof, 1930, 1936+* ‖ *no line space 1936 proof 1ˢᵗ reading* ‖ *new page so line spacing indeterminate 1933*

III 22 *as also* 23 **Lord,**] Lord *tsAW, tsIIIa, Commerce*

III 23 **worthy**] worthy. *tsIIIa 1ˢᵗ reading* ‖ worthy, *4to 1st proof, 4to 2nd proof*

III 23 ^ 24] *line space 1930, 1936, US 1963* ‖ *no line space tsIIIa (where 24 is a ms addition), tsIIIb, Commerce, 1963+* ‖ *no line space 4to 1st proof but with chevron and "another space" by TSE*. The line space in *1936* was made possible on a tight page by reducing the depth of the three previous line spaces in III. This was not done in *1963*, leaving no room for a line space here, but the line space was retained on the deeper page of *US 1963*.

III 24] *not tsAW, tsIIIa 1ˢᵗ reading*   **only.**] only *tsIIIb, Commerce (although facing translation has stop)*

IV

Part title IV] *1930+* ‖ VESTITA DI COLOR DI FIAMMA *tsAW*

IV 4 **Going**] Who walked *tsAW*   **colour,**] colour *tsAW*

IV 5 **Talking**] And talked *tsAW*

IV 6 **eternal**] perpetual *tsAW*

IV 7 **moved**] mover *(mistyping) tsAW*   **others**] othr *tsAW 1ˢᵗ reading* ‖ others, *2ⁿᵈ reading*   **as they walked,**] those who walked *tsAW*

IV 8 **Who then made strong**] She who made new *tsAW*

IV 9 **cool**] fresh *tsAW*   **made firm the**] the barren *tsAW*

IV 10 **colour,**] colour *tsAW*

IV 11 **Sovegna**] Soe *tsAW 1ˢᵗ reading* ‖ Sovvegna *4to 2nd proof (following a printer's suggestion on 4to 1st proof which TSE did not delete)*   **vos**] vos al pasada folor *tsAW*

IV 14 **moves in the time between sleep and waking**] walks between season and season *tsAW*

IV 15 **folded.**] folding the flame and green *tsAW* ‖ folded; *4to 2nd proof*

IV 15 ^ 16] *new page so line spacing indeterminate 1930 ltd ed., 1930 US*

IV 16–29] *tsAW*:

> Clothes that now clothe her, while the flowers rejoice
> In the blessed face
> And the blessed voice
> Of one who has heard the unheard, seen the unseen.
> Desire chills, and the hidden thoughts outrace   [5]
> The way of penance to the means of grace.
>
> Poi s'ascose nel foco and
> After this our exile

with After *in the last line typed over* And

IV 21 ^ 22] *line space 1930 ltd ed., 1936+* ‖ *new page so line spacing indeterminate 1930, 1933, US 1936*

IV 23 ^ 24] *end of page 1936, 1963, Sel Poems repr. 1954* (*causing erroneous line space in some later printings*)

IV 24] publisher's memo to printer, 12 Feb 1948, revoking an instruction to emend: "We have now discovered that the correct version is as it is now printed, i.e. 'signed' and not 'sighed'" (Faber archive). "Secretary to Mr. T. S. Eliot" to J. Posener, 9 Apr 1948: "In your previous letter I believe you suggested that in Section IV of *Ash Wednesday*, line 24 si<u>gn</u>ed should read si<u>gh</u>ed. I referred the matter to Mr. Eliot and he agreed. The other day Mr. Eliot was sending a copy of his *Poems* to a friend and asked me where this misprint occurred so that I could correct it. I told him and he then said that the original si<u>gn</u>ed was correct! Evidently he wasn't thinking when I queried him the first time about it!"

V

Part title V] LA SUA VOLUNTADE *tsAW* (see note to *A Cooking Egg* 24).

V 1–2] *tsAW*:

> If the lost word is lost, if
> The spent word is spent, if the unheard, unspoken

V 5–6] The Word within the world, and for the world, *tsAW*

V 8 **Word**] *all texts prior to 1936, US 1936, 1936 18th imp.* (*1961*), *1963+* ‖ World *1936* (*see Commentary*). *Corrected three times by TSE: in Curtis's 1936, TSE's 1949 and Washington copy 1954.* TSE confirmed on 22 May 1936, to the American publisher of *1936*, Donald Brace, that Brace had "found one glaring error in our edition. The text of *Ash-Wednesday* that you have is certainly correct. The line should read: 'Against the Word the unstilled world still whirled'. I shall be glad at least to have this correct in the American if not in the London edition." Brace, 4 June: "I am relieved to hear that that line in *Ash-Wednesday* is correct as we have printed it. I couldn't believe that it could be correct as printed in your edition, so I took the liberty, not without a good deal of hesitation, of adopting the reading which happily turns out to be the correct one." The error persisted in British editions, including *Sesame, Penguin* and *Sel Poems* (1954). David Bland of Faber to the Pitman Press, concerning a reprint of *Sesame*, 13 Apr 1962: "We have the following correction which is probably not included in those recently sent to you. This correction should appear in *Ash-Wednesday*: The sentence reading 'Against the World the unstilled world still whirled' should be read as 'Against the Word the unstilled world still whirled'" (Faber archive). *Beare* 35 notes the persistence of this error, its appearance in an American paperback edition, and even its translation into other languages.

V 9 **of**] oft *Guild*

V 9 ^ 10] *no line space tsAW* ‖ *two-line space (to avoid widow at the head of following page) 1933*

V 10 **people,**] people *tsAW*   **thee.**] thee! *4to 1st proof with exclamation mark changed to stop by TSE* ‖ *thee 4to 2nd proof (misreading TSE's instruction)*

V 11–37] *not tsAW*

V 11 **will the word**] will the *Sesame 1954 imp. (later corrected)*

V 24 **darkness?**] darkness *4to 1st proof 2nd reading (after question mark del by TSE), 4to 2nd proof*

V 27 **oppose**] oppose? *4to 1st proof with question mark del TSE*

V 28 **thee.**] thee! *4to 1st proof with exclamation mark changed to stop by TSE* ‖ *thee 4to 2nd proof (despite instruction)*

V 30 **Yew trees**] Yew-trees *4to 1st proof with hyphen del TSE, 1930 ltd ed., US 1930.* At VI 23, "the yew-tree" has a hyphen which TSE did not delete in *4to 1st proof.* Rather than a distinction between singular and plural forms, the inconsistent hyphenation in the published poems may be due to his sensitivity to rhythmic differences: "birch-trees", *Mr. Apollinax* 3; "mango-tree", *The Hippopotamus* 14; "pine trees", *The Waste Land* [V] 356; "yew trees", *Animula* 36; "juniper-tree" *Ash-Wednesday*, II 1, 48; "palmtrees" but *"bamboo tree", Sweeney Agonistes: Fragment of an Agon* 24, 42; "palmtree", *Coriolan* I. *Triumphal March* 33; "apple-tree", *Landscapes* I. *New Hampshire* 12; "fir trees" but "yew-tree", *The Dry Salvages* I 26, V 49; "yew-tree" and "apple-tree", *Little Gidding* V 19, 35.

V 35 **apple-seed.**] apple- | seed? *4to 1st proof 1st reading (broken at line-end) with question mark changed to full stop by TSE* ‖ *apple- | seed 4to 2nd proof (despite instruction)*

V 35 ^ 36] *no line space 4to proofs (there being no room on the page below)*

V 36] *very deep indent 4to proofs, 1930 ltd. ed., US 1930*   **people.**] people! *4to 1st proof with exclamation mark changed to full stop by TSE* ‖ *people 4to 2nd proof (despite instruction)*

VI

Part title. **VI**] *not tsAW, which runs directly from* V 10 *to* VI 11 *without break or line space between* V *and* VI.

VI 6 **dreamcrossed**] dream-crossed *4to 1st proof 1ˢᵗ reading*

VI 7 **me father)**] me, Father), *4to 1st proof 1ˢᵗ reading*

VI 11 **And**] If *tsAW*

VI 12 **lilac**] lilies *tsAW 1ˢᵗ reading* ‖ lilacs *tsAW 2ⁿᵈ reading*

VI 12 ^ 13] *indented* O my people what have I done unto thee. *tsAW*

VI 13] If the lost spirits quicken and rebel *tsAW*

VI 14 **bent golden-rod and the**] lost roses, sweet peas, *tsAW*   **smell**] smell, *tsAW*

VI 15 **Quickens**] If the lost ear quickens *tsAW*

VI 16 **whirling**] lost sea *tsAW*

VI 17 **And the blind**] If the lost eye *tsAW*

VI 18 **The empty forms**] The quickening form *tsAW*

VI 19–35] *tsAW*:

> O my people what have I done unto thee
> In this pool all the waves are silent
> In this pool all the seas are still
> All the waves die against this island
> Our life is in the world's decease   [5]
> Our peace
> In his will.
> Suffer me not to be separated
> O my people

VI 19 ^ 20] *new page so line spacing indeterminate 4to 1st proof, 4to 2nd proof, but line space confirmed by TSE in a memo about Later Poems (Faber archive RdlM 80)*

VI 22 ^ 23] *no line space 4to 1st proof but with chevron and "Double space" by TSE* ‖ *single line space 4to 2nd proof* ‖ *no line space 1930 ltd ed., 1930 (to avoid isolated line at head of page), US 1930, 1936+ (in TSE's 1949, TSE added a marginal chevron to indicate space; see also next note)* ‖ *new page so line spacing indeterminate 1933*

VI 24 ^ 25] *line space 1930, US 1936, Later Poems* ‖ *new page so line spacing indeterminate 1936, 1963* ‖ *no line space Sesame, Penguin, 1969, various later printings.* A proofreader's query about *Later Poems* asked whether the spaces VI 19 ^ 20 and 24 ^ 25 were correct. TSE responded "Yes" (Faber archive).

VI 29 **rocks,**] rocks: *4to 1st proof with colon del by TSE* ‖ rocks *4to 2nd proof*

VI 34 ^ 35] *single line space 1930+* ‖ *single line space 4to 1st proof but with chevron and "more space" by TSE* ‖ *two-line space 4to 2nd proof*

VI 35 **my**] me *1936 proof, corrected TSE*

Ariel Poems

Editions collated for the series: *Ariel* (the original pamphlets), *1936*, *Penguin*, *Sel Poems 1954*, *1963*, *US 1963*.

Section-title page] *1936+*

Journey of the Magi

Published as Ariel Poem 8, with drawings by E. McKnight Kauffer, 25 Aug 1927 (and with 350 numbered copies on hand-made paper, 23 Nov). To secure the US copyright, an edition of 27 copies was printed by William Edwin Rudge, Mount Vernon, NY, Dec 1927. (The poem was not otherwise printed in the US until *1936*.) Included in *The Faber Book of Modern Verse* with text as *1936*. Then *1936+*, *Penguin* and *Sel Poems 1954*.

ts1 exists in two versions:

> *ts1a* (sold Bonhams, 10 Apr 2013): single page ribbon copy with ms revisions in ink, initialled at foot. Text and revisions as *ts1b*. (Facsimile in Bonhams' catalogue, *The Roy Davids Collection Pt. III*.)

> *ts1b* (Houghton): carbon, sent to his mother, with revisions in pencil, apparently before those in *ts1a*.

Ariel proof (Eton College): page proof, emended by TSE, who has written on the front cover "Rough Proof only without decorations", then "Corrected T. S. E." As *Ariel* except where noted.

ms Signet (Texas): ms copy for Harvard's literary society, on Faber & Faber notepaper, endorsed "Fair copy made 24 July 1961 by T. S. Eliot for *The Signet*" on each of the three pages. TSE had been elected to the society, in Dunster Street, Cambridge, in March 1909.

Valerie's Own Book: fair copy, with two-line spaces 20 ^ 21 (see below) and 31 ^ 32.

3 **journey,**] journey *ts1*   **journey:**] journey. *ts1*

4 **sharp,**] sharp; *ts1*

5 **winter."**] winter". *ts1*, *ms Signet*

9 **terraces,**] terraces *ts1*

11 **Then**] What with *ts1 1st reading*

13 **night-fires**] nightfires *ts1*

15 **prices:**] prices; *ts1* (*punctuation apparently written over a colon*)

17 **night,**] night *ts1*

19 **With**] And *ts1*, *Ariel proof 1st reading*

20 **this was all**] all this was *ts1 1st reading*

20 ^ 21] *line space 1936+* ‖ *no line space ts1* ‖ *new page so line spacing indeterminate Ariel, US 1927* ‖ *new page but with line spaces at foot and head Valerie's Own Book*

21 **valley,**] valley *ts1*

22 **vegetation,**] *Washington copy 1954 emendation, 1963* ‖ vegetation; *ts1, printings prior to 1963, Valerie's Own Book* ‖ vegetation: *ms Signet*

23 **water-mill**] watermill *ts1, ms Signet*   **beating**] beating in *ts1 1ˢᵗ reading*

24 **low**] *apparently written over* s *ms Signet*   **sky.**] *Washington copy 1954 emendation, 1963* ‖ sky line, *ts1 1ˢᵗ reading* ‖ sky, *ts1, printings prior to 1963, Faber Bk Mod V, ms Signet, Valerie's Own Book*

25 **meadow.**] meadow, *ms Signet 1ˢᵗ reading*

26 **tavern**] tavern, *ts1*   **vine-leaves**] vine leaves *ts1*

28 **wine-skins**] wineskins *ts1, Valerie's Own Book*

30 **soon**] soon, *ts1*

31 **satisfactory.**] satisfactory *1936 17th imp.* (1959) (*presumably broken type*), *corrected 1936 18th imp.* (1961)

32 **remember,**] remember *ts1*

33 **again,**] again *ts1*

34] *not ms Signet*   **down**] down, *Ariel proof 1ˢᵗ reading*

36 **Death**] death *Valerie's Own Book 1ˢᵗ reading*

38 **different; this**] different. This *ms Signet* ‖ different: this *Valerie's Own Book*   **Birth**] birth *ms Signet 1ˢᵗ reading*

A Song for Simeon

Published as Ariel Poem 16, with Drawing by E. McKnight Kauffer, 24 Sept 1928 (and 500 signed large-paper copies, 24 Oct). Reprinted in *The Modern Muse: Poems of To-day British and American* (English Association, 1934). Then *1936+* and *Penguin / Sel Poems*.

ms1 (King's): "earliest draft, written at Chester Terrace SW1" (Hayward note); 1–18 only, in pencil. Three large boxes are pencilled over the poem (possibly representing sub-divisions, or pre-existing on the leaf before the poem was begun). With list on verso by TSE: "Moore | Bank [?] | Walden | presents [?] | office [?]"

ts1: two versions of a typing on two leaves, with "T. S. ELIOT" typed at foot.

> *ts1a* (Texas): ribbon copy, with "2 copies" pencilled alongside 3–5 in TSE's hand and then del. On the verso of fol. 2, another hand has written in blue crayon: "An old Jew who after having seen the Messiah in the temple intoned ~~the~~ a canticle:" This is probably the ts sent to McKnight Kauffer on 30 May 1928.

> *ts1b* (Houghton): carbon with ms revisions, apparently sent to his mother, with note at head: "'Ariel Poems' for 1928". This was pencilled beside the title evidently at the same time as the note at the head of *Ash-Wednesday*

tsIa (the position and angle both matching). The two, apparently pinned together, were probably sent in May or June 1928 (see *ts1a*).

Valerie's Own Book: fair copy, with two-line spaces 7 ^ 8, 16 ^ 17 (with 16 being at the foot of a page), 24 ^ 25.

Title] *not ms1* ‖ *spread across the two pages on which the poem appears Ariel*

1 **Lord,**] Lord *ms1*

2] *not ms1 1ˢᵗ reading* ‖ *joined by loop to 4 ms1 2ⁿᵈ reading*   **creeps by**] halts on *ms1*   **hills;**] hills *ms1*

3 **stubborn**] bitter *ms1*   **has made stand.**] is at a stand *ms1* ‖ had made stand. *1969, 1974*

4 **light**] very light *ms1 2ⁿᵈ reading*   **waiting for**] upon *ms1 1ˢᵗ reading*   **death**] dead *ms1*   **wind,**] wind *ms1, ts1*

5] *not ms1*

6] Light ⊲ dead *ms1 1ˢᵗ reading*   **Dust in sunlight**] With dust *ms1 2ⁿᵈ reading*

6 ^ 7] Waiting for the *ms1 1ˢᵗ reading*

7] Blooming at this season toward the dead land. *ms1*

8] *not ms1*

9 **walked**] walked the *ms1*   **city,**] City *ms1*

10 **poor,**] poor *ms1*

11] Enjoyed respect ⊲ honour among the people *ms1*   **ease.**] ease; *ts1*

12 **door.**] door *ms1*

13 **remember**] inhabit *ms1*   **house**] over c *ms1*   **shall live**] *not ms1*   **live**] *final "e" over illegible letter Valerie's Own Book*

14] After the destruction of the City *ms1*   **come?**] come *ts1*

15 **to**] *not ms1*   **goat's**] goats *ms1*   **and the fox's home,**] into rocky places *ms1*   **home,**] home *ts1*

16 **from**] *not ms1*   **swords.**] swords *ms1*

16 ^ 17] *two-line space ms1*

17 **Before the time of**] There will be *ms1*   **Before**] *written over A Valerie's Own Book (perhaps for "After")*

19–37] *not ms1*

19 **desolation,**] desolation *ts1*

20 **sorrow,**] sorrow *ts1*

21 **Now**] *written over B Valerie's Own Book (presumably for "Before")*   **decease,**] decease *ts1*

22 **Word,**] Word *ts1*

24 **to-morrow**] tomorrow *ts1*

25] *new leaf ts1, with " > space" pencilled at head in ts1b*

27 **derision,**] derision *ts1* ‖ derision. *Valerie's Own Book*

29 **ecstasy**] exstasy *ts1 1ˢᵗ reading*   **prayer,**] prayer *ts1*

32 **heart,**] heart *ts1*

33] *indented one space ts1*   **also.)**] *Ariel, Later Poems ("inside" endorsed by TSE in response to a proof query, Faber archive), US 1936, US 1952* ‖ *also). ts1, Later Poems proof, 1936, Penguin, 1963+, Valerie's Own Book*

34 **me,**] me *ts1*

35 **me.**] me, *Valerie's Own Book*

36 **depart,**] depart *ts1*

Animula

Published as Ariel Poem 23, with engravings by Gertrude Hermes, 9 Oct 1929 (and 400 signed large-paper copies, 28 Oct). First printed in US in *Modern Things*, ed. Parker Tyler (1934). Then *1936+* and *Penguin* and *Sel Poems*.

ts1 (Faber archive): two leaves with ms corrections. The first thirty-one lines are double-spaced, then after a line of space, the last six are single-spaced.

ts2 (Faber archive): carbon of secretarial typescript, sent to Gertrude Hermes. The first thirty-one lines are double-spaced then after a line of space, the last six are single-spaced.

Ariel proof (Pierpont Morgan): proof copy with four leaves (as opposed to two in finished copies). Frontispiece uncoloured and with one variant (35).

ms Abernethy (untraced): TSE to Milton Abernethy, 18 Nov 1936: "I have only one copy of *Animula* by me, but when I can get the time I will copy it out for you as it is very short."

Valerie's Own Book: fair copy (two pages).

14] Content with playing cards and with Kings and Queens, *Modern Things*

19 **"is and seems"**] "is" and "seems" *Valerie's Own Book*

20] *ts1*:

> And may and may not, fear of ridicule and shame,
> Of real and unreal, desire and control.

may and may not,] "may" and "may not", *Valerie's Own Book*

22 **window seat**] leather chair *ts1 1ˢᵗ reading*

23] *all roman tss*   **Encyclopaedia**] *1936+* ‖ *Encyclopædia Ariel, US 1936 (as title-page of Encyclopædia Britannica)*

26 **fare forward**] resign *ts1 1ˢᵗ reading*   **retreat,**] to insist, *ts1 1ˢᵗ reading*

29 **in**] of *Modern Things*

31 ^ 32] *two-line space Valerie's Own Book*

34 **fortune,**] fortune *tss*

35 **one**] one, *tss, Ariel proof*

Marina

Published as Ariel Poem 29, with drawings by E. McKnight Kauffer, 25 Sept 1930 (and 400 signed large-paper copies, 6 Oct). In proof copies, the words "DATTA | DAYADHVAM | DAMYATA" (penultimate line of *The Waste Land*) appear in light blue across the torso of McKnight Kauffer's illustration. In Gallup's proof copy (Yale), Kauffer has noted that the words were deleted at TSE's request. TSE to Kauffer, 8 Aug 1930: "My criticism was not of the drawing at all, but merely meant that I don't want what I write now to have *The Waste Land* stamped upon it." First printed in the US in *The New Poetry: An Anthology of Twentieth-Century Verse in English* ed. Harriet Monroe and Alice Corbin Henderson (rev. ed. 1932). Reprinted in the US in *An "Objectivists" Anthology*, ed. Louis Zukofsky (1932), where the editor takes TSE to task: "The point, however, would be not to proffer solemnly or whiningly confusions to the confused, but to indicate by energetic behavior how certain information may be useful to other information* [*footnote:* Mr. Eliot's poetic use of facts about ships, in *Marina*, is, it cannot be said an elementary but a good example]." *Marina* was reprinted in Britain in *The Modern Muse: Poems of To-day British and American* (English Association, 1934). Then *1936+* and *Penguin | Sel Poems*.

To Michael Sadler (Master of University College, Oxford), 9 May 1930, enclosing *ms1, ts1* and the carbon of *ts2*: "I have not forgotten that I promised to fake for you a manuscript copy of *Ash Wednesday*. So, as earnest, and as something which I think has relatively more interest, I am sending you herewith, meanwhile, the *genuine* manuscript, (2) my own altered typescript (3) final typescript, of my 'Ariel' poem for next autumn (*Marina*). If I make alterations in the proof (and I have an uneasy feeling that the poem is still only half baked) I will send you that too to complete the document."

ms1 (Bodleian): two leaves, in pencil on lined paper.

ts1 (Bodleian): two leaves, with pencil corrections. "2 copies" pencilled at head in unknown hand, perhaps a direction to a typist.

ts2 (Faber archive): two leaves, with " *T. S. Eliot* ?̶ Kauffer" in pencil at head. Probably the ts given to Richard de la Mare, Faber's production editor. Bodleian has an unannotated carbon of this.

ts3: two versions of a third typing, on two leaves. Probably a secretarial copy of *ts2*, apparently made to send to the poem's illustrator, E. McKnight Kauffer.

> *ts3a* (Texas): ribbon copy on two leaves formerly pinned together, signed by TSE at foot.

> *ts3b* (Faber archive): carbon of *ts3a*. Accompanied by a letter from Richard de la Mare to Kauffer, 29 July 1930, praising his drawings for the poem and expressing a wish to buy them.

ts Brace (untraced): post-publication ts. To Donald Brace, 31 Dec 1935: "I can't send a printed copy of *Marina* because it is out of print, so I am sending a typed copy instead."

Ariel proof (identical copies, Beinecke and Texas): the text appearing on fols. 1*v.* and

2r. (facing pages), rather than *2r.* and *2v.* (as published). As *Ariel* except where noted.

Title] *not ms1*

Epigraph] *as one line (being a single line of Seneca) tss, Ariel, New Poetry, Modern Muse,*
  "Objectivists" Anth, Faber Bk Mod V , US 1936, Sesame, Later Poems ‖ *not ms1* ‖
  above title ts1 1ˢᵗ reading ‖ *as two lines (" · · · quae | regio · · ·") not centred but*
  equally indented 1936+. (*In 1936, where the poem began on a recto, the page fell*
  short, with the line space 21 ^ 22 at the foot. Presumably to fill the page and prevent
  the poem from appearing to end with 21, the compositor set the epigraph as two
  lines.)   **quae** · · · **quae**] quæ · · · quæ *New Poetry, "Objectivists" Anth* ‖ *qual* · · ·
  qual 1936 proof, corrected TSE   **plaga?**] *plaga. 1963 proof*

1 **seas**] seas, *ms1*   **shores**] shores, *ms1*   **rocks**] rocks, *ms1*   **islands**]
  islands, *ms1*

2] *indent ms1*   **the**] *not ts3*

3 **pine**] pine, *ms1*   **woodthrush**] wood thrush *ms1*

3 ^ 4] (Off Roque Island) *ms1*

4 **images**] old forgotten images *ms1* ‖ image *ts3a 1ˢᵗ reading, ts3b*

5] And form themselves around—   O my daughter (*with extra space*) *ms1* ‖ And
  reform around—   O my daughter. (*with extra space*) *ts1, ts2* ‖ And reform
  around—O my daughter. *ts3, Ariel proof*   **daughter**] *written over* r (*uncertain*)
  ms1

5 ^ 6] *line space ts2, ts3* ‖ *two-line space ms1* ‖ *one and a half line space ts1* ‖ *new page*
  so line space indeterminate New Poetry

6–13] *ms1 1ˢᵗ reading:*

> Those who sharpen the tooth of the dog,
> Death
> Those who suffer the ecstasy of the animals,
> Death
> Those who glitter with the glory of the peacock,
> Death
> Those who fail in the stye of contentment,
> Death

  with meaning *then added to 6, 8, 10 and 12*

8 **hummingbird**] humming-|bird (*turned across line*) *US 1936* ‖ humming bird
  Faber Bk Mod V

10 **sty**] *1963* ‖ stye *ms1, tss, Modern Muse, 1936* (*emended in TSE's 1949*), *Sesame,*
  Penguin ‖ style *New Poetry* ‖ eye *Sel Poems 1954, Sel Poems 1961 pbk* (*corrected to*
  sty *in later printings*)

14 **Are become**] These are now *ms1*   **unsubstantial**] unsubstancial *ts3*

15 **pine,**] pine *ms1*   **woodsong**] wood song *ms1*

16] The world in chase diminished from place *ms1*

16 ^ 17] *no line space ts3* ‖ *new page so line spacing indeterminate Sesame*

17–19] *ms1:*

> What is this, less firm and firmer
> Where the pulse beats, less strong ⌀ stronger

with pulse *over an indecipherable false start*

17 **face,**] face *Faber Bk Mod V*

19 **eye**] hand *tss, Ariel proof*

19 ^ 20] *new page so line spacing indeterminate ts2, ts3, Ariel* ‖ *no line space New Poetry, "Objectivists" Anth, Faber Bk Mod V*

20–21] *ms1:*

> The whispers and the lap of waves and small laughter and running feet
> Under sleep, where the many ways ⌀ waters meet
>
> The old forms reform, in a new world

with new leaf after first line and line spaces after second and third

21] *tss, Ariel proof:*

> Under sleep, where all the waters meet
> The forms reform.

(*"no space here" after first line in ts1, where the second line begins a new leaf*)

before 22] *line space ms1, tss, Ariel, Faber Bk Mod V* ‖ *new page so line spacing indeterminate "Objectivists" Anth, 1936, 1963* ‖ *no line space Sesame, Later Poems, Penguin, Sel Poems 1954*

22] *indent Penguin, US 1952, 1963 (not 1963 proof, US 1963), 1969*   **Bowsprit**] Bow *ms1 1ˢᵗ reading*   **cracked with ice**] broken with ice *ms1*   **paint**] sides *ts1 1ˢᵗ reading*   **with heat.**] by heat. *ms1* ‖ with heat *Modern Muse*

23 **made**] have made *ms1*

24] And have remembered *ms1 1ˢᵗ reading* ‖ And now remember *ms1 final reading*

25 **rigging**] cording *ms1 1ˢᵗ reading*

26 **September.**] September *ms1*

27 **half conscious,**] *not ms1*   **own.**] own; *ms1*

28 **strake**] streak *ms1, ts1 1ˢᵗ reading*   **leaks, the**] leaks and the *ms1, ts1 1ˢᵗ reading*   **seams**] seems *ts3*   **need caulking.**] uncaulked *ms1 1ˢᵗ reading* ‖ wide open *ms1 2ⁿᵈ reading* ‖ are open. *ts1 1ˢᵗ reading*

30] Living beyond me; let me *ms1*

31 **Resign**] Rev *ms1 1ˢᵗ reading (uncertain)* ‖ Lose *ts1 1ˢᵗ reading*   **speech**] word *ms1, tss, Ariel proof*   **that**] the *ms1*   **unspoken,**] unspoken *ms1*

32 **awakened**] just awaked *ms1 1ˢᵗ reading* ‖ just awakened *ms1 2ⁿᵈ reading*   **ships.**] ships *ms1*

32 ^ 33] *two-line space ms1*

33 **towards my timbers**] *not ms1*

35] O my daughter. *ms1*

The Cultivation of Christmas Trees

Published as an Ariel Poem (new series), illustrated by David Jones, 26 Oct 1954, and in a US edition with "typography, binding, and decorations" by Enrico Arno, 8 Oct 1956 (the envelope stating: "A new poem by T. S. Eliot"). Then *1963+*.

VARIANT READINGS IN PRINT

galley (Pierpont Morgan, call no. 128379): galley proof on which Faber's production manager, David Bland, has written "Miss Fletcher Will you please show to Mr Eliot? DB"; then endorsed "Corrected | TSE 3. 6. 54". Facsimile in Bloomsbury Book Auctions catalogue 145 (6 Sept 1990).

11 **pretext;**] pretext. *galley 1ˢᵗ reading (following ts8–ts9)*

26 ^ 27] *line space galley (following tss)* ‖ *new page so line spacing indeterminate Ariel, US 1956* ‖ *no line space 1963*

VARIANT READINGS IN DRAFTS

Drafts at King's:

ms1: initial outline, in pencil on single ruled leaf.

ms2: initial draft, in pencil on two ruled leaves, heavily worked over.

ts1: ribbon copy; double-spaced on two leaves with ink corrections.

ts2: ribbon copy; double-spaced on two leaves, corrected in pencil.

ts3: ribbon copy apparently from an electric typewriter; double-spaced on two leaves of India paper, corrected in pencil.

ts4: ribbon copy apparently from an electric typewriter; single-spaced on a leaf of India paper

ts5a: ribbon copy; single-spaced on two leaves with a few pencil notes and queries, responding to comments on *ts5b*

ts5b: carbon of *ts5a* (bound preceding it), with pencil comments by Hayward.

ts6: ribbon copy; single-spaced on single leaf, repaired with tape.

ts7a: ribbon copy; single-spaced on single leaf, with two lines revised in ink

ts7b: carbon of *ts7a* with one line revised in ink. A second carbon, with the same revision, was sent to Geoffrey Curtis with a letter of 28 Dec 1953 (see notes).

Typescripts in Valerie Eliot collection:

ts8: single leaf with ink corrections.

ts9: single leaf, probably a carbon of the ts sent to printer. The text reaches its final form, except for the full stop at end of 11. With an identical carbon.

Title] *not mss* **The Cultivation of**] A Preamble to *ts1* ‖ A Comment upon *ts2* ‖

A Note on the Cultivation of *ts3 1st reading* ‖ How to Cultivate *ts3 2nd reading* ‖
The Cultivation of *ts3 final reading* (*uncertain, trimmed by binder leaving only
traces of the tails of letters*)
   ms1 (the initial outline):

> I am again bidden to write a poem
> for this season
>
> It is over 20 yrs since I have attempted
> such a task.
>
> There are several attitudes towards the   [5]
> Xmas season
>
> Ones attitude sh^d be dift. every year.
>
> Let us approach it with fear etc.
>
> Remembering St. Lucy etc.
>
> Is this the kind of Xmas card you   [10]
> hate to receive?

*The final version is so different from the early drafts that to use it to collate them would
be impracticable. So the earliest continuous version of the first full draft, ms2, is here
reproduced with a collation of subsequent typescripts (ts1–ts9), with line numbers in bold
(1–41). Corresponding line numbers in the published poem are in square brackets:*

> Since I am bidden to compose these verses
> Twenty years after—suitable to the season
> Or at least not wholly inappropriate, at Xmas,
> For an unknown giver to an unknown recipient,
> 20 yrs & more after, when the images are fainter   5
> And the mind more discursive, let me say how I feel about it.
> For a point of attention, take the Xmas tree.
>
> There are several responses to the Xmas season   [1]
> Some of which may be disregarded
> For my present purpose, the childish,   10
> (Not to be confused with the childlike: [5]
> Which is one of wonder, when the gilded angel
> Spreading its wings over the tree
> Is not merely a toy, but also an angel)
> The childish, I say, as well as the rowdy,   15
> The sodden, and the patently commercial.
> But, of the genuine responses
> To the feast as an event, and not as a pretext,   [11]
> We should omit none, preserving the earliest
> Glittering wonder, the rapture of the first   20
> Continued to the 80th Xmas tree.
> So that the early rapture, the merriment,
> The surprises, delight in new possessions,
> The expectation of the goose or turkey   [16]
> And the hush when it appears: so the proper levity   25
> May never be lost, in the later experience
> Of disillusionment, the sorrow,
> The separations, in the consciousness

> Of failure, or deterioration
> Or in the attitude of the new convert   30
> Sometimes tainted with a self-conceit   [23]
> (An offense before God ⊄ before the children).
>
> Thus at the last, at the 80th Festival
> Or more or less, whichever is the last,
> The resolution may be a great joy   35   [30]
> Which is also a great fear—that fear
> Experienced by the observer at Pentecost.
>
> But let me in passing, remember St Lucy
> Her carol, and her crown of flame.
>
> Is this the kind of message you want to send?   40
> Is it the kind that you care to receive?

ms2, ts1–ts9:

1–7] *not ts6–ts9*

1] *indented ts4, ts5*   **Since**] Seeing that *ms2 alt*   **bidden**] bidden once more *ts3 2nd reading, ts4, ts5*   **compose these verses**] *with "X" ms2* ‖ compose more verses *ms2 2nd reading* ‖ compose a poem *ms2 3rd reading* ‖ compose again, *ms2 final reading* ‖ compose again *ts1, ts2, ts3 1st reading* ‖ compose *ts3–ts5*

2 **Twenty years after—**] At *ms2 2nd reading* ‖ A set of verses *ms2 3rd reading (with* of verses *del), ts1–ts5*

2–3 *variant* **the season ··· unsuitable at**] *bracketed by Hayward ts5b*

3 **Or**] (Or *ts1 2nd reading, ts2*   **wholly inappropriate**] unsuitable *ms2 1st reading* ‖ wholly unsuitable *ts1–ts5*   **at Xmas**] for Christmas *ts1, ts2 1st reading* ‖ for Christmas, *ts2 2nd reading* ‖ at Christmas, *ts3–ts5*

4 **For**] And *ts1 2nd reading, ts2 1st reading*   **to**] to send to *ts1 1st reading* ‖ and *ts1 2nd reading, ts2–ts5*   **recipient,**] recipient *ts1 1st reading* ‖ recipient) *ts1 2nd reading, ts2*

5 **20 yrs ⊄ more after,**] Tenty years, and more, after: *ts1 (mistyping)* ‖ Twenty years and more after, *ts2* ‖ Twenty years and more later, *ts3 1st reading* ‖ Twenty-odd years later, *ts3 2nd reading, ts4, ts5* ‖ Twenty years, or so, later, *ts3 marginal alt*   **images are fainter**] imagery is fainter, *ts1, ts2 2nd reading* ‖ imagery is fainter *ts2 1st reading* ‖ fancy is less fertile, *ts2 3rd reading, ts3–ts5*

6 **And the**] The *ts1–ts5*   **discursive, let**] discursive ... Let *ts1* ‖ discursive: let *ts2–ts5*

6 ^ 7] *line space ts1–ts5*

7] As a point of attention, take the Xmas tree. *ts2 2nd reading* ‖ As a point of departure, let us take the Christmas Tree *ts1–ts5, indented ts5 and with first five words underlined with "?" Hayward ts5b*

8] *indented ts4, ts5*   **responses to the Xmas season**] responses to the Christmas season, *ts1, ts2 1st reading* ‖ forms of Christmas behaviour, *ts2 2nd reading* ‖ attitudes toward Christmas *ts2 additional alt* ‖ attitudes towards Christmas, *ts3–ts9*

9 **may be disregarded**] may be disregarded: *ts6 1st reading* ‖ we may disregard: *ts6 2nd reading, ts7–ts9*

10 **my**] this? *Hayward ts5b*   **For my present purpose**] *bracketed with* my *ringed and* this? *ts5a*   **purpose,**] purpose, such as *ms2 2nd reading* ‖ purpose—such as *ts1–ts5*   **childish,**] childish *ts3–ts5*

11 **identified**] confused *Hayward ts5b*   **(Not to be confused with**] (Not to be identified with *ms2 2nd reading, ts1–ts4, ts5 with* confused? *alt* ‖ To be clearly distinguished from *ms2 3rd reading*   **the childlike:**] the childlike *ts1* ‖ the child's response *ts2 1st reading with* response[s] *underlined here as in 8 and 17, each with a marginal mark* ‖ that of the child *ts2 2nd reading, ts3 2nd reading, ts4* ‖ that of the child, *ts3 1st reading*

10–11] *ts6–ts9:*

> The social, the torpid, the patently commercial,
> The rowdy (the pubs being open till midnight),   [2]
> But most of all the childish. Which is not that of the child

     [2] **pubs**] pub *ts7 1st reading (error)*   **midnight),**] midnight) *ts8 1st reading*

     [3] **But most of all**] And especially *ts6 2nd reading, ts7 (with "X" in ts7b), ts8 1st reading* ‖ And *ts8 2nd reading, ts9*   **childish. Which**] childish—which *ts8, ts9*   **child**] child, *ts8 1st reading*

12 **Which is one of wonder**] Which is one of ecstasy *ms2 2nd reading, ts1, ts2 1st reading with* ecstasy *underlined* ‖ When the candles are stars *ts2 2nd reading* ‖ When a candle is a star *ts2 3rd reading, ts3–ts5* ‖ For whom the candle is a star *ts6–ts9*   **when**] and *ts7–ts9*

13 **over**] at the summit of *ms2 2nd reading, ts1–ts9*

14 **merely**] only *ts6 2nd reading, ts7–ts9*   **toy**] decoration *ts1–ts9*   **also**] not *ts8, ts9*   **angel)**] angel. *ts6–ts9*

15 **I say**] *underlined with "?" Hayward ts5b* ‖ *ringed for del ts5a*   **rowdy,**] rowdy *ts1, ts2 1st reading*

15–16] *ts6–ts9:*

> The child wonders at the Christmas Tree,
> And the spirit of wonder is the spirit of Christmas.   ·   [2]

     [1] **Tree,**] Tree: *ts7a 2nd reading then line del, ts7b 2nd reading, ts8, ts9*

     [2] Let nothing interrupt the development of this wonder. *ts7a 2nd reading* ‖ Let nothing interrupt the progress of his wonder. *ts7a 3rd reading, ts7b 2nd reading* ‖ Let nothing interrupt the progress of our wonder. *ts7a 4th reading* ‖ Let him continue in the spirit of wonder *ts8, ts9*

15 ^ 16] *ts1 1st reading:*

> (for the pubs are open until midnight,
> on Christ's birthnight, we may remark in passing)

with second line del ‖ *ts1 2nd reading, ts2 1st reading:*

> (For the pubs are open until midnight)

ts2 2nd reading:

> The sodden (the pubs are open until midnight)

ts3, ts4, ts5:

> The sodden (for the pubs are open till midnight)

with for *ringed, and* are *del* with being ? *by TSE ts5a, and with* pubs being open *by Hayward ts5b.* (See **10–11** for *ts6–ts9.*)

16 **The sodden]** The social *ts2 2ⁿᵈ reading, ts3–ts5*   **and]** the well fed, *ts1, ts2 1ˢᵗ reading* ‖ the fed, and *ts2 2ⁿᵈ reading* ‖ the torpid *ts2 additional alt, ts3–ts5*

17 **]** *not ts8, ts9*   **But]** So *ts6, ts7 with "X" ts7b* ‖ Therefore *ts7a 2ⁿᵈ reading*   **of the]** of all the *ts1–ts7*   **genuine]** successive *ts6, ts7*

18 **]** *ms2 2ⁿᵈ reading, ts6, ts7*:

> To the Feast as an event, and not as a pretext,

ts1: (with is *1ˢᵗ reading for* being), *ts2–ts5*:

> To the Feast as an event (an event being something
> Of importance in time) and not as a pretext,

ts8 1ˢᵗ reading:

> At the Feast as an event, and not accept it as a pretext.

ts8 2ⁿᵈ reading, ts9:

> At the Feast as an event not accepted as a pretext.

19 **]** *not ts8, ts9*   **We should]** Let us *ms2 2ⁿᵈ reading, ts1–ts6, ts7a 1ˢᵗ and final readings, ts7b* ‖ Let him *ts7a 2ⁿᵈ reading*   **omit]** forget *ts1* ‖ abandon *ts2 2ⁿᵈ reading, ts3–ts7*   **preserving the earliest]** preserve even the earliest *ts3 1ˢᵗ reading* ‖ but preserve the early *ts3 2ⁿᵈ reading, ts4, ts5* ‖ but perpetuate *ts6, ts7*

20 **rapture]** delight *ts1 2ⁿᵈ reading* ‖ amazement *ts2–ts5*   **of]** at *ts2 2ⁿᵈ reading*   **first]** first remembered *ts1 1ˢᵗ reading*

21 **Continued to]** Still throbbing in *ts1* ‖ Still awaiting *ts2 1ˢᵗ reading* ‖ Still greeting *ts2 2ⁿᵈ reading* ‖ Still aroused by *ts2 3ʳᵈ reading* ‖ Surviving to *ts3 1ˢᵗ reading* ‖ To glorify *ts3 2ⁿᵈ reading, ts5*   **80ᵗʰ Xmas tree.]** eightieth Christmas Tree; *ts1–ts5*

20–21 **]** *ts6–ts9*:

> The glittering rapture, the amazement
> Of the first-remembered Christmas Tree;

> [1] **The]** So that the *ts8, ts9*

> [2] Of the first-remembered, to the final Tree *ts6 1ˢᵗ reading*   **Tree;]** Tree, *ts8, ts9*

22 **]** *not ts6–ts9*   **that]** *not ms2 2ⁿᵈ reading*   **early]** *not ts3 2ⁿᵈ reading, ts4, ts5*

23 **The]** So that the *ts6–ts9*   **surprises]** surprise *ts3*   **delight]** the delight *ms2 1ˢᵗ reading, ts3*   **possessions,]** possessions *ts1–ts5, ts8, ts9* ‖ *with comma and slash superimposed ts6*

23 ^ 24 **]** Each of which comes with a new smell, *ts1 1ˢᵗ reading* ‖ (Each one with its peculiar ~~delightful~~ smell) *ts1 2ⁿᵈ reading* ‖ (Each having its peculiar, exciting smell) *ts2, ts3 without comma* ‖ (Each one with its peculiar exciting smell) *ts4–ts7* ‖ (Each one with its peculiar and exciting smell), *ts8, ts9*

25 **hush]** awe *ms2 alt* ‖ expected awe *ts1, ts7–ts9*   **when it appears:]** at its appearance: *ms2 2ⁿᵈ reading* ‖ at its appearance, *ts1, ts3–ts7, ts8 1ˢᵗ reading* ‖ at its appearance *ts2* ‖ on its appearance, *ts8 2ⁿᵈ reading, ts9*   **so the proper levity]** *not ts1–ts9*

25 ^ 26 **]** So that the early reverent levity *ts1* ‖ So that the original reverent levity

ts2 ‖ So that the reverence and the levity *ts3–ts7* ‖ So that the reverence and the gaiety *ts8, ts9*

26 **May never**] May not *ts1–ts9*   **lost, in the**] lost in *ts2, ts6 1ˢᵗ reading* ‖ forgotten in *ts3–ts5, ts6 2ⁿᵈ reading, ts7–ts9*   **experience**] experience, *ts1, ts2, ts4–ts9* ‖ experience— *ts3*

27 **Of**] The *ms2 2ⁿᵈ reading* ‖ In the *ms2 3ʳᵈ reading, ts1*

27] *not ts2 1ˢᵗ reading* ‖ In bored habituation, recurrent tedium, *ts2 2ⁿᵈ reading* ‖ In the bored habituation, recurrent tedium, *ts2* ‖ In the bored habituation, the recurrent tedium, *ts3–ts7* ‖ In the bored habituation, the fatigue, the tedium, *ts8, ts9*

28 **The separations, in**] In memories of *ms2 1ˢᵗ reading* (*false start*) ‖ In the separations, in *ts1–ts2*

29 **or**] shame, *ms2 2ⁿᵈ reading* ‖ shame and *ts1, ts2*

28–29] The consciousness of death, of shame and of failure, *ts3 1ˢᵗ reading* ‖ The awareness of death, the consciousness of failure, *ts3 2ⁿᵈ reading, ts4–ts9* (*with terminal dash replacing comma ts6, ts7*)

30 **attitude**] piety *ms2 2ⁿᵈ reading, tss*   **new**] *del ts2* ‖ *not ts3–ts9*

31 **Sometimes**] (Sometimes *ms2 2ⁿᵈ reading* ‖ Which may be *ts1 1ˢᵗ reading, ts6–ts9* ‖ (Which may be *ts1 2ⁿᵈ reading, ts2–ts5*

32 **(An offense before God ⊄ before the children).**] *ms2 3ʳᵈ reading* ‖ For which *ms2 1ˢᵗ reading* (*false start*) ‖ (which is also an offense against the children *ms2 2ⁿᵈ reading* ‖ (An offense before God ⊄ before the children). *ms2 3ʳᵈ reading* ‖ (An offense before God ⊄ before the children). *ms2 4ᵗʰ reading* ‖ Offensive towards God and towards the children; *ts1 1ˢᵗ reading* ‖ Offensive towards God and towards the children). *ts1 2ⁿᵈ reading, ts2* ‖ Offensive to God and disrespectful to the children); *ts3–ts5* ‖ Offensive to God and disrespectful to the children *ts6, ts7* ‖ Displeasing to God and disrespectful to the children *ts8, ts9*

32 ^ 33] *before a line space:*

> (And here I remember also with gratitude
> St. Lucy, her carol, and her crown of fire);

ts6, ts7 and, with colon instead of semi-colon, ts8, ts9 (*see* 38–39)

33–35] *ms2 2ⁿᵈ reading:*

> Thus at the last, at the 80ᵗʰ Festival
> That is to say at whichever is the last,
> These may all be resolved into a great joy

ts1:

> Thus, at the last, at the eightieth Festival
> (That is to say, at whichever is the last)
> All the accumulated experience
> May be resolved into a great joy

ts2 1ˢᵗ reading:

> Thus, at the last, at the eightieth Festival—
> That is to say, at whichever is the last—
> All the accumulation of experience
> May be resolved into a great joy

ts2 2ⁿᵈ reading:

> So that, at the last, at the eightieth Festival—
> By "eightieth" I mean, ~~at~~ whichever may be final—
> All the accumulation of experience
> May be resolved into a great joy

ts2, incomplete redrafting at foot:

> So that before the 80ᵗʰ Festival—
> By 80ᵗʰ I mean
> The accumulation of ~~the~~ annual emotions
> May be simplified into a great joy

ts3:

> So that towards the end, at the eightieth Christmas
> (By "eightieth" I mean, whichever is the last)
> All the accumulation of annual emotion

[1] *in the margin*: "[ ] And"   **towards the end, at**] before the end, before
2ⁿᵈ reading

[2] **"eightieth" I mean,**] "eightieth", I mean *2ⁿᵈ reading*

[3] *in the margin*: "Let . . ."   **All the**] The *2ⁿᵈ reading*   **accumulation**]
accumulated memories *2ⁿᵈ reading*

ts4, ts5:

> So that before the end, before the eightieth Christmas
> (By "eightieth", I mean whichever is the last)
> The accumulated memories of annual emotion   [3]
> May be simplified into a great joy

[1] **So that**] *ringed along with the same words in 22, 25 ^ 26, and with* That *by*
Hayward *ts5b* ‖ *ringed ts5a*   **before · · · before**] *each ringed, with marginal*
"X" *ts5a*

[2] **I mean**] meaning *ts5a 2ⁿᵈ reading*

[3] ^ [4] *marginal arrow with* "St L[ucy]?" *ts5a*

ts6–ts9:

> So that before the end, the eightieth Christmas
> (By "eightieth" meaning whichever is the last)
> The accumulated memories of annual emotion
> May be simplified into a great joy

[2] **"eightieth"**] eightieth *ts8 1ˢᵗ reading* (*error*)

[4] **simplified**] concentrated *ts8, ts9*

36–37] *ts1–ts9*:

> Which is also a great fear
> When fear came upon every soul,
> Because reminder of the beginning is reminder of the end,   [3]
> And the first coming of the second coming.

[1] **is**] shall be *ts5–ts9* (*typed over is ts8*)   **fear**] fear, as on that occasion
ts2–ts7 ‖ fear, as on the occasion *ts8, ts9*

[2] **soul,**] soul: *ts2–ts9*

[3] **Because reminder of**] Because *ts1 2nd reading* ‖ *ts2–ts9*   **is reminder**] is a reminder *Hayward ts5b* ‖ shall remind us *ts6–ts9* ‖ should remind us *ts8 1st reading*   **end,**] end *ts2–ts9*

38–41] *not ts6–ts9*

38] *indented ts4, ts5*

38–39 But let me] Let me *ms2 2nd reading* ‖ And let me *ms2 3rd reading* ‖ But let me, *ts1, ts2* ‖ Let me, *ts3, ts4* ‖ And let me, *ts5* ‖ And let us, *with "?" Hayward ts5b 2nd reading* ‖ And here I remember, *ts5a alt (with* let me *ringed)*   **passing**] concluding *ts3 1st reading* ‖ conclusion *ts3 2nd reading, ts4 1st reading, ts5*   **remember St Lucy | Her**] remember with gratitude | St. Lucy, her *ms2 2nd reading, ts1 2nd reading, ts2 1st reading, ts3–ts5* ‖ remember St. Lucy | With *ts1 1st reading* ‖ include with other memories, | St. Lucy, her *ts2 2nd reading*   **crown of flame.**] lighted crown. *ms2 2nd reading* ‖ crown of fire. *ts1–ts5*

40] *indented ts4, ts5*   **message**] greeting that *ms2 2nd reading, ts1–ts5*   **want**] wish *ms2 2nd reading, ts1–ts5*

41] *ts1 1st reading*:

> Think well before you choose it. Is it the kind
> That you care to receive? And if not,
> How will you retaliate upon the giver?

all del ‖ *ts1 2nd reading*:

> Is it the kind that you care to receive?

with the *emended to* a

41 Is] And is *ms2 2nd reading*   **the**] a *ms2 2nd reading, ts2–ts5*

Unfinished Poems

Fragment of a Prologue and *Fragment of an Agon* had been published together as *Sweeney Agonistes* (1932) before they were collected in *1936*. By contrast, *Triumphal March* and *Difficulties of a Statesman* appeared together as *Coriolan* for the first time in *1936*.

Section-title page] 1936+

Sweeney Agonistes

The drafts at King's begin with a typescript of possible titles and epigraphs on a typed leaf which has been cut in half, and a carbon (later endorsed: "My typing. probably precedes the fragments themselves T. S. Eliot"), which is shown in facsimile in *Homage to T. S. Eliot* (1965).

HOMAGE TO ARISTOPHANES: A FRAGMENT
by T. S. Eliot

These are the gloomy companions of a disturbed imagination; the melancholy madness of poetry, without the inspiration.—JUNIUS.

Hence the soul can only be endowed with divine union, when it has divested itself of the love of created beings.—ST. JOHN OF THE CROSS.

Be absolute for death, either death or life
Shall thereby seem the sweeter: reason thus with life—
MEASURE FOR MEASURE.

Casey Jones was a fireman's name:
In the red-light district he won his fame.
OLD BALLAD.

FRAGMENT OF A MELOCOMIC MINSTRELSY
by T. S. Eliot

Oreste: *Vous ne les voyez pas, vous, mais, moi, je les vois. Elles me pourchassent, je ne puis plus rester.*—LES CHOEPHORES, trad. Paul Mazon.

The Commentary headnote, 6. *THE SUPERIOR LANDLORD* prints the two ruled leaves of a Manuscript Synopsis (which were shown in facsimile in *Homage to T. S. Eliot*), followed by a scenario in two parts with an interlude. The Commentary headnote 10. PREMIÈRE IN AMERICA: ENTER AN OLD GENTLEMAN prints a later addition never incorporated into the published text.

For the published text:

ts1 (King's): foolscap ribbon copy and carbon of a draft of *Fragment of a Prologue*, and carbon only of *Fragment of an Agon*, all bound with *The Superior Landlord*. First leaf of ribbon copy of *Fragment of a Prologue* numbered by TSE "147".

ts Morley (Berg): "Prompt copy" from the archive of the Group Theatre, with note by Robert Medley relating it to a production in the mid-1950s at Morley College, Lambeth. Twelve pages, interleaved with ms diagrams and stage directions (thought to be by Rupert Doone), duplicated ts and programme. As this has no textual authority, variants are not recorded below.

Criterion: *Fragment of a Prologue* in *Criterion* Oct 1926, and *Fragment of an Agon. From "Wanna Go Home, Baby?"* in *Criterion* Jan 1927.

Also collated: *Sweeney Agonistes* (*Sw. Ag.*, also 2nd ed. 1933), *1936* and later editions. *1936* and *1963+* inadvertently omitted *Fragment of a Prologue* 107.

The pirated printings in *Two Worlds Monthly*, NY, of *Fragment of a Prologue* (Jan 1927) and *Fragment of an Agon* (as *Wanna Go Home Baby?* / *Fragment of an Agon*, May–June 1927) are not collated.

Subsection title page **Sweeney Agonistes | Fragments of an Aristophanic Melodrama**] *1936, 1963*. Like *Coriolan*, *Sweeney Agonistes* is listed as a poem rather than a section in the Contents, and this subsection title page is set in smaller type than "Unfinished Poems" on the section-title page. The epigraphs also appear on this subsection title page.

Fragment of a Prologue

"Don't", "can't", "wouldn't", "won't", "shan't" have no apostrophes in *ts1*. *Guild* treats stepped lines as new lines, ranged left (except 96: "Well I *never.*")

Epigraphs] *not ts1. Both epigraphs printed at the top of each part in Criterion. Also in Profile printing of the second part (roman except for attributions). Roman with italic for attributions and speaker's name Sw. Ag., Later Poems.*

Title] Prologue *ts1*

Stage direction] Doris playing patience. Dusty on the piano-stool: occasionally she strikes a few bars, and sometimes both of them sing a few bars. *ts1 but not carbon, so a later addition*

24 TELEPHONE] *Doris ts1 1ˢᵗ reading*

25 DUSTY: That's Pereira] *not ts1*

26 Well can't] Cant *ts1* (*stepped from* 25)

27 say?] *1963+* ‖ *say! ts1* ‖ say! *printings prior to 1963, 1963 proof, US 1963 and later American printings*

45 All right] Allright *Criterion*

47 ^ 48] *line space ts1*

48] *indented after end of 47 ts1*

51 Clubs] Spades. *ts1*

56–58] *not inset ts1*

57 Of] "Of *ts1*

59 that] that? *ts1 1ˢᵗ reading*

68 ^ 69] *line space ts1*

70 **two of spades**] *ts1*, *printings prior to 1963* ‖ *two of spades 1963+. (The exclamation mark is roman except in Criterion, Sw. Ag., US 1936, Guild, where it is italic)*

72 **do?**] do! *ts1*

94 ^ 95] What was I saying a minute ago? *ts1*

96 **never**] *1936+* ‖ never! *ts1, Criterion, Sw. Ag.*

97 **are**] *1936+* ‖ are *ts1, Criterion, Sw. Ag.*

99] *indented as continuation of 98 ts1*

101] *continuation more deeply indented ts1*   **dear**] *1936* ‖ dear! *ts1, Criterion, Sw. Ag.*

103 **there?**] there *ts1*

106] *indented as continuation of 105 ts1*

107] *not 1936+*

108] *indented as continuation of 107 ts1*   (**to**] (to *ts1*

110] *prefixed with stage direction: Wauchope's Knock ts1*

110–114] *inset ts1*

114 ^ 115] *line space, no stage direction ts1*

119 **on**] in (?*mistyping*) *ts1 1ˢᵗ reading*   **business.**] business— *ts1*

122 **pleased**] pleased indeed *ts1*

123 **Extremely**] I'm extremely *ts1*

127 **war**] War *ts1*

129 **we**] we all *ts1*

141 **Miss—er—uh—**] *1936+* ‖ Miss Dorrance, *ts1* ‖ Miss—er—uh *Criterion, Sw. Ag.*

145 **it**] it it *1936 (corrected from 7th imp., 1944), Guild*

151 **Don't**] You mustn't *ts1*

after 159] (*To be continued*) *Criterion*

Fragment of an Agon

Also collated: *Profile: Ezra Pound: An Anthology Collected in MCMXXXI* (Milan, 1932).

"Won't" and "don't" have no apostrophe in *ts1*. *Criterion* spells "won't" without an apostrophe on all five occasions, and "don't" with an apostrophe on its first three appearances after the epigraph but without one on the further eight. *Sw. Ag., US 1936, US 1952* all spell "dont" and "wont" without an apostrophe. *US 1963* has the apostrophe consistently in "won't" but not in "dont". The British editions *1936, 1963, 1969* insert all the apostrophes except at 76.

Title] *1936+* ‖ *Fragment of AGON ts1* ‖ Fragment of an Agon. [From *Wanna Go Home, Baby?*] *Criterion, Profile* ‖ FRAGMENT OF AN AGON *Sw. Ag.*

Opening stage direction] *not ts1*

9 **you**] you *ts1*

28 **copulation,**] *US 1936, Later Poems (endorsed by TSE in response to a proof query, Faber archive RdlM 80), US 1952, US 1963* ‖ copulation *1936, Later Poems proof, 1963*

33 **I'd be bored.**] *indented to align with "You'd be bored", 32 Profile.*

39 ^ 40] *two-line space then* Snow and Swarts on banjos, Wauchope and Horsfall in low voices. *then line space ts1* ‖ *line space above and below stage direction Profile*

40–70 *as also* 73–89] *roman ts1* ‖ *roman with no line spaces Profile*

48 ^ 49 *as also* 60 ^ 61] *two-line space ts1*

54 **tree.**] *tree 1963, US 1963, 1969*

70 ^ 71] *three-line space ts1* ‖ *no line space Later Poems*

72 ^ 73] *three-line space then* Snow and Swarts on banjos, Klipstein and Krumpacker in low voices. *then two-line space ts1* ‖ *line space above and below stage direction Profile*

73–89] *all roman Profile*

76 **won't**] *1974+* ‖ wont *ts1 and printings prior to 1974*

84 **noontime**] *ts1, printings prior to 1963, US 1963 and subsequent US printings (and matching 88)* ‖ *noontide 1963+*

89 ^ 90] *two-line space ts1* ‖ *line space Criterion*

97 **SWARTS:**] WARTS: *1936 12th–16th imps. (1948–57), corrected by TSE in Washington copy 1954)*

100 ^ 101] *line space ts1*

102 **assure you,**] assure, *ts1*   **interested**] *ts1, Criterion, Sw. Ag., 1936 1st–9th imps. (to Jan 1946), US 1963+* ‖ interested *1936 from 10th imp. (Sw. Ag. 1946; the roman es being visibly inserted into standing type), 1963+*

102 ^ 103] *line space ts1*

105 **wants**] or wants *ts1*

119 **couple of**] coupla *ts1*

125 **do!**] *1936+* ‖ do? *ts1, printings prior to 1936*

136 **they both were**] they were both *1969, 1974 (later corrected)*

155 ^ 156] *two-line space,* Full chorus: Wauchope, Horsfall, Klipstein, Krumpacker, in loud voices. *line space ts1* ‖ *line space above and below stage direction Profile*

157 **on**] *ts1, Criterion, Sw. Ag., US 1936, Later Poems, US 1952* ‖ in *1936, Later Poems proof, 1963+. TSE emended 1936 proof to "on" but the change was not implemented. He also endorsed the change to "on" in response to a proof query about Later Poems (Faber archive RdlM 80).*

167–73] *ts1:*

> Ha
> Ha
> But you wait for the knock and the turning of the lock for you know that somebody's coming for you.
>
> *Pereira's Knock*   Knock knock knock
>   Knock knock knock
>   Knock

Knock
Knock

Doris goes off into hysterical screams of laughter.

Pereira's Knock   KNOCK KNOCK KNOCK
KNOCK KNOCK KNOCK
KNOCK
KNOCK
KNOCK

Coriolan I. Triumphal March

ts1 (U. Maryland): ribbon copy on two leaves of lightweight typing paper, with two holograph corrections. An untraced carbon copy sold by Glenn Horowitz in 1990 (cat. 22, item 50) has the same emendation of the title (in unknown hand) and "one pencil correction"; sold again, Sotheby's, 16 Dec 1996.

ts2 (Texas): secondary carbon copy on two leaves, headed "TRIUMPHAL MARCH | By T. S. Eliot". Second leaf signed "T. S. Eliot" at foot.

proof (untraced): single sheet folded once to make four pages, printed on three, with some variations of line spacing. An unknown hand has pencilled on the other page: "Mr. Eliot didn't like this type, so Mr. Simon is consulting with Mr. Kauffer before he sets it up again" (Oliver Simon was typographer at the Curwen Press; see headnote). Sold by Horowitz and then Sotheby's, with *ts1*.

Subsection title page **Coriolan**] *1936, 1963+. Coriolan*, like *Sweeney Agonistes*, is listed as a poem rather than a section in the Contents, and this subsection title page is set in smaller type than the section-title page "Unfinished Poems".

Title] I. Triumphal March *1936+* ‖ CORIOLAN: Part I *ts1 1ˢᵗ reading* ‖ *without numeral tss, Ariel, Modern Things, Faber Bk Mod V*

1 **oakleaves,**] oakleaves *US 1936*

6 **temple**] Temple *Modern Things*

7 **day?**] day. *ts2*

8] *two lines, the second indented (misreading Ariel, where the line is turned at "eagles. | And") Recent Poetry, Faber Bk Mod V* ‖ *lineation indeterminate 1936, 1963* ‖ *single line US 1936, US 1952, 1969*   **coming?**] coming. *tss*

12 **first?**] first. *tss*   **see?**] see. *tss*

13 ^ 14 *as also 23 ^ 24*] *no line space tss*

14–23] *single spaced and so tighter than the surrounding poem, which is typed with 1½-line spacing tss* ‖ *similarly set tighter Ariel, 1936 (not US 1936)*

19 **aeroplanes,**] aeroplanes *ts2 1ˢᵗ reading*

21 **now**] *ranged left and followed by space 1936, 1963+ (not US eds.)*

23 **bakeries.**] bakeries, *tss*

29 **his**] *1936+* ‖ those *tss, printings prior to 1936*

34 ^ 35] *two-line space Guild*

41 ^ 42] *line space 1936+* ‖ *two-line space Guild* ‖ *no line space tss, Modern Things, Recent Poetry, Faber Bk Mod V* (*where* 41 *is first line on page*) ‖ *new page so line spacing indeterminate Ariel*

42 **That**] This *1974 and some reprints of 1969*

45 **crumpets.)**] *crumpets. ts1 1ˢᵗ reading*

47 **Please,**] Please *1974*   **you**] you ~~give~~ *ts2*

Coriolan II. Difficulties of a Statesman

ms1 (King's): pencil on rectos only of six numbered leaves from a small ruled notebook, inscribed on fol. 2: "for J. H. from T. S. E. (20. 2. 48) First Draft." The paper size allowed sometimes only four words per line, so some verse lines occupy three physical lines. This makes it hard to judge the intended lineation, and may have influenced the very varied line-lengths in the finished poem. First and last pages shown in facsimile in *March & Tambimuttu eds.* (plate after 116).

ts1 (Brotherton Library, Leeds): ribbon copy on three leaves, with a note at head in the hand of Bonamy Dobrée: "Typescript by T. S. E. Given me as I sailed for U.S.A. c. 1929".

ts2 (Texas): carbon on three leaves. Parts of lines on the first leaf that have been mechanically duplicated in error are here ignored.

ts Turner (untraced): TSE wrote to the voice teacher J. Clifford Turner on 8 Mar 1935 promising "copies of *Mr. Pugstyles* and *The Difficulties of a Statesman* as soon as I have time to make copies, or have copies made."

Commerce set the whole poem in italics, with every line indented other than turns, which begin at the margin.

H&H: *Hound and Horn* Oct–Dec 1932. TSE to Harriet Monroe, 10 Aug 1932: "I have only one poem or part of a poem which I care to publish at the moment in any form, and I have given it to the *Hound and Horn* about six weeks ago. So now I am afraid there is literally nothing which I would care to offer to the readers of *Poetry.*"

First publication in a volume, *The Faber Book of Modern Verse* (a month before publication of *1936*).

Title] II. Difficulties of a Statesman *1936+* ‖ *not ms1* ‖ *without numeral Commerce, H&H, Faber Bk Mod V*

1 **CRY**] Cry *Faber Bk Mod V*

3 **The**] *not ms1 1ˢᵗ reading*   **Cavaliers,**] Cavaliers *ts2*

5 **Eagle**] Eagle, *ts2 1ˢᵗ reading with the opening bracket that follows then typed over the comma, without word space*   **class),**] Class) *ms1* ‖ class) *ts1*

8 **committees:**] Committees, *ms1*

9 **consultative councils, the**] *not ms1*   **standing committees**] Standing Committees *ms1*

14 **thirty shillings at Christmas**] 30/- at Xmas *ms1*

15 ^ 16 *new page H&H*

16 **committee**] commissioner *ms1*   **nominate**] ~~ap~~ *1ˢᵗ reading ms1 (uncertain reading, perhaps for* appoint)

17 **Water**] ~~water~~ *ts1 1ˢᵗ reading*

19 **chiefly**] primarily *ms1, tss, Commerce, H&H, Faber Bk Mod V* ‖ ~~especially~~ *ts2 1ˢᵗ reading*   **rebuilding**] renewing *ms1*

24 **marches**] marshes *1936 (corrected by TSE in John Hayward's copy of 1936 and Curtis 1936, as from 11th imp., 1947), US 1936 (corrected by TSE in William Yeo's copy of the 1947 imp., U. Virginia), Guild, Later Poems*

25 **in**] on *ts2 1ˢᵗ reading*   **marshes**] marches *ts2 1ˢᵗ reading*

26 **lightning**] lightening in the night of July. *ms1 1ˢᵗ reading* ‖ lightening in the nights of July. *ms1 2ⁿᵈ reading* ‖ lightning in nights of July. *ts2, Commerce* ‖ lightning, *H&H, Faber Bk Mod V*

32 **under the . . . Hidden under the . . . Where the**] *Commerce, 1936+, also US 1952 with* Where *turned as though to begin an indented new line* ‖ under the hidden under the Where the *ms1* ‖ under the   Hidden under the   Where the *ts2, H&H, Faber Bk Mod V*   **dove's**] doves *ms1*   **moment,**] moment *ms1*

34 **breast feather**] feather *ms1 1ˢᵗ reading*

36 **not among**] *1936+* ‖ not, happily, one of *ms1 1ˢᵗ reading* ‖ not one of *ms1 2ⁿᵈ reading, tss, printings prior to 1936*   **busts,**] *1936+* ‖ busts *ts2, printings prior to 1936*   **all**] *not ms1 1ˢᵗ reading*

37 **tired**] *not ms1*   **heads**] weary heads *ms1 2ⁿᵈ reading*

39 **wind**] ~~south~~ wind *ms1 2ⁿᵈ reading*

41 **time**] times *Guild*   **almost**] *not ms1 1ˢᵗ reading*

42 **immolations,**] *not ms1*   **oblations,**] oblations and *ms1*   **impetrations,**] *1936+* ‖ impetrations *ms1, tss, printings prior to 1936*

44 **not**] then *ms1 (? written over* n)

46 **silent**] silence of the *ms1*

47] *first words over illegible erasure ms1*   **with the sweep of**] *looped, as though to move last word to first place ms1* ‖ *in under ms1 alt*   **little bat's**] small bat's *ms1*   **firefly**] fire fly *ms1*   **or**] or the *ms1 1ˢᵗ reading* ‖ (or *ms1*   **lightning bug,**] lightening bug *ms1 1ˢᵗ reading* ‖ lightning bug) *ms1*

48 **and**] or *ts2 1ˢᵗ reading*

49 **chirp**] *apparently filling a blank left when the line was first written ms1*   **thinly through**] in *ms1*   **through the night**] *1936+* ‖ in the night *ms1, tss, printings prior to 1936*

52 **representative**] thoroughly representative *ms1*

52 ^ 53] *line space ms1*

53] *indented ts1* ‖ *centred US 1936, US 1952, US 1963*

53] *wide word spacing tss, Commerce, H&H, US 1936, US 1952, US 1963*

53] *ending with full stop ms1, ts2, Commerce, H&H*

Minor Poems

Section-title page] 1936+.

Eyes that last I saw in tears

ms1 (Texas): fair copy in pencil on a single leaf of lined paper without watermark. Facsimile in *An Exhibition of Manuscripts and First Editions of T. S. Eliot* (Texas, 1961). Probably sent to Ottoline Morrell late in 1924 (see textual headnote to *The Hollow Men ts1*).

ts1 (King's): carbon headed "DORIS'S DREAM SONGS" and with *Eyes that last I saw in tears* as "I" and *The wind sprang up at four o'clock* as "II". Foolscap leaf without watermark formerly folded three times to fit an envelope, endorsed "An early version typed by myself. T.S. Eliot". With pencil draft of *The Hollow Men* Part III lengthwise on verso (evidently written later).

Valerie's Own Book: fair copy. Facsimile in the programme for the Stage Sixty Theatre Club's *Homage to T. S. Eliot* (1965).

ts Virginia (U. Virginia): later typing not by TSE but endorsed in his late hand. As this has no independent authority, it is not collated here.

4 **The golden**] When the *ts1 1st reading*

5 **I**] *not 1963, though present in proof so published line spaced accordingly (corrected 5th imp., 1970)*

6 **affliction**] *Criterion, Chapbook, 1936, 1963, US 1963+* ‖ affliction. *Am. Poetry 1925, 1969, 1963 5th imp. (1970), 1974+*

6^7] *two-line space Valerie's Own Book*

12 **this,**] *printings prior to 1974, US 1963* ‖ this *ts1, 1974+*

The wind sprang up at four o'clock

Included in *The Year's Poetry 1936: A Representative Selection* ed. Denys Kilham Roberts and John Lehmann ([1936/7]). No variants.

ts1 (King's): carbon headed "DORIS'S DREAM SONGS" with I and II (see *Eyes that last I saw in tears ts1*, above).

ts Virginia (U. Virginia): later typing not by TSE but endorsed in his late hand. As this has no independent authority, it is not collated here.

Valerie's Own Book: fair copy with no variants.

  1 **at**] and broke *ts1 1ˢᵗ reading*

  5 **echo**] memory *ts1 1ˢᵗ reading*

10 **spears.**] spears *ts1*, *Chapbook*, *Am. Poetry 1925*

Five-Finger Exercises

Published in *Criterion* Jan 1933, then *1936+*.

Title] no hyphen in Contents list on *Criterion* cover ‖ Five-finger exercises *Later Poems Contents* ‖ *Five finger exercise Index to 1963 (corrected 1974)*

I. Lines to a Persian Cat

ms1 (Magdalene): manuscript addition to typed letter to I. A. Richards, 2 Mar 1932, with *Lines to a Persian Cat*, with the comment "Composed in the Underground. Too obvious Blake ⊲ Hopkins to be useful."

ts1 (U. Maryland): single leaf, double spaced, with typed title (without numeral) and single ms correction. Typed date at foot: "T. S. E. 29. 2. 32."

On 24 May 2000, Bloomsbury Book Auctions sold four slipcases enclosing 24 decorated manuscripts by Frederic Prokosch, catalogued as dating from 1932–36, and containing verse by TSE (mostly extracts). Among these manuscripts in "Butterfly Book" style, was *Lines to a Persian Cat*, to which Prokosch had added a note: "Eliot sent me a typescript of this poem in late June 1935: this is a copy of this version, with the word 'only' in the sixth line." No such typescript has been traced.

  2 **Square.**] Sq. *ms1* ‖ Square *Criterion*

  9 **will**] does *ts1 2ⁿᵈ reading*

II. Lines to a Yorkshire Terrier

ts1 (U. Maryland): single leaf, double spaced, with typed title (without numeral) and ms corrections. On the verso are written the words "'For Annie' by E. A. Poe", probably not in TSE's hand. Formerly folded with *Lines to a Persian Cat ts1*.

  1 **In a brown**] On a bare *ts1*

  2 **crookt and dry.**] cramped and bowed. *ts1*

  3 **In a black sky, from**] Natural forces, in *ts1 1ˢᵗ reading*

  4] *not ts1 1ˢᵗ reading*   **shriek'd**] shrieked *ts1*

  5] Cracked, shrieked and muttered restlessly. *ts1 1ˢᵗ reading* ‖ Cracked, rattled, muttered restlessly. *ts1 2ⁿᵈ reading*

7 a] the *Criterion*   **eiderdown,**] eiderdown; *ts1*
8 **Yet**] But *ts1*   **cracked**] dry *ts1* 2nd *reading*
9 **cramped**] crookt *ts1*
14 **paws,**] paws; *ts1* ‖ paws. *Criterion*

III. *Lines to a Duck in the Park*

A Butterfly Book printing for Frederic Prokosch, entitled *A Duck in the Park* and purportedly of three copies, "Ghent, Easter 1936", was actually printed in 1969. Its title has no authority, and it is not collated here.

Title **the Park**] a Park *1936 Contents* (*all impressions, but not US*), *corrected by TSE in Curtis 1936 and Washington copy 1954*
13 **shall**] must *Criterion*

IV. *Lines to Ralph Hodgson Esqre.*

The title, capitalisation and shape of the poem presented a more harlequin appearance in the *Criterion*:

> IV— FOR RALPH HODGSON ESQRE.
>
> How delightful to meet Mr. Hodgson!
>   (Everyone wants to know *him*).
> With his Musical Sound
> And his Baskerville Hound
>   Which, just at a Word from his Master   5
>   Will follow you Faster and Faster
>   And Tear you Limb from Limb.
> How delightful to meet Mr. Hodgson!
>   Who is Worshipped by all Waitresses
> (They regard him as Something Apart);   10
>   While on his Palate (fine) he Presses
>   The Juice of the Gooseberry Tart.
> How delightful to meet Mr. Hodgson!
>   (Everyone wants to know *him*).
> He has 999 Canaries   15
> And round his Head Finches and Fairies
> In Jubilant rapture Skim.
>   How delightful to meet Mr. Hodgson!
>   (Everyone wants to know *him*).

ts1 (Beinecke): typescript headed by a drawing (in ink over pencil) of Hodgson with pipe in hand and his bull terrier breaking from its leash to chase a tailcoated figure off the edge of the leaf (see Commentary). Cream paper with large double circle watermark: "AT THE CANDLESTICKS | IN THE OVLD BALY 1649". *ts1 has initial capitals on the same words (when they appear) as the Criterion printing, as also* 1] Delightful 2] Wants · · · Know *Him* 8] Delightful 17] Rapture 18] Delightful 19] Wants · · · *Him.*

Title] *not ts1* ‖ FOR RALPH HODGSON ESQRE. *Criterion*

1, *as also* 18, 19 **meet**] Know *ts1*

2] *no indent 1963+* ‖ *indent 1936* ‖ *triple indent US 1936, US 1952, US 1963*

5–6] Who, moving Faster & Faster | Will, just at a Word from his Master *ts1*

7 **And**] *not ts1*

8 **meet**] know *ts1*

8 ^ 9] *[indented]* (Everyone Wants to know *Him*). *ts1*

9 **Who is worshipped**] Adored *ts1*

10] *not ts1*

11 **While on**] Upon *ts1*   **fine**] (fine) *ts1*

13–14] *not ts1*

14, *as also* 19] *triple indent US 1963*   **him.**]] *Later Poems (endorsed by TSE in response to a proof query. Faber archive RdlM 80)* ‖ him). *printings other than Later Poems*

15 **999**] 99999999999999999999999 *ts1*

16 **round**] around *ts1*   **finches**] the finches *ts1*

V. *Lines for Cuscuscaraway and Mirza Murad Ali Beg*

ts1 (Beinecke): matching the typescript of *Lines to Ralph Hodgson*, with profile at head of wide-eyed TSE wearing a hat, drawn by himself (see Commentary). The two tss were sent to Hodgson on 16 Aug 1932 (Aurelia Hodgson to Valerie Eliot, 4 Aug 1974), and both appear in facsimile in Stanford S. Apseloff, *T. S. Eliot and Ralph Hodgson Esqre* in *Journal of Modern Literature* June 1983.

ts Manwaring (untraced): in his typed collation (King's), Beare mentions seeing, thanks to Gallup, a typescript "with corrections in Mr. Eliot's hand, bearing the inscription 'With the author's compliments to Miss Elizabeth Manwaring. T. S. Eliot. 18. 10. 32'."

ms Cournos (Beinecke): untitled fair copy in black ink on a single leaf, dated 24. ii. 33 and signed. With a later exhibition catalogue note by Gallup: "Eliot's imitation of Edward Lear, written out [for John & Helen Cournos at New Haven] 24 February 1933. Eliot stayed with the Cournoses on the occasion of his lecture at Yale on *The English Poets as Letter Writers*. (This was my first glimpse of Eliot in person, although we did not meet.)" Gallup's catalogue of his own collection notes: "Purchased Gotham Book Mart, Feb 1937." In this authorial transcript, 2, 5–7, 9–12 and 14 are inset.

ts Texas (Texas): later, untitled copy by TSE on a single leaf with letterhead "T. S. ELIOT | B–11 ELIOT HOUSE | CAMBRIDGE", which he used during his time at Harvard in 1932–33. *Sackton:* "Corrections and revision added as a joke, but the text finally restored to that of the [final] published version." Described in a letter from Angela Miles, TSE's secretary 1960–61, to F. Warren, 24 Apr 1961 (Texas): "He deliberately put it on the letter paper headed 'Eliot House, Cambridge' · · · the poem was [originally] written sometime prior to his stay at Eliot House." Illustrated in *An Exhibition of Manuscripts and First Editions of T. S. Eliot* (Texas, 1961). The text before correction is printed (so far as it can be determined) below the collation of other versions, and has a collation of its own.

The title, capitalisation and shape of the poem again presented a more harlequin appearance in the *Criterion*:

V— For Cuscuscaraway and
Mirza Murad Ali Beg

How unpleasant to meet Mr. Eliot!
  With his Features of Clerical Cut,
And his Brow so Grim
And his Mouth so Prim
  And his Conversation, so Nicely   5
Restricted to What Precisely
And If & Perhaps & But.
How unpleasant to meet Mr. Eliot!
  With a bobtail Cur
  In a Coat of Fur   10
  And a Porpentine Cat
  And a wopsical Hat;
How unpleasant to meet Mr. Eliot!
  (Whether his Mouth be Open or Shut).

Title] *not ts1* ‖ For Cuscuscaraway and Mirza Murad Ali Beg *Criterion*

  1, *as also* 8, 13] **unpleasant to meet**] Unpleasant to know *ts1*

  2–4] *inset ts1*

  2 **features of clerical cut,**] Coat of Clerical Cut,] *ts1* ‖ features of Clerical Cut; *ms Cournos*

  3 **brow so grim**] Face so Grim *ts1* ‖ brow so Grim, *ms Cournos*

  4 **mouth so prim**] Mouth so Prim *ts1* ‖ mouth so Prim, *ms Cournos*

  5 **conversation, so nicely**] Conversation so Nicely *ts1* ‖ Conversation, so Nicely *ms Cournos*

  7] *indent ts1*   **If**] if *ms Cournos* 1st *reading*   **and Perhaps and**] & Perhaps and *ts1*

  9–12] *inset ts1*

  9 **bobtail**] bobtailed *ts1* ‖ bob-tail *ms Cournos*   **cur**] Cur *ts1, ms Cournos*

  10 **coat**] Coat *ts1*   **fur**] Fur *ts1, ms Cournos*

  11 **porpentine cat**] Porpentine Cat *ts1, ms Cournos*

  12 **wopsical**] Wopsical *ts1*   **hat:**] Hat. *ts1* ‖ Hat; *ms Cournos*

14] *triple indent US 1936, US 1952, US 1963+*   (Whether]Whether *ts1*   mouth]
Mouth *ts1*   open] Open *ts1, ms Cournos*   shut).] Shut. *ts1* ‖ Shut.
ms Cournos ‖ shut.) *Later Poems (endorsed by TSE in response to a proof query.*
Faber archive RdlM 80) ‖ shut) *1936 18th imp.* (*1961; presumably broken type*).
The triple indent in American editions aligns "(Whether his mouth be open or
shut)." with "(Everyone wants to meet *him*)." in *Lines to Ralph Hodgson* (2, 14, 19)
to comic effect.

ts Texas 1ˢᵗ reading:

> How unpleasant to meet Mr. ██████ █████
> With his figure of corpulent size
> And his face inflamed
> And his manners untamed
> And his Conversation, so n [*illegible*]   5
> Restricted to x [*illegible*] x [*illegible*]
> And his sly and watery eyes.
> How unpleasant to meet Mr. ██████ █████
> With a bobtail cur
> In a coat of Fur   10
> And a porpentine Cat
> And a wopsical Hat,
> How unpleasant to meet Mr. Eliot
> Whether his Mouth be Open or Shut.

1 **unpleasant]** *1ˢᵗ and final reading* ‖ pleasant *2ⁿᵈ reading* ‖ delightful *3ʳᵈ*
reading   **meet]** met *1ˢᵗ reading*   ██████ ██████] *blotted deletions as*
though of names 1ˢᵗ reading ‖ *another blotted deletion 2ⁿᵈ reading* ‖ ~~Eliot~~ with "stet"
final reading. (*None of the blots appears actually to cover a typed or ms name.*)

2 **figure]** belly *2ⁿᵈ reading* ‖ Features *final reading*   **corpulent size]** Clerical Cut
final reading

3 **face]** nose *2ⁿᵈ reading* ‖ brow *final reading*   **inflamed]** so grim *final reading*

4 **manners untamed]** ways so courtly *2ⁿᵈ reading* ‖ mouth so Prim *final reading*

5 **n[*illegible*]]** nicely *final reading.* (*The deletions in this line and the next appear not*
to have been of real words.)

6 **x[*illegible*] x[*illegible*]]** what Precisely *2ⁿᵈ reading* ‖ what precisely *final reading*

7 **]** And If ⊲ Perhaps ⊲ But. *final reading*

8 ██████ ██████] *blotted deletions as though of names 1ˢᵗ reading* ‖ *another*
blotted deletion 2ⁿᵈ reading ‖ Eliot *final reading*

11 **Cat]** *1ˢᵗ and final reading* ‖ cat *2ⁿᵈ reading* (C *struck through with* "~~l.c.~~" *then* "stet")

12 **wopsical]** wposical *1ˢᵗ reading*

Landscapes

The manuscripts and typescripts of each piece are listed here below a late manuscript copy of all five, and the first printings.

ms Congress (Library of Congress): fair copies by TSE of the five poems on five leaves, each signed and dated 1959, presented to the library by Henry Sobiloff, 12 Nov 1959. Written out by TSE to be sold at a private auction on 7 Nov for the benefit of the Modern Poetry Association in Chicago, after a dinner in his honour. The catalogue includes a facsimile of *Usk*. The general title *Landscapes* and the numerals are omitted.

Valerie's Own Book: fair copies of the five poems on five pages, interrupted by other poems (see Textual History headnote 6. *VALERIE'S OWN BOOK*).

First printings:

I. *New Hampshire* and II. *Virginia*

The two, as *Words for Music*, in *Virginia Quarterly Review* Apr 1934; reprinted under the same title in *The Best Poems of 1934* ed. Thomas Moult.

Words for Music: "Twenty copies" of this Butterfly Book, privately printed for Frederic Prokosch, Bryn Mawr, 1934 (no copies for sale). TSE's letter to Prokosch, 20 Feb 1935, thanking him for his "kind gift" (see headnote) indicates that Prokosch had printed the poems without asking permission. He had probably come across them in *Best Poems*, published in Sept 1934. TSE to Stephen Spender, 22 Feb 1935: "I haven't the slightest idea who Prokosch is, but he seems a very amiable person." The texts of a proof copy corrected by Prokosch (Texas) and of two decorated manuscript copies made by Prokosch, *Butterfly ms1* (BL) and *Butterfly ms2* (McCue collection), are as printed copies except where noted.

Further printings for Prokosch of *Words for Music* in 1951, and of each poem as a separate Butterfly Book in 1968, were all falsely dated "1934" (often since erased and overwritten); see *Barker* 214–18. They are not collated here.

III. *Usk*

Not printed individually.

IV. *Rannoch, by Glencoe*

New English Weekly 17 Oct 1935 (no variants).

V. *Cape Ann*

New Democracy (NY) 15 Dec 1935.

III. *Usk* and V. *Cape Ann*

Two Poems: "Twenty-two copies" of this Butterfly Book, privately printed for Frederic Prokosch by Cambridge U. Press, Christmas 1935 (no copies for sale), with

Cape Ann preceding *Usk*. TSE to Prokosch, 17 Dec 1935, on receipt of *Two Poems* and referring also to *Words for Music*: "Thank you so much for the copies of the poems which you have had made for me, which I am sure will be as much admired as the previous ones which I have shown to friends."

The typeface of *Two Poems* is Perpetua, but Texas has a "Proof in Centaur type. One of two copies" (as a note by Prokosch describes it) with text as printed copies. Later printings for Prokosch of each poem as a separate Butterfly Book were falsely dated "1935". They are not collated here.

In the proof of *1936* the constituent titles were set the same size as those of *Five-Finger Exercises* (smaller than the main title), but with four differences: each part began a new page, the numerals were roman rather than italic, with no full stops, and the words were set beneath rather than alongside the numerals. In the printed volume, the titles were increased in size to that of individual poems throughout the book and the numerals were set in italics with full stops. The general title *Landscapes* was separated from that of the first poem by an asterisk (omitted in *Later Poems*). This remained the style in *1963*. In *US 1936*, where titles are generally all in capitals, the titles of the constituent parts of both *Five-Finger Exercises* and *Landscapes* are in type of the same size as the main title, but in upper and lower case italics, with numerals in roman type. Also in *US 1936*, the constituent parts of *Five-Finger Exercises* run on, whereas the *Landscapes* each begin a new page.

I. *New Hampshire*

ts1 (U. Virginia): ribbon copy of I and II, entitled *Words for Music*, sent to *Virginia Quarterly Review* (see headnote). Single leaf with pencilled instructions to printer.

ts2 (untraced): single leaf, headed "*New Hampshire*", and signed. Sold at Swann Galleries, 12 Jan, 1984 (*American Book Prices Current*). The sale of both this and *ts2* of II. *Virginia* at the Swann Galleries suggests that they were originally a pair.

Title] *ranged right without numeral ts1, Virginia Quarterly Review, Best Poems, Words for Music*

1 **Children's**] CHILDREN'S *Virginia Quarterly Review* (*house style*)

2 **blossom-**] blossom - *Words for Music proof* ‖ blossom *ms Congress*

7 **To-day**] Today *Words for Music*   **to-morrow**] *1936+* ‖ tomorrow *ts1, Virginia Quarterly Review, Words for Music, ms Congress*

8 **light-in-leaves;**] *1936+* ‖ light-in-leaves. *ts1, Virginia Quarterly Review, Best Poems, Words for Music*

9] *not Butterfly ms1*

II. *Virginia*

ts1 (U. Virginia): see I. *New Hampshire.*

ts2 (untraced): single leaf, headed "II. *Virginia*", and signed. Sold at Swann Galleries 6 Nov 1986 (*American Book Prices Current*).

Title] *ranged right without numeral ts1, Virginia Quarterly Review, Best Poems, Words for Music*

 5 **mocking-bird**] mockingbird *Valerie's Own Book*

 9 **living**] *typed over* L *ts1*

 13 **river, river.**] red river *Words for Music* (*corrected by TSE in copy IV, sent to I. A. Richards 20 Feb 1935, now Magdalene*), *Butterfly ms1* ‖ red river. *Butterfly ms2*

III. *Usk*

ms1 (Houghton): on verso of *ts1* of *Mr. Pugstyles.* Gift of TSE's brother.

ts1 (Texas *Sackton* F9), single leaf sent to Frederic Prokosch in summer 1935. With Prokosch's instruction to printer "Set in Perpetua 239/10" added at head. (The number refers to the Monotype typeface series number and size.)

ts2 (Magdalene, Box 44): sent (with *Cape Ann*) to I. A. Richards, 9 June 1935.

ms Spender (Lizzie Spender collection): post-publication fair copy in Stephen Spender's poetry autograph book, now with Lizzie Spender. (Unavailable to editors.)

ms White (formerly Roy Davids collection): post-publication fair copy in Eric W. White's poetry autograph book, which TSE directed his secretary to return to White, 4 Aug 1964, "hoping that you will be pleased with the verses that he has chosen". Sold Bonhams, 8 May 2013 (lot 331).

Title] Usk Valley. Brecon *ms 1st reading* ‖ Usk Valley *ms 2nd reading, ts2* (*ranged right*)

 1 **branch, or**] branch *ms1* ‖ branch or *ms White*

 3 **hart**] hind *ms1 1st reading* ‖ hart *with* ~~hind~~ *braced below ms1 2nd reading* **behind**] beside *ms1 1st reading* ‖ beyond *ms1 2nd reading* ‖ behind *ms1 final reading* **well.**] well *ms1*

 4 **aside,**] asideways, *ms1 1st reading* **not for**] *ms1 final reading+* ‖ cup and *ms1 1st reading* ‖ for cup and *ms1 2nd reading*

 5 **Old enchantments**] Ancient mantrams *ms1 alt added and del*

 6 **"Gently**] "Gebtly *ts1 1st reading* **not**] no *ts2 1st reading* (*mistyping*) **deep",**] deep". *ms1, ts1, Two Poems, ts2, ms White* ‖ deep," *US 1936*

 7 **Lift**] *ms1 1st and final reading* ‖ When you lift *ms1 2nd reading* **eyes**] eyes and *ms1 1st reading* (*very uncertain*)

8 **Where the**] *ms1 1ˢᵗ and final reading* ‖ Where *ms1 2ⁿᵈ reading*   **where the**] *ms1 1ˢᵗ and final reading* ‖ where *ms1 2ⁿᵈ reading*

10 **grey**] *word reinforced in ms1, possibly over "gray".*   **green**] grey *ms Congress 1ˢᵗ reading*   **air**] air, *ms1, ts2*

Rule beneath last line, after which is written and del Rannoch. (Shepherds of Glencoe) *ms1*

IV. *Rannoch, by Glencoe*

ms1 (Houghton): notebook leaf with blue rules, folded in four for posting and accompanied by an envelope addressed to Henry Eliot, postmarked 1937. Also photograph of this ms with typed transcript by Henry Eliot (Houghton). On her photocopy of the ms leaf, Valerie Eliot wrote "(Shepherds of Glencoe)".

ms Cheltenham (Cheltenham College): fair copy made at the request of C. Day Lewis, 1956. No variants. Writing to Day Lewis, 23 Oct 1956, to agree to "transcribe a page of my verse for Cheltenham College", TSE added "I have just done a poem for Rupert Hart-Davis's book, and saw that you had already done the same." This has not been identified.

Frank Morley said that he was handed a copy of this poem by TSE, presumably in ms or ts (see Commentary). Not present among Morley's papers at Haverford College.
    A Butterfly Book printing for Frederic Prokosch, purportedly of five copies, "Salzburg 1936", was actually printed in 1968. It is not collated here. In a note in copy delta, Prokosch wrote: "in the typescript which Eliot sent me there was no comma in line 4" (*Barker* 224–35). No such typescript has been traced.

Title] *not ms1*

1 **patient**] humble *ms1 alt*

2 **soft**] high *ms1 1ˢᵗ reading*

3 **soft**] low *ms1 1ˢᵗ reading*

4 **Substance crumbles, in the thin air**] And the thin air *ms1 with* Substance crumbles. *alt added.* See also note to "Butterfly Book" above

5] *overhanging step after* hot. *with* The *indented beneath* moon *ms1*

6 **war,**] war *US 1936*

7 **Languor**] Langour *US 1963 (error, from "Clangour"?)*   **broken**] the broken *ms1 1ˢᵗ reading*   **steel,**] steel. *ms1*

8 **confused**] old *ms1 1ˢᵗ reading*

9 **strong**] long *ms1 1ˢᵗ reading*

10 **Beyond**] In *ms1*

11 **long**] grim *ms1 1ˢᵗ reading*

V. Cape Ann

ts1 (Texas): single leaf of Colne Valley Parchment, sent by TSE to Frederic Prokosch in summer 1935. With Prokosch's instruction to printer "Set in Centaur 252/10" added at head.

ts2 (Magdalene): sent (with *Usk*) to I. A. Richards, 9 June 1935.

Title] *ranged right tss*

  1 **hear**] here *ms Congress*   **song-sparrow,**] song sparrow, *Valerie's Own Book*

  2 **Swamp-sparrow, fox-sparrow,**] Swamp sparrow, fox sparrow, *Valerie's Own Book*   **vesper-sparrow**] vesper-sparrow, *ts2* ‖ vesper sparrow *Valerie's Own Book*

  4 **to**] the *ts2 1st reading* (*mistyping*)

  6 **bob-white**] bobwhite *ts2*

  7 **bay-bush**] baybush *ts1*, *Two Poems*, *ts2*, *New Democracy* ‖ bay bush *Valerie's Own Book*

  8 **water-thrush**] water thrush *Valerie's Own Book*

10 **Sweet**] Some are archaic. Sweet *ts2*

12 **true**] last *ts1 1st reading*   **sea-gull**] seagull *Valerie's Own Book*

12 ^ 13 *line space*] *added by TSE Washington copy 1954, printed 1963+* (*not US 1963 or later US printings*) ‖ *not ts1, Two Poems, ts2, ms Congress, Valerie's Own Book, printings prior to 1963*

Lines for an Old Man

Published *NEW* 28 Nov 1935, then *1936+*.

ts1 (Houghton): nine typed lines, beneath which is pencilled drafting of four additional lines, with a loop to indicate that these are to precede the penultimate typed line.

ts2 (Houghton): 13 typed lines with last two deleted and three more added in pencil, apparently after *NEW* publication.

A Butterfly Book printing for Frederic Prokosch, entitled *Old Man's Song* and purportedly of five copies, is falsely dated "Salzburg 1936" but was printed later. In copy alpha, Prokosch wrote: "In the typescript which Eliot sent me this poem was titled (in pencil) *Old Man's Song*." No such typescript has been traced, and this title has no other authority. The Butterfly Book is not collated here.

Title] *not ts1, ts2 1st reading* ‖ WORDS FOR AN OLD MAN. *ts2, NEW* ‖ Lines for an old man *Later Poems Contents*.

Dedication] *to Stéphane Mallarmé. (first accent missing) ts2 ringed and del*

8–11] *not ts1 1ˢᵗ reading, but added in pencil:*

> My hate is more than hate of hate,
> More bitter than ~~the~~ the love of youth
>
> The hissing ~~of~~ over the flattened tongue
> Is inaccessible to the young.

[2] **More bitter**] *1ˢᵗ and 3ʳᵈ reading* ‖ *And bitterer 2ⁿᵈ reading* ‖ *More selfish final reading*   **the love of**] *1ˢᵗ and final reading* ‖ *love in 2ⁿᵈ reading*

[3] **The hissing**] *1ˢᵗ and final reading* ‖ *My hissing 2ⁿᵈ reading*

ts2 1ˢᵗ reading:

> The hissing over the flattened tongue
> Is more affectionate than hate,
> More bitter than the love of youth,
> And inaccessible to the young.

[1] **flattened**] *archèd 2ⁿᵈ reading*

[4] **to**] *by 2ⁿᵈ reading*

following 11] *ts1, ts2 1ˢᵗ reading:*

> Garlic [Thunder *ts1 1ˢᵗ reading*] and sapphires in the mud
> Clot the bedded axle-tree.

(the last typed lines, ending the poem until pencil addition in ts2 of 12–14), ringed and del ts2. These lines became Burnt Norton II 1–2.

12–14] *not ts1, ts2 1ˢᵗ reading, NEW*

13 ^ 14] *line space added by TSE Washington copy 1954, printed 1963+ (not US 1963 or later US printings)* ‖ *no line space ts2, printings prior to 1963*

14 **glad!**] glad? *ts2 (uncertain reading)*

Choruses from *"The Rock"*

Sesame prints only Choruses I and X (numbering the latter II). *Penguin* omits IV, V, VI and VIII.

ms1, ts1 (Bodleian): manuscript and heavily annotated combination of typescript and carbon, bound together in page sequence numbered by TSE. The bound volume also includes correspondence from those involved in creating the pageant, with "A Provisional Scheme for Spectacle of London Church Building" by E. Martin Browne and his "scenario" with light annotation by TSE, and a typed page of extracts from discourses by Robert Browne, "father of Congregationalism" (*fl.* 1550–1633) on a sheet of TSE's notepaper from Eliot House, Harvard. Since the sequence of the volume is erratic, folio numbers are given before each chorus below. In typescript, "GOD" appears as "GOD", and "LORD" as "LORD". (TSE to Geoffrey Curtis, 16 June 1943: "for a book not of a purely devotional character it is better to print God in the usual way instead of GOD all capitals.") The style "GOD" and "LORD" in *The Rock* (1934) became inconsistent in later printings, including *1963*, with "GOD" and "LORD" being more common. The style of *The Rock* has been preferred throughout the Choruses in the present edition.

ts2 (Bodleian): a later mixture of typescript and carbon, bound together in page sequence numbered by TSE. He has also written line numbers (every ten lines, in a single sequence) against the Choruses and some other passages in verse (totalling 743 lines). The bound volume also includes correspondence and papers by others concerning *The Rock*. (Sometimes the distinction between draft and fair copy typescripts is uncertain.)

ms Yale (Beinecke): first complete draft of the final chorus, on four leaves, and, on a fifth, the pageant's closing speech by "The Rock, now St. Peter", signed and dated March 1934. Sent by TSE to Toynbee Hall (presumably to be sold). To Mrs. L. M. Case, 27 Apr 1934: "The attached pencil manuscript of five pages is the first draft of a final chorus for *The Rock*, a pageant play written for performance at Sadler's Wells for the benefit of the Forty-five Churches Fund." To Gallup, 12 Feb 1948: "I cannot think where the five pages of manuscript of *The Rock* came from. I thought that all of the preparatory script for *The Rock* was included in what I gave to the Bodleian." Lacks terminal punctuation in the following lines: 12, 13, 14, 20, 26, 37, 39, 40, 41, 43, 45.

ts Chamb (Lord Chamberlain's Papers, BL): carbon of a typescript made by Marshall's Typing and Translations (4 Apr 1934), entitled *"The Rock: A Pageant Play* by T. S. Eliot" and sent for licensing. TSE to I. A. Richards, 20 Apr 1934: "The Lord Chamberlain and the Bishop of London have both passed my text, rather to my surprise, so I feel more cheerful."

proof: bound proof of *The Rock* (U. Virginia).

ts letter to Theodore Spencer, 7 Nov 1933 (Houghton): two lines from VI, and one from V. See headnote to *Choruses from "The Rock"*.

Sesame was presumably set from *1936*. *Penguin* was set from *1936* (as the error at IX 17 shows). *Sel Poems* was set from an emended copy of *Penguin* (the arrangement of IX 42–44 remaining the same), and in the collation below, *Sel Poems* is as *Penguin* except where noted.

In *The Rock* all verse is inset, as are the names of speakers, so that in these Choruses only stage directions begin at the left margin. The verse is also inset in *1936*, but stage directions and speakers' names both begin at the margin. *Penguin* and *Sel Poems 1954* inset paragraphs after the first stage direction in I, inset the entire text of III and inset the text of VII before the first stage direction, thereafter indenting the first line of some speeches.

Section-title page **Choruses from "The Rock"**] *1936+*

Title] *on section-title page, with numeral alone above first line 1936+ (matched only by Ash-Wednesday)*

Section numbers] *roman type US 1936, US 1952, Sesame, Penguin, 1969*

Stage directions] *square brackets not round, with stops not colons Rock, US Rock*

I

The Rock (1934) 7–11.

ts1: fol. 89, draft of 1–45 (carbon). Mention is made below of fol. 88, a preliminary outline ms.

ts2: fols. 17–21, double-spaced later version of entire Chorus (carbon).

ts Chamb 1–4.

Heading **I**] OPENING CHORUS. *with stage directions* Semi-Chorus of the Church *before* 1 *and* Semi-Chorus of Prophets: *before* 19 *ts1, also ts2 where both stage directions are del*

I 8 **Brings**] Bring *ts1, ts2, proof*

I 13 **no**] not *ts1 1ˢᵗ reading*

I 23 **Church**] church *ts1*

I 33 **the pleasant countryside**] ~~agricul~~ *ts1 1ˢᵗ reading*

I 34 **now**] *not ts1*   **only fit**] *not ts1 1ˢᵗ reading*

I 35 **And**] Only *ts1 1ˢᵗ reading*

I 40 **perhaps**] answer *ts1 1ˢᵗ reading, typed over*

I 46] The lot of man is ceaseless labour, ⊄ he must not expect the harvest for himself. *ms1* fol. 88

I 56] But one thing does not change. *Guild (compositor's eye-skip from* 61)

I 63–64] But the struggle merely changes its form. *ms1* fol. 88

I 65, 69] Two points: neglect of shrines ⊄ churches. neglect of the desert *ms1* fol. 88

I 66 **men**] things *ts2 2ⁿᵈ reading*

I 72^73] Squeezed like tooth-paste in the tube-train next to you, *ts2, ts Chamb* (*without terminal comma*), *Rock*. TSE deleted the line in most presentation copies of the 1st imp. It was removed from the 2nd imp., *US Rock* and later printings

I 75] I will show you some of the things that are being done, ๙ remind you of some that have been done. *ms1* fol. 88

I 79–124] *roman ts2, ts Chamb*

I 91 **Church**] church *ts Chamb, proof*

I 93^94 *stage direction*] CHANT OF UNEMPLOYED *ts2 1ˢᵗ reading*   **Now a**]   A *ts2*   **farther away,**] further away *ts2*

I 101 **plough**] plow *ts2 1ˢᵗ reading*

I 108^109 *stage direction*] CHANT OF WORKMEN AGAIN *ts2*

I 109 **turn**] *1963+* ‖ turn, *ts2, ts Chamb, printings prior to 1963*

II

The Rock (1934) 19–22.

ts1: fols. 119–20, draft with annotation (ribbon).

ts2: fols. 32–34, double-spaced later version (carbon).

ts Chamb 11–13.

Heading **II**] *CHORUS AA. ts1* ‖ *CHORUS. ts2*

II 1 **your**] our *ts1*   **were made**] became *ts1, ts2 1ˢᵗ reading*

II 4 **But you**] But *you ts2 2ⁿᵈ reading, with* "(*to the audience strictly*)"   **you** · · · **you** · · · **you**] we · · · we · · · we *ts1*   **well**] ill *ts1, ts2*   **helpless**] idle *ts2 1ˢᵗ reading* ‖ not *ts Chamb*

II 4–6] Have we built ill, that we are thus helpless, when many are born to idleness, to live and die in squalour, and those who would build and save know not what to do. *with* "*Perhaps begin with this theme referring to what was done in old days.*" *ms1* fol. 81.

II 5 **squalid deaths**] deaths of squalor *ts1 1ˢᵗ reading*   **in**] and *ts1 1ˢᵗ reading*

II 6 **for alms to be**] where alms are *ts1 1ˢᵗ reading*   **urn to be**] urn is *1ˢᵗ reading ts1*

II 7 **Your**] Our *ts1*   **building**] buildings *ts1, ts2 1ˢᵗ reading* ‖ body *2ⁿᵈ reading*   **framed**] joined *ts2 2ⁿᵈ reading*   **you sit**] we sit *ts1, ts2 1ˢᵗ reading*   **you may**] we may *ts1*   **which moved**] that moved *ts1*

II 8 **For love**] when we have only *ts1 1ˢᵗ reading* ‖ for love *ts1*   **as desire**] so desire *ts1*   **our labour to give**] to give our labour *ts1 1ˢᵗ reading*   **required.**] required *ts1*

II 9, 10] 10, 9 *ts1 1ˢᵗ reading, with loop to transpose*

II 9 **We wait**] Waiting *ts1*   **nobody**] no one *ts1*   **sung;**] sung." *ts1* ‖ sung: *Guild*

II 10 **Waiting**] And we wait *ts1 1ˢᵗ reading* ‖ We wait *ts1*

II 10^11] *line space Rock, Penguin, Sel Poems 1954, US 1952+* ‖ *line space very tight 1936, 1963* ‖ *no line space US 1936, Guild, 1969, 1974+* (*see McCue 2012 Proposal 2*)

II 11 **You** · · · **you** · · · **you**] We · · · we · · · we *ts1*   **well**] ill *ts1, ts2*

II 13 **that]** this *ts1 1ˢᵗ reading*   **for your]** of our *ts1*

II 14 **your]** our *ts1*   **fathers]** father *1974 (later corrected)*

II 19] Exporting cotton, coal and c *ts1 1ˢᵗ reading*

II 22] *ts1 1ˢᵗ reading*:

> Everything except the Word of GOD;
> Keeping the latter for ourselves exclusively
> Even

The second of these lines may have been typed after the first was del.

II 24] *ts1 has stop changed to semi-colon with added line*:

> And had abroad done better, had things been better done at home

II 25 **Of]** For *ts2 1ˢᵗ reading*   **you]** we *ts1*

II 26 **being]** not *ts1*

II 27 **deed]** deed done *ts2 2ⁿᵈ reading*

II 28 **neglect]** for neglect *ts1 1ˢᵗ reading*

II 30 **we]** you *ts1*

II 35–37] Church perpetually building ◁ perpetually subject to decay within and attack from without | In time of prosperity the people neglect the temple, in time of adversity they defame it. | All must pay the penalty for sin — sloth, avarice, gluttony, lust. *ms1 fol.81.*

II 32 **upon]** on *ts1*   **you · · · you]** we · · · us *ts1*

II 33 **you · · · you · · · your]** we · · · we · · · our *ts1*

II 34 **And all]** All *ts1 1ˢᵗ reading*   **you · · · your]** we · · · our *ts1*

II 36 **you]** we *ts1*   **while]** in *ts2 1ˢᵗ reading*

II 37 **they]** that *ts1 1ˢᵗ reading*   **decry]** defame *ts1 1ˢᵗ reading*

II 38 **you · · · you]** we · · · we *ts1*

II 39 **no]** not *ts1 1ˢᵗ reading*

II 40 **community]** community that is *ts1 1ˢᵗ reading*

II 41 **Even]** For even *ts1*

II 42 **whom]** him *ts1 1ˢᵗ reading*

II 44 **you]** we *ts1*

II 49 **about]** not *ts1*

II 51 **away]** ~~on~~ *ts1 1ˢᵗ reading*

II 52 **down,]** down, and *ts1*

II 54 **let the saw]** the chisel *ts1 1ˢᵗ reading* ‖ let the chisel *ts1 2ⁿᵈ reading, ts2, ts Chamb, proof*

II 55 **Let]** and *ts1*

III

The Rock (1934) 29–31.

ts1: fols. 128–29, draft with annotation (ribbon).

ts2: fols. 44–47 double-spaced fair copy (carbon).

ts Chamb 20–22.

Heading **III**] *Chorus I ts1 1ˢᵗ reading* || *Chorus A 2ⁿᵈ reading (see note)* || CHORUS. *ts2*

before III 1 *stage direction*] *Chorus of Prophets. ts1, ts2 (with colon), del*

III 5 **proceeds**] stratagems *ts1 1ˢᵗ reading*

III 12 **speculation**] speculations *ts1*

III 18 **me**] *not ts1 1ˢᵗ reading* || Me *2ⁿᵈ reading*

III 19 ^ 20 *stage direction*] *1st Prophet. ts1* || *First Prophet: ts2 1ˢᵗ reading* || *First Male Voice 2ⁿᵈ reading*

III 22 **forgetful**] forgetting *ts1 1ˢᵗ reading*

III 23 **labour**] stupour *ts2 1ˢᵗ reading*   **and delirious**] and forgetful *ts1 1ˢᵗ reading* || delirious *ts1*

III 24–25] The broken chimney, the peeled hull, a pile of rusty iron *ts1 1ˢᵗ reading* with There shall be left *added and a slash after* chimney, *to form two lines*

III 27, *as also* 30 **My**] *ts1, Later Poems proof, all other eds.* || my *Later Poems (endorsed by TSE in response to a proof query, Faber archive)*

III 27 ^ 28 *stage direction*] *2nd Prophet. ts1* || *Second Prophet: ts2 1ˢᵗ reading* || *Second Male Voice 2ⁿᵈ reading*

III 29 **City;**] city. *ts1*

III 35 **asphalt**] asphalte *ts1, ts2*

III 36 ^ 37 *stage direction*] *Chorus of the Church. ts1, ts2 1ˢᵗ reading (with colon)* || *Chorus 2ⁿᵈ reading*

III 38 **City**] city *ts1*

III 40 **you go.**] to go. *ts1 1ˢᵗ reading*

III 41 **colony**] tribe *ts1 1ˢᵗ reading*

III 48 **while**] where *ts2 1ˢᵗ reading*

III 51 **your**] you *1936 proof corrected TSE*

III 57 **prepared**] ready *ts1*

III 58 ^ 59 *stage direction*] *Chorus of Prophets. ts1, ts2 1ˢᵗ reading (with colon), del with chevron for line space*   **line space**] *not ts Chamb*

III 63 **and the**] and *ts2 1ˢᵗ reading*

III 70 **vacancy**] empti *ts1 1ˢᵗ reading (typed over)*

IV

The Rock (1934) 35.

ts1: fol. 133, double-spaced fair copy of a shorter version (ribbon).

ts2: fol. 51, double-spaced version of the full chorus (carbon).

ts Chamb 25–26.

Heading **IV**] CHORUS. *ts1, ts2 (with "A" added above)*

IV 4] *ts1* ‖ *not ts2+ (the omission was probably an accident when retyping)*

IV 3 ^ 4] When he built the wall and restored the Temple *ts1 (the omission in ts2 and later texts was perhaps accidental)*

IV 5–14] *not ts1*

IV 6 **king**] King *ts2, ts Chamb, Rock, US Rock*

IV 15 **to destroy him,**] who encompassed them, *ts1*

IV 16 **And**] There were *ts1*

IV 17] *not ts1*

IV 18 **So**] Wherefore *ts1*   **must**] must always *ts1*

V

The Rock (1934) 38–39.
ts1: fol. 135, double-spaced (ribbon).
ts Chamb 29–30.

Heading **V**] CHORUS B. *ts1*

V 1 **intention**] intentions *ts1*   **above**] in *ts1 1st reading*

V 3 **me**] me also *ts1*

V 4 **Prophet**] prophet *ts1*

V 7 **justified**] righteous *ts1*

V 8 **vain and**] profound an *ts1 1st reading*   **for silence:**] in silence; *ts1 1st reading*

V 10 **The**] But the *ts1 1st reading*

VI

The Rock (1934) 41–42.
ts1: fol. 137–39, early draft with annotation (ribbon).
ts2: fols. 60–61, double-spaced fair copy (carbon).
ts Chamb 30–32.

Heading **VI**] CHORUS C. *ts1* ‖ *CHORUS. ts2*

VI 10 **whatever**] all that *ts1 1st reading*

VI 13 **hardly**] long *ts1, ts2, ts Chamb, proof*

VI 14 **teeth**] teeth twice *ts1 1st reading*

VI 17] *first word of line preceded by* ~~Whyte~~

VI 27] *ts1 1st reading:*

> The blood of the Saints was not shed once for all
> The

Martyrs] martyrs *ts2 1st reading, printings prior the present ed.*

VI 29 **always**] always, *ts1*

after VI 34] *line space (new leaf in ts1) then:*

> But come, let us not lose hope in the world, prematurely;
> The world is not quite given up to diplomacy,
> Combinations and finding of formulas.
> There are always the young, the devoted,
> The enthusiasts, breakers of fetters.
> And some such I now see approaching
> With aloft their gay banner of sunrise.

[5]

ts1, ts2, Rock (subsequently dropped from this Chorus)

[2] **is not quite**] cannot be *ts1 1ˢᵗ reading* ‖ is not *quite ts1 2ⁿᵈ reading*

VII

The Rock (1934) 49–51.

ms1 fol. 85: the earliest sketch of this Chorus, a single leaf of the Bodleian drafts (Bodleian MS Don. d. 44):

> History of the world from the Creation. Gradual struggle ⋴ striving together towards the true Faith. Rise and Fall of Religions. Each carrying a race to a certain point of development ⋴ then arrest ⋴ decay. Xtianity alone seemed capable of leading man to greater ⋴ greater heights. But is man now failing Xtianity? Decay of the whole world.
>
> Stichomatheia of 2 Chorus leaders M. ⋴ F.

ms1 fols. 86–87: early pencil draft of 1–17. Turned lines are not indented.

ts1: fols. 142–43, double-spaced draft (ribbon).

ts2: fols. 70–72, double-spaced fair copy (carbon).

ts Chamb 1–2.

Heading **VII**] PART II. OPENING CHORUS *ts1, ts2* (*with* OPENING *del*) ‖ PART II. CHORUS *ts Chamb*

VII 1 **world. Waste**] world, waste *ms1*

VII 2 **towards**] toward *ms1*

VII 3 **Blindly**] Blind *ms1 1ˢᵗ reading immediately emended*   **seed upon**] feather on *ms1 1ˢᵗ reading* ‖ seed on *ms1*   **wind:**] wind *ms1*   **driven**] Driven *ms1* (*starting new line*)   **and that,**] or that *ms1*   **lodgement and**] lodgment and *ms1, ts1* ‖ lodgment or *ts1 1ˢᵗ reading*

VII 4 **forward**] not *ms1*

VII 5 **crying**] Crying *ms1* (*starting new line*)   **life**] this life *ms1, ts1 1ˢᵗ reading*   **for**] ~~and~~ for *ts2*

VII 7 **And**] *starting new line ms1*   **water.**] waters. *ms1, ts1* ‖ waters: . *ts1 1ˢᵗ reading* (*mistyping*)

VII 8 **turned towards**] knew *ms1*

VII 9 **Religions; and**] Religions. And *ms1*   **Higher Religions were**] H R were *ms1*

VII 10 **men**] them *ms1*   **Good**] good *ms1*   **Evil.**] evil *ms1* ‖ Evil; *ts1*

VII 11 **their**] the *ms1*   **light**] light ~~⋴ the~~ *ms1 2ⁿᵈ reading*   **and shot with** darkness] with darkness *ms1 1ˢᵗ reading* ‖ and shot with darkness of death *2ⁿᵈ reading*

VII 12 **air**] water *ms1 1ˢᵗ reading* ‖ water *ts1 1ˢᵗ reading* **temperate**] the *ms1 1ˢᵗ reading (overwritten)* **still dead breath**] still dead cold *ms1 1ˢᵗ reading* ‖ dead cold breath *2ⁿᵈ reading* **Current;**] current *ms1*

VII 13 **stirred with**] keeping *ms1* ‖ stirred by *ts1* **life,**] life *ms1*

VII 14 **they came to**] not *ms1* **the**] a *ms1, ts1 1ˢᵗ reading* **of a**] like a *ms1, ts1 1ˢᵗ reading*

VII 15–17] *ms1 (with or del)*:

> Prayerwheels, worship of the dead, denial of this world,
> or affirmation of empty rites
> In the sand and the windy places.
> W ᵈ V   W ᵈ V

VII 15 **affirmation**] and affirmation *ts1, ts2*

VII 16 **or the hills where the**] *ts2+* ‖ or the mountains where the *ts1 1ˢᵗ reading with first deletion reinstated* ‖ or in mountains where the *ts2 1ˢᵗ reading, ts Chamb, proof*

VII 21 **Then**] When *ts2 2ⁿᵈ reading* **must**] might *ts1* **light of the Word**] light, in the Word *ts1*

VII 24 **resuming**] returning *ts1 1ˢᵗ reading*

VII 26 **that has never**] that never *ts1*

VII 27 **Men have left GOD not for other gods, they say, but for**] Men say they are following no other gods, but *ts1* **no god;**] no gods: *ts1* ‖ no god: *ts2, ts Chamb*

VII 28] That men worshipped a god saying it was no god, professing first Reason, as in seventeen hundred and eighty nine, *ts1 with last seven words del*

VII 29 **And then**] And *ts1* **or**] or else *ts1*

VII 32 ^ 33 **VOICE**] VOICES *ts1*

VII 37 ^ 38 **(more faintly):**] *(Afar off). ts1*

VII 41 **mankind ··· mankind**] the World ··· the World *ts1* ‖ the world ··· the world *ts2 1ˢᵗ reading*

VIII

The Rock (1934) 56–57.

ms1: 2pp autograph with ts transcript presumably by Henry Eliot (Houghton). Sent by TSE to J. McG. Bottkol on 8 Feb 1934, along with *Usk*: "Here are a few scraps, if you want *genuine* manuscript. I could easily fake—i.e. write out a finished poem—which would be neater and more legible. And of course real ms. is not the finished form of anything, as after this stage it proceeds by typewriter (vide verso of one page). If this is not what you want, be more specific. With all good wishes, Yours sincerely, T. S. Eliot. All this is recent—*inédits*." On 4 Feb 1937 he wrote again to Bottkol: "I am sending, dispersed over several mails, a few more scraps of manuscript etc. and a couple of copies of the *Little Review* that remain in my possession to my brother. He will presumably hand over part or all of these to you to deal with for the Library."

ts1: fol. 153–54, draft (carbon). By pencilling "F" and "M" in the margin here, TSE allotted 1–3, 6 and 8–26 to the women of the Chorus and 4–5, 7 and 27–49 to the men.

ts2: fols. 76–78, double-spaced fair copy (carbon).

ts Chamb 7–8.

Heading **VIII**] CHORUS D. THE CRUSADES. | (To Blomfield): *ts1* ‖ CHORUS: *ts2*

VIII 2 **will**] shall *ms1*

VIII 3] *not ms1*   **Remembering**] Considering *ts1*

VIII 4 **inheritance,**] inheritance *ms1*

VIII 5 **temple**] holy temple *ms1*

VIII 6 **Edom?**] Edom | With dyed garments from Bosra? *ms1*

VIII 7] *not ms1*   **He has**] I have *ts1, ts2*

VIII 13 **who were neither.**] were neither *ms1*

VIII 16 **Some went who**] Some because they *ms1 1st reading* ‖ Some *ms1*

VIII 17 **and**] or *ms1*

VIII 18 **Many**] Some *ms1 1st reading*   **left their bodies to the kites of**] came never back from *1st reading* ‖ left their bodies *ms1*

VIII 19 **sea-strewn**] sea strewed *ms1*

VIII 20–21] Many lived on in Syria | Sunken in moral corruption *ms1*

VIII 22 **well broken**] half broken *ms1* ‖ well-broken *ts1 1st reading*

VIII 23 **and beggared,**] dispossessed or *ms1*

VIII 24 **in possession:**] *not ms1* ‖ in possession, *ts1* ‖ in possession; *ts2*

VIII 25 **Came home**] *not ms1*

VIII 26 ^ 27] *line space Rock* ‖ *new page so spacing indeterminate 1936, 1963, 1974* ‖ *new page, indenting 27 US 1952* ‖ *no line space 1969, CP2002*

VIII 30 **faith**] word *ts1*

VIII 31 **that was**] which is *ms1*   **tales**] tale *1936 17th and 18th imps. (1958, 1959), Sel Poems pbk (1961)*

VIII 33 **the**] their *ms1*   **it;**] *1963+* ‖ it. *ms1* ‖ it, *ts2, ts Chamb, Rock, 1936*

VIII 35 **many.**] many | No faith of none. *ms1*

VIII 37 **gluttony,**] *not ms1*

VIII 38 **that**] *not ms1*

VIII 40 **took men from home**] sent them out *ms1* ‖ took them from home *ts1 1st reading*

VIII 42 **virtue**] virtues *ms1*

VIII 43 **vice**] vices. *ms1* ‖ vice; *ts1*

VIII 45 **Because**] For *ts1 1st reading (typed over)*   **will**] would *ts2*   **never**] not *ms1*

VIII 46 **impossible,**] impossible *Guild*

VIII 47 **men**] those *ms1 1ˢᵗ reading*

VIII 49] *not ms1*

IX

The Rock (1934) 76–78.

ts2: fols. 95–96, double-spaced draft (carbon).

ts Chamb 28–29.

IX 10 **market**] markets *ts2 1ˢᵗ reading*

IX 11 **secular meetings**] public ~~occasions places.~~ *ts2 1ˢᵗ reading (deciphered by Katherine Hawkins)*

IX 12 **good**] well *ts2 1ˢᵗ reading*

IX 17 **unites**] *printings prior to 1936, 1969* ‖ united *1936–61, US 1936, Penguin (and Sel Poems until 1976 or later), 1963 emended to "unites" from 2nd imp.* TSE memo to Peter du Sautoy, 28 Apr 1964 (of "united"): "I think this is a misprint; in any case I think the original text is preferable" (Faber archive).

IX 20 **new**] comes new *ts2 1ˢᵗ reading*

IX 26 **our**] the *ts2 1ˢᵗ reading*

IX 33 **as**] with *ts2 1ˢᵗ reading*

IX 43 ^ 44] *no line space Penguin (but 44 is indented, like 42 and 43, as a new paragraph)*

X

The Rock (1934) 83–85.

ms draft: an early version of this Chorus, on the final two leaves of the Bodleian drafts (ms Don. d. 44 fols. 164, 164v., 165), is given here first. The text is the earliest legible reading, with variants listed below. New lines are given as in the ms (and numbered as such), but those presumed to be turned lines are indented (as are some of them in the ms). Two groups of lines defying lineation remain unindented.

Strophe

The church built, adorned, dedicated,
 wedded to Christ. One light burns
 in the darkness. What of the future?
Shall the Church vis. ⊄ invis. go forth
 to Conquer the world?   [5]

Antistrophe

The great snake lies low at the
 bottom of the pit of the world, curled
round the Tree. From time to time
awakens, famished, and reaches his
neck to devour. Let me not look
into the pit ⊄ seek to plumb the   [10]

Mystery of Iniquity. What fellowship
hath Righteousness with Unright-
eousness, ᴄↃ light with darkness?

—Wherefore come out from among them   [15]
    and be ye separate.

[new page]

Strophe

Let us therefore in the light meditate
on the Light.

Oh Light invisible
Too bright for mortal sight   [20]
We thank thee for the little light the
    light of altar ᴄↃ sanctuary
Light of the hermit in the deepest meditation
Light through the window
Sun lighting front of English   [25]
    church at evening. Moon and
Starlight faint light, where the
    bat squeaks over the pool.
Light through water showing the
    seagods the passing shadow of Argo.   [30]
Light from stones, light from coloured
    mosaic, fresco, silk curtains.

In the rhythm of earthly life we are glad
    when the day ends, when the play ends, we
    tire of worship ᴄↃ sleep ᴄↃ are glad to sleep   [35]
Controlled by the blood, ᴄↃ the day ᴄↃ night ᴄↃ seasons
And the candle must be extinguished
    the candle must be relighted

[new page]

We forever here light ᴄↃ quench the flame
Children who are quickly tired ᴄↃ fall asleep   [40]
    in the middle of play
We are tired children watching the fireworks
    late in the night, and can endure only a
    little light.
Therefore we thank thee for the little light,   [45]
    that Thou hast not made the light too
    great for us.
We thank Thee who has inspired us to
    build, finding life through our fingers,
    and that when we have built an altar   [50]
to the Invisible Light, we may set thereon
    the little visible lights suitable to our vision
And we thank thee for darkness to remind
    us of light.

[6] **at**] sleeping at *2ⁿᵈ reading*

[17] **meditate**] *over illegible reading*

[23] **hermit**] solitary *2ⁿᵈ reading*   **deepest meditation**] *uncertain reading*

[25] **front**] west front *2nd reading with "?"*

[26] **evening.**] evening. Crossing the farrow *2nd reading*

[28] *with, in the margin, "glowworm" and*

Glowworm showing the reach
ᴑ spread of a dozen blades of grass

[28] **squeaks**] *with* fluttering *added above*

[31] **Light from**] Light returned from precious *2nd reading* ‖ Light returned and scattered from precious *3rd reading*　　　**from**] *over illegible reading*

[35] ᴑ **sleep**] ᴑ we sleep *2nd reading*

[44] **little**] *over* light

[45] **thee**] Thee *2nd reading*

[49] **life**] *over illegible reading*

[53] **thee**] Thee *2nd reading*

ms Yale (see above).

ts2: fols.106–108, double-spaced draft (carbon).

ts Chamb 34–36.

X 1　**house**] church *ms Yale 1st reading*

X 2　**it is**] is it *ms Yale, ts2 1st reading*

X 4　**dark**] dark, *ms Yale*

X 5　**all we can build?**] singly enough? *ms Yale*

X 7　**half awake,**] half sleeping *ms Yale 1st reading* ‖ somnolent *2nd reading* ‖ half awake *final reading*

X 8　**and to left**] ᴑ left *ms Yale* ‖ and left *ts2 1st reading*　　　**prepares**] keeps *ms Yale 1st reading (uncertain)*

X 10　**those**] them *ms Yale*

X 11　] The worshippers and dedicated victims of the snake, take *ms Yale*

X 17　**we praise Thee!**] too bright for mortal vision *ms Yale 1st reading*

X 19　**praise**] thank *ms Yale 1st reading*

X 22　**over stagnant**] on the face of *ms Yale*

X 23　] *not ms Yale 1st reading* ‖ Moonlight ᴑ starlight, owl ᴑ moth light *ms Yale in margin without indication of where it is to go, apparently written over false start* S *(for "Starlight"?)*

X 24　**Glow-worm**] The glowworm *ms Yale* ‖ Glowworm *ts2, ts Chamb*　　　**glowlight**] glow light *ms Yale*　　　**grassblade.**] soaring grassblade *ms Yale*

X 25　**worship**] thank *ms Yale, ts Chamb*

X 26　**lights**] light *ms Yale, ts2 1st reading*

X 27　**The**] For *ms Yale*　　　**light**] lights *ts2 final reading*

X 28　**lights**] light *ms Yale 1st reading*　　　**those**] one *ms Yale 1st reading*　　　**meditate**] meditates *ms Yale*

X 29 **lights**] light *ms Yale, ts2 1ˢᵗ reading*

X 30 **light**] lights *ts2 final reading*

X 31 **fresco.**] fresco *ms Yale* ‖ frescoes. *ts2* ‖ fresco, *ts Chamb*

X 33 **that fractures**] filtered ⍺ broken *ms Yale*   **unquiet**] *over false start, perhaps*
und- *ms Yale*

X 34 **see not whence**] see not the sun from which *ms Yale* ‖ not the Sun from whence
ts2 1ˢᵗ reading

X 35 ^ 36] *two-line space ms Yale*

X 36 **ends,**] ends *ms Yale*   **is too much**] destroys with *ms Yale*

X 37 **who are**] *not ms Yale*   **and fall**] we fall *ms Yale 1ˢᵗ reading* ‖ who fall *2ⁿᵈ reading*

X 39 **rhythm of**] *not ms Yale*   **and day and the night and**] and the day ⍺ night and
ms Yale

X 42 **light, that is dappled with shadow.**] light *ms Yale* ‖ light, this is dappled with
shadow. *1969*

X 43 **to forming**] forming life *ms Yale*   **fingers and**] fingers, the *ms Yale*

X 44 **And**] Then *ms Yale*   **for**] to *ms Yale 1ˢᵗ reading*   **bodily**] *not ms Yale 1ˢᵗ*
reading   **made.**] formed *ms Yale 1ˢᵗ reading* ‖ made *2ⁿᵈ reading*

X 45 **reminds us**] reminds of *ms Yale 1ˢᵗ reading (overwritten)*

X 46] *line stepped at* Thee | thanks *ts2*

Four Quartets

See individual headnotes to each poem for drafts, proofs and printings relating to the separate poems. Editions of *Four Quartets* collated: *US 1943* (the first collected ed.); *1944* (first collected UK ed.); *1959 pbk* (first paperback ed.); *Mardersteig* (set from 9th imp. of *1944*, 1952); *Folio* (Folio Society, 1968); *1979* (new ed.); *1995* (new ed.); *Rampant Lions* (Rampant Lions Press, 1996); *2001* paperback ed.

US 1943 galley proofs a & b (untraced):

> *galley a*: ten leaves (dated 18 Jan)

> *galley b*: seventeen paginated leaves.

Glenn Horowitz catalogue 22 (1990), item 103: "While textually identical, the two states differ in composition and pagination, the earlier state being entirely unpaginated. In the later state, apparently the final setting prior to publication, the pages have been numbered, divisional titles printed and justified, and stanzas broken to accommodate the design of the pages." TSE was evidently sent *galley b*, for he wrote to Frank Morley: "My corrections are so few that it seems better to list them than to return the proof you so kindly sent me", and then referred to them by page number. The corrections all appear as requested in *US 1943*, and are listed below (one in *Burnt Norton*, four in *East Coker* and six in *The Dry Salvages*). TSE's letter continued: "I do not spot anything in *Little Gidding*. The very few errors seem to come from having used the *N.E.W.* text instead of the Faber."

Hayward to Frank Morley at Harcourt, Brace, 7 Sept 1942: "If and when you decide to set the four poems in type, you might remember me if you should have a spare set of proofs. I should like to preserve a set with the four typescripts I have." Hayward did not, however, receive a set.

1944 author's proof (King's): unbound page proofs of the UK ed. corrected by TSE and sent to Hayward on 12 June 1944; later bound for Hayward. Text as *1944* except where noted. The roman numeral part numbers are not letter-spaced in proof.

1944 author's proof (b) (untraced): unbound page proofs date-stamped by the printer 26 May 1944 on the half-title, where TSE has added "Corrected | TSE | 2.6.44". Sold by the executors of the Faber designer Berthold Wolpe, Bloomsbury Book Auctions, 6 Sept 1990, to Bernard Quaritch Ltd, whose catalogue 1160 (1993) confirms that TSE's changes were identical to those of the proofs now at King's.

1979, prepared under Valerie Eliot's supervision, appears to have been set from *US 1963*, leading to the omission of the stop in *East Coker* II 21. While *1979* avoids the errors of *US 1963* at *East Coker* III 26 and V 32, it erroneously omits line spaces at *East Coker* I 23 and *Little Gidding* III 16–17. Reference may have been made to *Mardersteig*, the only edition before *1979* to remove the brackets around the note preceding *The Dry Salvages*.

The immediate source of *1963* and *US 1963* is uncertain. For instance, their settings of *Little Gidding* III 16–17 are different; *1963* has an error at *East Coker* III 3 not made by *US 1963*; *US 1963* has an error at *East Coker* III 26 not made by *1963*, and the two disagree at *Burnt Norton* II 23–24.

The type from Faber's original settings of the four poems, used in *Four Quartets* since 1944, was melted down in 1968, on the advice of the printer, Stephen Easton, after 72,000 copies had been printed from it (Easton to David Bland, 19 Jan 1968); even more copies had been taken from the *Burnt Norton* pages (see below).

Proposed readings by others are attributed:

> [2] **change**] change, *Hayward ts3*

Likewise comments:

> II 80, 81] *transposed with "?" Hayward ts10b*

VOLUME VARIANTS

Section-title page **Four Quartets**] *collected eds of TSE from US 1952, 1963+* ‖ *Burnt Norton with epigraphs beneath 1936, Later Poems.* (Within *US 1952* section titles were afforded only to *Collected Poems 1909–1935* plus the subsequent separate volumes, *Four Quartets, Old Possum's Book of Practical Cats, Murder in the Cathedral, The Family Reunion* and *The Cocktail Party*.)

Acknowledgement] *present in editions entitled Four Quartets, but omitted from editions also containing other poems (US 1952 and subsequent US eds, 1963+). American editions read:*

> I wish to acknowledge a particular debt to Mr. John Hayward for general criticism and specific suggestions during the composition of these poems. | TSE.

on the recto of a page before Contents, US 1943.

British editions read:

> I wish to acknowledge my obligation to friends for their criticism, and particularly to Mr John Hayward for improvements of phrase and construction

on Contents page 1944 ‖ *on verso of epigraphs (i.e. following them) 1979, Rampant Lions* ‖ *on recto page between Contents and section-title 1959 pbk, Folio (all capitals).*
TSE to Frank Morley, 20 Feb 1943: "I wonder how you feel about a preliminary note of acknowledgement. The only person concerned is John Hayward, but he gave me so much and such valuable help, both of criticism and of suggestion of alternative words & phrases a number of which I accepted, that I should like to say: 'I wish to acknowledge a particular debt to Mr. John Hayward, both for general criticism of these poems during their composition, and for suggesting words and phrases which have found their way into the final text.' I prefer to leave this to your decision, knowing that you will accept it unless you are forcibly struck by some objection of a kind unlikely to have occurred to my own mind."

Paragraphing Following the practice of *1959 pbk* (the first paperback *Four Quartets*), *1963* indents the first line of second and subsequent paragraphs in several sections, and it does the same with the first line of two of the four poems (*East Coker* and *The Dry Salvages*). Yet while there are indents for "Where is there an end of it" and "Lady, whose shrine stands on the promontory" (*The Dry Salvages*

II and IV), there are none for "The wounded surgeon plies the steel" (*East Coker* IV) or "Ash on an old man's sleeve" or "The dove descending" (*Little Gidding* II and IV). The practice was abandoned in the resetting of the paperback by Jarrold, and by *1979*. The present edition therefore follows the pamphlets (and *US 1943* and *1944*) in not indenting. (See "This Edition", and *Composition FQ* 97.) When the discrepancy was brought to Valerie Eliot's attention during the proofing of the Folio Society edition, she confirmed that she preferred the text without indents (Peter du Sautoy to Brian Rawson of the Folio Society, 5 Mar 1968). The indents remained, however, in *1974*. *Mardersteig* insets sections of text according to visual balance on each individual page, with the depth of insetting varying when paragraphs turn onto new pages.

Poem titles] *on individual title pages 1979, 1995, Rampant Lions* ‖ *on individual title pages and again above poems 1959 pbk*

Burnt Norton

Burnt Norton was published as the section concluding *1936*. It then became a long-standing anomaly, being in print both there and as a pamphlet (*BN*) in the years 1941–44. After that, it was both the last poem in reprints of *1936* and the first in *Four Quartets* (1944). The anomaly ended only with the absorption of the other three Quartets into the *Collected Poems* of 1963.

Although second in the sequence of Quartets, *East Coker* was the first to appear as a pamphlet, after its first publication in *NEW*. The pamphlet resembled Auden's *Spain* (1937), but the typesetting followed a different model. Richard de la Mare, Faber's production editor, wrote to the printer, 1 July 1940: "I am sending you copy for a short new book of Eliot's, a poem called *East Coker*. I propose to set it up in exactly the same style as was used for his *Collected Poems* · · · so that later on, if we wanted to, we could include this in that volume." The intention was to save the expense of re-setting.

East Coker was published in Sept 1940, with two reprints in two months, and the format yielded an unanticipated dividend. As it became clear to the author that *Burnt Norton* could be the pattern for a sequence of poems, so it became clear to the publishers that *East Coker* could be the model for a series of pamphlets. Rather than putting the new poem into reprints of *1936*, Faber decided to make a shilling pamphlet from *Burnt Norton* as well. In Nov 1940 de la Mare wrote to the printer that *Burnt Norton* was the first of "a series of four or five poems that Eliot is writing · · · and the others will also be published separately in pamphlet form".

The printer took the standing metal type for the *Burnt Norton* pages from *1936* and rearranged it slightly, adding the title to the top of the first page, to match the format of *East Coker*. This meant moving the poem down by five lines and turning lines from one page to the next. The last page had originally had only ten short lines, which for visual harmony had been inset by half an inch. Now five more lines were brought over to the head of this page, and they too were inset. The first impression of 4,000 copies of *Burnt Norton* sold promptly and 4,000 more were printed in 1942. There were five impressions in all, to Nov 1943. *The Dry Salvages* (pub. Sept 1941) and *Little Gidding* (pub. Dec 1942) were also commercially very successful.

For the first collected British edition of *Four Quartets*, in 1944, Richard de la Mare asked the printer to re-use standing type from the four pamphlets (to John Easton, 15 Feb). But this was not entirely straightforward, since new pagination would be required, and the epigraphs to *Burnt Norton* and the note on the title *The Dry Salvages* had to be moved. Easton to Richard de la Mare, 17 Feb: "The fact that we shall have to alter the folio numbers and also place the notes at the beginning of *Burnt Norton* and *The Dry Salvages* on the first page of each of the poems means that there is in fact a good deal of rearrangement of type involved." Easton therefore suggested "that we should make moulds from the type of the four poems so that they can be reprinted from stereos in future. This will enable us to get the type into its proper shape for the new volume and to keep it standing in that form" (as pamphlets). In the course of rearrangement of the type and its preparation for *1944*, the poems were apparently read against the American edition of the four poems, in accordance with which, as *1944 author's proof* shows, "summer" at *East Coker* I 25 was changed to "Summer" (TSE changed it back).

Despite the careful planning for future impressions, however, one Quartet, *Burnt Norton*, was still needed in its original configuration: not that of the pamphlet, but that of its appearance in *1936*. When a new impression of that collection was called for in 1941, the standing type of the poem was again re-used. The title was removed again from the head (since *Burnt Norton* had its own section-title page in *1936*), and five lines were taken back from each page to the previous. Unfortunately, the compositor did not remove the quads (blank types) used to inset the five lines moved back from the last page, and these lines appeared puzzlingly inset in *1936* 4th imp. (1941). They remained inset until 1961, through fifteen impressions of *1936*, though always correct in *Four Quartets*.

Burnt Norton was published in *1936*; then in the Faber pamphlet *Burnt Norton*, 20 Feb 1941 (first separate publication; five impressions to Nov 1943); *Later Poems* (May 1941); then *1943, 1944+*. (TSE was mistaken when he wrote to Frank Morley, 13 Feb 1941, "I do not think this is a very good time for bringing out my Sesame book in New York because it contains *Burnt Norton*, and we want to save that for the volume" [*Four Quartets*]. The poem was not in *Sesame*. He may have been thinking of *Later Poems*, to be published by Faber in May 1941, in which *Burnt Norton* does appear.)

tsMinC (Hornbake Library, U. Maryland): draft of *Murder in the Cathedral* including thirteen lines written for the Second Priest to succeed Thomas's speech "Temporal power, to build a good world" (30). Not used in the play, the lines became the opening of *Burnt Norton* (see *Composition FQ* 15–16, 82). The lines are given in the Commentary to *Burnt Norton*: headnote, 2. GENESIS.

Lines for an Old Man ts1, ts2 both include *Burnt Norton* II 1–2.

ts1: ribbon copy and carbon of the printer's typescript.

ts1a (King's) = D in *Composition FQ*: printer's typescript for *1936* on eight leaves, with emendations by TSE, who has added the Greek epigraphs and references below the title in ink. Endorsed by TSE on a flyleaf of the bound volume: "*Burnt Norton* printer's copy from the T. S. Eliot bequest to John Hayward Esq." At the head of parts II–V, the printer has specified "Not a new page". Bound together with *ts1a add leaf*: four typed drafts of V 20–22.

ts1b (Houghton): carbon of *ts1a*, sent to Frank Morley, with emendations by TSE, who has again added epigraphs and references. Not recorded in *Composition FQ*.

Printer's BN 5th imp. (Pierpont Morgan): printer's marked copy of *Burnt Norton* (pamphlet), 5th imp., Nov 1943, with one textual emendation at II 18. On the cover are written the print-run and a date: "2,320 copies, 6.12.43". The marks were intended for further impressions of the pamphlet, rather than *Four Quartets* as a book, but no further impressions were issued.

Epigraphs] The status of these has long been ambiguous. In the form in which they originally appeared on the section title page to *Burnt Norton* in *1936* and in *Later Poems*, and as stationed below the title of that poem in *US 1952* and *1963*, they applied to it alone. Yet they were omitted from all five impressions of *Burnt Norton* as a pamphlet (1941–43), despite an instruction to the printer to set them on a preliminary recto. In *US 1943*, which has a title page for each

Quartet, they were printed for the first time on the *Burnt Norton* title page. Perhaps because of wartime paper shortages, the British *Four Quartets* (*1944*) has no title pages for the individual poems. In the Faber proofs, the epigraphs were set below the title *Burnt Norton* at the head of the text (in a large type), but TSE ringed them for transfer to the facing page (verso of the Contents), adding "and put in smaller type, as in American edition" (*1944 author's proof*). In that arrangement, as printed, the epigraphs might still be taken as relating to *Burnt Norton* alone, but were more naturally to be taken as prefixed to the sequence. Faber introduced individual title pages into *Four Quartets* in *1959 pbk*, where the epigraphs were printed on the verso facing the *Burnt Norton* title page. The new hardback edition of 1979 also has individual title pages, but here the epigraphs change places with the acknowledgement to John Hayward, and appear first. The epigraphs are prominent on the recto, followed by the acknowledgement (verso), the *Burnt Norton* title page (recto), a blank (verso) and then the poem (an arrangement followed by the Rampant Lions edition in 1996).

By moving the epigraphs further forward (in two steps), British editions of *Four Quartets* have given increasing warrant for supposing that they prefix the whole sequence. All the while, however, American editions, beginning with *US 1943* and including the collections *US 1952* and *US 1963*, have attached the epigraphs to *Burnt Norton* alone, and this was the case also when TSE incorporated *Four Quartets* into his *Collected Poems*, in the British edition of *1963*. There and in *1974*, the epigraphs appear beneath the title *Burnt Norton* at the head of the text, just as they did in *1936*. Faber subsequently reset the *Collected Poems* with the epigraphs below the section-title *Four Quartets*. Differences of spacing and the use of roman and italic faces are not recorded here.

Epigraph quotations πολλοί] *1944, 1963* ‖ πολλοὶ *ts1, 1936* (*although it was queried by the proofreader for Later Poems, that volume and all imps. of 1936 printed the grave accent* (ὶ). *Alongside the epigraphs on a proof sheet from US 1952, TSE wrote "Check this!!" and on a memo he added, ambiguously, "Correct Greek" (Faber archive)*

Epigraph references I.] *1. 1963* ‖ *l. 1969*

Epigraph attribution (**Herakleitos**).] Herakleitos). *1969*

I

I 1] *all capitals Mardersteig*

I 2 **time future,**] the future. *tsMinC* ‖ time future *1974*

I 3 **And time future**] Time future is *tsMinC*

I 4 **present**] present, *tsMinC*

I 6 **an abstraction**] a conjecture *tsMinC*

I 7 **perpetual**] permanent *tsMinC*

I 13] *not tsMinC*

I 14 **My words echo**] *not tsMinC*

I 37 **of heart**] of the heart *Later Poems*. Asked to check a list of proof corrections in *Later Poems*, TSE made no comment here, presumably taking "p.149 fourth line" to refer to the fourth line of verse (the next line, with "in the pool") rather than the fourth line of type.

II

II 1–2] *see Textual History, Lines for an Old Man, following* 11

II 1 **Garlic**] Thunder *Lines for an Old Man ts1 1ˢᵗ reading*

II 5 **Appeasing long**] *1936 7th imp. (Dec 1944)*+ ‖ And reconciles *ts1, 1936 until 6th imp. (Mar 1944), 1944 author's proof 1ˢᵗ reading (emended to* Appeasing long *by TSE), BN, Later Poems, US 1943*

II 10 **above**] about *recording 1946–47*

II 16] *indent US 1952, 1958 pbk, 1936 17th imp. (1959) only*

II 18 **fixity,**] *1936 7th imp. (Dec 1944)*+ ‖ fixity. *ts1, 1936 until 6th imp. (Mar 1944), US 1936, BN (emended Printer's BN 5th imp.), Later Poems.* TSE to Frank Morley, 20 Feb 1943, listing proof corrections for *US 1943*: "Comma after fixity."

II 22 **where**] where *ts1 1ˢᵗ reading*

II 23 ^ 24] *line space ts1, 1936 until 6th imp. (Mar 1944), Later Poems, BN and US 1943, US 1952, US 1963* ‖ *new page so line spacing indeterminate 1944 author's proof* ‖ *no line space (accidental omission when lines were moved in proof) 1944, 1936 from 7th imp. (Dec 1944), presumably to conform with 1944, Mardersteig (see McCue 2012a, Proposal 9).*

II 24] *indent US 1952*

II 33 **Yet the**] The *ts1 1ˢᵗ reading, ts1b*

II 35 **Protects**] Protect *ts1 1ˢᵗ reading*

II 37 **a little**] little *Mardersteig*

II 39 **But only**] *ts1a 2ⁿᵈ reading, ts1b, 1936*+ ‖ Yet it is *ts1 1ˢᵗ reading* ‖ Yet only *ts1a final reading*   **can**] that *ts1 1ˢᵗ reading*

II 42 **Be**] Can only be *ts1 1ˢᵗ reading*

III

III 20 ^ 21] Fuddled with images of picture papers, *ts1 del*

III 22 **Campden**] *"p" underlined with "X?" (probably by the printer) ts1a. See Commentary.*

III 30] *indent 1958 pbk (starting new page), 1936 17th imp. (1959) only, 1963 (not 1963 proof, US 1963), 1969*   **Desiccation**] Dessication *ts1*

IV

IV 5 ^ 6] *new page so line spacing indeterminate ts1, BN, 1944* ‖ *line space 1958 pbk, Folio*

IV 6] *indent 1958 pbk, 1936 17th imp. (1959) only.* An attempt was made throughout *1958 pbk* to clarify by indenting—as though for new paragraphs—the first line of subsections (except those beginning each part). In *1944* a new page begins with IV 6, and *1958 pbk* mistook this, and added a line space and indented the line. The text of *Burnt Norton* in the *Collected Poems (1936)* was then checked against *1958 pbk.* Three new indents were adopted (II 18, III 24, IV 6) in *1936* 17th imp. (1959) only, although the line space IV 6 ^ 7 was not adopted, leaving the one-word line "Chill" puzzlingly indented. All three indents were removed in *1936* 18th imp. (1961), the final impression.

IV 6–10] *printed as opening lines of* V *in 1944 9th imp.* (*1952*), *Mardersteig.* The standing type of *1944* having been disturbed, a compositor apparently looked to see where to replace the roman numeral, but was misled by the different disposition of lines in *1936*, where the numeral appeared correctly at the top of the page (because the title *Burnt Norton* does not appear above the first line of I). He therefore erroneously inserted the numeral at the top of his page. Although half of the 10,000 copies of the 9th imp. were corrected with a cancel leaf, one of the uncorrected copies was followed when *Mardersteig* was set (see *Gallup* A43c).

V

V 8 **lasts,**] lasts. *Mardersteig*

V 17 **stay**] say *1979*

V 21–22] Crying shadows and disconsolate chimeras. *ts1a add leaf 2nd draft*

V 21 **crying shadow in**] circling fury and *ts1a add leaf 1st draft* ‖ crying shadow and *3rd draft*

V 22 **lament of the**] lament, the sweet *ts1a add leaf 1st draft*

V 25–39] *erroneously inset in printings of 1936 beginning with 4th imp.* (*1941*). *See headnote.*

V 30 ^ 31] Under which all things are relative *ts1 del*

V 39] *ts1 1ˢᵗ reading*:

Stretching before and after

Light   [2]

[new leaf]

~~Light~~

~~Light of light~~

~~Gone~~   [5]

This deletion makes the final leaf superfluous, and it was discarded from ts1a but in ts1b it survives. ‖ *ts1a final reading, following the addition of* Gone *in pencil*:

Stretching before and after.

~~Light~~

~~Gone~~

ts1b final reading, following the addition of Gone *in pencil*:

Stretching before and after.

Light

Gone.

East Coker

Published in *NEW* 21 Mar 1940 (referred to as a "Supplement", the poem occupied the central four pages so as to be readily detachable, and some extra copies of these four pages were printed afterwards); *Partisan Review* May-June 1940 (first American printing, although V 1–18 had been quoted from *NEW* in *Poetry* May 1940, with no variants). The first printing with its own title page was *NEW leaflet* (see below), followed by the Faber pamphlet *East Coker* 12 Sept 1940 (*EC*; six impressions to Feb 1942); then *US 1943, 1944+*.

NEW leaflet: eight pages, stapled, "*East Coker* | A Poem by | T. S. Eliot | Reprinted from the Easter Number | of the *New English Weekly*, 1940." Although at 8¼" x 6½" the leaflet is in a smaller format than *NEW*, the same setting of type was used, newly paginated (3–8). Text as *NEW*. TSE to Gallup, 7 Oct 1946: "I don't think that the *New English Weekly* could be said to have published a separate edition of *East Coker*. I gave them the poem to be published as a kind of insert and I think that they sold a number of extra copies of that issue to people who wanted the poem. This was part of my design in giving them the poem." And 1 Nov 1946: "Thank you very much for your letter of October 28th and for sending me the leaflet of *East Coker* produced by the *New English Weekly*. I had forgotten all about this, but I must have authorised its printing as I am personally interested in the *New English Weekly* and therefore concerned with its support · · · one of the three weeklies in London which are worth reading."

ms Gallup (Beinecke; photostats at Houghton): four leaves from a ruled notebook, with undated pencil jottings for part IV. Accompanied by a letter to Hugh Walpole, 19 Apr 1940, sending them to be sold on behalf of the Red Cross: "Well, here are the scraps. As they appear so cryptic, I have attached a marked copy of the poem to which they belong, for identification. I shall be surprised if you get five shillings for them: the only point is the extreme rarity of any ms. verse of mine." Four days previously, TSE had written to Walpole: "If you want manuscripts I am the most difficult person to get them from, because I never write anything out fully in long hand, but do everything on the typewriter. I can give you two or three pencilled pages of rough notes for my last poem, if you like. But anyone would have to be an almost maniacal collector of my work to want to buy them. Any previous manuscripts, or near manuscripts, have gone to Oxford and Harvard." The "scraps" were bought at the Red Cross sale by C. A. Stonehill Inc. for Donald Gallup, and were published in *Composition FQ* 94–95.

fol 1:   1. The wounded surgeon—

fol 2:   our only health ~~is the~~ disease
          2) The dying nurse

fol 3:   3) ~~Singing is silence~~

          4)   ill of love—
          The Lover

          hospital the earth

          bankrupt ~~banker~~

              millionaire

[the second group of lines running diagonally uphill]

fol 4:   I am cold
      —must be consumed in fire
             I faint with heat
      —must be frozen in the lonely North,
      the chill   freeze
      the fever

      sharp Enigma of our fever chart

      The surgeon
      the nurse
      the hospital
      & final.

[all but the first four lines running diagonally uphill]

Five tss, from different stages of composition, and a marked proof of *NEW* were sent together by TSE to Hayward on 23 June 1940: "I can now report that I have discovered the early drafts of *East Coker*, and as there are five copies all of which appear to have different alterations, I might as well send you the lot. There is also the proof from the *N.E.W.* authenticated by a letter from Mairet. There was no ms. except of section IV, and that I gave to Hugh Walpole to try to sell for the Red Cross" (*Composition FQ* 8–9; for the ms, see *ms Gallup* above). All five are now bound together, the drafts representing three discrete typings. (Those initially retained by TSE as working copies are described as "retained by TSE", although later he gave them to Hayward.)

To signal the relation between versions of the same typing, and to make the notation of the composition's successive stages clear and economical, Helen Gardner's designations for the drafts have been changed as follows:

	This ed.	*Hayward vol*		*Composition FQ*
First typing:	*ts1a*	bound first	(retained by TSE)	*D1*
	ts1b	bound second	(sent to Fr. Hebert)	*D2*
Second typing:	*ts2a*	bound third	(sent to Hayward)	*D3*
	ts2b	bound fourth	(retained by TSE)	*D4*
Third typing:	*ts3a*	bound fifth	(printer's ts)	*D5*
	ts3b	—	(sent to Morley)	

ts1: two versions of first typing of Parts I–IV on eight leaves, with two add. leaves for Part V:

> *ts1a* (retained by TSE): carbon on eight leaves.

> *ts1b* (sent to Hebert): ribbon copy on eight leaves, folded and sent to Fr. Gabriel Hebert, of Kelham Theological College, a Faber author whose "incisive but temperate criticism" was commended by TSE in *Liberal Manifesto* (1939). During binding, the first leaf of this ribbon copy (reading "tattered", 13, and with TSE's line numbering) and the first leaf of *ts2a* (reading "tatterred" and without line numbering) have inadvertently been exchanged. They are here treated as though in their original positions. (Gardner proposes that the recipient was Herbert Read and describes the hand that made the comment against 58–60 as very like his. Yet a letter to Read of 18 Sept 1942 suggests that he was not privy to the next Quartet, *The Dry Salvages*, in draft. By contrast, TSE had relied for some years on Fr. Hebert's opinion of theological submissions, and on 1 Aug 1939 invited his criticisms while completing *The Idea of a Christian Society*. The name "Hebert" is twice clearly typed. See note to I 3 *variant*.)

> *ts1 add. leaves* (retained by TSE?): ribbon copy of Part V, on two leaves, without line numbering and without typed part or page numbers. At some stage these leaves have been folded with *ts1b*, perhaps for posting, but they bear no marks by other hands, and the second leaf especially is much less tidy than other drafts that TSE sent to friends at this time.

ts2 two versions of second typing; all five Parts on nine leaves:

> *ts2a* (sent to Hayward): ribbon copy, posted apparently in Feb 1940 (*Composition FQ* 9, 17), and with Hayward's pencilled annotations, some of which are now almost invisible.

> *ts2b* (retained by TSE): carbon with a few annotations and pencilled line numbering by TSE.

ts3 two versions of third typing; all five Parts on nine leaves:

> *ts3a*: typescript for printer with instructions from editor "10pt. Please keep exactly to spaces shown" and, braced against 29–34, "Printer to copy the spelling exactly".

> *ts3b* (Berg): secondary carbon with line numbering every five lines, probably by TSE (acquired by Berg with Frank Morley's papers; not listed in *Composition FQ*). With a few emendations and notes in an unknown hand. Accompanied by a list of "corrigenda" bringing readings into line with the final text. The corrigenda are not listed below.

ts Texas (Texas): single leaf, headed "From *East Coker* by T. S. Eliot". Not typed by TSE. I 14–23 only, with "the warm" for "a warm" (I 20).

Matthews 144 claimed that TSE sent a ts of *East Coker* to Emily Hale "before the poem was published", but this is untraced.

NEW 1st proof (King's): corrected by TSE. With a compliments slip from the editor, Philip Mairet, noting: "Shocking bad proofs. I've asked them to send you better ones, as these show breaks in the lines owing to faulty bedding. But these would do for corrections." As *NEW* except where noted.

NEW 2nd proof (Texas): adopting the changes marked in *NEW 1st proof* and with later changes and comments by TSE. Sent to Montgomery Belgion, and with "M. B. from T. S. E." on the first page. Sold by Belgion's widow to Bertram Rota Ltd. in 1974. Another copy (Harvard U. Archives), has a single variant at III 32, and is inscribed "to Mrs. Irving Babbitt from T. S. Eliot" on the first page. As *NEW* except where noted.

V 1–18 were quoted from *NEW* in *Poetry* (Chicago) May 1940, with no variants.

BBC script (Beinecke): six mimeographed pages of a professional transcript, headed *Literature in the West | 12: East Coker | Read by T. S. Eliot*, with dates of transmission (17 Mar 1946, 10.38–10.53pm) and repeat (18 Mar 1946, 4.15–4.30pm), and the announcer's words: "This is the West of England Home Service. Tonight listeners in the Scottish Home Service are joining us to hear T. S. Eliot read his poem *East Coker*. East Coker is a small village in Somerset from which Mr. Eliot's ancestors came. This is the last programme in our first series of *Literature in the West*." The part numbers are not marked, and parts I and II are run on. In I 13, "silent" appears in inverted commas (which may have been marked by TSE for aural emphasis). Having no independent authority, other variants are not recorded.

Valerie's Own Book: four pages (I 1 to II 23), then eight pages headed "*East Coker* continued" (II 24 to V 19), then a final page, headed "*East Coker Continued*" (V 20–38); in the contents list at the end of the first exercise book, the last becomes "*East Coker* (completed)". The thirteen pages are interrupted by eight other poems (see Textual History headnote, 6. *VALERIE'S OWN BOOK*).

No paragraph indents NEW, Partisan.

I

I 1] *indent 1963* (*not 1963 proof, US 1963*), *1969*

I 2 **extended**] rebuilt *ts1, ts2 1ˢᵗ reading, ts2b*

I 3 **restored**] replaced *ts1, ts2 1ˢᵗ reading, ts2b* ‖ restored / supplied *ts2a alt 2ⁿᵈ readings. The words* replaced *and* place *underlined with "?" by Hebert ts1b and, with "?", by Hayward ts2a. To Hayward, 27 Feb 1940*: "*Replaced* and *place*. It was intentional, but Hebert also objects, so I had better do something about it."

I 4 **by-pass**] *ringed with "?" by unknown hand ts3b*

I 12 **wainscot**] wainscoat *ts1, ts2. The words* wainscoat *and* field-mouse *underlined with "X" by Hayward ts2a*

I 13 **arras**] *EC*+ ‖ aresse *ts1–ts3, NEW, Partisan, underlined with* arras? *by Hayward* *ts2a, ringed with* ? arras *by unknown hand ts3b, changed to* arras *by TSE in NEW 2nd proof after publication* (*see Commentary*)

I 13 ^ 14, *as also* 46 ^ 47] *two-line space Valerie's Own Book*

I 15 **field**] fields *ts1–ts3, NEW 1st proof*   **deep**] dark *ts3, NEW 1st proof 1st reading*

I 19 **electric**] *underlined with "X" by Hayward ts2a.* To Hayward, 27 Feb 1940: "*Electric. I will think about alternatives.*"

I 21 **not**] but *ts1 1st reading* (*typed over*)   **refracted**] refected *Valerie's Own Book 1st reading*   **by**] by the *Valerie's Own Book*

I 23 **owl.** ^ **In**] *new page so step indeterminate ts1–ts3, EC, 1944, Folio* ‖ *stepped with extra word space but with no line space Partisan* ‖ *stepped but with no line space or word space US 1943, 1959 pbk, Mardersteig, 1979, 1995, Rampant Lions.* (The "open field" of the stepped phrase is a repetition from 4 and 15, as the stepped phrase "If you came this way" at *Little Gidding* I 20 and 39 appears also at 23.)

I 25 **summer**] May *ts1–ts3a 1st reading, ts3b* ‖ Summer *Partisan, US 1943, 1944 author's proof 1st reading* (*emended to* summer *by TSE*), *US 1952*

I 28–33] *beside these lines: "N.B. This is a quotation (1531)" NEW 2nd proof* (*after publication*)

I 29 **matrimonie—**] matrimonie *ts1, ts2*

I 30] *not ts1, ts2* (*but see 45–46*)

I 35 **rustic**] *ts1* ‖ solemn *ts2 1st reading, ts3 1st reading, ts3b*

I 36 **shoes,**] *US 1943+* ‖ shoes *ts1–ts3, NEW, Partisan, EC.* TSE to Frank Morley, 20 Feb 1943, listing proof corrections for *US 1943*: "Comma after shoes."

I 44 **man and woman**] men and women *ts1*

I 45–46 **And that of beasts. Feet rising and falling. | Eating and drinking. Dung and death.**]

> And that of beasts. Eating and drinking,
> Dung and death. Feet rising and falling.

ts1, ts2 ‖ *transposed to final sequence ts2b*   **falling.**] falling: *ts2*

I 46 ^ 47] A most dignified and commodious sacrament. *ts1, ts2* ‖ *bracketed for possible deletion by Hebert ts1b* ‖ *bracketed and ringed to move after 29 by TSE ts2b.* To Hayward, 27 Feb 1940: "*Dignified. Hebert also objects. I think this line is out of its place, and I can't think why I put* most. *It looks as if* daunsinge *and not* matrimonie *was the sacrament. I will deal with this.*"   **most**] *underlined with "X" by Hayward ts2a* ‖ *del ts2b*

I 47] *with "X" by Hayward ts2a*   **points, and another**] points and the star fades, and another *ts1, ts2* ‖ points. Another *ts2a 2nd reading.* To Hayward, 27 Feb 1940: "*Star fades. You are right.*" Gardner: "Probably Hayward pointed out that the morning star does not fade at dawn" (*Composition FQ* 99).

I 48–49 **Out at sea** · · · **slides**] Out at sea the little | Dawn wind slides. *ts1, ts2 1st reading, ts2b* ‖ Out at sea | The dawn wind slides [wrinkles *alt*] *ts2a 2nd reading* (*undeleted*) ‖ And the dawn wind | Wrinkles the sea *ts2a alt 2nd and final reading*

I 50 **my**] the *ts1, ts2*

II

II 6] *line bracketed with "?" by Hebert ts1b*   **down]** down, *ts1a, ts1b 1st reading*

II 7 **snow?]** snow. *ts1a, ts1b 1st reading (emended perhaps by Hebert)*

II 8–10] *bracketed with "reminiscent of something? Burnt Norton II, 4–5" by Hebert ts1b (referring to "Sings below inveterate scars | Appeasing long forgotten wars.")*

II 13 **and]** the *NEW 1st proof 1st reading*

II 15–17] *upside down on ts1b fol. 5v:*

> Alone—the ice cap
> Separated from the surfaces of human beings
> To be reunited in the Communion

(Composition FQ 111 has reunited *and in its transcription of the third line, corrected Moody 331.)*

II 16 **that]** *underlined (perhaps by Hebert) with* its? *alt (perhaps by Hebert) ts1b* ‖ the *ts2a 2nd reading*

II 17 **Which burns before the]** Before the patient *ts1, ts2*

II 17 ^ 18, *as also* 48 ^ 49, 49 ^ 50] *two-line space Valerie's Own Book*

II 18 **satisfactory:]** satisfactory— *ts1, ts2*

II 19 **fashion,]** fashion: *ts1, ts2*

II 21 **matter.]** *ts1–ts3, printings prior to 1946, US 1950, 1963, Folio, 1969* ‖ matter *1944 4th imp. (1946) and later printings of Four Quartets (incl. Mardersteig, Rampant Lions, 1979), 1963 proof, US 1963*

II 22 **expected.]** expected: *Valerie's Own Book*

II 24 **serenity]** serenity, *ts1*

II 25 **us,]** *1963* ‖ us *tss, printings prior to 1963, Mardersteig, Valerie's Own Book, 1979, 1995*

II 27 **receipt]** *underlined with "X" by Hayward ts2a*

II 32 **At best,]** None, or *ts1* ‖ None, or *bracketed (perhaps by Hebert) ts1b* ‖ At best, *ts1b alt*

II 33 **knowledge]** knowledge ~~that is merely~~ *ts1b 2nd reading*   **experience.]** experience— *ts1*

II 35 **moment]** movement *ts1*

II 39 **way]** way, *ts1 1st reading*

III

III 2 **vacant,]** vacant: *EC*

III 3 **letters,]** letters. *1963 (not US 1963), 1969 (error)*

III 5 **chairmen]** chairman *1963 (corrected 1974), 1969*

III 6 **dark,]** dark *EC*

III 7 **Sun and Moon]** sun and moon *Valerie's Own Book 1st reading*

III 13 **God. As]** God.—As *ts1–ts3* ‖ God.   As *Partisan, US 1943, US 1952*   **in a]** in *ts3 1st reading, ts3b*

III 15 **wings,**] wings. *ts1 1ˢᵗ reading*

III 16 **and the**] and *Valerie's Own Book*   **trees,**] trees, and *ts1, ts2 1ˢᵗ reading, ts2b*

III 17 **rolled**] taken *ts1, ts2 1ˢᵗ reading, ts2b*

III 18 **as,**] as *ts1*

III 19 **into silence**] away *ts1 1ˢᵗ reading*

III 20 **mental emptiness deepen**] mental activity fail *ts1, ts2* ‖ image activity fail
ts2a 2ⁿᵈ reading, against which Hayward wrote "X". ‖ mental image fail *ts2a final
reading.* To Hayward, 27 Feb 1940: "*Mental image* is right: I crossed out the
wrong word."

III 24 *as also* 25 **thing;**] thing: *ts1*

III 25 **there**] wait *Valerie's Own Book 1ˢᵗ reading*

III 26 **faith and the**] faith and *US 1963*   **love**] hope *ts1, Valerie's Own Book 1ˢᵗ
reading*   **hope**] love *ts1*   **all**] *not ts1*

III 28 **So the**] So that the *ts1* ‖ But the *ts2*

III 28 ^ 29 *line space*] *ts1–ts3, NEW, Partisan, US 1943, US 1952* ‖ *new page so line
spacing indeterminate EC, 1944, 1963, 1974* ‖ *no line space 1959 pbk, Mardersteig,
Valerie's Own Book, 1969, Folio, 1979+*

III 29 **Whisper**] Whispers *ts1, ts2*   **lightning,**] *ts1–ts3, NEW, EC* ‖ lightning.
Partisan, US 1943, 1944+, Valerie's Own Book. Helen Gardner: "The comma is
obviously right and should be restored" (*Composition FQ* 105).

III 31 **echoed**] shadowed *ts1a, ts1b 1ˢᵗ reading*   **ecstasy**] *NEW 2nd proof+* ‖ ecstasy,
ts1 ‖ ecstacy *NEW 1st proof*

III 32 **lost,**] lost; *NEW 2nd proof (Texas), punctuation emended to a comma in NEW 2nd
proof (Harvard)*

III 33] *stepped but with no line space ts1, ts3, NEW 1st proof, US 1952* ‖ *with "<" ts2a
(indicating eye-skip from 33 to 35 and omission of* You say · · · it again?*)* ‖ *stepped
with a half-line space and exaggerated horizontal space NEW* ‖ *stepped with no line
space and exaggerated horizontal space Partisan, US 1943* ‖ *two-line space Valerie's
Own Book*   **birth.**] birth *ts1–ts3, NEW, Partisan*

III 33–35 **You say · · · it again?**] *not ts1, ts2 (so that* III 33 *continues with* In order to
arrive there,*)*

III 34 **before.**] before? *Valerie's Own Book*

III 35 **again?**] here and now? *ts3a 2ⁿᵈ reading, NEW, Partisan.* Copies of *NEW*
inscribed to Richard Jennings on "Ascension Day [2 May] 1940" (Eton) and to
I. A. Richards, 4 June 1940 (Magdalene) were both emended by TSE to "again?",
as were the copies of *NEW 2nd proof* sent to Belgion and Mrs. Babbitt. See
Commentary.

III 37, *as also* 39, 41, 43] *no indent Valerie's Own Book*

III 38 **not**] *typed over* kno *ts3*

III 39] *double indent EC*

III 42 **what**] where *ts1, ts2 1ˢᵗ reading*

III 45] *not Valerie's Own Book*

IV

IV 3 **Beneath**] Under *ts1b alt del, ts2a 2nd reading, ts3, NEW 1st proof 1st reading*

IV 4 **compassion**] *ringed with* compunction?? *NEW 1st proof*

IV 5 **Resolving the**] And faint below the strict *ts1, ts1b 1st reading, ts2 1st reading* ‖ And faint beneath the strict *ts1b alt* ‖ Below the strict *ts1b final reading, ts2, ts3, NEW 1st proof 1st reading*

IV 6 **disease**] disease, *ts1, ts2*

IV 7 **nurse**] nurse, *ts1*

IV 9 **Adam's**] to Frank Morley, 20 Feb 1943, listing proof corrections for *US 1943*: "Delete comma after 'Adam's' (Adam's Curse)."

IV 10 **sickness**] suffering *ts1* ‖ malady *ts2b, ts2a 1st reading* with ailment *above perhaps as alt (both del) and with* sickness? *by Hayward* ‖ sickness *ts2a 3rd reading*. To Hayward, 27 Feb 1940: "Sickness. I will make this alteration" (*Composition FQ* 109).

IV 10 ^ 11] *no space 1995*

IV 12 **ruined**] bankrupt *ts1a, ts1b 1st reading*

IV 15 **leave us,**] let us be, *ts1a, ts1b 1st reading, ts2 1st reading*   **prevents**] *EC+* ‖ must torment *ts1a, ts1b 1st reading, ts2 1st reading* ‖ torments *ts1b, ts2, ts3, NEW (emended to* prevents *in copy sent to Richards and in NEW 2nd proof sent to Belgion), Partisan*. To Frank Morley, 20 Feb 1943, listing proof corrections for *US 1943*: "Read *prevents* instead of *torments*."

IV 15 ^ 16] 21–24 *written and cancelled in Valerie's Own Book*

IV 22 **food:**] food, *ts1*

V

All ts1 readings are from ts1 add. leaves except as specified in V 2.

V 1 **So here**] Here *ts1*

V 2] 20 yrs | l'entre 2 guerres | 20 yrs. or 600 upwards| Home is where we start from. *slantwise ts1b fol. 7v (the last becoming* V 19)   **Twenty years**] Twenty years, *ts2*   **the years of**] *ts1* ‖ *not ts1 1st reading* ‖ of *ts1 2nd reading*   *l'entre deux guerres*] l'entre deux guerres *ts1 1st reading*   **guerres—**] guerres *1959 pbk* ‖ guerres, *Valerie's Own Book*

V 4 **different kind of**] wholly fresh *ts1*

V 6–8] *ts1 1st reading:*

> For the things one no longer has to say, so each venture
> Is a new beginning, a raid on the inarticulate

perhaps an eye-skip—after which so each venture *was del and the missing words* or the way in which | One is no longer disposed to say it, and so each venture *were inserted*

V 7 **it. And**] it, and *ts1 2nd reading*

V 9 **shabby equipment**] worn-out equipment, *ts1, ts2, ts3a 1st reading.* (*See Commentary.*)

V 15 **fight**] task *ts1* ‖ urge *ts2*, *ringed in ts2a*   **recover**] recover, *ts1*

V 16 **again:**] again; *ts1*

V 17 **loss.**] loss: *ts1*

V 18 **us,**] us *ts1*   **trying. The**] effort. The *ts1 1st reading* ‖ trying: the *ts2*   **our business.**] ours. *ts1 1st reading*

V 18 ^ 19] *two-line space Valerie's Own Book*

V 19 **we grow**] one grows *ts1*

V 22 **Isolated,**] Isolated in a lifetime, *ts1*

V 23 **moment**] moment, *ts1*, *ts2*

V 27 **A**] And a *ts2b 2nd reading*

V 28 **(The**] The *ts1*, *Valerie's Own Book 1st reading*   **album).**] album *ts1*

V 29–38] *ts1 has two drafts on the same page. 1st draft (all finally struck through):*

> Here or there does not matter. We must be still
> And be still moving. The mind must venture
> Where it has not been, be separated
> For a further union, a deeper communion,
> Aranyaka, the forest or the sea   [5]
> The empty cold with the desolation
> With the ~~knowledge~~ understanding and the consolation
> Of the petrel and the porpoise. In my end is my beginning.

[7] The wave cry, the wind cry, and the consolation *2nd reading (with* understanding *accidentally not del). Gardner reads the intention differently (Composition FQ 112), taking "The wave cry, the wind cry" as an extra line, but this overlooks the deletion of "With the", which would leave a line consisting of only "understanding and the consolation".*

2nd draft:

> Love is itself unmoving
> But love is most nearly itself
> When now and now cease to matter.
> Here or there does not matter.
> We must be still and still moving   [5]
> Into another intensity
> For a further union, a deeper communion,
> Through the empty cold with the desolation,
> The wave cry, the wind cry, the vast waters
> Of the petrel and the porpoise.   [10]

[2] **But**] And *2nd reading*

[3 ^ 4] Old men ought to be explorers *2nd reading*

[8] **empty cold with the**] dark cold and the empty *2nd reading*

[10] **porpoise.**] porpoise. In my end is my beginning *2nd reading*

V 29] Love is itself unmoving | But love is most nearly itself *ts2 1st reading, with ts2a having "X" against the first line, which is then del in ts2a and ts2b.* ‖ Love is most nearly itself *ts2a final reading* ‖ And Love is most nearly itself *ts2b final reading*

V 32 **or**] *EC, 1974+* ‖ and *US 1943, 1944, US 1952, 1959 pbk, Mardersteig, 1963, US 1963, Valerie's Own Book, 1969, Folio*

V 33 **still and**] still, and *ts2a 2ⁿᵈ reading*

V 38 **porpoise.** ^ In] *four-character space US 1943, US 1952*

The Dry Salvages

Published in *NEW* 27 Feb 1941; *Partisan Review* May–June 1941 (first American printing). Separately as a Faber pamphlet 4 Sept 1941 (*DS*; four impressions to Feb 1944); then within *Four Quartets* in *US 1943, 1944+*.

Daedalus: Journal of the American Academy of Arts and Sciences Spring 1960 follows *US 1952* except in omitting the note beneath the title and the numeral "I"; reading "intractable" (I 2), inserting a line space (I 16 ^ 17), adding a stop after "seine" (I 22), and removing the erroneous stop after "union" (V 33).

Drafts of sections of *The Dry Salvages* appear in *msA* at Magdalene, which is described leaf by leaf in *Composition FQ*, Appendix B.

The earliest outline of the poem is *msA* fol. 65, a leaf (later) headed "Notes", with jottings about each of the five sections:

　　1. Sea picture　　—general
　　2.　　　　　　　　—particular
　　　　　　　　　　problem of permanence
　　　　　　　　　　of past pain
　　3. Past error can only be reconciled
　　　　in eternity. Arjuna ⊄ Krishna.
　　4. Invocation to the B.V.M.
　　　　　　　　meaning of "mother" ⊄ "father".
　　5. *Generalisation*: Liberation from
　　　　　　　　the past is liberation from the
　　　　　　　　future. To get beyond time ⊄
　　　　　　　　at the same time deeper into
　　　　　　　　time — the Spirit ⊄ the Earth

The next extant leaf is *msA* fol. 68:

	sailing
	lowers
	oceanless
	wastage
unflyable	liable
	destination
scaling	hailing
	ours
	~~devotionless~~
dockage	trackage
	~~reliable~~
	consummation

msA fols. 70–72 have drafts of the opening of III and the whole of IV (shown in the variants below).

There were five principal ts drafts (*ts1–ts5*):

ts1 (Magdalene): "1st draft"; all five parts on eleven leaves heavily corrected.

ts2 two versions of second typing on ten leaves:

> *ts2a* (Magdalene): ribbon copy, designated "2nd draft" (written in crayon over the same in pencil). Pencilled line numbers by TSE every ten lines, and total (232) at foot.

> *ts2b* (King's): carbon sent to Hayward (at the end of Dec 1940: *Composition FQ* 19), with some corrections by TSE matching those on *ts2a*, and pencilled marks by Hayward. TSE's corrections are mostly in ink, but the deletions at V 16 are in pencil, apparently by TSE at another time. For *Hayward's Queries* on receipt of *ts2*, see Commentary headnote to *The Dry Salvages*, 3. COMPOSITION.

ts3 two versions of third typing, on ten leaves:

> *ts3a* (Magdalene): "3ᵈ Draft", ribbon copy.

> *ts3b* (Texas): carbon of *ts3a*, with ms changes by TSE. Sent to Philip Mairet, 5 Jan 1941.

ts4 (Magdalene): "3ᵈ 4th Draft", with smaller type-height than previous typings. Carbon on ten leaves, sent to Geoffrey Faber, 21 Jan 1941.

ts5 (Faber archive, Geoffrey Faber papers): incomplete carbon (nine leaves of ten) of a typing with further revisions. Not listed in *Composition FQ*. An untraced copy, perhaps made by a Faber secretary from *ts5*, was sent to Frank Morley in the USA (and may be related to *ts Richards*). TSE to Morley, 13 Feb 1941: "Geoffrey will have sent you an imperfect text of the *Dry Salvages*. I hope he made it clear that this was not for immediate publication, because I had not finished working on it. It was sent merely for safe-keeping and for your own improvement. You will be receiving shortly the text as it will appear in the *New English Weekly* and on receipt of that you will know that I want you to peddle it for copyright." (10 Mar: "my cable will now have informed you that the final draft, that is to say, copies of the *New English Weekly*, are now on the way." Accordingly, the text in *Partisan* was set from *NEW*, repeating the error at II 20.)

ms Mairet (Texas): final eighteen lines of the poem, on cardboard, with blue crayon at the head: "One more version of the end! T.S.E.", and at the foot: "Please incorporate" (ringed). TSE's name has been added at the foot by another hand, then deleted. Apparently sent to Philip Mairet for *NEW*, of which he was editor. Not listed in *Composition FQ*.

ts Mairet (Texas): final eight lines of the poem, in a letter of 15 Feb 1941 to Mairet (illustrated in *An Exhibition of Manuscripts and First Editions of T. S. Eliot*, Texas, 1961). Not listed in *Composition FQ*. "I am wondering whether you got my corrected proof. I hope so, because I made a number of alterations, and I don't want the poem to appear without them. Also, by the time I had finished the pages had become such a griffonage that they were almost illegible, and

I am particularly [*word omitted?*] to get the last six lines right: which was why I asked for another pull. In case, here are the last lines again: ['For most of us ··· significant soil.'] It is important, because, however I have tried it, it turns out to be something to which people will give a topical allusion—not part of the fundamental intention—and if so, then it must not be a wrong twist which will put the rest of the poem out of joint."

ts Richards (Magdalene, Richards box 44): typed on airmail paper, originally folded in two and subsequently in three. Probably typed by a professional secretary and apparently sent to Eliot's brother, Henry, and thence to I. A. Richards, then teaching at Harvard. He in turn lent it to James Johnson Sweeney (whose letter returning it is also contained in the wallet with Henry Eliot's address sticker). The text is close to *ts4* or *ts5*. A secondary carbon of this, also on airmail paper and folded in two, is additionally present. Another carbon (Houghton, bMS Am 1691 [15]) was sent to Henry Eliot and emended by him after publication ("The changes are those made by T. S. Eliot before publication. Not his writing—mine, HWE", with a note at the end adding that the changes are to give the "published words"). These typescripts are not listed in *Composition FQ*. Only readings from *ts Richards* are given here.

NEW proof (Magdalene): corrected proof dated "Jan. 29 [1941]". As *NEW* except where noted.

TSE's NEW (Valerie Eliot collection): TSE's corrected copy of *NEW*. Not listed in *Composition FQ*.

Printer's DS 4th imp. (Pierpont Morgan): printer's marked copy of this impression (Feb 1944). On the cover are written the print-run and a date: "2,350 copies, 22.2.44". Another note on the cover, dated 12 Mar 1945, reads: "See correction (circled in blue) on p.7 ['hermit', I 19]. This will need to be made on the plate when a reprint is ordered." The marks in this copy were intended for further impressions of the pamphlet, not for *Four Quartets* itself, but no 5th imp. was issued.

	This ed.	Composition FQ	
First typing:	*ts1*	M1	(retained by TSE)
Second typing (*ts2*):	*ts2a*	M2	(retained by TSE)
	ts2b	D	(sent to Hayward)
Third typing (*ts3*):	*ts3a*	M3	(retained by TSE)
	ts3b	T	(sent to Mairet)
Fourth typing	*ts4*	M4	(sent to Geoffrey Faber)
Fifth typing	*ts5*	—	(Faber archive)
Airmail typing for USA	*ts Richards*	—	(probably secretarial)
Eighteen lines	*ms Mairet*	—	(sent to Mairet)
Eight lines	*ts Mairet*	—	(letter to Mairet)

Comments by Geoffrey Faber in the margins of *ts4* caused TSE to reconsider a number of lines, which he marked there with "X" in brown crayon. Some of the comments by Faber and by Hayward are discussed in the Commentary.

No paragraph indents, NEW, Partisan, DS, US 1943, 1944, US 1963, Folio, 1979, 1995, Rampant Lions

Title] not ts1 ‖ THE DRY SALVAGES. *ts3, with quotation marks added before and after ts3a*

Prefatory note] not ts1, ts2 ‖ (*Les trois sauvages*) *ts3, del ts3a* ‖ *with additional sentence*: The Gloucester fishing fleet of schooners, manned by Yankees, Irish or Portuguese, has been superseded by the motor trawlers. *ts4, ts5, NEW and Partisan* (*without the before motor in the printings, TSE having deleted it in the NEW proof*). TSE to Frank Morley, 20 Feb 1943, listing proof corrections for *US 1943*: "Delete the sentence 'The Gloucester fishing fleet · · · etc.' from the prefatory note."   **N.E.**] north-east *DS* (*emended to N.E. in Printer's DS 4th imp.*)   **assuages**] rampages *ts4, ts5, NEW proof 1st reading*

The whole note bracketed ts4, ts5, NEW, DS, US 1943, 1944, 1959 pbk, 1963, Folio ‖ *without brackets Mardersteig, 1979+*

Hayward to TSE, 5 Mar: "*The Dry Salvages* with its revisions and additions—particularly the extra lines where I hoped you might add something—is a splendid piece and I long to see it dressed up to match *Burnt Norton* & *East Coker* · · · When the poem is published separately I think the note should be removed to the verso of the leaf facing the first page of the text." The note appeared as a paragraph on its own verso before the poem in *DS* and *Rampant Lions*; on the section-title page below the title in *US 1943* and *Mardersteig* (justified) and *Folio* (unjustified); and on the section title page below the title in *1979* and *1995* (unjustified in both). Because of the chance arrangement of the paragraph in *1979*, where both "Salvages" and "Groaner" happen to begin a line, *1995* and *Rampant Lions* set it as three unjustified paragraphs, without paragraph indents.

I

I 1] *indent 1963* (*not 1963 proof, US 1963*)

I 2 **god—**] god: *ts1, ts2* ‖ god; *ts3*

I 3 **to some degree**] *ts1 3rd reading, ts2+* ‖ to all appearance *ts1 1st reading* ‖ to some appearance *ts1 2nd reading* ‖ *underlined Geoffrey Faber ts4, with "possibly not the finally satisfactory expression?"*   **at first recognised**] known for a time *ts1 1st reading, ts2a 2nd reading+* ‖ recognised for a time *ts1 2nd reading, ts2*

I 6 **solved,**] solved, then *ts1–ts5, NEW proof 1st reading. In ts4 Geoffrey Faber ringed* then *in this line and the previous with "? perhaps the repetition might be considered further—but I don't know. I think it is needed."*   **the**] a *ts4 1st reading, ts Richards*   **almost**] *not ts1–ts5, NEW proof 1st reading*

I 7 **ever, however**] *underlined Geoffrey Faber ts4, with "is this intentional? Yes, it must be. Not quite sure I get the exact significance of 'however' in that case. One reads it at first as = 'Always, nevertheless'. Does it then mean, rather 'Always, whatever happens'?"*

I 11 **was**] i *ts3 1st reading* (*typed over*)   **present**] *ts1 final reading+* ‖ present, is present, *ts1 1st reading* ‖ present underneath *ts1 2nd reading*

I 12 **In**] *ringed ts1, ts3 1st reading*   **rank ailanthus**] efflorescence *ts1 1st reading* ‖ rank ailantus *ts1 3rd reading, ts2–ts5, NEW proof 1st reading*   **ailanthus**] *underlined Geoffrey Faber ts4, with "one of the words I don't know! tho' I feel I ought to" (this comment marked "X" by TSE; see Commentary)* **of**] in ts3 *1st reading (typed over)* **dooryard**] ts1 *3rd reading, ts2+* ‖ suburbs ts1 *1st reading* ‖ garden ts1 *2nd reading* ‖ backyard *with "?" ts1 alt 3rd reading* s

I 13 **In the**] The ts1 *1st reading*

I 15 **us;**] us, ts1

I 18] *marked by Geoffrey Faber ts4, with "ITS INTS ... SI ST.NS ? onomatopoeia but, if so, isn't the effect possibly too much muffled by the middle part of the line?"* **creation:**] existence, ts1 ‖ existence: *ts2–ts5, NEW proof 1st reading*

I 19 **horseshoe**] hermit *ts1–ts5, NEW, Partisan, DS (emended to* horseshoe *in Printer's DS 4th imp.), US 1943 (corrected long after), 1944 (corrected 3rd imp., Aug 1945), US 1952 (see Commentary)* **crab, the**] crab, and *ts Richards*

I 20 **offers to**] nourishes for *ts1, ts2 1st reading*

I 22] *with "X" Hayward ts2b* **up**] us *ts1, with* up *as alt* **torn seine**] broken fishnet *ts1 1st reading*

I 25, 26] *stepped lines more deeply indented NEW* ‖ *steps indented to align with "The" of 24 (creating a subsidiary triplet) Partisan*

I 25 **on**] in *ts1 1st reading*

I 28] *with "X" Hayward ts2b* ‖ *first three words underlined Geoffrey Faber ts4, with "Don't much like this order of the words"* **heard:**] heard; *ts1–ts5, NEW*

I 29 **menace and caress**] soothing menace *ts1–ts5 (ts4 with TSE's "X" against Geoffrey Faber's comment: see Commentary I 28–32), NEW proof 1st reading* ‖ menace and caress and *NEW proof 2nd reading with last word del* **wave that**] wave o *ts1 1st reading (typed over)*

I 30 **rote**] *underlined with "?" ts3b* ‖ *underlined Geoffrey Faber ts4, with "this meaning of 'rote' is new to me—which isn't to say anything against it!"*

I 32] *with "X" Hayward ts2b*

I 34 **under the oppression**] *ts4 alt, NEW proof 3rd reading+* ‖ heard in the stillness *ts1–ts5 (ts4 with TSE's "X" against Geoffrey Faber's comment: see Commentary), NEW proof 1st reading* ‖ heard in the calmness *NEW proof 2nd reading*

I 36 **rung by the unhurried**] ringing to *ts1 1st reading*

I 37–38] *one line US 1952 proof (despite capital on* Older)

I 41 **unweave**] penetrate *ts1 1st reading*

I 42 **future,**] future *tss*

I 43 **when**] and *ts1 1st reading*

I 44 **before the morning watch**] and at the same time *ts1, ts2 1st reading (Hayward's Queries: "at the same time (tricky pun)")* ‖ while in the night watch *ts2a 2nd reading* ‖ while in the morning watch *ts2a 3rd reading*

I 45 **When time**] Time *ts1, ts2* ‖ When times *ts5*

I 46] And through the fog the pretemporal ground swell *ts1–ts5 (ts4 with TSE's "X" against Geoffrey Faber's comment: see Commentary)* ‖ And through the firtrees *ts1 alt erased*

I 47 **Clangs**] Rings *ts1 1st reading*

II

II 2 **flowers**] flowers d *ts Richards*

II 4 **to**] for *ts1*

II 8 **Consequence**] consequence *1959 pbk*

II 11 **what was believed in**] that which persisted *ts1 1st reading* || that which had persisted *ts1 2nd reading, ts2* || that which was believed in *ts3, ts4 1st reading with TSE's "X" against Geoffrey Faber's comment (see Commentary), ts5, NEW proof 1st reading*   **believed in as the most reliable**] *underlined Geoffrey Faber ts4, with "I feel that this is a little short of its context—I mean in the form of expression."*

II 14 **Pride or**] Lack of *ts1 1st reading*   **at**] of *ts1 1st reading* || at *ts1 2nd reading* || in *ts1 alt 2nd reading*

II 15] *with "I stick a little over this line, somehow—only over the elliptical grammar, not the sense or sound. But not seriously." Geoffrey Faber ts4*

II 19 **Where**] What *ts1*

II 20 **cowers?**] cowers— *ts1* || cowers *NEW proof 1st reading, NEW (TSE's proof correction was overlooked; he also corrected TSE's NEW), Partisan. To Frank Morley, 20 Feb 1943, listing proof corrections for US 1943: "Insert question mark after cowers."*

II 22–23] *Hayward's Queries: "4 ᴓ 5 f. b." (apparently referring to these lines, which are four and five of ts2 fol. 4, and to "forever bailing", II 25)*

II 25 **as**] not *ts1 1st reading*   **bailing,**] bailing *ts1 1st reading*

II 27 **unchanging**] unshifting *ts1 2nd reading, ts2*

II 28 **Or drawing**] Drawing *ts1 1st reading*   **money**] pay *ts1 1st reading*   **dockage;**] dockage *ts1 1st reading* || dockage: *ts1 2nd reading, ts2–ts5*

II 29 **as**] not *ts1 1st reading*

II 30 **bear**] *underlined Geoffrey Faber ts4, with "Do you mean this in the usual sense of not repaying examn? or do you mean 'that never will undergo examn'? The latter sense seems to be suggested—if so is 'bear' the right word?"*   **examination.**] examination *ts1 1st reading*

II 31 **the**] that *ts4 1st reading*   **wailing,**] wailing *ts1 1st reading*

II 32 **flowers,**] flowers *ts1 1st reading*

II 33 **motionless,**] motionless *ts1 1st reading*

II 35 **hardly, barely**] *underlined Geoffrey Faber ts4, with "Is the extra tension of the 2nd adverb so much needed as to warrant the sudden lengthening of the line? (That's a question, not a criticism.)"*

II 36 ^ 37] *Geoffrey Faber in ts4: "Why do you not make a formal break here? It would ease the reader's acceptance of the sudden change of tone." Beside the single line space in NEW proof, TSE wrote "double this space", and the space was increased slightly in NEW. Subsequent editions have had only a single space (1995 being indeterminate because of a new page). See Composition FQ 133.*

II 37–72] *Hayward's Queries: "I—One—We" (of the shifting pronouns).*

II 37 **It**] *ts1 1st reading*:

> One has to repeat the same thing in a different way
> And risk being tedious: it

with line to indicate step after tedious: *plus marginal symbol and "?"*
ts2:

> One has to repeat the same thing in various ways
> And risk being tedious.
>   It

the two full lines then del ts2a

II 38 **pattern, and**] pattern. It *ts1 1st reading*

II 39 **development**] a mere "development" *ts1 1st reading* ‖ "development" *ts1 2nd
reading, ts2a 2nd reading, ts3, ts4 with Geoffrey Faber's "X (inverted commas)"
prompting their deletion, ts5, NEW proof 1st reading* ‖ a "development"
ts2   **partial**] cheerful *ts1–ts5, NEW proof 1st reading*   **fallacy**] fallacy, *US
1943, 1944 author's proof 1st reading (comma del by TSE), US 1952.* To Frank
Morley, 20 Feb 1943, listing proof corrections for *US 1943*: "Insert comma after
fallacy".

II 40 **evolution,**] *1944+* ‖ Evolution *ts1–ts5, NEW proof 1st reading* ‖ evolution *ts1
1st reading, NEW, DS (comma added in Printer's DS 4th imp).* In his list of proof
corrections for *US 1943*, sent to Frank Morley, 20 Feb 1943, TSE asked for the
comma to be added.

II 41 **Which becomes, in the popular mind, a means of disowning**] Which is
but, in the popular view, cremation of *ts1, ts2 (Hayward's Queries: "view, but
cremation")* ‖ Which is thought of as a sort of cremation of *ts2a 2nd reading* ‖
Regarded as a sort of cremation of *ts2a final reading*

II 42 **not**] *ts2a 2nd reading+* ‖ I don't mean *ts1, ts2 (Hayward's Queries: "I don't mean
. . .? = not merely")*

II 45 **We**] One *ts1, ts2 1st reading*

II 48 **assign to happiness.**] attach to "happiness". *ts1–ts3* ‖ assign to "happiness".
*ts4 with Geoffrey Faber's "X (inv. commas)" prompting their deletion, ts5 (with the
last two words run together)* ‖ assign to "happiness." *ts Richards, NEW proof 1st
reading*   **I have said before**] I have suggested also *ts1–ts5 (with underlining
and "X" Geoffrey Faber in ts4 prompting TSE's own "X"), NEW proof 1st reading.
Hayward's Queries: "I have suggested also . . .?"*

II 51 **not forgetting**] *Geoffrey Faber in ts4: "is the grammatical structure quite right
here? Who does the 'not forgetting'?"*

II 52 **that**] which *ts1*   **probably**] *underlined Geoffrey Faber ts4, with "I don't like
'probably'."*

II 53 **behind**] beyond *ts1–ts3*

II 54 **recorded**] recordable *ts1, ts2*

II 56 **Now, we come to discover**] Now I would say, *ts1, ts2* ‖ Now the point is, *ts2a 2nd
reading, ts3* ‖ Now, the point is *ts4 (underlined Geoffrey Faber with "X"), ts5, NEW
proof 1st reading*

II 58 **hoped**] hopes *1969*

II 59 **not in question**] beside the point *ts1, ts2* ‖ not the question *1969*   **permanent**]
eternal *ts1 1st reading*

II 60 **We appreciate this better**] One appreciates this better *ts1, ts2a 1ˢᵗ reading, ts2b, ts4 (underlined Geoffrey Faber with "X")*

II 62 **ourselves**] oneself *ts1, ts2*   **our**] *ts2a 2ⁿᵈ reading+* ‖ one's *ts1, ts2*

II 63 **our**] *ts2a 2ⁿᵈ reading+* ‖ one's *ts1, ts2*   **covered by the currents**] covered by the ~~tides~~ *underlined ts1 1ˢᵗ reading with* sea / waters / compulsion of / currents *alts*

II 64 **remains**] is *ts1 1ˢᵗ reading*

II 65 **attrition.**] attrition; *ts1 1ˢᵗ reading*

II 66–69] *not ts1 1ˢᵗ reading* ‖ *ts1 2ⁿᵈ reading*:

> People change, ⅋ smile: but the agony remains:
> Time the destroyer is time the preserver,
>
> The fruit and the bite in the fruit

    [1] **remains**] *emended to* abides

    [2] **destroyer**] *with* The River? *and* (Like the river with its cargo of dead negroes, [stiff *added*] cows and chicken coops)

    [3] **The ^ fruit**] bitten / bitter *alts added*

II 68 **negroes**] Negroes *Partisan, US 1943, US 1952 (see Commentary)*

II 70 **restless**] moving *ts1, ts2*

II 74 **by:**] *ts1 3ʳᵈ reading+* ‖ by; *ts1 1ˢᵗ reading* ‖ by, *ts1 2ⁿᵈ reading*   **sombre**] sullen *ts1–ts3 1ˢᵗ reading*

II 75 **that**] the *ts1 1ˢᵗ reading (typed over)*   **fury, is:** *in ts4, Geoffrey Faber inserted a caret before "is", with "I admit I want the 'it' again here"*

II 75 ^ III] *line space then* Now about the future. *ts1* ‖ Now about the future. *ts2a 1ˢᵗ reading (del), ts2b*

III

III 1 **wonder**] wonder, I wonder *msA*   **is**] was *msA*

III 2 **things—**] things *msA*   **thing:**] thing *msA*

III 4] *not msA*

III 5–7] *msA (ending here)*:

> Pressed ~~in the~~ between leaves of a keepsake and that the past   [1]
> Is a pit for us still to explore: and the way up is the way down
> The way forward is the way back, and the light is the darkness,
>   the darkness is light.   [3]
> You cannot think long at a time, but one thing is sure
> That time is no healer. Time can only distract
> And not even time can show the right judgement or else the mistaken
> For what alters the past to fit the present, can alter the present
>   to fit the past.

    [1] **keepsake, and that the past**] forgotten book which has not yet been read *alt*

    [3] **back,**] back. *where the line originally ended. The second part, written at the foot of the leaf, but at the same time, is joined by a line.*

III 5 **opened**] read *ts1 1ˢᵗ reading*

III 7 **steadily]** *ts2a 2ⁿᵈ reading+* ‖ for long at a time *ts1, ts2*   **this]** one *ts1.*

III 11–12] *Hayward's Queries (of ts2 fol. 6): "last two lines begin 'And'".*

III 11 **(And]** *ts1 2ⁿᵈ reading, ts2 (with* And *del then stet ts2a), ts3+* ‖ And *ts1 1ˢᵗ reading*   **platform)]** platform, *ts1 1ˢᵗ reading*

III 12 **Their]** *ts2a 2ⁿᵈ reading+* ‖ And their *ts1, ts2*   **relief,]** relief *1979, Rampant Lions*

III 13 **sleepy]** *not ts1 1ˢᵗ reading*   **rhythm]** monotone *ts1 1ˢᵗ reading*   **hours.]** hours— *ts1, ts2*

III 14 **travellers!]** travellers, *ts1 1ˢᵗ reading*

III 15 **future;]** future: *ts1*

III 16 **that]** one *ts1 1ˢᵗ reading*

III 18 **narrowing]** narrow(ing) *ts1 2ⁿᵈ reading*

III 19 **And on]** Or from *ts1 1ˢᵗ reading*   **liner]** liner, *ts1, ts2*

III 24 **Is a voice descanting]** Are the voices singing *ts1 1ˢᵗ reading*

III 25 **time,]** time) *ts1 1ˢᵗ reading (typed over)*

III 26 **that]** *not ts1*

III 28 **will]** *not ts1*

III 29 **farther]** *US 1943+, 1944* ‖ further *ts1–ts5, NEW, Partisan, DS (emended to* farther in *Printer's DS 4th imp.)* To Frank Morley, 20 Feb 1943, listing proof corrections for *US 1943:* "I rather think that 'farther shore' would be better than 'further shore'."

III 37 **shall]** should *DS (emended to* shall *in Printer's DS 4th imp.)*   **lives]** souls *ts1, ts2*

III 40 **come]** came *1974 (later corrected)*

III 41 ^ 42] The way up etc. *ts1 added then del*

III 42 **Or]** And *ts1 1ˢᵗ reading*   **this]** *not ts1 1ˢᵗ reading*

III 44 **Not fare well,]** *not ts1 1ˢᵗ reading* ‖ not stepped *ts1 2ⁿᵈ reading*

III 45] *not ts1 1ˢᵗ reading*

IV

IV 1 **Lady,]** Lady *msA*   **stands]** is *msA*

IV 2 **for all]** for *msA*   **who are in ships]** in the ships *msA, ts1 1ˢᵗ reading* ‖ who are in the *NEW proof 1ˢᵗ reading*

IV 3 **business]** *underlined, with* occupation *in margin, TSE's NEW*

IV 4 **concerned with every]** about their *msA, ts1 1ˢᵗ reading* ‖ about every *ts1 2ⁿᵈ reading*   **traffic]** traffic, ~~and~~ *msA* ‖ affairs *msA alt*

IV 5 **conduct]** defend *msA*

IV 6 **Repeat a prayer]** Accept this intercession *msA* ‖ Transmit our prayer *ts1 1ˢᵗ reading* ‖ Compose a prayer *ts1 alt, ts2*

IV 7] Women waiting on the hither shore | Those who see their sons & husbands *msA*   **or]** and *ts1 with* or *as alt*

IV 9 **Figlia**] Tu, figlia *msA* **tuo**] *US 1943, 1944+* ‖ suo *msA, ts1–ts5, NEW, Partisan, DS (emended to* tuo *in Printer's DS 4th imp.*). To Frank Morley, 20 Feb 1943, listing proof corrections for *US 1943*: "Read 'Figlia del tuo figlio' . . . an error in our text." **figlio,**] figlio. *msA*

IV 10 **Queen**] Bride *msA, ts1 1ˢᵗ reading*

IV 11 **pray**] *not msA* ‖ we pray *ts1 1ˢᵗ reading* **in**] in the *msA*

IV 12 **Ended their**] ~~Find their~~ | ~~Cease~~ | End their *msA* ‖ End their / Ended their *ts1 alts*

IV 13 **which**] that *ts1 alt del* **them**] them, *msA*

IV 14] *with "X" Hayward ts2b* **Or wherever**] *ts1 final reading+* ‖ Where *msA* ‖ And *ts1 1ˢᵗ reading* ‖ Where *ts1 2ⁿᵈ reading*

V

V 2 **report**] verify *ts3 1ˢᵗ reading* **behaviour**] appearance *ts1, ts2* ‖ convolutions *ts3a 1ˢᵗ reading, ts3b* ‖ behaviour *underlined with* appearance *TSE's NEW*

V 3 **haruspicate or scry**] *ts2a 2ⁿᵈ reading+* ‖ divine in sand *ts1 1ˢᵗ reading* ‖ haruspicate in sand *ts1 2ⁿᵈ reading* ‖ haruspicate with sand *ts2, with "X" Hayward ts2b* **scry**] *underlined Geoffrey Faber ts4, with "I didn't know this word, either. But the C.O.D. [Concise Oxford Dictionary] (which failed me over ailanthus) does."*

V 4 **Observe**] Define *ts1, ts2* **signatures**] signature *ts4 1ˢᵗ reading*

V 5 **from**] in *ts1, ts2*

V 6–7] *ts1, ts2*:

> And tragedy from fingers; realise omens
> By crystal gazing, riddle the inevitable

[1] **from**] in *ts1 2ⁿᵈ reading, ts2* **realise omens**] release omens *ts1 2ⁿᵈ reading, ts2* ‖ use sortilege, or peer *ts2a alt*

[2] **By crystal gazing**] From the bottom of tea cups *ts2a 2ⁿᵈ reading* ‖ At the bottom of a tea cup *ts2a 3ʳᵈ reading*

V 8 **With playing**] By laying *ts1, ts2* **pentagrams**] *ts3a 2ⁿᵈ reading+* ‖ pentagons *ts1–ts3*

V 9 **acids**] forces *ts1 1ˢᵗ reading*

V 10 **The recurrent**] Recurrent *ts1 1ˢᵗ reading* **image**] dreams *ts1 1ˢᵗ reading*

V 11 **tomb, or dreams;**] tomb: *ts1 1ˢᵗ reading* ‖ tomb or dreams: *ts1 2ⁿᵈ reading* **dreams**] *Geoffrey Faber, ts4: "It's perhaps an unfair comment to say that psychoanalysis is a very new addition to the list."*

V 12 **press:**] press. *ts1 1ˢᵗ reading*

V 13 **And**] Have been and *ts1, ts2 1ˢᵗ reading* **some of them**] and *ts1, ts2 1ˢᵗ reading*

V 15 **in**] *not ts1*

V 16 **past**] the past *ts1, ts2 1ˢᵗ reading* **future**] the future *ts2 1ˢᵗ reading*

V 17 **that**] this *ts1* **apprehend**] attend to *ts1, ts2, ts3 1ˢᵗ reading* ‖ be aware of *ts3 2ⁿᵈ reading, ts4 (where Geoffrey Faber underlined of in this line and twice in 18 with "? too many 'ofs'", prompting TSE's "X"), ts5, NEW proof 1ˢᵗ reading*

V 18 **point of**] unheeded *ts1, ts2*

V 17–23] *Hayward's Queries* (of *ts2 fol. 9*): *"last five lines weakly expressed".* (The five lines became seven.)

V 20 **No occupation either**] And not an occupation *ts1*

V 21–22] *not ts1, ts2*

V 24 **Moment**] *ts2a 2nd reading+* ‖ Rare moment *ts1, ts2*

V 25 **distraction fit**] *underlined Geoffrey Faber ts4, with "?"*

V 25–50] *leaf missing from ts5*

V 26] *not ts1 1st reading* the] *not ts1 2nd reading*

V 29 **lasts.**] lasts, the spell lasts. *ts1, ts2 with last three words then bracketed in ts2a* **These are only hints**] Hints *ts1, ts2*

V 30 **and the rest**] but our ultimate term *ts1, ts2*

V 31–32] And ultimate gift, is Incarnation. *ts1, ts2*

V 32 **half guessed**] unguessed *ts3, ts4, NEW proof 1st reading* **half understood**] not understood *ts3, ts4 (for Geoffrey Faber's note see Commentary), NEW proof 1st reading*

V 32 ^ 33] *new page so line spacing indeterminate 1979* ‖ *line space 1995*

V 33 **union**] meeting *ts1–ts4, NEW proof 1st reading* ‖ union. *US 1952*

V 34] Of worlds becomes actual, *ts1 1st reading* ‖ Of existences becomes actual, *ts1 2nd reading*

V 35 **the**] both *ts1–ts4, NEW proof 1st reading*

V 36 **reconciled,**] reconciled *ts2, ts3* ‖ reconciled. *ms Mairet*

V 36 ^ 37] *ts1–ts3, del ts3a:*

> And here is implied Atonement
> And Atonement makes action possible

V 37 **Where**] When *ts1, ts2* **were otherwise**] had been but *ts1* ‖ had been only *ts2–ts4, NEW proof 1st reading. In ts4, Geoffrey Faber underlined "had been", with "I suppose this means that in the material world, without incarnation of the spirit, there would have been no spontaneous or willed movement? I'm not sure whether 'had been' is factual or hypothetical."*

V 39 **And**] (And *ts1, ts2* **movement—**] movement, *ts1, ts2*

V 40 **dæmonic**] *ms Mairet (the only ms), NEW, DS, 1944+ (British eds.)* ‖ daemonic *tss, US 1943, US 1952*

V 41 **Powers.**] Powers). *ts1, ts2*

V 42 **future also.**] future, from time. *ts1–ts3* ‖ future also— *ts3a 2nd reading, ts4* ‖ future also *NEW proof 1st reading*

V 44 **here to be**] to be quite *ts1, ts2* ‖ here quite *ts3, ts4, NEW proof 1st reading* **realised;**] *NEW proof 1st reading, NEW+* ‖ realised: *ts1–ts4, ms Mairet, ts Mairet, NEW proof final reading* ‖ realised. *NEW proof 2nd reading* ‖ realised, *emendation in TSE's NEW*

V 45–47] We content and should be *ts1, ts2 (with "X" Hayward ts2b), ts3a 1st reading, ts3b* ‖ We content in the end / We content at last *ts3a alt 2nd readings (not del)* ‖ *ts3a 3rd reading, ts4, NEW proof 1st reading:*

> We content and should be
> If we have gone on trying;   [2]
> We content at last

[3] **at last**] and should be *ts4, NEW proof 1st reading* ‖

NEW proof 1st redrafting (ink):

> We must learn serenity
> Which is to be found in trying;   [2]
> We content and should be

[1] **learn**] find the *2nd reading*

[2] **to be**] *not 2nd reading*   **trying**] the act of trying *2nd reading*

NEW proof 2nd redrafting (pencil):

> We must find the contentment
> That is found in going on trying;   [2]
> We, content at the last,

[3] *over erasure* (*perhaps* and should be,)

NEW proof 3rd redrafting (ink):

> We are undefeated
> If we have gone on trying;   [2]
> We, content at the last,

with the *added* (*in pencil*) *after second word. NEW proof 4th redrafting (ink) reads as final text*

V 47 **We,**] We *ms Mairet*

V 48] If the temporal aspect of the soul *ts1* ‖ If the temporal aspect nourish *ts2 1st reading* ‖ If the temporal conclusion nourish *ts2 2nd reading* ‖ If the temporal reversion nourish *ts2a 3rd reading*

V 49 (**Not**] Nourish (not *ts1*

Little Gidding

Published in *NEW* 15 Oct 1942. Separately as a Faber pamphlet 1 Dec 1942 (*LG*; three impressions to Sept 1943); then within *Four Quartets* in *US 1943* (first American printing), *1944+*.

The Magdalene manuscripts are described leaf by leaf in Appendix B of *Composition FQ*. The folio numbers given there are also used below. Helen Gardner used the manuscripts before they were bound. Her designations MS A to MS D are here *msA* to *msD*:

msA: 22 leaves of a "Scribbling Pad" with drafts of both *The Dry Salvages* and *Little Gidding*. Nine leaves remain in the pad, N.5.4 (b), while the rest have been bound together with *msB*, *msC* and *msD* as N.5.4 (a). TSE to Francis Turner, Librarian of Magdalene, 27 June 1945: "I have just discovered the enclosed scribbling block with scrawls of what appear to be still earlier versions than any of those sent. While I daresay that I should be well advised in the interest of my own reputation to destroy these scribbles, I feel that in doing so I should be committing a kind of fraud at the expense of the College. So if you care to add these to the pages in your possession, please do so. I enclose the block just as I found it. It appears to include a draft of a letter to *The Times* on the death of Evelyn Underhill but I have not bothered to remove that." Facsimiles of fols. 85r. and 86r. (drafting *Little Gidding* II 1–24) appear (enlarged) in *Autograph Poetry in the English Language* ed. P. J. Croft (1973), and fol. 85r. is also shown in *1979*.

msB: four leaves from a similar pad, with drafts of *Little Gidding* II.

msC: four leaves from a narrower pad, with drafts of *Little Gidding* V, II, IV.

msD: two leaves, possibly from the "Scribbling Pad" (see *msA*), with notes for *Yeats*, a memorial lecture delivered in Dublin in June 1940, and with second and third drafts of *Little Gidding* IV on versos. These appear to date from some two years later; TSE was probably re-using old paper (during wartime rationing of paper).

In 1963, I. A. Richards sent Hayward a xerographic copy of the Magdalene mss. On the envelope Hayward wrote: "This exercise book was handed by TSE to W. Mc. [Francis] Turner, when the latter was College Librarian as a present from an hon. fellow. It was found after Turner's retirement, stuffed into a drawer and evidently forgotten along with TSE's Nobel Prize ~~medal~~!" (The illuminated manuscript of TSE's Nobel Prize is now in Magdalene Old Library.)

msA fol. 77 has probably the earliest notes for *Little Gidding* (*Composition FQ* 157):

> Winter scene. May.
>
> Lyric—air earth water end ⊄ ⊄
> daemonic fire. The Inferno.
>
> They vanish, the individuals, and
> our feeling for them sinks into the
> flame which refines. They emerge
> in another pattern ⊄ recreated ⊄
> redeemed, having their meaning to-
> gether not apart, in a unison
> which is of beams from the central
> fire. And the others with them
> contemporaneous.
>
> Invocation to the Holy Spirit.

[8]

[8] **redeemed**] reconciled *alt*

[9] **unison**] union *Composition FQ* (*error*)

Magdalene also has 13 ts drafts, retained by TSE, now bound together in a second separate volume, and three *NEW* proofs, bound in a third separate volume.

King's has Hayward's cognate versions of five of the tss, annotated by him in pencil, as well as correspondence concerning the poem, proofs of *NEW* and *LG*, leaves with the printed poem from *NEW*, and other notes. These documents were left to King's by Hayward, despite what he had previously suggested to TSE, who wrote on 16 Oct [1942]: "I have never expressed my appreciation of your wish to bequeath your Eliot remains to Magdalene. That of course would please me more than any other disposition you could make: and I will, as you request, keep the information buried in my breast. Magdalene is already, and will be further, the possessor of those of your letters which have been written to assist *The Dry Salvages* and *Little Gidding*, which are included with the manuscripts of those poems."

Composition FQ gives priority to the tss which TSE sent to Hayward, but the collation below gives priority instead to the tss retained by TSE (see table below). The 13 retained drafts (designated *a* when there is a cognate version) are bound together in a single volume at Magdalene (N.5.4 [e]), with pagination as given in the table below. The folio number is pencilled on the verso of each leaf.

	This ed.	Composition FQ	
First typing: (Part I)	*ts1*	*M1*	(retained by TSE; Magd. vol. fols. 1–3)
Second typing (Parts I–V)	*ts2*	*M2*	(retained by TSE; Magd. vol. fols. 4–17)
Third typing (Parts I–V)	*ts3a*	*M3*	(retained by TSE; Magd. vol. fols. 18–29)
	ts3b	*D1*	(sent to Hayward, 7 July 1941; printed, with Hayward's marks in *Composition FQ*, Append. A)
"additional fragments"			(sent to Hayward, 14 July 1941; untraced)
Fourth typing (Parts I–V)	*ts4a*	*M4*	(retained by TSE; Magd. vol. fols. 30–40)
	ts4b	—	(Geoffrey Faber's copy)
Fifth typing (Parts I–V)	*ts5*	*M5*	(retained by TSE; Magd. vol. fols. 41–51; an untraced carbon may have been sent to Bonamy Dobrée before 6 Aug 1941)
Sixth typing (Part III)	*ts6*	*M6*	(retained by TSE; Magd. vol. fols. 52–53)
Seventh typing (Part II, 2nd section)	*ts7*	*M7*	(retained by TSE; Magd. vol. fols. 54–55)
Eighth typing (Part II, 2nd section)	*ts8*	*M8*	(retained by TSE; Magd. vol. fols. 56–58)
Ninth typing (Parts II–III)	*ts9a*	*M9*	(retained by TSE; Magd. vol. fols. 59–69)
(Parts I, V)	*ts9b*	*D2*	(sent to Hayward, 17 Aug 1942)
			(sent to Hayward, 27 Aug 1942)
Tenth typing (Part II)	*ts10a*	*M10*	(retained by TSE; Magd. vol. fols. 70–74)
	ts10b	*D3*	(sent to Hayward, 27 Aug 1942)
Eleventh typing (Part III)	*ts11*	*M11*	(retained by TSE; Magd. vol. fols. 75–77)
Twelfth typing (Parts I–V)	*ts12a*	*M12*	(retained by TSE; Magd. vol. fols. 78–89)
	ts12b	*D4*	(sent to Hayward, 2 Sept 1942)
Thirteenth typing (Parts I–V)	*ts13a*	*M13*	(Faber printer's copy; Magd. vol. fols. 90–100)
	ts13b	*D5*	(sent to Hayward, 19 Sept 1942)

ts1 (Magdalene): ribbon copy on three leaves, with emendations, Part I only, headed "Draft". Line numbers every ten lines by TSE as far as 40.

ts2 (Magdalene): ribbon copy, on fourteen leaves, headed "Little Gidding | 1. Draft

2", with extensive annotation of various kinds. Part II has the earlier, "Poitiers" conclusion, which was retained until *ts5*. Two drafts of Part IV within this ts are designated *ts2(i)* and *ts2(ii)*: TSE worked on both, as though unsure which was closer to what he wanted. Line numbers every ten lines in Part I by TSE, with totals per part at foot of leaves.

ts3: two copies.

> *ts3a* (Magdalene): ribbon copy on 12 leaves, with light annotation. Line numbers pencilled by TSE every ten lines to end of III.

> *ts3b* (King's): carbon of *ts3a*, described by Hayward as "First Complete Draft", sent to him 7 July 1941 (and so dated by him on three leaves). With "first draft for consideration. | Not sure." in TSE's hand. Bound for Hayward in HB/V12 with the following page nos. in his hand on rectos and versos: Part I: 5, 9, 13. Part II: 19, 25, 31, 39. Part III: 43, 47. Part IV: 49. Part V: 53, 57. Before Hayward had time to reply, TSE "pushed on with *Little Gidding*" and sent "provisional results" on 14 July. Hayward acknowledged "additional fragments of the pome" on 22 July.

"additional fragments": revisions of *ts3* sent to Hayward but untraced. See Commentary headnote, 2. COMPOSITION.

ts4: two copies of a typing made before TSE wrote to Hayward on 28 July 1941 to say he had cut a stanza from IV.

> *ts4a* (Magdalene): ribbon copy of retyping of *ts3* on 11 (surviving) leaves, with extensive revision. TSE's pencilled line numbering throughout. Part II on same page as the end of I. Missing fol. 10.

> *ts4b* (McCue collection): carbon of *ts4a* on 12 leaves, lacking most of its revisions and comments. This carbon provides the *ts4* readings for fol. 10 (IV 1–7, V 1–16). Sent to Geoffrey Faber, who later noted in crayon some lines that were altered before publication. Accompanied by Faber's "First rough notes" on three separate leaves, with the later comment "But I never gave him my comments! I saw that they weren't good enough. G. F." Despite Faber's disclaimer, he made some of his thoughts known, as TSE's correspondence with Hayward shows. Some of his comments are given here and in the Commentary as *Geoffrey Faber's notes*.

ts5 (Magdalene): ribbon copy on eleven leaves of retyping of *ts4*, incorporating its preliminary corrections.

ts6 (Magdalene): ribbon copy on two leaves of retyping of Part III from *ts4*, incorporating some of its revisions and making others. On the verso of the first leaf, upside down, is the page number "3." and, on the verso of the second leaf, upside down, are the words "And elsewhere" (see II 67–96, *Second venture in verse* [13]).

ts7 (Magdalene): ribbon copy, considerably annotated, of a retyping of Part II 25–*c.* 74. Two leaves, with another probably missing, since the final line ("~~In the strength and weakness of the English tongue~~") has no terminal punctuation.

ts8 (Magdalene): ribbon copy on three leaves of the second section of Part II, including a first draft of the "gifts reserved for age" conclusion (see II 76–93). With extensive changes in typing and annotation.

ts9: two copies.

> *ts9a* (Magdalene): 11 leaves, mixing ribbon copy of Parts I and V with carbon of Parts II and III. These ribbon copies and carbons (on pink paper) are reciprocal with *ts9b*.

> *ts9b* (King's): 11 leaves, designated "First Revision" by Hayward, mixing ribbon copy of Parts II and III (sent 17 Aug 1942) with a secondary carbon of Parts I and V (sent 27 Aug 1942). These ribbon copies and carbons are reciprocal with *ts9a* (together constituting two complete copies). Bound for Hayward in HB/V12 with the following page numbers in his hand on rectos and versos: Part I: 4, 8, 12. Part II: 18, 24, 30, 38. Part III: 42, 46. Part V: 52, 56.

ts10: two copies.

> *ts10a* (Magdalene): ribbon copy on five leaves of Part II with some annotation in response to Hayward.

> *ts10b* (King's): carbon of *ts10a*, described by Hayward as "Second Revision. Part II. 27 August 1942". Bound for him in HB/V12 with page nos. 16, 22, 28, 36, 34 (the last two thus transposed).

ts11 (Magdalene): ribbon copy of retyping on three leaves of *ts9* Part III.

ts12: two copies.

> *ts12a* (Magdalene): ribbon copy of new typing of entire poem on 12 leaves, retained by TSE whose emendations adopt some of Hayward's suggestions seen in *ts12b*.

> *ts12b* (King's): carbon of *ts12a*, described by Hayward as "Second Complete Draft. 2 Sep. 1942". Bound for him in HB/V12 with the following page nos. in his hand on rectos and versos: Part I: 74, 78, 82. Part II: 82, 86, 90, 94, 98. Part III: 98, 102, 106. Part IV: 108. Part V: 108, 112, 116.

ts13: two copies.

> *ts13a* (Magdalene): ribbon copy of a new typing on 11 leaves, used as printer's copy for Faber's pamphlet *LG*. With the name "John Easton" (of the printers R. MacLehose) at head, not in TSE's hand (despite *Composition FQ* 154). Sent from Faber to MacLehose on 24 Sept 1942 and acknowledged (as "the MS of this poem") on 29 Sept (Faber archive). This ts omits the line "Summer beyond sense, the inapprehensible" (19 ^ 20), which does not appear in *LG* or later printings, although when TSE corrected the first proofs of *NEW* on 28 Sept, and the two subsequent proofs, he allowed it to stand. (Similarly, the emendation on *NEW* proof from "which" to "that" at III 25 was not followed in the *LG* pamphlet.)

> *ts13b*: carbon of *ts13a*, described by Hayward as "Final Recension. 19 Septem^r. 1942". Bound for him in HB/V12 with the following page nos. in his hand on rectos and versos: Part I: 75, 79, 83. Part II: 83, 87, 91, 95, 99. Part III: 99, 103, 109. Part IV: 109. Part V: 113, 117.

NEW "First proof" (printed on versos of auctioneer's stationery), endorsed "Corrected | T.S.E. | 28. ix. 42". Text as *NEW* except where noted. Magdalene bound vol. of the successive proofs, N.5.4 (f), fols. 1–5.

> King's also has a "First proof" of *NEW* (printed on versos of five leaves of auctioneer's stationery), endorsed by TSE: "Corrected | T.S.E. | 28. ix. 42". Early

emendations in pencil (some probably by the printer) are followed by TSE's final emendations in ink.

A third copy of the first proof, with a few pencil corrections in an unknown hand, but no variants, is at Princeton.

As Helen Gardner explained, the text set up by the printer is a text lying between *ts12* and *ts13*. Eliot corrected it to the readings of *ts13* but with further alterations (*Composition FQ* 27, 155).

NEW "Second proof" (printed on versos of auctioneer's stationery). Magdalene bound vol. fols. 6–10.

NEW "Final Proof". Sewn gathering with typeset page numbers 213–220, with compliments slip from TSE. Magdalene bound vol. fols. 11–14.

NEW printing, emended by TSE (King's): three leaves extracted from *NEW* (two conjugate and one loose, all formerly stapled), with the poem on the first five pages and other magazine material on the sixth. Sent to Frank Morley at Harcourt Brace, 22 Oct 1942, with a note from TSE's secretary: "Mr Eliot has asked me to send you the enclosed second copy of *Little Gidding*. He sent you a previous copy last Saturday asking you to cable its receipt."

LG proof (King's): proof copy of the pamphlet, date-stamped by MacLehose 15 Oct 1942, corrected by TSE and inscribed to Hayward. Text as *LG* except where stated.

Sibyl Colefax's birthday book (Bodleian): entry of 22 lines beginning "With the drawing of this love and the voice of this calling". No variants from published text. TSE inscribed a copy of *Four Quartets* "to Sybil Colefax with the author's sentiments", the first name misspelt (*ODNB*). He spelt her name correctly when writing to Hayward on 21 July 1942.

Valerie's Own Book: fair copy on fifteen pages of the second exercise book.

Re-examination of the drafts has led to a small number of revisions of readings in *Composition FQ*, mainly of punctuation.

Title] *not ts1, ts3* ‖ *pencilled (later) at head of ts2* ‖ *added in brackets by Hayward ts3b*
Author's name] *not tss, not NEW 1st proof 1st reading*
Part numbers] *followed by full-stop NEW*

I

I 1–2] *"Does JH like sundown?" ts9a*

I 1 **spring**] summer *ts1, ts2 1st reading*

I 2 **towards sundown**] at the day's end *ts1 1st reading* ‖ toward the day's end *ts1 2nd reading* ‖ towards the day's end *ts2–ts5, underlined with "X" and* sun's end / sunfall / sundown *ts4a alts*

I 3 **pole**] cold *ts1 1st reading*   **tropic.**] heat, *ts1 1st reading* ‖ tropic, *ts1 2nd reading, ts2 1st and final reading, ts3–ts5*

I 4 **short**] brief *ts1 2nd reading (reverting then to* short)   **brightest**] lightest ts1   with frost] ice *ts1 1ˢᵗ reading*   fire,] fire *ts1*, *ts2 1ˢᵗ reading* ‖ fire. *ts2 2ⁿᵈ reading, ts3–ts5*

I 5, 6] *transposed ts1*

I 5   brief] short *ts1 1ˢᵗ reading* ‖ brief *underlined with "cf brief ⋪ facile II, 3" by Hayward ts9b (referring to this phrase at II 67 as it then stood, on the third leaf of Part II)*

I 6   **In windless]** Windless *ts1 1ˢᵗ reading* ‖ Of Windless *ts1 2ⁿᵈ reading*   **heart's]** soul's *ts1*, *ts2 1ˢᵗ reading*   **heat,]** heat. *ts1*

I 7   **Reflecting in]** N̶o̶t̶ ̶m̶e̶l̶t̶i̶n̶g̶,̶ ̶b̶u̶t̶ making *ts1*   **mirror]** film *ts1 1ˢᵗ reading*

I 8]   **A glare · · · afternoon:** *Geoffrey Faber's notes: "I am not quite sure about this line. There is something flat about it. But the flatness does help the image of blinding reflection off a still flat surface."*

I 8   A] Of *ts1*   **glare]** light / glare *ts1 alts*   **blindness]** blindness, *ts1* ‖ brightness *ts5 1ˢᵗ reading (typed over)*   **afternoon.]** *ts9a 2ⁿᵈ reading+* ‖ afternoon, *ts1– ts5* ‖ afternoon *ts9*

I 9   **glow]** fire / blaze *ts1 alts del and replaced by* glow   **blaze]** *ts1 3ʳᵈ reading+* ‖ that *ts1 1ˢᵗ reading* ‖ fire *ts1 2ⁿᵈ reading*   **branch, or brazier,]** branch or brazier *ts1 1ˢᵗ reading*

I 10   **Stirs]** Warms *ts1 1ˢᵗ reading* ‖ Which stirs *ts2 1ˢᵗ reading*   **dumb]** animated / numbed / awakened *ts1 alts*   **spirit]** mind *ts1 alt del*

I 12–13]   *Geoffrey Faber in ts4b: "Isn't there a distinctive smell, though, that I can't describe (or even certainly recall)? (Must wait 6 months or so to be sure!)"*

I 14   **covenant]** *ts9a 2ⁿᵈ reading+, the revised line ticked by Hayward ts12b* ‖ recurrence *ts1–ts5, ts9*

I 15   **Is blanched]** Glitters *ts1–ts4, underlined with* Glisters / Whitens *Hayward ts3b* ‖ Glitters / Blanches / Is blanched *ts5 alts*   **an hour]** a moment *ts1*, *ts3 1ˢᵗ reading (typed over)*, *ts4 1ˢᵗ reading (typed over)*, *ts5 1ˢᵗ reading (typed over)*   **blossom]** snow *ts1 1ˢᵗ reading*

I 19 ^ 20]   Summer beyond sense, the inapprehensible *ts1 (last word over* una*), ts2–ts12, NEW.* A possible ghost of this line appears in the final ts, *ts13*, where "Zero" is typed over "S" (see Commentary).

I 20, 39]   *second part of each of these lines much more deeply indented, the two being horizontally aligned NEW*

I 20   **Zero]** *underlined with "X" by Hayward ts3b*   **summer? ^ If]** *two-line space 1963+* ‖ *stepped with single line space ts1~ts12* ‖ *instruction to printer: "wide space" and, ringed, "2 lines blank" ts13* ‖ *stepped without line space, with arrow by printer to move two lines of space from 20 ^ 21 NEW 1st proof* ‖ *1½-line space LG, US 1943, 1944* ‖ *single line space US 1952, 1969, Mardersteig, 1974, 1979, 1995, Rampant Lions* ‖ *end of page but with line space evident 1959 pbk* ‖ *stepped without line space Valerie's Own Book.* See East Coker Textual History note to I 23.

I 20 ^ 21, *as also* 45 ^ 46, 68 ^ 69, 91 ^ 92, 117 ^ 118, 143 ^ 144, 190 ^ 191]   *instruction to printer at foot of page: "no space" ts13*

I 21   **route]** road *Valerie's Own Book 1ˢᵗ reading*   **would be]** are *ts2 1ˢᵗ reading*

I 22   **come]** start *ts1~ts12, NEW, Valerie's Own Book*   **from,]** from *ts1*

I 24   **sweetness.]** sweetness, *ts1 1ˢᵗ reading*

I 24 ^ 25] In the may time, the play time of the wakened senses, *ts1, ts2 without final comma, ts3, ts4 1st reading* ‖ *with "X" by Hayward ts3b* ‖ *with* play time *underlined and "X" ts5*. Hayward to TSE, 1 Aug 1941: "this is a rather dangerous conjunction, maytime and playtime (cf. *Baby* & *Maybe*) being a favourite stand-by in Tin Pan Alley. I should feel happier if this jingle were omitted." TSE, 5 Aug: "I agree about the playtime jingle: I wanted the Children hint again: but perhaps it is too close to the Playbox Annual." See also I 41.

I 25] There is human joy, but no greater glory. *ts1 with* glory *del and* rejoicing / rapture *alts*   journey,] journey. *ts2–ts4 1st reading, ts4b, ts5*

I 26 at] by *ts1, ts2*

I 27 day] day, *ts1*   not knowing] and knew *ts1 1st reading*

I 28 when you leave the rough road] where you leave the rough road *ts1* ‖ at the end of the journey *ts5 1st reading (error, copying 25, typed over)*

I 29 pig-sty] pig-stye *ts1~ts13, NEW (emended on final proof, perhaps retrospectively, and on pages from NEW sent to Morley), LG proof 1st reading*   façade] facade *ts12*

I 32 which the] the the the *ts1 1st reading*   breaks] breaks, *ts1, ts2 1st reading*   when it is fulfilled] when it is summoned, *ts1, ts2* ‖ *underlined with "X" ts4a*

I 33 Either] Whether *ts4 1st reading (typed over), ts9 1st reading (typed over)*

I 35 fulfilment] fulfillment *ts13 1st reading*

I 36 sea jaws] sea's jaw *ts1*

I 37 in a desert or] or dominating *ts1 1st reading* ‖ concealed in *ts1 2nd reading* ‖ within *ts1 3rd reading (uncertain)*

I 38 nearest] *underlined with "to what?" by Hayward ts3b.* Hayward to TSE, 1 Aug 1941: "nearest to what, or to whom? I think I understand you, but I am puzzled to know what an American reader would make of it."

I 39 Now and in England.] Tragedy and glory. *ts1 1st reading* ‖ Tragedy transcending *ts1 alt with* Now ⳩ in England *added in margin*   England. ^ If] *stepped with single line space ts5, 1944+* ‖ *overhanging step with single line space Valerie's Own Book* ‖ *stepped without line space ts1–ts4, ts9~ts13, LG* ‖ *new page so line spacing indeterminate NEW (1st proof has two lines of space and printer's instruction to turn second part of line to new page)*   way,] way *ts1, ts2*

I 41 At any time or at any season,] *ts4a 2nd reading+* ‖ *ts1–ts5*:

At any time, the day time or the dark time,
Or at any season, the dead time or the may time,

with "X" by Hayward against each line ts3b ‖ *with all but the first of the five occurrences of* time *underlined by TSE with "X" ts4a* ‖ *Geoffrey Faber's notes:* "a little jingly?" Hayward to TSE, 1 Aug 1941: "There is just a faint suggestion here, I think, of your parodying yourself. (*v. supra* Hayward on Jingles)." See I 24 ^ 25.

I 42 same: you] same. You *ts1 1st reading*

I 43 verify,] verify *ts5*

I 44 Instruct] Inform *ts1–ts3*   inform] cancel *ts1–ts3, underlined with "δ T.S.E." Hayward ts3b* ‖ instruct *ts3a 2nd reading.* To Hayward, 14 July 1941: "You will observe that I have had to remove 'cancel' from Part I, because I wanted the word further on" (the first stanza of IV then ended "Or cancelled by the Paraclete").

I 45–46] Or carry report. And prayer is more *ts1*

I 46 **has**] hads *ts2 1st reading*

I 47 **an order of words**] the meaning of the words learnt *ts1* ‖ an order of the words, or *ts3 1st reading*

I 48 **mind**] soul *ts2*   **praying.**] praying, *ts5 1st reading* ‖ praying; *ts5 2nd reading*

I 51 **is tongued with fire beyond**] exceeds *ts1 1st reading* ‖ does not speak in *ts1 2nd reading*   **tongued**] touched *ts2 1st reading* ‖ fringed / tongued *ts2 alts*

I 51 ^ 52] *ts1*:

> And the speech of the living is wind in dry grass
> And the living have no communication with each other

ts2–ts5, finally del ts4a:

> The words of the living are wind in dry grass,
> The communion of the dead is flame ~~beyond~~ on the wind: [2]

[2] **flame on the wind:**] *underlined with "X" ts4a* ‖ flame on the heart *ts4a alt*

I 51 ^ 52] "< 2 lines omitted" *added in margin by Hayward ts9b*

I 52 **Here,**] And *ts1*

I 53 **nowhere.**] nowhere: *ts1 2nd reading*   **Never and always.**] Nowhere and always *Valerie's Own Book*

II

msA fols. 85–86 (which have been separated when binding) contain the first verse draft of the lyric section of Part II.

II 1–2] *braced with "?" ts5*

II 1 **Ash**] Dust *msA, ts2 1st reading*   **an old man's**] *alt msA* ‖ a threadbare *msA 1st reading*

II 2] *with "X" Hayward ts3b*   **all**] *del in msA*   **ash**] dust *msA, ts2 1st reading*   **burnt**] *not msA 1st reading*

II 4 **story**] *msA alt* ‖ history *msA 1st reading*

II 5 **was**] is *msA, ts2 1st reading*   **house—**] house: *msA, ts2 1st reading*

II 6 **wainscot**] wainscote *msA* ‖ wainscoat *Valerie's Own Book*   **mouse.**] mouse, *msA, ts2 1st reading*

II 7 **despair,**] despair— *msA* ‖ despair. *ts2 1st reading*

II 8 **air.**] ‖ air *Valerie's Own Book*

II 8 ^ 9, *as also* 16 ^ 17, 24 ^ 25 *two-line space Valerie's Own Book*

II 9 **There**] Here *msA alt, ts2*   **are**] *ts12a 2nd reading+* ‖ is *msA~ts12*   **drouth**] drouth: *msA*

II 10 **Over**] On *msA 1st reading*   **mouth,**] mouth *msA* ‖ mouth. *ts2–ts4*

II 12 **Contending**] Competing *msA, ts2*   **hand.**] hand *msA*

II 13 **parched**] scorched *msA~ts5* ‖ scorched *underlined with* parched *by Hayward* *ts3b* ‖ annealed *ts9*   **eviscerate soil**] and unemployable soil *msA~ts5* ‖ and unemployable soil *with each "o" underlined by Hayward, with "X" (as again in ts9b) and* acarpous / unavailing / unserviceable *Hayward ts3b* ‖ and unemployable soil *with* and *bracketed and* fruitless / emasculate / ~~sexless~~ / eviscerate *ts9a* alts. *Upside down on the verso of the final leaf of ts12a is written* eviscerate dusk. Hayward to TSE, 1 Aug 1941: "'unemployable soil': this sounds ugly when read aloud to my ear. (Possibilities: acarpous, unavailing, unserviceable)." TSE, 5 Aug: "I like 'unemployable' because the word has a special significance in contrast to 'unemployed' in relation to 'derelict areas' and I wanted the assimilation of the soil to the human material."

II 15 **Laughs**] And laughing *msA 1st reading* ‖ *underlined with* Smiles *by Hayward ts3b* ‖ *underlined with* Grins *by Hayward ts9b.* Hayward to TSE, 1 Aug 1941: "I should prefer 'smiles'. It is easier, I think, to conceive of a smile without mirth than a laugh without mirth, for all that people speak of a hollow laugh &c. And it's easier and more convincing, I feel, to imagine the soil as smiling than as laughing. An inanimate object can appear to be smiling; it can hardly be thought of as laughing. In any case, you can't gape *and* laugh at the same time—I've just tried to in the mirror—and you can gape and smile without mirth at the same time."

II 16 ^ 17] *no line space Folio Soc*

II 18 **weed.**] weed *msA* ‖ weed; *ts2*

II 20 **sacrifice that**] scarred foundations *msA, ts2 1st reading* ‖ marred foundations *ts2 2nd reading* ‖ skeletons that *ts2 final reading (transposed from* II 22), *ts3– ts5*   **denied.**] denied *msA*

II 21 **shall rot**] win by lot *msA 1st reading*

II 22 **marred foundations**] skeletons that *msA, ts2 1st reading (transposed from* II 20) ‖ deep foundations *ts5*   **forgot,**] forgot *msA* ‖ forgot— *ts2~ts9, with dash changed to comma in ts9a*

II 23] The broken or entire *msA* ‖ The maimed or the entire *msA alt* ‖ The broken or entire. *ts2–ts4* ‖ The crumbled or entire. *ts4a 2nd reading, ts5~ts9* ‖ Of chantry and choir. *ts9a alt, changed to* The chantry and the choir. ‖ Of sanctuary and choir. *ts9a 2nd alt+*

II 24 ^ 25] *msA, ts2:*

> Fire without and fire within
> Shall purge the unidentified sin.   [2]
> This is the place where we begin.

inset as preceding lines in ts2 then del

[2] **Shall purge**] Purge *msA* ‖ Expel *msA alt*   **sin.**] sin *msA*

II 24 ^ 25 *line space*] *two-line space ts2 1st reading* ‖ *new leaf so line spacing indeterminate ts3* ‖ *two-line space ts4, ts5, ts12*

msA fols. 87–89 *contain the first verse draft of* II 25–63.

II 25–96] *line of space after each tercet with no indents msA, ts2* ‖ *slight leading between tercets NEW (introduced on 2nd proof to fill the page)* ‖ *line space after each tercet Valerie's Own Book*

II 25–27] *tercet inset US 1952*

II 25–26] *with "X" Hayward ts13b*

II 25 **In**] At *msA, ts10* **hour**] moment *msA* **before the morning** *ts9, ts10, with* the? *inserted between the words and "(cf before the morning watch)" by Hayward ts10b (referring to The Dry Salvages* I 44*)*

II 26–29] *underlining by Hayward ts3b*: ending ··· interminable ··· incredible end ··· unending ··· dark ··· incomprehensible *and with* incomprehensible descension *separately underlined with "X".* Hayward to TSE, 1 Aug 1941: "I don't like the mouthful (and earful) 'incomprehensible descension'." TSE, 5 Aug: "I had been particularly unhappy about Part II. As for 'incomprehensible', I think that can be bettered: re-reading the poem in the train yesterday ··· I noticed too many IBLES at the beginning. 'Descension' I mean to clong to cling to: for it means the disappearance of a star or planet below the horizon (the American freshwater college sleuth would here discover some innuendo about Spender & Connolly, but none intended) O.E.D. But I still think that this Part needs some sharpening of personal poignancy: a line or two might do it." A year later, 27 Aug 1942: "I was sorry to surrender the word 'descension' which you will discover from the O.E.D. is an astronomical term but I do think a simpler line at this point is desirable. I hope I have got rid of the unpleasant terminations without any sacrifice of sense."

II 26 **Near the ending**] In the final stillness *msA, ts2 1st reading* || Toward the ending *ts2 2nd reading, ts3–ts5* || Towards the ending *ts7~ts12* **interminable**] the restless *msA*

II 27 **recurrent**] incredible *msA~ts8 and underlined, with* recurrent *alt and marginal line ts9a*

II 28 **dark**] black *msA*

II 29] Had made his incomprehensible revelation *msA* || Had made his incomprehensible descension *ts2~ts9, with* incomprehensible *underlined and* inexplicable / indescribable *by Hayward ts9b (marked "X" by TSE, who then underlined* incomprehensible *in ts9a)* **below**] *ts10a 2nd reading+* || beyond *ts10, underlined with* below *and "(cf descension)" Hayward ts10b*

II 31 **asphalt**] asphalte *msA~ts12, with* asphalte *with "no (e) ασφαλτος – cf form origin" Hayward ts12b* **where**] whence *ts12a alt del* **was**] came *ts12a alt del*

II 32] *wavy underline with "?" ts4* **districts**] angles *msA–ts5* || corners *ts7*

II 33 **and**] but *ts2* **loitering and hurried**] hurried & yet unhurried *msA* || loitering and ~~un~~hurried *ts4*

II 34 **As if blown towards me**] But more as if blown, *msA* **towards**] toward *ts2, ts5*

II 35 **urban**] little *msA, ts2 1st reading* **dawn**] *ringed, as also at* II 38, *with "morn (cf morne)" Hayward ts9b* **unresisting.**] unresisting *msA*

II 36–38] *braced, with rule and "X" after* dawn, *Hayward ts3b* || *msA~ts8*:

And as I scrutinised the downturned face
With the pointed narrowness of observation [2]
By which we greet the first-met stranger at dawn,

[1] *indented ts3~ts8* **downturned**] down-turned *ts8*

[1 ^ 2] *no line space ts3~ts8*

[2] **the**] that *ts2 2ⁿᵈ reading, ts3~ts8*

[3] *indented ts3~ts8*   **By which we greet**] Which we turn upon *ts2 1ˢᵗ reading* ‖ We turn upon *ts2 2ⁿᵈ reading, ts3~ts7* ‖ With which we meet *ts8 1ˢᵗ reading (typed over* We t) ‖ With which we face *ts8 2ⁿᵈ reading*   **first-met**] first met *msA*   **dawn,**] dawn *msA, ts7*

ts9, ts10:

> And as I scrutinised the down-turned face
> With that pointed narrowness of observation   [2]
> We bear upon the first-met stranger at dawn

[1–2] And as I peered into the . . . With that pointed scrutiny . . . *Hayward ts10b (his ellipses)*

[1] **And as I scrutinised**] And as I bent upon *ts9a alt, ts10,* with bent *underlined with "bend a scrutiny?" and* scrutinized *by Hayward ts10b* ‖ As I directed to *ts10a 2ⁿᵈ reading*   **down-turned**] *underlined with* down-cast? *by Hayward ts9b (see Commentary)*

[2] That pointed narrowness of observation *ts9a 2ⁿᵈ reading* ‖ That pointed scrutiny w. wh we challenge *ts9a 2ⁿᵈ reading alt* ‖ That pointed scrutiny with which we challenge *ts10 with a loop from* scrutiny *to "Is this O.K? only since 1798 (F. Burney) C. Bronte" ts10a*

[3] **We bear upon the**] We bend upon the *ts9a 2ⁿᵈ reading* ‖ With which we greet the *ts9a 2ⁿᵈ reading alt* ‖ *with* bear *underlined and* turn *Hayward ts9b* ‖ The *ts10*   **at dawn**] *with* dawn *ringed by Hayward ts9b* ‖ in the first faint light *ts10, with* daybreak *and "X" Hayward ts10b.* (To Hayward, 2 Sept 1942: "I see yr points about *daybreak* and *waves* but can think of nothing which would not overstress." Again, 7 Sept: "I cannot yet improve the daybreak." Probably "waves" refers to the gesture, rather than "waves of the sea" V 38.)

ts12:

> As I directed to the down-turned face
> That pointed scrutiny with which we challenge
> The first-met stranger in the first faint light   [2]

[1–2] **As ··· scrutiny**] *with* And as I turned upon | The lowered face the enquiring look *Hayward ts12b*

[1] **As I directed to**] And as I fixed upon *ts12a 2ⁿᵈ reading*

[2] **That**] The *ts12a 2ⁿᵈ reading before reinstatement of* That

[3] **first faint** *underlined ts12a*   **in the first faint light**] after lantern-time / after lantern-end / after lantern-out *(ticked) ts12a 2ⁿᵈ reading alts* ‖ *with* faint half-light *Hayward ts12b*

[3] *line and alts ringed and redrafted:* A stranger in the antelucan hour *ts12a 3ʳᵈ reading* ‖ The stranger at the antelucan hour *ts12a 4ᵗʰ reading with* ~~dark~~ / ~~dusk~~ / ~~dark~~

(*See Commentary for TSE's discussions with Hayward.*)

II 39 **caught**] met *msA, ts2 1st reading* || drew *ts2 2nd reading, ts3–ts5*   **some dead master**] the dead masters *msA* || *with* some *ringed with "X" and a lost ts4a*

II 40 **forgotten,**] forgotten *msA*   **half recalled**] and recalled *msA* || half-recalled, *ts2–ts5* || half-recalled *ts7–ts10* || half recalled, *NEW*

II 41 **many;**] many— *msA* || many: *ts2–ts5*   **the**] those *msA*   **brown baked**] scorched brown *msA* || brown scarred *ts2 1st reading*

II 42] *no indent 1969 (error)* || The remoteness of a vague familiar ghost *msA*   **a**] some *ts2~ts8 1st reading*   **ghost**] ghost, *ts2–ts5*

II 43] *indent 1969 (error)* || The very near, and very inaccissible *msA* || **Both**] The *ts2–ts4 1st reading, ts5* || Both? *ts4a 2nd reading* || **intimate**] very near *ts2–ts5* || **unidentifiable**] wholly inaccessible *ts2–ts4* || not identifiable / unidentifiable *ts4a alts*

II 44] And I becoming other, so I cried *msA (with* becoming *written over* beg) || And I, becoming other and many, cried *ts2–ts5* || And I, becoming also many, cried *ts7*   **So I**] I too *ts13, with "too" in margin and again at II 51 Hayward ts13b (pointing to repetition), LG proof 1st reading*   **a double**] another *ts8*

II 45–93] *single quotation marks US 1943, despite double quotation marks in The Dry Salvages III (with single quotation marks within)*

II 45 **And heard another's voice cry: "What! are *you* here?"**] *ts12+* ||
And heard my voice: "Are you here, Ser Brunetto?" *msA* ||
And heard my voice: Are you here, Ser Brunetto? *ts2, ts3* ||
And heard my voice: "are you here, Ser Brunetto?" *ts4, ts5, ts7 1st reading (with* Andheard *run together)* ||
And heard my altered voice exclaim: you too? *ts7 2nd reading (with* question *as* alt *for* exclaim) ||
And heard my altered voice question: "are *you* here?" *ts7 final reading* ||
Hearing another's voice cry: "What! are you here?" *ts8* ||
And heard another's voice cry: "What! are *you* here?" *ts9, with first word underlined with* But *and* "(or Hearing . . .)" *by Hayward, who also wrote "Ser Brunetto" after the line ts9b* ||
And heard another's voice cry: "what! are *you* here?" *ts10, with "w" underlined and "W" by Hayward ts10b*

II 46 **we were**] it was *msA*   **still the same,**] often dead, *msA* || always dead, *ts2~ts12* || still the same *ts13 1st reading, ts13b* || always dead *NEW 1st proof 1st reading*

II 47 **Knowing myself yet being someone other—**] *ts13 2nd reading, LG+* || Often revived, and always something other, *msA* || Always revived, and always something other, *ts2–ts5, with* revived *underlined ts4a* || And still alive, and always something other, *ts7, ts10–ts12, NEW 1st proof 1st reading* || And still alive, and always someone other, *ts8, ts9* || Yet recognised myself as someone other— *ts13 1st reading* || Knowing myself, yet being someone other, *TSE's revision of NEW 1st proof, NEW 2nd proof* || Knowing myself yet being someone other, *NEW final proof, NEW*

II 48 **still forming;**] changing, *msA* || changing: *ts2–ts5* || changing; *ts7–ts12, NEW 1st proof 1st reading* || still forming, *NEW 1st proof 2nd reading, NEW 2nd and 3rd proofs, NEW*

II 49] For recognition where was no acquaintance *msA–ts7 1ˢᵗ reading (with recognition, msA)* ‖ For recognition of a new acquaintance *ts7 2ⁿᵈ reading*   **preceded]** pretended *ts8–ts10, with* portended *and "(i.e. presumed) not profess falsely" Hayward ts10b* ‖ *underlined with* predicted *(underlined with "X") /* portended *alts by Hayward ts12b* ‖ portended / intended *with "?" ts12a alts del*

II 50] Driven together by *ts8 1ˢᵗ reading (false start)*   **And so, compliant]** In step together, *msA*   **And so,]** And no identity, *ts2~ts7 1ˢᵗ reading* ‖ Raised from the past, *ts7 2ⁿᵈ reading (but with* identity *not del)* ‖ And so *ts8 2ⁿᵈ reading, ts9 (with comma added ts9b, probably by TSE, though attrib. to Hayward Composition FQ 180), ts10, with comma added by TSE ts10a*   **compliant to the]** blown by one *msA~ts7* ‖ consenting to the *ts8 1ˢᵗ reading*   **common]** airless *msA~ts7 1ˢᵗ reading* ‖ lifeless *ts7 2ⁿᵈ reading (see note below at III 38)*   **wind,]** wind *msA, NEW 1st proof 1ˢᵗ reading*

II 51] *opening words written after a line space (mistaking lineation of the terza rima) then erased and rewritten above msA*   **misunderstanding,]** cross of purpose *msA 1ˢᵗ reading* ‖ a cross of purpose *msA* ‖ any cross of purpose *ts2~ts7 1ˢᵗ reading* ‖ any cross of purpose, *ts7 2ⁿᵈ reading, ts8~ts12a* ‖ any crossed intention, *ts12a 2ⁿᵈ reading*

II 52 **In concord]** But intimate *msA–ts5* ‖ Communing *ts7 1ˢᵗ reading* ‖ Accepted *ts7 2ⁿᵈ reading* ‖ Consenting *ts8 1ˢᵗ and final reading, ts9~ts12* ‖ Compliant *ts8 2ⁿᵈ reading*   **at this]** as *msA* ‖ at the *ts2 1ˢᵗ reading, ts7* ‖ in the *ts2 2ⁿᵈ reading, ts3–ts5* ‖ to this *ts8~ts12* ‖ with this *NEW 1st proof 1ˢᵗ reading*   **intersection]** intersecting *msA–ts5*

II 53 **Of]** A *msA 1ˢᵗ reading* ‖ And *msA*   **after,]** after *msA, ts2 1ˢᵗ reading, ts8*

II 54 **We trod the pavement]** ~~We~~ *msA 1ˢᵗ reading* ‖ In tacit observance *msA* ‖ Stepping together *ts2~ts7* ‖ We strode together *ts8~ts13 (with "? trod" Hayward ts13b), NEW 1st proof 1ˢᵗ reading*   **in a dead patrol]** of a shared patrol, *msA (with* shared *written over* ch)

II 55 **"The]** "the *msA, ts2, ts4~ts10, with "T" Hayward ts10b (calling for a capital)*   **easy,]** easy *ts2~ts8*

II 56 **Yet]** And *msA~ts8 1ˢᵗ reading*   **Therefore speak:]** Speak to me. *msA (over erasure, perhaps* Do you speak) ‖ Therefore speak. *ts2~ts9* ‖ Therefore speak, *ts10~ts12*

II 57 **comprehend]** understand *msA~ts12, NEW 1st proof 1ˢᵗ reading* ‖ comprehand *ts13 1ˢᵗ reading (error, affected by "understand"?)*   **remember."]** remember". *msA~ts4, ts7*

II 57 ^ 58] *caret (perhaps for line space) and new leaf ts5*

II 58 **rehearse]** recall *msA, ts2 1ˢᵗ reading*

II 59 **thought]** thoughts *1963, 1974 (later corrected)*   **theory]** practice *ts7, ts8*   **forgotten.]** forgotten *msA* ‖ forgotten: *ts2~ts4, ts7, ts8* ‖ forgotten; *ts5*

II 60 **purpose: let]** turn, so let *msA (Composition 182 reads as* turn. so let) ‖ purpose; let *ts2, ts7, ts8* ‖ ~~turn so let~~ *ts12a 2ⁿᵈ reading* ‖ purpose. Let *Valerie's Own Book*   **be.]** be *msA*

II 62 **pray]** ask *msA~ts10*

II 63 **Both**] Bood *ts2 1ˢᵗ reading (mistyping of "Both good")*   **bad and good.**] good
and bad. *msA~ts8*   **eaten**] eaten. *msA* ‖ eaten, *ts3–ts5, NEW*

II 64] *not msA (but see msB in next note)* ‖ *begun in line space, del and retyped ts2*

II 66 ^ 67] *ts7, del*:

> Then changing form and feature, and becoming
> Another company, speaking in another chime
> In another mode and to another purpose:

Evolution of II 67–96:

A) *Remember rather the essential moments* (First venture in verse)
First, TSE wrote in manuscript an ending in twenty-four lines ("Remember
rather the essential moments · · · At which I started: and the sun had risen").
This appears in *msA* fols. 92–93 (the first two of the leaves he did not remove
from his working pad) and then in *ts2–ts5*. It differs substantially from the
eventual text.

B and C) *Then, changing face and accent* (Prose exposition)
Second, in *msB*, TSE wrote a prose exposition on one leaf ("Then, changing face
and accent"), with, on a second leaf, a rough verse fragment of half-a-dozen
lines with filaments to the eventual "Last season's fruit" (II 63), "fullfed" (II 64)
and "bitter tastelessness of shadow fruit" (II 80).

D) *Then, changing form and feature* (Second venture in verse)
Third, also in *msB*, he recast the prose exposition in twenty-five lines of verse
beginning "Then, changing form and feature". After much redrafting, this was
to become II 65–75, 91–93.

E) *Consider what are the gifts of age—* (Prose draft of intervening passage)
Fourth, in *msC*, he drafted in prose what became the intervening passage,
II 76–90, which appeared in typescripts from *ts8*, along with the final lines,
II 91–96.

These are given in turn below, each with its variant readings.

A) *Remember rather the essential moments*

First venture in verse, given here in its first typescript form (ts2):

> Remember rather the essential moments
> That were the times of birth and death and change
> The agony and the solitary vigil.
>
> Remember also fear, loathing and hate,
> The wild strawberries eaten in the garden,   [5]
> Remember Poitiers, and the Anjou wine,
>
> The fresh new season's rope, the smell of varnish
> On the clean oar, the drying of the sails,
> Such things as seem of least and most importance.   <

So, as you circumscribe this dreary round,   [10]
Shall your life pass from you, with all you hated
And all you loved, the future and the past.

United to another past, another future,
(After many seas and after many lands)
The dead and the unborn, who shall be nearer   [15]

Than the voices and the faces that were most near.
This is the final gift on earth accorded—
One soil, one past, one future, in one place.

Nor shall the eternal thereby be remoter
But nearer: seek or seek not, it is here.   [20]
Now, the last love on earth. The rest is grace."

He turned away, and in the autumn weather
I heard a distant dull deferred report
At which I started; and the sun had risen.

msA, ts2–ts5. (Composition FQ 183–84 prints ts3, which in common with ts4 and ts5 has no line spaces but indents every second and third line). The passage is braced then del in ts4a.

[1] **essential**] unchanging *ts4 (underlined in red crayon, as is change in next line), ts5*

[2] **the**] your *msA*   **birth and death**] death ⌗ birth *msA*   **change**] change; *ts3a 2ⁿᵈ reading* ‖ change, *Hayward ts3b, ts4* ‖ chance, *ts5* (Hayward to TSE, 1 Aug 1941: "Insert comma after 'change' and so avoid a possible Empsonism.")

[3–8] **The agony · · · the sails:** Hayward to TSE, 1 Aug 1941, "a trifle overpacked with definite articles—a difficulty in catalogues—and something might be done to tighten this passage. (The first thing that occurred to me—forgive the impertinence—was 'The walls of Poitiers, *la douceur angevine*')" . See Commentary on first venture in verse.

[3] *msA alt, ts2–ts5 (with terminal stop ts3–ts5)* ‖ The dark night in the solitary bedroom *msA*

[4] Remember fear, and jealousy and hate *msA 1ˢᵗ reading* ‖ Remember even fear, loathing and hate *msA*

[5] **The**] *ringed with "? δ" (meaning "? delete") by Hayward ts3b, where he also ringed the ten other occurrences of the word between* [3] *and* [8]   **in**] *not msA 1ˢᵗ reading (error)*   **garden,**] garden *msA*

[6] **Remember**] The walls of *ts3–ts5*   **Poitiers,**] Poitiers *msA*   **the Anjou wine,**] the Anjou wine *msA* ‖ with "*la douceur angevine*" [the Angevine sweetness] *Hayward ts3b*

[7] **season's**] seasons *msA*

[8] **sails,**] sails *msA*

[9] *no indent ts3 1ˢᵗ reading*   **Such things as seem**] And all that seems *msA (over erasure)* ‖ And things as seem *ts2 1ˢᵗ reading*   **and**] or *msA*

[10] **So, as you circumscribe**] Remember, as you go *msA*

[11] **Shall your life**] So shall time *msA*   **with all you**] all things *msA 1ˢᵗ*
reading ‖ ⊄ all things hated *msA*

[12] **And all you**] Or *msA 1ˢᵗ reading* ‖ Or all things *msA*   **past.**] past *msA*

[13–14] *msA*:

>   United to one past and to one future
>   (Borne over many seas and many lands)

[16] **near.**] near *msA*

[17] **on**] of *ts2 2ⁿᵈ reading, ts3–ts5*   **accorded—**] accorded, *msA (over erasure)*

[18] **place.**] place *msA*

[19] **remoter**] ~~less~~ remoter *msA*

[21] **Now,**] This is *msA*   **on**] is *ts4a 2ⁿᵈ reading, ts5*   **grace."**] grace. *msA,
ts2 1ˢᵗ reading*

[22–24] *wavy line ts4a*

[22] **in the autumn weather**] with his motion of dismissal *msA 1ˢᵗ reading* ‖
with his movement of dismissal *msA*   **autumn weather**] *underlined with
"X" by Hayward ts3b*

[23] **I heard**] There came *msA*

[24] **At**] *over erasure msA*   **started;**] started, *msA* ‖ started: *ts3–ts5*

B) *Then, changing face and accent*

Prose venture, II 67–93 (*msB* fol. 1. *Composition FQ* 186):

>   [Th]en, changing face and accent, he
>   declared with another voice:
>   These events draw me back to the
>   streets of the speech I learned early
>   in life. I also was engaged in the   [5]
>   battle of language. My alien people
>   with an unknown tongue claimed
>   me. I saved them by my efforts—
>   you by my example: yet while I
>   fought ~~some evil~~ the darkness I also fought the   [10]
>   ~~good~~ light, striving against those who
>   with the ~~wrong~~ false condemned the ~~right~~ true.
>   Those who have known purgatory
>   here know it hereafter—so shall you
>   learn when enveloped by the coils   [15]
>   of the fiery wind, in which you
>   must learn to swim.

[1] **[Th]en**] *first two letters partially torn away*   **face**] *over* form

[7] **an unknown**] a dying? *alt*

C) *msB* fol. 2 *has a rough verse fragment* (*Composition FQ* 188), *apparently the germ of
"Last season's fruit", "fullfed" and "bitter tastelessness of shadow fruit"* (63, 64, 80):

>   For the old rooted sin puts forth again
>   Even in exhausted soil, after many seasons,
>   When the starved growth shows still more foul   <

Without luxuriance. All time is in a moment
And a moment is all time.   [5]
When all is won or lost. Therefore success
Is preparation towards a greater danger.

[1] **For**] *ringed*   **For the**] [For y]ou shall know 2*nd reading, very doubtful* (*corner of leaf torn away*)

[3] **growth**] unflowering growth 2*nd reading* (*the first word emended from, perhaps,* unflowered)

[7] **preparation towards**] precipitation towards / preparation for 2*nd reading braced alts* || the introduction to *additional alt, also braced*

D) *Then, changing form and feature*

Second venture in verse, much revised in manuscript (*msB fols. 3–4. Composition FQ 186–88*):

Then, changing form and feature, he returned,
As another man, speaking with an alien voice
On another theme and to another purpose:

These desolations draw my pilgrimage
To streets and doors I thought not to revisit   [5]
When my spirit parted from the southern shore

But at these times the path is short ⪽ easy
To the spirit unappeased and peregrine;
For the two worlds draw nearer to each other.

I also was engaged, as you must know,   [10]
In fighting for language: here, where I was tutored
In the strength and weakness of the English tongue

And elsewhere: when the political fire had regressed
My alien people with an archaic tongue
Claimed me. I, and another, saved them   [15]

As you, by my example, you may learn.
Yet while I fought with darkness, fought the light
As who, in imperfection, can avoid?

Striving with those who still defend the darkness
And even with the true defend the false   [20]
And with the eternal truth the local error?

Those who knew purgatory here shall know
Purgation hereafter: so shall you learn also,
In the embraces of that fiery wind

Where you must learn to swim ⪽ better nature."   [25]

[1] **he returned,**] he continued, *Composition FQ* || he became 2*nd reading* || and becoming 3*rd reading*

[2] **As another**] Another 2*nd reading*   **speaking**] he spoke 2*nd reading*   **an alien**] a foreign *alt* (*with an alien voice itself written over an erasure*)

[2] Another ~~group of men~~ company, with another [~~an alien~~ *alt*] chime of tongues *alt* (*upside down on msB fol.* 1v, *connected by a line; Gardner, Composition FQ* 188, *takes this to be an alternative to* [14])

[3] **On another theme**] In another mode *2nd reading*

[4] **draw my pilgrimage**] bring my footsteps back *alt*

[5] **and doors I thought not to**] I never thought I should *alt*

[6] **my spirit parted from the southern**] I left my body on a distant *2nd reading* || I buried my body on a distant *3rd reading*

[7] **these times**] this time *2nd reading*   **the path**] [the?] transit *2nd reading* || the passage *3rd reading*

[8] **peregrine;**] peregrine, *2nd reading*

[9] **For the two worlds**] Between conditions *2nd reading*   **draw nearer to**] draw closer to *alt and with* draw *emended to* drawn *2nd reading* || so much alike *3rd reading* || much alike *4th reading*

[10] **must**] should *2nd reading*

[10–11] As you should know, I spent my life contending by my efforts *at foot of leaf, linked to three lines written vertically in margin*:

> I spent my life in that unending fight
> To give the a people speech:
> I too was one of those in that unending fight who for a
> lifetime strove

[11] **In fighting for language**] *ringed along with alts*   **fighting for**] the fight for / battle of *2nd reading alts*   **here**] both here *2nd reading*

[12] **tongue**] phrase *2nd reading*

[13–15] *large marginal "X"*

[13] **when the political fire had regressed**] when the political flame had dampened *alt ringed along with first reading*

[14] **My**] Another *2nd reading*

[16] **As you**] From which *1st reading*   **by my**] for your *alt*

[17] **with**] the *2nd reading*

[18] **avoid?**] avoid, *2nd reading*

[20] **And**] *written over* As   **true**] real *2nd reading*

[21] **truth**] truth maintain *2nd reading*

[21 ^ 22] *caret in margin for unknown insert*

[23] **Purgation**] The same *alt*

[24] **In the embraces of that**] Caught in the coils of that strong *alt*

[24 ^ 25] *illegible erasure*

[25] Moving like a dancer through the desolation *at an angle at foot of leaf, perhaps as alt for this line*   **better nature**] swim rejoicing *alt del*

E) *Consider what are the gifts of age—*

Prose draft of intervening passage, II 76–93 (*msC* fol. 3. *Composition FQ* 189):

> Consider what are the gifts of age—
> The cold craving when the sense is
> gone which kept the soul & body to-

gether; the angry impatience with
human folly & turpitude & pusillanimity   [5]
with the knowledge of the futility
of protest; the doubt of self which
springs from retrospection of past
motives, the awareness of the
fact that one was moved while   [10]
believing oneself to be the mover

For all these ills that the enraged
spirit strives to overcome by pro-
gressing into new and greater sin—
there is only the one remedy, pain   [15]
for pain, in that purgative fire
which you must will, wherein
you must learn to swim and
better nature.

Notes to published poem resume. (The rest of Part II is not in drafts earlier than ts7.)

II 67–69] *after 72 ts7*

II 67 **But, as**] But at this time *ts7* ‖ But as *ts12, ts13*   now] *not ts7*   **presents
no hindrance**] is brief and facile *ts7* ‖ is brief and facile, *ts8–ts10, with* "(*cf. brief
sun I*)" *Hayward ts10b (see I 5)* ‖ is quick and facile, *ts10a 2ⁿᵈ reading* ‖ is short
and facile *ts12, with* short *underlined and* swift *with* "X" *Hayward ts12b, and with*
short *underlined and* swift / quick / soft *ts12a alts by TSE* ‖ is quick and easy
ts12a final reading (ticked) ‖ presents no barrier *ts13, 1st proof of NEW 1ˢᵗ reading.
In ts13b, Hayward suggested* ? hindrance, *which TSE adopted on NEW 1st proof
(2ⁿᵈ reading), and this is the reading of NEW 2nd proof. However, NEW 3rd proof and
NEW revert to* barrier. *TSE changed this again to* hindrance *in the pages from NEW
which he sent to Morley, and again, definitively, on the proof of LG. To Hayward,
7 Sept 1942:* "'Swift' might do: but it suggests great rapidity of movement, as if
in a car. What about 'quick' or 'soft', or the more colloquial 'quick and easy'?"
2 Oct 1942 (after *NEW* "First proof"): "I changed 'barrier' to 'hindrance' but
I am thinking of changing it back again, because it seems a little insolite [OED:
Obs. rare: "unusual, unaccustomed, strange"] to speak of a *hindrance between*
two points, doesn't it? And the freedom of movement was not in one direction
only, but to and fro." 10 Oct: "I have retained 'barrier' · · · one of the purposes
of this interim publication is to give an opportunity for alterations in the Faber
text. But are you still assured that it is proper to speak of a hindrance *between*
two termini?"

II 68 **peregrine**] peregrine, *ts7–ts12*

II 69 **worlds**] states *ts7*   **become much like**] *ts12a 2ⁿᵈ reading+* ‖ so much alike
ts7 ‖ now so like to *ts8 1ˢᵗ reading* ‖ become alike *ts8 2ⁿᵈ reading* ‖ become so
like *ts9~ts12*

II 70] "This interruption brings my footsteps back *ts7*   **So I find**] I now have *ts8
1ˢᵗ reading* ‖ Now I find *ts8 3ʳᵈ reading*

II 70–71] **thought · · · thought**] *underlined with* "X", *as also* "X" *by Hayward ts12b. (See*
II 75.) *TSE to Hayward, 7 Sept 1942:* "Thought: this I have not solved yet."

II 71 **In**] To *ts7*   **revisit**] revisit, *ts7*

II 72 **left**] buried *ts7 1ˢᵗ reading*

II 73 **concern**] regard *ts8*

II 74] *typed in line space, del and retyped ts8*

II 75 **urge**] *typed over* i *ts13*   **mind**] conscious mind *ts8~ts12* (*with* conscious ~~life~~
ts12a 2ⁿᵈ reading), *NEW 1st proof 1ˢᵗ reading*   **aftersight and foresight,**] *ts13a
2ⁿᵈ reading, NEW 2nd proof 2ⁿᵈ reading*+ ‖ be more conscious *ts8, ts9* ‖ thought
more conscious *ts10* ‖ thought more conscious, *ts10a 2ⁿᵈ reading, ts12 with
first word ringed with* be *and "original version but weak" and "X" Hayward ts12b* ‖
life more conscious, *ts12a 2ⁿᵈ reading* (*line ticked*), *NEW 1st proof 1ˢᵗ reading* ‖
afterthought and foresight, *ts13 1ˢᵗ reading*

II 73–75] *ts7* (*which ends here*), *del*:

> I also was engaged (as you should know)
> To give the people speech: both here where I was tutored
> In the strength and weakness of the English tongue

II 76–90] *For Prose draft of intervening passage* (**Consider what are the gifts reserved
for age**) *in msC, see above, "Evolution of II 67–96". The subsequent evolution of the
passage appears in typescripts from ts8 onwards* (*here by comparison with the final
text*):

II 76] Reflect *ts8 1ˢᵗ reading* (*false start*)   **age**] age, *ts9~ts12*

II 77 **To set a crown upon your**] The utmost prizes of the *ts8 1ˢᵗ reading* ‖ The
final prizes of the *ts8 2ⁿᵈ reading* ‖ The final prizes of your *ts9~ts12, with first
vowels of* final, prizes *and* lifetime's *underlined with "X X X" and* crowning *with
"finis coronat opus" Hayward ts12b* ‖ The crown to consummate your *ts12a
2ⁿᵈ reading* ‖ That put a period to a *ts12a 3ʳᵈ reading* ‖ These put a period to
your *ts12a 4ᵗʰ reading* ‖ To put a period to *ts12a 5ᵗʰ reading* ‖ The final crown
upon your *ts12a 6ᵗʰ reading* ‖ That set a crown upon your *ts12a final reading.* To
Hayward, 7 Sept 1942: "In any case, I now think 'prizes' is rather heavy-handed
after 'gifts'. I propose 'Let me disclose the gifts reserved for age, | That put a
period to your lifetime's effort.'"   **lifetime's effort.**] life for language *ts8 1ˢᵗ
reading* ‖ lifetime's effort: *ts8 2ⁿᵈ reading*

II 78 **friction**] ful (*perhaps for* fulfilment) *ts8 1ˢᵗ reading* ‖ craving *ts8 2ⁿᵈ
reading*   **expiring**] exhausted *ts8 1ˢᵗ reading* ‖ expired *ts8 2ⁿᵈ reading* ‖
expiring *ts8 3ʳᵈ reading*

II 79] *line erroneously indented ts12 1ˢᵗ reading*

II 79] For what, if given, would give no more pleasure, *ts8* (*with last two words
run together*), *ts9, ts10, with* more *underlined and* further *by Hayward ts10b* ‖
Without enchantment, with no expectation *ts10a 2ⁿᵈ reading, ts12 1ˢᵗ reading,
with* expectation *underlined and "?" ts12a* ‖ Without enchantment, offering
no prospect *ts12a 2ⁿᵈ and final reading* ‖ Without enchantment, offering
the enjoyment *ts12a 3ʳᵈ reading*   **enchantment**] allurement *Hayward
ts13b*   **promise**] promise, *comma added by TSE at the quotation of this line in*
G. Jones

II 80, 81] *transposed with "?" Hayward ts10b*

II 80 **But**] The *ts8* ‖ O̶f̶ *ts12a 2ⁿᵈ reading*

II 81 **As**] When *ts8–ts9, ts10a 1ˢᵗ reading, ts10b*   **body**] both *Valerie's Own Book 1ˢᵗ reading (uncertain)*   **fall**] fade *ts8*

II 82 **conscious**] growing *ts8~ts12, NEW proofs 1–2 although ringed with* conscious *by TSE on Hayward's 1st proof, LG proof 1ˢᵗ reading*   **impotence**] importence *ts8 1ˢᵗ reading*. To Hayward, 2 Oct 1942 (after *NEW* "First proof"): "I think of changing 'growing impotence' to 'conscious impotence' as being rather stronger, and having removed 'conscious' elsewhere [II 75] it is possible."

II 83 **folly**] baseness and folly, *ts8~ts12, NEW 1st proof 1ˢᵗ reading*   **and the laceration**] turpitude and folly, *ts8 1ˢᵗ reading* ‖ lethargy and folly, *ts8 2ⁿᵈ reading, ts9 1ˢᵗ reading, with* "ulterius cor, lacerare nequit" *Hayward ts9b* ‖ and the rending pain *ts9a alt, ts10~ts12, with* laceration *Hayward ts12b* ‖ and the dying spasm *ts12a 2ⁿᵈ reading* ("dying" *and* "spasm" *written separately*) ‖ And the laceration *ts12a 3ʳᵈ reading*. To Hayward, 2 Sept 1942: "I am sorry that *rending pain* can't stand. My metric requires a feminine termination there." 7 Sept: "Laceration: yes, I like this" (with "rending pain" being transferred to II 85).

II 84 **Of**] And *ts8 1ˢᵗ reading* ‖ And of *ts8 2ⁿᵈ reading, ts9 1ˢᵗ reading with* And *ringed*

II 85] And last, the doubt of self in retrospection *ts8–ts12 1ˢᵗ reading, with* retrospection *underlined and* r̶e̶c̶o̶l̶l̶e̶c̶t̶i̶o̶n̶ *ts12a* ‖ and last in retrospect self-doubting *Hayward ts12b alt* ‖ And last, the pain of memory's re-enactment / And last, the rending pain of re-enactment *ts12a alt 2ⁿᵈ readings* ‖ And last, the pain of memory's re-enactment *ts12a final reading*. (To Hayward, 7 Sept 1942: "I find 'self-doubting' rather weak. The best I can do at, the moment is 'And last, the rending pain of re-enactment'.")

II 86 **done, and been;**] been and done, *ts8~ts12a 1ˢᵗ reading* ‖ done, and been, *ts12a 2ⁿᵈ reading* ‖ done, and been: *ts12a 3ʳᵈ reading, ts13, NEW*. To Hayward, 9 Sept 1942: "by the way, we both missed something I have just picked up—'Of all that you have been and done' ··· Why whatever was I thinking of, to have been and done that? Read 'Of all that you have done, and been:'" (OED "be" 6c. "*been and* (*gone and*)—: vulgar or facetious expletive amplification ··· used to express surprise or annoyance", quoting *Pickwick Papers* ch. XXVI: "Lauk, Mrs. Bardell.. see what you've been and done!")

II 88] *indent 1969 (error)*   **and**] then *ts8 1ˢᵗ reading*   **to others' harm**] in all assurance *ts8 1ˢᵗ reading*

II 89 **Which**] When *ts8 1ˢᵗ reading*   **took for**] thought were *ts8~ts12 1ˢᵗ reading, with* thought *underlined with* "X" *and* felt? / took? *by Hayward ts12b*. (TSE to Hayward, 7 Sept 1942: "*Felt* is not strong enough: I mean not simply something not questioned, but something consciously approved.")   **virtue.**] virtue: *ts8*

II 90 **Then**] And *ts8 1ˢᵗ reading*   **stains**] *ts10a 2ⁿᵈ reading+* ‖ shames *ts10a 1ˢᵗ reading, ts10b*

II 91 **From wrong to wrong**] *ts12a 2ⁿᵈ reading+* ‖ Progress from wrong *ts8 1ˢᵗ reading* ‖ From ill to worse *ts8 2ⁿᵈ reading, ts9* ‖ From wrong to worse *ts10–ts12*

II 93] Where you must learn to swim, and better nature. *ts8, ts9 1ˢᵗ reading with* m̶o̶v̶e̶ *added above* swim *in ts9a and with marginal mark and* swim *and* better nature *underlined by Hayward ts9b* ‖ Where you must learn your measure, like a dancer. / Where you must move in measure. *ts9a alts at foot of leaf*

II 94 **The day was breaking.**] This you shall learn." *ts8, ts9* ‖ This you shall know." *ts9a 2nd reading* ‖ The day was glimmering *ts10 1st reading, with* glimmering underlined by Hayward with "?" prompting TSE's emendation to breaking *ts10b*   **In the disfigured street**] *with "X" Hayward ts12b* ‖ And down the shabby road *ts8 1st reading* ‖ Down the shabby road *ts8 2nd reading* ‖ In the decaying street *ts8* ‖ Down the dismantled street *ts9, with* dismantled *underlined and* demolished *Hayward ts9b* ‖ Down the disfigured street *ts9a 2nd reading, ts10a 1st reading, ts10b*

II 95 **left**] passed *ts9, ts10a 1st reading, ts10b*   **me**] on *ts9b alt, with* with *by Hayward*   **valediction**] salutation *ts8~ts12, with "X" Hayward ts10b* ‖ valediction? *ts12a 2nd reading, then rewritten without question mark*

II 95–96] *with* passed on v̲ passed me *and* The day / east was lightening / brightening *(with first pair of alts braced together) Hayward ts10b at foot of leaf (with "Part IV?", which he had not seen in revised form)*

II 96] *with* "and the sun had risen" *Hayward ts9b*   **faded**] vanished *ts8~ts10, with* "vanished *(also Hamlet)* ⪫ fading already 'neither budding nor fading' I" *Hayward ts10b (referring to I 17)*   **on**] with *Hayward ts9b (suggested to avoid potential repetition from II 95)*

III

msA fol. 94: prose draft of III *(Composition FQ 197).*

> The use of memory, to detach oneself
> from ~~the~~ one's own past.—they vanish ⪫ return
> in a different action, a new relation-
> ship. If it is here, ⪫ now, why regret it?

>   [*Insert*]   Detachment ⪫ attachment only a hair's width apart.
>   Air ⪫ air
>   earth —   Anima Christi
>   water —
>   fire ⪫ perfect fire.

> If I think of three men on the   [5]
> scaffold it is not to revive dead political
> issues, or what might have happened —
> Can a lifetime represent a single mo-
> tive? The symbol is the fact, and
> one side may inherit the victory, another   [10]
> the symbol. This means the moment
> of union, an eternal present.

[2] **one's**] *uncertain reading (Composition FQ reads* ones)

[4] **+ now**] then *Composition FQ (reading corrected Moody 336)*

[*Insert*] *diagonally at the foot of the leaf, with a line to indicate position. A question mark alongside the list of elements was written earlier than* Anima Christi. *Composition FQ transcribes slightly differently.*

[8] *with* For *added before* can

msA fols. 96–98 have the first verse draft of the whole of III, collated here with subsequent drafts and printings.

III 1–16] *with "1st para. Too didactic? | needs fusing." Hayward ts3b ‖ braced ts5*

III 1 **conditions**] conditions, *msA, ts2 ‖* conditions, three *msA 2ⁿᵈ reading* **which**] *not ts3–ts5 ‖* which *with "?" ts4a 2ⁿᵈ reading ‖* which can *with "?" ts4a 3ʳᵈ reading* **often look alike**] differ completely, *msA (see note to III 1–2) ‖* look very much alike *ts2 ‖* look very much alike, *ts3–ts5.*

III 1–2] *The turn of the line in msA originally read* completely, | Yet grow very *which was revised first to* completely, yet grow | Very *and then back again.*

III 2] Yet grow very close together, like the ~~life~~ affinities of the hedgerow *msA* **Yet differ**] And differ *ts2, ts4a 3ʳᵈ reading, ts6~ts9, with* And *del and* Yet *substituted by Hayward ts9b ‖* Differ *ts3–ts5 ‖* Which differ *ts4a 2ⁿᵈ reading* **completely,**] completely, and they *ts4a 2ⁿᵈ reading ‖* completely, *ts4a 3ʳᵈ reading ‖* completely; they *ts4a 4ᵗʰ reading* **hedgerow**] hedge-row *NEW*

III 3 **self and to**] *not msA, ts2–ts5, Valerie's Own Book* **self**] thi *ts12 1ˢᵗ reading (typed over)*

III 4 **self and from**] *not msA, ts2–ts5* **persons;**] persons, *msA, ts2* **and,**] and *msA, ts3* **growing between them, indifference**] last indifference, *msA 1ˢᵗ reading (with* last *over illegible word) ‖* third, indifference *msA 2ⁿᵈ reading ‖* thirdly, indifference *msA final reading* (third, *Composition FQ*) **growing**] grown *ts4 1ˢᵗ reading (typed over)* **between**] close by *ts2–ts5* **them, indifference**] *turned to new line NEW 1st proof, with printer's instruction to move back*

III 5 **life,**] life *msA, ts2, ts3, ts6*

III 6–7] Being between two lives. This is the use of memory, *msA (with* Being *written perhaps over* Beg), *ts2–ts5 with* memory:

III 7 **The live and the dead nettle**] *ts9a 2ⁿᵈ reading+ ‖* The live and dead nettle *ts6~ts9, with* The live nettle and the dead *Hayward ts9b (see Commentary)*

III 8 **For liberation—**] In liberation, *msA* **less**] loss *msA (uncertain reading; Composition FQ reads* less) **expanding**] *ts12a 2ⁿᵈ reading+ ‖* extension *msA ‖* expansion *ts2~ts12*

III 9 **beyond**] *ts5 alt, ts6+ ‖* in the death of *msA ‖* in the end of *ts2–ts5* **and so**] so, *msA*

III 10 **Thus,**] So *msA*

III 11 **as**] in *msA ‖* as an *1974 (corrected in later printings)* **attachment to**] love of *msA ‖* dependence upon *ts2–ts5, underlined with "?" ts4a* **field of action**] activities, but reaches completion *msA* **field**] *underlined with* chance? *ts4a*

III 12–16] *msA:*

> In finding their unimportance—and this is not indifference
> So, they vanish, the faces ⊄ places,
>> with the self which we loved and which loved them
> To be seen to be represented, in another pattern.

III 12 **comes**] grows *ts2 1ˢᵗ reading*

III 13–14] Though never indifferent. So, now they vanish, *ts2 1ˢᵗ reading (one line)* **History may be servitude, | History may be freedom.**] History is servitude | History is also freedom. *ts2 2ⁿᵈ reading, ts5* || *also with colon after* servitude *ts3* || *also with* may be ··· may be *as alt to* is ··· is also *ts4a* || ~~His~~ History may be servitude | But also freedom. *ts6* See] So *ts2*

III 15–35] *the following (only, and in this order) appear in msA: 15–16, 20–21, 23–24, 33–35 [line space] 26–27, 31–32, with arrow from 26 to move some lines above 33*

III 15 **which,**] which— *ts2~ts12*   **could,**] could— *ts2~ts12*   **them,**] them: *ts2~ts6*

III 16 **renewed**] renowned *1959 pbk (corrected after a memo from TSE, 29 Aug 1963)*

III 16 ^ 17 **line space**] *ts6~ts11, US 1943* || *new leaf or page so line spacing indeterminate ts4, LG, 1959 pbk* || *three-line space ts5* || *two-line space ts12, Valerie's Own Book* || *new leaf with instruction to printer "wide space" ts13a* || *no line space 1944, 1963+ (in 1944 a new page begins with 16, which would have been left isolated by a line space)*

III 17–19] *not msA, ts2, ts3, ts4, ts5* || *"< Julian" ts4a 2ⁿᵈ reading (calling for quotation to be inserted), after which the lines are added in pencil*

III 17] *indent US 1952*   **Sin**] "Sin *ts12a 2ⁿᵈ reading*   **Behovely**] behovely *ts4~ts12, Valerie's Own Book 1ˢᵗ reading*

III 19, *as also III 48, V 43* **thing**] things *1974 (corrected in later printings)*   **well.**] well." *ts12a 2ⁿᵈ reading*

III 20] If I think of a king at nightfall, *NEW 1st proof 1ˢᵗ reading (error, copying III 26)*   **If**] But if *ts6 1ˢᵗ reading*   **think, again,**] think last *msA* || think, last, *ts2~ts6* || think, again and last, *ts9~ts12*

III 21 **And**] *written over erasure, perhaps O msA*   **commendable,**] commendable *msA*

III 22] *not msA*   **immediate**] *underlined with "X" ts4a*

III 23 **genius,**] genius *ts2*

III 24] *not Valerie's Own Book*   **All**] And *ms4, ts2*   **genius,**] genius *ts2 1ˢᵗ reading* || genius; *ts2 2ⁿᵈ reading, ts3~ts5*

III 25] *not msA, ts2~ts5*   **which**] *tss, NEW 1st proof 1ˢᵗ reading, LG+* || that? *Hayward ts13b* || that *NEW proofs 1–3, NEW. Composition FQ 205:* "Eliot wrote on 10 October 'I have definitely accepted your THAT (was it Swift or Defoe who wrote a plea for WHICH?)'. He corrected 'which' to 'that' on the *NEW proof* and the text in *NEW* reads 'that'. But his conversion to 'correct English' did not last. He made no correction of the text of [*ts13b*] for the printing of *LG* and *Four Quartets*, which both have the idiomatic 'which'."

III 26 **nightfall,**] nightfall *msA, ts2~ts4, ts6*

III 27 **men, and more,**] *msA alt, ts6+* || men in turn *msA 1ˢᵗ reading* || men and more *ts2* || men, or more, *ts3~ts5*

III 28–30] *not msA*

III 28 **a few**] one or two *ts2, ts3* || two or three *ts4, ts5*   **forgotten**] quietly *ts2, ts3, ts4a 1ˢᵗ and final reading, ts4b, ts5* || obscurely *ts4a 2ⁿᵈ reading*

III 28] (One who died blind and quiet) *ts4a alt, with arrow to move below III 40*

III 29 **and**] or *ts2 2ⁿᵈ reading, ts3~ts9*

III 30] *not ts2–ts4 (but see III 28), ts5, ts6 1ˢᵗ reading (so that after its insertion, the typing of 29–31 appears single-spaced)* **of one]** *one ts6 2ⁿᵈ reading* **blind]** *blind, ts6 2ⁿᵈ reading* **quiet,]** *quiet 1959 pbk, Folio, Valerie's Own Book*

III 31–32] *after 35 msA*

III 31 **we celebrate]** *ts3b 2ⁿᵈ reading+* ‖ *a man lament msA, ts2, ts3*

III 32 **These dead men]** *The dead any msA, ts2 1ˢᵗ reading* ‖ *The dead men ts2 2ⁿᵈ reading, ts3 2ⁿᵈ reading, ts6* ‖ *Dead people ts3 1ˢᵗ reading*

III 33 **bell]** *bells msA, ts2–ts5*

III 34 **Nor is it]** *It is not msA, ts2 1ˢᵗ reading*

III 35 **summon]** *raise up Hayward ts3b, ts5 alt* **spectre]** *ghost msA, ts2–ts5, with spectre ts4a alt* **Rose]** *rose msA, ts2, ts3 (with "R?" ts3a)*

before III 36] *msA, ts2 (circled for possible deletion):*

> No one is wholly alive
> No man is free from sin
> And sordid or petty weaknesses   [2]

[1] **alive]** *right ts2 2ⁿᵈ reading*

[2] **man]** *one ts2*

[3] **weaknesses]** *weakness ts2*

III 37 **restore]** *revive ts2 1ˢᵗ reading (error, copied from previous line)*

III 38 **an antique]** *the antique msA* ‖ *a broken ts2 1ˢᵗ reading* **drum.]** *drum 1995*

III 39 **men,]** *men msA, ts2~ts9* **them]** *them, ts2, ts3*

III 40 **opposed]** *opposed, ts2, ts3*

III 41] *Consenting to a common silence, msA* **Accept the]** *Consent to ts2 1ˢᵗ reading*

III 42] *preceding III 41 msA 1ˢᵗ reading* ‖ *with rule and "X" Hayward ts3b* **And are]** *Are msA* **single party.]** *common silence ts2 1ˢᵗ reading* **single]** ~~common~~ *ts4 1ˢᵗ reading. For TSE to Hayward on this change, see description of ts4.*

III 42 ^ 43] *msA:*

> The victory no longer a victory
> But only a neutral fact.
> No life had a single motive

with a loop, subsequently erased, to move the third line before the first ‖ *ts2 1ˢᵗ reading, del:*

> No longer defeat and victory
> But only a neutral fact.

III 43] *We have our bequest from the victors, msA (over illegible erasure)* **fortunate]** *victors ts2 1ˢᵗ reading* ‖ *victors, ts2 2ⁿᵈ reading, ts3–ts5*

III 44 **We have taken]** *Receiving msA*

III 45 **leave]** *give ts6 1ˢᵗ reading* **symbol:]** *symbol msA* ‖ *symbol, ts6 2ⁿᵈ reading*
III 46] *not ts9~ts12*
III 46–50] *msA:*

> The symbol created by death
> The life only death can bequeathe

In death the perfection of the motive
Which the moment of death attained.

[1] **death**] *apparently changed from* dead *in mid-formation*

[4] **attained.**] *over illegible erasure*

ts2–ts5, finally all del ts4a:

> The symbol created by death,
> The life only death transmits, [2]
> The perfection of the motive
> Which the moment of death brings to life. [4]

[1] **death,**] death *ts3–ts5*

[1 ^ 2] (Created by such a death) *ts3–ts5*

[3] **perfection**] purification *ts4, ts5*

[4] Which assent to death perfects. *ts4* ‖ Which consent to death perfects.
ts4a 2nd reading, ts5

2nd draft (beside 1st) ts4a (Composition FQ 209):

> The symbol of the defeated. the crown on the hedge—the Duke with his iron
> shutters. We must keep the symbol but not confuse it with the use we make of it.
> Who survives the test of victory?

3rd draft (upside down on verso of previous leaf) ts4a:

> The damaged crown on the thornbush
> The Duke with his iron shutters
> Have the dignity of the defeated
> In a world in which, as it happens,
> Only the defeated have dignity, [5]

[1] **damaged**] battered *2nd reading*

[5] The victors seldom keep dignity. *2nd reading*

ts6:

> The symbol of the defeated—
> The crown hanging in a thornbush
> And the Duke with his iron shutters—
> In the purification of the motive
> In the ground of our beseeching. [5]

[2–3] *not 2nd reading*

[4] **In**] With *2nd reading*

III 47 **And all shall be well and**: Hayward to TSE, 18 June 1944: "I suggested, by the
way, to Dick [de la Mare] that he should try to bring back a line to page 41 (I
think it is) so that the page shouldn't end with the broken phrase 'And all shall
be well and' which looks very gauche and is jarring to the reader." Instead, the
line which jarred in *LG* was taken forward to the top of 42 in *1944*.

III *after* 50] *msA~ts4:*

> Soul of Christ, inspire them
> Body of Christ, make their bodies good soil
> Water from the side of Christ, wash them,
> Fire from the heart of Christ, incinerate them.

[1–4] *inset ts3, ts4* ‖ *braced with "cut by T.S.E." Hayward ts3b* ‖ *braced with "?" then del ts4a*

[1] **inspire them**] sanctify them, *ts2–ts4*

[2] **make their bodies good soil**] let their bodies be good earth, *ts2–ts4*

TSE to Hayward, 28 July 1941: "I have I think improved the poem a little by cutting out the second stanza of Part IV and also the Anima Christi lines at the end of Part III (too heavy, I think)."

IV

IV *Genesis of the first published stanza.*

msA fol. 100 has a draft in two stanzas, the second of them finally struck through (*Composition FQ* 213):

> The dove descending breaks the air
> With breath of crepitative fire
> Its tongues declare
> The culmination of desire,
> Of expectation, doubt, despair.   [5]
>   Beneath those never resting feet
>   All aspirations end and meet.
>
> The marked invisible watery cross,
> The further mark of delegated hands,
> But emphasise our loss,   [10]
> Transformed into the sign that brands
> The votary of Soledos
> The gambler between death ↄ birth
> Whose climax is a pinch of earth

[2] **breath**] tongues *1st reading*

[3] **Its**] Where / While / Of which the *alt 2nd readings*

[5] **Of expectation**] Expectancy, hope *2nd reading*

[9] **further**] forgotten *Composition FQ*   **The further mark**] The unseen impress *2nd reading* ‖ The touch *final reading*

[12] *3rd reading* ‖ The miserable athanatos *1st reading* ‖ The votaries of thanatos *2nd reading*

[13] **The gambler between**] Who gambled *2nd reading*

[14] **Whose**] *written over* T

msA fol. 100v. has a revised draft of the second of these stanzas:

> Between the invisible watery sign
> And climax of a pinch of earth
> Our slippery hearts decline
> To pay the dues of death ↄ birth
> And mark the debt beneath the line   [5]
>   The deficit which is complete
>   Or cancelled by the Paraclete.

[3] **slippery hearts**] false accounts *2nd reading*

[4] **pay**] square *2nd reading* || show / set *alt 3rd readings*

[6–7] *over illegible erased lines, not indented*

msA fol. 99v. has three lines that contribute to another stanza (later abandoned):

> This death shall call the bailiffs in
> With all our patrimony spent
> Or lost in worthless shares, we win

with "a | b | a | b" and "a" written below. (The first word—read here, as by Composition FQ 213, as "This"—is so like "Till" that TSE may have misread it when he first typed these lines, in *ts2*.)

When TSE began to type the whole poem, Part IV consisted, from *ts2* until *ts4*, of three stanzas, two of them later abandoned.

IV.

> Between the invisible watery sign
> And climax of a pinch of earth
> We in our false accounts decline
> To square the dues of death and birth
> And mark the debt below the line: [5]
>   The deficit that is complete
>   Or cancelled by the Paraclete.
>
> Till death shall bring the bailiffs in
> To value all our worthless treasures:
> *Unprofitable Sin*,   [10]
> *Comforting Thoughts*, and *Sundry Pleasures*,
> The assets that we think to win
>   By *Prudence*, and by *Worldly Cares*
>   Figure as gilt-edged stocks and shares.
>
> The dove descending breaks the air   [15]
> With breath of crepitative terror
> Of which the tongues declare
> The culmination of desire.
> The only hope, or else despair
>   Is, like the bird upon the pyre   [20]
>   To be revoked from fire by fire.

ts2 (two drafts), *ts3*, *ts4 (leaf missing from ts4a, so readings are from ts4b)*, *ts5 (first stanza only)*.

In the margin of *ts2(i)*, shown above in its earliest state, TSE numbered the stanzas 2, 1, 3, and in *ts2(ii)* and *ts3* he typed them in the new order. Hayward therefore first saw this part, in his carbon of *ts3*, as three stanzas: "Till death", "Between the" and "The dove descending". But TSE had already decided to restore the stanzas' original order, so among other marks on Hayward's carbon he again numbered them 2, 1, 3, with "Perhaps omit 2?" beside "Till death". He typed *ts4* with the three stanzas in original order, but on Geoffrey Faber's carbon of this, he again asked of the second, "Perhaps omit this stanza?" To Hayward, 28 July: "I have I think improved the poem a little by cutting out the second stanza of Part IV and also the Anima Christi lines at the end of Part III (too heavy I think)." Accordingly, against "Till death", Hayward wrote "Cut by T. S. E." in *ts3b*. Hayward also braced the remaining two stanzas with "IV obscure ⊲ too little of it. non-sequiturish?" He amplified these doubts in a letter of 1 Aug (see Commentary, headnote to *Little Gidding*, 2. COMPOSITION) and perhaps in response to this TSE struck through both "Between the" and "Till death" in his own copy of *ts4*, writing to Geoffrey Faber, 22 Aug: "I think Part IV will have to be completely recast."

[1] **invisible**] *underlined with "?" and* initial *ts2(ii) 2ⁿᵈ reading* ‖ initial *ts3–ts5*

[2] **And ^ climax**] the *ts2(i) 1ˢᵗ reading*   **earth**] earth, *ts2(ii)–ts5*

[3] **We in our**] Our *ts2(i) 2ⁿᵈ reading, ts3–ts5*

[4] **square the dues**] *underlined ts2(i)* ‖ show the dues *ts3–ts5*   **death**] birth *ts4 1ˢᵗ reading (typed over)*

[5] **And**] Or *ts3, ts4*

[6, 7] *no indent ts2(ii), ts3*

[6] **complete**] complete, *ts3 2ⁿᵈ reading*

[8–10] *typed on ts2(ii)v.:*

> Till death shall bring the audit in
> To value all our worthless treasures:
> Unprofitable Sin

before TSE turned over and reversed the leaf.

[8] **bailiffs**] audit *ts2(i) alt, ts2(ii)–ts4*

[9] **worthless**] hoarded *ts2(i) alt, ts2(ii)–ts4*   **treasures:**] treasures— *ts3 2ⁿᵈ reading, ts4*

[10–11] Unprofitable Sin | Sundry Pleasures *jotting on inside lower cover of msA*

[10] *Unprofitable*] The *Profitable ts2(ii)–ts4*   *Sin*] sin *ts2(i) 1ˢᵗ reading*

[11] *Comforting*] Cosseting *ts2(ii), ts3 1ˢᵗ reading* ‖ Consenting *ts3, ts4*   *Pleasures,*] Pleasures; *ts2(ii) 2ⁿᵈ reading, ts3 1ˢᵗ reading* ‖ Pleasures: *ts3, ts4*

[12] **assets**] ventures *ts2(i) 2ⁿᵈ reading* ‖ prizes *ts2(ii)–ts4*   **to**] we *ts2(i) 1ˢᵗ reading (error)*

[13, 14] *indented ts4*

[13] *Cares*] Cares, *ts3, ts4*

[14] **gilt-edged**] gilt-edge *ts2(ii)–ts4*

[16] **breath**] flame *ts2(i) 2ⁿᵈ reading–ts4*   **crepitative**] *underlined with "?" and* incandescent *as alt ts2(ii)* ‖ incandescent *ts3, ts4*

[18] The one restorative from error. *ts2(i) 2ⁿᵈ reading* ‖ The one discharge from mortal error. *ts2* ‖ The one discharge from sin and error. *ts3, ts4*

[20] Lies in the choice of pyre or pyre *ts2(i) 2ⁿᵈ reading* ‖ Lies in the choice of pyre or pyre— *ts3, ts4*

[21] **revoked**] redeemed *ts2(i) 2ⁿᵈ reading, ts3, ts4*   **from fire by fire**] by fire from fire *ts3, ts4*

IV 6] *no indent Valerie's Own Book 1ˢᵗ reading (then marked with caret)*

IV 7 ^ 8] *four-line space at the foot of page after first stanza US 1943* ‖ *two-line space Valerie's Own Book*

IV 8–14] *Genesis of the second published stanza.*

msC fol. 4 has an initial draft (*Composition FQ* 216):

> Who heaped the brittle rose leaves? Love.
> Love put the match; and blew the coals.
> Who fed the fire? Love.
> To torture and to temper souls
> In that consumption from above   [5]
> Where all delights ⅋ torments cease
> The will is purified to peace.

    [5] Endless consumption, which is love *written below stanza, probably as alt for this line*   **In**] With *alt*

Second and third drafts appear in *msD* (*Composition FQ* 217; the leaf bearing the *3rd draft* is now bound before the *2nd draft*); *2nd draft*:

> Who then devised the torture? Love.
> He laid the train, and fixed the cure.
> And he it was who wove   [3]
> The insupportable shirt of fire

    [1] **devised**] designed *alt*

    [2] **train, and**] fuel, *2ⁿᵈ reading*   **the**] *over illegible letter or letters*

    [3] He also wove *1ˢᵗ reading del (false start)*   **he**] He *2ⁿᵈ reading*

Below this *2nd draft* is a further jotting:

> He set the ambush
> He kindled the encircling fire
>
> Who then designed the torture? Love.   [3]
> Love is the unfamiliar name
> Of Him, below, above,

    [1] *del*

    [5] **Him**] what *1ˢᵗ reading*

3rd draft:

> Who then devised the torture? Love.
> Love is the unfamiliar name
> Of what, before Eden, wove
> The insupportable shirt of flame
> Which we must wear, and not remove   [5]
> But always live, and still expire,
> Consumed by either fire or fire.

    [1] **torture?**] torment? *alt*

    [2] **unfamiliar**] unspeakable *alt*

    [3] Of what, in the beginning, wove *alt* ‖ Of what, before time, wove *2ⁿᵈ reading* ‖ Behind the power that wove *alt 2ⁿᵈ reading with* power *then*

changed to loom ‖ Written by the hands that wove *additional alt* ‖ Behind the hands that wove *further additional alt*

[5] **we must wear, and not**] human kind cannot *2nd reading*

[6] **But always**] We only *2nd reading*   and still] only *2nd reading*

The two stanzas that were eventually printed appear together first in *ts12*, which Hayward dated 2 Sept 1942.

IV 7 ^ 8] *no line space NEW 1st proof with rule and "< space if possible" ‖ new page in 2nd and 3rd proofs, NEW*

IV 8] *indent US 1952, 1959 pbk*   **devised**] designed *ts12*   **torment**] torture *ts12a 1st reading, ts12b*

IV 14] *no indent NEW proofs 1–2, emended on 1st proof probably by printer*

IV ^ V] *no line space NEW 1st proof, with instruction to add space probably from printer*

V

msC fols. 17–18 have a *verse draft* of V:

> What we think a beginning is often an end
> And to make an end is to make a beginning.
> The end is where we start from. For every moment
> Is both beginning and end. So every phrase,
> When it is right, when every word has power   [5]
> To sustain the others, to do its part
> In subservience to the phrase,
> Is the end and the beginning. The only obituary
> Is written in every word of the man who writes it:
> Every poem is its own epitaph every action   [10]
> A step on the scaffold, to the fire, to the sea.
> And that is the beginning.   *[new leaf]*
>   The dying die for us
> And we die with them. But to speak of regret
> Is to outlive regret. The moment of the rose   [15]
> And the moment of the yew tree are equally moments
> And so must vanish to become eternal
> So, they return: and the winter sunlight
>
> Freedom past and future
> Is union with past & future   [20]

[1] **often**] *over illegible false start*

[5] **right,**] the right one— *2nd reading*

[7] **phrase,**] phrase— *2nd reading*

[8] **obituary**] *1st and final readings (though the word looks more like* obituaries*)* ‖ epitaph *2nd reading*

[12] **beginning**] *written over illegible false start*

[12 ^ 13] *new leaf*

[15] **to**] *written over* no *(perhaps for* not*)*

[18] **they**] these *alt*

[19] **Freedom**] Freedom from *2ⁿᵈ reading*

V 1–16] *leaf missing from ts4a so ts4 readings are from ts4b*

V 1 **call**] *ts12b 2ⁿᵈ alt with "?", with marginal tick (crossed through)* ‖ think *ts2~ts9,* ‖ suppose? *Hayward ts9b* ‖ mark as *ts9a 2ⁿᵈ reading, ts12* **beginning**] beginnin *LG proof 1ˢᵗ reading* **is**] if *1969 (later corrected)* **the end**] an end *msC, ts2*

V 2] *msA fol.* 95 consists of this line alone (without terminal stop) beneath "V".

V 3 **And every phrase**] For every moment *msC*

V 3 ^ 4] Is both beginning and end. So every phrase, *msC*

V 4 **And**] Or *ts2–ts5, ts12, NEW* **right**] right, *ts2* **(where**] (which *ts2 1ˢᵗ reading* **home,**] home in *ts2 1ˢᵗ reading*

V 5 **Taking its place**] Doing its part *ts2~ts9* **support**] sustain *ts2*

V 6 **ostentatious**] ostentations *ts3 1ˢᵗ reading, ts12 1ˢᵗ reading, ts13, LG proof 1ˢᵗ reading*

V 8 **common**] new *ts2 1ˢᵗ reading* **exact**] simple, *ts2 1ˢᵗ reading* ‖ precise *ts2 2ⁿᵈ reading* ‖ exact *ts2 3ʳᵈ reading with* precise? *in margin*

V 9 **formal**] old *ts2 1ˢᵗ reading* **precise**] formal, *ts2 1ˢᵗ reading* ‖ exact *ts2 2ⁿᵈ reading* ‖ precise *ts2 3ʳᵈ reading* **but not pedantic,**] without pedantry, *ts2 1ˢᵗ reading, ts3 2ⁿᵈ reading~ts9* ‖ without pedantry) *ts2 2ⁿᵈ reading, ts3 1ˢᵗ reading* ‖ but not pedantic, *ts9a 2ⁿᵈ reading* ‖ yet not pedantic, *ts9a 3ʳᵈ reading*

V 8–9] *Hayward marks stresses:* witho͞ut vulga͞rity *adding his own* bu͞t unpeda͞ntic *ts9b*

V 10] *not ts2*

V 11 **Every**] So every *ts2 1ˢᵗ reading* **and every sentence**] not *ts2 1ˢᵗ reading* ‖ and sentence *ts2 2ⁿᵈ reading, ts4, ts5* ‖ or sentence *ts2 3ʳᵈ reading, ts3* **an end and**] an end or *ts3 1ˢᵗ reading* ‖ and end and *1969 (later corrected)* **beginning,**] beginning. *ts2 1ˢᵗ reading*

V 11–13] to Hayward, 7 Sept 1942 (between sending *ts12* and sending *ts13*):

> Every phrase and every sentence is an end and a beginning,
> Every poem an epitaph. And any decision
> Is a step . . . (*or,* May be a step?)
>
> (Composition FQ 221)

V 12] *ts2 1ˢᵗ reading*:

> So every poem is its own epitaph
> And that of the writer. Every action

ts2 2ⁿᵈ reading, ts3~ts12:

> Every poem its own epitaph. And every action

(*in emending ts2, TSE originally put a comma after* epitaph *then crossed it through for a full stop*) ‖ Every poem an epitaph. And any decision *ts12a 2ⁿᵈ reading* **Every**] Evey *1979*

V 12–13 **And any action | Is a step**] And all our actions | Are steps *Hayward, with "cf. of all our exploring" ts12b (referring to* V 27)

V 13 **Is a**] A *ts2 1ˢᵗ reading* ‖ ~~May be~~ *ts12a 2ⁿᵈ reading* **to the block**] on the scaffold *ts2* ‖ up the scaffold *ts3–ts5* **fire, down**] fire, to *ts2* **throat**] throat, *ts2*

V 14 **Or to an illegible stone:**] *not ts2 1ˢᵗ reading* ‖ Or to an illegible stone. *ts2 2ⁿᵈ reading* **and**] And *ts2*

V 15] The dying die to us, *ts2 1ˢᵗ reading* ‖ We die with the dying, *ts2 2ⁿᵈ reading, ts3*

V 16 **them.**] them; *ts3–ts5*

V 17–18] *not ts2*

V 17 **are born**] return *ts3 1ˢᵗ reading* **dead:**] dead, *ts3*

V 18 **them.**] them: *ts3*

V 20 **people**] nation *ts2*

V 21 **time,**] time. *ts4 1ˢᵗ reading* **for history**] and history *ts2*

V 22 **moments.**] moments, *1944 7th–9th imp. (1949–52)*

V 23 **winter's**] winter *ts2~ts9, with* winter's *ts9a and Hayward ts9b* **chapel**] chapel, *ts2, ts5*

V 23 ^ 24] *two-line space at foot of verso, so as to move 24 to head of recto US 1952 (see V 24 ^ 25)*

V 24 ^ 25 *two-line space] ts13 (with instruction to printer "wide space" ts13a), LG, 1963, Valerie's Own Book ‖ single line space NEW, Mardersteig, US 1963, 1969, 1974, 1979, 1995, Rampant Lions ‖ new page so line spacing indeterminate US 1943, 1959 pbk, Folio ‖ no line space, so as to prevent 24 being a widow, but with the effect of isolating 24 and 25 together at the head of the recto US 1952. Moody 258 urges a double space to indicate the relation of subsequent lines to all four Quartets (although Moody 304 and Moody 309 advocate triple spacing 24 ^ 25 and double spacing 25 ^ 26).*

V 25] *not ts2–ts5 ‖ 26 begins new leaf after two-line space ts2, ts5 ‖ 26 begins new leaf with line spacing indeterminate ts3 ‖ two-line space 24 ^ 26 ts4*

V 25] *indent 1959 pbk, Folio*

V 25] *with "X" Hayward ts9b ‖ with "'x'" Hayward ts12b, prompting TSE to enclose line in inverted commas before deleting them ts12a* **Love · · · Calling**] love · · · calling *ts9, ts12, with L and C (for capitals) Hayward ts12b*

V 25 ^ 26] *line space ts13, with instruction to printer "space, not so wide" ts13a ‖ two-line space Valerie's Own Book*

V 26] *indent 1959 pkb* **shall**] must *ts2*

V 28 **Will be**] Is *ts2* **Will**] Shall? *Hayward ts12b* **where**] with "*or* whence? (*at* where)" *Hayward ts9b*

V 29] *not ts2*

V 31 **of earth**] place *ts2*

V 32 **which**] where *ts5* **beginning;**] beginning *ts2, ts3 ‖* beginning: *ts4*

V 35] *not ts2*

V 37 **stillness**] *ts12a 2ⁿᵈ reading+ ‖* silence *ts2~ts12, with* stillness *and "X" Hayward ts12b (see Commentary)*

V 38 **Between two waves of the sea.**] *ts9, with "X" Hayward ts9b, ts12 with* Between the / trough / valley *Hayward ts12b alts, ts13+ ‖* Of distant lands and seas. *ts2–ts5* (TSE to Hayward, 2 Sept 1942: "I see yr points about *daybreak* and

waves but can think of nothing which would not overstress." For *daybreak* see
II 36–38.)   **of the sea**] on the shore *ts12a 2ⁿᵈ reading with "?"*

V 39–46] *not ts2*

V 39 **Quick**] Quick, *ts3 1ˢᵗ reading*

V 40 **condition**] matter *ts3 1ˢᵗ reading*   **complete**] utter *ts4a 2ⁿᵈ reading* ‖ final
ts4a 3ʳᵈ reading, ts5

V 42–43] *not ts3, ts5* ‖ *not ts4 but with* And all manner of thing shall be well *added
after* V 46 *in ts4a with* "? ···?" *before and after*

V 44 **tongues of flame**] burning tongues *ts12a 2ⁿᵈ reading (with 1ˢᵗ reading
then reinstated), with* "?" *ts12b alt* ‖ tongues of flames *1974 (error, later
corrected)*   **in-folded**] infolded *ts3, ts12a 1ˢᵗ reading, ts12b*

V 45 **knot**] rose? *ts4a alt* ‖ rose *ts5*

V 46 **one.**] the same. *ts3~ts12 with* as one Hayward *ts12b, where he (or perhaps TSE)
underlined* flame ··· same (V 44, 46) *with* "?" *TSE to Hayward, 7 Sept 1942:* "Very
well then, 'And the fire and the rose are one.'"

Occasional Verses

ts Occasional Verses (Washington U.): 11 leaves, professionally typed, but apparently not all at the same time. Consisting of ribbon copies, on at least two different papers, numbered 1–6 by TSE, beginning with a topsheet headed "Occasional Poems" and giving the prefatory notes to be inserted at the head of the section's first four poems, followed by the five poems themselves; then further followed by carbons of all these leaves except "4", *To the Indian Soldiers who Died in Africa* (so titled). Prepared in connection with *Washington copy 1954* (see headnote to Textual History, 3. KEY TO EDITIONS), with which it was bought from Bertram Rota Ltd. in 1970. The carbons are unannotated, except for the deletion of a stop, probably not in TSE's hand, at the end of *A Dedication to My Wife* 9. On the ribbon copy of *The Defense of the Islands* (so spelt), a pencilled note after the title has been erased but apparently referred to the American spelling. TSE also used pencil to correct "position" in the last line of this poem, to delete his name and the date at the foot, and to write out the date in fuller form. He then deleted and erased this, before pencilling the date in again, in slightly different form. Subsequently he used pen to delete this too. This suggests that the pencil corrections on these leaves precede those in ink. David Bland, whose ballpoint instructions appear also in *Washington copy 1954*, wrote on the topsheet "Each of the above notes to precede the verses attached". TSE pencilled two asterisks beside this, and 1–4 beside the notes. Then on the ribbon copies of the poems he added chevrons in pencil (sometimes with a number) to indicate where the notes should be inserted. (The collation below treats this as having been done.) His other annotations on the topsheet are in ink: two changes of wording and a correction in the first note (see below), and the addition of dates of publication for the books mentioned in the other three. The spelling "Defense" appears also in TSE's additions to the Contents of *Washington copy 1954*. The folder also contains a foolscap leaf listing TSE's books for the half-title verso of what it calls "*Collected Poems, 1909–1960*" (the terminal date emended in pencil, perhaps in TSE's hand, to "1962"). The leaf itself is dated by the typist "JL/ab 1.3.63". The folder also contains TSE's lists of poems to read at Boston College and Massachusetts Institute of Technology (4 and 13 Dec 1961) and with "Poetry Center 25.11.61" crossed out (referring to another reading).

Section-title page] 1963+

Defence of the Islands

Published in *Britain at War* (1941), then *1963+*.

The numerous typescripts are mostly by others and are so similar that their order here can only be tentative.

ms1 (Pierpont Morgan): working draft on a single leaf, with later presentation inscription "for Marion Dorn | in remembrance of | June 7–10, 1940 – | T. S. Eliot". A capital is used at the beginning of each "clause" (TSE's term: see Commentary headnote). Reproduced in facsimile in *Autograph Letters & Manuscripts: Major Acquisitions of The Pierpont Morgan Library 1924–1974* (1974). Line endings are not recorded here.

ms2 (private collection; unavailable to editors): pencil ms on two leaves dated 9. vi. 40. Catalogued in *Works of T. S. Eliot in the Thomas Shelton Collection* (Quill & Brush), item 168.

ts1 (King's): sent to Hayward with covering letter dated "Tuesday" with Hayward's tentative "[June 1940] 11 June" in pencil. Text in narrow column on right-hand side of leaf, with typed description, bracketed, to the left of each clause.

ts2 (Haverford College): typescript dated at foot "T. S. ELIOT | 9. vi. 40" among Frank Morley's papers. Each clause has a typed number in the left margin ("1." to "7.") and beneath this, in an unknown hand, are written descriptions: "Poetic England", "Home defense", "Navy", "Air Force", "Army", "Home Defense", "final". The paper is American. Two identical carbons are in the Berg collection, where the title and publication details have been added on the first, presumably by Morley.

ts3 (Pierpont Morgan): carbon copy, untitled, with numbered clauses and dated "T. S. ELIOT | 9.vi.40."

ts4 (Museum of Modern Art): carbon of another typing, with numbered clauses, again dated at foot "T. S. Eliot | 9.vi.40". With ms heading in unknown hand: "Poem to Photographic Exh. by T. S. Eliot", and, in another hand, "Defense of the Islands" and "Museum exhibition and catalog".

ts5 (Berg): ribbon copy, with title, and dated "T. S. ELIOT | 9. vi. 40". Single leaf in Frank Morley papers. American spelling "Defense" in title and [5].

ts6 (Valerie Eliot collection): fair copy of a double-spaced typing, dated "T. S. Eliot 9/vi/40". American spelling.

ts7 (Magdalene): ribbon copy and carbon of another typing, with explanatory subtitle, dated "T. S. Eliot | 9th June 1940".

ts Occasional Verses: see above. After the final line, this ts originally had "T. S. Eliot | 9. vi. 40", which TSE deleted and replaced with "June 9th June 1940", in turn erased and struck through.

Broadside: *Lines Written by T. S. Eliot to Accompany This Exhibition of Photographs*, about fifty copies for posting in the exhibition. Printed at a hand-press, "[London, Printed for H. M. Government] 1940" (*Gallup* E2d). No variants except title. On the Beinecke copy, descriptive notes have been added beside the clauses: "Views of Peaceful England", "Home Defense", "Navy", "Air Force", "Army", "Home Defense", "Types of Service People".

Britain at War ed. Monroe Wheeler (New York, 1941). American spelling.

No Mean Heritage ed. S. N. Ritchie (Melbourne, 1946). Arranged as paragraphs which ignore TSE's lineation. Followed by a note as requested by TSE. On 22 Feb 1945, TSE wrote to Sylvia Ritchie, in Mansfield, Victoria (following her version of the title):

> In view of your special plea, I have no objection to your publishing *The Defence of the Island*, if you will print, either at the head or as a footnote, the following explanation: "These lines were not intended by the author to be either poetry or verse. They were written to accompany an Exhibition of Photographs of National Defence Work, which was exhibited in New York in 1940. The 'we' of the lines is, therefore, the Army, Navy, Air Force or Civil Defence forces, accompanying the appropriate group of photographs." I should be obliged if you would send me a copy of the book when published, as I have no copy of the lines myself. They were written on request in the course of an afternoon, and I do not wish any literary pretence to be made for them.

The extensive variants, including the running together of the first two clauses, are not recorded here. After receiving the book, TSE wrote again on 23 May 1946, so as

> to point out a few errors of punctuation which very likely were in the text as it came to you, but which I should like very much to see corrected if the book runs to another edition. There should be no punctuation after *Island* at the end of the first clause; there should be a comma, not a full stop after *floor* at the end of the second clause; there should be a comma, not a full stop after *fire* at the end of the third clause, and after *weapons* at the end of the fifth clause there should be a colon. In the first clause there should be a dash after *instrument* to correspond to the dash before *music's*. In the fourth clause there should be a semi-colon after *France*. The sixth clause should read as follows: "To say of the past and the future generations of our kin and of our speech, that we took up our positions, in obedience to orders."

Even then, the punctuation would not quite have matched the text used in New York.

Valerie's Own Book: later fair copy (two pages), dated at foot: "T. S. Eliot | 9. vi. 40". With two-line spaces between clauses. American spelling.

The lineation varies slightly in the drafts and published texts, and is probably unimportant, although the present edition follows the lineation of *Britain at War* and *1963*, in both of which "de- | feat" is broken across two lines. The word is likewise broken in *ts4*, but it is not known whether this precedes or follows its appearance in *Britain at War*. Although compositorial chance is more likely, it is conceivable that the very word "defeat" was not to be contemplated in 1940. (In *Valerie's Own Book*, it is "darkness", 12, that breaks across two lines.) The line breaks of other clauses are evidently happenstance, only those of the fifth clause, beginning with *ts2*, are recorded below (15–16, 16–17, 17).

The American spelling "Defense" is used in title and text in *ts5, ts6, Britain at War, ts Occasional Verses, US 1963, Valerie's Own Book. Broadside* has "defence" (in text only).

Title] *not ms1, ts1, ts2, ts3, ts4 as typed (added in another hand), No Mean Heritage* ||
Lines Written by T. S. Eliot | To accompany the exhibition of photographs in the war exhibit | in the British Pavilion at the New York World's Fair *ts7* || Lines Written by T. S. Eliot | to Accompany this Exhibition of Photographs *Broadside*

Note] *not ms1-ts7, Valerie's Own Book*　　*Islands*] islands *ts Occasional Verses, US 1963*　　*makes*] make *ts Occasional Verses 1st reading*　　*McKnight*] Edward McKnight *ts Occasional Verses 1st reading*　　*They were*] It was *ts Occasional Verses 1st reading*　　*York,*] York *1963*

1–2 **stone—music's enduring instrument,**] stone, music's grey timeless instrument, *ms1* || stone, *ts1* || stone—music's enduring instrument— *Valerie's Own Book 2nd reading*

1–4] *with "(Views of Canterbury, countryside, Stratford on Avon etc.)" ts1*

2–3 **many centuries of patient**] of the generations *ms1*

5–6] *with "(Home Defence preparations)" ts1*　　**with the**] in *ms1*　　**of this defence of the islands**] with the defence of this Island by those who dwelt there *ms1 1st reading* || with those of the defence of this Island by us who dwelt there *ms1 2nd reading* || with those of the defence of this Island *ms1 final reading*　　**defence**] *with "s" added above in unknown hand ts4*

6 **islands**] island *ts1*

7 **the memory of those**] by those who were *ms1 1st reading* || by us who were *ms1*

7–10] *with "(Navy)" ts1*

8] ships, ~~the battle cruiser, destroyer,~~ battle ship, merchant seaman, trawler, *ms1*

9 **their share to the ages' pavement**] to the centuries' store *ms1*

11 **of**] by *ms1*　　**those**] us *ms1 2nd reading*　　**man's**] the world's most *ms1 1st reading* || the world's *ms1*　　**form of**] *not ms1*

11–13] *with "(Air Force)" ts1*

12 **fight**] fought *ms1*

12–13 **air and fire**] fire and air *ms1* || air and fire, *ts1*

14–17] *with "(Army)" ts1* ||

> And those from century to century destined
> to release some of their number to rest
> in Flanders & in France, unchanged in
> everything but their weopons

ms1 1st reading, with revisions to the first line probably as follows: And those who for [*rest of line illegible*] *ms1 2nd reading* || And those like their forebears destined *ms1 3rd reading* || And by us like our forebears destined *ms1 final reading*

15–16 **in de- | feat, unalterable** (*line break*)] *ts4, ts6* || in | defeat, unalterable *ts2, ts3, Valerie's Own Book* || in defeat, | unalterable *ts5, ts7*

16–17 **changing nothing | of their ancestors'** (*line break*)] *ts3–ts6* || changing | nothing of their ancestors' *ts2* || changing nothing of their | ancestors' *ts7* ||

17 **weapons**] *on new line ts2* ‖ *weapons,* ms1, ts1

18–19] *with "(Home Defence forces)" ts1*   **those**] *by us* ms1 2nd *reading*   **paths**]
field ms1 1st *reading* ‖ *fields* ms1 *final reading*   **glory**] *honour* ms1   **are the
lanes and the streets of Britain:**] *is a field at home—* ms1 1st *reading* ‖ *are the
field and streets of our homes—* ms1 2nd *reading* ‖ *are the field and towns of our
homes—* ms1 *final reading*

20–22] *with "(Over the Exit)" ts1* ‖ ms1 *1st draft of these lines,* 1st *reading*:

> Let these tell the English, and their kin,
> and those who speak their speech,
> that we

ms1 2nd *reading*:

> Let these tell the English generations of past and future, and our kin,
> and those who speak our speech,
> that we

TSE then substituted our *for the English before deleting this draft and writing* ms1
2nd draft:

> Let these memorials say to the generations
> of past ⊄ future that for their sake
> we took up our positions, in obedience to orders.

22 **positions**] *position* ts *Occasional Verses* 1st *reading*   **instructions.**] *orders.
with "At the end: would this be better: 'we took up our places, in obedience to
instructions'? What I wanted to say was: 'we took up our positions, in obedience to
instructions', but you can't have two –ions so close together." ts1 (see Commentary)*

A Note on War Poetry

Published in *London Calling*, ed. Storm Jameson (New York, 1942), then 1963+.
  ms1 (King's): pencil on two ruled leaves from a small notebook.

ts1 (Leeds U.): with letter to Bonamy Dobrée, 13 July 1942. Dated at foot: "July '42."

ts2 (King's): carbon, on pink paper, of a fair copy typescript. A second carbon on pink
paper, pasted into the Morley family scrapbook, has a typed addition at the foot:
"P.S. This is NOT a Poem: it is a SET OF VERSES" (for a similar caution in TSE's
letter to Dobrée, see Commentary to "Occasional Verses", headnote).

ts3 (Valerie Eliot collection): fair copy, with 14–15 protruding into margin by one
character. With "(1942)" added after title by TSE, but apparently not from his
usual typewriter and perhaps dating from considerably later.

Title] Notes on Poetry in Wartime ms1 1st *reading* ‖ A Note on Wartime Poetry ms1
2nd *reading*

Note] 1963+   **New York, 1942).**] New York). ts *Occasional Verses* 1st *reading*

1 **emotion**] emotions ms1 1st *reading* ‖ emotions, ms1 2nd *reading with comma del*

2] What is the residue of all these experiences? ms1 1st *reading* ‖ Imperfectly
recorded in the daily papers .. ms1 2nd *reading (with* in *changed to* by)

3 **Where**] And where *ms1 2ⁿᵈ reading with* And *del*   **merely**] *not ms1 1ˢᵗ reading*

5 **an action**] something *ms1 1ˢᵗ reading underlined* ‖ an action *ms1 alt with* "?"   **merely**] not only *ms1 1ˢᵗ reading*

6 **To create the**] But *ms1 1ˢᵗ reading*   **originate a symbol**] to generate a symbolism *ms*

7 **impact**] contact *ms1 1ˢᵗ reading* (*the emendation to* impact *is followed by an illegible erasure*)   **This**] this *ms, ts1, ts2*

9 **forces**] force *ms1 alt with* "?"   **control by experiment—**] *ms1 alt* ‖ direction, the intersection *ms1 1ˢᵗ reading* ‖ control by experiment: *ts1* (*where* by *is typed over* of), *ts2, London Calling*

10 **Mostly**] *not ms1 1ˢᵗ reading* ‖ Here, *ms1 2ⁿᵈ reading* ‖ Now, / Mostly *ms1 alt 3ʳᵈ readings, each with* "?" ‖ Mostly, *ts1, ts2, London Calling*   **the**] The *ms1 1ˢᵗ reading*

11 **large**] great *ms1*   **Our**] The *ms1 1ˢᵗ reading*

13 **In**] With *ms1 1ˢᵗ reading*   **effort**] struggle *ms1 alt with* "?"   **day and night**] two lives *ms1 1ˢᵗ reading*

17] This is both too large ⋴ too small a pattern, *ms1 1ˢᵗ reading with* War *alt first word, undel but with* "?" ‖ And war is not a life. It is one problem, *ms1 2ⁿᵈ reading with final two words changed to* a situation,

18 **may**] can *ms1*   **accepted,**] accepted: *ms1 1ˢᵗ reading* ‖ be accepted; *ms1 2ⁿᵈ reading*

20 **scattered.**] *ms1 alt+* ‖ dispersed *ms1 1ˢᵗ reading*

21–25] *ms1 1st draft:*

> The true resolution is not yet possible
> And would not be acceptable. Meanwhile the effort
> To maintain the standard of universality
> In the particular, which we call "poetry"
> Can be affirmed in verse.   [5]

[1] The eternal is no substitute for the transient, *2ⁿᵈ reading with* eternal *changed to* enduring

[2] **And would not be acceptable**] And cannot do that job / Neither one for the other *alt 2ⁿᵈ readings*

[3] **standard**] *1ˢᵗ and final reading* ‖ highest standard *2ⁿᵈ reading del*

ms1 2nd draft:

> The true resolution is not yet possible
> And wᵈ not be acceptable. Meanwhile the standard
> Of particular experience at its highest intensity
> Becoming universal, wh. we call "poetry",
> Can be affirmed in verse.   [5]

[1] **yet**] here *2ⁿᵈ reading*

[2] **acceptable**] accepted *2ⁿᵈ reading*   **Meanwhile the standard**] The abstract notion *2ⁿᵈ reading* ‖ But the abstract notion *3ʳᵈ reading* ‖ Meanwhile the notion *alt 3ʳᵈ reading*

[3] **particular**] private *2ⁿᵈ reading*

[5] **Can**] May 2*ⁿᵈ reading* **affirmed**] found *uncertain 1ˢᵗ reading*

21 **not a**] no *ts1, ts2, London Calling*

after last line] 1942. *ts Occasional Verses del*

To the Indians who Died in Africa

Published in *Queen Mary's Book for India* (1943). Reprinted in *The Tiger Triumphs: The Story of Three Great Divisions in Italy* (1946).

ts1 (King's): carbon on pink leaf, sent to John Hayward, with "for favour of censure" pencilled at head.

ts2 (Valerie Eliot collection): ribbon copy, pinned to the letter from Lady Richmond of 13 Mar 1942 quoted in Commentary, headnote to this poem.

ms Clodd: manuscript in unknown hand, omitting third stanza. Three capitals added in final stanza by TSE, who noted: "Written for Miss Cornelia Sorabji for the Indian Red Cross Book (for the benefit of the Indian Red Cross)." Alan Clodd collection, sold Maggs 2004 (catalogue item 858).

Valerie's Own Book: fair copy (two pages). Probably following *ts1*, with subsequent emendations (in another ink) from another source.

Title] For the Indian Soldiers who Died in Africa *ts Occasional Verses, after which TSE pencilled and then erased the date* (1943), *Valerie's Own Book* ‖ *not Tiger Triumphs* **To**] For *ts1, Of Books and Humankind*

Note] *not ts1, QMB, Tiger Triumphs, Valerie's Own Book* **Died**] *died ts Occasional Verses, 1963 (not US 1963, 1969, 1974)* **Ltd., 1943).**] Ltd.). *ts Occasional Verses 1ˢᵗ reading* **Dobrée**] Dobree *ts Occasional Verses, 1963*

2 **fire,**] fire *Tiger Triumphs* **cooking;**] cooking, *Tiger Triumphs*

4 **neighbour's grandson,**] dog's great-grandson *ts1, ts2 1ˢᵗ reading, Valerie's Own Book* ‖ neighbours' grandson *Tiger Triumphs*. On the facing page in *Valerie's Own Book*, TSE added: "*Or* And see his grandson, and his neighbour's grandson".

5, 10, 15] *no indent ts1, ts2, QMB, Tiger Triumphs*

5 **Playing**] Play *ts2, QMB*

6 **secure,**] secure *Tiger Triumphs* **memories**] narratives *ts2 2ⁿᵈ reading, QMB*

7 **Which return**] (Which return *ts1, Valerie's Own Book 1ˢᵗ reading* ‖ To relate *ts2 2ⁿᵈ reading* ‖ To repeat *QMB* **conversation,**] conversation *ts2, QMB*

8 **(The warm**] The warm, *ts1* ‖ (The warm, *ts2, QMB* ‖ The warm *Valerie's Own Book 1ˢᵗ reading* **climate)**] *Tiger Triumphs, 1963+* ‖ climate)— *ts2* ‖ climate), *QMB, Of Books and Humankind*

11–15] *not Tiger Triumphs*

11 **destiny,**] destiny. *ts1, ts2, QMB*

14 **soil**] land *ts1 1ˢᵗ reading*

16 **your**] our *ts1 1ˢᵗ reading* **land,**] land *Tiger Triumphs* **or**] nor *ts1,*

ts2 1ˢᵗ reading, Valerie's Own Book 1ˢᵗ reading **ours]** yours *ts1 1ˢᵗ reading* **Midlands,]** Midlands *ts1, ts2, QMB, Valerie's Own Book*

17 **graveyard]** memories *ts2 2ⁿᵈ reading, QMB*

18 **you:]** you— *Tiger Triumphs*

20 **we]** I *ts1, ts2, QMB, Of Books and Humankind, ts Occasional Verses 1ˢᵗ reading emended in pencil*

21 **Know,]** Know *Tiger Triumphs* **judgment]** *QMB, 1969, 1963 4th and 5th imps. (1968, 1970)* ‖ moment *ts1, ts2 1ˢᵗ reading, 1963 1st–3rd imps. (to 1966), US 1963 and later US printings, Valerie's Own Book* ‖ judgement *ts2 2ⁿᵈ reading, Tiger Triumphs, 1974+ (see Commentary)*

22] *no indent ts1, ts2, QMB, Tiger Triumphs*

To Walter de la Mare

Printed first in *Tribute to Walter de la Mare on his Seventy-fifth Birthday* (ed. W. R. Bett, 1948). Reprinted in *Tiger's Eye* (NY), 15 Dec 1948. Collected in *1963*.

The bound proof of *Tribute* has no variants.

Valerie Eliot's collection contains a series of typed drafts, on 11 leaves, together with correspondence with the editor of *Tribute*, W. R. Bett:

ts1: two leaves, with a pair of sonnets, both finally struck through (given separately below). Lines from Sonnet I became 1–12 of the final poem, and lines from II became 16–21.

ts2: two leaves with a complete draft of the final poem, lightly emended.

frag a: single leaf, redrafting 28–32, probably later than *ts2* but earlier than *ts3*.

ts3: ribbon and carbon copies of a full draft, each on a single leaf and independently emended.

ts3a: ribbon copy with extensive emendations and two trial lines in ms on verso.

ts3b: carbon of *ts3a* with lighter emendation.

Then three leaves of fragmentary redraftings:

frag b: seven typed lines, redrafting 4–6.

frag c: 16 typed lines, redrafting 28–32.

frag d: 17 typed lines, further redrafting 28–32.

frag e: 17 typed lines, consisting of three further drafts of 28–32 (*e1–e3*)

ts4: single leaf with a fair copy of the whole poem, lightly emended.

ts Occasional Verses: no variants

Texas has a typescript made by another hand (with "T.S.Eliot O.M." at the foot), which is not collated below.

ts1 pair of sonnets:

I.

The children who explored the brook had found
A desert island with a sandy beach,
Quite inaccessible, but within reach,
A snug retreat, but very dangerous ground.

For here the capybara may abound   5
And shadowy lemurs glide from limb to limb;
But not a tiger. There's no room for him.
And surely, under that mysterious mound

Is Spanish Gold. We'll bring a spade next time.
And then, returning to the nursery tea,   10
After so long, were glad of English fare;
And having told of their exploits at sea
Demanded to be read to, please, the rhyme
You said was made by Walter de la Mare.

I I.

When the familiar scene is suddenly strange
Or when the strange is one already known,
And presences walk with us, when alone;
When two worlds intersect: what caused the change?

When cats are maddened for the moonlight dance   5
And dogs are frightened of the dark, and cower
Under the table; when at the midnight hour
The witches' sabbath of the maiden aunts

Is celebrated. What mysterious power
Directs the prodigy and works the charm?   10
Before the fire, in a Georgian chair
He sits. I do not think he means us harm:
It could indeed be no one else than our
Revered enchanter, Walter de la Mare.

II. 5 **moonlight**] midnight *1ˢᵗ reading*

Title] ts3+ ‖ *in ts Occasional Verses TSE pencilled* (1948) *after the title and then erased it*
Note] *1963+*   **Ltd., 1948),]** Ltd.), *ts Occasional Verses 1ˢᵗ reading*
  2 **cove**] shore— *ts2 1ˢᵗ reading* ‖ cove— *ts2*
  3 **(A hiding place)** A snug retreat *ts2 1ˢᵗ reading* ‖ (A snug retreat *ts2 2ⁿᵈ reading with* hiding place *added left*
  4 **here**] there *ts3 1ˢᵗ reading, ts3b*   **rove,]** rove *ts2, ts3 1ˢᵗ reading, ts3b*
  5, 6, 7] *three lines beginning* And *are each marked ts2*
  5] And here the capybara may be found *ts2 1ˢᵗ reading* ‖ And here the capybara may abound *ts2* ‖ And there the capybara may abound *ts3a 1ˢᵗ reading, ts3b* ‖ Coatis and capybara may abound *ts3a 2ⁿᵈ reading* ‖ And ~~bandi~~ jaguars and bandicoots abound *ts3a alt added right* ‖ Coatis and capybaras may abound *ts4 1ˢᵗ reading* ‖ Peccary and coatis may abound *ts4*

6] And mangabeys may haunt the mango grove *ts2, ts3 1ˢᵗ reading, ts3b* ‖ In the dark jungle of the mango grove *ts3a 2ⁿᵈ reading*

5–6] *ts3a alt at foot*:

> And jaguars and marmosets abound
> And capybaras haunt the mango grove

4–6] *further experiments, frag b*:

> For there

> For here the water buffalo may rove,
> Coatis and capybaras may abound
> In the dark jungle of the mango grove
> Where

> For here the water buffalo may rove,
> Or

7 **And**] When *ts3a 2ⁿᵈ reading*   **tree to tree—**] limb to limb *ts2 1ˢᵗ reading* ‖ tree to tree *ts2 2ⁿᵈ reading* ‖ tree to tree, *ts2*

8 **long-lost**] long-hid *ts2*   **treasure-trove)**] treasure-trove: *ts2 1ˢᵗ reading* ‖ treasure trove) *Tiger's Eye*

9 **at the**] over *ts2 1ˢᵗ reading, apparently del without replacement but with "X" in the margin, before the substitution of at the which is ticked*

10 **lamps are**] *three dots beneath the letters –s are with "?" ts2*

11 **be,**] be? *ts2, ts3 1ˢᵗ reading, ts3b*

12] *instead of a line space in the middle of this line, ts3 has a line space after* lawn, *so that it is the fourth stanza, not the fifth, that occupies four lines on the page*   **time for bed**] bed time hour *ts2 with "time for bed" in another hand*   **Or when**] When *ts2 1ˢᵗ reading*

13 **ghosts**] they *ts2 1ˢᵗ reading, apparently with the underline crossed through after the word itself was del and* ghosts *substituted*

15 **yearn;**] yearn *ts2 1ˢᵗ reading*

17] Or what we know is what we have to learn, *ts2 1ˢᵗ reading* ‖ Or the well known is what we have to learn, *ts2 2ⁿᵈ reading, ts3*

20] *with "?" ts2*   **bats,**] bats *Tiger's Eye*

21 **At the witches'**] At witches' *1963+*

23 **sleeper**] ~~answer~~ sleeper *ts2*   **by his call**] when he calls *ts2, ts3 with* cries / shouts *and "?" ts3b, which has a line to* No sleeper ~~by~~ with his call *at foot*

24 **house;**] house *ts2 1ˢᵗ reading*

27 **passage**] transit *ts2, ts3*

28 **you;**] yours, *ts2, frag a, ts3 1ˢᵗ reading, ts3b*   **by those deceptive**] and through those subtle *ts2, frag a, ts3a 1ˢᵗ and final readings, ts3b* ‖ and through your subtle *ts3a 2ⁿᵈ reading*

29 **Wherewith**] *ts3a 2ⁿᵈ reading, ts4 1ˢᵗ reading* ‖ By which *ts2, ts3 1ˢᵗ reading, ts3b* ‖ In which *frag a* ‖ Wherein *ts3a final reading, ts4*   **refined;**] *ts3 1ˢᵗ reading* ‖ refined, *ts2, ts3a final reading (after hesitations)*

30 **By**] And *ts2, frag a, ts3* ‖ Your *ts3a 2ⁿᵈ reading*   **conscious**] studied *1ˢᵗ reading*

ts2   **practised with**] endued with *ts2*, *frag a*, *ts3* ‖ assuming *ts3b alt* (*with line linking* with *to* with, 30–31)   **ease;**] ease, *ts2*, *ts3*, *ts4 1ˢᵗ reading* ‖ ease *frag a*

30 ^ 31] *no line space ts2, frag a, ts3*

31] So that we say of any poem one please, *ts2 1ˢᵗ reading* ‖ So we can say any poem you please *ts2*, *with* We know *in another hand* ‖ Compels us with insidious melodies *frag a 1ˢᵗ reading* ‖ Detains us with insidious melodies *frag a*, *ts3*

32] Is what one poet only could have signed. *ts2* ‖ Of the audible, invisible web you wind. *frag a 1ˢᵗ reading* ‖ In the audible, invisible web you wind. *frag a*, *ts3 1ˢᵗ reading*, *ts3b* ‖ The invisible web of melodies you wind. *frag a 1ˢᵗ alt* ‖ The audible, invisible web you wind. *frag a 2ⁿᵈ alt* ‖ Of the audible, [   ] you wind *ts3a 2ⁿᵈ reading with* ~~Entangled in~~ by the ~~invisible~~ audible thread *below*, *and* of the ~~delicate~~ audible, the *at foot* (*below redrafting of* 5–6), *and* Caught in the *vertically in right margin, and on verso*: In the [   ] invisible toils you wind *and* Engages us in the unseen toils you wind

28–32] *further experiments frag c*:

    By you; and through those subtle cadences
    Wherewith the common measure is refined,
    Your conscious art perfecting natural ease
    Your conscious art enlarging natural ease
    Completes the   [5]

    Compels us

    And
    The conscious art composed
               practised
    The conscious art informed with natural ease

    In the unresisted, unseen toils you wind.   [10]
    Compels our feet to follow
    Draws us to follow
    Into the unresisted toils you wind

    Compels our steps feet

    Engages us   [15]

    [2] **Wherewith**] Whereby *alt*

    [3] **perfecting**] *over* end

and frag d:

    By you; and by those subtle cadences
    Wherewith the common measure is refined,
    Thus conscious art practised with natural ease
    Compels us
    Forming   [5]
    Casting
    Detains the ear until its melodies

    Employs

    Weaving a web of

    Weaving   [10]
                                   <

Weaves unsuspected webs of melodies
Weaving its unseen web of melodies

Detains us among

Leads us by unsuspected sorceries
Into   [15]
Detains us in the unseen toils you wind.
Detains the

[3] **Thus]** *1ˢᵗ reading* ‖ Your *2ⁿᵈ reading* ‖ Where your *3ʳᵈ reading*
frag e consists of three attempts (e1–e3) at the same lines. The first two are given as variants of e3:

By you; by your deceptive cadences
Wherewith the common measure is refined;
By conscious art practised with natural ease,
The delicate, invisible web you wove—
The unexplainable mystery of sound.   [5]

[1] **by your deceptive]** and by those subtle *e1, e2*

[2] **refined;]** refined. *e2*

[3] **By]** The *e2*   **ease,]** ease. | Takes us | Detained among insidious
    melodies. *e1* (*which ends here*) ‖ ease *e2*

[3–4] line space *e2*

[4] By the audible, invisible web you wove | Detaining us *e2*

[5] The simple, inexplicable *e2 1ˢᵗ reading not del but with* [5] *beneath*

A Dedication to my Wife

A different text was published as *To My Wife*, the dedication to *The Elder Statesman* (1959) and reprinted (with identical text) at the head of that play in *Collected Plays* (1962). In each of these books, the lines are all italic. Within *1969, A Dedication to my Wife* appears in roman at the end of the *Collected Poems* and *To My Wife* appears in italic at the head of *The Elder Statesman*.

The first volume of *Valerie's Own Book* contains an intermediate version (collated below), while the second volume contains a further, rejected version, *Dedication II* (for which see "Uncollected Poems").

In *1963, To the Indians who Died in Africa* occupies a recto, 231, so that *To Walter de la Mare* would fall naturally on 232–33, with *A Dedication to my Wife* on the verso, 234, opposite the start of the *Index of Titles of Poems* on 235. However, in the first impression, 232 is left blank, so that the last two poems each begin on rectos. Then 236 is a further blank, facing the start of the index. This was presumably deliberate, to give due prominence to *A Dedication to my Wife* and to prevent it from appearing to be an afterthought. Neither the later impressions of *1963* nor *1974* have this arrangement. *US 1963*, which has no "Index of Titles of Poems", has *To the Indians who Died in Africa* on a recto, 217, with the verso blank, followed by *To Walter de la Mare*, 219–20, and *A Dedication to My Wife* also on a recto, 221.

Title] To My Wife *The Elder Statesman* ‖ A Dedication *contents list of Washington copy 1954, 1963 proof, Valerie's Own Book. In TSE's additions to Washington copy 1954, the date of composition was originally given as* 1959–1962 *but this was deleted along with the dates of the other Occasional Verses* ‖ A Dedication to My Wife *US 1963*

2 **wakingtime**] wakingtime, *Valerie's Own Book*

4] *double indent 1969*

5] Of lovers . . . *The Elder Statesman*   **other**] other, *Valerie's Own Book*

7 **meaning.**] meaning: *The Elder Statesman, Valerie's Own Book*

8–12] *The Elder Statesman*:

> To you I dedicate this book, to return as best I can
> With words a little part of what you have given me.
> The words mean what they say, but some have a further meaning
> For you and me only.

Valerie's Own Book:

> To you I dedicate this book, to return as best I can
> In words, some little part of what you have given me.
> The words mean what they say; but some have a further meaning
> For you and me only.

Uncollected Poems

A Lyric ("If Time and Space, as Sages say")

Published in *Smith Academy Record*, Apr 1905. Reprinted in *Early Youth 1950, 1967+* and in *Powel* in 1957.

Song ("If space and time, as sages say")

Published in *Harvard Advocate* 3 June 1907, then *Adv 1938, Adv 1948, Undergrad. Poems, Early Youth 1950+*.

As in *Early Youth* (*1950, 1967*) and *1969*, two texts of this poem are given in the present edition. When printed in the *Smith Academy Record*, the first immediately followed TSE's *A Tale of a Whale*. Beneath the printed date "June, 1907" in his copy of *Adv 1938* (King's), TSE pencilled "Written early in *1905.*"

To Hayward, 19 Aug 1943: "I enclose for your collection a curiosity which is, I fear, of biographical rather than literary interest · · · You will find enclosed the original draft of the first poem I ever wrote to be shown to other eyes. On the reverse you will find my name, the date and my mark for the poem. I remember that the English master, a certain Mr. Roger Conant Hatch, conceived great hopes of a literary career for me." In 1953: "Mr. Hatch, who taught English [at Smith Academy], commended warmly my first poem, written as a class exercise, at the same time asking me suspiciously if I had had any help in writing it", *American Literature and the American Language* 5. In 1963 TSE told Donald Hall that the first poem of his that had been preserved "is one which appeared first in the *Smith Academy Record*, and later in *The Harvard Advocate*, which was written as an exercise for my English teacher and was an imitation of Ben Jonson", *Paris Review* (1959).

A LYRIC

ms1 (King's): fair copy in black ink (now very faded) on a ruled leaf of school paper, endorsed on verso "Eliot | January 24 1905" and graded "A" by his English teacher, Roger Conant Hatch. Also in black ink but perhaps later, TSE has written at the foot "(Doggerel Licence No. 3,271,574)", see plate facing 116 in *March & Tambimuttu eds*. (OED gives "poetic licence" from 1530; many US states require dog owners to have licences.)
    Sent to John Hayward, 19 Aug 1943 together with *ts3* of *To the Class of 1905*. Hayward acknowledged receipt on 22 Aug 1943. A typed copy of this (including the Doggerel No., typed) is in the Linda Melton (Benson) collection at Houghton and was probably an unauthorised copy made by her while working as TSE's secretary, when the ms was sent to Hayward in 1943 (variants not recorded below). For her collection, see also *What O! Epitaff* in "Other Verses".

ms2 (Houghton): untitled, in Charlotte Eliot's hand and mounted on a leaf from her scrapbook.

ts1 (Houghton): carbon of a typescript made for TSE's mother: on which she has written "A school composition | Thos. S. Eliot", with later typed note: "The first (or first known) poem written by T. S. Eliot, at fifteen years of age. This is one of a number of copies which his mother had made at the time." Harvard also has two identical carbons. TSE's uncle, Thomas L. Eliot, was sent one of these by TSE's father, who wrote on it: "verses by Thomas Stearns Eliot for one of his classes in 'Composition'. *Good* for 16 yrs!"

ms1 has no indents in first stanza except 5; *ms2* has no indents; *tss* have no indents. In *Smith Academy Record*, title and text are all italic. Variants in *Powel* are not recorded here.

Title] *not mss, ts1*

  1 **Time**] time *ms2, Record*   **Space,**] Space *ms2* ‖ space, *Record*   **Sages**] sages *ms1 2ⁿᵈ reading (uncertain), ms2, Record*   say] *underlined in red by teacher with "?" ms1 (TSE reinforced the originally malformed "y")*

  2 **which**] that *ms2 2ⁿᵈ reading*   **be,**] be *ms2*

  3 **does not feel**] never knows *ms2*   **decay**] decay, *Record*

  4 **greater**] better *ms2*

  5 **So**] Then *ms2*   **Love**] love *ms2, ts1*

  6 **century?**] century *ms2*

  7 **that**] wh[ich] *ms2*

  9 **gave**] brought *ms2 1ˢᵗ and final reading* ‖ pluck *2ⁿᵈ reading*

  10 **vine**] *malformed word underlined in red by teacher with "?" ms1*

  12 **eglantine.**] eglantine *ms2*

  13 **So**] Then *ms2*   **to pluck**] ⁊ pluck *ms2*   **anew**] anew, *Record*

  14 **mourn**] grieve *ms2*   **pine,**] pine *ms2*

  15 **be few**] be few, *ms2* ‖ are few, *Record*

  16 **Yet**] O, *ms2*

SONG

  1 **say,**] say *Adv 1938*

A Fable for Feasters

Published in *Smith Academy Record* Feb 1905, signed "T. E. '05", then *Early Youth 1950+*.

ms1 (untraced): in a memo of 8 Oct 1969 to Eileen Brooksbank concerning the text of *1969*, Valerie Eliot wrote "I have checked the manuscript" and "checked against original manuscript" (Faber archive).

To the Class of 1905

Published in *Early Youth 1950+* under a provided title, *At Graduation 1905*.

ts1 (Valerie Eliot collection): two leaves. Untitled and with stanzas numbered II–XV, with space at head as though in anticipation of a new first stanza. This typescript is probably what Valerie Eliot had in mind when she wrote in a memo to Eileen Brooksbank, 8 Oct 1969 (Faber archive), that the "manuscript" was in her possession.

ts2 (Houghton): two-page carbon laid into scrapbook of Charlotte Eliot and apparently from her typewriter. Like *ts1*, this is untitled and has stanzas numbered II–XV, with space at head as though in anticipation of a new first stanza, but it is a fresh typing incorporating revisions from *ts1*, the final text of which it follows precisely.

ts3 (King's): carbon from an unknown source on four leaves, used by Hayward for *Early Youth 1950* and headed by him in faint pencil "[AT GRADUATION 1905]". TSE, sending it to Hayward, 19 Aug 1943: "I do not know who typed the poem and the original has completely disappeared."

ts4 (Washington U.): untitled ribbon copy on two leaves of turn-of-the-century paper. Discovered in 1964, tipped into Smith Academy yearbook 1904–05, and taken by Hayward to be identical to *ts3* when he was sent a xerographic copy (King's). Though the two were made on the same typewriter and match extremely closely, the horizontal position of the stanza numbers differs slightly, as does the text. A different typewriter has added the heading "Written by Thomas Stearns Eliot | Class of 1905 | Smith Academy", and the first leaf is stamped "Property of Chancellor's Office Washington University."

Stanza numbers] *followed by stops ts1–ts4*

Title **To the Class of 1905**]*from "Fiftieth Annual Graduating Exercises Smith Academy" (13 June 1905). This "Programme" lists a reading of the poem as item VII (Washington U.)* ‖ [At Graduation 1905]*printings prior to the present edition*

16 **to**] seek *ts1 1st reading*

21 **hopeful**] the hopeful *ts1 1st reading*

36 **bestow**] *Early Youth 1950+* ‖ bestow. *ts1–ts3, ts4 1ˢᵗ reading* ‖ bestow, *ts4 2ⁿᵈ reading*

64 **schools—a**] schools a *ts4*

70 **thy**] the *Early Youth 1967, 1969 (acknowledged as an error by Valerie Eliot in a memo to Peter du Sautoy, 23 Mar 1967)*

Song ("When we came home across the hill")

Published in *Harvard Advocate* 24 May 1907, then *Adv 1938, Adv 1948, Undergrad. Poems, Early Youth 1950+*. No ms or ts known.

5 **still,**] *Early Youth 1950+ (Hayward's emendation)* ‖ still *printings prior to Early Youth 1950*

Before Morning

Published in *Harvard Advocate* 13 Nov 1908, then *Adv 1938, Adv 1948, Undergrad. Poems, Early Youth 1950+*. No ms or ts known.

6 **dawn,**] dawn. *Adv 1948, Undergrad. Poems*

Circe's Palace

Published in *Harvard Advocate* 25 Nov 1908, repr. in *Cap and Gown: Some College Verse* (1931). Then *Adv 1938, Adv 1948, Undergrad. Poems, Early Youth 1950+*. No ms or ts known.

5 **stain**] strain *Cap and Gown (error)*

After 14] *additional lines:*

> Let us quickly gather and go:
> We shall not come here again.

pencilled into the copy of Adv 1938 sent by TSE to Hayward (King's).

On a Portrait

Published in *Harvard Advocate* 26 Jan 1909, then *Adv 1938, Adv 1948, Undergrad. Poems, Early Youth 1950+*.

ms1 (Houghton): blue ink, with emendations in black ink and pencil, and some awkward readings reinforced in pencil. Endorsed later: "Original MS. written by myself. T. S. Eliot 24. vi. 53", and, referring to his own name, in black ink: "(Name written in by Tinckom-Fernandez T. S. E.)". However, the hand of the poem is quite unlike that of *Song: The moonflower opens to the moth*, and may not be TSE's. A facsimile copy at Brown U. was made before the addition in 1953.

2 **brain**] brains *ms1 1st reading*

5 **goddess carved**] carved goddess *1969 (corrected in reprints)*   **of**] from *ms1 1st reading*

13 **spy,**] spy. *Advocate*

Song ("The moonflower opens to the moth")

Published in *Harvard Advocate* 26 Jan 1909, then *Undergrad. Poems, Early Youth 1950+*.

ms1 (Houghton): The title and stanza numbers I and II appear to be editorial additions. The signature at the foot has been changed from "T. S. E." to "T. S. Eliot", then deleted and replaced by "T. S. E." once more, these changes likewise perhaps editorial. A much later note beneath the signature reads: "Original ms. written by myself. I hope it will never be reprinted. Shd. have been rejected. T. S. Eliot 24. vi. 53". The annotations at 1, 3, 4, 5 are probably editorial. An accompanying sheet of comments shows that *Advocate* editors were divided about its merits. The manuscript was retrieved from the printers by Haniel Long along with that of *On a Portrait* (see *Crawford 2015* 104). On the back of a photograph showing the ms before 1953, Harford Powel notes the discrepancy in the last line (Hay Library, Brown U.).

1 **moonflower**] *second and third syllables of "moonflower" underlined later with both straight and wavy lines, with "monosyl.", itself del ms1 (see 5).*

3 **great**] *underlined, with wavy marginal line ms1*

4 **alder**] *underlined later, with "Why 'alder'" ms1*

4 ^ 5] *no line space Undergrad. Poems*

5 **flowers,**] flowers *underlined with caret to note, "dissyl.", itself del ms1* ‖ flowers *Advocate*   **Love,**] *ms1+* ‖ which *ms1 1st reading* ‖ that *2nd reading*

8 **lips**] *ms1* ‖ life *printings prior to the present edition*

Ballade of the Fox Dinner

Recited 15 May 1909. Published in *Fifty Years: William R. Castle* (1949) and repr. in *Soldo* (both without variants).

ms1 (Valerie Eliot collection): three leaves. Fair copy with filing note at head in another hand, "Thos. S. Eliot '10". Beneath the Envoi, TSE has written: "This is the original manuscript of the *Ballade of the Fox Dinner* which I wrote at the behest (I think) of Charles Wilkins Short. But I think that someone has dated it wrongly. Leland, McNeill and Short (as well as Talbot, who however only managed to stay in college two years) were all of the class of 1908. Bowen and Devereux (Nick) were 1909. I should date this 1908. I give it to my beloved Valerie. T. S. Eliot. 6 May 1958."

Jonathan H. Morgan, Undergraduate Secretary of the Fox Club, to TSE, 3 Apr 1958: "In browsing through the Fox Club archives, I was suddenly struck by a letter written by you some ten years ago in which you enquired about the manuscript of the *Ballade of the Fox Dinner*, written May 15, 1909. I thereupon browsed further back among the archives and there it was, and here it is · · · It once appeared in print that you were a Fox because you had been ensnared by the 'drinking crowd.' Alas, the wiles of Bacchus still prevail · · · It would be most wonderful if you could come to the Club during your sojourn here in Cambridge this spring, say for cocktails from 5 to 7 or so." TSE to Morgan, 10 Apr 1958: "I shall be delighted to have the MS. of my *Ballade* of 1909 and my wife will be still more pleased to have such a curiosity to add to her collection. Please keep it until we meet. I should be delighted to come in to have a few drinks with members one afternoon while we are in Cambridge · · · When I was in Cambridge two years ago, I passed the Club several times and wondered whether to walk in and introduce myself to anybody present or not. Sometimes an old buffer who has not been seen for a long time feels as timid as the newest member!"

After this correspondence in 1958, his dating of the manuscript to 1908 on giving it to Valerie may have been influenced by a wish to celebrate a half-century.

23 **will**] still *ms1 1st reading*

Nocturne

Published in *Harvard Advocate* 12 Nov 1909. After being reprinted in *Adv 1938*, the poem appeared in a non-Harvard publication, *Time* 2 Jan 1939, without a title and against TSE's wishes. Then *Adv 1948*, *Undergrad. Poems*, *Early Youth 1950+*.

1 **sérieux**] *Early Youth 1950+* ‖ serieux *Advocate, Adv 1938, Adv 1948, Undergrad. Poems*

12 **forever**] Forever *Time*

First Caprice in North Cambridge

Published in *March Hare* (with facsimile 97).

ms1 (Berg): *March Hare* Notebook 4; blue ink. No variants. For details of the Notebook and accompanying leaves, see headnote to *Prufrock and Other Observations* in Commentary.

Second Caprice in North Cambridge

Published in *March Hare*.

ms1 (Berg): Notebook 6; blue ink.

4 **rack**] haunt *1st reading*
8 **débris**] debris *1st reading*
12 **fields**] lots *1st reading*
15 **an unexplained**] a quite unknown *1st reading*

Opera

Published in *March Hare*.

ms1 (Berg): Notebook 8; blue ink.

5 **love**] *probable reading*; life *possible reading*

Humouresque

Published in *Harvard Advocate* 12 Jan 1910, then *Adv 1938*, *Adv 1948*, *Undergrad. Poems*, *Early Youth 1950+*. *March Hare* published the text of *ms1*, whereas the text of the present edition follows *Early Youth 1967*.

ms1 (Berg): Notebook 46. Black ink, indenting even-numbered lines 2–16.

Title] *Advocate*, *Adv Anth*, *Early Youth* (*1950*, *1967*) ‖ Humoresque *Adv 1938*, *Adv 1948*,
    Undergrad. Poems
(AFTER J. LAFORGUE)] *not ms1* ‖ *upper and lower case italics Advocate*, *Adv Anth*, *Early*
    Poems I ‖ *without brackets, as if first line of text Adv 1948*, *Undergrad. Poems*
4] *not bracketed ms1*   **frame).**] frame), *Adv 1948*, *Undergrad. Poems*
5 **deceasèd**] deceased *Adv 1948*, *Undergrad. Poems*
6 **liked: a common face,**] liked—I liked his face *ms1*
7] *not bracketed ms1*   **we forget**] you forget, *ms1*
8 **Pinched**] Locked *ms1*
9] Half-bullying, half-imploring air *ms1*
10 **Mouth twisted to**] And mouth that knew *ms1*
11 ^ 12] *line space ms1*

12 **moon.**] moon *ms1*

13 **useless**] cast-off *ms1*

14 **set him there;**] fancy him there *ms1*

15 **fashion since last spring's,**] fashion, just this spring's *ms1*

16 **"The**] The *ms1* **style,**] cry *ms1* ‖ style *Adv 1938, Adv 1948, Undergrad. Poems, Adv Anth* **swear.**] swear." *ms1*

16 ^ 17] *no line space Adv 1948, Undergrad. Poems*

17 **class?**] class" *ms1*

18 **(Feebly**] (And here *ms1* **nose),**] nose) *ms1* ‖ hose), *Advocate, Adv 1938 (corrected in TSE's copy and that sent to Hayward), Adv 1948, Undergrad. Poems*

20 **"Now**] Now *ms1* **York—"**] York—" *ms1* ‖ York"— *printings prior to the present ed.* **goes.**] goes ‖ *ms1*

21 **a marionette's,**] —a marionette's *ms1*

22 **premises; yet**] premises—but *ms1*

23 **hero!**] life! **Where**] but where *ms1* *1st reading* ‖ and where *ms1* **he**] it *ms1*

24 **But, even at that,**] And after all— *ms1* **mask**] masque *ms1* ‖ mark *Advocate, Adv 1938 (corrected in TSE's copy and that sent to Hayward), Adv 1948, Undergrad. Poems* **bizarre!**] bizarre! *ms1* ‖ bizzarre! *Adv 1948, Undergrad. Poems*

Convictions (Curtain Raiser)

Published in *March Hare*.

ms1 (Berg): Notebook 2–3; blue ink.

2 **intense!**] intense: *1st reading*

11 **The**] *1st and final reading* ‖ And The *2nd reading*

24 **One who**] Who shall *alt, but without consequential change to "appreciate"*

Spleen

Published in *Harvard Advocate* 26 Jan 1910, then *Adv 1938, Adv 1948, Undergrad. Poems, Early Youth 1950+.* No ms or ts known.

1 **Sunday:**] Sunday ‖ *Adv 1948, Undergrad. Poems*

12, 13] *transposed Undergrad. Poems (despite being a re-impression from the type of Adv 1948)*

14 **of**] to *Adv 1948, Undergrad. Poems*

First Debate between the Body and Soul

Published in *March Hare*.

ms1 (Berg): both sides of a loose leaf watermarked "Harvard Co-operative Society", accompanying Notebook. Pencil, which is hard to decipher, so that several readings, especially deletions and alternatives, are doubtful and here differ slightly from *March Hare*.

Heading] Reflections in a Square *added above title then del*

Title **Debate**] Reconciliation (*uncertain reading*) *ms1*

  1 **down**] up *1ˢᵗ reading*

  2] A blind old man   groans and mutters *1ˢᵗ reading*

  3 ^ 4] *four- or five-line space with pencil marks as though for a couplet ms1*

  6 **The**] In the *1ˢᵗ reading*

  9 **One sits**] Sits one *1ˢᵗ reading*

  10 **the blind inconscient**] their every leering *1ˢᵗ reading* ‖ their disconcerting *2ⁿᵈ reading*

  11] A score of houses that exude *1ˢᵗ reading, not del*   **leering**] battered *1ˢᵗ reading*   **houses**] housefronts *alt*

  12 **turpitude**] ~~conscious~~ turpitude *1ˢᵗ reading with* leering *above* ~~conscious~~ *but ringed to move to 11* ‖ conscient turpitude *2ⁿᵈ reading*

  14] ~~That are~~ hinting: "Accept ~~this~~ position"— *1ˢᵗ reading*

  17 **wheeze**] wheeze. *March Hare* (*error*)

  22 **eye**] brain *1ˢᵗ reading*

  23 **brain**] intellect *1ˢᵗ reading*

  24 **Nor distils**] Will not distil *1ˢᵗ reading*

  26] The muddy emphasis of sense! *alt*

  27] *1ˢᵗ reading, after which readings proliferated:*

                            Eternal. Here's
                            Cosmic, immense

    marginal alts   **cosmic**] *1ˢᵗ reading del* ‖ indifferent / careless *2ⁿᵈ reading alts* ‖ callous *further alt, ringed to move to replace* enormous

  28] *following 25 there had been a version of this line, erased:* [*indecipherable*] goes on posting bills.

  29 **soul**] sanctuary of the soul *1ˢᵗ reading*   **soul**] *1ˢᵗ and final reading* ‖ brain *alt del*   **And always come**] *originally a new line*

  30–31] The street pianos through the trees | Whine and wheeze. *1ˢᵗ reading* ‖ Whine and wheeze | And street pianos through the trees *2ⁿᵈ reading*

  36 **Absolute! complete**] *a line looped under these two words*   **idealist**] *with "assist"* (*see* 40)

37 **supersubtle**] supersensitive *1st reading*

38 **(Conception**] (No *1st reading*

40 **the**] thy *1st reading*

44] And life evaporating in a smile *1st reading*

49 **Defecations**] or desquamations *added (presumably as alt)*

Easter: Sensations of April

Published in *March Hare*. Part II had appeared in *Letters* (1988), with a facsimile of the page from the Notebook.

ms1 (Berg): part [I]: Notebook 14; title and first three lines in blue ink, then twelve lines in pencil, the final one deleted. Part II: leaf laid into Notebook; pencil. It is unclear whether (a) the poem was to begin and end with lines about "The little negro girl"; or (b) TSE, when he took up his pencil, started the poem again with "Geraniums" and concluded by adapting what had been the opening; or (c) at the end he was starting the poem again, in revision. The move from ink to pencil is germane. In favour of (b), beginning with "Geraniums" and the heat, is the parallel then with the beginning of part II, with "Daffodils" and the heat. In favour of (a) is the fact that TSE did not delete the opening lines about "The little negro girl", or delete—as possibility (c) would have asked—the first twelve lines.

after [I] 14] She is very sure of God. *ms1 del*

Ode ("For the hour that is left us Fair Harvard")

Published in *Harvard Class Day*, programme of events for Commencement Day, 24 June 1910, and in *Harvard Advocate* the same day. Also published in *Boston Evening Transcript* and *Boston Evening Herald*. Repr. in *Adv 1948, Undergrad. Poems, Early Youth 1950+*.

No ms or ts known.

Text as *Harvard Advocate* and *Early Youth 1950+*.

Title] The Ode *Harvard Class Day*

Author's name] not *Adv 1948*

1 **us Fair**] us, fair *Harvard Class Day*

7 **From the**] The *Harvard Class Day*

8 **past as we**] past, as we *Harvard Class Day* ‖ past we *Adv 1948, Undergrad. Poems*

9 **these years**] the years *Harvard Class Day*

Silence

Published in *March Hare*.

ms1 (Berg): Notebook 9. Blue ink. No variants

Mandarins

Published in *March Hare*.

ms1 (Berg): Notebook 10–13; blue ink with pencil additions. Each part begins on a new page.

1 7 **Of**] For *1ˢᵗ reading*

3 4 **nose;**] nose— *1ˢᵗ reading*
3 8] *bracketed probably for reconsideration* ‖ Attentive intuitionist *alt del*   idealist] intellectualist *alt del*

4 2 **Though**] But *1ˢᵗ reading*
4 3] How few (of even those who think) *1ˢᵗ reading* ‖ But few (of even those who think) *2ⁿᵈ reading*
4 4] Are conscient of what they mean. *1ˢᵗ reading* ‖ Arrange and comprehend the scene. *2ⁿᵈ reading* ‖ Arrange their outlines on the screen *3ʳᵈ reading*
4 5 **find**] think *1ˢᵗ reading*
4 7 **demoiselles**] stately dames *1ˢᵗ reading* ‖ all our dames *2ⁿᵈ reading* (*second word uncertain, third word del*)

Goldfish (Essence of Summer Magazines)

Published in *March Hare*.

ms1 (Berg): Notebook 18–21, black ink and pencil; plus excised leaf in pencil only (supplying IV 18–37; Beinecke). Parts III and IV finally all cancelled.

I 7 **nights and**] *not 1ˢᵗ reading*
I 12] For meanings that we not discern. *1ˢᵗ reading* ‖ For meanings we cannot discern. *2ⁿᵈ reading*

II 1 **its**] his *1ˢᵗ reading*
II 9 **must**] should *1ˢᵗ reading*

II 10 **should**] do *1ˢᵗ reading*

III 5 **eternal**] immortal *1ˢᵗ reading*

III 21–22] Bays and rose. *1ˢᵗ reading (one line)*

IV 7 **which October**] all the answ *1ˢᵗ reading (uncertain)* ‖ all the senses (?) *March Hare*

IV 9 **headed**] labeled *1ˢᵗ reading*

IV 10] *opening quotation marks apparently not closed.*   **Along**] Among *1ˢᵗ reading (uncertain)*

IV 14] *added*   **winds**] waves *1ˢᵗ reading*

IV 19 **beg**] humbly beg *ms 1ˢᵗ reading*

IV 29 **At**] And *1ˢᵗ reading (uncertain)*

IV 36 **—I am off**] And lay my course *1ˢᵗ reading*

IV 37] *one or two indecipherable words written above* street *may be* off *for* from the previous line

Suite Clownesque

Published in *March Hare.*

ms1 (Berg): Notebook 24–27, plus excised leaf (supplying the last line of III and the whole of IV; Beinecke); black ink. *Fragments* ("There was a jolly tinker came across the sea") appears on the verso.

Title] Suite *1ˢᵗ reading*

I 8 **Impressive**] Infinite *alt, with both readings apparently del, but* sceptic *not accordingly capitalised*

I 9 **The most**] Most *1ˢᵗ reading*   **expressive, real**] *ringed*

I 11 **without**] that lacks *1ˢᵗ reading*

I 13 **Just while he**] The while the *1ˢᵗ reading*

I 18 **still continue**] are always *1ˢᵗ reading*

II 4] *brackets added*

II 8 **stools**] a stool *1ˢᵗ reading*

II 15 **When**] *written over* And *(uncertain reading)*

III 10 **time**] world *1ˢᵗ reading*

III 11] Improvement on the high sublime *1ˢᵗ reading*

III 12 **in**] at *1ˢᵗ reading*

III 12 ^ 13] Seen from the depths of a New York street, *added then del*

III 14 **It's**] Its *ms1*

III 16] *erroneously* III 19 *in March Hare (now corrected by Jayme Stayer)*   **girls**] little girls *1ˢᵗ reading*

III 20] *originally written* 16^17, *then bracketed, del and reinstated, with arrow indicating new position, perhaps replacing a line that had been added and del:* (I'm such a rover)

III 21] *with "?"*

IV 3 **smiling**] Broadway *1ˢᵗ reading*   **rattan**] the rattan *1ˢᵗ reading*

IV 9] *not 1ˢᵗ reading*

IV 10 **And the**] The *1ˢᵗ reading*

IV 10^11] And *del*

IV 12 **falls**] leans *1ˢᵗ reading*

IV 15] *brackets added*

The Triumph of Bullshit

Published in *March Hare.*

ms1 (Beinecke): leaf excised from Notebook. Dated Nov 1910.

1 **Ladies**] Critics *1ˢᵗ reading*   my attentions have] ~~my~~ *1ˢᵗ reading* ‖ I have patiently *2ⁿᵈ reading*

2 **If you**] Those who *1ˢᵗ reading*   **are**] too *1ˢᵗ reading*

16 **your**] my *1ˢᵗ reading*

16, 24, 28 **Christ's**] Christs *ms1*

17 **me unduely**] I am merely *1ˢᵗ reading*

21] Teddy bears carnivorous, engines califerous *1ˢᵗ reading*

23 **only**] merely *1ˢᵗ reading*

26 **Theories scattered**] guests star-scattered *1ˢᵗ reading* ‖ Theories, star-scattered *alt* ‖ Theories, ~~scatter~~ scatteredly *2ⁿᵈ reading*

27 **Take up my good intentions**] Then take my good intentions *1ˢᵗ reading* ‖ Take up this set of verses *2ⁿᵈ reading*

28] You have the right to stick them up my ass. *1ˢᵗ reading*

Fourth Caprice in Montparnasse

Published in *March Hare.*

ms1 (Berg): Notebook 5; black ink.

Title **Montparnasse**] North Cambridge *1ˢᵗ reading*

6 **mass**] mess *perhaps*

10 **unpaid**] all their *1ˢᵗ reading*

12 **derided.**] derided, ~~chided~~; *ms1*

13] *not 1ˢᵗ reading*

15] **But why**] Why *1ˢᵗ reading*

after 15] *1ˢᵗ reading*:

> The world is full of journalists,
> And full of universities.

with And *ringed* || *2ⁿᵈ reading*:

> And the world is full of journalists,
> Full of universities.

then all del

Inside the gloom

Published in *March Hare*.

ms1 (Berg): pencil on the verso of a loose leaf accompanying Notebook. Couplets are scattered down and across the page, and then numbered for reordering.

1 **gloom**] tomb *1ˢᵗ reading*

2 **garret**] furnished *1ˢᵗ reading*

4 **Took up**] Assumed *alt*

5–6] *before 3–4, then transposed*

7 **Scorpion**] scorpion *1ˢᵗ reading*

11–12] *added*

13 **Major Bear**] dancing bear *1ˢᵗ reading*. (*TSE may have intended to delete* The *when making the revision.*)

14 **Balanced**] Stood on *1ˢᵗ reading*

15–16] *added*

15 **direction**] effect *alt*

16 **intellection**] intellect *alt*

18 **scheme**] notion (*or perhaps* nature *?*) *1ˢᵗ reading*

19 **too**] then *1ˢᵗ reading*

21 **while the debate was rife**] with a fork and knife *alt*

25 **Said**] Cried *1ˢᵗ reading*   **all**] *del and restored*

27 **So they**] They *1ˢᵗ reading*

Entretien dans un parc

Published in *March Hare*.

ms1 (Berg): Notebook 39–40; black ink.

Title] Situation *1ˢᵗ reading*

  1–2] *TSE's square brackets*

  4 **uncertainties**] certain uncertainties *1ˢᵗ reading*

  13 **as if, perhaps,**] perhaps as if *1ˢᵗ reading*

  26 **broken**] *1ˢᵗ and final reading* ‖ tumbling (*doubtful reading; possibly* trembling) *2ⁿᵈ reading*

  34 **opening out**] laying out / laying open *alts*

Interlude: in a Bar

Published in *March Hare*.

ms1 (Berg): Notebook 48. Pencil.

Bacchus and Ariadne: 2nd Debate between the Body and Soul

Published in *March Hare*.

ms1 (Berg): loose leaf of lightweight wove typing paper, accompanying Notebook; formerly folded together with *The smoke that gathers blue and sinks*. Pencil, with some readings doubtful.

Title] *preceded by* Fragment (*overlooked by March Hare*). See textual headnote to *He said: this universe is very clever.*   **Ariadne:**] Ariade *ms1*

  3 **might have broken**] might have happened / should have broken! *alts*

  4 **unknown**] suppressed *1ˢᵗ reading*

  5 **drums**] floods *1ˢᵗ reading*

  8 **insights**] incidents *1ˢᵗ reading* ‖ intuitions *alt*   **marched**] moved *1ˢᵗ reading* (*uncertain*)

  11] The life that breathed across had left no trace *1ˢᵗ reading, with* life *revised to* wind   **wind**] winds *March Hare* (*error*)

  12] The world began again its even slow *1ˢᵗ reading* ‖ I saw the world begin again its slow *2ⁿᵈ reading* ‖ And I saw that Time began again its slow *3ʳᵈ reading*

  13 **Attrition**] Rasping *1ˢᵗ reading* (*uncertain*)

14 **burst**] spring *alt del*　　**pure**] fresh and pure *1ˢᵗ reading*

15 **triumph**] *alt to a deleted word possibly* victory (*although it is also possible that* triumph *was intended as alt to* it is *and that the deletion leaves the line* Surprised, but knowing—triumph unendurable to miss!)　　**unendurable**] not endurable *March Hare* (*with* "unendurable *perhaps*")

15 ^ 16] For purity is not *del*

16] To have found free the purity that springs *1ˢᵗ reading*

18 **meditates**] *underlined with* "?"

18, 19] *originally in reverse order*

20 **sure**] *1ˢᵗ and final reading* ‖ sure that *2ⁿᵈ reading*　　**like**] *not 1ˢᵗ reading*

The smoke that gathers blue and sinks

Published in *March Hare.*

ms1 (Berg): loose leaf of lightweight wove typing paper, accompanying Notebook; formerly folded together with *Bacchus and Ariadne: 2nd Debate between the Body and Soul.* Pencil.

7 **die**] stop *1ˢᵗ reading*

7 ^ 8] Machinery *del*

8 **Stifled**] Choaked up *1ˢᵗ reading.* TSE continued to be uncertain of this spelling, writing "choaked" in a letter to Robert Waller, 21 Sept 1942, before emending to "choked".

12 **Some attraction?**] Here's the attraction *1ˢᵗ reading*

21 **that's quite**] that ought to be *1ˢᵗ reading*

He said: this universe is very clever

Published in *March Hare.*

ms1 (Berg): loose leaf of lightweight wove typing paper, accompanying Notebook. Pencil, with "Fragment" written diagonally in the top right-hand corner and a head sketched upside down. Paper and writing match *Bacchus and Ariadne: 2nd Debate between the Body and Soul.* The indenting of even numbered lines to 12 is imprecise but probably intentional, although *March Hare* indents only 2.

3 **goes on working out its law**] has its Place in Life *alt*

5 **it is**] it's *1ˢᵗ reading*

6 **like a syphilitic**] *with* flattened (*perhaps for* flattened like *or* as *alt to* syphilitic)　　**syphilitic**] spongy *1ˢᵗ reading* (*uncertain*) ‖ bloated *2ⁿᵈ reading*

8 **ourselves**] our lives *1st reading* (*uncertain*)

8 ^ 9] *TSE's rule*

9 **"this**] they *1st reading* ‖ "that *alt*

10 **on officechairs**] upon [*indecipherable*] chairs *1st reading* ‖ in wearing out of chairs *alt del*

12 **six abysmal**] three unending *alt del*

Interlude in London

Published in *March Hare* (facsimile 99).

ms1 (Berg): Notebook 7; black ink.

10 **broken**] timid / furtive *alts del* (*uncertain readings*)

Ballade pour la grosse Lulu

Published in *March Hare*.

ms1 (Beinecke): leaf excised from Notebook. Dated July 1911. The stanzas are arranged in a square and were numbered subsequently:

I	IV
III	II

That is, the order of composition was probably I, III, IV, II. They are printed according to the roman numerals. Stanzas I and IV were finally cancelled. The first line of each stanza was originally "The papers give an interview"; when TSE revised it to "The Outlook . . .", he made the consequential change to "gives" in 1 but neglected to do so in the other stanzas.

ms McCouch (Huntington): st. II only, on the notepaper and in the hand of Conrad Aiken's friend Dr. Grayson P. McCouch. A note in another hand adds that it is "from a letter to C. A. which he sent on to McCouch".

1 **Outlook gives**] papers give *ms1 1st reading*

6 **call,"**] call;" *March Hare* (*error*)

7 **But, My Lulu**] But, I say *ms1 1st reading*

10 **Booker T.**] Edward Bok *ms1 1st reading*

11–12] Called 50 kinds of Irish Stew | And "How to fill a Christmas Sock" *ms1 1st reading*

11 **Stew!"**] Stew *ms1, ms McCouch*

12 **Or "How**] Or How *ms McCouch*   **nigger free!"**] Nigger free" *ms McCouch*

13 **papers say "the**] Outlook said the *ms McCouch*

14 **Key,]** Key *ms McCouch*   **stall."]** stall *ms1* ‖ stall. *ms McCouch*
15 **My Lulu "Put"]** *I* say "Put *ms1 1ˢᵗ reading* ‖ I say: put *ms McCouch*
16 **Whore House Ball!"]** whore house ball! *ms McCouch*
23 **My Lulu]** I say *ms1 1ˢᵗ reading*

The Little Passion: From "An Agony in the Garret"

Published in *March Hare*.

ms1 (Berg): leaf laid into Notebook (with 17–21 on verso). Pencil. The hand resembles that of poems from Paris, 1911. (In *March Hare*, this draft, beginning "Of those ideas in his head", is printed beneath *ms2* rather than in the textual apparatus.)

ms2 (Berg): Notebook 52. Black ink. No variants. The hand resembles that of poems of 1914–15 (*Afternoon, Suppressed Complex* and *Morning at the Window*). Presumably TSE's distillation of *ms1*, "Of those ideas in his head".

Text from *ms2*.

Title] *not ms1*
ms1:

> Of those ideas in his head
> Which found me always interested
> Though they were seldom well digested—
> I recollect one thing he said
> After those hours of streets and streets   5
> That spun around him like a wheel
> He finally remarked: "I feel
> As if I'd been a long time dead."
>
> Upon those stifling August nights
> I know he used to walk the streets   10
> Now diving into dark retreats—
> Or following the lines of lights
>
> Or following the lines of lights,
> And knowing well to what they lead
> To some inevitable cross   15
> Whereon our souls are spread, and bleed.
>
> And when he leaned across the bar
> Twisting a hopeless cigarette
> I noticed on his withered face
> A smile which I cannot forget   20
> A washed-out, unperceived disgrace.

1 **those]** *uncertain reading* ‖ these *Gallup 1968*
4 **recollect]** remember *ms1 1ˢᵗ reading*
12 **the lines]** a line *ms1 1ˢᵗ reading*

14 **And knowing**] Knowing *ms1 1ˢᵗ reading*   **they lead**] it leads *ms1 1ˢᵗ reading*

16] Whereon his soul is spread, and bleeds. *1ˢᵗ reading ms1* ‖ Whereon our soul are spread and bleed *ms1*

21] A thin, unconscious half-disgrace *ms1 alt*   **unperceived**] infinite *ms1 1ˢᵗ reading with* ~~barely~~ *(uncertain) and then* and *written above, and* ~~not~~ unperceived *below*

The Burnt Dancer

Published in *March Hare*.

ts1 (Berg): loose leaf of typing paper, accompanying Notebook. Ribbon copy with the French refrain typed in red. Paper and typing match *Oh little voices of the throats of men ts1*.

4 **heedless flight**] hidden flight *1ˢᵗ reading (with the final reading typed over, then del)* ‖ little flight *1ˢᵗ reading in March Hare (error)*

14 *as also* 29 **danse mon**] danse *1ˢᵗ reading*

19 **us**] *not 1ˢᵗ reading*

20 **Children's**] Childrens' *ts1 (compare The Death of Saint Narcissus 17)*   **little**] hidden *1ˢᵗ reading*

23 **delight?**] delight *1ˢᵗ reading*

28 **not with**] with *1ˢᵗ reading*

32 **pain,**] pain *1ˢᵗ reading*

33 **sinews,**] sinews *1ˢᵗ reading*

34 **fire,**] fire *1ˢᵗ reading*

35 **those**] these *1ˢᵗ reading*   **toss,**] toss *1ˢᵗ reading*

Oh little voices of the throats of men

Published in *Letters* (1988) with text from *ts1*; then *March Hare* with text from *ts2*.

ts1 (U. Maryland; now Hornbake Library; formerly, like other TSE tss, McKeldin Library): sent to Aiken 25 July 1914. Ribbon copy on two leaves also containing *The Love Song of St. Sebastian*. Text differs from *ts2* in having no terminal punctuation to 2, 9, 10, 12, 13, 15, 16, 17, 18, 22, 25, 28, 29, 31, 38, 41, 42, 44, 46, 48.

ts2 (Berg): ribbon copy with 6 added in pencil, on a loose leaf of "Marcus Ward's" typing paper accompanying Notebook. Later than *ts1*.

ts Aiken (Huntington, AIK 479): fair copy transcript of *ts1* typed by Aiken on two leaves, treating this poem and *The Love Song of St. Sebastian* as one. That title is transferred to the head of this poem, and a row of dots is introduced at the foot of the first leaf, with *The Love Song of St. Sebastian* following on, without separate title, on the second leaf. TSE's annotations are typed in the margins. His emendation of the verbs in "I should remember" and "I should for a moment" (28, 29) was misunderstood so that these appear as "Shall I remember" and "Should I for a moment". (The rearrangement may have been an editorial intervention intended to help TSE, or an attempt to create from the fragments a single poem to set beside *The Love Song of J. Alfred Prufrock* so as to increase the value of the material to a collector. When *ts1* was sold by Sotheby's, NY, in 1972, it was catalogued as a single poem entitled *The Love Song of St. Sebastian*.) At the time of this typing, probably 1930/31, Aiken also folded into these two leaves a further transcript of *Suppressed Complex* and *Afternoon* on a leaf of the same paper (perhaps for safekeeping or to send to Maurice Firuski). As this transcript has no independent authority, its variants are not recorded below.

ts *Quinby* (Huntington, AIK 478): carbon of a transcript of *ts1* (both this poem and *The Love Song of St. Sebastian*), typed by Jane Quinby, with TSE's annotations transcribed in her hand. The first half of 25 is conflated with the second half of 26 to form a single line. As this ts has no independent authority, its variants are not recorded below. See description of Quinby's transcript of *The Love Song of St. Sebastian*.

Text as *ts2* and *March Hare*.

1–14] *braced with "Introduction. To be amplified at the end also." ts1*

6] *not ts1, ts2 1ˢᵗ reading*

7 **hell**] hell Sha *ts1 1ˢᵗ reading (starting 8)*

8 **paths**] ways *ts1, ts2 1ˢᵗ reading*

8 ^ 9] *no space ts1*

9 **roads**] ways *ts1*

11 **balance pleasure**] measure joy *ts1*

14 ^ 15] *five line space with rule across page added ts1*

15–34] *with marginal note "This theme to recur twice, in variations" ts1*

18 **led**] lead *ts1, ts2 (and March Hare)*

19 **unvaried**] unvarièd *ts1*

20 **Intolerable interminable**] Interminable intolerable *ts1*

25 **Appearances, appearances,**] Appearances appearances *ts1*

27 **yet**] but *ts1*

28 **whether**] Whether *ts1*

30 **word**] truth *ts1 1ˢᵗ reading, ts2 1ˢᵗ reading*   **paths you tread**] ways you keep *ts1*
1ˢᵗ reading

31 **true**] truth *ts1*   **be, when all is said:**] be (when all is said) *ts1*

34 **but**] than *ts1*   **than**] but *ts1 2ⁿᵈ reading*

37–49] *new leaf, with marginal reminder "finale to the foregoing" ts1*

37 **plumes**] plumes the *ts1 1ˢᵗ reading*

40 **light**] *not ts1 1ˢᵗ reading (error, miscopying?)*

43 **on**] *in ts1, ts2 1ˢᵗ reading*

44 **morning**] *daylight ts1*

47 **in**] ~~at~~ *ts1 1ˢᵗ reading*

49 **known**] *not ts1 1ˢᵗ reading (error, miscopying?)*

The Love Song of St. Sebastian

Published in *Letters* (1988) with text from *ts1*; then *March Hare* with text from *ts2*.

ts1 (U. Maryland; now Hornbake Library; formerly McKeldin Library): sent to Aiken 25 July 1914. Differs from *ts2* in having no terminal punctuation to 3, 4, 8, 11, 15, 25, 26, 27, 31, 32, 33. Subsequently in the collection of Urling Iselin of New York, along with Aiken's ts of *The Love Song of J. Alfred Prufrock*. A letter to Aiken from Mrs. Iselin's assistant, Jane Quinby, 24 Nov 1948, asking to buy TSE's original accompanying letter, is in the Huntington.

ts2 (Berg): loose leaf of "Marcus Ward's" typing paper, accompanying Notebook. Untitled, and beginning so high on the leaf as to look like a continuation of *Oh little voices of the throats of men*. Later than *ts1*.

ts Aiken (Huntington, AIK 479): transcript by Aiken of *ts1*. See textual headnote to *Oh little voices of the throats of men*.

ts Quinby (Huntington, AIK 478): transcript by Quinby of *ts1*. See textual headnote to *Oh little voices of the throats of men*. Only 1–11, 22–23, 28–29 and 34–38 of *The Love Song of St. Sebastian* are given, with rules separating the extracts. This transcript appears to have been made in 1948 to send to Aiken, the original owner of *ts1*. He had written to Maurice Firuski of the Housatonic Bookshop, Connecticut, 11 Sept 1930: "Would I have a chance of selling, for example, a typescript of the Prufrock poem, typed by T.S.E. himself, with corrections in his handwriting, and signed? It looks good. I also have a letter from him which contains three poems never published. One of them, long, unfinished, with marginal comments. Could anything be done with this . . ?" Firuski, 25 Mar 1931: "As to the T. S. Eliot ms—*do I dare catalogue it?* It would be a swell stunt. I shall not do so till I get your permission. Your name would not figure in it. Are the other poems unpublished? I can't seem to figure out what to ask for the stuff. Give me more dope on it. Why is the name M. D. Armstrong (of fragrant memory) on the *Prufrock*? are the comments to him or to you? What draft of *Prufrock* is it actually? Early? Late? Revised? *I need material for a selling talk.* Let me know and there will be cold cash." (Both letters, Huntington.) Aiken then sold his drafts of *The Love Song of J. Alfred Prufrock, Oh little voices of the throats of men, The Love Song of St. Sebastian, Suppressed Complex* and *Afternoon*, which Firuski himself sold "quite promptly" (*Gallup 1998* 295) to Mrs. Iselin. When her assistant Jane Quinby wrote to TSE about them, he replied, 6 Apr 1948: "I think that the most likely explanation of the manuscript which has come into your hands is that these were all the original property of Conrad Aiken. I should think that it is likely that the pencil address in the upper right hand corner of *The Love Song of J. Alfred Prufrock* would turn out to be in Mr. Aiken's writing, since Mr. M. D. Armstrong was Mr. Aiken's friend and not mine. I suspect that this is a copy which I gave to Conrad Aiken in 1912 or 1913 to take to London with him and which he unsuccessfully attempted to place at that time on my behalf with several English periodicals." Then, on 3 May: "I have your letter of April 25th with the fuller transcription of the unidentified verses. I am afraid I must admit the likelihood that the fragments entitled *The Love Song of St. Sebastian, Suppressed Complex*, and *Afternoon* were written by myself. I cannot swear that the first page [*Oh little voices of the throats of men*] is not by myself either. But whether the lines are by Conrad Aiken or by me I think it is a great pity that any of them have been preserved because they all strike me as very bad indeed." After Mrs. Iselin's death, *The Love Song of J. Alfred Prufrock, Oh little voices of the throats of men* and *The Love Song of St. Sebastian* were sold on 31 Oct 1972 at Sotheby's, NY (see *The Times* 2 Nov), where they were bought by The House of Books for U. Maryland. The auction contained two other TSE lots. The first, lot 261, contained four letters to Quinby about these materials from 1948: two from TSE and two from Aiken. It must have been bought by a dealer, for the lot was split, with TSE's letters going to Maryland and Aiken's to the Huntington (which in 1975 bought his papers, probably including the transcriptions sent by Quinby in 1948).

Text as *ts2* and *March Hare*.

Title] *added in pen ts1* ‖ *not ts2*

2 **lamp**] little lamp *ts1*

4 **bled**] bleed *ts1 1ˢᵗ reading*

7] *with arrow and question to Aiken: "does this mean anything to you? I mean stand all about in a pool on the floor" ts1*   **lamp**] light *ts1 1ˢᵗ reading, ts2 1ˢᵗ reading*

9 **arise your neophyte**] arise, your neophyte, *ts1 2ⁿᵈ reading*

11] **To**] And *ts1 1ˢᵗ reading*   **led**] lead *ts1 with "preterite! not present", ts2 (and March Hare)*

18 **in without**] in to your bed without *ts1*

23 **beneath my knees**] between my knees *ts1 1ˢᵗ reading* ‖ below my knees. *ts1 2ⁿᵈ (final) reading*

28 **shall**] should *ts1 1ˢᵗ reading*

29 **should**] shall *ts1 1ˢᵗ reading, ts2 1ˢᵗ reading*

31 **beneath**] between *ts1*

32 *as also* 33 **would**] will *ts2 1ˢᵗ reading*

33 **be nothing more**] not be one word *ts1*

34 **would · · · should**] will · · · shall *ts2 1ˢᵗ reading*

35 **infamy;**] infamy. *with second "m" del and "Not to rhyme with 'mammy'" ts1*

36 **should · · · had**] shall · · · have *ts2 1ˢᵗ reading*

37–38] *one line (to fit leaf) with stroke indicating division ts1*

Paysage Triste

Published in *March Hare*.

ts1 (Berg): leaf laid into Notebook.

2 a] the *1ˢᵗ reading*
3 **Who**] The girl who *1ˢᵗ reading*
16 **my**] your *1ˢᵗ reading*

Afternoon

Published in *Letters* (1988); then *March Hare*.

ms1 (Berg): Notebook 49; black ink.

ms2 (untraced): folded leaf with *Afternoon* and *Suppressed Complex* on fols. 1 and 3 respectively. Sent to Aiken with TSE's letter of 25 Feb [1915], later owned by Mrs. Iselin, but not sold at Sotheby's, NY, in 1972 when her (Aiken) tss of *The Love Song of J. Alfred Prufrock*, *Oh little voices of the throats of men* and *The Love Song of St. Sebastian* were sold. *Gallup 1998* 295 implies that *ms1* was a copy from this leaf, but without stating whether Gallup had ever seen the leaf itself.

ts Aiken (Huntington, AIK 484): fair copy by Aiken of *Suppressed Complex* followed by *Afternoon* on a single leaf. Typed at the same time and on the same paper as the two leaves of his copy of *Oh little voices of the throats of men* and *The Love Song of St. Sebastian* (*ts Aiken*) and folded together with those.

ts Quinby (Huntington, AIK 483): carbon of a transcript of *Suppressed Complex* and *Afternoon* typed by Jane Quinby, with description of the source, *ms2*, typed at head: "Autograph manuscript on 1st and 3rd pages of single folded sheet:". A note by Quinby at the foot reads: "(This is all in the same handwriting as the notes and corrections on the typescript)", meaning that *ms2* is in the same hand as that seen on the ts of *Oh little voices of the throats of men* and *The Love Song of St. Sebastian*. Quinby also typed for Donald Gallup copies, themselves now untraced, of "the Iselin poems" (*Gallup 1998* 297).

Text from *ms1*.

2 **Museum.**] Museum *ts Quinby*
4 **overshoes**] shoes *ts Quinby*
7 **statuary**] statuary, *ts Aiken*
8 **lawn**] lawn, *ts Aiken*, *ts Quinby*
9 **unconscious,**] unconscious *ts Quinby*   **absolute**] absolute. *ts Aiken*, *ts Quinby*

Suppressed Complex

Published in *Letters* (1988), then *March Hare*, both with text from *ms1*.

ms1 (Berg): Notebook 50; black ink.

ms2 (untraced): folded leaf with *Afternoon* and *Suppressed Complex* on fols. 1 and 3 respectively. See description of *Afternoon ms2*.

ts1 (Beinecke): ribbon copy on the top third of a leaf of Croxley Manifest Bank. Enclosed, along with an untraced "copy of the Lady" (*Portrait of a Lady*), in TSE to Pound, 2 Feb 1915 (a ms letter on the same paper). "I enclose one small verse. I know it is not good, but everything else I have done is worse. Besides, I am constipated ⅋ have a cold on the chest. Burn it."

ts Aiken (Huntington, AIK 484): see description of *Afternoon ts Aiken*. Alternate lines indented.

ts Quinby (Huntington, AIK 483): see description of *Afternoon ts Quinby*.

Text from *ts1*.

   2 **think.**] think *ms1*, *ts Quinby*, *March Hare*

   5 **fingers**] fingers. *Letters* (1988) 87 (*erroneous transcript of Notebook*)

   7 **morning**] l *ts1 1ˢᵗ reading*   **shook**] stirred *ts Quinby*, *ts Aiken*

   8 **out through**] through *ts1 1ˢᵗ reading, emended in ink in unknown hand*

In the Department Store

Published in *March Hare*.

ts1 (Berg): leaf laid into Notebook. No variants.

Do I know how I feel? Do I know what I think?

Published in *March Hare*.

ms1 (Berg): pencil on both sides of a loose leaf of blue ruled paper, accompanying Notebook. The leaf has been punched for filing.

   6 **would he tell me**] he would know *1ˢᵗ reading*   **and feel**] *probably added when revising* 9

   8 **or**] of *1ˢᵗ reading*   **more"—**] more— *ms1*

   9] And yet I dread what I know he will not say *1ˢᵗ reading*

10 **we**] I *1ˢᵗ reading*

12 **or stifled in**] in neurasthetic *1ˢᵗ reading*

13 **can**] has the heart to *alt*

15 **There is**] *written over* I have (*uncertain reading*)

16 **something**] water *1ˢᵗ reading*

17 **his**] the *1ˢᵗ reading*

18] Will investigate *1ˢᵗ reading* (*anticipating next line*)

20 **Would**] As he pulls back the skin, would *1ˢᵗ reading*

23 **in**] like *1ˢᵗ reading*

The Death of Saint Narcissus

Published in *Early Youth* (1950, 1967), then *WL Facs.* Lines 1–5 printed in *Kenner* 33. Probably written in 1915; submitted to *Poetry* by Pound, 29 May 1916 (see Commentary headnote to this poem).

ms1 (Berg; *WLFacs* 90–93): rough pencil draft on both sides of a single leaf of Excelsior Fine British Make paper, matching that of *Mr. Apollinax ms1*.

ms2 (*WLFacs* 94–97): fair copy on both sides of a leaf of blind-ruled laid paper, matching that of *The Engine ms2*. The paper is similar, but not quite a match for, that of the "Fresca couplets" *ms1924* (see *The Waste Land*, Textual History, 5. THE "FRESCA COUPLETS").

ts Poetry (U. Chicago): purple carbon sent to *Poetry* and marked up for the printer by H. B. Fuller, with the general heading "POEMS" added by him above the title. Assigned to 1915 by *Rainey* 198. For details of the submission by Pound of five poems by TSE to *Poetry* on 29 May 1916, see Textual History headnote to *Morning at the Window*.

galley (U. Chicago): galley-proof pulled for *Poetry*, to appear on two pages, but all finally scored through with "kill" on each half, and with Harriet Monroe's later comment at head: "This poem never pub'd T. S. Eliot". John Hayward claimed to have followed this text in *Early Youth 1950*, but printed the colon from *ts Poetry* in 5.

Except for the removal of editorial indents, the text is as *Early Youth 1950*, which presumably had the imprimatur of TSE.

Title] *not ms1*   **Death**] death *ms2*   **Saint**] a Saint *ms2 1ˢᵗ reading*

1, *as also* 8, 21, 24, 28, 33] *no indent mss, ts Poetry 1ˢᵗ reading* ‖ *indent ts Poetry 2ⁿᵈ reading* (*editorial?*)+

1 **gray rock—**] *ts Poetry 2ⁿᵈ reading* (*editorial?*)+ ‖ grey rock *mss* ‖ gray rock *ts Poetry 1ˢᵗ reading*

2 **in**] <and sit> *ms1 1ˢᵗ reading. The angle brackets, which are TSE's, may have been added to mark these words for consideration, prior to their deletion*   **gray rock,**] *ts Poetry 2ⁿᵈ reading* (*editorial?*)+ ‖ grey rock *mss* ‖ gray rock *ts Poetry 1ˢᵗ reading*

3 **something**] a shadow *mss*

5 **leaping**] huddled *ms1*   **behind**] by *ms1, ms2 1st reading*   **red rock:**]
redrock. *ms1* ‖ red rock; *galley*

6 **cloth**] coat *ms1 2nd reading*   **limbs**] green limbs *ms1 1st reading* ‖ bloodless
limbs *ms1 2nd reading, del*

7 **gray**] blue *ms1 1st reading* ‖ grey *ms1 2nd reading, ms2*   **on**] between *ms1*

8 **once**] first *ms1*

9 **When**] Where *mss*   **limbs**] legs *mss*   **smoothly**] *not ms1 1st
reading*   **other**] other and his knees grasping each other *ms1 1st reading (last
three words del before the others)*

12 **soothed by his own rhythm.**] carried apart *ms1*

14 **his eyes**] his ~~own~~ eyes *ts Poetry (uncertain reading)*

15 **aware**] were aware *ms1*   **the pointed tips of his**] long *ms1* ‖ the tips of his *ms2*

15 ^ 16] *no line space mss, galley* ‖ *new page Early Youth 1950* ‖ *line space Early Youth
1967, 1969 (error)*

16] So because he was struck mad [down *alt added*] by the knowledge of his own
beauty *ms1*

17 **men's**] mens' *mss (error, compare The Burnt Dancer 20)*   **before**] to
ms1   **God.**] God *Early Youth 1967, 1969*

18 **streets**] streets, in the streets of Carthage *ms1*

19 **faces**] pale faces *ms1 1st reading* ‖ many faces *ms1 2nd reading (first word
uncertain)*   **convulsive**] convulsed *ms2 1st reading*   **thighs and knees.**]
ms1 3rd reading ‖ thighs. *ms1 1st reading* ‖ knees. *ms1 2nd reading*

20 **under**] to live under *mss*

20 ^ 21] *new leaf so line spacing indeterminate ms2*

21 **was sure**] wished *ms1*   **tree,**] tree *mss*

22 **Twisting**] To push *ms1*   **other**] other, *ms1 (probable reading, although WLFacs
has a full stop)*

23 **And**] and *ms1 1st reading*   **tangling**] tangle *ms1*   **other.**] other *ms1*

24 **knew**] wished *ms1*

25 **held tight in**] caught between *ms1 1st reading* ‖ held between *ms1 2nd
reading*   **his own**] his own *ms2*   **fingers,**] fingers *ms1*

26 **Writhing**] To have writhed *ms1*   **ancient**] *not ms1*   **beauty**] beauty caught
in the net of his own beauty *ms1 1st reading* ‖ beauty caught in his own beauty
ms1 2nd reading

27] *not ms1 (but see 26 for elements of the line)*

28 **he**] he wished he *ms1*

30 **Knowing at the end**] To have known at the last moment, *ms1*   **taste**] full
taste *ms1*   **his**] her *mss*

31] *indented ms1 (inadvertent?)*   **his**] her *mss*   **smoothness,**] smoothness.
ms1

32] *not ms1*

33 **became a dancer**] devoted himself *ms1*

34 **burning**] penetrant *ms1*

37] *ms1*:

> He surrendered himself and embraced them
> And his whiteness and redness satisfied him.

37 ^ 38] We each have the sort of life we want, but his life went straight to the death he wanted. *del ms1*

38 **green,**] green *ms1 del*

To Helen

Published in *March Hare* from *ms1*.

ms1 (Berg): black ink on a loose leaf accompanying Notebook. Untitled.

ms2 (Beinecke): black ink on a loose leaf not from the Notebook. The presence of the title suggests this was subsequent to *ms1*.

Text from *ms2*.

Title] *not ms1, March Hare*

  3 **bananas,**] bananas *ms1*

  5 **impatient**] restless *ms1*

  6 **large**] wide *ms1*

  7 **finger bowl**] finger-bowl *ms1*

  8 **Till**] Until *ms1*   **around the corner**] beneath the table *ms1*

  9 **And twitched**] *ms2* ‖ The t *ms1* (*apparently before writing the last two words of* 8) ‖ The *ms2 1ˢᵗ reading*   **crumbs.**] crumbs *ms1*

After the turning of the inspired days

Published in *WLFacs*. Date uncertain: see Commentary headnote.

ms1 (Berg; *WLFacs* 108–109): black ink on squared paper, widely punched for filing and folded in four for posting (along with *I am the Resurrection and the Life* and *So through the evening, through the violet air*).

  1 **the inspired**] a thousand *1ˢᵗ reading*

  2 **praying**] praying and crying *1ˢᵗ reading. TSE added square brackets around and crying before deleting the words*   **crying**] sighing

  4 **kept**] *not 1ˢᵗ reading*   **withered**] the withered *1ˢᵗ reading*

  8 *as also* 10] *indented?*

13 **world seemed futile**] *3rd reading, braced with earlier readings* || world was ended *1st reading* || show was ended *2nd reading*

I am the Resurrection and the Life

Published in *WLFacs*.

ms1 (Berg; *WLFacs* 110–111): black ink on paper matching that of *After the turning of the inspired days*. No variants.

So through the evening, through the violet air

Published in *WLFacs*.

ms1 (Berg; *WLFacs* 112–15): black ink and pencil on both sides of a single leaf of paper matching that of *After the turning of the inspired days*.

2 **One**] *alt 3rd reading and final reading* || A *1st reading* || Some *2nd reading and alt 3rd reading* **dragged**] led *alt*

3 **from which**] wherefrom / whereof *alts* **seemed**] had / was *alts*

6 **When**] *enclosed in square brackets* **trees**] withered trees *1st reading; TSE enclosed* withered *in square brackets before deleting the word*

7 **one essential**] *not 1st reading* **that**] *1st and final reading* || which *2nd reading*

8] *perhaps added* **that**] which *1st reading*

9 **This**] To the *1st reading* || When to the *2nd reading* **wrinkled ^ road**] withered *twice added and del* **which**] that *1st reading* **winds and**] *not 1st reading*

11 **whereof**] of which *1st reading, the second word then linked to* which *in the next line by a double-headed arrow* **gone**] lost *1st reading*

12 **we**] I *alt* **alone:**] along *alt*

15 **shrill**] *WLFacs reads as* Shrill

16 **Whining**] Sobbing *1st reading*

17 **distorted**] *2nd reading* || one withered *1st reading* || contorted *2nd reading alt*

19 **I saw him creep**] Such a one crept *alt*

22 **there were**] *enclosed in square brackets*

22 ^ 23] *no line space WLFacs transcript*

23–27] *added in pencil*

23 **impulsions**] *2nd reading* || impulsion *1st reading* || impulses *alt 1st reading, undel*

24 **cried**] said *1st reading*

26 **world**] world" *1st reading*

27 **It**] The world *1st reading* **strange**] such *1st reading (not WLFacs*

transcript)   **revolutions since I died**] catalepsies since I died *1ˢᵗ alt* ‖ revolutions; let me bide *2ⁿᵈ alt* ‖ revolutions; I abide *3ʳᵈ alt*. (*The word "revolutions" in 2ⁿᵈ and 3ʳᵈ alts is followed by a semi-colon, not the colon given in WLFac transcript.*)

27 ^ 28] *turn of leaf, so line spacing uncertain in ms1, although the space after the lines in ink (to 22), in which 23–27 were added in pencil, suggests a discontinuity or even possibly that a new poem begins at 28*

28 **As**] Like *1ˢᵗ reading*   **deaf mute**] blind man *1ˢᵗ reading*

30 **surf is**] surface *1ˢᵗ reading*

Introspection

Published in *March Hare*.

ms1 (Berg): black ink on the fourth page of a loose double leaf of Waldorf Club Newton Mill paper, accompanying Notebook. Prose poem, written only on the left half of the page. The lineation (including hyphenation) is preserved in the present edition. No variants.

The Engine

Published in *March Hare*.

Two manuscripts on loose leaves accompanying Notebook:

ms1 (Berg) = *March Hare A*: pencil first drafts on fourth and second pages of a folded leaf of notepaper headed U.S.M.S. *St. Louis* (with a flag), titled I *The Engine* and II *Machinery: Confetti*, the second changed to II *Machinery: Dancers*.

ms2 (Berg) = *March Hare B*: blind-ruled laid paper matching *The Death of Saint Narcissus ms2*. Fair copy in black ink, with the two parts together now entitled *The Engine* and simply numbered as paragraphs.

Text from *ms2*.

I

hummed] leapt *ms1 1ˢᵗ reading*   **Flat**] The flat *ms1 1ˢᵗ reading*   **along the tiers of chairs in one plane,**] in tiers along *ms1 1ˢᵗ reading* ‖ in one plane along the tiers of chairs, *ms1 2ⁿᵈ reading* ‖ in one plane along the tiers of chairs *ms2 with* deck- *added and del before* chairs   **six-penny**] six penny *ms1*   **The machine was hard, deliberate, and alert; having chosen with motives and ends unknown to cut through the fog it pursued its course;**] The machine was hard, deliberate and alert, cutting through the fog *ms1 1ˢᵗ reading* ‖ The machine having chosen to cut through the fog with motives and ends unknown was hard, deliberate and alert *ms1* ‖ The machine was hard, deliberate, and alert; having chosen ~~for~~ with motives ⁊ ends ~~of its own~~ unknown to cut though the fog it pursued its course; *ms2*   **stirred · · · surface**] *illegible in ms1*   **certain and sufficient as a**] more and more *ms1 1ˢᵗ reading* ‖ certain and self-sufficient eternal [*illegible*] a *2ⁿᵈ reading* ‖ certain self-sufficient ~~like~~ as a *final reading*   **bush,**] bush; *ms1*   **indifferently · · · parasite.**] justifying and accounting for the parasitic aphis. *ms1*   **aimless**] *added ms2*

II

while] as *ms1*   **scuffle**] shuffle *ms1 1ˢᵗ reading (uncertain)*   **The**] *ms1 1ˢᵗ reading, ms2* ‖ And the *ms1*   **ceased**] stopped *ms1 1ˢᵗ reading*   **from the steerage**] *following* tune *ms1 1ˢᵗ reading*   **only to see on the wall a spider taut as a drumhead**] and saw a spider *ms1 1ˢᵗ reading* ‖ to see a spider on the wall at my feet *ms1 2ⁿᵈ reading* (*the added words* on the wall *may have been written after* at my feet *not as an alt, but reiterating that the speaker is in bed*) ‖ to see at my feet a spider on the wall *ms1 final reading* ‖ and saw on the wall a ~~taut~~ spider taut as a drumhead *ms2 1ˢᵗ reading*   **endless**] all the *ms1 1ˢᵗ reading*   **a small**] one small black *ms1*   **drowsily**] confusedly *ms1*   **But**] ~~An~~ But *ms2*   **faces . . ."**] *ms1* ‖ faces . . . *ms2*   **then**] *added in ms1*   **the feet**] then the feet *ms1*

Hidden under the heron's wing

Published in *March Hare*.

ms1 (Berg): pencil on a loose leaf accompanying Notebook.

1 **wing**] wings *1ˢᵗ reading*
2 **lotos-birds sing**] lotos-bird sings *1ˢᵗ reading*
8 **housemaid's**] maid with *1ˢᵗ reading*   **crimson**] scarlet *alt del*

O lord, have patience

Published in *March Hare*.

ms1 (Berg): pencil on lightweight Merchants Pure Bond paper (Carter Rice & Co, Boston), accompanying Notebook. The top two-thirds of the ms page are given to the three widely spaced lines of Dante, each underlined, with TSE's quatrain immediately following the third of these. TSE may have intended to supply verses to follow each of Dante's three lines.

In silent corridors of death

Published in *March Hare*.

ms1 (U. Maryland; now Hornbake Library; formerly McKeldin Library): pencil on ruled leaf. No date assigned by *Rainey*.

7] *not 1ˢᵗ reading*
8–9] *underlined (perhaps for reconsideration)* ‖ *then below the poem, at an angle:*

Suffused light—light from where?
Stifled scent—scent of what?   [2]

Stifled sighs and sighing breath
In vacant corridors of death.   [4]

[4] **vacant**] stifling *alt*

Airs of Palestine, No. 2

Published in *March Hare*.

ts1 (Berg): loose leaf of lightweight typing paper, accompanying Notebook. Ribbon copy annotated by TSE and Pound. With unannotated carbon on the same paper.

Valerie's Own Book: first and third stanzas only (presumably from memory), headed *Lines to the Editor of the Westminster Gazette* and with a note, "(Date uncertain)".

2 **"Take thou this Rod,**] "take thou thy rod *Valerie's Own Book*

3 **Rock";**] rock". *Valerie's Own Book*

5–8] *braced by Pound ts1* ‖ *not Valerie's Own Book*

9 **struck the living Rock,**] smote the living rock, *Valerie's Own Book*

10 **Rock was wet,**] rock was wet; *Valerie's Own Book*

11 **From which henceforth**] From which thenceforth *ts1 1ˢᵗ reading* ‖ And thence, each day *Valerie's Own Book*

13–40] *not Valerie's Own Book*

14 **crawl and writhe**] writhe and crawl *ts1 alt*

16] To Cannon St. and London Wall. *ts1 alt with* London Bridge *as alt to* Cannon St.

20 **Bubble**] They flow *ts1 1ˢᵗ reading*

21–24] *braced by Pound ts1*

23 **Troubling**] They stir *ts1 1ˢᵗ reading*

24 **Mounting**] And mount *ts1* *1ˢᵗ reading* ‖ They mount *March Hare* (*error in transcription of 1ˢᵗ reading*)

39–40] instead of scales to ~~cloud~~ shade their eyes, | They use Spender's gazette. *Pound ts1*

Petit Epître

Published in *March Hare.*

ts1 (Berg): ribbon copy with accents added by hand, on a loose leaf of lightweight typing paper, accompanying Notebook.

No attempt is made here to correct TSE's French.

6–7 **chacals? · · · mâle**] *braced, with "rhyme?"*

21 **aurais**] aurai *1ˢᵗ reading*

25 **promiscuité."**] promiscuité)." *ts1* (*but with no opening bracket*)

27 **qui sert**] par voie *1ˢᵗ reading*

31 **tous,**] tous *1ˢᵗ reading*

44 **dames**] *not TSE's hand* (*perhaps Dulac's?*) ‖ femmes *1ˢᵗ reading, braced with* réclame *in next line, with "rhyme?"* (*del after revision*)

50 **entends**] entend *1ˢᵗ reading*

Tristan Corbière

Published in *March Hare.*

ts1 exists in two copies:

> *ts1a* (Berg): loose leaf of lightweight typing paper, accompanying Notebook. Ribbon copy with accents added by hand.
>
> *ts1b* (Berg): loose leaf of lightweight typing paper, accompanying Notebook. Carbon of *ts1a* annotated by Pound, with, pinned to it, a scrap of paper with an alternative version, in TSE's hand, of 12–14. Accents added by hand.

No attempt is made here to correct TSE's French.

1 **cinquième**] *with "cinquième on the côte or in Paris?? or the mer in his d*[   ]*" Pound ts1b* (*leaf torn*)

3 **sa**] la *ts1, with "s" written over "l" ts1b* (*March Hare mistakes the order of these readings*)

5 **des**] de *Pound ts1b* (*correcting TSE's French*)

7 **quelques trous**] *del Pound ts1b* ‖ le verrou *alt ts1b*

10 **au Luxembourg**] aux jardins *alt, del in ts1b by Pound, who ringed* Luxembourg *with "Avenue Champs Elysèe, ou a L'Etoile—before the clubs in the C.E. next door to Pres. Fallieres back yard"*

11 **clignant**] lorgnant *alt ts1a (with* clignant *ringed). Beneath his marginal comment on* 10, *Pound wrote "or Cafè de la Paix if they are going to clign very heavily" ts1b*

12–14] *alt on scrap of paper:*

> Telle sur le boulevarde une ancienne grue
> Le Lieutenant Loti, très bien dans sa tenue
> Fait le trottoirs dans les pages des complaisants revues

13–14] *with "? promène au coin" Pound ts1b*

14] *ringed with arrow to move before* 12 *Pound ts1b*

Ode ("Tired. | Subterrene")

Published in *AraVP* but not *US 1920*. Reprinted in James E. Miller, *T. S. Eliot's Personal Waste Land: Exorcism of the Demons* (1977); Vicki Mahaffey in *American Literature* Jan 1979; H. A. Mason in *Cambridge Quarterly* Apr 1990; then *March Hare* (from *ts1*).

ts1 (Berg): ribbon copy and carbon, each on a single leaf of lightweight typing paper, accompanying Notebook. Some inadvertent indenting.

ts2 (Berg): purple carbon of a later version, on a loose leaf of lightweight wove typing paper, accompanying Notebook. Both paper and typing match *Gerontion ts2*.

Text from *AraVP*.

Title] Ode | on Independence Day, July 4th 1918. *ts1*

Epigraph] *not ts1*

1 ^ 2] *line space ts1*

5] *stepped but with no line space ts*

8 ^ 9] *line space ts1*

13 **Hymenæe**] Hymenaee *tss*

14] Sullen succuba suspired *ts1 1ˢᵗ reading*

15 ^ 16] *line space ts1*

The Death of the Duchess

Published in *WLFacs*.

ts1 (Berg; *WLFacs* 104–107): two loose leaves of lightweight typing paper with horizontal chainlines but no watermark (matching *Gerontion ts3*). Ribbon copy with annotations in ink (by TSE or possibly Vivien Eliot?), then in pencil by Pound. On verso of second leaf, in pencil:

Encounter

—

Imprisonment
Flight   Meeting
Afterwards

Giving these words in a footnote in *WLFacs* (where they are not shown in facsimile), Valerie Eliot added: "These words may refer to the plot of John Webster's *The Duchess of Malfi*." Previously, *Gallup 1968* had noted they were "possibly, as Mrs Eliot suggests, an outline for *La Figlia Che Piange*". Browning's *The Flight of the Duchess* (for which see Commentary to *The Death of the Duchess* II 7–10, 16–17) was followed by *Meeting at Night*.

Title] *added in ink in cramped capitals*

Part numbers] *added in pencil, perhaps by Vivien Eliot (though attrib. to Pound in WLFacs)*

I 1–8] **"have silk hats · · · last is gone | They"** *ringed with empty box above by Pound*

I 5 **feel**] feel a *1ˢᵗ reading*

I 10–13] *braced by Pound*

I 10 **for you and me**] *ringed by Pound*

I 12 **do**] *with "?" added*

I 13] *ringed by Pound*

I 14–15] *del by Pound*

I ^ II] *rule (perhaps by Vivien Eliot) with* II *and again* II. *in margin*

II 1] In the evening *and* people hang upon the bridge rail *marked for transposition, Pound*

II 5 **Dogs'**] Dogs *ts*   **eyes**] heads *1ˢᵗ reading*

II 6 **in**] *not 1ˢᵗ reading*

II 9] *ringed with "?" by TSE, then bracketed by Pound*

II 15–16] *braced by both TSE and Pound*

II 16 **and other bird things**] *within open box by Pound*

II 17 **but no wings.**] *within open box by Pound*

II 19 **floor**] *underlined with double loop by Pound*

II 22] *braced ts*   **into**] like *1ˢᵗ reading*

II 23 *cause*] *ringed in ts with "~~antiquated~~" Pound (Valerie Eliot reads: "~~anticipate?~~"?, adding "very doubtful reading" WLFacs)*

II 25 **were**] *within open box with "x" by Pound*

II 28 **tails—**] tails *1ˢᵗ reading*

II 31] *braced with "Pruf-" by Pound*

II 33] *braced with "cadence reproduction from Pr. or Por [Prufrock or Portrait of a Lady]" Pound*   **should we**] we should *Pound*

II 39 **with one more**] *underlined by Pound*

II 41 ^ 42] *chevron with "rhythm ?" by Pound*

II 44 **This and this**] *underlined with "?? particularize" and zigzag by Pound*

II 49 **Pressing**] *over earlier reading (perhaps Passing)*

II 54 **found**] *with "i" in ink above (for find) by TSE, del by Pound*

II 55 **turned**] *with "(?)" in pencil by TSE, del by Pound*

II 57–58] *bracketed and del by Pound*

Song ("The golden foot I may not kiss or clutch")

Published as *Song to the Opherian* in *Tyro* Apr 1921, with the pseudonym "Gus Krutzsch"; then *WLFacs* from *ts1*, where the typed title *Song for the Opherion* has been reduced to a single word, probably by Pound (though the deletion is assigned to TSE in *WLFacs*).

ts1 (Berg; *WLFacs* 98/99): loose leaf of British Bond laid paper. Ribbon copy with revisions by TSE and Pound.

ts Aiken (Huntington): fair copy in the Aiken collection, on Eaton's Corrassable Bond, a paper characteristic of the 1950s and 1960s. No variants from printed text.

The present edition gives not the text published in *Tyro* but that of *ts1* as it was subsequently left by TSE and Pound.

Title] Song to the Opherian *Tyro* ‖ Song for the Opherion *ts1, with last three words del probably by Pound*

  2 ^ 3] Perhaps it does not come to very much *Tyro, ts1 1st reading (bracketed and del by Pound ts1 with zigzag and "georgian")*

  5 ^ 6] *no line space Tyro*

  6] *short indent Tyro*   **Waiting a touch a breath**] Waiting that touch. *Tyro* ‖ Waiting that touch *ts1 1st reading* ‖ Waiting that touch that breath *ts1 2nd reading*

  7 **bells**] bells, *Tyro*

  9–10] *braced by Pound ts1 (although WLFacs takes the brace to cover 8–11 and erroneously gives the appearance of a line space 10 ^ 11)*

  11 **an alien**] the alien *Tyro* ‖ the sullen *ts1 1st reading with* sullen *ringed by TSE with* an alien? *as alt and with the* and sullen *each separately del by Pound* ‖ a Pound *ts1, perhaps itself del Pound. The marks and their order are uncertain, so intermediate combinations are possible. Pound's final reading is probably simply* a *and TSE's final reading (preferred in the present edition) is* an alien *but this itself is an alt*

  12 **campfire**] campfires *ts1 1st reading with last letter del Pound*   **spears**] spears. *Tyro*

after 12] *line space followed by*

> Waiting that touch
> After thirty years

ts1, with the lines del probably by Pound (the terminal stop in WLFacs is erroneous).
attribution] GUS KRUTZSCH *Tyro*

Elegy

Published in *WLFacs*.

ms1 (Berg; *WLFacs* 116/17). Small leaf of Hieratica Bond wove paper, torn from the same notebook as *The Waste Land ms2*, and apparently at the same time (*WLComposite* 429–74). See the Commentary headnote to *The Waste Land*, 1. COMPOSITION.

Title] *not 1ˢᵗ reading*

  2 **a**] *the 1ˢᵗ reading*

  3] *chevron before line*

  7 **Were't**] But *1ˢᵗ reading*   **a**] *the 1ˢᵗ reading*

  8 **always**] very *1ˢᵗ reading*

  10 **sepulchral**] *the 1ˢᵗ reading*   **flung**] thrown *1ˢᵗ reading*

  19 **poison**] interfere *1ˢᵗ reading*   **not**] not with *1ˢᵗ reading*   **present**] *not 1ˢᵗ reading* ‖ nightly *2ⁿᵈ reading*

  20 **charnel**] charnal *ms1 (not recorded in WLFacs)*

  23 **His**] The *1ˢᵗ reading*   **anger**] pity *1ˢᵗ reading* ‖ horror *2ⁿᵈ reading* ‖ passion *3ʳᵈ reading*   **desire**] of ire *1ˢᵗ reading*

  24 **Approach**] a *1ˢᵗ reading (written over)*

Dirge

Published in *WLFacs*.

ms1 (Berg; *WLFacs* 118/19): rough pencil draft on verso of *Elegy*.

ms2 (Berg; *WLFacs* 120/21): black ink fair copy on Pound's quad-ruled paper, marked by Pound "*??* doubtful". Paper, ink and hand match *The Waste Land ms5*, the fair copies of Part IV (*WLFacs* 54–61).

Text from *ms2*.

  3 **jew's**] jew's / man's *alt readings ms1, or possibly* Jew's / man's   **eyes!**] *exclamation mark apparently a second thought ms1*

4–5] *no indent ms1*

4 **eat**] nibb *ms1 1ˢᵗ reading*

6 **suffer**] suffers *ms1 1ˢᵗ reading*   **sea-change**] sea change *ms1*

9, 11–15] *no indent ms1*

10] *brackets perhaps added as a second thought ms1*

11 **stare**] lo *ms1 1ˢᵗ reading*

13 **Roll**] Stir *ms1 1ˢᵗ reading*

15 **gold in**] black yellow +

16 **Lobsters hourly**] Sea nymphs nightly *ms1 1ˢᵗ reading*   **keep close**] *ms1 final reading, ms2* ‖ *[two illegible words, the first perhaps beginning* wai-*] ms1 1ˢᵗ reading* (wai/tend his *very doubtful reading WLFacs*) ‖ keep the *ms1 2ⁿᵈ reading*

17 **Hark!**] Hark *ms1*   scratch   scratch   scratch] *no extra word spacing but with these words half a line lower than the rest of the line ms1*

Those are pearls that were his eyes. See!

Published in *WLFacs*.

ms1 (Berg; *WLFacs* 122/23): rough pencil draft on loose leaf of British Bond wove paper.

2 **clambers through**] shelters in *1ˢᵗ reading*   **big**] fat *1ˢᵗ reading*

3 **him,**] him, purple, red, *1ˢᵗ reading*

5 **and**] ℀ *ms1*

Exequy

Published in *WLFacs*.

ts1 (Berg; *WLFacs* 100–103): ribbon copy from second typewriter, with pencil and ink annotations by Pound and further rough drafting in pencil by TSE on verso. Loose leaf of Verona Linen paper (matching *The Waste Land ts3*, which is also annotated by Pound in both pencil and ink).

9 **lithe, forever**] gracious, ever *1ˢᵗ reading*

10 **shall**] sg *1ˢᵗ reading*

11 **maids;**] maids, *1ˢᵗ reading*

12 **cordial**] constant *1ˢᵗ reading with* "cordial OK." *Pound*

14 **but not**] nor yet *alt Pound*

15 **fountain**] *within open box Pound*

15–21] *verso of ts has pencilled lines originally considered "an untitled poem"* (*Gallup 1968*) *but later seen to relate to this stanza* (*WLFacs 102/103*). *Order of composition uncertain* (*but TSE presumably wanted seven lines rhyming ABBCACA*).
initial state:

> Where the m. waters fall
> In conduits led between the trees
> Down ornamental terraces

revised state:

> Pudibund, in the clinging vine
> The adepts grouped in 2ˢ and 3ˢ
> Are scattered underneath the trees
> Down ornamental terraces

with **adepts**] votaries *emendation del* ‖ mystics / adepts *2ⁿᵈ emendation alts* ‖ *final state*:

> Pudibund, in the clinging vine
> ~~Where the m. waters fall~~
> ~~The adepts grouped in 2ˢ and 3ˢ~~
> ~~In conduits led between~~ the trees
> Are scattered underneath [the trees]
> ~~Down ornamental terraces~~
> The smooth mel. waters fall,
> Where am. adepts recline

17 **Adepts twine**] *chevron added between words Pound*

18 **The**] In *with "In sacramental" Pound*

19–21] *bracketed with "This is Laforgue not XVIII" Pound*

20] *indented in ts*   **some**] an *Pound*

21 **Of ^ fireworks**] the (*perhaps to replace "Of"?*) *Pound*   **or**] *del Pound*   **waltz**]
WLFacs transcription ‖ walz *ts1*

24 **Shall**] *del Pound*

25 **The colour**] With colours *Pound* (*who ringed* The *and* the)

27 **Just at**] *ringed with* Upon *alt added TSE, with* Just at *then del Pound*   **he shall**]
ringed and del Pound

27] ⊲ (——) *at the c.[risis]* hear *alt Pound*

29 **SOVEGNA VOS A TEMPS DE MON DOLOR**] *1ˢᵗ reading, del but probably also the final reading* ‖ Consiros *vei* la pasada folor. *2ⁿᵈ reading del*   **A**] AL *ts*   **MON**]
SON *Pound*

The Builders

No. 107 in Cramer's Library of Unison and Part-Songs by Modern Composers, ed. Martin Shaw; words by T. S. Eliot, music by Martin Shaw.

ms1 (Bodleian): pencil drafts and typescripts of several versions, including three stanzas printed neither in *The Builders* nor in *The Rock*. Not collated here.

ts Chamb (BL): Lord Chamberlain's Papers (see Commentary to *Choruses from "The Rock"* headnote, 5. PERFORMANCE).

proof (U. Virginia): bound proof of *The Rock*.

The Rock (1934), where verses are inset.

theatre programme (1934).

St. Stephen: Gallup E4ac: *St. Stephen, South Kensington, S.W.7* service sheet (BL; King's). Each pair of lines in the verses is printed as a single line, losing a capital letter in each case, except "Churches" (12). The refrain is indented.

Text from Cramer's Library.

Subtitle] *ts Chamb, Rock* || *not ts Chamb, Rock, St Stephen*

   7 **Island**] *ts Chamb, Rock* || island *programme*   **Water**] Water, *Rock* || water *programme*

   8 **House**] *ts Chamb, Rock* || house *programme*   **our**] Our *Rock*

   9 **Church**] *ts Chamb, Rock* || church *ts Chamb*

  10 **even**] *ts Chamb, Rock* || ever *ts Chamb, proof* (*where the same reading is found in this refrain in the final line of the play*)

21–28] *ts Chamb, Rock*:

> Shall arms hang straight
> With fingers unbent
> While voices debate
> Of money misspent
> And the coverless bed
> And the fireless grate
> And the lamp unfed?
> How late shall we wait?

Mr. Pugstyles: The Elegant Pig

ts1 (Houghton): first three stanzas only, with ms corrections. With *ms1* of *Usk* on the verso, suggesting a date around June 1935. With a typed transcript by Henry Eliot.

ts2 (Houghton): first three stanzas only. Carbon fair copy from around the same time as *ts1* but on a different typewriter, with note in unknown hand "Unpublished poem by T. S. Eliot". Given to Harvard by Henry Eliot's widow, presumably having been sent to Henry.

ts3 (BL): the whole poem, on two leaves, sent to the Tandys. Undated.

ts4 (Valerie Eliot collection): the whole poem, on two leaves with some ms corrections. In the title and verses, "Mr. Pugstyles" is typed with a space between the words, unlike *ts1–ts3* (which have "Mr.Pugstyles"), so suggesting that *ts4* was made substantially later.

ts5 (Houghton): on two leaves, sent to Mary Trevelyan, 23 Dec 1946. "Mr. Pugstyles" typed with space between the words.

ms1 (Valerie Eliot collection): fair copy, dating from 1950s, on blanks and rear free endpaper of the copy of the *Practical Cats* first edition containing *emendations B*. No indents except at stepped lines and 19. With short rules between stanzas, and full stop occasionally missing after "Mr" (not specified below). Apparently copied from *ts4*.

ts Turner (untraced): TSE wrote to the voice teacher J. Clifford Turner on 8 Mar 1935 promising "copies of *Mr. Pugstyles* and *The Difficulties of a Statesman* as soon as I have time to make copies, or have copies made. The former is unpublished, and the latter has never been published in this country. Meanwhile, I am sending Miss Thirburn the only available copy of the former. Perhaps she would let you take a copy off that."

Both *ts1* and *ts2* indent alternate lines in each of their three stanzas, breaking the penultimate line of each stanza into two lines, both deeply indented.

Text from *ts5*.

Title] *ts4 2nd reading, ms1* ‖ Mr. Pugstyles *ts1–ts3* ‖ Mr. Pugstyles: The Worcestershire Pig *ts3, ts4 1st reading* ‖ *untitled ts5*

  2 **foreign bred**] foreign-born *ts1 1st reading* ‖ foreign-bred *ts1–ts3*   **pigs**] Pigs *ts1* ‖ pig *ts5*   **which**] what *ts3*   **disdains;**] disdains, *ts1, ts2, ms1* ‖ disdains— *ts3*

  3 **their · · · their**] your · · · your *ts3, ts4, ms1*

  4 **Their**] Your *ts3, ts4, ms1*   **and**] their *ts1, ts2* ‖ burly blonde *ts3*   **burly blond**] blond burly *ts1, ts2* ‖ burly blonde *ts3*

  5 **I**] *I ts3*   **says**] say *ts1, ts2*

  6 **defiles:**] defiles; *ts2, ms1* ‖ defiles. *ts3*

  7 **pig what**] Pig who *ts1, ts2*

  8 *as also* 31 **heavyweight,**] porker, our *ts1–ts3* ‖ champion, *ts4, ms1*

  9, *as also* 19, 61] *two lines ts3*

 10 **What a wonderful pig is**] Such an Elegant Pig is *ts1, ts2* ‖ Our Worcestershire porker, *ts3* ‖ Our Worcestershire champion, *ts4 1st reading* ‖ What an elegant pig is *ts4 2nd reading, ms1*

 11 **ends**] toes *ts1 1st and final reading, ts2–ts4, ms1* ‖ tips *ts1 2nd reading*

 12 **He's**] He is *ts1 1st reading*   **enough to make**] such as makes *ts1, ts2*   **other**] of his *ts4*   **champions**] porkers *ts1–ts3* ‖ rivals *ts4*

 13] He takes all the blue ribbons and all the gold medals *ts1 1st reading* ‖ He's won the blue ribbons, he's won the gold medals *ts1, ts2*

 14 **our grand**] at our *ts1 1st reading* ‖ our own *ts4*

 16 **underbred swine only**] heavyweight champions *ts1, ts2*

 17 **trim**] cut *ts1 1st reading, circled with* trim ? *ts1* ‖ cut *ts2*

 18 **perfections**] distinction *ts1, ts2* ‖ perfection *ts3*

 20 **Our Worcestershire heavyweight,**] What an elegant pig is our *ms1*   **heavyweight,**] porker, our *ts1–ts3* ‖ champion, *ts4*

21–24] *ts1, ts2*:

> Not in rural Chalk Farm or at Camberwell Green,
> Or at shady Nine Elms or in sweet Maida Vale,
> Or at Highbury Barn can such porkers be seen, [3]
> Or where cows graze in remote Notting Dale.

[4] **cows**] cattle *ts1 1st reading* ‖ the cows *ts1 final reading*

21 **Highbury Barn,**] shady Nine Elms *ts4, ms1*   **in sweet Maida Vale,**] in sweet Maida Vale *ts4 2nd reading, ms1* ‖ remote Notting Dale, *ts3* ‖ ~~in rural Chalk~~ *ts4 1st reading*

22 **shady Nine Elms**] rural Chalk Farm *ts4, ms1*   **such porkers**] his equal *ts4, ms1*

23 **rural Chalk Farm**] Highbury Barn *ts4, ms1*   **remote Notting Dale,**] remote Notting Dale *ts4, ms1* ‖ in sweet Maida Vale, *ts3*

24] Or where the pigs graze *ts4 1st reading*   **the cows**] cattle *ts4 1st reading*

25 **No**] No, *ts1–ts4, ms1*   **Old**] old *ts2*   **Jewry,**] Jewry *ts4*

27] Not in the sweet-smelling haunts of Old Drury, *ts1 1st reading* ‖ Not where the styes smell so sweet by Old Drury *ts1 2nd reading* ‖ Not in the sweet-smelling styes of Old Drury *ts1 2nd reading alt del* ‖ Not where the styes are so sweet by Old Drury *ts1*   **stys**] *ts4, ts5, ms1* ‖ styes *ts1–ts3*

28 **where the hogs roll**] where the Pigs trot *ts1 1st reading* ‖ little Pigs run *ts1 2nd reading* ‖ or where the shoats . . . *ts1 3rd reading* ‖ where the Hogs roll *ts1* ‖ where the pigs trot *ts2*   **Cheapside**] Cheapside, *ts1 1st reading, ts2*

29–30] *one line ts4, ms1*

29 **Can**] Will *ts1, ts2*   **find**] see *ts1–ts3*   **pig**] Pig, *ts1, ts2* ‖ pig, *ts4, ms1*

30 **No**] No, *ts2* ‖ no *ts4* ‖ no, *ms1*   **pig**] Pig *ts1, ts2*

32 **week,**] week— *ts3* ‖ week *ts4*

33 **do;**] do, *ts4*

34 **come**] came *ts4*   **speak**] speak: *ts3*

35, *as also* 36 **their selves**] themselves *ts3, ts4, ms1*

36 **croak.**] croak— *ts3* ‖ croak, *ts4* ‖ croak *ms1*

37 **So**] Then *ts3* ‖ Till *ts4, ms1*   **Wheatsheaf**] Angel *ts4, ms1*

38 **Angel**] Wheatsheaf *ts4, ms1*

39 **pint,**] pint *ts4, ms1*   **more,**] more *ms1*

40 **roar:**] roar *ms1*

41] "Mr Pugstyles! We want Pugstyles! *ms1* ‖ Mr. Pugstyles, ~~Mr Pug~~ *ts4 1st reading* ‖ Mr. Pugstyles! We want Pugstyles! *ts4*

42] We won't have any member but Mr Pugstyles!" *ms1 1st reading* ‖ The man for our money is Mr Pugstyles!" *ms1* ‖ The man for our money is Mr. Pugstyles"! *ts4*   **a wonderful**] an elegant *ts3*

43 **Then**] They *ts5*   **choke**] choak *ts3, ts4, ms1*

44 **Wheatsheaf**] Angel *ts3, ts4, ms1*

45 **Angel**] Wheatsheaf *ts3, ts4, ms1*   **Oak,**] Oak— *ts3* ‖ Oak; *ts4, ms1*

46 **come**] came *ts3*   **door;**] door— *ts3* ‖ door. *ts4, ms1*
47 **town hall**] Town Hall *ts3, ts4, ms1*
48 **miles,**] miles; *ts3*
49] And then suddenly somebody started to bawl: *ts3*   **bust out**] started *ts4, ms1*
50–52] *all capitals ts3*
50] *not ts4, ms1*   **Pugstyles.**] PUGSTYLES! *ts3*
51] MR. PUGSTYLES, | MR. PUGSTYLES, *ts3 (two lines)* ‖ "Mr. Pugstyles! We want Pugstyles! *ts4, ms1*
52 **Pugstyles".**] PUGSTYLES!" *ts3* ‖ Pugstyles!" *ts4, ms1*
53 **vote**] vote, *ts3, ts4*
54 **him, and**] him and *ts3, ts4, ms1*   **milk,**] milk *ms1*
55 **hat,**] hat *ts3, ts4, ms1*
57 **So**] And *ts4, ms1*   **quiet**] happy *ts4, ms1*   **alone**] alone, *ts3, ts4, ms1*
58 **wiles.**] wiles; *ts4*
59 **own,**] own *ts3, ms1*
62] Our WORCESTERSHIRE Porker, our Mr. PUGSTYLES. *ts3*   **heavyweight**] champion *ts4, ms1*

Bellegarde

ts1 (Houghton): two leaves, with pencilled additions on the first, which is then entirely cancelled.

Title] *not 1ˢᵗ reading*
4–7] *not 1ˢᵗ reading*
5 **imagination**] *edge of leaf, so a terminal comma may have been intended*
11] Too light for pleasure. *beside the line, perhaps as alt or to insert 10 ^ 11*
11 ^ 12] *new leaf, although more than half of the first is blank*

The Anniversary

ts1 (Beinecke): single leaf of Faber stationery, with ink addition in TSE's hand of "In memoriam | June 6th, 1935" at head, and signed at foot. Four pencilled variants, making the poem suitable for a different occasion, are probably but not certainly by TSE. Donald Gallup's catalogue of his own collection specifies: "Purchased Goodspeed's 1972."

5 **practised**] practiced *1ˢᵗ reading*
13 **the Dr.**] Miss Emily *pencil variant*

17 **him**] her *pencil variant*

19 **firkins**] pail *pencil variant*

20 **DOCTOR PERKINS**] Emily Hale *pencil variant*

A Valedictory

Forbidding Mourning: to the Lady of the House

Recited 28 Sept 1935.

ms1 (Bodleian): fair copy in ink addressed "To Mrs. John Carroll Perkins, Stamford House, Chipping Campden, Glos." and written on the versos of four leaves of her headed notepaper. Also present is a flyer for Mrs. Carroll Perkins's garden lectures "for the season of 1929–1930", one of which was "An Illustrated Garden Lecture for Children: Flowers; Fairies; Birds; Songs. Miss Emily Hale assisting." TSE to Donald Gallup, 15 Sept 1961: "I don't remember whether there was any holograph copy of those verses or not. I should think it quite likely that the verses in possession of the Bodleian library were as near to the original draft as there was. But I cannot think why Mrs. Perkins sent them to the Bodleian, or what reason there was for imposing any prohibition on their inspection. I would like to see a copy of them myself. [*Footnote*: Perhaps she never sent them to the Bodleian! But I covet a copy for Valerie's collection!]"

ts1 (Beinecke): ribbon copy on two leaves, folded in quarters. Inscribed in black ink at head: "(to Mrs John Carroll Perkins, | Stamford House, | Campden, Glos. | 28. ix. 35)", and signed by TSE at foot. Bought at Seven Gables Bookshop, June 1961, by Donald Gallup, who subsequently typed a copy to send to TSE "for Valerie's collection" (*Gallup 1988* 116).

ts2 (Beinecke): later typed copy with American spelling, by Mrs. Perkins, on three leaves, emended by TSE and signed "T. S. Eliot | for | Mrs. John Carroll Perkins | July 18, 1946." Bought by Gallup, Seven Gables Bookshop, June 1961. Evidently copied from *ts1*, from which "Your" (27) is taken, but then corrected by TSE to "Their". It has no independent authority, and several errors by Mrs. Perkins (mostly of punctuation) are not noted. Most were corrected by TSE, who also bracketed and then deleted 43–44, and bracketed the final couplet (taken from *ts1*). With a further typed copy using American spelling, on five small leaves, prepared by a member of the Perkins family (variants not noted here).

mss Perkins (Beinecke): rough pencil copy on three leaves, probably by Mrs. Perkins, noting in ink TSE's omission of 43–44 and the final couplet (taken from *ts1*) when reading aloud at Petersham, Massachusetts, 18 July 1946. Bought by Gallup, Seven Gables Bookshop, June 1961. With a further ms copy by Mrs. Perkins in green ink, on both sides of two notebook leaves. As these mss have no independent authority, variants are not noted.

Text from *ms1*.

Subtitle **Mourning:**] Mourning *ts2, with comma added by TSE*

   4 **yet**] yet. *ts1*

   9 **violas and**] dahlias and the *ts1 1ˢᵗ reading*

 11] *typed, then del, then retyped beneath ts1*

 16 ^ 17] Yet summer lingers with us still *ts1 del*

 20 ^ 21 *as also* 30 ^ 31] *line space only ts1*

 25 **they**] you *ts1 pencilled 2ⁿᵈ reading, erased*

 27 **Their**] Your *ts1 pencilled 2ⁿᵈ reading, erased*

 35 **stems**] roots *ts1 1ˢᵗ reading*

 36 **long**] *ts1 1ˢᵗ and final reading* ‖ dull *ts1 2ⁿᵈ reading*

 38 **calm**] long *ts1 1ˢᵗ reading*

 41 **Dare**] Will *ts1 1ˢᵗ reading*

 42 ^ 43] *new leaf so line spacing indeterminate ts1*

 44 **Remembers**] Remembers. *ms1*

 44 ^ 45] *line space, then* Green earth forgets, one says *all del, then another line space ts1*

 46 **memories;**] memories, *ts1*

 47 **ghosts**] ghosts, *ts1 1ˢᵗ reading*

 48 **Of dear and**] Remember *ts1 1ˢᵗ reading*

 51 **came,**] came *ts1*

 52 **same.**] same; *ts1*

after 58]

> In conclusion, I wish to express my grateful thanks
> For your patient attention, and forbearance with my pranks.

ts1 (with 1ˢᵗ reading ending endurance of my pranks.)*, ts2 (bracketed by TSE)*

Pollicle Dogs and Jellicle Cats

ts1 (Faber archive): typescript on four leaves with three other leaves of pencil sketches.

ts2 (Brotherton): to Bonamy Dobrée, 11 July 1934, closes with 1–5 (only), followed by three asterisks and then *I have teeth, which are False & Quite Beautiful*.

Text from *ts1*.

Title] *not ts1, ts2*

   1 **at**] in *ts2*   **The Princess Louise,**] *The Princess Louise, ts1* the Princess Louise *ts2*

   2, 4, 5] *indented ts2*

   3 **had ordered**] was eating *ts2*   **peas,**] peas; *ts2*

10 **I've**] have *ts1 1st reading*

15 **work**] trade *ts1 1st reading*

50–51] *typed at end of stanza as "variant" ts1*:

>   He will make lightning sketches without any labour,
>   Of slim Mr. Stewart or Stout Mr. Faber

64 **at**] with *ts1 1st reading*

The Country Walk

Published in *The Times* 6 June 2009 from *ts1*.

ts1 (Morley family album): sent to the Morleys and reproduced in "The Family News", as seen in BBC *Arena* documentary 2009. Signed at foot, "T. S. Eliot".

ts2 (Princeton): single leaf, with later comment at foot by E. H. [Emily Hale]: "Written, I think, the summer of '37 or '38, while visiting at Stamford House, Chipping Campden, Glos, where T. S. E. visited my uncle and aunt (Rev. & Mrs John Carroll Perkins D.D.) and where we often took long walks in the country about Gloucestershire." (Shown in Donald Gallup's exhibition of TSE's writings, Yale University Library, Feb–Mar 1937, though not listed in the catalogue.)

ts3 (BL): letter to Polly Tandy, dated "4 December [1936]", on *Criterion* stationery. "Mrs. Tandy ma'am here's a Poem I was just inspired to write; yes it came just like that, but as you will see it's only suitable for adults Cert A. [film classification "for Adults"] and when you read it you will see why. Anyway it will show you I do now & then write a poem for Adults. It is called "THE COUNTRY WALK. | In the form of an Epistle to a Lady."

ts4 (King's): signed typescript, apparently the last, sent to Hayward, 6 Dec 1936. In his next *London Letter*, Hayward wrote: "Mr. Eliot is composing nonsense verses and has written me a verse-epistle about cows", *New York Sun* 19 Dec 1936.

ms1 (Valerie Eliot collection): fair copy in fluent hand, probably late 1950s, omitting 5–8, 13–16, 21–24. Untitled.

ms2 (Valerie Eliot collection): fair copy from the 1950s, on flyleaf of the copy of the *Practical Cats* first edition which contains *emendations B*. Probably copied from *ms1*, and with the same omissions. An additional secretarial fair copy typescript is textually identical except in lacking the accent on "sanctúary" (33) and beginning the next line with a capital.

Valerie's Own Book: fair copy on two pages, with the same omissions as the other mss.

Text from *ts4*.

Title] not *ms1* ‖ Cows *ts1* ‖ The Cows: a Pastoral *ms2* ‖ Of Cows: A Poem *Valerie's Own Book*

Subtitle] not *ts1, mss* ‖ *last nine words not ts4 1st reading* ‖ An Epistle to Miss

E— H— with the humble Compliments of her obliged servant, the Author. *ts2* ‖
In the form of an Epistle to a Lady. *ts3*   **Tatlow,**] Tatlow. *ts4 1ˢᵗ reading*

1 **Of all**] Among *ts2*   **beasts**] Beasts *ms2*

2 **land**] land, *ts1, ts2, ms1*

3 **most of all**] cordially *ts3*   **dislike**] distrust *mss*   **Cows.**] Cows: *ts1, ms2,*
Valerie's Own Book ‖ Cows— *ts2, ts3*

4 **do not**] cannot *mss*   **understand.**] understand *ms1*

5–8] *not mss*

7 **bear—**] bear, *ts2*

11 **Bus**] Bus, *ts1–ts3* ‖ Bus— *mss*

12 **stare.**] stare! *ms2*

13–16] *not mss*

14 **scorns:**] scorns; *ts1*

17 **But**] And *ms1 2ⁿᵈ reading*   **I'm terrified**] I am afraid *ts1–ts3* ‖ I fear the Cows
ms1, Valerie's Own Book ‖ I fear the Cow *ms2*

18 **tweeds,**] tweeds *Valerie's Own Book*

20 **stopping to discuss the**] pointing out the different *ts2, ts3, mss*

21–24] *not mss*

21 **mild**] mild, *ts1, ts3*

22 **stone they throw,**] stick they throw; *ts1–ts3*

23 **City Child,**] town-bred child *ts1* ‖ town-bred Child *ts2, ts3*

25 **But**] BUT *ts2*   **in lanes alone**] in fields *alone ts1* ‖ in lanes *alone ts2* ‖ in lanes
alone *ts3* ‖ alone abroad *mss*   **stroll,**] stroll *mss*

26 **O then in vain**] Oh then in vain *ts1, ms2, Valerie's Own Book* ‖ In vain at me
ms1   **tossed,**] tossed; *ts2, ms1* ‖ tost. *Valerie's Own Book*

27 **their bloodshot**] their stupid *ms1, ms2* ‖ at me their *Valerie's Own Book*   **roll,**]
roll— *ts1, ts2, ms1, Valerie's Own Book* ‖ roll. *ms2*

28 **boast.**] boast! *ts2*

29 **wall,**] hedge *ts1–ts3, ms1, ms2* ‖ hedge, *Valerie's Own Book*   **five-barred**]
5 barred *ms1*   **gate,**] gate *ts3, mss*

30 **stray;**] stray, *ms1, Valerie's Own Book*

31] In vain their prongs may lie in wait, *ts1* ‖ Their deadly prongs in vain may
wait— *ts2* ‖ Their deadly prongs may lie in wait, *ts3* ‖ In vain for me they lie in
wait— *ms1, ms2* ‖ For me in vain they lie in wait— *Valerie's Own Book*

32 **But**] For *ts1, ts2, ms2, Valerie's Own Book*   **away!**] away. *ts3*

32 ^ 33] *line space Valerie's Own Book*

33–34] *indented ts1, mss*

33 **could**] can *ts1–ts3, mss*   **sanctuary**] sanctúary *ts1, ts3 (superimposed mark to
indicate four full syllables, as in TSE's recordings of Little Gidding II 23), mss*

34 **any**] friendly *ts2, ts3, mss*

I am asked by my friend, the Man in White Spats

ts1 (BL): letter to Alison Tandy, 6 Jan 1937.

11 **the Man in White Spats**] my friend *1ˢᵗ reading*

A Proclamation

ts1 (Valerie Eliot collection): sent to John Hayward, 27 Jan 1937, asking him to "Please return it with any marginal notes you think fit to make." The inked name "Roger Roughton" (with florid "R"s) is probably in TSE's disguised hand.

26 **bring down the sky;**] ~~proclaim,~~ *ts1*

A Practical Possum

Printed in an edition of eighty copies in 1947. Only sixty copies had been authorised, and twenty were subsequently destroyed at TSE's insistence (*Gallup 1988* 103; see Commentary). No lines indented.

ms1 (Houghton): pencil draft on four notebook leaves ruled in blue, folded roughly in four for posting. Formerly owned by Henry Eliot. The leaves are from the same notebook as the ms of *Rannoch, by Glencoe* sent by TSE to Henry in 1937. They are accompanied by a typed transcript by Henry, of no independent authority, so not collated below. The margin of *ms1* wavers, with only 10 and 12 indented.

ts1 (Houghton): 1–42 only on a single leaf, folded in four for posting, given to Harvard by Henry Eliot's widow, with "Unpublished poem by T. S. Eliot" in what is presumably her hand. Later, Valerie Eliot added: "It was printed in a private limited edition VE". A second leaf was presumably once present. The following lines (only) are inset: 5–8, 13–16, 22–23, 32–33. Date unknown.

ts2 (BL): fair copy on two leaves, with drawing at head of a satisfied possum in a pie-dish with a sandwich on a plate. Folded in six and sent to the Tandy family. Date unknown.

Text from *ts2*. (Both typescripts appear to be more revised than *1947*, but only *ts2* is complete and was certainly typed by TSE.)

Title] *not ms1, ts2* ‖ The Practical Possum *1947, ts1*
   1 **Pye,**] Pye* *ts1* (*asterisk perhaps for a footnote now lost*)
   3 **walked**] went *ms1, 1947, ts1*   **Glass**] glass *ms1, 1947, ts1*   **Eye**] eye *ms1, 1947, ts1*

4 **Clerical Hat**] clerical hat *ms1, 1947, ts1*   **gaiters.**] gaiters *ts1*

5 **For**] And *ms1 1st reading*

6 **observed;**] observed: *1947*

7 **said:**] said, *ms1, 1947, ts1*   **"What**] What *1947*   **Charming**] charming *ms1, 1947, ts1*   **Smile**] smile *ts1*

8 **And isn't he**] He's remarkably *ms1, 1947, ts1*   **Preserved!"**] Preserved". *ms1* ‖ preserved." *ts1* ‖ Preserved. *1947*

10 **Doing Himself**] doing himself *ms1, 1947, ts1*   **very**] Very *1947*

11 **that was**] not *ms1, 1947, ts1*

13 **wrong—**] wrong, *ms1, ts1* ‖ wrong *ts1*

15 **you'd wish**] you'd like *ms1 1st reading* ‖ ~~he'd~~ want *ms1 2nd reading (leaving line incomplete)* ‖ you'd want *1947, ts1*   **subtract—**] subtract *ms1, 1947* ‖ subtract, *ts1*

17 **No one could**] You could not *ms1, 1947, ts1*   **Pye,**] Pye *ms1, 1947*

18 **Possum**] ~~Practical~~ Possum *ms1*   **Soup.**] soup *ms1* ‖ soup, *1947, ts1*

19 **dry;**] dry. *ms1, 1947*

20 **coop,**] coop *ms1, 1947* ‖ coop. *ts1*

21 **measles or**] the mumps or the *ms1, 1947, ts1*   **croup,**] croup *ms1, 1947* ‖ croup— *ts1*

22 **let me**] I must *ms1, 1947, ts1*

23 **Smell**] smell *ts1*

24 **Grocer,**] Grocer *ms1, 1947, ts1*

25 **he**] not *ms1, 1947, ts1*   **Grocer:**] Grocer, *ms1, 1947, ts1*   **"O! Sir!**] "O Sir, *ms1, ts1* ‖ O Sir, *1947*

26 **Pye?"**] Pye? *1947*

27 **Grocer:**] Grocer, *ms1, 1947, ts1*   **"That**] That *1947*

29 **Onions**] onions *ms1, 1947, ts1*   **Spain,**] Spain *ms1, 1947, ts1*   **Cheese**] cheese *ms1, 1947, ts1*   **Gouda**] Gouda, *1947, ts1*

30 **And a**] And ~~som~~ *ms1 1st reading*   **Life Buoy**] Lifebuoy *ms1, 1947, ts1*   **Soap",**] Soap," *ts1* ‖ Soap *1947*   **Grocer,**] Grocer *ms1*

31 **"Will**] Will *ms1, ts2, 1947*   **Pye."**] Pye. *ms1, 1947*

32 **answered: "No! Sir!"**] answered No Sir *ms1* ‖ answered "No Sir," *ts1* ‖ answered, No Sir. *1947*

33 **he shut**] winked *ms1 1st reading* ‖ he closed *ms1 2nd reading, with* shut *alt* ‖ he winked *ts1*   **Other Eye**] other eye *1947, ts1*

34 **Cheroot**] Cheroot, *ts1*

35 **And he**] Then he *ms1 1st reading* ‖ And *ms1, 1947, ts1*

36 **he**] not *ms1, 1947, ts1*   **his**] the *1947, ts1*

37 **said: "I am willing to**] said, I will *ms1* ‖ said, "I will *ts1*

38 **cod liver**] codliver *1947*

39 **some**] not *ms1, 1947, ts1*   **Eno's**] Epsom *ms1 1st reading* ‖ Enno's *ts1*

40 **Spice**] spice *ms1, 1947, ts1*

41 **price.**] price; *ts1*

42 **The Smell",**] That, *ms1 1ˢᵗ reading* ‖ The Smell, *ms1, 1947*   **"will be very nice."**] will be Very Nice. *ms1, 1947*

43 **So**] And *ms1 1ˢᵗ reading*   **Sigh**] sigh *ms1, 1947*

44 **Other Eye.**] other eye *ms1, 1947*

46 **by now**] *not ms1 1ˢᵗ reading*   **Both Eyes**] both eyes *ms1, 1947*

47 **But**] And *ms1 1ˢᵗ reading*

48 **The**] A *1947*   **Lavender**] Practical *ms1 1ˢᵗ reading*

50 **Magical Bag**] magical bag *ms1, 1947*

51 **Pye.**] Pye *ms1, 1947*

53 **Possum**] P. *1947*

54 **"I**] I *1947*   **wrong;**] wrong, *ms1, 1947*

57 **Blossom.**] blossom *ms1, 1947*

58 **awake,**] awake *ms1, 1947*

59 **Pye,**] Pye *ms1, 1947*   **we must now suppose,**] as everyone knows *ms1 1ˢᵗ reading* ‖ we must suppose *ms1, 1947*

60 **Nose**] repose / Nose *ms1 alts*

61 **And**] From / And *ms1 alts*   **ears and**] ears to *ms1, with* and *alt braced to second word*   **toes."**] toes. *1947*

The Practical Cat

ts1 (BL): typescript enclosed with a letter to Alison Tandy, 15 Nov 1937, headed "This is a minor OPUSS which I had forgotten".

ts2 (BL): carbon of Geoffrey Tandy's broadcasting script.

22] And *here he is* in his best cravat! *with "(Shd. be a pixture here)" ts1*

The Jim Jum Bears

ts1 (Houghton): on notepaper of Eliot House, Cambridge, autographed, and with a note by Eleanor Hinkley: "Written at request of my grandmother, Susan Hinkley (who was cousin Tom's aunt), for my three sons ··· for her to put in a picture book she was making for her great-grandsons, for Christmas, I believe in 1937."

ts2 (Columbia U.): verso of leaf of notepaper of Barnard College, with a version of *Invitation to all Pollicle Dogs and Jellicle Cats to Come to the Birthday of Thomas Faber* on recto. First four lines in pencil, space apparently having been left for them when the rest of the poem was typed. No terminal punctuation to 5–8, 11–13, 15, 17–19.

Text from *ts1*.

Title] *this ed.* ‖ *not tss*
  1 **Tricks**] tricks *ts2*
  2 **have been**] are *ts2*
  4 **a**] the *ts2*
  6 **we're**] we're all *ts2*
  8–10] *inset, with* 9 *further indented ts2*
  8 **"It's**] It's *ts2*
  9 **Bears!**] Bears, *ts2*
10 **about!"**] about? *ts2*
12, 14, 16] *indented ts2*
14 **leave Dirty Marks**] make dirty marks *ts2*
15 **drop**] leave *ts2*   **down**] over *ts2* 1*st reading*
16 **muddy feet**] Muddy Feet *ts2*   **hall**] Hall *ts2*
18–20] *inset, with* 20 *further indented ts2*
18 **"The**] Those *ts2*
19 **The**] Those *ts2*
20 **all!"**] all. *ts2*

The Marching Song of the Pollicle Dogs

Published in *The Queen's Book of the Red Cross* (1939) with *Billy M'Caw: The Remarkable Parrot*.

ts1 (King's): carbon copy on a leaf headed by TSE in pencil "First version (Folio I)", formerly folded for posting. Bound for Hayward with his *Practical Cats* typescript. A second carbon (BL), has at the head "First draft only" and at the foot "What about *Troddling*??" and "N.B. Must do a Song for the Jock Russells of the West." This was sent to the Tandys on 2 Nov 1939, and reads as *ts1* except where stated.

ts2 (Houghton): ribbon copy on a leaf with typed note added at head: "(Copy: for the Lord Mayor's Red Cross Book)" and with printer's instruction to compositor "10pt Bask[erville]". The title is underlined in red, and the first word is typed in red. The printer has ringed the start, for a drop capital.

ts3 (Valerie Eliot collection): later fair copy ts on a leaf with "Who dares meddle with me!" added by TSE beneath the revised last line.

Qu Book proof (BL): galley proof of *Queen's Book*, stamped "30 Oct 1939 Rev. 12". At the head is pencilled "NB They have altered your punctuation on the copy Oh, dear, etc" in an unknown hand. As *Queen's Book* except where stated.

Qu Book proof 2 (Pierpont Morgan): revised galley proof, printed on both sides, with pencil ticks against each stanza.

Valerie's Own Book: fair copy (three pages, with corrections facing). No indents.

Text from *Qu Book*.

before 1] *ts1*:

> *My name it is little Tom Pollicle,*
> *And wha maun meddle wi' me?*

1 **nation,**] nation— *ts1*

3] *del Valerie's Own Book 2nd reading*   **Dalmatian**] Alsatian *ts1, Valerie's Own Book*

4–5] *omitted Valerie's Own Book 1st reading.* (Supplying these lines on the facing page, TSE braced them, with two arrows, for insertion 3 ^ 6. Probably he then noticed the repetition of "Alsatian" in 3 and 5, causing him to delete 3 entirely.)

4 **Spain;**] Spain. *ts1, Valerie's Own Book*

5 **Alsatian**] *ts1 1st reading, ts2+* ‖ Dalmatian *ts1 2nd reading*

7 **And**] Well *ts1*   **that**] who *ts1, Valerie's Own Book 1st reading*   **frisky and**] fresh and too *ts1*

8 **plain:**] plain—] *ts3*

9 *as also* 19, 29, 39 **Little**] little *ts1, Valerie's Own Book 1st reading*

11 **curious,**] curious. *ts1*

12 **drowsy**] sleepy *ts1, ts2 1st reading, Qu Book proof 1st reading emended TSE*

15 **frantic**] barky *ts1*   **furious—**] furious, *ts1*

16 **of**] to *ts1*

17] There are dogs that are rough and too rollicle: *ts1*

18 **plain:**] plain. *ts1*

19 **Pollicle—**] Pollicle. *Valerie's Own Book 1st reading*

20 ^ 21] *beginning a new page and a new stanza, TSE wrote* 21, 24 *and all but the last word of* 25 *before noticing the omission of* 22–23. *Deleting the three lines, he began again with* 21.

22 **freaky**] weakly *ts1*   **frail;**] frail. *ts1, ts2 1st reading*

24 **puny**] sickly *ts1*

25 **scrumpious,**] mumpious, *ts1* ‖ scrumpious *ts2 1st reading*

27 **amphibolical**] amphibolical, *ts1*

28 **plain**] plain, *ts1*

31 **still**] *not ts1*   ***cave canem—***] *recte et fortiter— ts1*

32 **cry**] word *ts1, Valerie's Own Book 1st reading*   **Clan,**] Clan. *ts1, ts2 1st reading*

33–36] *ts1*:

> We will bark it at every auditor,
> We will bark at dog, devil or man.
> We will bark at defamer or laudator,
> We will bark just as long as we can.

with loud ? *as alt for* long *in Tandy carbon*

36 **man.**] man, *Qu Book proof with comma changed to stop TSE*

37 **ye**] you *ts1*, *Valerie's Own Book 1ˢᵗ reading*

38 **be—**] be: *ts1*

39 **Pollicle,**] Pollicle— *ts1* ‖ Pollicle *ts2 1ˢᵗ reading*

40] *capitals for small capitals tss*   **And**] AND *Valerie's Own Book*   MAUN] DAUR
ts3 2ⁿᵈ reading ‖ DAUR *Valerie's Own Book*

Billy M'Caw: The Remarkable Parrot

Published in *The Queen's Book of the Red Cross* (1939) with *The Marching Song of the Pollicle Dogs*. To this text, the present edition adds 5 from *ts2* (apparently lost during retyping), and restores the deliberate spelling error in 38.

The text in *Cats: The Book of the Musical* (1981) was significantly rearranged (not collated here).

ts1 (Valerie Eliot collection): two leaves, with no indents, using the spellings "parret" and "Sattaday".

ts2 (Houghton): from correspondence with Mary Trevelyan. Undated but *c.* 1946 (perhaps enclosed with the postcard postmarked 15 Aug 1946 which reads simply "Here it is"). The form is close to *ms1*. No indents, and with "parrot" and "Saturday" properly spelt.

ts3 (BL): sent to the Tandy family. With indents only at the broken lines, and spelling "Bar" with a capital on every occasion.

ts4 (Houghton): two-page top copy, with title underlined in red and first word ringed by printer as for a drop capital (matching *ts3* of *The Marching Song of the Pollicle Dogs*).

Qu Book proof (BL): galley proof of *Queen's Book*, with the proof of *The Marching Song of the Pollicle Dogs*, which is stamped "30 Oct 1939 Rev. 12". As *Queen's Book* except where stated.

Qu Book proof 2 (Pierpont Morgan): revised galley proof, printed on both sides, with pencil ticks against each stanza. Text from *Queen's Book*.

ms1 (Valerie Eliot collection): fair copy, from 1950s, on rear blanks of Valerie Eliot's first edition of *Practical Cats* (containing *emendations B*). No indents except at stepped lines and 19. Short rules between stanzas. The spellings and the omission of 13 suggests that this was copied from *ts1*.

Text from *Qu Book*.

Title] *not ts2*   **Parrot**] Parret *ts1*, *ms1*

1 *as also 42* **Oh,**] Oh *ts1, ts2, ts4 1ˢᵗ reading, ms1* ‖ O *ts3*   **Bush,**] Bush *ts1–ts3*,
ts4 1ˢᵗ reading, ms1

2 **night—**] night, *ts1* ‖ night; *ts2, ms1*

3 **Where,**] Where *ts1, ts2, ms1*   **happened,**] 'appened *ts1* ‖ happened *ts2, ms1*   **rush,**] rush *ts1* ‖ rush— *ts3*

4 **he**] 'e *ts1*   **polite;**] polite *ts1* ‖ polite, *ts2, ms1* ‖ polite. *ts3*

5 *not ts3, ts4, Qu Book*   **he**] 'e *ts1*   **have**] 'ave *ts1*   **anythink**] *ts1, ms1* ‖ anything *ts2*

6 **Station**] station *ts1*   **being**] bein' *ts1, ms1* ‖ bein *ts3*   **near,**] near *ts1, ts2, ms1*

7 **what with the water**] the water what sometimes *ts1–ts3, ms1*   **into**] in to *ts2, ms1*

8] *line del ts1*

9, *as also 11* **House**] 'ouse *ts1* ‖ house *ts2, ts3, ms1*

9 **was**] Was *ts3*   **Oh**] Oh, *Qu Book proof with comma del TSE*   **dear!**] dear *ts2, ts4* ‖ Dear! *ts3* ‖ dear, *Qu Book proof with comma emended to exclamation mark TSE*

10 **garret**] garrett *ts3*

11 **parret—**] parret, *ts1, ms1* ‖ parrot, *ts2* ‖ parrott— *ts3*

12] *indented ts4 1ˢᵗ reading*   **parret, the parret**] parrot, that parrot *ts2* ‖ parrot, the parrot *ts3*   **M'Caw,**] M'Caw— *ts1, ms1*

13] *not ts1, ms1*

14] *not ts2*   **Ah!**] Ah, *ts1, ms1*   **Life**] life *ts1 2ⁿᵈ reading, ts3, ms1*   **bar.**] bar! *ms1*

15 **Of**] On *ts1 1ˢᵗ reading*   **night,**] night *ts1, ms1*   **feeling**] feelin' *ts1, ms1*   **bright,**] bright *ts1, ms1* ‖ bright. *ts4 1ˢᵗ reading*

16 **Rose—**] Rose, *ts1, ts2, ms1*   **Barmaid**] barmaid *ts1, ms1*   **was—**] was, *ts1, ts2, ms1*

17 *as also 28, 39*] *line not stepped ts1, ts2*

18 **bar!"**] bar". *ts2, ms1*

20 **had**] 'ad *ts1*   **her**] 'er *ts1*   **head;**] 'ead. *ts1* ‖ head. *ms1*

21 **have**] 'ave *ts1*   **no**] *ts4 1ˢᵗ and final reading* ‖ no, *ts4 2ⁿᵈ reading, Qu Book proof with comma del TSE*   **that much**] a word *ts1, ts2*

22 **argument**] argyment *ts1, ms1*   **dispute,**] dispute— *ts3*

23 **She'd**] She would *ts3*   **boot**] boot, *ts2, with comma pencilled then erased ts4*

24] *indented with pencilled alignment query ts4*   **her**] ~~your~~ *ts1 1ˢᵗ reading*

25 **when we was thirsty**] when we was tired *ts1, ms1* ‖ if we was tired *ts2*

26 **when**] if *ts2*   **happy**] cheery *ts1, ms1*

27 **had**] 'ad *ts1* ‖ had, *ts3*

28 **M'Caw!**] M'Caw! come give us a tune *ts2 1ˢᵗ reading*

29 **Come**] Go *ts3 1ˢᵗ reading (uncertain), ts4 1ˢᵗ and final reading* ‖ Come, *ts4 2ⁿᵈ reading, Qu Book proof with comma del TSE*   **flute!"**] flute"— *ts1* ‖ flute". *ts2*

31 **balmy**] happy *ts3*   **tear,**] tear *ms1*

32 **beer—**] beer, *ms1* ‖ beer; *ts1* ‖ beer. *ts2*

33–34] *song titles underlined ts1, ms1*

33, *as also* 36 **Bird**] bird *ts1–ts3, ms1*   **Adairs,**] *Adairs ts1, ms1*

34 **in the**] In The *ts3*   **Wapping**] *Wappin' ts1*   **Stairs,**] *Stairs ts1, ms1* ‖ Stairs *ts4 1ˢᵗ reading* ‖ Stairs— *ts3*

35 **eyes**] eye *ts1*   **would.**] would: *ts1, ts3, ms1*

36 **saying**] sayin' *ts1*

37 **feeling**] feelin' *ts1*   **tearful,**] tearful *ts1*

38 **say:**] say *ts2*   "**Now,**] "Now *ts1, ts3*   **somethink**] *ts1, ts3, ts4, ms1* ‖ something *ts2, Qu Book*   **cheerful!**] cheerful. *ts2*

39 **M'Caw**] M'CAW *ts3 1ˢᵗ reading*

40 **Come**] *ts4 1ˢᵗ and final reading* ‖ Come, *ts4 2ⁿᵈ reading, Qu Book proof with comma del TSE*   **guitar!"**] guitar". *ts1, ts2*

43 **came**] come *ts1*   **far.**] far; *ms1*

44 **House. From**] house, from *ts1, ts2, ms1* ‖ house. From *ts3*   **garret**] garret: *ts2*

45 **House**] house *ts2, ts3, ms1*   **Ah**] Ah, *ts1–ts3, Qu Book proof, ms1, with pencilled comma erased ts4*   **the**] that *ts2*   **parret**] parrot *ts2, ts3*

46 **The parret, the parret**] The parrot, that parrot *ts2* ‖ The parrot, the parrot *ts3*   **M'Caw,**] M'Caw *ts2, ts4 1ˢᵗ reading, ms1*

47 **Who**] That *ts1–ts3, ms1*

48 **Ah,**] Yes, *ts1* ‖ Ah. *ts3* ‖ Ah *ts4 1ˢᵗ and final reading*   **Life**] pride *ts1, ts2, ms1*   **bar.**] Bar! *ts3*

Grizabella: The Glamour Cat

Published as part of a song of this title in *Cats: The Book of the Musical* (1981).

ts1 (BL): letter to Polly Tandy, 13 Feb 1940: "The Glamour Cat, I am sorry to say, is not turning out a suitable subject for edifying my juvenile audience; in fact, she came down in the world pretty far. The story is very sad, and also a bit sordid. For ["She haunted many a low resort . . ."] No, I fear that the story had better not be told."

Valerie's Own Book: below the title, TSE wrote: "(the last 8 lines, all that was ever written. The history of Grizabella was too sad to be told to the children)." In the Contents list at the back of the first exercise book, the lines are referred to as "*Grizabella, the Glamour Cat* (Fragment)".

ts2 (Valerie Eliot collection): typescript following *Valerie's Own Book*, with TSE's typed initials but probably not by him.

Text from *Valerie's Own Book*.

Title] *untitled ts1 (but introduced as "The Glamour Cat" within the letter)*   **the Pollicles**] Pollicles *Valerie's Own Book Contents list 1ˢᵗ reading*

1 ... **She**] She *ts1*

2] In the dingy Road of Tottenham Court. *ts1*

3 **No Man's Land**] no man's land *ts1*

4] From the Rising Sun to the Friend at Hand. *ts1* ‖ From "The Rising Sun" to "The Friend at Hand". *ts2* ‖ From The Rising Sun to The Friend at Hand. *1981*

5 **scratched**] shook *ts1*

6 **really ha' thought she'd**] ha' thought that cat *ts1*   **dead—**] dead *1981*

7 *that*] *underlined twice Valerie's Own Book*, *ts2*

8 **Grizabella**] Grizzabella *ts1*   **Cat!"**] Cat? *ts1*

In Respect of Felines

Published in *Kenyon Review* Summer 1984 (see Commentary).

ts1 (private collection): letter to Miss B. R. Skinker dated 1 June 1940, on *Criterion* paper with address deleted. Initials in manuscript. Bought by Gekoski at Bonhams, 28 Mar 2006.

LINES

Addressed to Geoffrey Faber Esquire, on his Return from a Voyage to the Bahamas, and the Parts about New Spain

ts1 (King's): carbon on pink paper.

ts2 (Valerie Eliot collection): revised typescript, with one line emended in autograph, sent to Hayward (acknowledged 22 Aug 1943).

Title **on ^ his**] the Occasion of *not ts1*   **a Voyage to**] *not ts1*

2 **hell;**] hell, *ts1*

3 **people,**] people *ts1*

4 **frolicks**] frolics *ts1*

5 **quiring**] choir *ts1*

6 **His patient consort knew**] Penel'pe came to know *ts1, ts2 1st reading*

9 **Circe**] Circe, *ts1*

10 **stitch,**] stitch; *ts1*

11 **th' expected**] the proper *ts1* ‖ th' ap *ts2 1st reading* (*overtyped, perhaps for "th' appropriate"*)

Morgan Tries Again

ts1 (Princeton): two leaves of Croxley paper, formerly folded in four along with Emily Hale's ts of *The Country Walk*. The poem begins halfway down the first leaf, the top half of which has been cut away, leaving no date. *Matthews* 142 printed 11–12. Although introduced to TSE's readers only in 1952, Cat Morgan joined Faber & Faber in 1944 (see headnote to *Cat Morgan Introduces Himself*).

Montpelier Row

Published in *The Walter de la Mare Society Magazine* July 2002, with a facsimile of one of Walter de la Mare's copies of *ts2*.

ts1 (Faber archive): photocopy on two leaves.

ts2 (Valerie Eliot collection): on two leaves, possibly typed by de la Mare's secretary, headed "*Montpelier Row* a poem by T. S. Eliot with notes, February 1947". Follows *ts1*, letter for letter, except where some of its words had been run together. Three carbons (or the ribbon copy and two carbons) are among de la Mare's papers.

Valerie's Own Book: fair copy, with two-line spaces 4 ^ 5 and 8 ^ 9.

Title] Montpellier Row *ts1*, *ts2* (*one of the de la Mare copies being corrected*) ‖ *with* (Twickenham) *beneath and ranged right in* Valerie's Own Book, *followed by* Lines (unprinted) *written in February 1947 and sent to Walter de la Mare after a visit.*

1] De la Mare delicate *Valerie's Own Book*

4 **window pane**] windowpane *Valerie's Own Book*

12 **moment!**] moment, *Valerie's Own Book* ‖ moment: *WdlM Magazine*

Notes

Line 5.] Line 8. *Valerie's Own Book* (error)   **of doors**] doors *Valerie's Own Book* *1ˢᵗ reading*   **windows,**] windows *Valerie's Own Book*   **in The Memoirs of Sherlock Holmes**] (in *The Memoirs of Sherlock Holmes*) *Valerie's Own Book*   **rhyme, for,**] rhyme, *Valerie's Own Book*   **remote from**] remote than *Valerie's Own Book 1ˢᵗ reading*

Let quacks, empirics, dolts debate

Published in *Gala Day London* (1953). No drafts known.

AMAZ'D astronomers did late descry

Published in Laurence Whistler, *Engraved Glass 1952–1958* (1959), then *Matthews*.

ts1 (King's): single-spaced ts of this poem with, beneath, *VERSES: To Honour and Magnify Sir Geoffrey Faber Kt.* (headed "ALTERNATIVE —"). Dated "III Sunday in Lent 1954".

ts2 (King's): double-spaced carbon, headed "Original Drafts— | For the Goblet:—"

Whistler Notes: Laurence Whistler, *Engraved Glass 1952–1958* 22 ("Notes on the Plates"), where the verse is entirely italic.

Text from *ts2*.

   1 **AMAZ'D**] Amaz'd *ts1*

   4 **Name**] name *Whistler Notes, Matthews*

   5 **Sir Geoffrey**] SIR GEOFFREY *Whistler Notes, Matthews*   **be".**] be." *Whistler Notes, Matthews*   **word**] Word *Whistler Notes, Matthews*

   6 **Heav'ns**] heav'ns *Whistler Notes*   **and**] & *Whistler Notes*

VERSES

To Honour and Magnify Sir Geoffrey Faber Kt.

Folio broadsheet printed by Oxford University Press in Fell Types (1954), *Gallup* E2h, one of about 24 copies (King's, BL). Only this version uses the long-s.

ts1 (King's): headed "ALTERNATIVE —": see *ts1* of *AMAZ'D astronomers did late descry*.

ts2 (King's): this poem only. Carbon, with the footnote to 4 typed directly onto the leaf, and with pencil annotation.

proof (King's): broadsheet proof.

Title] *all roman, on a separate sheet, headed "Something to this Effect:" ts1*   **VERSES**] LINES *ts1, ts2 with "now altered to VERSES", proof*   2 **To Honour and Magnify**] Addressed to *ts1*   **Kt.;**] Kt., *ts1*   3 **Prefented**] *not ts1*   4 **faithful**] Faithful *ts1*   5 **to mark**] on *ts2*   6, 7] *transposed ts1 1st reading*   8 **Return,**] Return *ts1*   **Delivery from all**] Escape from the *ts1*   9 **by Land,**] of Land & *ts1* ‖ by Land *ts2*   9 ^ 10] in the Barbarous Parts of the Globe *ts1*   10 **We defire**] We here united wish *ts1*

   2] A hundred Crichtons' close epitome; *ts1*

   4 **Cunning**] Able *ts1*   **Court;**] Court, *ts1*

   4 *footnote*] *not ts1* ‖ *roman ts2*   **the St. Jamef's**] the Buck House *ts2 ringed with "now St. James's"*   **Bailey.**] Bailey.— ED. *ts2 2nd reading*

5–6] *in ts1 the eventual 7–8 are braced, with an arrow to these lines (at the foot) as an alternative, with "OR" and "perhaps better?"*

8 **As**] Be *ts1*   **patroon,**] patroon; *ts1 with* "N.B. *If the word 'patroon' errs by lack of familiarity, the following line may be substituted:* Be scholar, poet, bursar or tycoon. *But to those who have easy access to the O.E.D. 'patroon' may not seem too inapt.* 'Tycoon' is anything but exact." *Against the word in ts2 TSE has written:* "*this use of the word first in U.S.A. (1758) Dutch origin.*"

10 **Compoſt-land**] Sussex plains *ts1*

11 **wondering**] wond'ring *ts1*

12 **Man**] man *ts1*

14 **Lo! At laſt**] so at last, *ts1*

Long may this Glass endure, and brim with wine

ts1 (Faber archive): draft on a single leaf with author's corrections.

ts2 (Faber archive): fair copy on a single leaf as sent to Laurence Whistler.

1 **and**] to *ts1 1ˢᵗ reading*

2 **To**] And *ts1 1ˢᵗ reading*

3 **design**] design: *ts1 1ˢᵗ reading*

8 **penetrative**] penetrating *ts1 1ˢᵗ reading*

Beneath the verse, ts1 has, all del:

NOTE:

Chant. It is the wine, not the glass, that chants. Cf. Baudelaire: "l'âme du vin chantait dans la bouteille".

Honours. Refers also to a toast "with all the honours".

The gourmet cat was of course Cumberleylaude

ts1 (private collection): letter to Anthony Laude, 8 July 1964.

12 **salmon**] Salmon *ts*

How the Tall Girl and I Play Together

Valerie's Own Book: fair copy on two pages.

Sleeping Together

Valerie's Own Book: fair copy on one page, without title, except in the list of Contents at the end of the first exercise book.

How the Tall Girl's Breasts Are

Valerie's Own Book: fair copy on two pages (with no apostrophe in title above poem, although this is correct in the Contents at the end of the first exercise book).

Dedication II

Valerie's Own Book: fair copy on one page.

6,8] *ranged left ms*

Love seeketh not Itself to please

ms1 (Valerie Eliot collection): ruled leaf. TSE's late hand. The three stanzas appear in reverse order but are then numbered 3, 2, 1, and headed "Read from Bottom Up".

1 **seeketh**] that *1ˢᵗ reading*
2 **But**] And *1ˢᵗ reading*
10 **has**] takes *1ˢᵗ reading*
11 **joys**] joys only *1ˢᵗ reading*   **taking**] *not 1ˢᵗ reading*

Old Possum's Book of Practical Cats

Old Possum's Book of Practical Cats has appeared in many editions and, since 1940, with illustrations by Nicolas Bentley, Edward Gorey, Errol Le Cain and Axel Scheffler. During the 1940s and 1950s, unillustrated and illustrated editions were both kept in print. An extra poem, *Cat Morgan Introduces Himself*, was added to the unillustrated edition in 1953, though by 1959 it had not been added to the illustrated edition. The first paperback appeared in 1962, the first paperback with all of Bentley's illustrations not until 1974. Four known copies contain emendations by TSE (*emendations A–D*) and he sent others in memos to David Bland, Faber's production editor. Bland's own memos to the printers, attempting to achieve a stable text, continued after TSE's death.

But not all of the emendations from the copies marked up by TSE and the list referred to as *emendations E* can be incorporated, since some contradict others. For instance, in *Old Deuteronomy*, "My mind may be wandering but" is revised in *emendations B* to "My legs may be failing but yet", but in *emendations C, D* to "My sight may be failing but yet". If the second of these is adopted as probably the later, does this mean that only changes from *emendations D* should be incorporated? If so, it would mean not adopting from *emendations B, C* the (necessary) change later in the poem, from "My sight's unreliable but" to "I'm deaf of an ear now but yet". And if the principle were extended to the whole book, some twenty changes from *emendations A, B, C* would be ruled out. Alternatively, it would be possible to incorporate as many of the changes as possible, giving priority to those that appear to be the latest. Yet this would be to ignore the evidence that TSE had second and third thoughts about his emendations, as he had about pre-publication drafts. In *Skimbleshanks*, for instance, "You ought to reflect" is revised to "You'll have to admit" (*emendations B*), "You're bound to admit" (*emendations C*) and "You have to admit" (*emendations D*)—and a printed lifetime edition apparently later than any of these (the second impression *1964 pbk*) reads differently again: "You are bound to admit". So if a particular reading is called for on one occasion, but not repeated in later sets of emendations, it may be prudent to suppose that TSE had come to prefer the printed text. As elsewhere, the present edition has considered each case individually.

TYPESCRIPTS

No manuscripts of poems from *Old Possum's Book of Practical Cats* are known to survive. Most of the surviving typescripts were sent to friends. They are of two kinds: those sent individually as the poems were written, and those sent as more-or-less complete sheaves. John Hayward's archive of TSE includes both kinds. The principal collections and repositories are described first. The details of the typescripts of individual poems then refer to these sheaves, so that, for instance, the typescripts of *The Naming of Cats* designated *ts2a* and *ts2b* are cognate copies, found within Hodgson's *ts sheaf* and Hayward's *ts sheaf* (i).

The space between stanzas in the typescripts is sometimes two lines: this is noted only when single line spaces are also used in the same poem.

Tandy corresp. (BL): nine poems (plus *The Practical Cat*; see "Uncollected Poems") enclosed at various times in letters to the Tandy family, who were usually—perhaps always—the first audience. The nine are *The Old Gumbie Cat*, *Growltiger's Last Stand* (two versions), *The Rum Tum Tugger*, *Mungojerrie and Rumpelteazer*, *Old Deuteronomy*, *The Awefull Battle of the Pekes and the Pollicles*, *Mr. Mistoffelees*, *Macavity: The Mystery Cat*, *The Ad-dressing of Cats*. The poems are not bound consecutively, and their order does not reflect their order of composition or posting.

Faber corresp. (photocopies, Valerie Eliot collection): five poems enclosed at various times in letters to Enid Faber: *Mungojerrie and Rumpelteazer*, *Old Deuteronomy*, *Macavity: The Mystery Cat*, *Bustopher Jones: The Cat about Town*, *Skimbleshanks: The Railway Cat*.

BBC (BL): scripts for a reading by Geoffrey Tandy on "Regional" radio, 25 Dec 1937, 2.30–2.45 p.m. and perhaps other occasions. The poems were sent to Tandy by Ian Cox of the BBC in two batches. The first, preceded by introductory notes, included *The Naming of Cats*, *The Practical Cat*, *The Rum Tum Tugger* and *Old Deuteronomy*. The second, which Cox sent on 8 Dec "with apologies for leaving these out of the first batch", included *Macavity: The Mystery Cat*, *Skimbleshanks: The Railway Cat* and *The Ad-dressing of Cats*. *Growltiger's Last Stand* must also have been sent, as it is mentioned in a note on the verso of the title page for the Christmas broadcast. However, TSE had authorised the broadcast of "not more than five" poems on that occasion, and the exact composition of the broadcasts is not known.

Hodgson's ts sheaf (Beinecke): ribbon copy of a professional typing of all 14 poems in *1939*, on 25 leaves, including title page, Note of Acknowledgement (*i.e.* Preface) and Contents. Sent in 1938 to Ralph Hodgson, who was commissioned to illustrate the poems (see Commentary headnote, 6. WITH AND WITHOUT ILLUSTRATIONS). Ribbon copy except *Bustopher Jones: The Cat About Town*, carbon. Ink emendations by TSE. Contents list begins with "Epistle Dedicatory".

Hayward's ts sheaf (King's):

(i)   carbon of the book's first 11 poems, cognate with *Hodgson's ts sheaf.*

(ii) additional carbons of five poems sent individually (each of the first three being identified by Hayward as "a different typing"): *The Rum Tum Tugger*, *The Song of the Jellicles*, *Mungojerrie and Rumpelteazer*, *Macavity: The Mystery Cat*, *Gus: The Theatre Cat*. (Of these additional drafts, some are apparently earlier than *Hodgson's ts sheaf*, such as *Mungojerrie and Rumpelteazer ts3*, and others later, such as *Gus: The Theatre Cat ts2*).

(iii) carbons of three other poems sent individually: *The Ad-dressing of Cats*, *Bustopher Jones: The Cat about Town* (two versions, sent at the same time), *Skimbleshanks: The Railway Cat* (two successive drafts).

(iv) *The Marching Song of the Pollicle Dogs* (see "Uncollected Poems").

These category numbers—(i), (ii), (iii), (iv)—are used in the descriptions below to indicate the history of each typescript, although the poems from them are interspersed in a single volume bound for Hayward.

Hale's ts sheaf (Scripps College): secondary carbon of a professional typing of the 14 poems in *1939* on 25 leaves, including title page, Note of Acknowledgement and Contents. Inscribed below title "for Miss Emily Hale this not quite final text, from Old Possum 18. vii. 38". Some poems adopt TSE's revisions from *Hodgson's ts sheaf.*

PUBLISHED TEXTS AND POST-PUBLICATION EMENDATIONS

1939: first ed., without illustrations except line drawings by TSE on front and back of the jacket. Two impressions appeared before the illustrated edition of 1940, and this cheaper unillustrated alternative remained in print through ten impressions in all before the new edition of 1953. Later impressions adopted a few readings from *1940*. In 1948 when production was switched to new printers (Mardon, Son & Hall), Bentley's line drawings (though not the colour plates) were accidentally included in the ninth unillustrated impression.

US 1939: as *1939* except where noted.

1940: first illustrated ed., for which "Nicolas Bentley drew the pictures" (black-and-white and colour). As *1939* except where noted.

US 1952: TSE, *The Complete Poems and Plays*, the first collected edition to include *Old Possum's Book of Practical Cats.*

1953: *Old Possum's Book of Practical Cats* "New edition, 11th impression, 1953". A further impression of *1939* (from the same type) with the addition of *Cat Morgan*. As *1939* except where noted.

1962 pbk: first paperback ed., pub. 19 Apr, with Bentley's line drawings but not his colour plates. A new setting (with poem titles in upper and lower case), incorporating all the changes in *emendations A*, but not those that appear only in *emendations B, C, D*. An untraced marked copy of *1962 pbk* with new corrections was sent by David Bland to Maclehose (printers of the paperback) and a list of these was sent to Mardon (printers of the hardback unillustrated and illustrated eds.), 20 Aug 1962. These corrections were evidently from TSE, who then added "two more changes" in a memo to Bland of 8 Jan 1963 which was also relayed to both Maclehose and Mardon (Faber archive). The final lifetime text, that of *1964 pbk*, is therefore the first for which all authorial readings were available.

1964 pbk: second paperback imp., incorporating further changes, most of them probably from the marked copy of *1962 pbk* and including the two in TSE's memo of 8 Jan 1963 (to *Skimbleshanks* 59 and *Cat Morgan* 12). As *1962 pbk* except where noted.

1969: the British first collected edition to include *Old Possum's Book of Practical Cats.* As *1962 pbk* except where noted.

1974 pbk: first paperback with all of Bentley's illustrations.

Gorey: first ed. illustrated by Edward Gorey (1982). As *1964 pbk* except where noted. The reprint of the same year with Bentley's illustrations had a slightly different text (not noted below).

emendations A (Pierpont Morgan): author's emendations in a copy of *1953* 13th imp. (1960). All adopted in *1962 pbk*.

emendations B (Valerie Eliot collection): author's emendations in a copy of *1953*, repeating or further revising all of *emendations A*.

emendations C (Valerie Eliot collection): author's emendations, dating from 1950s, in Valerie Eliot's copy of *1939*, inscribed on the title page successively "Inscribed for Miss Valerie Fletcher by T. S. Eliot", "and for Valerie Eliot by T. S. Eliot", "and finally for my beloved Valerie, my darling, from her adoring Tom." On the free endpaper TSE wrote: "This is the copy I used in recording all the Cats for the British Council. Finished 18. vi. 57", and there are occasional pencilled ticks, chevrons and crosses throughout, presumably as aids to reading. The emendations to *Of the Awefull Battle of the Pekes and the Pollicles* 5–6 and to *Skimbleshanks* 51 appear to have been copied from *emendations B* where earlier attempts at revision are discernible, but some other emendations from there are ignored. This copy also contains in ms, on the front flyleaf, *The Cows: a Pastoral* (that is, *The Country Walk*) and, on the rear flyleaf and endpapers, *Billy M'Caw: The Remarkable Parrot* and *Mr. Pugstyles: The Elegant Pig*.

emendations D (photocopy): author's emendations in a copy of *1962 pbk*, "Inscribed for Miss Walton, Matron of Brompton Hospital and for George Brompton (whose portrait appears in the book) T. S. Eliot". (The silhouette of a cat on 47, opposite the end of *Gus: The Theatre Cat*, is identified by TSE as "George".) All the emendations are either repeated from or further revisions of *emendations B, C*, but other emendations from these are ignored.

emendations E (enclosed in the copy of *1939* bearing *emendations C*): undated memo to David Bland (production manager of Faber) calling for "Two more slight alterations to text of *Practical Cats*, if and when any edition is reprinted. Both in *Bustopher Jones*" (36 and 38). The alterations were listed in *emendations B, C, D*, but TSE may have thought better of them (the second strains the sense), for they were not printed in his lifetime. They appeared only in *1969*. (Also noted in the memo is a correction for the text of *Selected Essays*.)

A WORD ABOUT THE MUSICAL SETTINGS

For the musical *Cats* by Andrew Lloyd Webber (1981), Valerie Eliot gave permission for certain alterations to the poems of *Old Possum* specifically for the musical settings. Although *Cats: The Book of the Musical* printed the poems as published, the altered versions appeared on the record sleeve of the cast album and in the musical score. In addition to the *Old Possum* poems, the musical included *Grizabella: The Glamour Cat*, lines from *Billy M'Caw: The Remarkable Parrot*, from *The Marching Song of the Pollicle Dogs* (as part of *The Awefull Battle of the Pekes and the Pollicles*), and what was called *The Journey to the Heaviside Layer* (from the fragment in the letter to Geoffrey Faber of 6 Mar 1936 quoted in the Commentary headnote to *Pollicle Dogs and Jellicle Cats*). Other fragments of TSE's poetry were incorporated elsewhere, and into the two songs by other writers, *Memory* by Trevor Nunn and *Jellicle Songs for Jellicle Cats* by Richard Stilgoe.

Title] Old Possum's Book of | PRACTICAL CATS | with pictures supplied by | The Man in White Spats *Hodgson's ts sheaf, Hayward's ts sheaf, Hale's ts sheaf* ‖ BOOK OF PRACTICAL CATS *running head US 1952*

Preface title] *no heading US 1939* ‖ Note of Acknowledgement *Hodgson's ts sheaf, Hale's ts sheaf* ‖ Epistle Dedicatory *Hayward's ts sheaf, Hale's ts sheaf Contents list*

Preface] I wish to thank numerous friends who have given encouragement, criticism, and advice; and particularly Mr. T. E. Faber, Miss Alison Tandy, Miss Susan Wolcott, and the Man in White Spats. ¶ O.P. *Hayward's ts sheaf, Hodgson's ts sheaf* (*with* and *after semi-colon del*), *Hale's ts sheaf* (*omitting* and)

The Naming of Cats

ts1: single leaf of *BBC*.

ts2a and *ts2b*: cognate copies, on single leaves in *Hodgson's ts sheaf* and *Hayward's ts sheaf* (i).

ts3: single leaf of *Hale's ts sheaf*.

4] *unindented in all eds* (*error*)

8 *as also* 12 **sensible**] practical *tss*

28 **name**] Name *ts2* (*emended to* name *in ts2b*)

For additional lines in letter to Tom Faber, 7 Jan 1936, see Commentary.

The Old Gumbie Cat

ts1: letter to Alison Tandy, 10 Nov 1936, in *Tandy corresp.*

ts2a and *ts2b*: cognate copies with different emendations, on single leaves in *Hodgson's ts sheaf* and *Hayward's ts sheaf* (i).

ts3: single leaf of *Hale's ts sheaf*.

ts Perkins (Beinecke): single leaf, folded in six presumably for posting. The enclosing folder has a note by Gallup: "Typescript prepared for (& by?) Mrs John Carroll Perkins (has readings variant from printed text)." Bought by Gallup from Seven Gables Bookshop, 25 July 1961.

Title **The**] O (*mistyping*) *ts2 1st reading*

1–4] *transposed with* 13–16 *ts Perkins*

3 **mat:**] *1940+* ‖ mat; *ts1, ts2, 1939* ‖ mat. *ts Perkins* (*where as part of the second chorus this is* 15)

4, *as also* 16, 28 **sits—**] sits *tss*

4 **that's**] *that's ts Perkins* (*second chorus*)   **Cat!**] Cat!! *ts Perkins* (*second chorus*)

7 **family's**] fambly's *ts1, ts Perkins*

8 **slips down the stairs**] *ts3, emendations B, C & D, 1964 pbk* ‖ tucks up her skirts *ts1, ts2, ts Perkins, printings prior to 1964 pbk, 1969, recording 1957*   **to the basement to**] and downstairs will *ts1* ‖ to the kitchen to *ts Perkins*

9] There she must every night attend to the mice— *ts1*

11 **So**] And *ts2a 1st reading, ts2b*

15 **on the bed**] *ts1–ts3, ts Perkins* (*where as part of the first chorus this is* 3), *1939* ‖ in the sun *emendations A & B, 1962 pbk+.* (The emendation, thirty years after composition, is reversed in the present edition because of the repetition of "sits in the sun" from *Old Deuteronomy* 10.)   **on my hat:**] in my hat: *ts1* ‖ in my hat. *ts Perkins* (*first chorus*)

20 **diet;**] *ts2, ts3, 1939* ‖ diet. *ts1, ts Perkins* ‖ diet *1953+* (*probably broken type*)

22 **sets straight**] *ts1–ts3, ts Perkins, emendations B & C, 1964 pbk* ‖ sets right *printings prior to 1964 pbk and some subsequently, 1957 recording* ‖ sets *1969* (*error*)

23 **of**] with *ts1, ts Perkins*

24 ***beautiful***] beautiful *ts1, ts Perkins*

26 **curtain-cord**] window-cord *ts1, ts2a 1ˢᵗ reading, ts2b, ts Perkins*   **into**] up in *ts1*   **sailor-knots**] sailor knots *ts1* ‖ sailor- | knots (*broken across line*) *1939* (*but not US 1939*)

28 **that's**] THAT'S *ts Perkins*   **Cat!**] Cat!!! *ts Perkins*

32 **prevent**] preserve *ts1*

35 **a good deed to do—**] a great deal to do; *ts1* ‖ their good deeds to do— *ts Perkins*

37–38] *no indent 1962 pbk* (*error*)

37 ^ 38] (CHEER, please) *ts Perkins* (*as though a direction to an audience, not to be read aloud*)

Growltiger's Last Stand

ts1: two leaves in *Tandy corresp.* Sent to Tandy family before 10 Nov 1936. With "Griddletone" for "Griddlebone". The epigraph suggests composition after June 1935 when Sir John Simon became Home Secretary. A secondary carbon of the same typing, with a compliments slip from the vestry of St. Stephen's Church, is at the Berg, acquired with Frank Morley's papers.

ts2: two leaves in *Tandy corresp.* A revised version also sent to Tandy family, with identical carbon. Still with "Griddletone" for "Griddlebone".

ts3a and *ts3b*: cognate copies each on two leaves, in *Hodgson's ts sheaf* and *Hayward's ts sheaf*(i); with additional emendation in *ts3a* at 42.

ts4: two leaves of *Hale's ts sheaf.*

Epigraph] *"He was no better than a Pirate"*:—Sir John Simon, replying to a Question in the House during the Debate on the Growltiger Incident. *ts1 only*

1 **GROWLTIGER**] *1939, 1969* ‖ GROWLTIGER *ts1–ts3, US 1939* ‖ *Growltiger 1962 pbk*   **Bravo**] ruffian *ts1, ts2*   **travelled on**] *printings from 1946* (*see Commentary*), *recording 1957* ‖ grew up on *ts1, ts2* ‖ lived upon *1939*   **barge:**] Barge; *ts1, ts2* (*over b in ts2*)

2 **fact**] fact, *tss*   **cat**] Cat *ts1, ts2*

4 **title**] Title *ts1, ts2*

5 **His**] In *ts1, ts2*   **did not calculate to please;**] he was hardly made to please: *ts1, ts2*

6 **torn and seedy**] rough and shaggy *ts1 1st reading*

7 **tell you**] ask me *ts1, ts2*

8 **from**] with *ts1, ts2*   **eye.**] eye *late impressions of 1939 (error, corrected emendations B)*

9 **fame;**] *ts1, ts2, 1940+* ‖ fame, *ts3, ts4, 1939*

12 **LOOSE!**] LOOSE. *tss*

13 **cage;**] cage! *ts1, ts2*

14 **rage;**] *1940+* ‖ rage! *ts1, ts2* ‖ rage. *ts3, 1939*

15 **bristly**] boastful *ts1 1st reading*   **Bandicoot, that**] Bandicoot who *ts1, ts2*

16 **woe**] Woe *ts1*   **grips!**] grips. *ts1, ts2*

19 **Persian**] persian *ts2*

21 **seemed**] was *ts1, ts2*

22 **barge**] Barge *ts1, ts2*

23] In the balmy summer moonlight it was rocking on the tide, *ts1, ts2*

25 **bucko**] burly *ts1, ts2*

27 **his**] the *ts1, ts2*   **bosun**] Bosun *ts2*   **he too had**] he had also *ts1* ‖ had also *ts2*

29 **sate alone,**] sat alone *ts1, ts2*

31 **sleeping**] lying *ts1 1st reading*   **barrels**] not *ts2 1st reading (word missing)*

32 **As**] While *ts1, ts2*

33 **Griddlebone**] Griddletone *ts1, ts2*

35 **awaiting**] expecting *ts1, ts2*

36 **hundred**] *emendations A & B, 1962 pbk* ‖ thousand *tss, printings prior to 1962 pbk and some subsequently, recording 1957*   **bright**] fierce *ts1, ts2*

37 **And closer still and closer**] Now closer and still closer *ts1, ts2*

38 **was not heard a sound.**] did not come a sound; *ts1, ts2*

39 **duet, in danger**] love song, regardless *ts1, ts2*

40 **For**] But *ts1, ts2*   **cruel**] gleaming *ts1 1st reading*

42 **they**] *ts3a 2nd reading+* ‖ then *ts1, ts2, ts3*   **aboard.**] aboard; *ts1, ts2*

44 **the**] their *ts2 1st reading*   **on**] of *ts1 1st reading*

45 **Griddlebone**] Griddletones *ts1* ‖ Griddletone *ts2*   **screech**] shriek *ts1, ts2*

48 **serried**] stubborn *emendations B*

49] The stern determined foemen pressed forward, rank on rank, *ts1, ts2*   **stubborn**] serried *emendations B*

50] Growltiger found that he at last was forced to walk the plank: *ts1 1st reading* ‖ Growltiger found himself at last compelled to walk the plank: *ts1, ts2*

51 **hundred**] thousand *ts1, ts2*

52] He at the end of many crimes was made to go ker-flop. *ts1, ts2*

53 **in**] at *ts1, ts2*

55 **Brentford, and at Victoria Dock**] Deptford, as well as Boulter's Lock *ts1, ts2*

after 56] *two-line space then* BUT *then two-line space then* A deputation of Unemployed Cats from Bermondsey is to be received tomorrow by the Prime Minister, to protest against the march-past of Siamese Cats in uniform which took place at Hampton on Saturday last.—B.B.C. 6 p.m. News Bulletin. *ts1, ts2 (ts2 omitting final point)*

The Rum Tum Tugger

ts1: sent to Alison Tandy, "Epiphany 1937" [6 Jan], with the introductory lines *I am asked by my friend, the Man in White Spats* (see "Uncollected Poems"). In *Tandy corresp.* A carbon is in Frank Morley's papers (Berg).

ts2: carbon on a single leaf with a note by Hayward: "a different typing [11 Jan 1937]". Bound in *Hayward's ts sheaf* (ii).

ts3: single leaf of *BBC*.

ts4a and *ts4b*: cognate copies with matching emendations, on single leaves in Hodgson's ts sheaf and Hayward's ts sheaf (i).

ts5: single leaf of *Hale's ts sheaf.*

1 **Cat:**] Cat, *ts1*

3 **much prefer**] rather have *ts1, ts2*

4 **rather have**] much prefer *ts1, ts2*

5 **mouse**] rat *ts2*   **he only wants**] he'd rather have *ts1*   **rat,**] mouse, *ts2*

6 **rat**] mouse *ts2*   **he'd rather chase**] he only wants *ts1*   **mouse.**] rat. *ts2*

8 **call**] need *ts2*

12 **terrible bore**] terrible Bore *ts1* ‖ Terrible Bore *ts2*

13 **be**] get *ts3–ts5*

15 **he'd like**] he wants *ts1*

16 **bureau**] bottom *ts1, ts2*

19 **it isn't any use**] there isn't any cause *ts2*   **doubt**] scout *ts1*

23 **curious beast:**] Curious Beast, *ts1* ‖ Curious Beast: *ts2*

24 **disobliging**] exasperating *ts1* ‖ disagreeable *ts2*

25 **feast;**] Feast, *ts1*

26 **eat**] have *ts2*

27 **sniffs and**] only *ts1*   **sneers,**] sneers— *ts2*

28 **For he**] He *ts1, ts2*   **likes**] enjoys *ts1*   **finds**] takes *ts2*

29 **So**] But *ts2*   **catch**] find *ts1, ts2*

31 **artful**] observant *ts1, ts2*

34 **nothing**] nothing that *ts1 1st reading*   **horrible**] terrible *ts1* ‖ frightful *ts2*

36] **need**] call *ts2*

The Song of the Jellicles

ts1: carbon on a single leaf bound in *Hayward's ts sheaf* (ii), with a note by Hayward: "a different typing [25 Jan 1937]". Typed directly onto this carbon (presumably by TSE) is another note: "N.B. The word 'toilette' is pronounced with the accent strongly on the second syllable." Another carbon of the same typing was sent the same day to the Tandy family. A further carbon of the same typing is at Berg, acquired with Frank Morley's papers, and is accompanied by a typed note, formerly pinned to it:

> HOY! You Illustrator, try your 'and at this.
> (Composed tonight, after our having some
> words on the subject).
> You ought to be able to work as
> fast as I can.

ts2a and *ts2b*: cognate copies, on single leaves in *Hodgson's ts sheaf* and *Hayward's ts sheaf* (i).

ts3: single leaf of *Hale's ts sheaf.*

Even-numbered lines, except chorus, indented ts1

   1–4] *no chorus here, but typed in full after first stanza and abbreviated to "Jellicle Cats etc." after subsequent stanzas ts1*

   3 **bright—**] *bright:* ts1

  11 **like to practise**] practise away at *ts1*

  16 **and**] or *ts1*

  24 **moonlit**] moonlight *ts1*

  28 **by**] in *ts1*

  31 **stormy**] rainy *ts1*

Mungojerrie and Rumpelteazer

ts1: ribbon copy on two leaves, sent to Enid Faber, postmarked 22 Oct 1937. In *Faber corresp.*

ts2: carbon of a slightly revised version, sent to the Tandy family with a letter dated 21 Oct 1937 but postmarked the following day. In *Tandy corresp.*

ts3: ribbon copy on two leaves bound in *Hayward's ts sheaf* (ii), with a note by Hayward: "a different typing [22 Oct 1937]". A secondary carbon is in Frank Morley's papers (Berg).

ts4a and *ts4b*: cognate copies with different emendations, each on two leaves, in *Hodgson's ts sheaf* and *Hayward's ts sheaf* (i). (In Hayward's bound volume, *ts4b* is placed before *ts3*.)

ts5: two leaves of *Hale's ts sheaf.*

Title] MUNGOJERRIE AND RUMPELTEAZER | By the Author of | *"The Fantasy of Fonthill: or, Betjeman's Folly"* | and | *"John Foster's Aunt". ts3*

1, *as also* 6 **cats**] Cats *ts1–ts3*

4 **their centre of**] the centre of their *ts2, ts3*

6 **can**] could *ts1, ts2*

7–14, *as also* 21–27, 34–37] *not inset ts1–ts3*

9 **If**] Or *ts3*   **came**] was *ts1*

10 **presently**] suddenly *ts1*   **ceased to be**] stopped being *ts1–ts3*

11 **If**] Or *ts1–ts3*   **from**] of *ts1, ts2*

13 **after supper**] after dinner *ts1–ts3*

14 **Woolworth pearls:**] rope of pearls— *ts1–ts3*

15, *as also* 28 **Then the**] The *ts1–ts3*

15, *as also* 28, 38 **cat**] Cat *ts1–ts3*

16 **It was**] It's *ts2, ts1* ‖ "It is *ts3*

16 ^ 17] *line space tss, US 1939* ‖ *new page so line spacing indeterminate 1939, 1940, 1953, 1962 pbk* ‖ *no line space 1969*

17 **very unusual**] most remarkable *ts1* ‖ very remarkable *ts2*

18 **as well**] also *ts1, ts2*   **remarkably smart at a**] expert at business of *ts1–ts3*

19 **Grove. They**] Grove, but *ts1, ts2*

20 **fellows,**] fellows *ts1, ts2*   **and liked to**] and often were known to *ts1, ts2* ‖ would often *ts3*   **a friendly policeman**] police constables *ts1* ‖ police officers *ts2*

22] All ready to placate the man that's inner *ts1–ts3* ‖ All ready to comfort the man that's inner *ts4, ts5*

23 **On**] *1939+* ‖ With *tss*

24–25] *ts1 (with* Cook*), ts2, ts3:*

> Which were being made ready behind the scenes—
> And the cook would appear, and say with sorrow:

26 **and have dinner**] to dine till *ts1*   ***tomorrow!***] tomorrow, *ts1* ‖ TOMORROW! *ts2, ts3* ‖ *tomorrow! US 1939*

27 **For**] "For *ts3*   **oven**] larder *ts1*

29 **It was**] "It's *ts1* ‖ It's *ts2* ‖ "It is *ts3*

32 **oath**] oath— *ts1–ts3*

33 **Was it Mungojerrie—**] Was it Mungojerrie? *ts1* ‖ Was it Mungojerrie?— *ts2* ‖ It was Mungojerrie? *ts3*   **or could**] —or could *ts1* ‖ —could *ts2 1ˢᵗ reading*   **mightn't be**] might have been *ts1, ts2*

34 **dining-room**] drawing-room *ts1, ts2*   **smash**] crash, *ts1* ‖ smash, *ts2, ts3*

35 **there came**] would come *ts3*   **crash**] smash, *ts1* ‖ crash, *ts2, ts3*

36 **came**] come *ts3*   ***ping***] ping! *ts1–ts3*

37 **was commonly said to be**] the dealer had certified *ts1–ts3*

39 **It was Mungojerrie! AND**] It was Mungojerrie—AND *ts1*, *ts2* ‖ "It was Mungojerrie—AND *ts3*

Old Deuteronomy

ts1: ribbon copy sent with a letter to Alison Tandy, 15 Nov 1937. In *Tandy corresp.*

ts2: ribbon copy on a single leaf of a slightly revised version, sent to Enid Faber, 15 Nov 1937. In *Faber corresp.*

ts3: single leaf of *BBC.*

ts4a and *ts4b*: cognate copies with matching emendations, each on a two leaves, in *Hodgson's ts sheaf* and *Hayward's ts sheaf* (i).

ts5: single leaf of *Hale's ts sheaf.*

2 **has lived many**] is living nine *ts1*, *ts2*

4 **A long while**] For some years *ts1*, *ts2*

9 **that**] his *ts2*

10 **sits**] lies *ts1*, *ts2*

12, *as also* 27 **really!... No!... Yes!...**] really... No!... Yes! *ts1*, *ts2*

13-14, *as also* 28-29, 44-45] *not inset ts1*, *ts2*

13, *as also* 28, 44] Oh, why! *ts1* ‖ Ho! Hi! *ts2* ‖ Ho! hi! *ts3*, *ts4*

14, *as also* 29, 45] Oh my eye, *ts2*

15] *emendations B 1ˢᵗ reading, emendations C & D, 1964 pbk* ‖ My mind may be wandering, but I confess *tss, printings prior to 1964 pbk and some subsequently, recording 1957, 1969* ‖ My eyes may be failing, but yet I confess *emendations B final reading*

16 I] *I 1964 pbk*

18 **market day;**] market day, *ts1* ‖ Market Day; *ts2*

21 **cars**] Cars *ts1* **over**] up on *ts1*

23 **untoward may chance**] at all may occur *ts1*, *ts2*

25] His attention apparently fixed on astronomy— *ts1*

25 ^ 26] a line is missing, to rhyme with "of all..." (26)

30] *emendations B, C & D, 1964 pbk* ‖ My sight's not reliable, but I can guess *ts1*, *ts2* ‖ My sight's unreliable, but I can guess *ts3–ts5, printings prior to 1964 pbk and some subsequently, 1969*

31 **cause of the trouble**] interruption *ts1*

32 **lies**] sits *ts1*, *ts2*

37] ~~And I'll have the police if there's any uproar~~" — *ts2 1ˢᵗ reading (error)*

39 **shuffle**] creep *ts1*, *ts2* **a**] one *ts1*

43] Things... Can it be... Yes!... No! *ts1*, *ts2* **Yes!**] N *ts4 1ˢᵗ reading*

Of the Awefull Battle of the Pekes and the Pollicles

ts1: ribbon copy on two leaves sent to the Tandy family (date unknown). In *Tandy corresp.*

ts2a and *ts2b*: cognate copies with different emendations, each on two leaves, in Hodgson's ts sheaf and Hayward's ts sheaf (i).

ts3: two leaves of *Hale's ts sheaf*.

Valerie's Own Book: fair copy (four pages), reverting to the reading of *ts1* at 26 ^ 27.

An unauthorised printing Eden Press, Toronto, was included in the 1984 *Wayzgoose Anthology* in an edition limited to 120 copies, with 20 issued separately.

Title] *1940, later impressions of 1939 ‖ includes subtitle after colon, ts2, 1939 ‖ includes subtitle after semi-colon ts1 ‖ the whole set in three unjustified lines of capitals ts2 (with* INTERVENTION *del before* PARTICIPATION*), ts1 (with* FINAL *before* INTERVENTION*) ‖ the whole set as six justified lines 1939 ‖ the whole set in seven justified lines, the first starting in the left margin US 1939 ‖ with subtitle in three centred lines of smaller italics 1969.* The Pekes and the Pollicles *Contents page in Hale's ts sheaf and all eds*

4 **most people**] people may *ts1*

5 **will often display**] *emendations B, C, D, 1964 pbk+ ‖ yet once in a way, ts1 (without comma), ts2, ts3, printings prior to 1964 pbk and some subsequently (unchanged in emendations A), recording 1957, Valerie's Own Book*

6 **Every symptom of wanting to**] *emendations B 2nd reading, emendations C, emendations D (omitting* to*), 1964 pbk+ ‖ They will now and again tss, printings prior to 1962 pbk and some subsequently, recording 1957, Valerie's Own Book ‖ Or now and again, they emendations A, emendations B 1st reading, 1962 pbk and some subsequent printings including 1969*   **join in**] *emendations C, 1964 pbk+ ‖ join in to tss, printings prior to 1964 pbk and some subsequently (unchanged in emendations A, B, D), recording 1957, Valerie's Own Book*   **fray.**] *ts1, 1964 pbk+ ‖ fray ts2, ts3, printings prior to 1964 pbk and some subsequently including 1969, Valerie's Own Book*

7 ^ 8, *as also 21 ^ 22, 42 ^ 43] line space tss*

8] Bark bark bark bark ba *1st reading ts1*

9, *as also 23, 44* **Bark bark**] Bark Bark *ts1*   BARK BARK] BARK B A R K *ts1–ts3*

9 ^ 10, *as also 23 ^ 24, 44 ^ 45] line space tss*

10, *as also 24, 45] no indent Valerie's Own Book*

10 ^ 11, *as also 24 ^ 25, 45 ^ 46] two-line space tss, Valerie's Own Book*

12 **nearly a week**] almost a week— *ts1*

13 **(And]** And *ts1*   **Peke).**] Peke. *ts1*

16 **Bricklayer's**] *1964 pbk ‖ Wellington tss, printings prior to 1964 pbk, 1969, recording 1957, Valerie's Own Book ‖ Bricklayers' emendations B & C*

19 **retreat,**] retreat: *ts1*

20 **glared**] GR *ts1* *1ˢᵗ reading (uncertain, perhaps for* GROWLED?*)* ‖ GLARED *ts1* ‖ glared *Valerie's Own Book*

26 **Dog**] dog *Valerie's Own Book 1ˢᵗ reading*

26 ^ 27] *ts1, Valerie's Own Book*:

> And China (with all due respect to that Nation)
> Is known as a country of dense population.

27 **uproar**] Uproar *ts1*

28 **door;**] door— *ts1*

31 **huffery-snuffery**] huffery snuffery *Valerie's Own Book*   **Heathen**] heathen *ts1*   **Chinese**] chinese *Valerie's Own Book 1ˢᵗ reading*

36 **pipers**] Pipers *ts1*

37] Playing "When the Blue Bonnets Came over the Border. *ts1 1ˢᵗ reading, quotation marks then added after stop*   **Came Over**] came over *Valerie's Own Book 1ˢᵗ reading*

39 **roof,**] roof *Valerie's Own Book*

44 **bark**] Bark *Valerie's Own Book*

46 **Now**] So *ts2a 1ˢᵗ reading, ts2b*   **these bold**] all our *ts1*

47 **trembled,**] trembled. *Valerie's Own Book*

49 **Brigade.**] Brigade— *ts1*

51 **RUMPUSCAT.**] RUMPUSCAT! *ts1*

54 **area,**] area *Valerie's Own Book*

56 **And**] So *ts1*   **yawning,**] yawning *Valerie's Own Book*

58 **sky**] sky, *Valerie's Own Book*   **he**] the *Valerie's Own Book (error)*

59 **scattered**] vanished *ts1*   **sheep**] sleep *Valerie's Own Book 1ˢᵗ reading*

59 ^ 60] *two-line space Valerie's Own Book*

60 ***beat,***] beat *Valerie's Own Book*

60–61] *ts1*:

> And
>   (*very softly*)
>   when the Police Dog returned to his beat—
> There wasn't a single dog left in the street.

Mr. Mistoffelees

ts1: ribbon copy on two leaves sent to the Tandy family (date unknown). In *Tandy corresp.* No indents.

ts2a and *ts2b*: cognate copies with different emendations, each on two leaves, in *Hodgson's ts sheaf* and *Hayward's ts sheaf* (i).

ts3: two leaves of *Hale's ts sheaf.*

6 **There's**] there *ts2 1ˢᵗ reading*

9 **creating**] f *ts1 1ˢᵗ reading (perhaps beginning* for*?)*

12 **defy**] stand *ts1 1ˢᵗ reading*

24] From the tips of his ears to his tail; *ts1, ts2a 1ˢᵗ reading, ts2b 1ˢᵗ reading bracketed with final reading added as alt with "?"*

25 **crack,**] crack *1962 pbk+*

35 **and then**] the *ts1 1ˢᵗ reading (immediately overwritten)* ‖ the next *ts2 1ˢᵗ reading*   **gawn!**] *ts2 final reading+* ‖ gone, *ts1 1ˢᵗ reading, ts2a 1ˢᵗ reading, ts2b* ‖ gorn! *ts2a 2ⁿᵈ reading* ‖ gawn! *US 1939*

41 ^ 42] *three line space 1962 pbk (single line space 1969)*

45 **curled up**] asleep *tss*

46 **sometimes**] often *ts1*

48 (**At**] At *ts1*   ***heard***] heard *ts1*   **somebody who**] *emendations B & C, 1964 pbk* ‖ that somebody *tss, printings prior to 1964 pbk, 1969*   **purred**)] purred— *ts1*

52 **in from**] out in *ts2 1ˢᵗ reading*

55 **right**] from *ts1 1ˢᵗ reading*

58–59] Was there ever | A Cat so clever *ts1*

Macavity: The Mystery Cat

ts1: ribbon copy on two leaves sent to Tandy family (date unknown), with ink emendation at 2. In *Tandy corresp.*

ts2: two leaves sent to Enid Faber, 5 Feb 1938, in *Faber corresp.* A carbon sent to Hayward in *Hayward's ts sheaf* (ii).

ts3: single leaf of *BBC.*

ts4a and *ts4b:* two copies with matching emendations (all made during the writing), on single leaves in *Hodgson's ts sheaf* (ribbon) and *Hayward's ts sheaf* (i).

ts5: single leaf of *Hale's ts sheaf.*

2 **master criminal**] Master Criminal *ts2*   **can defy**] keeps inside *ts1 1ˢᵗ reading* ‖ lives beyond *ts3–ts5*

5 ^ 6, *as also* 17 ^ 18] There never was a criminal so cunning as Macavity, *ts1, ts2*

8 **And**] For *ts2*

9 **look up**] seek him *ts1, ts2*

13 **is deeply lined with**] has many lines of *ts1, ts2 1ˢᵗ reading (emended on carbon also)*

15 **sways**] moves *ts1, ts2, ts4 1ˢᵗ reading*   **with movements like**] as if he was *ts1, ts2*

16 **And**] You'd *ts1, ts2, ts4 1ˢᵗ reading*   **when you think he's**] think that he is *ts1, ts2*   **he's always**] but he is *ts1, ts2*

19 **You may**] You might *ts1* ‖ You will *ts2 1st reading (emended on carbon also)* ‖ You'll *ts2 2nd reading*   **may see**] might meet *ts1* ‖ will meet *ts2 1st reading* ‖ may meet *ts2 2nd reading (emended on carbon also)*

20 **discovered, then**] discovered— *ts1, ts2*

22 **And**] But *ts1, ts2, ts4 1st reading*

23 **jewel-case is**] jewels have been *ts1, ts2*

24–25] *ts1*:

> Or the greenhouse glass is broken, or another Peke's been stifled,
> Or when the milk is missing, or the trellis past repair—

24 **when**] the *ts4 1st reading*   **Peke's**] Peke *ts2*

27 **Treaty's**] Treaty *ts1, ts2*

29 **a scrap**] some scraps *tss*

31 **the**] a *ts1*   **loss**] crime *ts1, ts2*

32 **Macavity!"**] Macavity" *ts1, ts2*

33 **You'll be**] You are *ts1*   **a-licking of his thumbs**] a-twiddling of his thumbs *ts1, ts2 1st reading* ‖ a-licking of his gums, *ts2 2nd reading (emended on carbon also)*

36 ^ 37] There never was a criminal so cunning as Macavity. *ts1, ts2*

41 **agents**] Agents *ts1, ts2*

Gus: The Theatre Cat

ts1: carbon on two leaves in *Hayward's ts sheaf* (ii).

ts2a and *ts2b*: revised version, later than *ts1* and close to the published text, on two leaves of *Hodgson's ts sheaf* and *Hayward's ts sheaf* (i). A further carbon was sent to Enid Faber (6 Feb 1938).

ts3: two leaves of *Hale's ts sheaf.*

4 **call him just**] just call him *ts1*

5 **thin**] lean *ts1*

7, 8] *transposed ts1*

7 **youth**] time *ts1*

8 **But**] He's *ts1*

10 **Though**] But *ts1, ts2 1st reading (unemended on carbons)*   **time**] pr *ts1 1st reading*

11 **the**] their *ts1*

16 **He has**] He's *ts1*   **Irving**] Benson *tss*

18 **Where**] When *ts1*   **cat-calls.**] cat-calls *1939 later imp. (broken type)*

27 **that**] which *ts1*

30 **rung**] ring *ts2 1st reading (uncorrected on carbons)*

31 **flat,**] *printings prior to 1962 pbk, 1969* ‖ flat *1962 pbk+*

36 **Lynne.**] *Lynn: ts1 1ˢᵗ reading* ‖ *Lynne: ts1 2ⁿᵈ reading*

37 **At**] In *ts1, ts2 1ˢᵗ reading*

42 **Ghost**] ghost *ts1*

44 **rescue a child**] give the alarum *ts1 1ˢᵗ reading* ‖ give the alarm *ts2 1ˢᵗ reading*   **on fire**] afire *ts1*

47 **They never get**] They've never been *ts1*

48 **smart, just**] clever, *ts1*

50 **Theatre's**] theatre's *ts1*

Bustopher Jones: The Cat about Town

ts1a and *ts1b*: carbons of two versions, on single leaves sent together to Hayward, with ribbon copy of a title page: "BUSTOPHER JONES | Two Versions | The First perhaps only suitable for private circulation." Bound together in *Hayward's ts sheaf* (iii), though the poem is not mentioned in the contents list. Like the wording of the title page, the variant at 38 suggests that the "private" version *ts1a*, came first, although it has been bound after *ts1b*, the version for publication. "St.James's" is run together on both typescripts at each appearance (including title).

ts2: ribbon copy on a single leaf sent to Enid Faber, 28 Feb 1938, in *Faber corresp.* Attached was a note on paper headed The Vestry, St. Stephen's Church: "This is the unexpurgated version, for private consumption only." The text derives from *ts1a* with some readings from *ts1b*.

ts3: secondary carbon on a single leaf of *Hodgson's ts sheaf.* Ignoring *ts2*, the text derives from *ts1b*.

ts4: single leaf of *Hale's ts sheaf.*

Title] BUSTOPHER JONES: THE ST. JAMES'S STREET CAT. *ts1*

 6 **fastidious**] a fashionable *ts1a*

10 **Brummell**] Brummel *tss*

13, 16] *emendations B has an asterisk beside* 13 *indicating a note*:
　　　Originally

　　　　　One club that he's fixed on's the Wormwood ↻ Brixton . . .
　　　　　And the Joint Correctional Schools

13] One club he has fixed on's the *Wormwood and Brixton ts1a, ts2* (*with &*). See Commentary.

14 **And**] (For *ts1a* ‖ (And *ts1b* ‖ For *ts2*

15 **For**] That *ts2*   **one**] smart *ts1a*   **to belong**] should belong *ts2*

16 **Superior**] Correctional *ts1a, ts2*   **Schools.**] Schools). *ts1a* ‖ Schools: *ts1b*

18 **is found**] goes *ts1*   **at**] to *ts1* ‖ as *1969* (*error, corr. in reprints*)   **Blimp's;**] Blimp's). *ts1b* ‖ Blimp's. *emendations B 1ˢᵗ reading del with* "stet"

19 **But he's**] *emendations A & B, 1962 pbk* ‖ And he's *ts1a* ‖ He is *ts1b, ts3, 1939* ‖ And he *ts2*

20 **is famous for**] has excellent *ts1*

21 **ben'son**] benison *ts1, ts2*

24 **To drop in for a drink**] For a drink with the lads *ts1*

26 ***Glutton;***] *Glutton* ‖ *US 1939*

27 **lunched at**] been to *ts1, ts2*

28] With bishops and cabbage and mutton. *ts1a, ts2*   **On**] For *ts1b*

31 **cause**] *emendations B & C, 1964 pbk* ‖ be *tss, printings prior to 1964 pbk and some subsequently*

36 **so he'll**] he will *ts2* ‖ so he'd *emendations B, C, D & E, 1969*

37 **And (to put it in rhyme)**] *emendations B & C, 1964 pbk* ‖ Or to put it in rhyme: *ts1, ts2* ‖ Or, to put it in rhyme: *ts3, ts4, printings prior to 1964 pbk and some subsequently*

38 **word of**] word for *emendations B, C, D & E, 1969*   **stoutest**] sagest *ts1a 1ˢᵗ reading*   **Cats.**] Cats: *ts1, ts2*

Skimbleshanks: The Railway Cat

ts1: carbon on two leaves in *Hayward's ts sheaf* (iii), with "Rough Draft" pencilled at top by TSE. Not including 33–50.

ts2: slightly later version on two leaves sent to Enid Faber, 15 Mar 1938, in *Faber corresp*. Still not including 33–50. A carbon is in *Tandy corresp*.

ts3: two leaves of *BBC*.

ts4a and *ts4b*: cognate copies with different emendations, each on two leaves, in *Hodgson's ts sheaf* (emended in pencil and, at 54 and 56, in ink) and *Hayward's ts sheaf* (iii) (emended in pencil, then ink). The poem is not in the contents list to *Hayward's ts sheaf* (i), and *ts4b* was sent separately.

ts5: two leaves of *Hale's ts sheaf*.

1 **11.39**] 11.29 *ts1*

6 **searching**] hunting *ts1*

9 **At 11.42**] At 11.32 *ts1*   **then the signal's nearly due**] we're already overdue *ts1* ‖ the departure's nearly due *ts2* ‖ then the signal's overdue *1969, Bentley 1982*. (*No warrant for the posthumous readings is known.*)

14 **signal**] message *ts3–ts5*   **"All clear!"**] "all clear"; *ts1, ts2*

15 **for**] to *ts2*

20 **them**] us *ts2*

25 **He will watch**] He'll observe *emendations B & C*   **sees**] knows *tss, emended to final reading ts4a*

28 **When**] Q *ts1 1ˢᵗ reading* ‖ While *ts1 2ⁿᵈ reading, ts2*

29] He gives one shake of his long brown tail— *ts1, ts2*

30 **He's a Cat**] It's a tail *ts1, ts2*   **ignored;**] ignored! *ts1, ts2* ‖ ignored. *ts3–ts5*

31 **So**] And *ts1, ts2*   **Northern**] Midnight *ts1 alt added*

32 **aboard.**] aboard! *ts1, ts2*

33–50] *not ts1, ts2*

35 **newly folded**] clean and tidy *ts3–ts5*

38 **button**] *emendations A & B, 1962 pbk* ‖ handle *ts3–ts5, printings prior to 1962 pbk*   **turn**] press *emendations B alt* (*TSE del* handle that you turn *and wrote* button that you turn *then substituted* press *yet also put a dotted line beneath the printed words* that you turn)

39 **you're supposed**] you are meant *ts3–ts5*

43 **was**] is *ts4a 1st reading, ts4b*   **him,**] him. *1969*

47 **You are bound to admit**] *1964 pbk* ‖ You ought to think *ts3–ts5* ‖ You ought to reflect *printings prior to 1964 pbk and some subsequently* ‖ You'll have to admit *emendations B* ‖ You have to admit *emendations D* ‖ You're bound to admit *emendations C*

51 **middle**] *emendations B & C, 1964 pbk* ‖ watches *tss, printings prior to 1964 pbk and some subsequently* ‖ hours *emendations B 1st reading*   **bright;**] bright *ts1* ‖ bright, *ts2–ts5*

52] And the guard and he will have a cup of tea *ts1*   **Every**] And *ts2* ‖ Only *ts3, ts4a 1st reading, ts4b, ts5*

53 **watch,**] watch *ts2*

54 **stopping**] pausing *emendations B*   **here and there**] now and then *ts1, ts2, ts4 1st reading*

56 **walking**] striding *ts1, ts2* ‖ stalking *ts4a 1st reading, ts4b*

59 **summons**] *emendations B, C & D, memo 8 Jan 1963 (Faber archive), 1964 pbk, 1969* ‖ speaks to *tss and printings prior to 1964 pbk*

61 **get**] got *ts4 1st reading*   **there**] then *ts1, ts2*   **do**] did *ts4 1st reading*

63–65] *(inset) ts1*:

> And if your journey has been a success
>   And you'd like to take it again,
> Then you owe your thanks to no one less—
> To no one less you owe your thanks—
> You owe your thanks to Skimbleshanks—

(inset) ts2:

> And if your journey has been a success
>   And you'd like to take it again:
> You've a debt of gratitude more or less—
> More or less you owe your thanks—
> You owe your thanks to Skimbleshanks—

63 **wave**] shake *ts4b 2nd reading*

65 **You'll**] We'll *ts3–ts5*   **Mail**] Mail"— *ts4, ts5*

65 ^ 66] And you wave your thanks to Skimbleshanks *ts3–ts5*. *Presumably because*

this draft line repeated "wave" from 63, TSE experimented with "a shake of his long brown tail" there in ts4b, but decided against it and instead deleted this line.

66 **Train."**] Train! *ts1, ts2* ‖ Train. *ts3–ts5*

The Ad-dressing of Cats

ts1: carbon on two leaves, sent to the Tandy family. Date unknown, but now between *Macavity: The Mystery Cat* and *A Practical Possum ts2* in *Tandy corresp.*

ts2: two leaves of a secondary carbon in *BBC*.

ts3a and *ts3b*: cognate copies, each on two leaves, in *Hodgson's ts sheaf* and *Hayward's ts sheaf* (iii). The poem is not in the contents list to *Hayward's ts sheaf* (i), and *ts3b* was sent separately.

ts4: two leaves of *Hale's ts sheaf.*

1 **read of**] now met *ts1* ‖ heard of *emendations C* (*probably intended specifically for broadcast*)   **Cat,**] Cat— *ts1*

2] And I am of opinion that *ts1*

5 **You now**] For you *ts1*

9 **sane**] good *ts1*   **mad**] bad *ts1*

10 **good**] sane *ts1*   **bad**] mad *ts1*

14 **about their**] their really *ts1*

27 **much inclined**] very apt *ts1*

32 **or**] and *ts1*

46 **he**] it *ts1*

48 **comes to see me in**] calls upon me at *ts1*

50] *1964 pbk* ‖ His name, I have been told, is James— *ts1* ‖ I think I've heard them call him James— *ts2–ts4, printings prior to 1964 pbk, 1969* ‖ I've *heard* them call him James Buz-James, *emendations C*

51] We've not yet got to using names. *ts1*

56 **might**] could *ts1*

66] In time you may achieve your aim, *ts1*

Cat Morgan Introduces Himself

ts1 (Valerie Eliot photocopy): early draft with variant spellings, on Faber & Faber headed paper. A note in Valerie Eliot's hand about where she found the draft reads "FVM [Frank Morley] Next to 18. 10. 37". This date corresponds with a letter of condolence from TSE to Morley's mother when she was widowed, but Morgan the cat did not appear in Russell Square until 1944 (see Commentary).

ts2 (King's): "T. S. Eliot's original autograph typescript with his corrections"

(Hayward's pencil note), bound in a volume of "Essays, Addresses and Verses". Presumably once kept by Hayward in the folder he had made for *The Country Walk*, on the cover of which its title appears and is deleted.

ts3 (King's): carbon of a fair copy, with TSE's name at the end, bound in the same volume. A further carbon of this is in a private collection.

ts Harvey-Wood (untraced): sent to the younger daughter of Henry Harvey-Wood of the British Council in Paris in 1951 (*Tomlin* 160).

Texas has a ms copy in unknown hand (perhaps Frank Morley's) and a ts, each headed "*Morgan the Cat* (once a firewatcher with T. S. Eliot) His autobiography by T. S. Eliot". Not collated.

Faber Book News, duplicated sheet sent out with Faber's book catalogue for Autumn 1951.

The Animals' Magazine Sept 1952.

broadside: *Cat Morgan's Apology* "Set into type and 30 copies struck off in memory of Cat Morgan at the Bibliographical Press in New Haven, Connecticut, 1953", by Donald Gallup (E2g).

Title] Cat Morgan's Invitation *ts1* ‖ Cat Morgan's Apology through the pen of T. S. Eliot, O.M. *Animals' Magazine* ‖ Cat Morgan's Apology *broadside* ‖ Morgan, the Commissionaire Cat *recording 1957* (*where TSE begins*: Morgan speaking · · ·)

1–3] *ts1*:

> When I was a pirut what sailed the high seas,
> I knowed well them fellers what navigate junks;
> And if I hencountered a Dog Pekinese
> I'd skin him, and boil him, and eat him in chunks.

> But after my colours was struck from the mast
> I happlied for a job as a com-mission-aire:
> And that's how I found a snug harbour at last

3 **how**] why *ts2 1st reading*   **find**] see *ts2 1st reading*

4 **And keepin'**] A-keepin' *ts1*   **Square**] square *ts1*

5–8 *after* 9–12] *ts1*

5] I don't get no partridges, likewise no grouse, *ts1*

6 **And I favour that**] I don't get no *ts1* ‖ And I'm partial to *ts2 1st reading*

7 **'ouse**] house *ts1*

8 **o'**] of *ts1*

9 **me**] my *ts1*

10] And my get-up ain't what you would raly call smart; *ts1*

11 **And**] But *ts1*   **enough:**] emendations B, *1964 pbk* ‖ enough; *1953, 1962 pbk, 1969, Bentley 1982*

12 **'e's**] he's *ts1*   **kind**] *ts1*, emendations B, D & memo *8 Jan 1963, 1964 pbk* ‖ good *ts2, ts3, printings prior to 1964 pbk, 1969*   **'art."**] hart". *ts1* ‖ 'art. *ts2 1st reading*

14 **me**] my *ts1*

15 **can**] kan *ts2 1ˢᵗ reading* ‖ kin *emendations B 1ˢᵗ reading*   **I'm not one to**] ~~I guess~~
~~that~~ *ts2 1ˢᵗ reading*

17–20] *ts1:*

> So if you should be passin' along Russell Square,
> Just you ask for Morgan, the folks all know me.
> And I think I could find you a biscuit to spare
> And maybe a saucer of milk for your tea.

17 **'ave**] have *broadside*

19 **spare**] save *ts2 1ˢᵗ reading*

20 **door**] Door *ts2, ts3, Faber Book News, broadside*

Anabasis

TSE's Anabase (Bodleian): Exemplaire No. XII of 50 copies numbered I–L of the first edition total of 625 copies (1924), with some translations that were taken up in *ts1*. The cover is inscribed "T. S. Eliot 1926" (and, upside down, "Eliot"). The *ts1* translations are recorded below, but TSE's underlinings and marginal marks, and Perse's annotations, which make sense only with the French, are not recorded below.

ts1 (Bodleian): ts of the translation on 29 leaves, extensively annotated by Perse (given to the library by TSE, 17 Jan 1931). Another copy is at the Fondation Perse. The title page reads "ΑΝΑΒΑΣΙΣ | poem of | ST. J. PERSE. | Translated into English by | T. S. ELIOT". Perse emends to ANABASIS adding "better in *Latin* letters" and

> Le mot "anabase" neutralisé dans ma pensée jusqu'à l'effacement d'un terme usual, ne doit plus suggérer aucune association d'idées classiques.
> Rien à voir avec Xénophon.
> Le mot est employé ici abstraitement et incorporé au français courant avec toute la discrétion nécessaire—monnaie usagée et signe fiduciaire—dans le simple sens étymologique de: "expédition vers l'intérieur", avec une signification à la fois géographique et spirituelle (ambiguïté voulue)

> [The word "anabase", neutralised in my thinking to the point of effacing the usual term, ought no longer to suggest an association with classical ideas. Nothing to be found in Xenophon. The word is employed here abstractly and incorporated into current French with all the necessary discretion—money in circulation, fiduciary sign—in the simple etymological sense of: "journey into the interior", with a sense at the same time of the geographical and the spiritual (deliberate ambiguity)].

Criterion (Section I only): *From "Anabase"* in *Criterion* Feb 1928 (printed without Perse's French).

1930: *Anabasis* (Faber, 1930; reissued 1937).

US 1938: *Anabasis* (New York, 1938). *Gallup*: "Second edition (first American edition)".

Mirror: Part IV only, in *A Mirror for French Poetry 1840–1940* ed. Cecily Mackworth (1947), facing the French text. Headed *From "Anabasis"*. Text as *US 1938* except where stated.

US 1949: *Anabasis* (NY, 1949). *Gallup*: "Third edition, revised and corrected".

1959: *Anabasis* (Faber, 1959). *Gallup*: "English edition" with a new "Note to the Third Edition".

The asterisks between some paragraphs are absent from *ts1*, the *Criterion* and *1930*– *US 1949*. Varying numbers of stops in ellipses are not recorded but are standardised to three.

Text from *1959*.

PREFACE

Preface ts (Valerie Eliot collection): retained carbon from 1930. (Printed in the present edition in the Commentary to *Anabasis* headnote, 3. APROPOS OF PUBLICATION.)

Valery Larbaud] Valéry Larbaud *throughout all eds.* (*error, corrected passim*)   **the sequence of images**] the consequent images *Preface ts 2ⁿᵈ reading*   **"fundamental brainwork"**] "fundamental brain-work" *1930, US 1938* (the phrase is Rossetti's)   **no one word to separate**] no word to indicate *with* indicate *changed to* separate *ts Preface*   **only a very small**] the greater *ts Preface 1ˢᵗ reading*   **bad because it is prosaic**] prosaic verse *ts Preface 2ⁿᵈ reading*   **The ten divisions of the poem are headed**] The ten divisions of the poem Mr. Fabre describes *Preface ts final reading*   **I. Arrival of the conqueror · · · the navigator**] *see headnote for previous reading (1930–US 1949)*   **writing of the same importance**] writing of the same order of importance *Preface ts final reading*   **James Joyce**] Mr. James Joyce *1930, US 1938*   **He has, I can testify**] What inaccuracies remain are due to my own wilfulness, and not to my ignorance, which the author has corrected; and not to the author's ignorance, for he has, I can testify *1930*   **1930**] *date added US 1938+*

SONG

i **Under · · · to my liking**] *drafted in TSE's Anabase*   **foaled.**] foaled, under the bronze leaves. *TSE's Anabase, ts1*   **fruit**] bay *TSE's Anabase, ts1, 1930– US 1949*   **Stranger. Who**] Stranger. The Stranger Who *TSE's Anabase, ts1*   **Here**] And here *TSE's Anabase*   **comes news of other provinces to my liking.—**] to my liking is rumour of farther provinces. *TSE's Anabase* ‖ to my liking comes news of far provinces . . . *ts1* ‖ to my liking comes news of far provinces.— *1930*   **tallest tree**] most considerable of the trees *1930–US 1949*

ii **Stranger. Who**] Stranger. The Stranger who *ts1*   **tells us of an herb. O**] has spoken of grass and of tundra and steppe. To and *ts1*   **blow many winds. What ease to our way! how**] blows the wind? How comfortable to me are our tracks. How *ts1*   **way!**] ways, and *1930–US 1949*   **the feather revels in**] *not ts1* ‖ the feather adept of *1930–US 1949*   **great girl**] my daughter *ts1*   **ours."**] ours . . . . . ." *ts1*

iii **foaled.**] foaled, under the bronze leaves. *ts1*   **fruit**] bay *ts1, 1930–US 1949*   **Stranger. Who**] Stranger. The Stranger who *ts1*   **comes a great bruit**] came a confusion *ts1*   **in the**] of flute-players in the cool *ts1*   **O what ease in our ways**] How comfortable are our tracks *ts1*   **tales**] gestes *ts1, 1930–US 1949*   **Stranger to**] Stranger with *ts1*

I

i **honour**] strength *ts1, Criterion*   **great**] *not ts1, Criterion*

ii **Beautiful are bright weapons**] Our burnished arms are fair *ts1, Criterion, 1930, US 1938*   **fair.**] fair? *ts1*   **Given over to our horses this seedless earth**] *US 1949* ‖ This fruitless earth given over to our horses *ts1, Criterion* ‖ This husk of earth given over to our horses *1930, US 1938* ‖ Given over to our horses this seedless earth. *1959*

iii **delivers to us**] is more to us that *ts1* (*mistyping* than), *Criterion* (*error*)   **Sun**]

sun *ts1*   **not named**] unmentioned *ts1*, *Criterion*, *1930–US 1949*   **us.**] us *ts1*, *Criterion*, *1930–US 1949*

iv **presumption of the mind.**] pride of the spirit. *ts1*, *Criterion*

v **you**] who *ts1*, *Criterion*   **as we march in darkness . . .**] on our ways of bivouac and vigil. . *ts1* || on our ways of bivouac and vigil! . . . *Criterion* || on our tracks of bivouac and vigil. *1930, US 1938*   **day**] dawn *ts1*, *Criterion*   **our dream, older than ourselves?**] the primogeniture of dream. *ts1* || the primogeniture of dream? *Criterion* || our entail of dream? *1930, US 1938*

vii–viii] I shall not hail the people of another shore. I shall not trace || the diverse quarters of cities, I would simply live among you. *ts1* (*with blank after* trace) || I shall not hail the people of another shore. I shall not trace in sugar of coral the diverse quarters of cities on the slopes. I would simply live among you. *Criterion*

ix **at**] to *ts1*, *1930*   **idea pure as salt**] pure idea *ts1*, *Criterion*   **day light**] day. *ts1*, *Criterion* || light time *1930–US 1949*

x **in**] on *ts1*, *Criterion*   **commerce**] communication *ts1*, *Criterion*

xi **gale.**] wind. *ts1*, *Criterion*

xii **splendour . . .**] honour. *ts1*, *Criterion*   **"In the delight of salt the mind shakes its tumult of spears**] The spears of the spirit press toward the pleasure of salt *ts1*, *Criterion*   **desire!**] desire? *ts1*

xiii **He**] Him *1930–US 1949*   **a sallet**] a casque or sallet. *ts1* || casque or sallet, *Criterion*

xiv **I trust him little in the**] He knows little I think of the *ts1*, *Criterion*   **commerce of the soul**] soul's communion *ts1*, *Criterion*   **not named**] unmentioned *ts1*, *Criterion*, *1930–US 1949*

xv **creatures of dust**] dusty people *ts1*, *Criterion*   **ways**] devices *ts1*, *Criterion*, *1930–US 1949*   **men from the marches and those from beyond**] folk of the frontiers and foreign men *ts1*, *Criterion*, *1930, US 1938*   **O men of little weight in the memory of these lands**] O light folk blown by a breath of wind out of the memory of these places *ts1*, *Criterion*   **from the valleys and the uplands and**] of the valleys and of the plateaux and of *ts1*, *Criterion*   **to the ultimate reach of our shores;**] beyond our shores: *ts1* || beyond our shores; *Criterion* || to the shores' end; *1930, US 1938*   **Scenters**] seers *ts1*, *Criterion* || Seers *1930–US 1949*   **seeds, and**] sowings, *ts1*, *Criterion*   **winds**] gales *ts1*, *Criterion*   **followers of trails**] trackers of beasts *ts1*, *Criterion*, *1930, US 1938*   **watercourses**] water and watercourses *ts1*, *Criterion*

xvi **traffic**] traffick *ts1*, *Criterion*   **waken**] wake *ts1*

xviii **single robe and pure,**] comely robe *ts1*, *Criterion*, *1930–US 1949*   **year,**] year *ts1*, *Criterion*, *1930–US 1949*   **amongst**] among *ts1*, *Criterion*

xix **the seeds of time**] seedtime and harvest *ts1*, *Criterion*   **at its height**] that rests *ts1*, *Criterion*   **scales**] scale *ts1*, *Criterion*

xx **Mathematics**] Geometry *ts1*, *Criterion* || Calculations *1930–US 1949*   **floes**] veins *ts1*, *Criterion* || layers *1930*   **at the sensitive point**] *not ts1*, *Criterion*   **the most rapt god-drunken**] a whole people, the wildest *ts1*, *Criterion*

xxi] launching from our ways the keels ¶ unforgotten unforgettable. *ts1* (*two paragraphs*) ‖ drawing to our ways the keels ¶ unforgotten unforgettable. *Criterion* (*two paragraphs*)

II

iv **armpit**] axil *US 1938*

vi **us!... How**] us. How *1930, US 1938* ‖ us ... How *US 1949*

viii **pieces...**] pieces. *1930, US 1938*

III

i **imposing**] stressed *1930, US 1938*

iii **lies!...**] lies! *1930, US 1938*   **O Slinger**] mudslinger *1930, US 1938*   **splendour of the quicklime**] glare of the calcimine *1930, US 1938*   **"O great age!"**] O Senectus! *1930, US 1938* ‖ O Senectus! .. *US 1949*

v **ampler**] more generous *1930, US 1938*   **leaf shadows on**] frondage of *1930, US 1938*

vii **man**] the man *1930, US 1938*   **inspired**] excited *US 1938*   **man,**] man. *1959*

ix **showing the heel's yellow colour**] bending the yellow heel *1930, US 1938*   **captains with tonsillar voices**] hoarse-voiced captains *1930, US 1938*   **saddle ··· is**] stools ··· are *US 1938*

IV

iv **tracts of burnt-over land**] turf-burnings *1930, US 1938*

iv^v] *line space 1930, US 1938* ‖ *new page so line spacing indeterminate US 1949* ‖ *no line space 1959*

v **clear sounding**] holy *1930–US 1949*

vii **as we sit**] in our places *1930, US 1938*

viii **to**] is *US 1938* (*error, not copied by Mirror*)   **the sky**] heaven *1930–US 1949*

ix **where**] there *Mirror*

x **cluster**] tuft *1930, US 1938*   **wares of the druggist**] the chemical products *1930* ‖ the wares of the druggist *Mirror*   **rubbish.)**] rubbish) *1930, US 1938*   **one that**] that *1930*

xi **... Solitude**] Solitude *1930, US 1938*   **the bays**] the bay-leaves *1930, US 1938*   **littered**] laden *1930, US 1938*

xiii **practising**] trilling *1930*

xiv **shade**] shadow *Mirror*   **waist cloths**] camiknickers *1930* ‖ knickerbockers *US 1938* ‖ drawers *US 1949*

xv **... At**] At *1930, US 1938*

V

i **far-off**] far *1930–US 1949*   **an hundred fires revived in towns**] an hundred fires in towns wakened *1930* ‖ in towns an hundred fires revived *US 1938, US 1949*

iv **Leader**] Lord *1930*

v **Solitude! ... squadrons**] Solitude! squadrons *1930, US 1938*   **enlisting**]
engaging *1930, US 1938*   **from**] for *US 1938*   **homely star**]
domestic luminary. *1930* ‖ domestic luminary *US 1938*

vi **Confederate**] Allied *1930, US 1938*

viii **praised be**] praise to *1930*

xi **stale**] sick *1930–US 1949*

xii **was benighted**] put up for the night *1930* ‖ was held up for the night *US 1938*

xiv **immense**] huge *1930, US 1938* ‖ enormous *US 1949*   **in crowd on the earth—
arise in crowds and cry out**] all together and cry *1930, US 1938*

xv **extends**] stretches *1930*

xvi **sticky**] gummed *1930–US 1949*   **who has not yet, in dreams, stolen**] to whom
it does not yet occur to knock out *1930–US 1949*

xviii **saliva**] spittle *1930–US 1949*

VI

i–iv] *drafted in TSE's Anabase (between the printed lines), with the rest of this section
and the next heavily annotated. Many variant words listed here are not part of a
continuous translation, but isolated notes on difficulties.*

i–iii] Omnipotent in our great military governments, with our perfumed daughters
clothed in mist [*with* mist? breath] these silks scented | We ~~founded~~ set in high
places our traps for delight. | ~~Abundance~~ Plenty *⊄* well-being happiness so long
in our cups the ice sang like Memnon *TSE's Anabase*

iv **deflecting**] *with* leading astray *alt TSE's Anabase*   **to**] at *1930*   **held up by
the handmaidens**] in the hands of the handmaidens *with last word over an earlier
reading—perhaps* servants—*and with* slave girls *alt*   **at**] to *TSE's Anabase 1st
reading, 1930* ‖ on *TSE's Anabase*

v **came a year of wind in the west and,**] there was a year of west wind and *TSE's
Anabase* ‖ came a year of wind in the west, and *1930, US 1938*   **all the**] a
whole *TSE's Anabase, 1930, US 1938*   **bright**] brilliant *TSE's Anabase 1st
reading*   **the delight of wide spaces**] pleasure at large *TSE's Anabase*   **on
the crest of**] threading the *uncertain 1st reading TSE's Anabase* ‖ in the defiles of
TSE's Anabase   **feeding on**] stirring up *with "?" TSE's Anabase*   **sunshine**]
fine weather *TSE's Anabase*   **published**] issued *1930, US 1938*   **fiery
bulletin**] fervent report *1930, US 1938*

vi **shudder from afar of space**] shudder running through *TSE's Anabase* ‖ shudder
of space *1930–US 1949*   **tree! ...**] tree! *1930, US 1938*   **dissolute**] broken
TSE's Anabase   **auctioned**] bartered *alt TSE's Anabase*   **priced**] valued *alt
TSE's Anabase*

vii **sniffed**] scented *TSE's Anabase*   **business, not mine,**] business not mine *1930,
US 1938*   **caused at**] forced on *TSE's Anabase, 1930*

viii **race settled**] folk squatting *1930–US 1949*   **dismounted among the food
crops**] unhorsed, tillers of the earth *1930*   **absorbed**] devoured *TSE's
Anabase* ‖ consumed *1930* ‖ brought to fruition *US 1938*   **cluster**] grape *1930,
US 1938*   **abstemious**] docile *TSE's Anabase* ‖ staid *1930, US 1938*   **seeds**]
furrows *with "?" TSE's Anabase*   **exhausted countries**] faint lands *1930, US*

1938 **are to be remade**] must be refashioned *TSE's Anabase* **composed**] arranged *1930* **act**] do *1930–US 1949*

ix **their favourite tale**] the tale of their fashions *1930, US 1938* ‖ their favorite tale *US 1949* **holding aloft**] lifted on *TSE's Anabase 1st reading* ‖ held aloft *TSE's Anabase* **swearing fealty**] lavishing their *TSE's Anabase 1st reading*

x **nubile**] marriageable *TSE's Anabase, 1930, US 1938* **of purest ring**] pure-sounding *TSE's Anabase* ‖ clear clinking *1930, US 1938* **traffic of influence in the teeth of the rivers**] influence trafficking down to the river mouths *TSE's Anabase, with "en dépit de"* **daughters**] girls *US 1938, US 1949* **leaves of gold**] gold plates *1930* **boundary**] boundaries *TSE's Anabase* **lands roused to passion**] delighted lands *1930–US 1949* ‖ excited *TSE's Anabase* **floors**] tile work *TSE's Anabase* **rose red**] red *1930, US 1938* **honey rose jelly**] jellies [of] rose-honey *TSE's Anabase*

xi **breath, silken webs . . .**] breath of silken webs . . . *1930*

xii **—In**] In *1930, US 1938* **trodden**] trod *TSE's Anabase*

VII

i **pleasance**] playground *with "?" TSE's Anabase*

ii **hangs**] swings *TSE's Anabase* **terraces of climate**] climate-floors *TSE's Anabase with "superficies" in margin* **huge earth rolls on its surface**] earth huge on its area rolls *1930* **lone**] lonely *1930–US 1949*

iii **glittering with mica**] of stone of quartz *1930–US 1949* **barbs**] beard *TSE's Anabase, 1930* **—From**] From *1930, US 1938* **gillstained**] pitted [with] earholes *with "?" TSE's Anabase* **locusts**] acridians *1930* ‖ crickets *US 1938, US 1949*

iv **Like milch-camels**] Camels *1930* ‖ Milch-camels *US 1938, US 1949* **gentle**] mild *alt TSE's Anabase* **shears and**] shearing tonsure *TSE's Anabase* ‖ shears, *1930–US 1949* **scheme**] facts *1930–US 1949* **kneel**] kneeling *1930–US 1949* **smoke**] fantasy *US 1938, US 1949* **annihilate themselves**] find amend *TSE's Anabase*

v **fading blue**] cerulisations *TSE's Anabase* **doubtful**] fantastic *with "(or omit)" TSE's Anabase*

vi **gentleness**] mildness *1930–US 1949* **—my**] my *1930, US 1938* **make good likeness**] liken themselves well *TSE's Anabase*

viii **jujuba**] juniper *1930* **a breath sweeps smoking toward us**] swept away by a breath, to our feet *1930–US 1949* **nuptials**] union *with "?" TSE's Anabase*

ix **Raise · · · raise**] Erect · · · erect *1930–US 1949* **cavalcades of green bronze**] green-bronze groups of ~~equestrians~~ horsemen *TSE's Anabase*

VIII

iii **a marvellous**] an unknown *TSE's Anabase, 1930* ‖ a peculiar *US 1938*

v **beasts akin to none**] eremite beasts *1930–US 1949* **pure bred horses with**] horses with pure *1930* ‖ thoroughbred horses with *US 1938* **frontiers**] marches *1930–US 1949* **selucid**] seleucid *1930–US 1949*

vii **crested tits**] tomtits *1930–US 1949*   **—Man**] Man *1930*, *US 1938*

ix **starved**] famished *TSE's Anabase*   **lightning**] levin *1930–US 1949*

xi **ties**] bonds *TSE's Anabase*   **year without ties or anniversaries, seasoned**] boundless unreckoned year, squared out *1930*, *US 1938* ∥ unconfined unreckoned year, seasoned *US 1949* ∥ marked out? / squared out? *alts TSE's Anabase*   **heavenly fires**] fires *1930* ∥ camp fires *US 1938*   **Sacrificed, in the morning,**] Matutinal sacrifice of *1930–US 1949*

IX

ii **smoke . . .**] smokes . . . *1930–US 1949*

iii **nature**] soul *with "?" TSE's Anabase*

iv **crying**] keening *1930–US 1949*   **dissipation**] scattering *TSE's Anabase*

v **in the**] in *1930*   **seated**] squatting *1930–US 1949*

vi **lustre**] notoriety *1930–US 1949*

xi **a sap**] spittle *1930* ∥ a spittle *US 1938, US 1949*

xii **takes its pleasure from**] draws its pleasure at *1930* ∥ has its pleasure at *US 1938*   **womb**] breast *US 1938*

xiii **dairy produce**] milk *TSE's Anabase*

xvi **felicity of springs**] bounty of fountains *1930* ∥ felicity of fountains *US 1938, US 1949*

xix **the girl-tree**] the female tree *1930* ∥ the sapling *US 1938* ∥ virgin branches *US 1949*

xxii **the painted cloth of their**] their print *US 1938, US 1949*

X

i] *first line indented 1959*

v **pond**] pool *1930–US 1949*   **discovery of springs**] dousing of *TSE Anabase* ∥ water-dowsing *1930–US 1949*   **passes**] hills *1930*

vi **toward**] before *1930–US 1949*   **turning**] airing *TSE's Anabase* ∥ spreading *1930, US 1938*   **roofs, on the prongs of**] roofs with *1930, US 1938*   **rose red**] red *1930, US 1938*   **fatigue**] not *1930*   **zig-zag**] ribbon *1930*   **the invoicing**] bulletins *1930, US 1938*   **disbanding of escorts**] escort licences *1930, US 1938*   **sheds**] penthouse *1930–US 1949*   **protestation of bills of credit**] protests of rights of creditors *1930*   **making**] composition *1930*   **firesmoke of man**] smokes of mankind *1930* ∥ reek of mankind *US 1938* ∥ firesmoke of mankind *US 1949*

vii **smith,**] smith; *1930–US 1949*   **takes**] has *1930–US 1949*   **pitch**] sound *1930*   **fountains**] fresh water pools *1930*   **juggler**] player of the game of goblets *1930*   **delight**] pleasure *1930*   **maggots**] worms *1930*   **sniffs the odour**] noses the phosphorus scent *1930*   **sword blade**] blade *1930–US 1949*   **planted**] sealed and placed *1930, US 1938*   **suburbs**] quarters *1930*   **with hands like a girl's**] bedecked by the hands of girls *1930*   **warrior**] fighting man *TSE's Anabase*

viii **connexions**] alliances *1930*   **ravish**] abduct *TSEs Anabase* ix **on the way ··· on the way**] travelling ··· travelling *1930*   **unleavened**] the azyme of *1930*

ix^x] *line space US 1938* ‖ *new page so line spacing indeterminate 1930, 1959* ‖ *no line space in French*

xi **Who talks of building?**] *italicised 1930, US 1938*   **spread**] parcelled *TSE's Anabase, 1930–US 1949*   **heedless of**] estranged from *1930*

SONG

i–iii] *drafted entire in TSE's Anabase*

i **whistle**] breathe *alt TSE's Anabase*   **sweet**] pure *alt TSE's Anabase*   **banks**] shores *alt TSE's Anabase*   **morning**] morning are *TSE's Anabase*   **glory)** . . .] glory . . .) *1930, US 1938*

ii] Let a man be sorrowful ↄ heavy-laden, but let him arise before day, and bide circumspectly in the converse [communion *alt*] of an ancient tree [oak *alt*], lean on a fading star, he shall behold in the heavens great things [mysteries *alt*] and pure that turn [conduct / unfold *alts*] to delight *TSE's Anabase*   **delight** . . .] delight. *1930*

iii **whistle**] breathe *TSE's Anabase*   **sweet**] pure *alt TSE's Anabase*   **But tidings there are of my brother the poet**] But there are tidings of my brother the poet *with last five words then transposed to follow first word, TSE's Anabase*   **a song of great sweetness**] well *TSE's Anabase, 1930, US 1938*   **thereof** . . .] of it—— *TSE's Anabase*

Index to the Editorial Material
in Volume II

Index of Titles and First Lines